PRIVATE INTERNATIONAL LAW IN COMMONWEALTH AFRICA

This book provides a comprehensive and comparative examination of private international law in Commonwealth Africa. It offers an unrivalled breadth of coverage in its examination of the law in Botswana, Gambia, Ghana, Kenya, Lesotho, Malawi, Namibia, Nigeria, Sierra Leone, South Africa, Swaziland, Tanzania, Uganda, Zambia and Zimbabwe.

Drawing on nearly 1,500 cases decided by courts in these countries, and numerous national statutes, this book covers the four cornerstones of private international law: jurisdiction, choice of law, foreign judgments and arbitral awards enforcement, and international civil procedure. The book is clearly and logically structured – it is organised around broad themes or issues, with country reports, and accompanied by detailed commentaries. The author also provides an extensive bibliography of the literature on African private international law. Scholars and practitioners alike will find *Private International Law in Commonwealth Africa* invaluable and illuminating.

DR RICHARD FRIMPONG OPPONG is an assistant professor in the Faculty of Law at Thompson Rivers University in Canada. He was the Director of Studies in Private International Law at The Hague Academy of International Law in 2012. He has published numerous articles and books, and has been cited by the United States Court of Appeal for the Ninth Circuit and by the South African Supreme Court of Appeal.

PRIVATE INTERNATIONAL LAW IN COMMONWEALTH AFRICA

RICHARD FRIMPONG OPPONG

CAMBRIDGE
UNIVERSITY PRESS

CAMBRIDGE
UNIVERSITY PRESS

University Printing House, Cambridge CB2 8BS, United Kingdom

Cambridge University Press is part of the University of Cambridge.

It furthers the University's mission by disseminating knowledge in the pursuit of education, learning and research at the highest international levels of excellence.

www.cambridge.org
Information on this title: www.cambridge.org/9780521199698

First published 2013

A catalogue record for this publication is available from the British Library

Library of Congress Cataloguing in Publication data
Oppong, Richard Frimpong, 1978–
Private international law in Commonwealth Africa / Richard Frimpong Oppong.
pages cm
ISBN 978-0-521-19969-8 (Hardback)
1. Conflict of laws–Africa, English-speaking. I. Title.
KQC126.067 2013
340.9096′09171241–dc23 2013007045

ISBN 978-0-521-19969-8 Hardback

To
Mary Adjei
Maame, thank you.

CONTENTS

FOREWORD

The publication of *Private International Law in Commonwealth Africa* marks a significant milestone in the history and development of private international law in Africa. Its encyclopaedic analysis of fifteen national legal systems – which account for over 40 per cent of the continent's population yet over 70 per cent of its economic output – will go a long way to filling a gap in knowledge in respect of this important region of the world.

I have had the pleasure of getting to know Richard Frimpong Oppong in my work at the Hague Conference on Private International Law. The Hague Conference – the 'world organisation for cross-border cooperation in civil and commercial matters' – is the only intergovernmental organisation solely devoted to the study, development and global unification of private international law. While the organisation, whose origins lie in late-nineteenth-century continental Europe, has been effective in increasing its global coverage (it currently represents over 70 states from all continents and all major legal systems), the African continent remains regrettably under-represented. At present, the only Member States in Commonwealth Africa are South Africa and Zambia, although a handful of other such states are parties to one or more of the 'Hague Conventions' (i.e. the international treaties concluded at the Hague Conference).

I have been struck by how little there is by way of academic literature on private international law issues in Commonwealth Africa, with the possible exception of South Africa. To the extent that such literature does exist, it tends to paint the region in broad strokes. This often gives the impression that private international law issues are treated in a similar manner to how they are treated under English common law, the legal system on which the legal systems of Commonwealth African countries are principally founded. The comprehensive survey conducted in this book demonstrates that this is not necessarily the case. This suggests that Commonwealth Africa is not only a source for different solutions to private international law issues, but also new ground for the progressive unification of the rules of private international law. It stands to reason, therefore, that private international law in Africa is deserving of 'special attention'.

Private international law is bound to gain prominence right across the African continent in the coming years, particularly in view of the regional economic integration processes currently underway. The experiences of similar processes elsewhere in the world (for example, within the European Union, Mercosur and ASEAN) reveal the linkages between an attention to private international law issues and the facilitation of cross-border trade and investment, let alone promotion of fundamental human rights. One need only look to organisations such as ECOWAS (Economic Community of West African States) and the EAC (East African Community) to realise the potential for mechanisms for cross-border judicial cooperation, uniform rules on choice of forum and choice of law, and regimes for the cross-border enforcement of judgments. In some of these organisations, the necessary legal infrastructure is already in place to develop harmonised solutions to these key private international law issues. Now, more than ever, it is important for decision-makers involved in these processes to have access to accurate data to assess what further action is needed.

Over recent years, Richard has developed a close relationship with the Hague Conference. He has generously contributed information on private international law developments in Commonwealth Africa, including case law and commentary from the various jurisdictions. He has also contributed his subject-matter expertise to ongoing projects, bringing with him a unique and indispensable African perspective. Most recently, he has been a member of the working group established to develop a non-binding instrument on choice of law in international contracts (the 'Hague Principles'), in which he participated alongside other experts in the fields of private international law, international commercial law and international arbitration law.

Richard's earlier writings and research on private international law issues in Commonwealth Africa have been of great interest and benefit to the ongoing work of the Hague Conference. Indeed, we considered his paper entitled 'The Hague Conference on Private International Law in Africa: A Plea for Cooperation' (published in Volume VIII of the *Yearbook of Private International Law*) to be so important and valuable that we decided to translate it into French, and to use it in our ongoing efforts to improve the participation of African states in the work of the Hague Conference, thereby drawing in not only Commonwealth Africa, but also 'Francophone Africa'.

I am very confident that the Hague Conference will benefit tremendously from the book in our continued efforts to promote existing Hague Conventions in Africa and to include African perspectives in the development of future conventions. Further afield, the book will provide an invaluable reference tool to academics, students and legal practitioners in Commonwealth Africa who study and practise in the field of private international law issues. It will also be an indispensible resource for government officials, as well as regional and international organisations, in collecting the fundamental data needed to assess what further action is needed for reform in private international law, whether at a national, regional or multilateral level.

Ultimately, however, the book will be of greatest benefit to the individuals and businesses whose cross-border relationships with and within Africa engage aspects of private international law. I have no doubt that the book will serve its aim of 'filling the current void' and 'complementing the existing African legal infrastructure necessary for regulating international commercial and transnational personal relationships'.

Dr Christophe Bernasconi
Secretary General
Hague Conference on Private International Law

PREFACE

'Why should I ever have become involved in this conflict of laws?' This was the sobering question the celebrated A. V. Dicey posed to his friend, James Bryce, in a letter dated 1896. When I took on this project little did I know the amount of work it would entail!

The seed for this project was sown while working as a research assistant for my Ph.D. supervisor, Professor Joost Blom, on the unrelated subject of economic torts in Canada. Intrigued by the comprehensiveness of the database he was using to organise his cases, I conceived of the idea of using his approach to do a similar work on African countries in the field of private international law. It is with a profound sense of gratitude that I acknowledge the contribution of Professor Blom to the successful execution of this project.

Although the seed for this project was sown in the corridors of the University of British Columbia, what one reads now is the product of five years of research which took place in three other universities, namely: Lancaster University, Dalhousie University and Thompson Rivers University. The contributions of these institutions and especially their law librarians are sincerely acknowledged.

This book was written solely by me and therefore is my responsibility alone. But whoever has tried his or her hands at such a monumental project – a project which covers fifteen countries – would appreciate my indebtedness to many who, in differing qualities and in varying degrees, have been instrumental in its accomplishment. I am indebted to Solomon Amoateng, Danny Auron, Benedict Daminabo, Malebakeng Forere, Tiyanjana Mphepo, Killey Mwitasi, Lisa Niro, Prince Nyekwere, Banjugu Nyangado, Justice Osei-Afriyie, Gwen Park, Professors Christopher Forsyth, David McClean, Gordon Woodman, Elizabeth Edinger and Olugbenga O. Bamodu for their diverse contributions. I am very much indebted to Professor Vaughan Black of the Schulich School of Law, under whose able supervision I wrote parts of this book as a Killam Postdoctoral Fellow. His support secured me substantial funding for the post and this project and without his very penetrating reviews this work would have been poorer. I am equally grateful to Dr Christophe Bernasconi, Secretary General of the Hague Conference on Private International Law, for supporting this project.

This book would have been impossible without the immense support I received from my family. I am heavily indebted to my loving wife, Joyce Okofo Adjei, and 'my girls' Mary Adjei and Zoe Oppong Serwaa. Joyce's not so infrequent question 'Rich, is this the project you were working on in . . .?' constantly reminded me of Dicey's words and of the need for me to get this book published and out of 'our way' at the earliest possible time. Nana Ama, may your heart rejoice in realising that the book is indeed published! By cutting down on their play dates with me Mary and Zoe ensured that this work reached the world a little sooner!

I thank the staff at Cambridge University Press, including Finola O'Sullivan, Elizabeth Spicer, Amanda George, Mary O'Hara, Christina Sarigiannidou, and Sophie Rosinke for making this book possible. I acknowledge the very generous financial support I received from the Killam Trusts, Canada, which funded my postdoctoral fellowship at Dalhousie University, and the British Academy, which funded the initial material gathering phase of the project.

Dr Richard Frimpong Oppong
Kamloops, British Columbia, Canada
4 May 2013

TABLE OF CASES

Botswana

Gambia

Ghana

Kenya

Lesotho

Weng v. *Weng*, CIV/T/351/99 (High Court, Lesotho, 1999) 14, 200
Western Credit (Africa) (Proprietary) Ltd v. *Mapetla* 1965 ALR Comm. 361 132

Malawi

AA Mirza v. *AMI (Malawi) Ltd*, Civil Cause No. 59 of 1999 (High Court, Malawi, 2007) 96
Atupele Haulage Ltd v. *Carbomoc* [1991] 14 MLR 18 434
Bauman Hinde v. *David Whitehead*, MSCA Civil Appeal No. 17 of 1998 (Supreme Court, Malawi, 2000) 402, 403
Bauman, Hinde & Co. Ltd v. *David Whitehead & Son Ltd*, Civil Cause No. 2107 of 1996 (High Court, Malawi, 1998) 402, 403
Bond v. *Bond* [1984–6] 11 MLR 87 31, 193
Brown v. *Brown*, Matrimonial Cause No. 9 of 2002 (High Court, Malawi, 2002) 31, 193
Chanthunya v. *Ngwira* [1987–9] 12 MLR 133 96
Chidzero v. *Chidzero* [1978–80] 9 MLR 22 196
Commissioner for Taxes v. *A Ltd* [1973–4] 7 MLR 211 15
Coombe v. *Coombe* [1923–60] ALR Mal. 115 31
Cromar v. *Cromar* [1991] 14 MLR 60 258
Dorrington v. *Dorrington* [1993] 16(1) MLR 73 31, 193
Gouveia v. *Gouveia* [1923–60] ALR Mal. 239 15, 187
Gray v. *Gray* [1923–60] ALR Mal. 160 31
Heyns v. *Demetriou*, Civil Cause No. of 2001 (High Court, Malawi, 2001) 316, 317, 326, 332, 346, 353
In re. Chitaukire [1975–7] 8 MLR 38 236
In re. David Banda (A Male Infant), Adoption Cause No. 2 of 2006 (High Court, Malawi, 2008) 223
In re. Osman Hussein; Ali v. *Osman* [1923–60] ALR Mal. 276 280, 293
In the Estate of Barretta [1984–6] 11 MLR 110 15, 281
In the Matter of CJ (A Female Infant), Adoption Cause No. 28 of 2009 (Supreme Court of Appeal, Malawi, 2009) 223
In the Matter of CJ (A Female Infant) of C/O Mr Peter Baneti, Zomba, Adoption Case No. 1 of 2009 (High Court, Malawi, 2009) 223
Investment and Development Bank of Malawi v. *Gredean Africa (Pvt) Ltd* [1993] 16(2) MLR 531 429
Jervis v. *Jervis* [1968–70] ALR Mal. 119 31
Kalilombe v. *Kalilombe* [1987–9] 12 MLR 170 194
Kamcaca v. *Nkhota* [1966–8] ALR Mal. 509 15
Kamcaca v. *Nkhota (No. 2)* [1966–8] ALR Mal. 518 15
Kaunda v. *Kaunda* [1993] 16(2) MLR 545 31, 193
Landell Mills Associates Ltd v. *Marshall* [1991] 14 MLR 175 96
Magennis v. *Malawi Press Ltd (No. 2)* [1961–63] ALR Mal. 584 8
Maseko v. *Maseko* [1973–4] 7 MLR 310 15, 187

Namibia

Nigeria

Sierra Leone

South Africa

Foize Africa (Pty) Ltd v. *Foize Beheer BV* [2012] 4 All SA 387 102
Francis & Graham Ltd v. *East African Disposal Co. Ltd* 1950 (3) SA 502 459
Frank Wright (Pty) Ltd v. *Corticas 'BCM' Ltd* 1948 (4) SA 456 75
Frankel's Estate v. *The Master* 1950 (1) SA 220 187
Friend v. *Friend* 1962 (4) SA 115 446
G & P Ltd v. *Commissioner of Taxes* 1960 (4) SA 163 20, 23
Gabelsberger v. *Babl* 1994 (2) SA 677 321, 332, 337
Gallo Africa Ltd v. *Sting Music (Pty) Ltd* 2010 (6) SA 329, [2011] 1 All SA 449 277
Gardener v. *Walters* 2002 (5) SA 796 270
Ghomeshi-Bozorg v. *Yousefi* 1998 (1) SA 692 79
Godbeer v. *Godbeer* 2000 (3) SA 976 237
Government of the Republic of Zimbabwe v. *Louis Karel Fick*, Case CCT 101/12 (Constitutional Court, South Africa, 2013) 315
Government of the Republic of Zimbabwe v. *Louis Karel Fick*, Case No. 657/11 (Supreme Court of Appeal, South Africa, 2012) 315
Granoth v. *Granoth* 1983 (4) SA 50 196
Grant v. *Grant* 1949 (1) SA 22 446
Great River Shipping Inc. v. *Sunnyface Marine Ltd* 1992 (4) SA 313 101
Greater Services (Pty) Ltd v. *Du Toit* 1975 (1) SA 260 80
Grindal v. *Grindal* 1997 (4) SA 137 33
GS v. *AH*, Case No. 11592/05 (High Court, South Africa, 2006) 244
Guggenheim v. *Rosenbaum (1)* 1961 (4) SA 15 446
Guggenheim v. *Rosenbaum (2)* 1961 (4) SA 21 5, 133, 184, 203
Gwambe v. *Gwambe* 1950 (2) SA 643 34
H v. *R* 2001 (3) SA 623 237
Halfon v. *Halfon* 1952 (4) SA 260 100
Harnischfeger Corp. v. *Appleton* 1993 (4) SA 479 17, 18
Harris v. *Rees* [2010] 4 All SA 603 75
Hassan v. *Hassan* 1998 (2) SA 589 18, 189
Hay Management Consultants (Pty) Ltd v. *P3 Management Consultants (Pty) Ltd* 2005 (2) SA 522 79, 80
Henry v. *Branfield* 1996 (1) SA 244 146
Hermes Versekeringsmaatskappy v. *Dartnell* 1980 (4) SA 279 79
Hespel v. *Hespel* 1948 (3) SA 257 446
Hibbs v. *Wynne* 1949 (2) SA 10 33
Hillard v. *Hillard*, Case No. 1464/2007 (High Court, South Africa, 2008) 33
Himelsein v. *Super Rich CC* 1998 (1) SA 929 80
Hind v. *Boswell Bros Circus (Pty) Ltd* 1952 (2) SA 158 446
Hirschowitz v. *Hirschowitz* 1965 (3) SA 407 213
Hlophe v. *Mahlalela* 1998 (1) SA 449 18
Hockeman v. *Hockeman* 1954 (1) SA 37 438
Holland v. *Holland* 1973 (1) SA 897 195, 200
Holz v. *Harksen* 1995 (3) SA 521 18, 332

Swaziland

Tanzania

Uganda

Zambia

Zimbabwe

Non-Commonwealth African countries

Foreign cases

ABBREVIATIONS

Law reports

ALR	African Law Reports (Commercial Series)
ALR Mal.	African Law Reports (Malawi Series)
All NLR	All Nigeria Law Reports
BLLR	Butterworths Labour Law Reports
BLR	Botswana Law Reports
BSC	Bophuthatswana Law Reports
Div. Ct.	Gold Coast Divisional Court Reports
EA	East Africa Law Reports
EAP LR	East African Protectorate Law Reports
EACA	East African Court of Appeal Reports
eKLR	Electronic Kenya Law Reports
FNLR	Federation of Nigeria Law Reports
FSC	Federal Supreme Court (Nigeria)
GBR	Ghana Bar Reports
GLR	Ghana Law Reports
GR	Gambia Law Reports
ILR	International Law Reports
KLR	Kenya Law Reports
Kam. LR	Kampala Law Reports
LAC	Lesotho Appeal Cases
LLR	LawAfrica Law Reports
LLR-LB	Lesotho Law Reports and Legal Bulletin
LRC Comm.	Law Reports of the Commonwealth, Commercial Law Division
LRNR	Law Reports of Northern Rhodesia
MLR	Malawi Law Reports
NCLR	Nigeria Commercial Law Reports
NR	Namibia Law Reports
NWLR	Nigeria Weekly Law Reports
R & N	Rhodesia and Nyasaland Law Reports
Ren.	Renner's Reports
RLR	Rhodesian Law Reports

SA	South Africa Law Reports
SC	Supreme Court Reports (Nigeria)
SCGL	Supreme Court of Ghana Law Reports
SLJR	Sudan Law Journal and Report
SLR	Sudan Law Reports
Sw. LR	Swaziland Law Reports
TLR	Tanzania Law Reports
WACA	West African Court of Appeal
WALR	West African Law Report
WRN	Weekly Reports of Nigeria
ZLR	Zimbabwe Law Reports
ZR	Zambia Law Reports

Books

James Facwcett and Janeen M. Carruthers, *Cheshire, North & Fawcett Private International Law*, 14th edn (Oxford University Press, 2008) [Hereinafter, *Cheshire, North & Fawcett*]

Lord Collins of Mapesbury et al. (eds.), *Dicey, Morris and Collins on the Conflict of Laws*, 15th edn (London: Sweet & Maxwell, 2012) [Hereinafter, *Dicey, Morris & Collins*]

Christopher Forsyth, *Private International Law – the Modern Roman Dutch Law including the Jurisdiction of the High Courts*, 5th edn (Lansdowne: Juta & Co Ltd, 2012) [Hereinafter, Forsyth]

INTRODUCTION

> We should always be willing to compromise preferred solutions in order to achieve justice for the individuals involved. But there is no need for us unthinkingly to accept foreign solutions or approaches to the problems of private international law. There is no need for us to be like the weather-vane flipping one way or the other as the winds from abroad blow. The truth is that the challenges we face are those of resources and interest.
>
> C. Forsyth[1]

This book is about private international law or conflict of laws in Commonwealth Africa.[2] In academic terms, it is a study in comparative private international law. It is also meant to be a practitioner's guide – a first stop – on private international law issues in Africa. It examines the law in fifteen countries – Botswana, Gambia, Ghana, Kenya, Lesotho, Malawi, Namibia, Nigeria, Sierra Leone, South Africa,[3] Swaziland,[4] Tanzania, Uganda, Zambia and Zimbabwe[5] (hereinafter, 'the countries under study').[6]

[1] 'The Provenance and Future of Private International Law in Southern Africa' (2002) *Journal of South African Law* 60 at 68.

[2] For similar comparative works on the Commonwealth, see V. Black, *Foreign Currency Claims in the Conflict of Laws* (Oxford: Hart Publishing, 2010); J. D. McClean, *Recognition of Family Judgments in the Commonwealth* (London: Butterworths, 1983); K. W. Patchett, *Recognition of Commercial Judgments and Awards in the Commonwealth* (London: Butterworths, 1984); and H. E. Read, *Recognition and Enforcement of Foreign Judgments in the Common Law Units of the British Commonwealth* (Cambridge: Harvard University Press, 1938).

[3] South Africa has what is, perhaps, the oldest and most advanced system of law reporting in the countries under study. In this book I have focused mainly on cases from the South African Law Reports, 1947 to date.

[4] Swaziland is the most under-represented in this book. I have been unable to access legislation and law reports from the country.

[5] Zimbabwe is currently not a member of the Commonwealth, but is included in the study.

[6] There are occasional references to some old cases from Somalia and Sudan, which historically had an encounter, either directly or indirectly, with English common law.

Private international law deals with claims which involve a foreign element. For a number of reasons, Africa provides an interesting but unexplored forum for the study of this subject. At present there are serious efforts aimed at expanding international economic activity within Africa. This is reflected in the emergence of multiple, regional economic integration arrangements[7] and unilateral national drives to promote trade, investment and the free movement of persons. The quest for 'greener pastures', combined with national civil conflicts, has also led some countries to experience significant inflows of foreigners. Private international law is a key aspect of the legal infrastructure necessary to facilitate international commercial activity and to regulate transnational personal relationships, and hence the economic development of a country. However, given the previously low levels of international commercial contacts and historically modest inflow of foreigners into African countries, the role of a sound private international law regime to economic development has not attracted serious attention. In general, it can be said that Africa is saddled with a private international law regime which is still developing, but will increasingly be called upon to address largely *res nova* issues.

The research, study and practice of private international law in Africa have stagnated and this is reflected in the absence of academic texts across most of the continent. Indeed, this proposition is equally true for all aspects of private law in Africa, such as contracts and torts. Historically, interest in private international law in Africa was evident up to around the late 1970s. The African Law Reports Commercial Law Series and Commonwealth Law Reports regularly reported African private international law cases. Articles on the subject appeared in leading journals. However, very few monographs or treatises were written, and those that were concentrated on internal conflict of laws problems – problems resulting from the pluralist nature of legal systems of many African countries. At present, it can be argued that it is only in South Africa that the subject enjoys systematic academic attention. Existing African works, mostly very dated, are also jurisdictionally constrained; they tend to focus purely on one country. Furthermore, there have been no attempts to produce a genuinely African-based or African-influenced private international law treatise, i.e. a treatise which, while not discounting the importance of non-African sources, takes its principal sources of

[7] R. F. Oppong, *Legal Aspects of Economic Integration in Africa* (Cambridge University Press, 2011).

law (case law, legislation and academic commentary) from Africa and remains oriented towards meeting the challenges now facing the continent. These challenges include regional economic integration, the promotion of international trade and investment, immigration, globalisation and legal pluralism.

Despite the stagnation of private international law in Africa, it has all the characteristics of an emerging research subject. The editors of the *Yearbook of Private International Law* suggested that Africa was 'an entire most promising continent' when it came to the study of private international law. A chronicle of African private international law cases in the 2007 volume of the *Yearbook* was characterised in the foreword as 'unique' and deserving of 'special attention'. Recently, a few research papers on isolated issues in African private international law have been published in leading journals. These papers aim at satisfying a growing international demand for knowledge on private international law jurisprudence in Africa. For example, the celebrated English work on the subject – *Dicey, Morris & Collins on the Conflict of Laws* – has cited recent cases from Africa. Moreover, articles on conflict of laws in Africa have become a regular feature of the *Journal of Private International Law*, and the *American Journal of Comparative Law* recently published a bibliography of private international law articles written in African law journals.[8] All these are manifestations of the growing international interest in private international law in Africa.

However, the growth of the subject in Africa is currently constrained by the absence of relevant texts and the difficulty of accessing cases, legislation and commentary. A legal practitioner, academic or policy-maker seeking to investigate a private international law issue in many of the countries under study would be amazed at the absence of text of the subject. This book aims at filling the current void and complementing the existing African legal infrastructure necessary for regulating international commercial and transnational personal relationships.

To write a book covering fifteen countries and dealing with a subject likely to evolve rapidly in the future[9] necessarily presents challenges. These challenges include access to materials, and adopting an approach that would appeal to different audiences (legal practitioners, academics,

[8] R. F. Oppong, 'Private International Law Scholarship in Africa (1884–2009) – A Selected Bibliography' (2010) 58 *American Journal of Comparative Law* 319.

[9] R. F. Oppong, 'Private International Law in Africa: The Past, Present and Future' (2007) 55 *American Journal of Comparative Law* 677.

researchers, students, law- and policy-makers, as well as institutions), and which will be susceptible to regular updating in order to reflect changes in the laws of the countries under study. The approach adopted by this book is, accordingly, shaped by practical and pragmatic considerations: it is a compromise directed towards meeting the needs of many audiences, and with a view to facilitating future revisions and updates.

The book is organised around broad themes or issues. Each chapter begins with a brief explanation of the topic or issues addressed in the chapter in general terms. These introductions are directed mostly at readers who may not be familiar with the subject matter.[10] The chapters are divided into sections founded on broad themes. Under each theme there are alphabetically arranged country reports with accompanying commentary on the reports.[11] The country reports are presented in the form of bare statements of law or legal principles supported by authority (statute and case law). There is little or no attempt to comment on or discuss them – that is reserved for the commentary sections. In other words, the country reports focus on what the law *is*. The nature of the existing jurisprudence and legislation implies that, under each theme, cases and statutes may be addressing different aspects of the same issue. When dealing with the same aspect of the same issue it is remarkable the extent to which laws as similar in the countries under study. The effect of this is that some parts of the book may appear repetitive. However, a reader should be aware that, in reality, this book is 'fifteen books in one jacket'! Read together, the country reports would often provide a comprehensive treatment of the chosen theme. Read in isolation, each country's report may leave many issues unaddressed.[12] Indeed, for some

[10] In general, this book should not be read as if it were a 'textbook'. To a large extent it assumes prior knowledge of private international law and is mainly directed at helping those who, possessed of such knowledge, want the specific answers the countries under study would give to defined issues.

[11] I depart from this approach in a few areas dominated by legislation of almost similar content, such as on the grounds of allowing for the service of writs abroad, jurisdiction in matrimonial causes, and the enforcement of foreign judgments and arbitration awards under statute. In these areas, the common statutory provisions are presented in the text and countries with relevant provisions stipulated in footnotes.

[12] Two foreign books cited most often in the decided cases – albeit to older editions – are *Dicey, Morris & Collins* and *Cheshire, North & Fawcett*. Both books may be resorted to for persuasive authority on unaddressed issues, especially in Gambia, Ghana, Kenya, Malawi, Nigeria, Sierra Leone, Tanzania, Uganda and Zambia. For Lesotho, Namibia, South Africa, Swaziland and Zimbabwe, C. F. Forsyth, *Private International Law: The Modern Roman-Dutch Law Including the Jurisdiction of the High Court*, 5th edn (Cape Town: Juta & Co, 2012) is indispensable.

themes, I may not have found any relevant decided case or statute in certain countries, in which case there is no respective report on the law. Time and space do not allow detailed analysis of the law in each country, or a discussion of individual cases and statutes. Instead, the commentary sections attempt to pull together and discuss significant aspects of the jurisprudence in the country reports. Their focus is usually on issues of convergence, divergence, gaps, underdevelopment or inconsistency in law and, finally, reform.

Given how the book is organised, those readers who wish to find out about the law in specific countries, or who are interested in more general or comparative knowledge, can easily find what they want. However, because of the limitations of an academic project of such range and scope, whatever is found should, in most cases, be considered merely a starting point for inquiry, and not necessarily the end.[13]

[13] For some recent and more detailed country-focused works, see R. F. Oppong, *Private International Law in Ghana* (Alphen aan den Rijn: Kluwer Law International, 2012); E. Schoeman and C. Roodt, 'South Africa' in B. Verschraegen (ed.), *Private International Law* in R. Blanpain (gen. ed.), *International Encyclopedia of Law* (Alphen aan den Rijn: Kluwer Law International, 2007); I. O. Agbede, 'Nigeria' in B. Verschraegen (ed.), *Private International Law* in R. Blanpain (gen. ed.), *International Encyclopedia of Law* (Alphen aan den Rijn: Kluwer Law International, 2004); C. Schulze, *On Jurisdiction and the Recognition and Enforcement of Foreign Money judgments* (Pretoria: University of South Africa Press, 2005); Forsyth, *Private International Law*; and J. Kiggundu, *Private International Law in Botswana, Cases and Materials* (Gaborone: Bay Publishing Ltd, 2002).

PART I

Preliminary matters

1

Conceptual issues in choice of law

The choice of law process is often preceded or interrupted by very abstruse and highly technical questions. Prior to determining the appropriate rule for the choice of law and thus ascertaining the applicable law, a judge may have to determine the juridical nature of the question that requires decision. There may be uncertainty about the scope or reach of the category which forms part of any choice of law rule. The choice of law rule may itself be clear and well established, but it may be uncertain whether the matter disputed in a particular case falls within the category to which the rule applies. The judge may have to determine whether a given set of facts or rule of law raises a question about the proprietory consequence of marriage or succession, or whether it founds an action for breach of contract or tort. This is the domain of characterisation or classification.

In addition to the main issue, a private international law case may place a subsidiary issue before the court, which may require its own choice of law rule for resolution. This is the field of the incidental question. Furthermore, in some cases, the selection of the applicable law leads to a further question – what is meant by the applicable 'law'? Is it a reference to the internal law of the applicable law, or does it include the country's private international law rules? What if it includes the private international law rules and those rules refer the judge to the law of a different country? This potentially unending process of reference from the law of one country to the law of another is the domain of the doctrine of *renvoi*, the seed of which is sown by differences in choice of law rules. Finally, it is not every aspect of a claim involving a foreign element that is governed by foreign law – some matters are treated as questions of procedure to be governed by the *lex fori*, and others are held to be questions of substance and governed by the *lex causae*. The distinction between substance and procedure is thus important in determining the applicable law. The above issues are the subject matter of this chapter.

Characterisation, incidental question and *renvoi*

Botswana

A reference to Botswanan law in a foreign judgment recognised in Botswana is a reference to the laws of Botswana, including its private international law. In a divorce decree, a Tanzanian court directed that matrimonial property located in Botswana should be distributed in accordance with 'the law obtaining in Botswana'. Both former spouses were domiciled in Tanzania. Under Botswanan private international law, the distribution of matrimonial property (movable and immovable), in the absence of special circumstances, is governed by the law of the domicile of the parties. It was held that the reference in the Tanzanian decree to the laws of Botswana included Botswana's private international law and, accordingly, the assets of the parties located in Botswana should be distributed in accordance with the law of Tanzania, as outlined in section 114 of the Law of Marriage Act 1971.[1] It is implicit in the judgment that the distribution was carried out in accordance with the law of Tanzania, excluding its private international law.

Ghana

A reference to the *lex situs* does not simply mean the domestic law of the *situs*, but also its private international law, which may refer to some other system of domestic law.[2] In *Youhana* v. *Abboud*,[3] two Lebanese domiciled men died intestate with immovable properties in Ghana. On the issue of the law governing succession to their properties, it was held that it should be *lex situs*, including its private international law. Under these rules, the properties should devolve in accordance with the law of the domicile of the deceased. It is unclear from the judgment whether the reference to Lebanese law included its private international law, or what would have happened if those rules referred the matter back to the *lex situs*. Indeed, prior to the judgment, the properties had been distributed by a Lebanese court without any reference to Ghanaian law.

Lesotho

In Lesotho, the preferred approach to dealing with issues of characterisation is one midway between characterisation by the *lex fori* and the *lex*

[1] *Mtui* v. *Mtui* 2001 (2) BLR 333.
[2] *Akoto* v. *Akoto* [2011] 1 SCGLR 533. [3] [1974] 2 GLR 201.

causae, with the ultimate objective of producing a policy-oriented decision. In *Mohapi* v. *Motleleng*,[4] the court had to resolve the issue of whether a widow's claim to inherit her late husband's estate rested on a right to matrimonial property, or to a right of succession. The couple were married in South Africa, the property was situated in Lesotho, and it was unclear whether they were domiciled in South Africa or Lesotho. After taking into account both South African and Lesotho law, the court held that the claim should be characterised as one relating to matrimonial property.

South Africa

South African courts have shown a preference for the *via media* approach to characterisation. According to this approach, the rules of the forum relating to conflict of laws should be construed from a cosmopolitan or worldwide point of view, so as to permit the application of foreign domestic rules. In so doing, the courts regard both the *lex fori* and the *lex causae* before characterising an issue and full attention is paid to the 'nature, scope and purpose' of the foreign rule in its context of foreign law. The first step is to make provisional characterisation in relation to both applicable systems of law. This is followed by a final characterisation, which takes into account policy considerations.[5]

Deciding a private international law issue (governed by foreign law) may involve determining a prior, subsidiary and independent private international law matter, which could be governed by the conflict of laws rules of either a foreign or domestic forum, although with potentially different results. *Phelan* v. *Phelan*[6] illustrates this. In an action for divorce and ancillary relief, the defendant raised the defence that the parties' marriage, concluded in Australia, was invalid. The defendant had previously been married. He had obtained a divorce in the Dominican

[4] *Mohapi* v. *Motleleng* [1985–6] LAC 316.

[5] *Society of Lloyd's* v. *Price* 2006 (5) SA 393 (on appeal from *Society of Lloyd's* v. *Price* 2005 (3) SA 549); *Society of Lloyd's* v. *Romahn* 2006 (4) SA 23; *Laurens NO* v. *Von Hohne* 1993 (2) SA 104; *Monokandilos* v. *Generale Des Carriers et Des Mines SA*, Case No. 11261/2001 (High Court, South Africa, 2010), but see *Laconian Maritime Enterprises Ltd* v. *Agromar Lineas Ltd* 1986 (3) SA 509, where, after providing various justifications, it was held that classification is to be carried out in terms of the *lex fori*.

[6] 2007 (1) SA 483. See also *Guggenheim* v. *Rosenbaum (2)* 1961 (4) SA 21, in which the court had to determine whether the validity of a contract to marry entered into in New York, the plaintiff having previously obtained a decree of divorce in the State of Nevada, would be recognised in New York.

Republic at a time when he was ordinarily resident in the Republic of Ireland. The defendant's contention was that, since his Dominican divorce decree would not be recognised in Australia, their marriage was invalid. Thus, to determine the validity of the Australian marriage, the court had to determine the prior, subsidiary and independent question of whether the defendant was still married to another when the marriage to the plaintiff took place in Australia. If this was the case, then the marriage could not be permitted under Australian law. The court did not expressly acknowledge that it was confronted with an incidental question, but after examining Australian law, it was held that the defendant had discharged the onus of establishing that the Dominican Republic divorce decree would not be recognised in Australia and, accordingly, the marriage between the plaintiff and the defendant was void.

Zimbabwe

It has been held that the traditional approach in private international law is for the *lex fori* to characterise according to its own law, and not the *lex causa*. The better approach, however, especially in cases of gap, is to apply a *via media* approach which allows the court to exercise judicial discretion in relation to choice of law, taking into account the consequences of deciding cases one way or the other. This enables the court to decide cases with a view to achieving international comity and a balance of justice and convenience.[7]

Comments

Problems of characterisation occur in private international law systems, such as those found in Africa, which are based on categories and connecting factors. It is a problem inherent in the application of multi-lateral choice of law rules. It has given rise to very engaging writings in which various approaches have been espoused.[8] However, it appears there have not been many African cases on the issue or, rather, it has not been seriously discussed in cases. Indeed, in some cases, courts fail to

[7] *Coutts & Co.* v. *Ford* 1997 (1) ZLR 440.

[8] C. Schulze, 'Formalistic and Discretionary Approaches to Characterization in Private International Law' (2006) 123 *South African Law Journal* 161; C. Forsyth, 'Characterisation Revisited: An Essay in the Theory and Practice of the English Conflict of Laws' (1998) 114 *Law Quarterly Review* 141.

appreciate the existence of a characterisation problem.[9] It is only recently that the Lesotho, South Africa and Zimbabwe courts have acknowledged and discussed the issue.

One of the thorniest problems in characterisation is what is actually being characterised: is it an issue, a rule of law or a set of facts? In South Africa, it has been held that it is rules of law which are characterised.[10] Another issue is whether characterisation should be performed in accordance with the *lex fori*, the *lex causae*, the *via media* approach (which pays attention to both the *lex fori* and *lex causae*) or with some other approach. In Lesotho, South Africa and Zimbabwe, the courts have preferred the *via media* approach.

The problem of *renvoi* arises when a reference to the law of a foreign country in conflict of laws rules is taken as a reference to the law of that country, including its conflict of laws rules, and the conflict rules of that country refer the issue at stake to the 'law' of a third country or the 'law' of the forum (country hearing the case). Even though there have been decisions which concede that a reference to the law of a foreign country could encompass the latter's conflict of laws rules, the courts have not provided any guidance on how they resolve problems resulting from this. In South Africa, statute has restricted the scope of problems of *renvoi* in the context of choice of law rules which rely on domicile as the connecting factor. Under the Domicile Act, if a court, when applying choice of law rules, finds that a question before it should be decided in accordance with the law of a foreign state or territory on account of a person's domicile, it shall decide the question in accordance with that law, even though a court of that state or territory, in the application of its choice of law rules, would have found South African law or any other law to be applicable with respect to the question concerned.[11]

Substance and procedure

Kenya

Kenya's law on limitation of actions, generally contained in the Limitation of Actions Act 1967, applies to actions before Kenyan courts,

[9] See, e.g., *Powell* v. *Powell* 1953 (4) SA 380; *Anderson* v. *The Master* 1949 (4) SA 660.

[10] *Laconian Maritime Enterprises Ltd* v. *Agromar Lineas Ltd* 1986 (3) SA 509 at 517.

[11] Domicile Act 1992, s. 4. Another area where *renvoi* is statutorily excluded is testamentary succession. See Ch. 15.

regardless of where the cause of action has arisen. However, in proceedings brought before a Kenyan court where a foreign law bars either the right or the remedy with respect to a cause of action arising outside Kenya, the action is barred.[12]

Lesotho

Under Lesotho law, questions of prescription are matters of substance and are governed by the *lex causae*. For example, in an application for the attachment of a *peregrinus* defendant's assets, for the purpose of founding jurisdiction, the applicant relied on an alleged unlawful detention of the applicant's vehicle in South Africa as his cause of action. This cause of action was prescribed in South Africa. It was held that prescription was governed by the *lex causae* and, as the action was prescribed under South African law, there was no prima facie case against the respondent to merit attachment.[13]

Malawi

Estimating the costs of litigation is a matter of procedure governed by the *lex fori*. The Malawi courts have found no reason in principle why lawyers litigating in Malawi should be remunerated using foreign scales and principles.[14]

Namibia

It is for the *lex fori* to decide if a right created in a foreign country gives rise to relief in Namibia. Thus, whether the rights of a foreign bond holder will be recognised and granted any relief in Namibia is a matter for the *lex fori*.[15]

[12] Limitation of Actions Act 1967, s. 40(1). See generally *Athman bin Mahomed* v. *Abdulhosein Karimji* [1917–18] KLR 5; *Shadi Ram Mohindra* v. *BC Mohindra* [1954] KLR 89; *Doshi* v. *Patel* [1953] 26 KLR 15.

[13] *Lepota* v. *Hyland*, CIV/APN/280/87 (High Court, Lesotho, 1991).

[14] *Preferential Trade Area Bank* v. *ESCOM*, Civil Cause No. 238 of 2000 (High Court, Malawi, 2003). But also see *Magennis* v. *Malawi Press Ltd* (No. 2) [1961–3] ALR Mal. 584, which held that a foreign lawyer's bill ought to be taxed on the scale of charges appertaining to the country where he or she practises.

[15] *Banco Exterior de Espana SA* v. *Government of the Republic of Namibia* 1996 NR 1, 1992 (2) SA 434.

South Africa

Under South African law, the *lex fori* governs all matters of procedure, while matters of substance are governed by the *lex causae.*[16] Whether a rule is substantive or procedural is decided by the *lex fori.*[17] It has been held that the order of priority in ranking claims,[18] quantification of damages,[19] recognition of a claim as giving rise to a maritime lien,[20] sufficiency of evidence[21] and rules relating to *res judicata*[22] are all matters of procedure governed by the *lex fori*. On the other hand, the extinction (or creation) of a right by prescription is a matter of substance and, accordingly, governed by the *lex causae.*[23]

Tanzania

The Law of Limitations Act applies to proceedings in Tanzania on rights of action arising outside Tanzania in the same way as it applies to rights of action arising within Tanzania. However, where foreign law bars either the right or the remedy in respect of a right of action arising outside Tanzania, but which is pursued in a Tanzanian court, the proceedings are barred.[24]

Zimbabwe

The remedy available to a person to recover a claim by action at law is a matter of procedure that is governed by the *lex fori.*[25] However, prescription is a matter of substance and governed by the *lex causae.*[26]

[16] *Minister of Transport, Transkei* v. *Abdul* 1995 (1) SA 366.

[17] *Kuhne & Nagel AG Zurich* v. *APA Distributors (Pty) Ltd* 1981 (3) SA 536 at 521.

[18] *MV Guzin S (No. 1) Hamburgische Landesbank-Girozentrale* v. *Fund created by the sale of the MV Guzin S* 2002 (6) SA 113; *Transol Bunker BV* v. *MV Andrico Unity* 1989 (4) SA 325.

[19] *Santam Ltd* v. *Gerdes* 1999 (1) SA 693.

[20] *Transol Bunker BV* v. *MV Andrico Unity* 1989 (4) SA 325; *Transol Bunker BV* v. *MV Andrico Unity* 1987 (3) SA 794; *Brady-Hamilton Stevedore Co.* v. *MV Kalantiao* 1987 (4) SA 250. On the nature of a maritime lien, see *Southern Steamship Agency Inc.* v. *MV Khalij Sky* 1986 (1) SA 485.

[21] *Ex p. Heinmann* 1952 (3) SA 149.

[22] *Laconian Maritime Enterprises Ltd* v. *Agromar Lineas Ltd* 1986 (3) SA 509.

[23] *Kuhne & Nagel AG Zurich* v. *APA Distributors (Pty) Ltd* 1981 (3) SA 536; *Society of Lloyd's* v. *Price* 2006 (5) SA 393 (on appeal from *Society of Lloyd's* v. *Price* 2005 (3) SA 549); *Society of Lloyd's* v. *Romahn* 2006 (4) SA 23.

[24] Law of Limitations Act 1971, s. 42(1).

[25] *Timms* v. *Nicol* [1967] RLR 386.

[26] *Coutts & Co.* v. *Ford* 1997 (1) ZLR 440.

Comments

In private international law, a distinction is drawn between matters of substance and procedure. The former is governed by the *lex causae* and the latter by the *lex fori*. The difficult task, however, is often trying to determine which matters are substantive, and which are procedural. The principles that issues of procedure are governed by the *lex fori* and matters of substance by the *lex causae* are well accepted.[27] The list of matters of procedure is not closed; the courts have not provided an exhaustive list of what they would characterise as procedural. To date, it has been held that the sufficiency of evidence, recognition of rights created abroad, remedies available to a party, quantification of damages, priority in ranking claims and the assessment of costs of litigation are all matters of procedure. It could be argued that it is important to place a lid on the scope of matters treated as procedural by the courts – an expanding list of such matters undermines the purpose of choice of law rules and conflict of laws in general. Indeed, there is arguably a move in the common law world towards restricting the scope of matters characterised as procedural.[28]

Whether limitation periods should be characterised as procedural or substantive has been subject to debate.[29] In Lesotho, South Africa and Zimbabwe, prescription has been characterised as substantive and governed by the *lex causae*. The position in Kenya and Tanzania (where foreign law which bars either the right or the remedy in respect of a foreign right of action prevails) is consistent with the approach adopted in Lesotho, South Africa and Zimbabwe. However, unlike in Lesotho, South Africa and Zimbabwe, it does not matter in Kenya or Tanzania how the *lex causae* characterises its rule of prescription (i.e. as substantive or procedural) – it just has to be applied. This avoids the gap experienced in some Southern African cases. This problem arises where the *lex fori*

[27] See also *Coal Export Corp.* v. *Notias George* [1962] EA 220, which held that questions of priorities attaching to claims for moneys in the nature of wages are to be determined by the *lex fori*; and *George Michailides* v. *Nerves Yacoub* [1900–31] 1 SLR 190, questioning whether the *lex loci contractus* prevails over the *lex fori* as to questions of procedure and prescription.

[28] *John Pfeiffer Pty Ltd* v. *Rogerson* (2000) 203 CLR 503; *Harding* v. *Wealands* [2006] UKHL 32; United Kingdom – Foreign Limitation Periods Act 1984; *Tolofson* v. *Jensen* [1994] 3 SCR 1022; *Castillo* v. *Castillo* [2005] 3 SCR 870.

[29] See generally the interesting Nigerian case of *Rhein Mass Und See Schiffahrskontor Gmbh* v. *Rivway Lines Ltd* (1998) All NLR 565, [1998] 5 NWLR 265 on the distinction between action and cause of action for the purpose of the law on limitations.

characterises prescription as substantive and the *lex causae* characterises it as procedural. Traditionally, the common law draws a distinction between a statute which merely bars a remedy and that which extinguishes a right or cause of action. Only the latter is treated as an issue of substance governed by the *lex causae*. The distinction between remedy barring and cause of action which extinguishes statutes is often difficult to make. Whether other African countries will continue to adhere to the distinction remains to be seen, but there is a strong case for treating all limitation periods as matters of substance.

2

Foreign law

To a large extent the subject matter of private international law is foreign law. Unlike comparative law which compares foreign law, private international law investigates the extent to which foreign law may be applied in another legal system. The application of foreign law can arise in any context, although it is particularly relevant in the field of choice of law.

There are a number of issues that can arise before or during an inquiry into whether foreign law should apply to a particular question. These issues include: whether foreign law should be treated as a question of fact or law; who is qualified to prove foreign law; the mode of proof; what standard of proof must be met and the consequences of not meeting that standard; what the roles of the judge, parties, and in some cases jury, are in ascertaining the content of foreign law; when so ascertained whether foreign law is automatically then applicable or may be excluded from application on any ground; and the extent to which an appellate court will review a trial court's determination on foreign law. The issues and related matters are the subject matter of this chapter.

Nature, existence and proof of foreign law

Botswana

Foreign law is a fact that must be proved by expert evidence.[1] The courts do not take judicial notice of foreign law. Like other factual averments in a case, it requires evidence given by an expert witness, who could be a lawyer practising in the respective foreign country. In applying these principles, it is immaterial whether the foreign country shares the same legal tradition as Botswana, especially in cases where the court is dealing

[1] *Mtui* v. *Mtui* 2000 (1) BLR 406 at 413; *Garmroudi* v. *The State* 1987 BLR 409. See generally Evidence (Commonwealth Statutes) Act 1923; Evidence (Commonwealth and Foreign Acts of State and Judgments) Act 1910.

with a foreign statute.[2] In addition to proof from expert evidence, and subject to the existence of a convention between the two countries, a Botswanan court may make reference to a superior court in a foreign country in order to ascertain the law applicable to the facts of a case pending before it.[3]

Gambia

Whenever a Gambian court has to decide a point of foreign law, the opinions of especially skilled persons (experts) in the foreign law are deemed relevant facts. Such opinions are admissible evidence. The experts may also produce books which they consider works of authority on the foreign law. After receiving books on foreign law and expert opinion thereon, the court is entitled to construe them for itself. In other words, the court is not bound by expert opinion or pronouncements in books tendered in evidence.[4]

Ghana

Foreign law is treated as fact.[5] A person who relies on foreign law must prove it with evidence. Although it is a question of fact, it is not determined by the jury; the determination of foreign law is for the court.[6] Proof of foreign law must be provided by an expert witness[7] whose competence is a question of law for the judge.[8] A local counsel who has never practised in Indiana, USA before is not a competent expert on Indiana law.[9] On the other hand, a priest of the Maronite Roman Catholic Church could be regarded as an expert witness on the matrimonial laws of Lebanon.[10] Merely presenting a judge with the text of a foreign law and leaving him to draw his own conclusions does not satisfy the requirements of proof by evidence.[11] Where a party fails to meet the

[2] *Point Trading (Pty) Ltd* v. *The Attorney General* 2004 (1) BLR 75.
[3] Commonwealth and Foreign Law Ascertainment Act 1910.
[4] Evidence Act 1994, ss. 57 and 58.
[5] *Davis* v. *Randall* [1962] 1 GLR 1; *In re. Canfor (Deceased); Canfor* v. *Kpodo* [1968] GLR 177; Evidence Act 1974, s. 1(2).
[6] Evidence Act 1974, s. 1(2).
[7] *Godka Group of Companies* v. *PS International Ltd* [1999–2000] 1 GLR 409.
[8] *Huzaifeh* v. *Saba* (1939) 5 WACA 181.
[9] *Godka Group of Companies* v. *PS International Ltd* [1999–2000] 1 GLR 409.
[10] *Khoury* v. *Khoury* [1958] 3 WALR 52.
[11] *Godka Group of Companies* v. *PS International Ltd* [1999–2000] 1 GLR 409.

requisite standard of proof, which is proof on the balance of probabilities, the court will apply the presumption that the foreign law is the same as Ghana law.[12] Although the concept of foreign law is not defined in any statute, it can be inferred from the Evidence Act that it encompasses the law of 'an organisation of states to the extent that such law is not part of the law of Ghana' and the laws of foreign states or their sub-divisions.[13] In other words, both unincorporated international laws and foreign state laws are treated as foreign law.

Kenya

When a Kenyan court has to determine a point of foreign law, opinions upon that point are admissible if given by persons especially skilled in such foreign law.[14] In the field of the administration of estates, the Probate and Administration Rules provide that, where evidence of foreign law is required on an application for a grant, the affidavit of any person who practises, or has practised, as a barrister, solicitor, advocate or other legal practitioner in that country and who is conversant with its law, may be accepted by the court. The court may dispense with this rule in special circumstances if it is satisfied that a person who does not possess similar qualifications sufficiently possesses knowledge of the foreign law.[15]

Lesotho

Lesotho courts do not ordinarily take judicial notice of foreign law. It must be proved by the evidence of an expert witness, who may be either a professional lawyer or the holder of an office which requires legal knowledge or at any rate gives him special opportunities to become acquainted with the law.[16] In the absence of such proof, foreign law is presumed to be the same as the *lex fori*.[17] However, in

[12] Evidence Act 1974, s. 40; *Moubarak* v. *Holland West Afrika Lijn* [1953] 14 WACA 262; *Godka Group of Companies* v. *PS International Ltd* [1999–2000] 1 GLR 409.

[13] Evidence Act 1974, s. 1(2). [14] Evidence Act 1963, s. 48.

[15] Probate and Administration Rules 1981, s. 30.

[16] *Serobanyane* v. *Serobanyane*, CIV\APN\290\91 (High Court, Lesotho, 1991).

[17] *Serobanyane* v. *Serobanyane*, CIV\APN\290\91 (High Court, Lesotho, 1991); *Weng* v. *Weng*, CIV/T/351/99 (High Court, Lesotho, 1999); *Ndlovu* v. *Employment Bureau of Africa Ltd*, CIV/APN/142/98 (High Court, Lesotho, 2002); *Mutua* v. *Matholoane*, CIV/APN/183/94 (High Court, Lesotho, 1994).

appropriate cases, a Lesotho judge may take judicial notice of foreign law – in this instance, South African law.[18]

Malawi

Foreign law is treated as a fact and must be proved by expert evidence.[19] This principle extends to customary laws of African countries.[20] And, for that purpose, a person who has lived in Rhodesia (Zimbabwe) and studied customary law by attending court cases will be considered as an expert witness on Rhodesian customary law.[21] Similarly, a notary versed in Italian law,[22] and an advocate practising at Tete in Portuguese East Africa (Mozambique)[23] have been held as qualified to give evidence on Italian and Portuguese law, respectively. The burden of proving foreign law lies with the party who bases a claim or defence on it. When foreign law is not proved, the court will apply the *lex fori.*[24]

Namibia

Namibian courts treat foreign law as fact that must be proved by expert evidence.[25] A Namibian court cannot – as it must in the case of Namibian law – take judicial notice of foreign law (in this instance English law). It must be proven by the evidence of an expert witness – normally by lawyers practising in the courts of the country whose law the Namibian courts want to ascertain. Once proven by the evidence of duly qualified experts, the court is constrained to accept it as a correct statement of the foreign law and must apply it as such.[26]

It has been held that a professor at the University of London who had already taught courses on the legal systems of the Commonwealth of Independent States, including the legal system of the Ukraine, with a few

18 *Mohapi* v. *Motleleng* (1985–9) LAC 316.

19 *Commissioner for Taxes* v. *A Ltd* [1973–4] 7 MLR 211.

20 *Kamcaca* v. *Nkhota* [1966–8] ALR Mal. 509 at 516.

21 *Kamcaca* v. *Nkhota (No. 2)* [1966–8] ALR Mal. 518 at 523.

22 *In the Estate of Barretta* [1984–6] 11 MLR 110.

23 *Gouveia* v. *Gouveia* [1923–60] ALR Mal. 239 at 241.

24 *Maseko* v. *Maseko* [1973–4] 7 MLR 310.

25 *Westdeutsche Landesbank Girozentrale (Landesbausparkasse)* v. *Horsch* 1992 NR 313 at 314, 1993 (2) SA 342 at 344.

26 *Dowles Manor Properties Ltd* v. *Bank of Namibia* 2005 NR 59.

years of law practice experience in a law firm where he was responsible for practice in the Commonwealth of Independent States, and had frequently given evidence before English courts on aspects of Soviet law, including Ukrainian law, was qualified to give expert evidence on Ukrainian law. It was not necessary for his knowledge and experience to embrace specific branches of Ukrainian law.[27] When proving foreign law, there is no inflexible rule either regarding the production of foreign statutes or the duty of the court itself to examine them. Both matters depend on the circumstances of a case – the governing factor is whether it is necessary to examine the foreign statutes in order to reach a satisfactory conclusion on them.[28]

Where a party seeks to rely on foreign law, the onus lies upon him to prove what the law is. Failing such proof the court must apply Namibian law, adopting the fiction that the foreign law is the same as the law of Namibia. This presumption does not only apply to the common law, but also to law governed by a statute.[29]

Nigeria

Foreign law is a fact that must be pleaded and proved – if one fails to do so, the court will apply Nigerian law.[30] This rule does not extend to laws of states within the Nigerian federation; statute compels Nigerian courts to take judicial notice of laws of states within the federation.[31] Under the Evidence Act 2011, when a court has to decide a point of foreign law, the opinions upon that point of persons especially skilled in such foreign law (experts) are considered relevant facts. The opinions of experts who are acquainted with such law in their profession are regarded as admissible evidence. Such experts may produce before the court, books which they declare to be works of authority upon the foreign law in question. After receiving all necessary explanation from an expert, the court may construe the books for itself. Any question as to the effect of evidence given

[27] *MFV Kapitan Solyanik Ukrainian-Cyprus Insurance Co.* v. *Namack International (Pty) Ltd* 1999 (2) SA 926, 1997 NR 200.

[28] Ibid.

[29] *Dorbly Vehicle Trading & Finance Co. (Pty) Ltd* v. *Nekwaya*, Case No. A 191.98 (High Court, Namibia, 1998).

[30] *Murmansk State Steamship Line* v. *Kano Oil Millers Ltd* [1974] (3) ALR Comm. 192; *Ogunro* v. *Ogedengbe* [1960] 5 FSC 137.

[31] Evidence Act 2011, s. 122(2), *Peenok Ltd* v. *Hotel Presidential Ltd* (1982) 12 SC 1; *Benson* v. *Ashiru* [1967] 1 All NLR 184.

with respect to foreign law is decided by the judge.[32] In determining whether a person is 'especially skilled', the test is always the knowledge and experience of the particular witness and whether the evidence justifies the conclusion that he or she is especially skilled. This means no more than special knowledge, training or experience in the matter in question.[33] In line with this, it was held that a Russian lawyer and head of the legal department of Sovfracht, a state-operated firm of Shipping Brokers in Russia, qualified as an expert on Russian law.[34]

South Africa

To a South African court, each aspect of foreign law – the law of a state recognised by South Africa[35] – is a factual question and evidence on any aspect thereof should emanate from someone with the necessary expertise.[36] However, it is not a factual question whether foreign law applies – that is a question of law.[37] A senior consultant in a tax and legal unit of an accounting firm in Maputo, who was legally qualified and possessed extensive experience of the Mozambican legal system, qualified as an expert witness.[38] The onus rests on the person who relies on foreign law to prove it.[39] Unless it is otherwise adequately proven to the satisfaction of the judge, the foreign law is presumed to be the same as South African law.[40] This presumption is of general application; it applies to both statute and common law.[41] However, the courts have cautioned against its unthinking invocation.[42]

[32] Evidence Act 2011, ss. 68 and 69; *Melwani* v. *Chanhira Corp.* [1995] 6 NWLR 438; *Bhojwani* v. *Bhojwani* [1995] 7 NWLR 349.

[33] *Ajami* v. *The Comptroller of Customs* (1952–5) 14 WACA 34; *Ajami* v. *The Comptroller of Customs* (1952–5) 14 WACA 37.

[34] *Murmansk State Steamship Line* v. *Kano Oil Millers Ltd* 1974 (3) ALR Comm. 192.

[35] *Ocean Commodities Inc.* v. *Standard Bank of SA Ltd* 1978 (2) SA 367 at 376; *Standard Bank of SA Ltd* v. *Ocean Commodities Inc.* 1980 (2) SA 175 at 181 and 183.

[36] *Schlesinger* v. *Commissioner of Inland Revenue* 1964 (3) SA 389 at 396; *Atlantic Harvesters of Namibia (Pty) Ltd* v. *Unterweser Reederei Gmbh of Bremen* 1986 (4) SA 865.

[37] *Burchell* v. *Anglin* 2010 (3) SA 48 at 54–9.

[38] *Skilya Property Investments (Pty) Ltd* v. *Lloyds of London Underwriting* 2002 (3) SA 765.

[39] *Anderson* v. *The Master* 1949 (4) SA 660.

[40] *Rogaly* v. *General Imports (Pty) Ltd* 1948 (1) SA 1216; *Harnischfeger Corp.* v. *Appleton* 1993 (4) SA 479; *Estate H* v. *Estate H* 1952 (4) SA 168; *Bank of Lisbon* v. *Optichem Kunsmis (Edms) Bpk* 1970 (1) SA 447; *Deutsche Bank* v. *Moser* 1999 (4) SA 216.

[41] *Bank of Lisbon* v. *Optichem Kunsmis (Edms) Bpk* 1970 (1) SA 447; *Rogaly* v. *General Imports (Pty) Ltd* 1948 (1) SA 1216.

[42] *ITT Continental Baking Co.* v. *Registrar of Trade Marks* 1980 (2) SA 127.

When proving foreign law, it is not enough for an expert merely to refer to the decision of a foreign court where an interpretation of the meaning and effect of a statute has been given. The expert should at least state the *ratio* of the decision on which he or she relies. The court is not bound to apply a foreign decision as evidence of foreign law if it is satisfied, on all the evidence, that the decision does not accurately represent the foreign law. Where the expert does not justify his or her interpretation of a foreign statute, the court is free to apply its own interpretation, or at least apply the presumption that the rules of interpretation under the foreign law would be the same as in South Africa.[43] Put more emphatically, a South African court is not bound by expert opinion on foreign law; it can look at the text of foreign law and make its own judgment as to its meaning.[44]

Section 1(1) of the Law of Evidence Act 1988 empowers the court to take judicial notice of foreign law insofar as it can be 'ascertained readily and with sufficient certainty'.[45] Access to authoritative sources is an important consideration when applying this provision.[46] Relying on the provision, courts have taken judicial notice of the Family Law (Scotland) Act 1985 as the law regulating the proprietary consequence of marriage in Scotland,[47] prescription in Greece,[48] as well as aspects of English and German civil procedure.[49]

Swaziland

Where a transaction is governed by foreign law, it must be proved as a fact by a practitioner duly admitted in that country.[50]

43 *Continental Illinois National Bank* v. *Greek Seamen's Pension Fund* 1989 (2) SA 515 at 544.

44 *Atlantic Harvesters of Namibia (Pty) Ltd* v. *Unterweser Reederei Gmbh of Bremen* 1986 (4) SA 865 at 874; *Standard Bank of South Africa Ltd* v. *Ocean Commodities Inc.* 1983 (1) SA 276 at 294.

45 *Harnischfeger Corp.* v. *Appleton* 1993 (4) SA 479; *Hlophe* v. *Mahlalela* 1998 (1) SA 449; B. S. C. Martin, 'Judicial Notice of Foreign Law' (1998) 31 *Comparative and International Law Journal of Southern Africa* 60; B. Martin, 'The Ascertainment of Foreign Law by Means of Judicial Notice' (1997) 8 *Stellenbosch Law Review* 377; A. J. Kerr, 'Judicial Notice of Foreign and Customary Law' (1994) 111 *South African Law Journal* 577.

46 *Harnischfeger Corp.* v. *Appleton* 1993 (4) SA 479.

47 *Hassan* v. *Hassan* 1998 (2) SA 589.

48 *Monokandilos* v. *Generale Des Carriers et Des Mines SA*, Case No. 11261/2001 (High Court, South Africa, 2010).

49 *C. Hoare & Co.* v. *Runewitsch* 1997 (1) SA 338; *Holz* v. *Harksen* 1995 (3) SA 521.

50 *Bonham* v. *Master Hardware (Pty) Ltd*, Civil Trial 294/08 (High Court, Swaziland, 2009); *Southern Textiles (Pty) Ltd* v. *Taga Investments*, Civil Case No. 4223/2007 (High Court, Swaziland, 2009).

Tanzania

Foreign law is a matter of fact and cannot be invoked without pleading it.[51] Under the Evidence Act 1967, when a court has to determine a point of foreign law, the opinions of persons possessing special knowledge, skill, experience or training in such foreign law (experts) are taken as relevant facts.[52] It has been held that the 'German law' current in Tanzania prior to and/or during the occupation by British forces was not foreign law to be proved by expert evidence, but lay within judicial notice of the court. Under German law, the court referred to laws prevailing in Tanganyika (now Tanzania) at the time when Tanzania was under German administration.[53]

Uganda

When a Ugandan court has to decide a point of foreign law, opinions on that point are admissible if given by persons especially skilled in such foreign law.[54] As regards the law of England, the court may dispense with the need for proof by expert evidence, and instead rely on recognised treatises on English law such as the *Halsbury's Laws of England*.[55]

Zambia

In *Mwiba* v. *Mwiba*,[56] the issue of the nature of a marriage fell to be decided by Rhodesian law. However, there was no proof of that law. The court embarked on its own research and took judicial notice of the fact that marriages among indigenous Africans, particularly in Central Africa, do not resemble Christian marriages and were potentially polygamous.

Zimbabwe

Under section 25 of the Civil Evidence Act, a Zimbabwean court shall not take judicial notice of the law of any foreign country or

[51] *Auto Garage Ltd* v. *Motokov* [1972] 1 ALR Comm. 17.
[52] Evidence Act 1967, s. 47(1).
[53] *Land Officer* v. *The Motor Mart and Exchange* [1953–7] TLR 295.
[54] Evidence Act 1909, s. 43; *Amrit Goyal* v. *Hari Chand Goyal*, Misc. App. No. 649 of 2001 (High Court, Uganda, 2003).
[55] *F. L. Kaderbhai* v. *Shamsherali Zaver Virji*, Civil Appeal No. 10 of 2008 (Supreme Court, Uganda, 2010).
[56] (1980) ZR 175.

territory,[57] nor shall it presume that such law is the same as Zimbabwean law.[58] Any person who, in the opinion of a court, is suitably qualified to do so on account of his/her knowledge or experience, shall be competent to give expert evidence as to the law of any foreign country or territory, whether or not he/she has acted, or is entitled to act, as a legal practitioner there. Thus, an affidavit from a certified family law specialist in California, USA, who is very familiar with the California laws pertaining to marital dissolutions and related actions, is admissible in terms of the Act in proof of those laws.[59] Section 25 does not render Zimbabwean courts incompetent to interpret foreign laws without resort to expert evidence. Accordingly, the Supreme Court of Zimbabwe is competent to interpret a New Zealand statute without the aid of an expert on New Zealand law.[60] Section 25 further provides that, in considering any issue as to the law of any foreign country or territory, a court may have regard to: any finding or decision purportedly made or given in any court of record in that country or territory where the finding or decision is reported or recorded in citable form;[61] any written law of that country or territory, and any decision given by the High Court or the Supreme Court of Zimbabwe as to the law of that country or territory.

Comments

Foreign law, or law other than that of the forum, is at the heart of private international law. Surprisingly, it often receives only marginal treatment in academic works on private international law.[62] Whether or not a dispute involving foreign elements goes to trial, issues related to foreign

[57] Historically, the courts could take judicial notice of foreign law. See *Grauman* v. *Pers* 1970 (1) RLR 130 at 133, where the court took judicial notice of the South African Rules of Court.

[58] *Walker* v. *Industrial Equity Ltd* 1995 (1) ZLR 87.

[59] *G* v. *G* 2003 (5) SA 396, 2002 (2) ZLR 408.

[60] *Registrar-General of Citizenship* v. *Todd* 2002 (2) ZLR 680. See also *G & P Ltd* v. *Commissioner of Taxes* 1960 (4) SA 163 (the court interpreted UK tax legislation without expert evidence); *Mandimika* v. *Mandimika* 1997 (2) ZLR 352 (the court embarked on its own research on the nature of Ghanaian marriage).

[61] A finding or decision shall be taken to be reported or recorded in citable form only if it is reported or recorded in writing in a report, transcript or other document which, if it has been prepared in connection with legal proceedings in Zimbabwe, could be cited as an authority in legal proceedings in Zimbabwe.

[62] See generally R. Fentiman, *Foreign Law in English Courts* (Oxford University Press, 1998); S. Geeroms, *Foreign Law in Civil Litigation, A Comparative and Functional Analysis* (Oxford University Press, 2004).

law are likely to feature prominently in the parties' assessments of their legal positions. In court, the bar and bench are often confronted with difficult questions, including the nature of foreign law, how it should be proved and what happens if it is not satisfactorily proved.

The principle that foreign law is a fact is well entrenched in all the countries under study.[63] From it are derived two other principles, namely that foreign law must be pleaded and proved by evidence. Although foreign law has not been expressly defined in any statute, it is implicit in decided cases that it refers to the laws of other states. Ghana has gone beyond this definition to include the laws of 'an organisation of states to the extent that such law is not part of the law of Ghana'.[64] To treat international law in the same way as national law appears to be a departure from the English common law position – the position of the legal system on which the legal systems of Commonwealth African countries are founded.[65] Indeed, other than the statutory language, there is no decided case that supports the view that courts in Ghana (and indeed in any of the other countries) treat international law as a category of fact which must be pleaded and proved by expert evidence. This is a sound position the courts have taken. Unlike foreign law, judges learn international law as part of their legal education and international law is not country-specific. It cannot therefore be presumed that judges are not cognizant of principles of international law. It also remains to be decided into which category – fact or law – non-state law, such as the *lex mercatoria* and other principles developed by private organisations, would be placed. Non-state law is likely to be treated as fact which must be pleaded and proved with evidence.

The fact that foreign law has to be pleaded implies a judge cannot of his/her own motion introduce foreign law, let alone embark on independent research to ascertain it. In other words, unless foreign law is pleaded, the courts will decide a case as a purely domestic one. An exception to this appears in Botswana. A Botswanan court is given the discretion, wherever it considers it 'necessary or expedient for the proper disposal of any action', to remit the facts of the case for the opinion of the

[63] See also the Supreme Court of Somalia case of *Adan Deria Gedi* v. *Sheikh Salim El Amoudi* 1964 (1) ALR Comm. 385.

[64] Evidence Act 1974, s. 1(2).

[65] *Trendtex Trading Corp.* v. *Central Bank of Nigeria* [1977] 2 WLR 356 at 377; I. A. Hunter, 'Proving Foreign and International Law in the Courts of England and Wales' (1977–8) 18 *Virginia Journal of International Law* 665.

appropriate Commonwealth or foreign court.[66] However, there is no reported case in which this discretion has been exercised.

Expert evidence is required to prove foreign law in all the countries under study. It remains within the courts' power to determine who qualifies as an expert. However, neither the courts nor statutes have insisted on any special qualifications: academics, legal practitioners and persons with legal knowledge acquired through experience or observation have all been held to qualify as experts. This flexibility is appropriate as courts are not bound by expert opinion and remain ultimate judges of what constitutes foreign law. There is no limit on the scope of materials that could be relied on by experts when proving foreign law – statutes, judicial decisions, textbooks, journal articles and affidavits have all been held admissible, provided they meet the requisite national rules on admissibility.

There is a rebuttable presumption (codified by statute in Ghana) that foreign law is the same as the *lex fori*. This presumption has been criticised,[67] and in Zimbabwe, statutorily abrogated.[68] The presumption operates as the fall-back rule in cases where a party who relies on foreign law has been unable to satisfactorily prove it, that is, on the balance of probabilities, or where foreign law cannot be ascertained.[69] On the other hand, in appropriate cases, such as where the court is of the opinion that the application of a presumption would occasion injustice, or that it would be wholly artificial to apply the *lex fori*, it is open to the court to decide that the party on whom the burden of proof lies has failed to establish his case – a failure to prove foreign law is a failure to discharge the burden of proof.

There is division among the countries under study as to whether a court can take judicial notice of foreign law. Courts in South Africa are allowed by statute to do that, but Zimbabwe courts are statutorily prevented from doing so.[70] In Lesotho, there is judicial support for courts

[66] Commonwealth and Foreign Law Ascertainment Act 1910.

[67] See, e.g., *Dicey, Morris & Collins*, para. 9–025. But see *Bank of Lisbon* v. *Optichem Kunsmis (Edms) Bpk* 1970 (1) SA 447 at 451.

[68] Civil Evidence Act 1992, s. 25(1).

[69] E. Khan, 'What Happens in a Conflicts Case when the Governing Foreign Law is Not Proved?' (1970) 87 *South African Law Journal* 145; C. Wesley, 'The Presumption that Foreign Law is the Same as the Local Law: An Absolute Tradition Revised' (1996) 37 *Codicillus* 36.

[70] Historically, this position had judicial support in South Africa. See *Schlesinger* v. *Commissioner of Inland Revenue* 1964 (3) SA 389 at 396.

taking judicial notice of foreign law, or at least South African law, but the Botswanan courts have cautions against doing that, even in respect of South African law. There is merit in courts taking judicial notice of foreign laws, especially the laws of legal systems with which they have much in common.[71] Many aspects of South African law would be familiar to a Botswanan judge because both countries share the Roman-Dutch legal tradition. Similarly, aspects of English common law will not be unfamiliar to a Ghanaian or Nigerian judge. It was observed in *G & P Ltd* v. *Commissioner of Taxes* that 'the reason for the rule requiring evidence to prove foreign law is the lack of familiarity of a local court with foreign law. The more familiar the local court is with the relevant topic of foreign law, so the need for evidence diminishes in inverse ratio.'[72]

However, law always displays its own unique domestic subtleties and nuances that are likely to be unfamiliar to an external observer. It may not always be appropriate for a judge to make authoritative pronouncements about foreign law and proceed to base a decision on it without recourse to the opinion of persons well tutored in it, or until after an adversarial inquiry to test the soundness of such opinion. Indeed, even in South Africa where courts are allowed to take judicial notice of foreign law, this can only be done in instances where foreign law can be 'ascertained readily and with sufficient certainty'. Similarly, in *Mohapi* v. *Motleleng*,[73] Justice Schutz observed: 'I think it would be the height of unreality for judges sitting in Lesotho who ordinarily practise in South Africa not to take judicial notice of South African law. But I should not be taken as holding that Lesotho judges should at all times and in all circumstances take judicial notice of South African law'.

Exclusion of foreign law

Ghana

A court in Ghana may exclude the application of foreign law where its application or the results thereof would be inconsistent with the public policy of Ghana. In *In re. Kariyavoulas (Deceased); Donkor* v. *Greek Consul-General*,[74] the deceased, a Greek national, had married a

[71] F. Tsikata, 'Proving Familiar Foreign Law' (1987–8) *Review of Ghana Law* 249; E. Khan, 'Proving the Laws of our Friends and Neighbours' (1965) 82 *South African Law Journal* 133.
[72] 1960 (4) SA 163 at 168. [73] [1985–6] LAC 316 at 321–2. [74] [1973] 2 GLR 52.

Ghanaian woman under customary law while resident in Ghana. They had two children. In an application for letters of administration, it was argued that the marriage was void under Greek law (the law of the domicile of the deceased). It was held that, even if this was the case, the court would uphold the validity of the marriage on the grounds of public policy. The court held that allowing the law of the domicile of a foreign man who has married a Ghanaian woman in Ghana to defeat the marriage would adversely affect the latter and, in such a situation, it is important for the court to protect citizens of Ghana. In this instance, this involved excluding the application of foreign law.

South Africa

Public policy provides a basis for excluding application of the *lex causae*. However, the mere fact that a foreign statute embodied concepts not recognised by South African law did not of itself constitute grounds for refusing to enforce it.[75] Accordingly, it was held that there was nothing contrary to South African public policy in enforcing a foreign judgment given on the basis of an Israeli statute that required a party to pay compensation for not negotiating in good faith.[76]

Courts in South Africa will not enforce foreign revenue laws. In *Commissioner of Taxes, Federation of Rhodesia* v. *McFarland*,[77] a case on the enforcement of a foreign judgment, it was held that the courts had no jurisdiction to entertain legal proceedings involving the enforcement of the revenue laws of another state. It was reasoned that the fact of allowing a foreign state, whether directly or indirectly, to obtain a judgment in another country for taxes imposed on all those it considered as sharing in its economic or social life, would amount to judicial intervention in the direct derogation of that state's territorial supremacy.[78] It has, however, been held that the foreign revenue rule does not apply where a liquidator, an official assignee, or trustee of an insolvent estate is seeking to recover property which would, in due course of administration, benefit ordinary creditors as well as a state's revenue authorities. In such a case, a foreign trustee, liquidator or assignee is not in substance seeking to enforce the revenue laws of a foreign country.[79]

[75] *Eden* v. *Pienaar* 2001 (1) SA 158. [76] *Eden* v. *Pienaar* 2001 (1) SA 158.
[77] 1965 (1) SA 470. [78] See also *Jones* v. *Borland SSC* 1969 (4) SA 29.
[79] *Priestley* v. *Clegg* 1985 (3) SA 955.

A South African court will not directly or indirectly enforce the exchange control regulations of another state.[80] Foreign law will not be recognised so as to give it extra-territorial application or effect. Accordingly, foreign exchange control legislation cannot invalidate property transfer transactions that are subject to South African law as the *lex situs*.[81]

Comments

It is not in all cases that a court, after finding the applicable law and its content, will go ahead and apply it.[82] Statute and the common law define situations in which a court may exclude the application of foreign law.[83] There have been relatively very few cases decided on this subject. One reason for this could be that cases where courts in the countries under study have been confronted with the actual application of foreign law are relatively few compared with cases dealing with issues such as jurisdiction in international matters. The principle that a court will not enforce foreign revenue law or foreign law whose application would contravene domestic public policy appears well entrenched in the common law tradition. For example, Ghanaian and South African decisions support this. Furthermore, it is unlikely that other countries will depart from this when confronted with an appropriate case.[84] There is, however, no comprehensive definition of the concepts of 'public policy' and 'revenue law', although admittedly, defining both concepts to delimit their scope is not an easy task.[85] The absence of definition leaves open the prospect that they could be inappropriately invoked.

[80] *Ocean Commodities Inc.* v. *Standard Bank of SA Ltd* 1978 (2) SA 367; *Standard Bank of SA Ltd* v. *Ocean Commodities Inc.* 1980 (2) SA 175.

[81] *Standard Bank of SA Ltd* v. *Ocean Commodities Inc.* 1980 (2) SA 175.

[82] See generally E. Spiro, 'Must Foreign Law be Applied?' (1979) 12 *Comparative and International Law Journal of Southern Africa* 319.

[83] Statutory exclusions of foreign law are also dealt with in other parts of this book, e.g. limitations on party autonomy, applicable law in matrimonial causes, and the recognition and enforcement of judgments and awards.

[84] But see T. A. Ijohor, 'Foreign Revenue Laws and the Nigerian Conflict of Laws' (2003) 2 *Benue State University Law Journal* 107.

[85] In *Dale Power Systems Plc* v. *Witt & Busch Ltd* [2001] 8 NWLR 699, [2001] 33 WRN 63, the Nigerian court defined public policy as the community sense and common conscience extended and applied throughout the state to matters of public morals, health, safety, welfare and the like.

The propriety of the foreign revenue rule is open to question. Indeed, the policy rationales for the rule have not been critically discussed by the courts.[86] It is suggested that in cases of tax evasion, it would be inappropriate for courts to side with the tax evader and not assist a foreign government to recover the taxes due. To assist a taxpayer to evade his/her legal obligation is, arguably, a negation of international comity. However, it may be the case that, rather than the judicial abrogation of the rule or the adoption of a case-by-case approach to its application, a more appropriate course would be for states to conclude treaties that allow for recovering taxes in their respective jurisdictions.[87] As Justice Vieyra observed, 'if it is in the modern world desirable that the tax-gatherer be permitted to pursue his claims beyond the domestic confines ... such must be sought by way of conventions and treaties'.[88]

[86] R. D. Leslie, 'The Non-Enforcement of Foreign Revenue Laws' (1976) 93 *South African Law Journal* 46; E. Khan, 'Enforcement of Foreign Revenue Law' (1954) 71 *South African Law Journal* 275.

[87] See, e.g., *Joint Council of Europe – OECD Convention on Mutual Administrative Assistance in Tax Matters*, 25 January 1988, 28 ILM 1160 (1988).

[88] *Commissioner of Taxes, Federation of Rhodesia* v. *McFarland* 1965 (1) SA 470 at 474.

3

Domicile

Multilateral conflict rules are a key aspect of the private international law regimes in the countries under study. Such a rule consists in two parts, namely the category and the connecting factor. The category presents the issue to be decided, such as the validity of a marriage or the capacity to enter into a contract. The connecting factor points to the legal system whose law should be used to resolve that issue. Connecting factors act as signposts to the appropriate legal system.

Domicile is one such important signpost. The question of whether a natural or legal person is domiciled in a named country can be important in many fields of private international law, but particularly so in the areas of jurisdiction, family and property law. Among the issues addressed in this chapter are the different categories of domicile, when a person can be said to be domiciled in a country or a particular place, what must be established to prove such domicile, and whether a person can change their domicile and how.

Domicile of origin and domicile of choice

Botswana

The legal position[1] is well summed up in *Naude* v. *Naude*.[2] Whether a person has abandoned his domicile of origin is a question of fact to be proved on a balance of probabilities. To determine whether a person has succeeded in establishing a domicile of choice, the court takes into account several factors, including the length of time the person has lived in the country of his/her alleged domicile of choice; how frequently he/she has

[1] See generally J. Kiggundu, 'The Law of Domicile in Botswana: The Need for Reform' (1990) 2 *African Journal of International and Comparative Law* 626; A. J. G. M. Sanders, 'The Expatriate Contract Worker and the Acquisition of a Domicile of Choice – The Botswana Position' (1983) 100 *South African Law Journal* 705.

[2] 2002 (1) BLR 30. See also *Dance* v. *Dance* 1975 (2) BLR 39; *Dance* v. *Dance (2)* 1976 BLR 43.

visited the country whose domicile he/she alleges to have abandoned; whether he/she owns any movable property in the country of his/her alleged domicile of choice; his/her level of investment in that country, and whether he/she retains any ties with, or has any property in, the country whose domicile he/she alleges to have relinquished. The court has to look at all factors before it can be satisfied that it is safe to accept such evidence.

A person who claims to have acquired a Botswanan domicile of choice must demonstrate a settled intention to remain there permanently,[3] but it is not necessary for there to be the intention never to change the new country of domicile.[4] A temporary right of residence in a country is not an automatic bar to acquiring domicile there,[5] but neither citizenship nor continuous residence per se is sufficient basis for claiming the domicile of a particular state.[6] Evidence of a plaintiff's state of mind is an important, albeit inconclusive, factor. Thus, where a party to proceedings where the issue of domicile is involved gives evidence in positive and unequivocal terms regarding the abandonment of his/her domicile of origin and the intention to acquire a new domicile, that evidence should not be rejected on the sole grounds that there is a strong motive for giving it, provided he/she appears to the court to be a credible witness and there is no conduct that is inconsistent with their testimony.[7]

Gambia

Gambian law recognises two main classes of domicile – domicile of origin, which is acquired at birth, and domicile of choice, which could be acquired at any time. To acquire a Gambian domicile of choice, it should be affirmatively shown that the *propositus* is resident in Gambia with an intention to reside there indefinitely. Residence alone, without that state of mind, is insufficient. In other words, residence that is temporary, involuntary, and unaccompanied by any intention to make Gambia one's permanent home will not suffice to enable a person to acquire a Gambian domicile of choice.[8]

Ghana

Ghanaian courts have emphasised the distinction between domicile and nationality. A person's nationality, apart from naturalisation, depends on

[3] *Jeffreys* v. *Jeffreys* 1973 (1) BLR 42.
[4] *Kenyon* v. *Kenyon* 1974 (1) BLR 2.
[5] *Sergeant* v. *Sergeant* 1983 BLR 61.
[6] *Ucanda* v. *Ucanda* 1989 BLR 21.
[7] *Scarr* v. *Scarr* 1971 (2) BLR 44.
[8] *Siwingwa* v. *Siwingwa* [1994] GR 276.

the place of birth or parentage, but domicile is constituted by residence in a particular country *animo manendi*. A person may be a national of one country but domiciled in another.[9] Accordingly, a naturalised American does not automatically lose his or her Ghanaian domicile of origin.[10] Whether a person is domiciled in Ghana is determined by the *lex fori*.[11] A person whose domicile is the object of inquiry must prove *animus manendi*; he or she must have formed a fixed and settled purpose of making their home in the country of residence.[12] An assertion that one has applied for Ghanaian citizenship is not enough evidence of an intention to live permanently in Ghana,[13] nor will a mere statement of intention from a petitioner, without any supporting evidence of extraneous facts, suffice to prove a change of domicile of choice.[14] Long residence – in this instance twenty-three years – does not equate to acquisition of domicile: residence and domicile are distinct concepts.[15]

Kenya

Kenya's law on domicile is largely codified in statute.[16] Under it, no person may have more than one domicile at any time and no person shall be deemed to be without a domicile.[17] Although a person may have left the country of his or her domicile with the intention of never returning, that domicile persists until a new domicile is acquired.[18] Where a person, who is not under a disability, takes up residence in a country other than that of their domicile, with the intention of making it their permanent home, or where, being resident in a country other than that of their domicile, they decide to make that country their permanent home, they shall, as from the date of so taking up residence or of such a decision (as the case may be), acquire domicile in that country and cease to have their former domicile.[19] A person may intend or decide to make a country his

[9] *Republic* v. *Mallet, Ex p. Braun* [1975] 1 GLR 68.
[10] *Amponsah* v. *Amponsah* [1997–8] 1 GLR 43.
[11] *Omane* v. *Poku* [1972] 1 GLR 295 upheld in *Omane* v. *Poku* [1973] 2 GLR 66.
[12] *Abu-Jaudeh* v. *Abu-Jaudeh* [1972] 2 GLR 444. See also *Davis* v. *Randall* [1962] 1 GLR 1.
[13] *Abu-Jaudeh* v. *Abu-Jaudeh* [1972] 2 GLR 444.
[14] *Simpson* v. *Simpson* [1960] GLR 105.
[15] *Abu-Jaudeh* v. *Abu-Jaudeh* [1972] 2 GLR 444.
[16] Law of Domicile Act 1970.
[17] Law of Domicile Act 1970, s. 10(1).
[18] Law of Domicile Act 1970, s. 10(2).
[19] Law of Domicile Act 1970, s. 8(1). Mere residence in a country is not enough to confer domicile, but it has to be accompanied by requisite intention, which in turn has to be proved by evidence or necessary inference (*Ender* v. *Ender* [2008] 2 EA 105).

or her permanent home even though they would contemplate leaving it should circumstances change.[20]

The courts always view change from domicile of origin to domicile of choice as a serious matter. The standard of proof required is, accordingly, a high one; the intention to acquire a new domicile must be proved with perfect clearness.[21] On the other hand, to require that a change in domicile of origin must be proved with 'perfect clearness' is not to demand too high a standard of proof. The meaning to be attached to the phrase 'with perfect clearness' may be a matter of opinion. The standard of proof depends in some measure on the allegation.[22]

Lesotho

A person is domiciled in the country where, for legal purposes, he or she is presumed to be present at all times. A person of full juristic capacity can freely choose where he or she wants to be domiciled. To give effect to that choice, they must actually take up residence in the chosen country and form a fixed intention of residing there permanently, of abandoning the existing domicile, and acquiring a new one. Thus, the mere fact that a person takes up residence in another country to secure medical treatment does not mean that he or she has abandoned his or her domicile of origin.[23]

A party's *ipse dixit* does not usually suffice on the issue of domicile; it must be shown at least that the probabilities support the claim.[24] A person's residence in a country is prima facie evidence that he or she is domiciled in that country and there is a rebuttable presumption that domicile grows in strength with the length of residence. The burden of proving a change of domicile lies upon the person who alleges that a change of domicile has occurred. If the evidence before the court conflicts to the point that it cannot elicit with certainty what the resident's intention is, the court will decide in favour of the existing domicile.[25]

[20] Law of Domicile Act 1970, s. 8(1).

[21] *Schiratti* v. *Schiratti* [1976–80] 1 KLR 870; *Field* v. *Field* [1964] EA 43.

[22] *Field* v. *Field* [1964] EA 43.

[23] *Maphathe* v. *Maphathe*, CIV/APN/479/02 (High Court, Lesotho, 2004).

[24] *Binns* v. *Binns* (1980–4) LAC 14, 1980 (1) LLR 18; *Fischer* v. *Fischer*, CIV/T/302/85 (High Court, Lesotho, 1985).

[25] *Lepelesana* v. *Lepelesana* [1977] LLR 190; *Mokoena* v. *Mokoena*, C of A (CIV) No. 2 of 2007 (Court of Appeal, Lesotho, 2007).

Malawi

The domicile of origin adheres to a person and prevails until it is plain *de animo et facto* that he or she has acquired a domicile of choice. It requires nothing short of the strongest evidence to show that a person's domicile of origin has been displaced by a domicile of choice, with a clear, unequivocal and fixed intention of permanently abandoning one's domicile of origin.[26] The existence of a clearly foreseen and reasonably anticipated contingency to force the *propositus* back to the country of one's domicile of origin may defeat a claim that one has abandoned that domicile.[27] The courts have cautioned against placing undue emphasis on the element of permanency in relation to residence; the intention to reside should be unlimited in period, but not irrevocable in character.[28] Nor should courts treat a *propositus*'s word as conclusive proof of change in domicile.[29] A person does not become domiciled in Malawi solely by virtue of being employed there.[30] However, twenty-three years of residence, coupled with an intention not to leave Malawi, has been held sufficient to acquire a Malawian domicile of choice.[31]

Namibia

Under Namibian law a person is always free to choose his *domicilium*.[32] Domicile and the place of a person's residence are closely connected.[33] Residence is presumptive evidence of domicile, but only if accompanied by the necessary *animus*. The person claiming a change in domicile bears the burden of proving it on the balance of probabilities.[34] Whether residence is accompanied by the necessary *animus manendi* is to be inferred from the facts of a case. The *animus manendi* requirement of domicile may consist of an intention to reside permanently or for

[26] *Brown* v. *Brown*, Matrimonial Cause No. 9 of 2002 (High Court, Malawi, 2002). See also *Whitelock* v. *Whitelock* [1978–80] 9 MLR 43; *Bond* v. *Bond* [1984–6] 11 MLR 87; *Gray* v. *Gray* [1923–60] ALR Mal. 160; *Kaunda* v. *Kaunda* [1993] 16(2) MLR 545.

[27] *Whitelock* v. *Whitelock* [1978–80] 9 MLR 43.

[28] *Jervis* v. *Jervis* [1968–70] ALR Mal. 119.

[29] *Coombe* v. *Coombe* [1923–60] ALR Mal. 115.

[30] *Msindo* v. *Msindo*, Civil Cause No. 67 of 2006 (High Court, Malawi, 2006).

[31] *Dorrington* v. *Dorrington* [1993] 16(1) MLR 73.

[32] Sections 22 and 23 of the Immigration Act 1993 contain specific rules on the acquisition and loss of domicile for the purposes of the Act.

[33] *Oliver No* v. *Insolvent Estate D Lidchi* 1998 NR 31.

[34] *Main No* v. *Van Tonder No* 2006 (1) NR 389 at 394.

unlimited time in the country of choice and it does not require an intention never to change the new country of domicile.[35]

A person lacks capacity to acquire a domicile of choice in Namibia for as long as his or her residence remains unlawful.[36] An illegal immigrant cannot, as long as he continues to be unlawfully resident in the country of choice, acquire the domicile of that country.[37] A court has observed that the view of the Roman-Dutch authorities, which recognises the possibility that a person could have more than one domicile, has not been rejected in modern case law and probably still reflects the position at common law.[38]

Nigeria

The onus of proving a domicile has been chosen in substitution for the domicile of origin lies upon the party who asserts that fact, which must be established with perfect clearness, while taking into account all the facts. Accordingly, a decision on the question of domicile of choice requires detailed analysis and an assessment of the available facts to discover the mind of the party concerned. For that purpose, residence and domicile are distinct concepts.[39] A domicile of origin is not lost until a domicile of choice is acquired; indeed, it is never destroyed, but remains in abeyance when a new domicile is chosen, and revives when the new domicile is abandoned.[40] A court has cast doubt on the view that a person cannot have more than one domicile at any given time.[41]

South Africa

Issues of domicile, including the capacity to acquire a domicile, are determined by the *lex fori*.[42] By statute, every person aged 18 years and above and every person who, by law, has the status of a major (excluding any person who does not have the mental capacity to make a rational choice) is competent to acquire a domicile of choice, regardless of sex or

[35] *Gravato NO* v. *Redelinghuys*, Case No. A 401/2009 (High Court, Namibia, 2012).
[36] *Government of the Republic of Namibia* v. *Getachew* 2008 (1) NR 1 at [42]–[56].
[37] *Minister of Home Affairs* v. *Dickson* 2008 (2) NR 665.
[38] *Main No* v. *Van Tonder No* 2006 (1) NR 389 at 395.
[39] *Bhojwani* v. *Bhojwani* [1995] 7 NWLR 349. See also *Osibamowo* v. *Osibamowo* [1991] 3 NWLR 85; *Omotunde* v. *Omotunde* [2001] 9 NWLR 252.
[40] *Bhojwani* v. *Bhojwani* [1995] 7 NWLR 349.
[41] *Odiase* v. *Odiase* [1965] 2 All NLR 91.
[42] *Ex p. Jones: In re. Jones* v. *Jones* 1984 (4) SA 725.

marital status.[43] Domicile of choice is acquired by a person when he or she is lawfully present at a particular place and has the intention to settle there for an indefinite period.[44] A person shall not lose his or her domicile until they have acquired another one, whether by choice or by operation of law,[45] but no person's domicile of origin shall be automatically revived; the doctrine of revival of domicile is not part of South African law.[46]

Whether a domicile of choice has been acquired or lost is determined on a balance of probabilities.[47] The onus of proving acquisition of domicile of choice is discharged once physical presence is proved and a fixed and deliberate intention to abandon one's previous domicile and settle permanently in South Africa is established. The contemplation of a certain or foreseeable future event at which residence would cease excludes such an intention. If the *propositus* entertains any doubt as to whether or not they will remain, intention to settle permanently is likewise excluded.[48]

There is no absolute rule that debars persons in particular professions from acquiring domicile at the place they are stationed; whether a domicile of choice has been established depends upon the facts of each case. Accordingly, members of the armed forces,[49] consuls of foreign governments[50] and seamen[51] are all capable of acquiring a South African domicile during their period of service in South Africa. Similarly, a prohibited immigrant is not by virtue of mere prohibition debarred from acquiring a South African domicile. However, the possibility that the power of deportation may be exercised renders precarious the character of their residence and could undermine their intention to remain permanently.[52] Indeed, deportation extinguishes the deportee's acquired

43 Domicile Act 1992, s. 1(1).
44 Domicile Act 1992, s. 1(2).
45 Domicile Act 1992, s. 3(1).
46 Domicile Act 1992, s. 3(2); *Grindal* v. *Grindal* 1997 (4) SA 137.
47 Domicile Act 1992, s. 5; *Ley* v. *Ley's Executors* 1951 (3) SA 186; *Senior* v. *Commissioner for Inland Revenue* 1960 (1) SA 709; *Hillard* v. *Hillard*, Case No. 1464/2007 (High Court, South Africa, 2008).
48 *Eilon* v. *Eilon* 1965 (1) SA 703. See also *Smith* v. *Smith* 1952 (4) SA 750; *O'Mant* v. *O'Mant* 1947 (1) SA 26.
49 *Nicol* v. *Nicol* 1948 (2) SA 613; *Hibbs* v. *Wynne* 1949 (2) SA 10; *Ex p. Readings* 1958 (4) SA 432.
50 *Naville* v. *Naville* 1957 (1) SA 280.
51 *Ex p. Pekola* 1951 (3) SA 793.
52 *Van Rensburg* v. *Ballinger* 1950 (4) SA 427. The fact that an immigrant is engaging in activities contrary to the conditions of his residence will, in addition, not automatically undermine his ability to acquire a South African domicile; *Toumbis* v. *Antoniou* 1999 (1) SA 636.

South African domicile, regardless of the intention of the deportee to return.[53] A *propositus* should be capable of exercising their intention to remain permanently, independent of the control of any authority.[54] The fact that the *propositus* continues to owe allegiance to a foreign government and pay taxes to it does not affect their ability to acquire a new domicile.[55]

Tanzania

A person who alleges they have acquired a Tanzanian domicile of choice bears the burden of proving it.[56] The possibility that an enemy alien would be compelled to leave Tanzania after a war does not affect the validity of their current *animus manendi* and, hence, their capacity to acquire a Tanzanian domicile of choice.[57] Long residence alone will not suffice to acquire a Tanzanian domicile of choice. Accordingly, in *Gordon* v. *Gordon*,[58] it was held that the fact that a petitioner had been resident in Tanganyika (now Tanzania) for eighteen years, had most of their interests and ties there, and could indeed be said to have 'joined a new society' fell short of establishing, or even raising a presumption, that they had abandoned their English domicile of origin.

Uganda

The domicile of origin prevails until a new domicile is acquired.[59] A new domicile continues until the former domicile has been resumed or another has been acquired.[60] A man acquires a new domicile by taking up his fixed habitation in a country which is not the domicile of origin. On the other hand, someone may not be considered to have taken up fixed habitation in Uganda merely because they reside there in the exercise of a profession or calling.[61] The burden of proving a change from domicile of origin to domicile of choice is not light; the change must be proved with 'perfect clearness'.[62] There must be sufficient evidence of a settled intention on the part of the *propositus* to remain

[53] *Drakensbergpers BPK* v. *Sharpe* 1963 (4) SA 615.
[54] *Ex p. Glass et Uxor* 1948 (4) SA 379. [55] *Gwambe* v. *Gwambe* 1950 (2) SA 643.
[56] *Taylor* v. *Taylor* [1921–52] 1 TLR 746. [57] *Reinhard* v. *Reinhard* [1921–52] 1 TLR 749.
[58] [1965] EA 87. [59] Succession Act 1906, s. 8.
[60] Succession Act 1906, s. 12. [61] Succession Act 1906, s. 9.
[62] *Santhumayor* v. *Santhumayor Ferris* [1959] EA 204.

in Uganda permanently before the court will hold that they have acquired a Ugandan domicile of choice.[63] However, not having Ugandan nationality does not affect the *animus manendi* to acquire Ugandan domicile of choice.[64]

A person may acquire domicile in Uganda by making and depositing in a designated office a declaration in writing under their own hand of the desire to acquire such domicile, provided they have been resident in Uganda for one year immediately preceding the time the declaration is made.[65] A person who is appointed by the government of a country to be its ambassador, consul or other representative in another country does not acquire a domicile in the latter purely on the basis of residing there in pursuance of the appointment; nor does any other person acquire such domicile solely by reason of residing with that person as part of his or her family or as a servant.[66]

Zambia

The onus is on a person who claims a change in domicile to prove it with evidence of residence and an intention to remain permanently. The court must examine evidence of declarations of intent with great care.[67] It is essential in establishing the acquisition of a domicile of choice that one is 'settled' in the country – to be present in a country merely because it offers better pay is a preference for pay, and not for the country.[68]

Zimbabwe

In Zimbabwean law,[69] domicile is a question of fact, and the facts giving rise to domicile must be placed before the court. A person is domiciled in the place that he or she regards as their permanent home, which is not

[63] *Thornhill* v. *Thornhill* [1964] EA 616; *Aslanidis* v. *Aslanidis* [1967] EA 10.

[64] *Thornhill* v. *Thornhill* [1965] EA 268.

[65] Succession Act 1906, s. 10. It has been held that this provision is relevant only to matters of intestate or testamentary succession; *Santhumayor* v. *Santhumayor Ferris* [1959] EA 204 at 206.

[66] Succession Act 1906, s. 11. [67] *Healy* v. *Healy* 1963 R & N 278.

[68] *Russell* v. *Russell* [1949–54] NRLR 756.

[69] Section 3 of the Immigration Act 1979 contains special rules on domicile for the specific purposes of the Act. For cases discussing the provision, see *Principal Immigration Officer* v. *O'Hara* 1993 (1) ZLR 69; *In re. Hoggart* 1992 (1) ZLR 195; *Baxter* v. *Chief Immigration Officer* 1989 (2) ZLR 320.

necessarily where they reside.[70] Acquisition of domicile of choice is established on the balance of probabilities.[71] To acquire a domicile of choice, what matters is an intention to remain permanently; it does not really matter that there may be obstacles to realising that intention.[72] Thus, mere liability to be deported as an alien does not make it impossible to acquire a domicile of choice, but it is impossible for a person *sui juris* to acquire a domicile of choice in Zimbabwe if their initial entry and residence is unlawful under statute at all times thereafter.[73] A new domicile is not acquired until there is a fixed intention of establishing permanent residence in some other country and this intention has been carried out by actual residence there. Residence in a country without an intention to remain permanently is insufficient for replacing one's existing domicile.[74] A change of domicile requires both an intention to reside indefinitely in a new country *animus manendi* and residence in that country.[75] Thus, where a plaintiff has left their domicile of choice without any intention of settling in another country permanently, they cannot be said to have abandoned that domicile.[76] Moreover, someone can be domiciled in a particular state of Australia, but not in Australia.[77]

Comments

Domicile connects a person[78] to a system of law under which a number of his or her legal relationships are regulated. It is an important connecting factor in the private international law regimes in the countries under study, especially in the areas of choice of law and jurisdiction.[79] The country reports above have focused on the general law on domicile. In

[70] *De Jager* v. *De Jager* 1998 (2) ZLR 419.
[71] *Howard* v. *Howard* [1966] RLR 182, 1966 (2) SA 718.
[72] *Boswinkel* v. *Boswinkel* 1995 (2) ZLR 58.
[73] *Smith* v. *Smith* 1962 R & N 469, 1962 (3) SA 930; E. Spiro, 'Domicile of Illegal Immigrant' (1963) 12 *International and Comparative Law Quarterly* 680. See also Immigration Act 1979, s. 3(2)(3).
[74] *Baxter* v. *Chief Immigration Officer* 1989 (2) ZLR 320.
[75] *Nunes* v. *Nunes* 2003 (1) ZLR 14.
[76] *Mandlbaur* v. *Mandlbaur* 1983 (1) ZLR 26.
[77] *Smith* v. *Smith* 1970 (1) SA 146.
[78] 'Person' here refers to a natural person. Statutes sometimes use domicile in relation to legal persons, such as companies. For a case dealing with the domicile of a company, see *Silverstone (Pty) Ltd* v. *Lobatse Clay Works (Pty) Ltd* 1996 BLR 190, which held that, where a company is incorporated in Botswana and has its registered office in Botswana, it is domiciled in Botswana for jurisdictional purposes.
[79] On domicile as an issue in enforcing foreign judgments, see *Chinatex Oriental Trading Co.* v. *Erskine* 1998 (4) SA 1087.

some of the countries under study, such as Namibia and Zimbabwe, there are special statutory rules on domicile in specific contexts, such as immigration.

The principle that whether a person is domiciled in a particular place is a question for the *lex fori* appears common to all the countries under study. Thus, a person may be considered by a South African court as domiciled in Utopia, even though under the laws of Utopia, he or she is not domiciled there; indeed, the concept of domicile may be unknown to Utopia.

In general, the courts have held – indeed it is codified in statute in South Africa – that acquisition and change of domicile should be proved on the balance of probabilities. However, the courts have used various concepts, such as 'perfect clearness' and 'strongest evidence', which convolute what is entailed in the standard of proof. On this, two things stand out in the jurisprudence. Firstly, it requires stronger evidence to prove abandonment of domicile of origin. Secondly, courts pay attention to all facts relevant to establishing the intention to remain permanently; indeed, deciding whether a domicile has been acquired is a highly factual determination. In addition to the fact that it was borrowed from English jurisprudence, judicial reluctance to readily accept abandonment of domicile of origin could be explained in terms of Africa's colonial history. Most of the older cases deal with the expatriate community in Africa. One can legitimately entertain the suspicion that for such persons, the courts were reluctant to countenance holding they had acquired a domicile of choice in the colonies and therefore have applied to them the laws of a colony.[80]

Even though the notion of intention is at the heart of decisions on acquisition of domicile of choice, the courts have not clearly or definitely specified which test – objective or subjective – is used in assessing that intent. There are *dicta* suggesting that the test is subjective.[81] An important issue, on which there is divergence in approach, is what happens between the time a person loses his or her domicile and the time they acquire a new one. The doctrine of revival of domicile, which holds that

[80] Indeed, Dicey, Morris and Collins note that there is a presumption against the acquisition of a domicile of choice by a person in a country whose religion, manners and customs differ widely from those of his own country. *Dicey, Morris & Collins*, para. 6–050 and the cases cited there.

[81] *Sergeant* v. *Sergeant* 1983 BLR 61 at 63 ('there can be little doubt that the enquiry involved in a case such as this is a subjective one').

on losing a domicile of choice, the domicile of origin revives, has been rejected by statute in Kenya, South Africa and Uganda in favour of the doctrine of persistence. There are, however, no cases or legislation favouring this position in the other countries.

There is some divergence or uncertainty on the influence of illegality of residence or conduct on the capacity to acquire domicile.[82] In South Africa, neither the status of a prohibited immigrant, nor the fact that an immigrant is engaged in activities inconsistent with his or her residence permit, automatically debars them from acquiring a South African domicile of choice. However, in Zimbabwe and Namibia, illegal entry or residence in Zimbabwe and Namibia prevents an immigrant from acquiring a domicile of choice there. It is arguable whether illegality of residence in a foreign country prevents the acquisition of domicile there.[83]

There is further divergence on whether a person can have more than one domicile at any given time. In Kenya, a person cannot have more than one domicile.[84] Similarly, in Uganda, a person can have only one domicile for the purpose of succession to his or her movable property.[85] However, courts in Nigeria and South Africa have cast doubt on the proposition that one cannot have more than one domicile. Indeed, to some commentators, it is useful for a person to be considered domiciled in different places for different purposes.[86] It is also arguable whether African courts should adopt a context-sensitive approach to the meaning of domicile, such that its meaning would vary depending on the purpose for which it is needed.

An important issue that remains largely undecided is that point in time when domicile of choice is acquired. Domicile of origin and dependency are acquired at easily ascertainable periods, such as at birth, marriage or adoption. That is not the case with domicile of choice. Whether it is the date of first residence, forming the intention to remain permanently, or the time a court declaration of a new domicile has been acquired, remains largely uncertain. It appears that it is only in Kenya where this issue is addressed by statute; there, either the date of taking up residence, or of deciding to remain permanently,

[82] The House of Lords has held that illegal residence does not prevent a person from acquiring domicile in England; *Mark* v. *Mark* [2006] 1 AC 98; C. Forsyth, 'The Domicile of the Illegal Resident' (2005) 1 *Journal of Private International Law* 335.

[83] To hold that illegality of residence in a foreign country prevents the acquisition of domicile there would amount to enforcing the public laws of a foreign country.

[84] Law of Domicile Act 1970, s. 10(1). [85] Succession Act 1906, s. 5.

[86] E. Khan, 'Multiple Domiciles' (1965) 82 *South African Law Journal* 147.

suffices.[87] The answer to this question could be particularly important in cases where there have been significant changes in the conflicts rule, or in the substantive law of the *lex causae*.

Significant aspects of the existing law, such as the principles on domicile of origin and domicile of married women, remain unsatisfactory or uncertain. However, except in Kenya, Lesotho, Namibia, South Africa and Uganda there have been no significant attempts at legislative reform. Indeed, the very idea of domicile as a connecting factor has come under attack and alternatives, such as residence, habitual residence and nationality, have been suggested. As will be noticed in parts of this book, various statutes adopt these alternative connecting factors for specific purposes. However, it is unlikely that domicile will lose its pre-eminence in the determination of personal law in the countries under study. While there have been statutory interventions, especially as regards jurisdiction in matrimonial causes, the law on domicile still remains largely dominated by received common law rules, with occasional judicial and academic outcry on specific aspects.

Domicile of dependency

Botswana

A married woman assumes the domicile of her husband on marriage. This assumption of the husband's domicile is by operation of law, and she cannot contract out of it.[88] An order of judicial separation does not change this rule so as to allow the wife to acquire a new domicile.[89] As regards jurisdiction in matrimonial matters, there has been statutory intervention to ameliorate the effect of the rule, but it remains part of Botswanan law despite calls for it to be abolished on the grounds that it is discriminatory.[90]

Kenya

A woman acquires the domicile of her husband on marriage.[91] However, where a marriage is voidable, the wife's domicile is unaffected by the domicile of the husband.[92] An adult married woman is capable of

[87] Law of Domicile Act 1970, s. 8(1).
[88] *Egner* v. *Egner* 1974 (2) BLR 5; *Ucanda* v. *Ucanda* 1989 BLR 21.
[89] *Egner* v. *Egner* 1974 (2) BLR 5.
[90] *Nku* v. *Nku* 1998 BLR 187.
[91] Law of Domicile Act 1970, s. 7.
[92] *Dobbs-Johnson* v. *Dobbs-Johnson* [1950–1] KLR 55.

acquiring an independent domicile of choice.[93] Acquisition of a domicile of choice by a married man does not, of itself, change the domicile of his wife, but the fact that she is present with her husband in the country of his domicile of choice at the time when he acquires that domicile, or subsequently joins him in that country, raises a rebuttable presumption that she has also acquired that domicile.[94]

Every person is deemed to have acquired, at the date of his or her birth, if born legitimate, or deemed to be legitimate, the domicile of their father. If born posthumously, a person acquires the domicile that his or her father had at the date of his death. If a person is born illegitimate, he or she acquires the domicile of the mother.[95] An infant who is a foundling acquires domicile in the country where he or she is found.[96] An infant who is legitimated by the marriage of his or her parents acquires the domicile of the father at the date of the legitimation.[97] An infant whose adoption has been authorised by a court of competent jurisdiction, or recognised by a declaratory decree of a court, acquires the domicile of the adopter or, where they have been adopted by two spouses, that of the husband, as from the date of the order or decree.[98]

The domicile of an infant changes with that of the father, where the infant is born legitimate, is deemed to be legitimate, or has been legitimated, and if the father is dead, with that of the mother.[99] Where the infant is illegitimate, the domicile corresponds to that of the mother. Where the custody of an infant has been entrusted to his mother by decree of a court of competent jurisdiction, his or her domicile shall change with the mother's domicile.[100] Furthermore, the domicile of an infant female who is married changes to that of her husband.[101] The domicile of an infant, other than a female who is married, and whose adoption has been authorised by a court or recognised by the declaratory decree of a court, changes to that of the adopter or, where he or she has been adopted by two spouses, to that of the husband, or, if the husband is dead, to that of the wife.[102]

Lesotho

The domicile of a married woman corresponds to that of her husband. However, where circumstances warrant, it shall be ascertained by

[93] Law of Domicile Act 1970, s. 8(3).
[94] Law of Domicile Act 1970, s. 8(4).
[95] Law of Domicile Act 1970, s. 3.
[96] Law of Domicile Act 1970, s. 4.
[97] Law of Domicile Act 1970, s. 5.
[98] Law of Domicile Act 1970, s. 6.
[99] *Jusab* v. *Gamrai* [2009] 1 EA 164.
[100] Law of Domicile Act 1970, s. 9(1).
[101] Law of Domicile Act 1970, s. 9(2).
[102] Law of Domicile Act 1970, s. 9(3).

reference to the same factors as are applied in the case of any other person capable of acquiring a domicile of choice, irrespective of the date on which the marriage was entered into.[103]

The domicile of a child is the place with which the child is most closely connected and where his or her interests are safeguarded. However, if, in the normal course of events, a child resides either with both parents or with just one of them, it shall be presumed, unless proven to the contrary, that the child's domicile is where the child resides.[104]

Namibia

The domicile of a married woman shall not solely by virtue of marriage be considered to correspond with that of her husband, but shall be ascertained by reference to the same factors as apply in the case of any other individual capable of acquiring a domicile of choice.[105]

The domicile of a child (including a child born outside of marriage[106]) shall be the place with which that child is most closely connected.[107] If, in the normal course of events, a child resides with his or her parents or with just one of them, it shall be presumed, unless indicated to the contrary, that such a child's domicile is where he or she so resides.[108]

Nigeria

By operation of law, a married woman takes the domicile of her husband on the day of marriage.[109] The domicile of a wife follows her husband's and she cannot have a different domicile while the marriage lasts.[110]

South Africa

Under South African law, every person – whether male or female – of the requisite age and providing they have no mental disability, is capable of

[103] Legal Capacity of Married Persons Act 2006, s. 13.

[104] Legal Capacity of Married Persons Act 2006, s. 14.

[105] Married Persons Equality Act 1996, s. 12. [106] Children's Status Act 2006, s. 18.

[107] Married Persons Equality Act 1996, s. 13(1)(a), but see *Main No* v. *Van Tonder No* 2006 (1) NR 389, which held that a legitimate child acquires the domicile of origin of the father at the time of birth. In the case of a child with mental incapacity, and consequently unable to form the necessary *animus manendi* to determine his or her own domicile, only the father has the legal capacity and competence to change the child's domicile.

[108] Married Persons Equality Act 1996, s. 13(1)(b).

[109] *Omotunde* v. *Omotunde* [2001] 9 NWLR 252.

[110] *Machi* v. *Machi* [1960] Lagos LR 103; *Adeyemi* v. *Adeyemi* [1962] Lagos LR 70.

acquiring a domicile.[111] A person outside the scope of this rule is domiciled at the place with which he or she is most closely connected.[112] If, in the normal course of events, a child has his or her home with both or just one of their parents, it shall be presumed, unless shown to the contrary, that the parental home concerned is the child's domicile.[113]

Uganda

A woman acquires the domicile of her husband through marriage.[114] During the subsistence of a marriage, a wife's domicile follows that of her husband. The domicile of a wife no longer follows her husband's if they are separated by the decree of a competent court.[115] An insane person cannot acquire a new domicile in any other way than by following the domicile of another person.[116]

The domicile of origin of every person of legitimate birth is the country where, at the time of the child's birth, the father is domiciled, or, if the child is born posthumously, in the country where the father was domiciled at the time of death.[117] The domicile of origin of an illegitimate child is the country, where at the time of his or her birth, the mother was domiciled.[118] The domicile of a minor follows the domicile of the parent from whom the minor derives his or her domicile of origin, but this does not change with that of the minor's parent if the minor is married, or holds any office or employment in the service of the government, or has set up, with the consent of the parent, in any distinct business.[119]

Zimbabwe

The change of domicile of a minor child depends more upon the intention of the guardian than of the custodian parent in cases where guardianship and custody are separated.[120]

[111] Domicile Act 1992, s. 1. [112] Domicile Act 1992, s. 2(1).
[113] Domicile Act 1992, s. 2(2). [114] Succession Act 1906, s. 14.
[115] Succession Act 1906, s. 15; *Joy Kiggundu* v. *Horace Awori* [2001] Kam. LR 374.
[116] Succession Act 1906, s. 17. [117] Succession Act 1906, s. 6.
[118] Succession Act 1906, s. 7.
[119] Succession Act 1906, s. 13. Except in this instance, a person cannot during minority acquire a new domicile: see s. 16.
[120] *Favard* v. *Favard* 1953 (3) SA 656.

Comments

In addition to domicile of origin and domicile of choice, the common law recognises domicile of dependency. It has been judicially doubted whether this constitutes a different type of domicile.[121] Domicile of dependency is domicile assigned by law to specific groups of people, such as children, wives and persons with mental disabilities.

If there is any aspect of the law of domicile which needs reform in Africa, it is the domicile of dependency. An example is the rule that a woman acquires the domicile of the husband on marriage and is prevented from acquiring an independent domicile during the subsistence of the marriage.[122] Kenya and South Africa have statutorily abrogated the rule and now allow a married woman to acquire an independent domicile. This is not the case in other countries,[123] despite the fact that many writers have been critical of the rule. Similarly, some courts have expressed disquiet with it, but have stopped short of judicially abrogating it.[124] The rule is anachronistic: the product of bygone years. With the spread and constitutional entrenchment of human rights in Africa, its continued application is untenable. It is a palpable violation of the fundamental right of gender equality. As a Nigerian writer long ago observed, 'it must be borne in mind that domicile is not a privilege. Even if it were, we are doing no more than extending to the wife a privilege hitherto enjoyed exclusively by the husband.'[125]

Another issue is the effect of judicial separation on the wife's capacity to acquire an independent domicile. In Botswana, an order of judicial separation does not affect the rule that the wife's domicile follows that of her husband. However, a different position is taken in Uganda.

With the rise of other forms of relationship outside the traditional notion of marriage (i.e. between men and women), and other modes of conceiving children outside a marriage relationship, there is the need to

[121] *Bhojwani* v. *Bhojwani* [1995] 7 NWLR 349 at 364; F. N. Ekwere, 'Is there Domicile of Dependence in Nigerian Conflict of Laws?' (2000) 12 *African Journal of International and Comparative Law* 616.

[122] On the effect of this rule in matrimonial proceedings and how their adverse effects have been ameliorated legislatively, see Ch. 12.

[123] Some countries have, however, created an exception specifically for the purpose of jurisdiction in matrimonial causes. See discussion in Ch. 12.

[124] In *Amponsah* v. *Amponsah* [1997–8] 1 GLR 43 at 45, the court described the rule as not 'progressive'.

[125] I. Oluwole Agbede, '*Lex Domicilii* in Contemporary Nigeria: A Functional Analysis' (1973) 9 *African Legal Studies* 61 at 93.

reconsider the law on the domicile of dependency, in line with the features of these developments. At present, it is only in South Africa that gay and lesbian relationships are legalised.[126] However, it is possible for a court in other countries to be invited to decide, for example, the domicile of two 'married' women or men. Assuming that such a marriage would be recognised, and against the underlying principle that the issues of domicile are determined by the *lex fori*, some interesting domicile-related questions could arise: Does one partner take on the domicile of the other on marriage? Which partner would that be? Do they maintain their independent domiciles?

[126] Civil Union Act 2006.

PART II

Jurisdiction

4

Bases of jurisdiction

An important issue in private international law is the ground or basis upon which a court will have jurisdiction to hear an action or claim. In all the countries under study, the jurisdiction of a court to adjudicate a claim is always conferred by statute. However, no matter how broadly that authority is statutorily phrased, a court cannot adjudicate every claim under the sun that is brought before it. The bases of jurisdiction enable courts to further define their competence, especially in claims involving a foreign element. The bases of jurisdiction may be the product of common law or statute. Moreover, they may be defined in respect of particular causes of action or parties to the action – different bases of jurisdiction may exist for actions *in personam* and actions *in rem* as well as for foreign plaintiffs and defendants.

This chapter deals with the grounds on which the courts in the countries under study will hear a claim involving a foreign element. The focus is on actions *in personam*, especially actions sounding in money. Because of the very distinct nature of the rules in the countries under study, these actions are stated and discussed separately for what may be characterised as 'common law countries'[1] and Roman-Dutch law countries.[2]

The common law countries

Gambia

The foundation of jurisdiction is service. Every suit shall be commenced by a writ of summons.[3] A Gambian court has jurisdiction in an action *in personam* where the defendant is present in Gambia.[4] As regards a

[1] Gambia, Ghana, Kenya, Malawi, Nigeria, Sierra Leone, Tanzania, Uganda and Zambia (hereinafter, 'common law countries').

[2] Botswana, Lesotho, Namibia, South Africa, Swaziland and Zimbabwe (hereinafter, 'Roman-Dutch law countries').

[3] Rules of the High Court, Ord. II, r. 1(1).

[4] *Solo Dabo* v. *Mohammed Abdalla Mousa* [1963–6] GR 22.

defendant outside the jurisdiction, the Rules of the High Court allow for such a defendant to be served outside the jurisdiction. Where the defendant is outside jurisdiction at the time a writ is issued, substituted service within the jurisdiction cannot be used as a means of circumventing the need for service out of the jurisdiction.[5] Service out of the jurisdiction of a writ, or notice of a writ, may be allowed by the court in the following situations where:[6]

(a) the whole subject matter of the action is land situate within the jurisdiction (with or without rents or profits), or the perpetuation of testimony relating to land within the jurisdiction;
(b) an act, deed, will, contract, obligation or liability affecting land situate within the jurisdiction is sought to be construed, rectified, set aside or enforced in the action;
(c) relief is sought against any person domiciled or ordinarily resident within the jurisdiction;
(d) the action is for the administration of the personal estate of a person who died domiciled within the jurisdiction, or for the execution (as to property within the jurisdiction) of the trusts of any instrument of which the person to be served is a trustee, which ought to be executed according to Gambian law;
(e) the action is brought to enforce, rescind, dissolve, annul or otherwise affect a contract or to recover damages or other relief for or in respect of the breach of a contract which: was made within the jurisdiction; was made by or through an agent trading or residing within the jurisdiction on behalf of a principal trading or residing outside the jurisdiction; or is governed by Gambian law. It can also be an action brought against a defendant in respect of a breach committed within the jurisdiction regardless of where the contract was made. This is so even though the breach was preceded or accompanied by a breach outside the jurisdiction which rendered impossible the performance of the part of the contract which ought to have been performed within the jurisdiction;
(f) an action is founded on a tort committed within the jurisdiction;
(g) an injunction is sought as to anything to be done within the jurisdiction or any nuisance within the jurisdiction is sought to be prevented or removed, regardless of whether damages are sought;

[5] *Blell* v. *Isaac* [1997–2001] GR 748.

[6] Rules of the High Court, Ord. VIII, r. 8(a)–(i).

(h) a person out of the jurisdiction is a necessary or proper party to an action properly brought against some other person duly served within the jurisdiction;
(i) the action is by a mortgagee or mortgagor in relation to a mortgage or personal property situate within the jurisdiction, and seeks relief in the form of a sale, foreclosure, delivery of possession by the mortgagor, redemption, reconveyance, delivery of possession by the mortgagee, but does not see any personal judgment or order for the payment of any money due under the mortgage.

These grounds, and the procedures for service out of the jurisdiction, have to be strictly complied with.[7]

Ghana

In actions *in personam*, the jurisdiction of the Ghanaian courts is determined and regulated by common law and statute. The foundation of jurisdiction in international matters is service. As long as the defendant can be served with a writ of summons, the Ghanaian courts will assume jurisdiction over him or her. Thus, the fact that a contract was executed and was to be performed abroad[8] or that a tort was committed abroad[9] does not deny jurisdiction to the courts.

Physical presence is a basis of jurisdiction in international matters. The fact that a defendant is present in Ghana, no matter how briefly, allows the Ghanaian courts to assume jurisdiction over him or her.[10] A defendant who submits to the jurisdiction of a Ghanaian court confers jurisdiction on it to hear a dispute between him or her and the plaintiff. Submission can be by conduct, or through a choice of forum agreement. Thus, a defendant who, on being served with a writ, enters appearance unconditionally and does not move the court to stay proceedings submits to the jurisdiction of the court through his or her conduct.[11]

Under Order 8 of the High Court (Civil Procedure) Rules 2004, no writ shall be served out of the jurisdiction. However, with leave of the

[7] Ibid., Ord. VIII, r. 9 and r. 10; *Joseph Sarjuka Jobe* v. *Jack Alderlifste* (2002–8) 2 GR 535.
[8] *Edusei* v. *Diners Club Suisse SA* [1982–3] GLR 809.
[9] *Wachter* v. *Harlley* [1968] GLR 1069.
[10] *Tafa & Co. (Ghana) Ltd* v. *Tafa & Co. Ltd* [1977] 1 GLR 422.
[11] *Polimex* v. *BBC Builders & Engineers Co. Ltd* [1968] GLR 168; *Moubarak* v. *Holland West Afrika Lijn* (1953) 14 WACA 262.

court, notice of the writ in a specified form can be so served.[12] Order 2, rule 7(5) of the High Court (Civil Procedure) Rules provides that 'no writ, notice of which is to be served out of the jurisdiction, shall be issued without leave of the Court'. One issue that arose under the predecessor of this Order was the time at which the application for leave should be made in cases where the plaintiff contemplates service outside the jurisdiction. In *Lokko* v. *Lokko*,[13] it was held that, where a plaintiff intended to proceed against a defendant resident outside the jurisdiction, the plaintiff had to first obtain leave of the court before issuing the writ. Accordingly, where the plaintiff issued a writ against a defendant resident in New York before obtaining leave, it was held that the writ was incurably bad and, thus, completely null and void.[14] However, in *Shirlstar Container Transport Ltd* v. *Kadas Shipping Co. Ltd*,[15] a modification of this principle was introduced in cases of multiple defendants. It was held that, where some of the defendants reside within the jurisdiction and others reside outside it, it is undesirable, unfair and unjust to require compliance with Order 2, rule 4 (now Order 2, rule 7(5)). In other words, in cases of multiple defendants – some within and others outside the jurisdiction – the plaintiff can issue a writ before obtaining leave to serve notice of the writ on those defendants who are abroad.

A person who seeks leave to serve notice of a writ out of the jurisdiction must make an application to the court. The application must be supported by an affidavit stating the grounds on which the application is made. It should also state that, in the deponent's belief, the plaintiff has a good cause of action. The affidavit must show the place or country where the defendant is, or could probably be found. A plaintiff's failure to state the grounds for making the application is not fatal if he or she files a comprehensive statement of claim together with the writ.[16]

[12] High Court (Civil Procedure) Rules 2004, Ord. 8, r. 1(1). A writ includes a writ of summons and a statement of claim or a petition in a cause or matter. Ord. 82, r. 3.

[13] [1989–90] 1 GLR 96.

[14] On appeal, the Court of Appeal agreed with the principle, but held that, given the facts, the writ was not intended for service out of the jurisdiction. The court reasoned that, where there is evidence of solicitors and attorneys within Ghana who are prepared to accept the service of a writ and to conduct the litigation on behalf of a defendant, in spite of a foreign address on the writ, and a clear indication that the writ is not the type intended for service out of the jurisdiction, in such a situation, the defendant is deemed to have waived the necessity for leave. His representatives would be presumed to have agreed to do all he would have done, as if he were within the jurisdiction. See *Lokko* v. *Lokko* [1991] 2 GLR 184.

[15] [1989–90] 1 GLR 401.

[16] *Shirlstar Container Transport Ltd* v. *Kadas Shipping Co. Ltd* [1989–90] 1 GLR 401.

The court will not grant leave to serve notice of a writ out of the jurisdiction unless it sufficiently appears to them that: (i) the case is a proper one for service out of the jurisdiction; and (ii) the case falls within one of the grounds in Order 8, rule 3.[17] Exercise of the power granted to the courts to order service out of the jurisdiction is discretionary, not mandatory. The courts must exercise this discretion with great care and resolve any doubt in favour of the prospective defendant.[18] This is because an application for service out of the jurisdiction is made and heard *ex parte*; the foreign defendant is neither notified nor heard. It is unjust to drag a person into Ghana to defend an action without substantial grounds and justification. In the words of Justice Griffiths-Randolph, 'the courts generally are not enamoured of putting parties resident outside their jurisdiction to the unnecessary expense involved in, and inconvenience that might be occasioned by answering frivolous claims before them'.[19] Indeed, the power to grant leave for the issuance of a writ for service out of the jurisdiction should be exercised carefully. The applicant must furnish plausible evidence to convince the court that he or she has a good cause of action, or that there is a real issue to be tried and that the other party does not have a proper defence to the claim.[5]

The following are grounds on which an applicant can make a case for service out of the jurisdiction if:[20]

(a) the whole subject matter of the action begun by the writ is immovable property situate within the jurisdiction (with or without rents or profits) or the perpetuation of testimony relating to any such property;
(b) an act, deed, will, contract, obligation or liability affecting immovable property situate within the jurisdiction is sought to be construed, rectified, set aside or enforced in the action begun by the writ;
(c) in the action begun by the writ, relief is sought against a person domiciled or ordinarily resident within the jurisdiction;
(d) the action begun by the writ is for the administration of the estate of a person who died domiciled within the jurisdiction or for any relief or remedy that might be obtained in any such action;

[17] High Court (Civil Procedure) Rules 2004, Ord. 8, r. 2(2).
[18] *Eboe* v. *Eboe* [1962] 1 GLR 453.
[19] *Signal Oil and Gas* v. *Bristow Helicopters* [1976] 1 GLR 371 at 374.
[20] High Court (Civil Procedure) Rules 2004, Ord. 8, r. 3.

(e) the action begun by the writ is for the execution, as to property situated within the jurisdiction, of the trusts of a written instrument, being trusts that ought to be executed according to the laws of this country and of which the person to be served with the writ is a trustee, or for any relief or remedy that might be obtained in any such action;[21]

(f) the action begun by the writ is brought against a defendant not domiciled or ordinarily resident within the jurisdiction to enforce, rescind, dissolve, annul or otherwise affect a contract, or to recover damages or obtain other relief in respect of the breach of a contract: that was made within the jurisdiction; that was made by or through an agent trading or residing within the jurisdiction on behalf of a principal trading or residing out of the jurisdiction; or that is by its terms, or by implication, governed by the laws of this country;[22]

(g) the action begun by the writ is brought against a defendant not domiciled or ordinarily resident within the jurisdiction, with respect to a breach committed within the jurisdiction of a contract made within or out of the jurisdiction, notwithstanding the fact that the breach is preceded or accompanied by a breach committed out of the jurisdiction that renders impossible the performance of so much of the contract as ought to have been performed within the jurisdiction;

(h) the action begun by the writ is founded on a tort committed within the jurisdiction;[23]

(i) in the action begun by the writ, an injunction is sought that orders the defendant to do or refrain from doing anything within the jurisdiction (whether or not damages are also claimed with respect to a failure to do or to the doing of that thing);

(j) the action begun by the writ is properly brought against a person duly served within the jurisdiction, but a person out of the jurisdiction is a necessary or proper party to it;

(k) the action begun by the writ is by a mortgagee of immovable property situated within the jurisdiction and seeks the sale of the property, foreclosure of the mortgage or delivery by the mortgagor of

[21] It has been held that where a defendant is sued as a trustee, in the absence of a written instrument, the court has no jurisdiction to grant leave for service out of the jurisdiction. See *Eboe* v. *Eboe* [1962] 1 GLR 453.

[22] *Sanyo Electric Trading Co.* v. *Quacoopome* [2001–2] GLR 198.

[23] *Signal Oil and Gas* v. *Bristow Helicopters* [1976] 1 GLR 371.

possession of the property, but not an order for payment of any moneys due under the mortgage;

(l) the action begun by the writ is by a mortgagor of immovable property situate within the jurisdiction and seeks redemption of the mortgage, discharge of the mortgage or delivery by the mortgagee of possession of the property, but not a personal judgment;

(m) the action begun by the writ concerns a contract that contains a term to the effect that the court will have jurisdiction to hear and determine any action with respect to the contract.

In instances where the contract was made through an agent resident in Ghana, the court can, on an *ex parte* application, make an order authorising service of the writ to commence an action that relates to the contract, to be effected on the agent instead of the principal.[24]

An important issue is whether a plaintiff can respectively combine actions falling outside and within the grounds in Order 8 and still obtain leave to serve out of the jurisdiction. It has been held that, if a writ of summons contains any claim with respect to which leave for service out of the jurisdiction cannot be granted, then even though it contains other claims with respect to which leave can be granted, the court cannot by reason of the former claims grant leave for service out of jurisdiction, as such a writ does not fall within any of the provisions of Order 11, rule 11 (now Order 8).[25]

A company resident in Ghana is subject to the jurisdiction of the Ghanaian courts. The test for residence is whether business is carried out at some definite and more or less permanent place in Ghana. Whether a company is resident in Ghana for the purposes of jurisdiction is to be determined by the facts as they exist at the commencement of an action.[26]

A company doing business in Ghana is subject to the jurisdiction of the Ghanaian courts.[27] Such a company need not have a permanent place of business in Ghana. It is enough if it sells its products or renders services in Ghana. It has been held that a foreign unincorporated partnership that is not carrying on business in Ghana cannot issue a writ of summons or sue in the name of the firm.[28] Such a foreign entity might

[24] High Court (Civil Procedure) Rules 2004, Ord. 7, r. 13.
[25] *Eboe* v. *Eboe* [1962] 1 GLR 453 at 457.
[26] *Ackerman* v. *Société Générale de Compensation* [1967] GLR 212 at 214.
[27] *Tafa & Co. (Ghana) Ltd* v. *Tafa & Co. Ltd* [1977] 1 GLR 422.
[28] *Attorney General* v. *Levandowsky* [1971] 2 GLR 58.

not possess any separate legal personality in its country of origin that could be recognised by the Ghanaian courts. A company incorporated in another country has the capacity to sue in Ghana. The Ghanaian courts will recognise legal personality conferred on a company by a foreign state. Such a company is, however, bound to disclose its place of incorporation in the writ of summons.[29]

Kenya

The foundation of jurisdiction in claims *in personam* is service. The presence of a defendant in Kenya confers jurisdiction on its courts. It was considered proper service to serve a writ on a defendant at the Eastleigh Airport, Nairobi, while he was in transit through Kenya.[30] Nor does it matter that the underlying transaction was entered into outside the jurisdiction, in this instance, via a contract made in Kigali, Rwanda.[31]

The Civil Procedure Rules 2010 make provision for serving a writ out of the jurisdiction.[32] In defined cases, an action lies in Kenya against an absent defendant provided he or she is duly served.[33] Service of a summons or notice of a summons out of Kenya may be allowed by the court whenever:

(a) the whole subject matter of the suit is immovable property situate in Kenya (with or without rents and profits);
(b) any act, deed, will, contract, obligation or liability affecting immovable property situate in Kenya is sought to be construed, rectified, set aside, or enforced in the suit;

[29] *Edusei* v. *Diners Club Suisse SA* [1982–3] GLR 809; *Kimon Compania Naviera SARP* v. *Volta Line Ltd (Consolidated)* [1973] 1 GLR 140.

[30] *Riddlesbarger* v. *Robson* [1958] EA 375.

[31] *Georgina Ngina* v. *Inter Freight East Africa Ltd* [2006] eKLR (the contract was to be performed in Kenya), but see *Sunrise Travel and Tours Ltd* v. *Wanjigi* [2002] LLR 5933, where the court held that despite the fact that a contrary position may well be a good thing in the era of increased globalisation, under existing Kenyan law, a contract wholly entered into and performed outside Kenya gives courts no jurisdiction, even if the defendant actually resides in Kenya.

[32] Civil Procedure Rules 2010, Ord. 5, r. 21(a)-(h). Order 5, r. 22 and r. 24 make further provision for service out of the jurisdiction, and for other processes, such as originating summons, originating notice of motion, petition or other originating proceedings.

[33] *African Mercantile Co. Ltd* v. *Patel* [1927–8] 11 KLR 69.

(c) any relief is sought against any person domiciled or ordinarily resident in Kenya;[34]

(d) the suit is for the administration of the personal estate of a deceased person who at the time of his death was domiciled in Kenya, or for the execution (as to property situate in Kenya) of the trusts of any written instrument, of which the person to be served is a trustee, which ought to be executed according to the law of Kenya;

(e) the suit is one brought to enforce, rectify, rescind, dissolve, annul or otherwise affect a contract or to recover damages or other relief for or in respect of the breach of a contract: made in Kenya; or made by or through an agent trading or residing in Kenya on behalf of a principal trading or residing out of Kenya; or by its terms or legislation to be governed by the laws of Kenya; or which contains a provision to the effect that any Kenyan court has jurisdiction to hear and determine that suit in respect of that contract, or is brought in respect of a breach committed in Kenya, of a contract, wherever made, even though such a breach was preceded or accompanied by a breach out of Kenya which rendered impossible the performance of the part of the contract which ought to have been performed in Kenya;[35]

(f) the suit is founded on a tort committed in Kenya;[36]

(g) any injunction is sought as to anything to be done in Kenya, or any nuisance in Kenya is sought to be prevented or removed, whether damages are or are not also sought in respect thereof; or

(h) any person out of Kenya is a necessary or proper party to a suit properly brought against some other person duly served in Kenya.

Service out of the jurisdiction has been described as an exceptional measure. Accordingly, an applicant applying for it must strictly meet the statutory requirements imposed for the exercise of such jurisdiction.[37] The granting of leave is discretionary, and even if an applicant is able to bring his or her application within the strict terms of the rule, there may be grounds which justify the court in refusing it, including the failure of the applicant to make full and fair disclosure or show a

[34] *Donnebaum* v. *Mikolaschek* [1964] EA 645.

[35] *Karachi Gas Co. Ltd* v. *Issaq* [1965] EA 42, 1965 ALR Comm. 35; *Nairobi Projectors Services Ltd* v. *Patricia Kabuleeta* [2006] eKLR; *Kenya School of Flying* v. *ACE INA UK Ltd* [2005] eKLR; *African Mercantile Co. Ltd* v. *Patel* [1927–8] 11 KLR 69.

[36] *Donnebaum* v. *Mikolaschek* [1964] EA 645; *Kenya School of Flying* v. *ACE INA UK Ltd* [2005] eKLR.

[37] *Assanand and Sons (Uganda) Ltd* v. *East African Records Ltd* [1959] 1 EA 360.

reasonable and probable cause of action.[38] Where personal service of a writ issued under an order for service out of the jurisdiction cannot at all be effected, the court may order substituted service.[39]

Residence of a company within the jurisdiction confers jurisdiction on the Kenyan courts. It has, however, been held that transactions by a foreign company's forwarding agent in a jurisdiction do not necessarily amount to transaction by the company through the forwarding agent, for the purposes of establishing the company's presence or residence within the jurisdiction.[40] A foreign company which does business within the jurisdiction can be sued.[41]

Nigeria

Submission constitutes a basis of jurisdiction in Nigeria. The Nigerian courts have jurisdiction to try an action relating to any contract made by parties which have voluntarily submitted to the jurisdiction of the court.[42] Submission may take the form of entering into a choice of forum agreement or may be inferred from conduct such as entering unconditional appearance to an action and taking further steps in the proceedings.[43] However, an appearance solely to protest against the jurisdiction does not constitute voluntary submission to jurisdiction.[44]

Similarly, residence within the jurisdiction is a basis of jurisdiction in Nigeria law. Thus, in an action to secure the repayment of a loan, the fact that a loan was contracted abroad does not prevent the Nigerian courts from assuming jurisdiction if it can be established that the debtor is resident within the jurisdiction.[45]

Nigerian law allows for the service of a writ outside the jurisdiction.[46] No writ, or notice of a writ, to be served out of the jurisdiction shall be

[38] *Paul Donnebaum* v. *Kurt Mikolaschek* [1966] EA 25.

[39] *Patel* v. *Mart* [1954] 27 KLR 40.

[40] *In re. Lowenthal and Air France* 1966 (2) ALR Comm. 301, [1967] EA 75; *Kanti & Co. Ltd* v. *Oriental Fire & General Insce Co. Ltd* [1973] 1 EA 203.

[41] *His Majesty's Principal Secretary of State for the Colonies* v. *Deutsche Ost-Afrika Linie* [1906–8] KLR 74.

[42] *Barzasi* v. *B Visinoni Ltd* 1973 (1) ALR Comm. 373, [1973] NCLR 373.

[43] *Grisby* v. *Jubwe* (1952–5) 14 WACA 637.

[44] *Holman Bros (Nigeria) Ltd* v. *Kigo (Nigeria) Ltd* [1980] FNLR 395 at 407.

[45] *First Bank of Nigeria Plc.* v. *Kayode Abraham* [2008] 18 NWLR 172 (reversing *First Bank of Nigeria Plc* v. *Kayode Abraham* [2003] 2 NWLR 31).

[46] In this chapter, I only focus on the rules of the Federal High Court. Each of the state High Courts has its own civil procedure rules which, on this issue, contain provisions similar to those of the Federal High Court (see, e.g., High Court of Lagos State (Civil Procedure)

served without leave of the court.[47] Service out of the jurisdiction of a writ of summons or notice of a writ of summons may be allowed by the court whenever:[48]

(a) the whole subject matter of the action is land situate within the jurisdiction (with or without rents or profits);
(b) any act, deed, will, contract, obligation or liability affecting land or hereditament situate within the jurisdiction is sought to be construed, rectified, set aside or enforced in the action;
(c) any relief is sought against any person domiciled, or ordinarily resident, within the jurisdiction;
(d) the action is one brought against the defendant to enforce, rescind, dissolve, annul or otherwise affect a contract or to recover damages or other relief for or in respect of a breach of a contract made within the jurisdiction, or made by or through an agent trading or residing within the jurisdiction on behalf of a principal trading or residing out of the jurisdiction, or by its terms or by implication to be governed by the law in force in the jurisdiction or is brought against the defendant in respect of a breach committed within the jurisdiction

Rules 2004, Ord. 8, r. 1; High Court of the Federal Capital Territory, Abuja (Civil Procedure) Rules, Ord. 12, r.13; High Court of Kaduna State (Civil Procedure) Rules 2007, Ord. 8, r. 1). Nigeria is a federal state and some of the issues discussed in this chapter have arisen in the context of intra-state conflict of laws. On this, see generally 'Gbenga Bamodu, 'In Personam Jurisdiction: An overlooked Concept in recent Nigerian Jurisprudence' (2011) 7 *Journal of Private International Law* 273.

[47] Federal High Court (Civil Procedure Rules) 2000, Ord. 6, r. 12(1). *Nwabueze* v. *Okoye* [2002] 10 WRN 123; *Broad Bank of Nigeria Ltd* v. *Olayiwola* [2005] WRN 101, [2005] 3 NWLR 434. It appears that Nigerian courts have not been entirely consistent in their decisions on the effect of failing to seek leave before serving out of the jurisdiction. Some have held that failure to obtain leave to issue a writ for service out of the jurisdiction, or to serve it out of the jurisdiction without leave, does not render the writ void, but merely voidable. And the court has power to retroactively grant leave to issue writs of summons for service out of the jurisdiction. *Aermacchi SPA* v. *AIC Ltd* [1986] 2 NWLR 443; *Caribbean Trading & Fidelity Corp.* v. *Nigerian National Petroleum Corp.* [2002] 34 WRN 11. Others, including the Supreme Court, have, however, held in recent decisions that non-compliance with the rules on service out is not a mere irregularity, but a fundamental defect which goes to the root of the jurisdiction and competence of the court. *Owners of the MV 'Arabella'* v. *Nigeria Agricultural Insurance Corp.* (2008) 2 All NLR 491; *Drexel Energy and Natural Resources Ltd* v. *Trans International Bank Ltd* (2008) 2 All NLR 224. See also *Nwabueze* v. *Okoye* [2002] 10 WRN 123; *United Bank for Africa Plc* v. *Odimayo* [2005] 2 NWLR 21; *AGIP (Nigeria) Ltd* v. *AGIP Petroli International* [2010] 5 NWLR 348 at 395; *Touton SA* v. *Grimaldi Compagnia di Naviga Zioni SPA* [2011] 4 NWLR 1.

[48] Federal High Court (Civil Procedure Rules) 2000, Ord. 13, r. 13.

of a contract wherever made, even though the breach was preceded or accompanied by a breach out of the jurisdiction which rendered impossible the performance of the part of the contract which ought to have been performed within the jurisdiction;[49]

(e) the action is founded on tort or other civil wrong committed within the jurisdiction;[50]

(f) any injunction is sought as to anything to be done within the jurisdiction or any nuisance within the jurisdiction is sought to be prevented or removed, whether damages are or are not also sought in respect thereof;

(g) any person out of jurisdiction is a necessary or proper party to an action properly brought against some other party within the jurisdiction;

(h) the action is by a mortgagee or mortgagor in relation to a mortgage of property situate within the jurisdiction and seeks relief of the nature or kind of the following, that is to say, sale, foreclosure, delivery of possession by the mortgagor, redemption, reconveyance, delivery of possession by the mortgagee; but does not seek (unless and except so far as permissible under paragraph (d) of this rule) any personal judgment order for payment of any moneys due under the mortgage; or

(i) the action is one brought under the Civil Aviation Act or any regulations made in pursuance of the Act or any law relating to carriage by air.

Every application for leave to serve a writ or notice on a defendant out of the jurisdiction shall be supported by affidavit or other evidence stating that, in the belief of the deponent, the plaintiff has a good cause of action and shows the place or country where the defendant is, or is likely to be found, and the grounds upon which the application has been made.[51] No such leave shall be granted unless it sufficiently appears to the court that the cause is a proper one for service out of jurisdiction.[52] This indicates the standard of proof to be applied when determining where

[49] *Cold Containers (Nigeria) Ltd* v. *Collis Cold Containers Ltd* 1977 (1) ALR Comm. 97, [1977] NCLR 97; *Nahman* v. *Allan Wolowicz* [1993] 3 NWLR 443; *Benworth Finance Ltd* v. *Ibrahim* 1969 (3) ALR Comm. 180; *Blaize* v. *Dove* [1936] 13 NLR 66; *Arjay Ltd* v. *Airline Management Support Ltd* [2003] 7 NWLR 577.

[50] See generally *Ezomo* v. *Oyakhire* [1985] 1 NWLR 195, (1985) 2 SC 260.

[51] Federal High Court (Civil Procedure Rules) 2000, Ord. 13, r. 14(1).

[52] Ibid., Ord. 13, r. 14(2).

the above grounds for service outside the jurisdiction have been fulfilled – it must sufficiently appear to him or her that it is a proper case for service outside. The proper test is whether, on consideration of all the admissible material, there remains a strong argument that the grounds have been satisfied: it is not sufficient for the plaintiff merely to show that he or she had a prima facie case against the proposed defendant, but neither is it necessary that the court be satisfied beyond reasonable doubt as to the existence of the grounds.[53] The restriction on a plaintiff's right to issue and serve a judicial process out of the jurisdiction is to enable the court (an agency of the state) to decide whether it is fitting in that particular case to exercise the judicial power of the state over a person in another country where its jurisdiction does not extend. Once the court has decided that it has jurisdiction to grant leave, whether it should then do so is a matter of discretion, although this discretion should be exercised with great care. Factors to be taken into account include: the *forum conveniens* for the trial of the action; comparative cost and convenience, and, if relevant, whether proceedings in respect of the same cause of action are already pending elsewhere.[54] Where, at the time of the issue of the writ, personal service cannot be effected in law on the defendant outside the jurisdiction of the court, substituted service should not be ordered.[55]

The Nigerian courts have jurisdiction over a company resident[56] or anyone carrying on business in Nigeria.[57] Residence is a question of fact, and the residence of a company is the place of its central management and control.[58] The phrase 'carrying on business' means more than casually dealing with customers, remote and away from a company's headquarters or head office. There must be something to show that the company really carries on business within the jurisdiction.[59] However, a foreign company may carry on business within the jurisdiction through

[53] *Cold Containers (Nigeria) Ltd* v. *Collis Cold Containers Ltd* 1977 (1) ALR Comm. 97, [1977] NCLR 97.

[54] *Nwabueze* v. *Okoye* [1988] 4 NWLR 664. See also *Cold Containers (Nigeria) Ltd* v. *Collis Cold Containers Ltd* 1977 (1) ALR Comm. 97, [1977] NCLR 97.

[55] *Kida* v. *Ogunmola* [2006] 13 NWLR 377.

[56] *University of Nigeria* v. *Orazulike Trading Co. Ltd* [1989] 5 NWLR 19. See generally Companies and Allied Matters Act 1990, ss. 78 and 54.

[57] *In re. Gresham Life Assurance Society (Nigeria) Ltd* 1973 (1) ALR Comm. 215, [1973] 1 All NLR (Part I) 617, [1973] NCLR 215; *In re. Gresham Life Assurance Society (Nigeria) Ltd* v. *Ochefu* [1970] NCLR 78.

[58] *University of Nigeria* v. *Orazulike Trading Co. Ltd* [1989] 5 NWLR 19.

[59] *Ezebube* v. *Alpin & Co. Ltd* 1966 (2) ALR Comm. 97.

an agent,[60] but a foreign company does not carry on business in Nigeria merely by owning the share capital in a Nigerian company.[61]

Sierra Leone

Sierra Leone law allows a plaintiff to serve a writ out of the jurisdiction. However, no writ of summons for service out of the jurisdiction, or of which notice is to be given out of the jurisdiction, shall be issued without the leave of the court.[62] Service out of the jurisdiction of a writ of summons, or notice of a writ of summons, may be effected with leave of the court in cases where:[63]

(a) a relief is sought against a person domiciled in Sierra Leone;
(b) an injunction is sought ordering the defendant to do or refrain from doing anything within Sierra Leone (whether or not damages are claimed in respect of a failure to do or the doing of that thing);
(c) the claim is brought against a person duly served in Sierra Leone or out of it and a person out of Sierra Leone is a necessary or proper party to the action;
(d) the claim is brought to enforce, rescind, dissolve or otherwise affect a contract, being (in either case) a contract which: was made in Sierra Leone; was made by or through an agent trading or residing outside Sierra Leone; or is by its terms or by implication governed by Sierra Leone law;
(e) the claim is brought in respect of a breach committed in Sierra Leone of a contract made in Sierra Leone and irrespective of the fact, if such is the case, that the breach was preceded or accompanied by a breach committed outside Sierra Leone that rendered impossible the performance of so much of the contract as ought to have been performed in Sierra Leone;[64]
(f) the claim is founded on a tort and the damage was sustained or resulted from an act committed in Sierra Leone;
(g) the whole subject matter of the action is land situate in Sierra Leone (with or without rents or profits) or the perpetuation of testimony relating to land so situate;

60 *Spiropoulos & Co. Ltd* v. *Nigerian Rubber Co. Ltd* 1970 (2) ALR Comm. 94, [1970] NCLR 94.
61 *Aluminium Industries Aktien Gesellschaft* v. *Federal Board of Inland Revenue* 1971 (2) ALR Comm. 121, [1971] 2 NCLR 121.
62 High Court (Civil Procedure) Rules 2007, Ord. 6, r. 8.
63 Ibid., Ord. 11, r. 1.
64 *Aboud* v. *Mandi* [1920–36] ALR SL 240.

(h) the claim is brought to construe, rectify, set aside or enforce an act, deed, will, contract, obligation or liability affecting land situate in Sierra Leone;
(i) the claim is made for a debt secured on immovable property or is made to assert, declare or determine proprietary or possessory rights, or rights of security in or over movable property or to obtain authority to dispose of movable property in Sierra Leone;
(j) the claim is brought to execute the trust of a written instrument, being a trust that ought to be executed according to Sierra Leone law and of which the person to be served with the writ is a trustee or for any relief or remedy which might be obtained in such action;
(k) the claim is made for the administration of the estate of a person who died domiciled in Sierra Leone or for any relief or remedy which might be obtained in such action;
(l) if the action begun by the writ is by a mortgagee of immovable property situated within Sierra Leone and seeks the sale of the property, foreclosure of the mortgage or delivery by the mortgagor of possession of the property but not an order for payment of any moneys due under the mortgage;
(m) if the action is by a mortgagor of immovable property situate within Sierra Leone and seeks redemption of the mortgage or delivery by the mortgagee of possession of the property but not a personal judgment; or
(n) if the action begun by the writ is in respect of a contract which contains a term to the effect that the court shall have jurisdiction to hear and determine any action in respect of the contract.

An application for the grant of leave shall be supported by an affidavit stating: the grounds on which the application is made; that in the deponent's belief the plaintiff has a good cause of action; in what place or country the defendant is or probably may be found, and in the case of an applicant invoking the 'necessary or proper party' ground, the grounds for the deponent's belief that there exists between the plaintiff and the person on whom a writ has been served, a real issue which the plaintiff may reasonably ask the court to try.[65] No leave shall be granted unless it sufficiently appears to the court that the case is a proper one for service out of the jurisdiction.[66]

[65] High Court (Civil Procedure) Rules 2007, Ord. 11, r. 3(1).

[66] Ibid., Ord. 11, r. 3(2).

Uganda

In an action *in personam*, the Ugandan courts have jurisdiction to determine disputes as long as the person served with the summons to file a defence is within Uganda.[67] Service out of the jurisdiction of a summons or notice of a summons may be allowed by the court whenever:[68]

(a) the whole subject matter of the suit is immovable property situate within the jurisdiction (with or without rents and profits);
(b) any act, deed, will, contract, obligation or liability affecting immovable property situate within the jurisdiction is sought to be construed, rectified, set aside or enforced in the suit;
(c) any relief is sought against any person domiciled or ordinarily resident within the jurisdiction;[69]
(d) the suit is for the administration of the personal estate of any deceased person, who at the time of death was domiciled within the jurisdiction, or for the execution (as to property situate within the jurisdiction) of the trusts of any written instrument, of which the person to be served is a trustee, which ought to be executed according to Ugandan law;
(e) the suit is founded on any breach or alleged breach within the jurisdiction of any contract wherever made which, according to the terms of the contract, ought to be performed within the jurisdiction;
(f) any injunction is sought as to anything to be done within the jurisdiction, or any nuisance within the jurisdiction is sought to be prevented or removed, whether damages are or are not also sought;
(g) any person out of the jurisdiction is a necessary or proper party to a suit properly brought against some other person duly served within the jurisdiction; or
(h) the suit is founded on a tort committed within the jurisdiction.

The Ugandan courts have jurisdiction over a company resident in Uganda. Thus, it has been held that the fact that a firm resides within the jurisdiction of the courts confers jurisdiction on the court to hear a

[67] *Eastern and Southern African Trade and Development Bank* v. *Hassan Basajjabalaba*, HCT-00-CC-CS-0512-2006 (High Court, Uganda, 2007). See generally *Ruby General Insurance Co. Ltd* v. *General Land and Insurance Agencies Ltd* [1963] EA 154.

[68] Civil Procedure Rules 1964, Ord. V, r. 22(a)–(h).

[69] *Alemayehu Degafa* v. *Kim Bowerman* [1994] Kam. LR 644.

dispute between it and a firm incorporated in another country, even though the contract in dispute is to be performed abroad.[70]

Zambia

The Zambian court has jurisdiction over a matter involving a contract to be performed abroad where the defendant is resident in Zambia, or where the defendant has submitted to jurisdiction.[71]

An action *in personam* is initiated with a writ.[72] Zambian law allows for the service of a writ out of the jurisdiction. Before such a writ can be issued, leave of the court must be obtained, and it is only after the court's leave has been obtained that the writ can be issued.[73] Service out of the jurisdiction of a writ of summons or notice thereof may be allowed by the court whenever:[74]

(a) the whole subject matter of the action is land situate within the jurisdiction (with or without rents or profits), or the perpetuation of testimony relating to land within the jurisdiction;
(b) any act, deed, will, contract, obligation or liability affecting land or hereditaments situate within the jurisdiction is sought to be construed, rectified, set aside or enforced in the action or matter;
(c) any relief is sought against any person domiciled or ordinarily resident within the jurisdiction;
(d) the action is for the administration of the personal estate of any deceased person, who at the time of his death was domiciled within the jurisdiction, or for the execution (as to property situate within the jurisdiction) of the trusts of any written instrument, of which the person to be served is a trustee, which ought to be executed according to the law of Zambia;
(e) the action is one brought to enforce, rescind, dissolve, annul or otherwise affect a contract or to recover damages or other relief for or in respect of the breach of a contract made within the jurisdiction; or made by or through an agent trading or residing within the jurisdiction on behalf of a principal trading or residing out of the

[70] *Wigglesworth Clearing Ltd* v. *Trago (U) Ltd* [1999] Kam. LR 758.
[71] *Commonwealth Development Corp.* v. *Central African Power Corp.* (1968) ZR 70, 1968 (3) ALR Comm. 416; *Fratelli Fasani SPA* v. *Zambital Ltd* (1983) ZR 129.
[72] High Court Rules, Ord. VI, r. 1(1).
[73] *Leopold Walford (Zambia) Ltd* v. *Unifreight* (1985) ZR 203.
[74] High Court Rules, Ord. X, r. 15.

jurisdiction; or by its terms or by implication to be governed by Zambian law; or it is one brought in respect of a breach committed within the jurisdiction of a contract wherever made, even though such breach was preceded or accompanied by a breach out of the jurisdiction which rendered impossible the performance of the part of the contract which ought to have been performed within the jurisdiction;

(f) the action is founded on a tort committed within the jurisdiction;[75]

(g) any injunction is sought as to anything to be done within the jurisdiction, or any nuisance within the jurisdiction is sought to be prevented or removed, whether damages are or are not also sought in respect thereof;

(h) any person out of the jurisdiction is a necessary or proper party to an action properly brought against some other person duly served within the jurisdiction; or

(i) the action is by a mortgagee or mortgagor in relation to a mortgage of personal property situate within the jurisdiction and seeks relief of the nature or kind following, that is to say, sale, foreclosure, delivery of possession by the mortgagor, redemption, re-conveyance, delivery of possession by the mortgagee; but does not seek (unless and except so far as permissible under paragraph (e)) any personal judgment or order for payment of any moneys due under the mortgage.

Comments

In an action *in personam*, presence, residence and submission are bases of jurisdiction in the common law countries. It has been held in Ghana and Kenya that the mere presence of the defendant within the jurisdiction, no matter how transient, gives the court jurisdiction to hear a claim involving that person. However, it is debatable whether mere presence is an acceptable basis of jurisdiction – it is open to abuse, undermines the legitimate expectation of parties, has been rejected in other jurisdictions and encourages forum shopping. That said, the harshness of the approach (particularly where the cause of action has little or no connection with the forum) is, in the common law countries, mitigated by the

[75] It has been held that an action to recover money paid by mistake of fact is not an action arising in any way from contract. Accordingly, the court will not make an order for service out of the jurisdiction in such an action. *Northern Rhodesia Tobacco Co-operative Society Ltd* v. *Baird* [1949–54] NRLR 387.

application of the doctrine of *forum non conveniens*, which allows a court to stay its proceedings for the claim to be heard in a more appropriate forum abroad.

Whether a person is resident within the jurisdiction is a question of fact to be determined on the circumstances of each case. The issue of residence is particularly problematic in respect of legal persons, such as companies. Legislation has a significant impact in determining whether a company is resident within the jurisdiction. Companies incorporated in the forum,[76] or which establish a 'place of business' within the forum under the respective national laws, will certainly be considered resident in the forum for jurisdictional purposes.[77] Indeed, special provision is made in most of the national legislation for service on what are variously described as 'external' or 'foreign' companies (i.e. companies incorporated outside the forum which have an established place of business within the jurisdiction)[78] and companies in general.[79] It is worth noting

[76] Some national laws allow a company to be incorporated in the country as a non-resident company. See, e.g., Gambia – Companies Act 1955, s. 364 (companies incorporated in Gambia which may not carry on business in, or be controlled from, Gambia).

[77] See generally Gambia – Companies Act 1955, ss. 348–57; Ghana – Companies Act 1963, ss. 302–17; Kenya – Companies Act 1962, ss. 365–75; Malawi – Companies Act 1986, ss. 306–20; Sierra Leone – Companies Act 2009, ss. 484–93; Tanzania – Companies Act 2002, ss. 433–49; Uganda – Companies Act, ss. 369–79; Zambia – Companies Act 1994, ss. 240–61. Except with a special exemption granted for the purpose Nigerian law does not allow a company incorporated abroad to have an established place of business in Nigeria. See Companies and Allied Matters Act 1990, s. 54. In general, in these countries, an established place of business means a branch, management, share, transfer or registration office, factory, mine or any other fixed place of business. It does not include an agency unless the agent has, and habitually exercises, a general authority to negotiate and conclude contracts on behalf of the body corporate or maintains a stock of merchandise belonging to that body corporate from which the agent regularly fills orders on its behalf. A body corporate does not have an established place of business in the forum merely because it carries on business dealings in the forum through a genuine broker or general commission agent acting in the ordinary course of business as a broker or general commission agent. Also, the fact that a body corporate has a subsidiary which is incorporated, resident or carrying on business in the forum, whether through an established place of business or otherwise, shall not of itself constitute the place of business of that subsidiary or an established place of business of that body corporate.

[78] Gambia – Companies Act 1955, s. 354; Ghana – Companies Act 1963, s. 306; Kenya – Companies Act 1962, s. 372; Malawi – Companies Act 1986, s. 311; Sierra Leone – Companies Act 2009, s. 488; Tanzania – Companies Act 2002, s. 440; Uganda – Companies Act, s. 376; Zambia – Companies Act 1994, s. 250.

[79] Gambia – Companies Act 1955, s. 380; Ghana – Companies Act 1963, s. 263; Kenya – Companies Act 1962, s. 391; Malawi – Companies Act 1986, s. 137; Nigeria – Companies and Allied Matters Act 1990, s. 78; Sierra Leone – Companies Act 2009, s.514; Tanzania – Companies Act 2002, s. 470; Uganda – Companies Act, s. 394.

that the civil procedure rules[80] in some of the common law countries also contain provisions on the service of legal process on companies. In most of the countries, the provisions in the Companies Acts prevail in cases of inconsistency.[81]

Submission to the jurisdiction can take the form of a jurisdiction agreement or may be inferred from the conduct of the defendant. The presence of a jurisdiction agreement has been treated as evidence of submission. Interestingly, there have been only a few instances in which the underlying contracts of an action have designated an African court as the forum for dispute settlement. The minimal use of African state jurisdiction agreements tells us a lot about individual perceptions of the adequacy of courts and laws in Africa to deal with the complex issues involved in cross-border transactions. These adverse perceptions of the ability of African courts and their legal systems to deal with complex issues of cross-border transactions will have to be addressed through institutional reform and the enhancement of resources (including personnel training), available to the judiciary.

In respect of contracts executed, or which were to be performed abroad, some courts have been unprepared to assume jurisdiction, even in those cases where one of the parties is resident within the jurisdiction. It is submitted that these patently wrongly decided cases confuse the existence of jurisdiction with its exercise. The service of a writ on a defendant present or resident within the jurisdiction certainly confers jurisdiction on its courts. In deciding whether or not to exercise the jurisdiction so created by service, the court may take into account the connection of the subject matter of the action with the forum as part of its *forum non conveniens* analysis. However, to deny the existence of jurisdiction merely because a contract was executed, or was to be performed, abroad (or that the cause of action arose abroad)[82] is not only analytically unsound, but also inconsistent with well-established authority in the common law countries.

Jurisdiction founded on service always creates problems in cases where the defendant is absent from the jurisdiction. At common law, service out

[80] See, e.g., Gambia – Rules of the High Court, Ord. VIII, rr. 3–4; Ghana – High Court (Civil Procedure) Rules 2004, Ord. 7, r. 5(1); Kenya – Civil Procedure Rules 2009, Ord. V, r. 2; Nigeria – Federal High Court (Civil Procedure) Rules 2000, Ord. 13, r. 8; Sierra Leone – High Court Rules 2007, Ord. 10, r. 4(2)(c); Zambia – High Court Rules, Ord. X, r. 11(3).

[81] See, e.g., *Dakar Ltd* v. *Industrial Chemical and Pharmaceutical Co. Ltd* [1981] GLR 453.

[82] See, e.g., *Capital Bancorp Ltd* v. *Shelter Savings and Loans Ltd* [2007] 3 NWLR 148.

of the jurisdiction has not been recognised.[83] To overcome this problem, legislation in each of the common law countries makes provision for serving writs on defendants abroad. These statutory provisions,[84] no doubt borrowed from England, are remarkably similar in wording. However, there have been relatively few cases to interpret them. In all the common law countries, a plaintiff is not entitled to have a writ issued for service abroad or to be served abroad – it is within the discretion of the court to so order[85] and it is a discretion which is exercised with care and caution. The courts have reasoned that this is necessary not only because of the seemingly 'extra-territorial' nature of the exercise of the respective jurisdiction, but in most cases, the application is also made *ex parte* and the defendant is not before the court. In the words of one Nigerian judge, the court owes a duty to determine whether the person sought to be served out of the jurisdiction can be conveniently tried elsewhere.[86] There have been cases where the courts have set aside the service of a writ on a defendant abroad on the sole basis that the plaintiff did not seek leave of the court before serving the writ. However, apart from recent decisions of the Nigerian Supreme Court to the contrary,[87] it appears to be generally accepted that such a failure does not render void the issue or service of the writ – it is rather a procedural irregularity, which in appropriate cases may be cured by the court.

The discretion to allow service out of the jurisdiction is not exercised in a vacuum. There are specific heads or grounds of jurisdiction which must be established before leave may be granted for such service. In this regard, the contract's head appears to be the most often invoked. In addition, the court has to be satisfied that the case is a proper one for service abroad. There has been surprisingly little discussion in case law

83 *Motibhai Girdharbhai* v. *Thomas King* [1959] EA 270 at 276.

84 Tanzania is the only common law country that appears not to have a similar provision in its law.

85 While in some of the countries, it appears that both the issue and service require the leave of the court, in others it is only service which so requires. Compare, e.g., Nigeria – Federal High Court Rules, Ord. 6, r. 12, which provides 'no writ which, or notice of which, is to be served out of the jurisdiction shall be served without leave of the Court', with Sierra Leone – High Court Rules 2007, Ord. 6, r. 8, which provides 'no writ of summons for service out of the jurisdiction or of which notice is to be given out of the jurisdiction shall be issued without the leave of the Court or a Judge'.

86 *Broad Bank of Nigeria Ltd* v. *Olayiwola* [2005] WRN 101, [2005] 3 NWLR 434.

87 *Owners of the MV 'Arabella'* v. *Nigeria Agricultural Insurance Corp.* (2008) 2 All NLR 491; *Drexel Energy and Natural Resources Ltd* v. *Trans International Bank Ltd* (2008) 2 All NLR 224.

on the standard of proof to be met by applications in order to serve out of the jurisdiction. In what is perhaps the most detailed case law discussion yet on the issue, it was held that the plaintiff must make it sufficiently apparent to the court that the action it proposes to bring is within the scope of the relevant head and that there is a strong case for argument.[88]

Given that the common law does not allow for service out of jurisdiction and with the growing complexity of international litigation, it is open to question whether the existing heads of service out of jurisdiction are adequate. Indeed, there is a strong case to be made that the list of grounds upon which such service may be allowed needs to be expanded. For example, there is currently no head which allows for a writ to be served out of the jurisdiction in respect of an action to enforce a foreign judgment or arbitral award. Furthermore, the tort and contracts heads are currently worded in such a way that they appear to exclude restitutionary claims. Indeed, a Zambian court has held that an action to recover money paid by mistake of fact is not an action arising in any way from contract[89] – it is also certainly not an action in tort and whatever cause of action it may be appears not to be covered under the current heads in any of the common law countries. The law in England, on which all the service out of jurisdiction provisions are based, has undergone significant changes since these common law countries borrowed from it.[90] The time has therefore come for the law in these common law countries to be updated to reflect current needs.

The Roman-Dutch law countries

Botswana

In Botswana, every action, other than the process of arrest of the defendant, shall, where service is to be effected within the jurisdiction, be commenced by a writ of summons signed by the Registrar and sealed with the seal of the court.[91] No writ of summons for

[88] The best discussion of the subject appears to be in the case of *Cold Containers (Nigeria) Ltd* v. *Collis Cold Containers Ltd* 1977 (1) ALR Comm. 97 at 116, [1977] NCLR 97.

[89] *Northern Rhodesia Tobacco Co-operative Society Ltd* v. *Baird* [1949–54] NRLR 387.

[90] See *Cheshire, North & Fawcett*, pp. 372–99.

[91] Rules of the High Court 1970, Ord. 6, r. 1(1). See also Order 10, which provides, among others, that except by leave of the court, no process or document whereby proceedings are instituted shall be served outside the republic.

service out of the jurisdiction of the court shall be issued without the leave of the court or a judge.[92]

The principle of effectiveness is a fundamental aspect of the rules on jurisdiction in Botswana. Indeed, it has been held that there is no reason why the principle of effectiveness should not also apply to arbitration – attachment to confirm jurisdiction can be extended to situations where a dispute is pending before an arbitrator.[93] Because of this principle, a Botswanan court will not assume jurisdiction in a matter which has nothing to do with Botswana and to which the court can give no effective implementation if judgment were granted.[94] However, in appropriate cases, the principle of effectiveness may yield to other public policy considerations. Thus, it has been held that while there have been important public policy considerations behind the requirement for effectiveness in court judgments, there were equally important ones behind the requirement that parties be held to their contracts.[95]

The character of the parties is important in determining the appropriate rules of jurisdiction to invoke. The law distinguishes between actions commenced by an *incola* and actions instituted by or between peregrines.[96] An asset of a *peregrinus* may be attached for the purposes of founding or confirming jurisdiction in an action between an *incola* and a *peregrinus*, or in actions between peregrines. An application for attachment *ad fundandam jurisdictionem* is only required where the respondent is a *peregrinus* and not an *incola*.[97] The courts do not lightly allow property to be attached, either to found or confirm jurisdiction. It is incumbent on the applicant to furnish the court with certain vital particulars of the property sought to be attached. Such vital particulars include, for instance, the nature, value and situation of the property. The nature of the property

[92] Rules of the High Court 1970, Ord. 6, r. 9. *Lifelinx Insurance Agencies (Pty) Ltd* v. *Chikowe* 2006 (2) BLR 435; *Gaam Associates (Pty) Ltd* v. *Ogbugo* 1995 BLR 683. On how to serve writs and order documents abroad, see Ord. 8, rr. 4–6.

[93] *Silverstone (Pty) Ltd* v. *Lobatse Clay Works (Pty) Ltd* 1995 BLR 669 at 681–2.

[94] *Cloete* v. *Brink* 1996 BLR 224; *Gaam Associates (Pty) Ltd* v. *Ogbugo* 1995 BLR 683; *Pretorius* v. *Sweiger* 1979–80 BLR 124.

[95] *MAK (Pty) Ltd* v. *St Paul Insurance Co. SA Ltd* 2007 (1) BLR 210.

[96] It has been held that a company incorporated in Botswana and which had its registered office in Botswana was domiciled in Botswana for jurisdictional purposes and, accordingly, also as an *incola* on the basis of *ratione domicili*. *Silverstone (Pty) Ltd* v. *Lobatse Clay Works (Pty) Ltd* 1996 BLR 190 (varying *Silverstone (Pty) Ltd* v. *Lobatse Clay Works (Pty) Ltd* 1995 BLR 669). However, carrying on business *simpliciter* does not make a company an *incola*. *Bezuidenhout* v. *Dominion Earth Works (Pty) Ltd* 1964–70 BLR 233.

[97] *Healthcare Management Services (Pty) Ltd* v. *Smith* 1996 BLR 301.

is necessary to satisfy the court that it does not include perishable goods, or that it is not exempt from execution by law. The cited value of the property is necessary to satisfy the court of its saleable value, or its value as compared with the value of the claim. The situation of the property is necessary to eliminate any mistake as to the identity of the property and so that those executing the order, if granted, would know where to find the property.[98] In the instance of a plurality of potential plaintiffs, a single asset may be attached to found jurisdiction, even if it is already attached for a similar purpose in another case. The value of the property to be attached may be trifling when compared with the plaintiff's claim.[99]

In an action between peregrines, the mere fact that an asset of the *peregrinus* defendant has been attached is not enough to give the courts jurisdiction – there must be an additional jurisdictional connecting factor (*rationes jurisdictionis*). Thus, where one peregrine has money claims contracted abroad against another peregrine, the mere fact that the latter is possessed of assets within the jurisdiction does not constitute for the court a *forum rei sitae.*[100] Similarly, as between peregrines the mere existence of a *rationes jurisdictionis* is not enough. There must be an arrest or attachment to confirm jurisdiction.[101]

Submission provides an alternative means of overcoming the challenges posed by the attachment of the assets of a *peregrinus*. The defendant's action in submitting or acquiescing to jurisdiction should be clearly made and if it is being inferred it must be from factors which point unequivocally to submission.[102] Submission alone without attachment is sufficient to confer jurisdiction in an action by an *incola* plaintiff against a *peregrinus* defendant. Such submission to jurisdiction by a *peregrinus* has been sufficient to give the court jurisdiction without an attachment of property *ad confirmandam* jurisdiction.[103] Even in an action between peregrines, submission alone is enough to give the courts jurisdiction. Thus, it has been held that in the age of intense international trade involving cross-border transactions, as well as with the existence of efficient mechanisms for the international enforcement of judgments,

[98] *Martex Trading (Pty) Ltd* v. *Yannoulis (No. 2)* 1991 BLR 346; *Martex Trading (Pty) Ltd* v. *Yannoulis* 1991 BLR 330.

[99] *Semele* v. *Montanus* 1977 BLR 110.

[100] *Pretorius* v. *Sweiger* 1979–80 BLR 124.

[101] *Pascoe* v. *Botswana Ash (Pty) Ltd* [2008] 2 BLR 540.

[102] *Cloete* v. *Brink* 1996 BLR 224 at 227; *Cloete* v. *Brink* 1995 BLR 275.

[103] *Bigzy Holdings (Pty) Ltd* v. *Eso Management (Pty) Ltd* 2002 (2) BLR 125. In this case, the contract was entered into within Botswana and performance of the contract was to be in Botswana. Thus, it was not only submission that connected the suit to Botswana.

there is no reason why peregrines who have, by their own agreement, submitted themselves to the jurisdiction of the court, should not be held to their obligations in terms of their agreement.[104]

The effectiveness of submission or consent as an alternative to attachment depends on when it was given. Where a submission or consent to jurisdiction by a *peregrinus* occurs before an order of attachment to confirm jurisdiction has been granted, the court will not grant an order of attachment, because the court's jurisdiction will already have been secured and the court will thereafter not concern itself with whether or not any possible judgment it could give would be effective. A submission coming after attachment has been executed would be too late and the court would not in such an event set aside the attachment.[105]

Lesotho

A Lesotho court may, on application, grant leave for the property of a *peregrinus* in Lesotho to be attached, in order to give the court jurisdiction in an action which the applicant intends to bring against such a *peregrinus*.[106] The applicant must satisfy the court that he or she has a prima facie cause of action against the *peregrinus*; that the property sought to be attached is the property of the *peregrinus*, or that the *peregrinus* has some right in the property;[107] and that the applicant him- or herself is an *incola* of Lesotho and the respondent is a *peregrinus*.[108] The *peregrinus* may at any time before judgment apply to the court, on notice to the plaintiff, to set aside the attachment on a good cause shown.[109] Similarly, if any person can show that the property attached is their property and not that of the *peregrinus*, such a person may apply to the court to set aside the attachment.[110]

Furthermore, on the application of an *incola* of Lesotho, the court may order the arrest of a *peregrinus* who is temporarily within the jurisdiction

[104] *MAK (Pty) Ltd* v. *St Paul Insurance Co. SA Ltd* 2007 (1) BLR 210.

[105] *Bigzy Holdings (Pty) Ltd* v. *Eso Management (Pty) Ltd* 2002 (2) BLR 125.

[106] High Court Rules 1980, s. 6(1).

[107] *Moggee & Du Toit* v. *Makhoza*, CIV/T/238/84 (High Court, Lesotho, 1985).

[108] High Court Rules 1980, s. 6(2). The applicant may in the same application apply for leave to serve the defendant by edictal citation. Section 5(1) provides that, except by leave of the court, no process or any document whereby proceedings are instituted shall be served outside Lesotho. On the procedure for serving documents outside Lesotho, see High Court Rules 1980, s. 5(3)–(9).

[109] High Court Rules 1980, s. 6(4). See generally *Lepota* v. *Ivan Hyland*, CIV/APN/280/87 (High Court, Lesotho, 1991).

[110] High Court Rules 1980, s. 6(6).

of the court.[111] The applicant must show that he or she has a good cause of action against the *peregrinus* and must also produce a certificate from an advocate who certifies that he or she has considered the information on the question given and from the document produced by the applicant, and that in their opinion, the applicant has a good cause of action against the *peregrinus*.[112] If the application is granted, the Sheriff will be ordered to arrest the *peregrinus* and bring him or her to court as soon as possible. The *peregrinus* can give security to ensure his or her release from custody.[113]

Namibia

In Namibia, attachment of the property of a *peregrinus* defendant or their arrest is an important aspect of the rules on jurisdiction in international matters. No attachment of person or property to found jurisdiction shall be ordered against an *incola* of Namibia.[114]

In order for the property of a *peregrinus* to be attached at the instance of another *peregrinus*, the court must have jurisdiction over the contemplated suit: either *rei sitae*, *loci contractus* or *loci solutionis*, or on the grounds of a delict committed within the court's jurisdiction. The attachment only strengthens the jurisdiction already possessed by the court – mere submission to jurisdiction by both peregrines is not sufficient to found jurisdiction.[115] In other words, the general rule is that consent or submission, whether express or implied, cannot vest the court with jurisdiction where there are no other grounds for jurisdiction, and where the plaintiff and defendant are peregrines.[116] In the words of Justice Brebner, 'the doctrine of prorogation of jurisdiction cannot apply where the Court has no jurisdiction over the subject matter of the suit . . . the consent of the parties cannot confer jurisdiction over the subject-matter of a suit by agreement'.[117] However, where several debtors, jointly liable for the same debt, are within different areas of jurisdiction,

[111] Ibid., s. 6(8). *Lesotho Express Delivery Services Ltd* v. *Ravin Panambalana*, CIV/T/634A/02 (High Court, Lesotho, 2006), which involved an unsuccessful application for the arrest of the defendant to found or confirm jurisdiction.

[112] High Court Rules 1980, s. 6(8)(a).

[113] Ibid., s. 6(8)(c).

[114] High Court Act 1990, s. 25; *Schiebler* v. *Kiss* 1985 (3) SA 489.

[115] *Slabber* v. *Blanco* 1991 NR 404 at 409. See generally *SOS-Kinderdorf International* v. *Effie Lentin Architects* 1990 NR 300, 1991 (3) SA 574.

[116] *Argos Fishing Co. Ltd* v. *Friopesca SA* 1991 NR 106 at 111, 1991 (3) SA 255 at 260; *New York Shipping Co. (Pty) Ltd* v. *Emmi Equipment (Pty) Ltd* 1968 (1) SA 355.

[117] *Brecher* v. *Brecher* 1947 (3) SA 225 at 229–30.

according to the *causae continentia* rule, they should nevertheless be amenable to the jurisdiction of a single court. This avoids a multiplicity of actions and the possibility of conflicting judgments. The application of the exception is reinforced where the defendants, by their conduct, are deemed to have tacitly consented to the court's jurisdiction.[118] Where a *ratio jurisdictionis* exists, submission or consent to jurisdiction may render unnecessary the need for attachment, but consent to jurisdiction by a *peregrinus* after an order of attachment has been executed is too late.[119]

An applicant seeking an order of attachment *ad fundandam* or *confirmandam jurisdictionem* must show that he or she has a prima facie cause of action against the defendant, that the defendant is a *peregrinus*, that the defendant is within the area of jurisdiction of the court, or that the property in which the defendant has a beneficial interest is within that area of jurisdiction.[120]

In respect of companies, the Namibian courts have jurisdiction over a foreign company which carries on substantial operations in Namibia, or where the relief being claimed arises from a contract entered into and executed in Namibia.[121]

The procedure of edictal citation allows a plaintiff to serve legal process on a person abroad. Save by leave of the court, no process or document whereby proceedings are instituted shall be served outside Namibia.[122]

South Africa[123]

Attachment is an essential aspect of the rules on jurisdiction in South Africa. However, no attachment of person or property to found

118 *New York Shipping Co. (Pty) Ltd* v. *Emmi Equipment (Pty) Ltd* 1968 (1) SA 355.

119 *Bourgwells Ltd (Owners of MFV Ofelia)* v. *Shepalov* 1998 NR 307.

120 *Bourgwells* v. *Shepalov*.

121 *Mahe Construction Ltd* v. *Seasonaire* 2002 NR 398; *Seasonaire* v. *Mahe Construction Ltd* 2002 NR 53.

122 High Court Rules 1990, s. 5. On the procedure for serving documents outside Namibia, see s. 4(3)–(5). See also generally *Cabinet of the Transitional Government of South West Africa* v. *Dagnin* 1990 NR 14, which held that a summons directed against a person resident outside the jurisdiction of the court should state the grounds on which the court has jurisdiction.

123 This section does not deal with jurisdictional issues that arise internally between South African courts. See generally Supreme Court Act 1959, s. 19(1)(c); *Ewing McDonald & Co. Ltd* v. *M & M Products Co.* 1991 (1) SA 252; *Koppe & Co.* v. *Accreylon Co. Inc.* 1948 (3) SA 591; *Kopelowitz* v. *West* 1954 (4) SA 296; *Bock & Son (Pty) Ltd* v. *Wisconsin*

jurisdiction shall be ordered by a South African court against a person who is resident in South Africa.[124] Historically, and by reason of the doctrine of effectiveness,[125] attachment to confirm jurisdiction has only been justified in cases sounding in money or claims relating to property, i.e. claims involving property or real rights to or in property. It has not had any application to matrimonial causes or actions *in personam* which do not have a monetary or property component.[126] Thus, in an application for a prohibitory interdict against a peregrine respondent, it has been found that all the delicts complained of were committed abroad and the South African courts had no control over the respondent, or over the cessation of the acts in question. It has therefore been held that, in such instances, the court lacks jurisdiction and this cannot be cured by an attachment to found jurisdiction.[127]

In a claim sounding in money against a *peregrinus* defendant, an order for the attachment of the property of a *peregrinus* defendant is essential. A South African court will not assume jurisdiction in an action sounding in money between peregrines unless there is both a *ratio jurisdictionis* and an attachment (or, historically, arrest) to confirm such jurisdiction.[128] A *peregrinus* plaintiff cannot secure the attachment of the property of a *peregrinus* defendant in order to found jurisdiction unless there is a *ratio jurisdictionis*.[129] In such actions, the mere fact that property belonging to one *peregrinus* lies within the jurisdiction of the court is not

Leather Co. 1960 (4) SA 767; *Ex p. Gerald B Coyne (Pty) Ltd* 1971 (1) SA 624. Jurisdiction involving legal persons raises special issues (such as when is a company resident within the jurisdiction? Or what amounts to doing business within the jurisdiction?) which are not addressed in this section. On these points, see generally *Leibowitz t/a Lee Finance* v. *Mhlana* 2006 (6) SA 180; *Appleby (Pty) Ltd* v. *Dundas Ltd* 1948 (2) SA 905; *Bisonboard Ltd* v. *K Braun Woodworking Machinery (Pty) Ltd* 1991 (1) SA 482; *Dairy Board* v. *John T Rennie & Co. (Pty) Ltd* 1976 (3) SA 768; *Spie Batignolles Société Anonyme* v. *Van Niekerk* 1980 (2) SA 441; *Skjelbreds Rederi A/S* v. *Hartless (Pty) Ltd* 1982 (2) SA 739; *ISM Inter Ltd* v. *Maraldo* 1983 (4) SA 112; *Joseph* v. *Air Tanzania Corp.* 1997 (3) SA 34.

124 Supreme Court Act 1959, s. 28(1). For a useful discussion of the concept of 'residence', see *Mayne* v. *Main* 2001 (2) SA 1239; *Terblanche* v. *Damji* 2003 (5) SA 489.

125 See generally *Makoti* v. *Brodie* 1988 (2) SA 569, [1984–7] 4 BSC 411.

126 *Simon* v. *Air Operations of Europe* 1999 (1) SA 217.

127 *Ex p. Hay Management Consultants (Pty) Ltd* 2000 (3) SA 501. See also *Di Bona* v. *Di Bona* 1993 (2) SA 682.

128 *Chong Sun Wood Products Ltd* v. *K & T Trading Ltd* 2001 (2) SA 651; *Siemens Ltd* v. *Offshore Marine Engineering Ltd* 1993 (3) SA 913.

129 *Chattanooga Tufters Supply Co.* v. *Chenille Corp. of South Africa (Pty) Ltd* 1974 (2) SA 10; *Berger* v. *Aiken* 1964 (2) SA 396.

enough.[130] Thus, the court has no jurisdiction to grant an order at the instance of a *peregrinus* plaintiff to attach the property of a *peregrinus* defendant to found jurisdiction so that a debt incurred under a contract entered into and performed outside South Africa can be recovered.[131] However, in an action by an *incola* plaintiff against a *peregrinus* defendant, attachment alone is sufficient to found jurisdiction: there is no need for a *ratio jurisdictionis*.[132]

The onus is on an applicant for attachment to show that it is possessed of rights of entitlement to claim an order of attachment.[133] The mere fact that the applicant is a cessionary who has received his or her right of action from a *peregrinus* does not disentitle him or her to bring an application to attach *ad fundandam jurisdictionem*.[134] Although the question of whether or not the respondent was a fugitive from justice was not crucial to the determination of the application for attachment to found jurisdiction, it was a relevant factor.[135] The property to be attached must be within the jurisdiction of the court.[136] For the purposes of attachment to found or confirm jurisdiction, the *situs* of a share is the place of registration of the shares.[137]

The defendant must have an attachable interest in the property to be attached – the property sought to be attached must belong to the *peregrinus*. There can be no justification for an attachment to confirm jurisdiction in an action against a *peregrinus* defendant (whether by an *incola* or a *peregrinus* plaintiff) of property or of any person other than the proposed defendant, and a fortiori if the plaintiff claims ownership of the property. This is because the purpose of an attachment is to render the jurisdiction of the court effective and this purpose cannot be achieved by such an attachment.[138] The onus is on the applicant to establish on a balance of probabilities that the respondent has an attachable interest in

130 *Frank Wright (Pty) Ltd* v. *Corticas 'BCM' Ltd* 1948 (4) SA 456.

131 *Maritime & Industrial Services Ltd* v. *Marcierta Compania Naviera SA* 1969 (3) SA 28. See also *Minesa Energy (Pty) Ltd* v. *Stinnes International AG* 1988 (3) SA 903.

132 *Kudu Granite Holdings Ltd* v. *Caterna Ltd* 2007 (6) SA 615.

133 *Skjelbreds Rederi A/S* v. *Hartless (Pty) Ltd* 1982 (2) SA 710.

134 *Kaffraria Property Co. (Pty) Ltd* v. *Government of the Republic of Zambia* 1980 (2) SA 709.

135 *Harris* v. *Rees* [2010] 4 All SA 603.

136 In this regard it does not matter where the property is located in South Africa. See Supreme Court Act 1959, s. 26(1).

137 *Uniroyal Inc.* v. *Thor Chemical SA (Pty) Ltd* 1984 (1) SA 381.

138 *Chong Sun Wood Products Ltd* v. *K & T Trading Ltd* 2001 (2) SA 651.

the assets sought to be attached.[139] The crucial moment for testing whether the respondent is the owner of the property sought to be attached is, generally, the moment when the judge, hearing the application for attachment, is requested to issue the order.[140] The courts will set aside an attachment where it is demonstrated that the *peregrinus* defendant does not have an attachable interest in the property sought to be attached.[141]

The categories of property which may be attached are not closed – it may be movable or immovable. Property which has been pledged or subject to a lien;[142] which has been sold to the respondent under a hire purchase agreement;[143] amounts due under a bill of lading;[144] a personal right to be paid a sum of money;[145] an order for cost;[146] and a member's interest (like a share in a company) in a closed corporation[147] have all been subjects of attachment. An existing claim (regardless of its value) by a prospective *peregrinus* defendant against a prospective *incola* plaintiff is attachable to found jurisdiction in a proposed action.[148] However, the obligation of a debtor is not property which can be attached.[149]

As a matter of principle and policy, courts are prepared to exclude certain forms of property from attachment. Thus, it has been held that it is not in the interests of international trade and banking for the buyer of

[139] *Sunnyface Marine Ltd* v. *Hitoroy Ltd* 1992 (2) SA 653; *Barlows Tractor & Machinery Co.* v. *Oceanair (Transvaal) Pty Ltd* 1978 (3) SA 175; *Degem Systems Ltd* v. *Government of the Republic of Bophuthatswana* [1989–90] 6 BSC 466; *American Cotton Products Corp.* v. *Felt and Tweeds Ltd* 1953 (2) SA 753.

[140] *Numill Marketing CC* v. *Sitra Wood Products Ltd* 1994 (3) SA 460.

[141] *Anderson & Coltman Ltd* v. *Universal Trading Co.* 1948 (1) SA 1277; *Jackson* v. *Parker* 1950 (3) SA 25; *Banco de Mocambique* v. *Inter-science Research and Development Services (Pty) Ltd* 1982 (3) SA 330; *Bominflot Ltd* v. *Kien Hung Shipping Co. Ltd* 2004 (2) SA 556.

[142] *Mercantile Bank of India* v. *Davis* 1947 (2) SA 723; *Hymore Agencies Durban (Pty) Ltd* v. *Gin Nih Weaving Factory* 1959 (1) SA 180.

[143] *BW Diesel Distributors (Pty) Ltd* v. *Byrne* 1957 (2) SA 29.

[144] *Araxos (East London) (Pty) Ltd* v. *Contara Lines Ltd* 1979 (1) SA 1027.

[145] *Meihuizen Freight (Pty) Ltd* v. *Transportes Maritimos de Portugal LDA* 2005 (1) SA 36; *Ferguson & Timpson Ltd* v. *African Industrial & Technical Services (Pty) Ltd* 1949 (4) SA 340.

[146] *Drop Inn Group of Liquor Supermarkets (Pty) Ltd* v. *Longman Distillers Ltd* 1988 (4) SA 35; *Drive Control Services (Pty) Ltd* v. *Troycom Systems (Pty) Ltd* 2000 (2) SA 722.

[147] *Schmidt* v. *Weaving* 2009 (1) SA 170. In such a case, actual notice of the attachment should be given to the corporation for it to be valid.

[148] *Thermo Radiant Oven Sales (Pty) Ltd* v. *Nelspruit Bakeries (Pty) Ltd* 1969 (2) SA 295. But see *Ex p. Usko Ltd: In re. Usko Ltd* v. *Cortinovis Spa* 1998 (4) SA 976.

[149] *MV Snow Delta Serva Ship Ltd* v. *Discount Tonnage Ltd* 2000 (4) SA 746.

an irrevocable letter of credit to be able to subvert that irrevocability through attachment, and the court would accordingly imply a term into the contract between the buyer and seller to the effect that the buyer will not undermine the irrevocable nature of that letter of credit by seeking to attach the seller's right to payment from the bank issuing the letter of credit.[150] It has also been queried whether a negative right, such as a copyright, is generally attachable to found jurisdiction.[151] Moreover, all property of a foreign state, including money held by it for public purposes in the area of the jurisdiction of the court, is immune from attachment.[152]

The property to be attached need not be of any particular value and certainly need not be equivalent to the value of the claim.[153] The fact that the value of the property to be attached to found jurisdiction might be insufficient to satisfy a judgment the court might subsequently give would not per se oust jurisdiction or render the attachment liable to be set aside.[154] If the property attached had a value when the attachment order was granted and served, the fact that it might thereafter become valueless will not affect the court's jurisdiction once it had been founded and confirmed by the attachment.[155] A *peregrinus* defendant may provide security in order to obtain release of property attached. However, the fact that the attachment of property of insignificant value is sufficient to found jurisdiction does not mean that a *peregrinus* is entitled to obtain the release of his or her property by providing security of equivalent value to that of the property attached.[156]

In addition to proving that the defendant has an attachable interest in the property which he or she seeks to attach, an applicant for attachment must demonstrate a prima facie cause of action. The requirement of a prima facie cause of action in relation to an attachment to found jurisdiction is satisfied where there is evidence which, if accepted, will show a

150 *Ex p. Sapan Trading (Pty) Ltd* 1995 (1) SA 218.

151 *Bieber* v. *Columbia Pictures Inc.* 1981 (2) SA 405.

152 *Parkin* v. *Government of the Republique Democratique du Congo* 1971 (1) SA 259.

153 *Yorigami Maritime Construction Co. Ltd* v. *Nissho-Iwai Co. Ltd* 1977 (4) SA 682.

154 *MV Snow Delta: Discount Tonnage Ltd* v. *Serva Ship Ltd* 1998 (3) SA 636 (*The MV Snow Delta Discount Tonnage Ltd* v. *Serva Ship Ltd* 1997 (2) SA 719).

155 *MT Tigr Owners of the MT Tigr* v. *Transnet Ltd* 1998 (3) SA 861. Jurisdiction once appropriately invoked cannot be displaced. *Coin Security Group (Pty) Ltd* v. *Smit NO* 1992 (3) SA 333 (reversing *Coin Security Group (Pty) Ltd* v. *Smit NO* 1991 (2) SA 315); *Cats* v. *Cats* 1959 (4) SA 375; *South African Railways and Harbours* v. *Chairman, Bophuthatswana Central Road Transportation Board* 1982 (3) SA 24.

156 *Yorigami Maritime Construction Co. Ltd* v. *Nissho-Iwai Co. Ltd* 1977 (4) SA 682.

cause of action. The mere fact that such evidence is contradicted does not disentitle the applicant to the remedy. Even where the probabilities are against him or her, the requirement will still be satisfied. It is only when it is quite clear that he or she has no action, or cannot succeed, that an attachment should be refused or discharged.[157] Indeed, the onus which rests upon an applicant for an order of attachment *ad fundandam jurisdictionem* is not a very heavy one.[158] This does not deny that attachment is an 'exceptional remedy'; the courts are expected to grant it with 'care and caution'.[159] Once all the requirements for attachment have been satisfied, a court has no discretion to refuse an attachment.[160]

The rationale underlying the need to attach the property of a *peregrinus* defendant in order to found or confirm jurisdiction lies in the doctrine of effectiveness. Where such effectiveness is otherwise open to attainment, the courts do not require an attachment. Accordingly, it has been held that there is no need to effect an attachment either to confirm or found jurisdiction in proceedings for the ejectment of a tenant from immovable property.[161]

Historically, as regards *peregrinus* defendants, the law holds that attachment or arrest (attachment of persons) is mandatory to found or confirm jurisdiction.[162] An *incola* is entitled as of right to an order for the attachment or arrest of a *peregrinus* for confirmation of jurisdiction and is under no obligation to appraise the *peregrinus* of his or her right to

157 *Bradbury Gretorex Co. (Colonial) Ltd* v. *Standard Trading Co. (Pty) Ltd* 1953 (3) SA 529; *Italtrafo SpA* v. *Electricity Supply Commission* 1978 (2) SA 705; *Butler* v. *Banimar Shipping Co. SA* 1978 (4) SA 753; *Inter-science Research and Development Services (Pty) Ltd* v. *Republica Popular de Mocambique* 1980 (2) SA 111; *Kaffraria Property Co. (Pty) Ltd* v. *Government of the Republic of Zambia* 1980 (2) SA 709; *MY Summit One Farocean Marine (Pty) Ltd* v. *Malacca Holdings Ltd* 2005 (1) SA 428 (*MY Summit One Farocean Marine (Pty) Ltd* v. *Malacca Holdings Ltd* 2003 (6) SA 94); *MV Lina Union Shipping and Managing Co. SA* v. *Lina Maritime Ltd* 1998 (4) SA 633; *Rees* v. *Harris* 2012 (1) SA 583.

158 *Yorigami Maritime Construction Co. Ltd* v. *Nissho-Iwai Co. Ltd* 1977 (4) SA 682.

159 *Ex p. Acrow Engineers (Pty) Ltd* 1953 (2) SA 319; *Hülse-Reutter* v. *Gödde* 2001 (4) SA 1336.

160 *Simon* v. *Air Operations of Europe* 1999 (1) SA 217; *Associated Marine Engineers (Pty) Ltd* v. *Foroya Banki PF* 1994 (4) SA 676.

161 *Sandton Square Finance (Pty) Ltd* v. *Biagi, Bertola and Vasco* 1997 (1) SA 258; *Manna* v. *Lotter* 2007 (4) SA 315. But see *Jackaman* v. *Arkell* 1953 (3) SA 31.

162 See generally *Ex p. Whitehead* 1950 (3) SA 429; *Jardine* v. *Stibbe* 1959 (2) SA 783; *Van Ryneveld* v. *Paxinos* 1964 (3) SA 754; *Tick* v. *Broude* 1973 (1) SA 462; *Small Business Development Corp. Ltd* v. *Amey* 1989 (4) SA 890; *Preisig* v. *Tattersall* 1982 (3) SA 1082; *Reilly* v. *Benigno* 1982 (4) SA 365.

submit to the jurisdiction of the court.[163] In *Bid Industrial Holdings (Pty) Ltd* v. *Strang*,[164] it was held that arrest to found or confirm jurisdiction infringed the right to freedom and security of the person involved and was therefore unconstitutional. In its place, it has been held that where attachment of property is not possible, a South African court would have jurisdiction, if the summons is served on the defendant while he or she is present in South Africa and if there is sufficient connection between the suit and the area of jurisdiction of the court concerned to ensure that disposal of the case by that court is appropriate and convenient.[165]

In appropriate cases, submission or consent to jurisdiction may serve as an alternative to attachment.[166] Only in cases where a *causa jurisdictionis* apart from the attachment exists, i.e. in the case of an attachment *ad confirmandam jurisdictionem*, can attachment become unnecessary as a result of submission to jurisdiction.[167] In this regard, the effectiveness of submission depends in large part on the character of the parties. In an action by an *incola* plaintiff against a *peregrinus* defendant, submission to jurisdiction renders an attachment neither necessary nor permissible.[168] In other words, in the case of an *incola* plaintiff, submission by a *peregrinus* defendant is sufficient to confer jurisdiction without an attachment *ad fundandam jurisdictionem*.[169] However, in a case where a *peregrinus* plaintiff sues a *peregrinus* defendant, the action cannot be entertained solely on the grounds that the defendant has submitted to the court's jurisdiction – in addition there have to be traditional grounds for jurisdiction, such as *ratione rei sitae*, *ratione res gestae* or *ratione contractus*.[170]

[163] *Naylor* v. *Jansen* 2006 (3) SA 546.

[164] 2008 (3) SA 355. [165] *Bid Industrial Holdings* v. *Strang*.

[166] *Transnet Ltd* v. *Owner of the MV 'Alina II'* [2011] 4 All SA 350. See generally *Njikelana* v. *Njikelana* 1980 (2) SA 808, which held that domicile without actual residence or physical presence for the time being is sufficient ground for jurisdiction in a claim sounding in money and that in such a case attachment of the person of the defendant is not necessary to give any future judgment effectiveness. See also *Nusca* v. *Nusca* 1995 (4) SA 813.

[167] *Ghomeshi-Bozorg* v. *Yousefi* 1998 (1) SA 692; *Briscoe* v. *Marais* 1992 (2) SA 413.

[168] *American Flag Plc* v. *Great African T-shirt Corp. CC* 2000 (1) SA 356; *Ex p. Jamieson: In re. Jamieson* v. *Sabingo* 2001 (2) SA 775; *Cinemark (Pty) Ltd* v. *Transkei Hotel* 1984 (2) SA 332; *Centner* v. *Griffin* 1960 (4) SA 798; *Du Preez* v. *Philip-King* 1963 (1) SA 801. But see *Slabbert* v. *Herbst* 1981 (4) SA 257; *Blue Continent Products (Pty) Ltd* v. *Foroya Banki PF* 1993 (4) SA 563.

[169] *Hay Management Consultants (Pty) Ltd* v. *P3 Management Consultants (Pty) Ltd* 2005 (2) SA 522.

[170] *Hermes Versekeringsmaatskappy* v. *Dartnell* 1980 (4) SA 279; *Veneta Mineraria Spa* v. *Carolina Collieries (Pty) Ltd (in Liquidation)* 1987 (4) SA 883; *Veneta*

To constitute submission to the jurisdiction of the court, the conduct which forms the subject matter of such an inquiry must be of such a nature that the court can say it is consistent only with acquiescence.[171] Submission does not have to take any particular form – in any particular matter it is a question of fact whether a respondent has consented to jurisdiction.[172] It may be written or oral, unilateral or bilateral, express or implied.[173] Neither the mere failure to oppose an application,[174] nor the fact that the defendant has appointed an address for service within the area of the court's jurisdiction in compliance with an order of the court, constitute submission to the court's jurisdiction.[175] However, it is a well-established principle that a plaintiff always submits to the court where he or she has brought their action.[176] A statement from the bar at a hearing that the respondent consented to jurisdiction has been held to be good submission.[177] Once made, submission to jurisdiction cannot be revoked.[178]

Time is an important factor in assessing the effectiveness of submission as an alternative to attachment. Submission to jurisdiction volunteered by a *peregrinus* after the attachment *ad confirmandam jurisdictionem* of his or her property has been ordered at the instance of an aggrieved *incola* does not, and cannot, have the effect of discharging the attachment.[179] However, submission before any order of attachment to confirm jurisdiction has been granted or prior to the execution of an order for attachment renders attachment unnecessary.[180]

Mineraria Spa v. *Carolina Collieries (Pty) Ltd* 1985 (3) SA 633; *Greater Services (Pty) Ltd* v. *Du Toit* 1975 (1) SA 260; *Towers* v. *Paisley* 1963 (1) SA 92.

171 *Van der Walt Business Brokers (Pty) Ltd* v. *Budget Kilometers* 1999 (3) SA 1149; *Du Preez* v. *Philip-King* 1963 (1) SA 801; *Blue Continent Products (Pty) Ltd* v. *Foroya Banki PF* 1993 (4) SA 563.

172 *Agro-grip (Pty) Ltd* v. *Ayal* 1999 (3) SA 126; *Bonugli* v. *Standard Bank of South Africa* 2012 (5) SA 202.

173 *Hay Management Consultants (Pty) Ltd* v. *P3 Management Consultants (Pty) Ltd* 2005 (2) SA 522.

174 *Leibowitz t/a Lee Finance* v. *Mhlana* 2006 (6) SA 180.

175 *JPS Nominees (Pty) Ltd* v. *Binstock* 1993 (1) SA 341.

176 *American Flag Plc* v. *Great African T-shirt Corp. CC* 2000 (1) SA 356.

177 *Agro-grip (Pty) Ltd* v. *Ayal* 1999 (3) SA 126.

178 *Centner* v. *Griffin* 1960 (4) SA 798.

179 *Kasimov* v. *Kurland* 1987 (4) SA 76; *Bettencourt* v. *Kom* 1994 (2) SA 513; *Himelsein* v. *Super Rich CC* 1998 (1) SA 929; *Tsung* v. *Industrial Development Corp. of SA Ltd* 2006 (4) SA 177.

180 *Jamieson* v. *Sabingo* 2002 (4) SA 49; *Rosenberg* v. *Mbanga* 1992 (4) SA 331; *Utah International Inc.* v. *Honeth* 1987 (4) SA 145.

The presence of a jurisdiction agreement in a contract constitutes submission prior to an order of attachment.[181]

South African law allows for legal process to be served abroad. However, except by leave of the court, no process or document whereby proceedings are instituted shall be served outside South Africa.[182] Granting leave to sue via edictal citation is within the discretion of the court. Before exercising such discretion in favour of an applicant, the court must not only be satisfied as to such an applicant's cause of action and its jurisdiction over the respondent, but also that the application is necessary, or cannot be avoided, in order to enable the applicant to achieve the relief claimed.[183]

Swaziland

An essential aspect of the rules on jurisdiction in Swaziland is the principle of effectiveness. A Swaziland court will attach the assets of a *peregrinus* defendant for the purpose of founding or confirming the jurisdiction of the court. The court will order the attachment of the person or property of a *peregrinus* at the instance of another *peregrinus* provided it has jurisdiction in the suit apart from attachment.[184] The onus which rests upon the applicant is satisfied if there is evidence which, if accepted, will establish a cause of action.[185]

Where the defendant consents to the jurisdiction of the court, they dispense with the need for attachment. However, consent of a *peregrinus* is consent to jurisdiction only over the person of the party. In law, it cannot represent consent to jurisdiction over the cause of action. In other words, by consenting to jurisdiction, a defendant subjects his or her person to the court's jurisdiction, but that is not enough – one or more of the traditional grounds of jurisdiction over the subject matter of the

[181] *Elscint (Pty) Ltd* v. *Mobile Medical Scanners (Pty) Ltd* 1986 (4) SA 552.

[182] Uniform Rules of Court, s. 5(1). See generally *Consani Engineering (Pty) Ltd* v. *Anton Steinecker Maschinenfabrik GmbH* 1991 (1) SA 823; *Rand Estate Agency (Pty) Ltd* v. *Lacey* 1949 (4) SA 83.

[183] *Steinberg* v. *Steinberg* 1962 (4) SA 321, but see *Orion Pacific Traders Inc.* v. *Spectrum Shipping Ltd* 2006 (2) SA 586, which held that, once it appeared prima facie that the court had jurisdiction and it was clear that the action was not vexatious and was properly before the court, the court had no discretion to refuse the relief as the applicant was entitled to the relief as of right.

[184] *De Hart* v. *Kleynhans* [1963–9] Sw. LR 373. See generally *Molly Kiwanuka* v. *Samuel Muwanga*, Civil Case No. 1506/98 (High Court, Swaziland, 1999).

[185] *Standard Bank of Swaziland Ltd* v. *Cassamo* [1979–81] Sw. LR 247.

dispute must also be present. Save for jurisdiction over a person, a party cannot consent to additional grounds for jurisdiction where the court does not have jurisdiction on such grounds to begin with.[186]

Zimbabwe

Attachment of property or the arrest of a defendant is an essential aspect of the rules on jurisdiction in Zimbabwe. At the instance of an *incola* plaintiff, a Zimbabwean court will attach the property of a *peregrinus* if the property is in its area of jurisdiction, so as to found jurisdiction in a claim sounding in money brought against a *peregrinus*, even if there are no other grounds for exercising jurisdiction.[187] Property owned by the prospective defendant, including immovables, can be attached.[188] Indeed, an interest in property, short of ownership, constitutes a right capable of being attached. Thus, the control which one company has over another and its assets may be of such great commercial value that it is amenable to attachment.[189]

Founding or confirming jurisdiction is not the only purpose of attachment; a further object is to furnish an asset on which execution may be levied in order to satisfy the judgment which may be given in favour of the person seeking attachment, so that the court's judgment will not be rendered nugatory.[190] Thus, in a case where the respondent was a resident of Zimbabwe before the action commenced, but left permanently after the service of the summons, she could not for practical purposes be regarded as an *incola* and attachment of her property (or the deposit with her legal practitioners of a sum of money equal to the value of the property) was necessary to confirm jurisdiction and to provide security for the judgment which might be given against her.[191]

[186] *AG Thomas (Pty) Ltd* v. *Grinaker Lta (Ltd)*, Case No: 1453/2004 (High Court, Swaziland, 2005).

[187] *Central African Airways Corp.* v. *Vickers-Armstrong* 1956 (2) SA 492, 1956 R & N 4; *Riseley* v. *Watt* 1965 (2) SA 664, [1965] RLR 82; *Ex p. Vulcan Trading Co. Ltd* 1951 (1) SA 355; *African Distillers Ltd* v. *Zietkiewicz* 1980 ZLR 135 at 136.

[188] *Ex p. Smith* 1956 (1) SA 252; *Ex p. Sletcher* 1947 (1) SA 549; *Ex p. Heald* 1952 (3) SA 740; *Ex p. Gregory* 1956 (1) SA 215.

[189] *Stanmarker Mining (Pvt) Ltd* v. *Metallon Corp. Ltd* 2004 (1) ZLR 45 (reversing *Stanmarker Mining (Private) Ltd* v. *Metallon Corp. Ltd*, HC 919/03 (High Court, Zimbabwe, 2003)).

[190] *Grobler* v. *Boshoff* 1988 (2) ZLR 447.

[191] *Grobler* v. *Boshoff*.

In any case where the High Court may exercise jurisdiction founded on, or which may be confirmed by, the arrest of any person or the attachment of any property, the court may permit or direct the issue of the process, within such period as the court may specify, for service either in or outside Zimbabwe, without ordering such arrest or attachment, if the court is satisfied that the person or property concerned is within Zimbabwe and is capable of being arrested or attached, and that the jurisdiction of the High Court in the matter shall be founded or confirmed, as the case may be, by the issue of such a process.[192] The purpose of this provision is to give the court discretion to confirm jurisdiction by the issue of process rather than by arrest or attachment. It does not relieve the plaintiff from the burden of having to show that the *peregrinus* was within the country or had property capable of attachment.[193] Accordingly, the court has no jurisdiction to entertain a suit against a *peregrinus* for damages arising from alleged breaches of a contract entered into and performed in Zimbabwe, where neither the *peregrinus*, nor any of his or her property, lies within the territorial jurisdiction of the court.[194]

The discretion to dispense with attachment or arrest is exercised in an equitable manner: the court is not bound to give the applicant preferential treatment, but can take into account the effect of the order upon third parties and can have regard to the balance of convenience in exercising the discretion.[195] However, the courts have been careful not to detail all the circumstances where an order for attachment may be made. Examples of the types of cases where orders of attachment have been made are those where the property sought to be attached is subject to the very dispute in question, or cases where it is quite clear that the only property the respondent has within the jurisdiction is that which is sought to be attached and there is a danger that, if it is not attached, he

[192] High Court Act 1981, s. 15; *Ex p. Mor-Tal Construction Co. (Pvt) Ltd* 1962 (2) SA 664, 1962 R & N 248; *Ex p. Mercer* 1969 (1) R & N 117, 1969 (2) SA 207; *Clan Transport Co. (Pvt) Ltd* v. *Government of the Republic of Mozambique* 1993 (3) SA 795; *Ex p. Coote* 1962 R & N 423. See generally *McGuire* v. *Fourie* 1962 R & N 420, 1962 (3) SA 302; *In re. Practice Note* 1963 (4) SA 165.

[193] *Monarch Steel (1991) Ltd* v. *Fourway Haulage Ltd* 1997 (2) ZLR 342; *Riseley* v. *Watt* 1965 (2) SA 664, [1965] RLR 82; *Stanmarker Mining (Pvt) Ltd* v. *Metallon Corp. Ltd* 2004 (1) ZLR 45.

[194] *African Distillers Ltd* v. *Zietkiewicz* 1980 ZLR 135. See also *Riseley* v. *Watt* 1965 (2) SA 664, [1965] RLR 82.

[195] *X & Y (Pvt) Ltd* v. *Z* 1974 (1) SA 195, 1973 (2) RLR 178; *Voicevale Ltd* v. *Freightlink (Malawi) Ltd* 1987 (2) ZLR 22.

or she will make away with that property, thus giving rise to the possibility that the court's judgment will be a *brutum fulmen.*[196]

Jurisdiction by consent or submission has been recognised in Zimbabwean private international law. In *Beverley Building Society* v. *De Courcy*,[197] the defendants, both *peregrini*, had been sued jointly and severally for an amount due under a deed of suretyship. Neither was domiciled or resident in Southern Rhodesia, nor had there been any attachment of their person or property to confirm jurisdiction. They had, however, chosen *domicilium citandi et executandi* in Salisbury. It was held that the choice by the defendants of the *domicilium citandi et executandi* more probably meant consent to jurisdiction than merely an address for service. Accordingly, the court had jurisdiction even though there had been no attachment either of person or property to found jurisdiction.[198]

Comments

Attachment of property or person (arrest) to found or confirm jurisdiction are essential features of the rules on jurisdiction in the Roman-Dutch law countries. Attachment serves a dual purpose, namely to found jurisdiction and afford security in order to satisfy the judgment of the court. Attachment is not a mere formality, but a substantive first step in obtaining a remedy for a cause of action. Indeed, attachment may be considered a remedy.[199] An attachment or arrest will found jurisdiction where no other basis of jurisdiction exists. Where a basis of jurisdiction already exists (for example, where the contract was made within the jurisdiction, or the cause of action arose within the jurisdiction), attachment or arrest merely confirms the court's jurisdiction.

The Roman-Dutch law countries distinguish between actions involving an *incola* plaintiff and a *peregrinus* defendant and actions between peregrines.[200] It is obvious from the nature of existing rules that special privileges or protections are accorded to *incolae* – their person and property

[196] *Ex p. Mor-Tal Construction Co. (Pvt) Ltd* 1962 (2) SA 664 at 665, 1962 R & N 248 at 249.

[197] 1964 (4) SA 264, 1963 R & N 208.

[198] See generally *Ex p. Adair Properties Ltd* [1967] RLR 56.

[199] To a large extent attachment to found or confirm jurisdiction in the Roman-Dutch law countries is very much like the pre-judgment attachment available in the common law countries, except that in the latter, it has no jurisdictional purpose.

[200] 'A peregrine is a person who is neither domiciled nor resident within the area of jurisdiction of the court and it has been held that either domicile or residence within

are immune from attachment and they can invoke the jurisdiction of the courts on the basis of principles unavailable to a *peregrinus*. As discussed below, this contrasts sharply with the approach in the common law countries. In the Roman-Dutch law countries, as between an *incola* plaintiff and a *peregrinus* defendant, arrest or attachment (without any *ratio jurisdictionis*[201]) is enough to found jurisdiction. In other words, the mere fact that the *peregrinus* defendant has an asset within the jurisdiction attached or where he or she has been arrested is enough to give the courts jurisdiction, regardless of the fact that the cause of action has no other connection with the forum and that the asset has no relation to the underlying cause of action. Although this law is now so settled, there were conflicting decisions in the Cape Colony until 1931.[202] As between peregrines, a recognised *ratio jurisdictionis*, as well as an attachment or arrest to found or confirm jurisdiction, is necessary for the court to assume jurisdiction.

An application for attachment or arrest has to basically meet the same requirements in all Roman-Dutch law countries. It has to be established on the balance of probabilities that the *peregrinus* defendant is, or has, assets within the jurisdiction and that there is a prima facie cause of action against the defendant. Once these are established, the plaintiff is entitled as of right to attachment or arrest. However, in Zimbabwe, legislation expressly empowers the court to dispense attachment or arrest, and instead order that process should be served on the defendant. In other words, in Zimbabwe, in cases where the defendant is within the jurisdiction or has property therein – i.e. where arrest or attachment is a possibility – the court has the discretion to dispense with the need for arrest or attachment, and instead order the issue of process to be served on the defendant.[203]

the area or jurisdiction of the court, of some permanent or settled nature, is sufficient to constitute a person an incola': *Healthcare Management Services (Pty) Ltd* v. *Smith* 1996 BLR 301 at 306. Citizenship does not per se enter the equation. *Sandton Square Finance (Pty) Ltd* v. *Biagi, Bertola and Vasco* 1997 (1) SA 258 at 260; *Klisser* v. *McGovern* 1963 (4) SA 483. On when a legal person is an *incola*, see *Silverstone (Pty) Ltd* v. *Lobatse Clay Works (Pty) Ltd* 1996 BLR 190 (varying *Silverstone (Pty) Ltd* v. *Lobatse Clay Works (Pty) Ltd* 1995 BLR 669); *Worldview Botswana* v. *World University Services of Canada* 1996 BLR 527; *Bezuidenhout* v. *Dominion Earth Works (Pty) Ltd* 1964–70 BLR 233.

201 That is, jurisdictional connecting factors, such as residence, domicile, the place where the contract was made or will be performed, and the place where a delict was committed.

202 *Central African Airways Corp.* v. *Vickers-Armstrong* 1956 (2) SA 492 at 493, 1956 R & N 4 for a discussion of the earlier conflicting decisions.

203 This has been described as 'vastly different from South African practice'. *Slabbert* v. *Herbst* 1981 (4) SA 257. Historically, this was not the case. Thus, in *Central African*

Almost any property of the defendant in the jurisdiction, including assets in the hands of third parties, is amenable to attachment. One of the most controversial attachable interests in this regard is the order for costs. The effect of an order for costs being amenable to attachment is that a foreign resident who successfully take steps to set aside an unmeritorious order for the attachment of goods, or who has successfully opposed an application for attachment to found or confirm the jurisdiction of a court, or who successfully defends an action brought against him or her, may, by obtaining an order for costs, find him- or herself exposed to an attachment of the costs order to found jurisdiction.[204] This demonstrates how harsh the law in Roman-Dutch law countries can be on *peregrinus* defendants.

Attachment may also have consequences for third parties. For them, the effect of the attachment often amounts to an interdict upon the property attached, preventing them from exercising such rights as they may have acquired (for example, by way of contract) over the property. Most of the cases in which third parties have intervened in cases of attachment have involved an argument that the property in question does not belong to the *peregrinus* defendant. It will arguably be rare for a court to set aside or decline an order of attachment on the sole basis that it will inconvenience a third party. However, because statute gives Zimbabwean courts discretion to grant attachment, it has been held that the court can take into account the effect of an order of attachment on third parties in deciding whether to grant the order.

Judges and academics have queried whether (as for arrest, which has been held as unconstitutional in South Africa, but remains part of the law in Botswana, Lesotho, Namibia, Swaziland and Zimbabwe) attachment of the property of a *peregrinus* to found or confirm jurisdiction is either constitutional or consistent with existing human rights norms, including freedom from discrimination – only assets of peregrines may be attached.[205] Like arrest, the effect of attachment on the rights of a

Airways Corp. v. *Vickers-Armstrong* 1956 (2) SA 492 at 494, 1956 R & N 4: 'It was also argued that . . . there was a discretion whether or not to grant the attachment at common law. This is not so.'

204 In at least one case, the defendant was forced to abandon any claim for an order for cost for fear that it would be attached. See *Drive Control Services (Pty) Ltd* v. *Troycom Systems (Pty) Ltd* 2000 (2) SA 722.

205 See, generally, *De Roeck* v. *Campbell* 1990 NR 126 at 133 on the impact of attachment to found or confirm jurisdiction and pre-judgment attachment on the right to property.

peregrinus can be grave. Attachment may impose hardship on a *peregrinus*. Any of the *peregrinus*'s property present within the jurisdiction can be attached. This represents a great challenge for *peregrinus* defendants: they cannot deal with the attached assets during the period. The fact that such a restriction on one's right to property is imposed on a *peregrinus* defendant merely by the *incola* plaintiff establishing a prima facie case is also problematic. An order which will deprive the respondent of his or her property for at least the duration of the trial should not be made merely through the establishment of a prima facie case. An equally effective remedy, but one which allows for closer scrutiny before assets are 'attached' and greater rights and protection after 'attachment', exists in the common law countries in the form of a pre-trial freezing injunction.[206] It is likely that one day, the whole question of attachments to found or confirm jurisdiction may have to be re-examined. For now, it remains an essential aspect of the rules on jurisdiction in all Roman-Dutch law countries, but courts acknowledge that it is an exceptional remedy and the jurisdiction to grant the remedy should be exercised with caution.

One way a *peregrinus* defendant may avoid attachment is by submitting to the jurisdiction prior to the granting of an order of attachment. In this regard, a controversial issue which divides the Roman-Dutch law countries is whether, in an action between peregrines, submission alone is enough to give the courts jurisdiction. For example, will a South African court assume jurisdiction over a contract where the sole connection with South Africa is a South African jurisdiction agreement? While Namibian and South African courts have answered this in the negative, in Botswana the courts have been prepared to assume jurisdiction in such cases. In other words, in Namibia and South Africa, it is impossible for a peregrine to sue another peregrine unless the cause of action has some connection with the jurisdiction other than their jurisdiction

[206] In order to obtain a freezing injunction, the claimant must establish: a good arguable case against the defendant on the merits of the case; that there is a serious risk that any judgment will go unsatisfied as the defendant is likely to dissipate his or her assets; and that, in the circumstances of the case, it is just and convenient to grant the relief and provide undertaking as to damages. Furthermore, the injunction is relief *in personam* and does not operate as an attachment on property. Accordingly, it allows the defendant to deal with the property in a limited number of cases (it does not give the plaintiff security rights in priority over other creditors and the defendant can usually pay his or her creditors in the normal course of business).

agreement.[207] A potential explanation for this may be found in the jurisprudence of the Swaziland court, which has held that, by consenting to jurisdiction, a defendant subjects his or her person (and not the cause of action) to the court's jurisdiction – the court must also have jurisdiction over the subject matter through the existence of one or more of the traditional grounds of jurisdiction. In contrast, in the common law countries, the presence of a jurisdiction agreement with nothing more will be enough to confer jurisdiction on the courts.

It is worth comparing and contrasting other aspects of the rules on jurisdiction in the common law and Roman-Dutch law countries. There are significant differences in their response to the issue of when a court will assume jurisdiction to hear a claim sounding in money. Recently, the South African Supreme Court of Appeal accepted that, in cases where attachment is not possible, presence plus service may be enough to give the courts jurisdiction in claims sounding in money. This somewhat aligns the position in South Africa with that of common law countries, where presence forms a basis of jurisdiction.[208] Until this decision, there was perhaps no other issue in jurisdiction where the rules in common law countries differed more from those in Roman-Dutch law countries. In the common law countries, jurisdiction is founded on service – service of the writ is the foundation of the court's jurisdiction to entertain an action *in personam*. A court will assume jurisdiction over a foreign defendant when the defendant is present within its jurisdiction, has submitted to its jurisdiction, or where leave to serve out of the jurisdiction has been granted to the plaintiff and service has been effected on the defendant. In the common law countries, the courts will neither attach the assets of a defendant nor arrest them for jurisdictional purposes.[209] This is so, regardless of the character of the defendant. Indeed, the distinction

[207] For a robustly critical commentary on this and other aspects of the law in the Roman-Dutch law countries, see C. Forsyth, 'The Impact of the Domestic on the International: Some Crucial Deficiencies in the South African Law of Jurisdiction with their Regional and International Consequences' (2006) 18 *South African Mercantile Law Journal* 1.

[208] However, it leaves a number of issues unaddressed. On this, see R. F. Oppong, 'Roman-Dutch Law Meets the Common Law on Jurisdiction in International Matters' (2008) 4 *Journal of Private International Law* 311.

[209] See *Michigan Trust Co.* v. *Ferry* 228 US 346, 353 (1913), where Justice Holmes held: 'Ordinarily jurisdiction over a person is based on the power of the sovereign asserting it to seize that person and imprison him to await the sovereign's pleasure. But when that power exists and is asserted by service at the beginning of a cause . . . we dispense with the necessity of maintaining the physical power . . . This is one of the decencies of civilization that no one would dispute.'

between an *incola* and *peregrinus* is unknown to the common law countries' rules on jurisdiction.

The Roman-Dutch law countries' response to the question of when a court will assume jurisdiction over a foreign defendant is more complicated. They distinguish between two types of action: actions between an *incola* and *peregrinus* defendant and actions between peregrines. In general, as discussed above, courts in the Roman-Dutch law countries will not assume jurisdiction over a *peregrinus* unless his or her assets within the jurisdiction have been attached to found or confirm jurisdiction or, aside from South Africa, unless he or she has been arrested for the same purpose. What informs this need for attachment or arrest is the doctrine of effectiveness. The doctrine expresses the idea that 'jurisdictional rules should ensure that the court is in a position to give a meaningful judgment'.[210] Although the doctrine has been much criticised,[211] it has been described as the basic principle of the rules on jurisdiction in all the Roman-Dutch law countries.

Both the Roman-Dutch and common law countries have rules for dealing with cases where the defendant is abroad. In the common law countries, on the bases of statutorily defined grounds and for the purposes of establishing the jurisdiction of the court, a plaintiff may be allowed to serve a writ out of the jurisdiction. In the Roman-Dutch law countries, after jurisdiction has been founded or confirmed through attachment, the court may allow the plaintiff to serve the process, whereby the proceedings are instituted on the defendant abroad. This procedure, known as edictal citation, provides machinery for the institution and prosecution of actions against those in respect of whom the court concerned has jurisdiction, but on whom the process of the court cannot be served because they are outside the jurisdiction of the court.[212]

[210] Forsyth, p. 159. [211] Ibid., pp. 170–5.

[212] In Zimbabwe, it appears that the procedure of edictal citation as a method of serving a summons on a defendant who is outside the jurisdiction has been abolished. Rather, where a person wishes to sue and the process has to be served on the defendant who is in a country outside Zimbabwe other than South Africa, or the neighbouring states of South Africa, the plaintiff must apply to a judge in Chambers asking for leave to effect service of a summons to the defendant: *Westwood* v. *Westwood* 1997 (1) ZLR 295. Although there is no difference in effect between the issue of summons and the issue of edictal citation, the two processes are different. A summons is addressed to the Sheriff, who is directed to command the defendant to answer the plaintiff's claim. An edictal citation, on the other hand, is addressed to the defendant. *McGuire* v. *Fourie* 1962 R & N 420 at 422, 1962 (3) SA 302 at 304.

Unlike the procedure for service out of jurisdiction in the common law countries, edictal citation does not establish the jurisdiction of the court. Rather, it notifies the defendant of an already established jurisdiction. Put differently, the courts in the Roman-Dutch law countries cannot issue such a citation unless preceded or accompanied by either the arrest of the defendant or attachment of any of his or her goods within the jurisdiction.[213]

[213] *Murphy* v. *Dallas* 1974 (1) SA 793.

5

Forum non conveniens, *lis alibi pendens* and forum selection agreements

The fact that a court has jurisdiction on the basis of one or more of the grounds discussed in Chapter 4 does not mean that it will go ahead to hear the case. Fundamental questions in this regard include whether a court has jurisdiction to decline to exercise jurisdiction it already possesses, on what grounds it can do that, and what factors it may take into account in so acting. While courts struggle with these issues, the parties to a contract may, by using jurisdiction and arbitration agreements, seek to give a court jurisdiction it would otherwise not possess, or 'take away' from the courts any jurisdiction they would otherwise have possessed. The inclusion of jurisdiction and arbitration agreements in contracts is an aspect of party autonomy and freedom of contract. The extent to which such agreements may be given effect by the courts is an important issue for parties of any international contract.

This chapter discusses the principles which allow courts in the countries under study to decline jurisdiction, and also the extent to which they may give effect to jurisdiction and arbitration agreements.

Botswana

If any party to an arbitration agreement commences any legal proceedings in any court against any other party to the agreement, in respect of any matter within the scope of the agreement, parties to such legal proceedings may at any time after appearance, before delivering any pleadings, or before taking any other steps in the proceedings, apply to that court to stay the proceedings. The court, if satisfied that there is no sufficient reason for the matter not to be referred in accordance with the submission, and that the applicant was, at the time the proceedings commenced, and still remains, ready and willing to do all things necessary for the proper conduct of the arbitration, may make an order staying the proceedings, subject to such terms and conditions as are considered just.[1]

A Botswanan court may also exercise its discretion and stay proceedings before it in favour of a foreign proceeding on the basis of a plea of *lis alibi pendens*.[2]

Gambia

A Gambian court will give effect to an arbitration agreement – the courts have a prima facie duty to act upon an agreement between the parties.[3] A court before which proceedings are brought in a matter which is the subject of an arbitration agreement shall, if a party so requests not later than the submission of his or her first statement on the substance of the dispute, stay those proceedings and refer the parties to arbitration. The court shall not stay proceedings if it finds that the agreement is null and void, inoperative or incapable of being performed, or if there is not in fact any dispute between the parties with regard to the matters agreed for referral.[4]

Ghana

The doctrine of *forum non conveniens* is an essential aspect of the rules on jurisdiction in international matters in Ghanaian law. The mere fact that the court has jurisdiction does not mean that this will be exercised. Thus, in an application for leave to serve a writ out of the jurisdiction, the mere fact that one of the heads of jurisdiction is satisfied is not enough. The power granted to the court to order service out of the jurisdiction of a writ of summons is discretionary and the connections of the cause of action and the parties with the forum influence the determination of whether it is the *forum conveniens*.[5] It has been held that the mere fact of the pendency of a similar suit does not constitute a criterion for determining the *forum conveniens*.[6]

[1] Arbitration Act 1959, s. 6(1).

[2] *Makgekgnene* v. *Makgekgnene* [2007] BLR 621.

[3] *ESB International Ltd* v. *Utilities Holding Corp.* [1997–2001] GR 297; *Lerr Group Ltd* v. *Ballast Nedam Africa*, Civil Suit No: HC/269/09/CO/082/D2 (High Court, Gambia, 2010).

[4] Alternative Dispute Resolution Act 2005, s. 12. This Act gives effect to the UN Convention on Recognition and Enforcement of Foreign Arbitral Awards 1958.

[5] *Shirlstar Container Transport Ltd* v. *Kadas Shipping Co. Ltd* [1989–90] 1 GLR 401.

[6] *Fattal* v. *Fattal* [1999–2000] 1 GLR 331 at 350.

Applications to stay proceedings have often been presented in cases where the parties have agreed to jurisdiction or arbitration agreement in their contract. It has been held that parties are free to enter into jurisdiction agreements – the case for giving effect to such agreements is even stronger in instances where the courts of the chosen forum are closely connected with the place and language in which the contract was made.[7] However, such an agreement does not oust the jurisdiction of the court. The particular circumstances of a case may dictate that effect should not be given to the agreement.[8] Reasonableness is usually the criterion for deciding whether or not a jurisdiction clause ought to be honoured. What is reasonable is a question of fact. Thus, in a contract for the carriage of goods where both parties were Ghanaian, the goods were delivered in Ghana, the bill of lading stipulated England as the choice of forum, and the court found that Ghanaian and English law on the matter did not differ in any material manner, it was held that this was not a proper case for staying the proceedings.[9] Indeed, a party's own conduct in taking steps in litigation may prevent it from invoking a jurisdiction agreement.[10]

A Ghanaian court will give effect to an arbitration agreement.[11] It has been held that an arbitration agreement is not rendered inoperative merely because the arbitration body initially agreed to have been wound up. It is within the court's discretion to appoint an arbitrator for the parties, taking into account the generality of the agreement.[12] However, in appropriate cases, the court may decline to give effect to an arbitration agreement.[13]

Kenya

In appropriate cases, the Kenyan court may exercise discretion and stay proceedings in favour of a foreign court. The onus for establishing a

[7] *CILEV* v. *Chiavelli* [1967] GLR 651. See also *CILEV* v. *Chiavelli* [1968] GLR 160.

[8] *CILEV* v. *Black Star Line* [1967] GLR 744.

[9] *Fan Milk Ltd* v. *State Shipping Corp.* [1971] 1 GLR 238.

[10] *Moubarak* v. *Holland West Afrika Lijn* (1953) 14 WACA 262.

[11] Ghana is a party to the UN Convention on Recognition and Enforcement of Foreign Arbitral Awards 1958. The Alternative Dispute Resolution Act 2010 gives effect to the Convention. See also s. 6 of the Act, which enables a party to apply to court for a stay of proceedings on the basis that the parties agree the dispute should be resolved through arbitration. *Republic* v. *High Court, Tema; Ex p. My Shipping Pvt Ltd* [2011] 1 SCGLR 237.

[12] *Paul Gyasi* v. *Abosso Goldfields Ltd*, Suit No. ANR 17/2004 (High Court, Ghana, 2004).

[13] *Polimex* v. *BBC Builders & Engineers Co. Ltd* [1968] GLR 168.

strong reason for avoiding the jurisdiction of the Kenyan courts is on the party who seeks to avoid that jurisdiction and that burden is a heavy one. In exercising its discretion, the court should take into account all circumstances of the particular case, such as: the country where the evidence on the issues of fact is situated or more readily available; whether and how differently the law of the foreign country applies; with what country either party is connected and how closely; whether the defendant genuinely desires trial in the foreign country or is only seeking a procedural advantage, and whether the plaintiff would be prejudiced by having to sue in the foreign country.[14] The mere fact that proceedings are pending abroad is not enough to compel the court to stay proceedings – an important consideration is the danger of inconsistent judgments.[15] Similarly, where there is concurrent jurisdiction in more than one country, the court will be guided by the principle of the balance of convenience between the parties.[16]

A Kenyan court will give effect to a jurisdiction agreement.[17] There is no conflict between so doing and the Constitution of Kenya, which gives the High Court unlimited jurisdiction in all civil matters.[18] However, in appropriate cases, the court may decline to give effect to parties' choice of forum agreement. Thus, where the subject matter of one dispute was a contract for the supply of motor vehicles with drivers, two earlier contracts between the parties contained Kenya's choice of forum clauses, the relevant evidence was in Kenya, the litigation would be convenient and less expensive in Kenya, Kenya was a common law country and the respondent would be greatly prejudiced if sued in Germany, and the German defendants were operating in Kenya and contracted with a

[14] *United India Insurance Co. Ltd* v. *East African Underwriters (Kenya) Ltd* [1985] KLR 898, [1976–85] 1 EA 579.

[15] *Owens* v. *Owens* [1959] EA 909; *Walker-Munro* v. *Walker-Munro* [2010] eKLR. See also the explanatory note to s. 6 of the Civil Procedure Act 1924, which reads: 'the pendency of a suit in a foreign court shall not preclude a court from trying a suit in which the same matters or any of them are in issue in such suit in such foreign court'.

[16] *Kanti* v. *South British Insurance Co. Ltd*, Civil Appeal No. 39 of 1980 (Court of Appeal, Kenya, 1981).

[17] *Fonville* v. *Kelly III* [2002] EA 71, [1995] LLR 2636; *Raytheon Aircraft Credit Corp.* v. *Air Al-Faraj Ltd* [2005] 2 KLR 47; *Areva T & D India Ltd* v. *Priority Electrical Engineers* [2012] eKLR. Exclusive jurisdiction can only be conferred on the courts of a particular country by clear and unequivocal statement in the contract. The mere stamping of an insurance contract in the United Kingdom does not make it subject to the exclusive jurisdiction of the English courts: *Kanti* v. *South British Insurance Co. Ltd*, Civil Appeal No. 39 of 1980 (Court of Appeal, Kenya, 1981).

[18] *Raytheon Aircraft Credit Corp.* v. *Air Al-Faraj Ltd* [2005] 2 KLR 47.

Kenyan businessman, the court declined to stay proceedings in favour of a German court.[19] The burden is on the party resisting a stay of proceedings on the basis of a jurisdiction agreement to show cause against it.[20] The party wishing to depart from the agreement must discharge a heavy burden of showing strong cause. The court has upheld an exclusive jurisdiction clause contained in a bill of lading vesting jurisdiction in the South African courts, even though the only connection of the contract with South Africa was that the defendant had its registered offices there.[21]

The Kenyan court will give effect to a choice of arbitration agreement.[22] A court before which proceedings are brought in a matter which is the subject of an arbitration agreement shall, if a party so applies not later than the time when they enter appearance or otherwise acknowledge the claim against which the stay of proceedings is sought, stay the proceedings and refer the parties to arbitration, unless it finds that the arbitration agreement is null and void, inoperative or incapable of being performed, or that there is not in fact any dispute between the parties with regard to the matters agreed for referral to arbitration.[23] In agreements where parties have agreed to refer disputes to arbitration, the jurisdiction to deal with substantive disputes and differences is given to the arbitrator, but the Kenyan courts retain residual jurisdiction to deal with peripheral matters and to see that any disputes or differences are dealt with in the manner agreed between the parties.[24] Thus, where a loan agreement between the plaintiff and defendant provided that disputes between them were to be settled under the Rules of Conciliation and Arbitration of the International Chamber of Commerce, it was held

[19] *Valentine Investment Co. Ltd* v. *Federal Republic of Germany* [2006] eKLR. The court also took into account the fact that the parties negotiated on level ground. See also *The Despina Pontikos* 1974 (3) ALR Comm. 329.

[20] *Ronning* v. *Société Navale Chargeurs Delmas-Vieljeux* [1976–85] 1 EA 513.

[21] *Friendship Container Manufacturers Ltd* v. *Mitchell Cotts Ltd* [2001] 2 EA 338, [1995] LLR 1282.

[22] See generally *Rift Valley Textiles* v. *Cotton Distributors Inc.* [1976–85] 1 EA 505. See also *Midland Finance & Securities Globetel Inc.* v. *Attorney General* [2008] KLR 650, which held that whether a dispute is capable of being referred to arbitration – arbitrability – is governed by the *lex arbitri* and not the law governing the contract. *Nedermar Technology BV Ltd* v. *Kenya Anti-corruption Commission* [2008] KLR 476; *Nedermar Technology BV Ltd* v. *Kenya Anti-corruption Commission* [2006] 2 KLR 678.

[23] Arbitration Act 1995, s. 6(1). See generally *The Despina Pontikos* 1974 (3) ALR Comm. 329 at 352–3, where the court declined to give effect to an arbitration agreement.

[24] *Tononoka Steels Ltd* v. *Eastern and Southern African Trade and Development Bank* [2000] 2 EA 536; *Indigo EPZ Ltd* v. *Eastern and Southern African Trade and Development Bank* [2002] KLR 1, [2002] EA 388; *Caneland Ltd* v. *John Deere (Proprietary)* [2011] eKLR.

that this did not prevent the courts from granting an injunction restraining the defendant from demanding repayment.[25]

Lesotho

A Lesotho court will not enforce a jurisdiction agreement if its enforcement contravenes the public policy of the forum. Thus, where the enforcement of a jurisdiction agreement for litigation in South Africa would deprive an employee working mostly in Lesotho of more favourable conditions under Lesotho law, it was held that the jurisdiction agreement was null, void and unenforceable.[26]

Malawi

A Malawian court will give effect to a jurisdiction agreement.[27] The jurisdiction to give effect to jurisdiction agreements is discretionary and, in appropriate cases, the court may decline to give effect to such an agreement.[28]

If a party to an arbitration agreement commences legal proceedings in any court against any other party to an agreement in respect of any matter agreed for referral, any party to those legal proceedings may at any time after appearance, and before delivering any pleadings or taking any other steps in the proceedings, apply to that court to stay the proceedings. The court, if satisfied there is no sufficient reason why the matter should not be referred in accordance with the agreement, and that the applicant was, at the time the proceedings commenced, and still remains, ready and willing to do all things necessary for the proper conduct of the arbitration, may make an order staying the proceedings.[29] In the case of a submission

[25] *Indigo EPZ* v. *Eastern and Southern African Trade and Development Bank*.

[26] *Khotle* v. *Metropolitan Life Insurance*, CIV/T/662/84 (High Court, Lesotho, 1985). The court also took into account the fact that giving effect to the jurisdiction agreement would have put the plaintiff to great personal expense and considerable inconvenience in instituting action in Cape Town where he was a foreigner. He may have been obliged to find security for the defendant's costs with the possible total frustration of his action, whereas the employer had its branch office in Maseru where the whole dispute had arisen. See also *Komane* v. *City Express Stores (Pty) Ltd*, LAC/CIV/A/5/2002 (High Court, Lesotho, 2006).

[27] *Landell Mills Associates Ltd* v. *Marshall* [1991] 14 MLR 175.

[28] *AA Mirza* v. *AMI (Malawi) Ltd*, Civil Cause No. 59 of 1999 (High Court, Malawi, 2007).

[29] Arbitration Act 1967, s. 6(1). The jurisdiction to uphold arbitration agreements extends to a *Scott* v. *Avery* clause and an application for a stay of proceedings may be founded on such a clause. See *National Insurance Co. Ltd* v. *Ngwira* [1993] 16(1) MLR 381; *Chanthunya* v. *Ngwira* [1987–9] 12 MLR 133.

to arbitration made in pursuance of an agreement to which the Protocol on Arbitration Clauses, 1923 applies, the court shall stay the proceedings, unless satisfied that the agreement or arbitration has become inoperative or cannot proceed, or that there is not in fact any dispute between the parties with regard to the matter agreed for referral.[30]

Namibia

The presence of a foreign exclusive jurisdiction clause in a contract does not automatically oust the jurisdiction of the Namibian courts. They retain discretion as to whether the action should be pursued in Namibia or in the chosen forum. In exercising discretion whether or not to hear the matter, a compelling consideration is the kind of relief which the applicant seeks. Where in breach of an exclusive Rotterdam jurisdiction agreement the applicant brought an action in Namibia seeking an interim order pending an action to be instituted at a later stage, and it was found that, given time constraints, it was practically impossible for the applicant to obtain the relief from the Rotterdam courts, and that even where relief was so obtained it could not be enforced in Namibia (because it was not final and conclusive), the court declined to exercise discretion in favour of litigation in Rotterdam.[31]

Nigeria

The doctrine of *forum non conveniens* is part of Nigerian law. A Nigerian court may stay proceedings before it on the grounds that there is a more appropriate forum abroad for the trial of the action. In so deciding, the courts take into account all the circumstances of the case. Thus, in one action for breach of contract, all the defendants were domiciled in the United States, the business the defendants conducted had no connection with Nigeria, the alleged breach occurred in the United States and all the documents necessary to resolve the dispute were located in the United States, and so it was held that the Lagos court was not the *forum conveniens* for trial of the action.[32] It has also been held that, where granting a stay of proceedings would spell injustice to the

[30] Arbitration Act 1967, s. 6(1).

[31] *Olympic Fruit* v. *Nagrapex Holdings*, Case No. A 278/2011 (High Court, Namibia, 2011).

[32] *Resolution Trust Corp.* v. *FOB Investment & Property Ltd* [2001] 6 NWLR 246. See also *Adel Kamel Barsoum* v. *Clemessy International* [1999] 12 NWLR 516.

plaintiff – such as where the action is already time-barred in the foreign court and granting the stay would amount to permanently denying the plaintiffs any redress – justice is better served by refusing a stay of proceedings.[33]

The mere fact that proceedings are pending abroad is not an automatic ground for staying proceedings. A plaintiff is entitled to institute action in two different countries in respect of the same subject matter, unless it can be proved by the applicant that bringing a second action will be vexatious. The applicant must provide a substantial case for vexation resulting from the identity of proceedings, remedies and benefits, or from the existence of some motive other than the bona fide desire to determine disputes.[34]

Nigerian courts will give effect to a jurisdiction agreement,[35] but a jurisdiction agreement only binds parties to it. As a contract term, it does not bind persons who are not privy to the contract.[36] In appropriate cases, the court may decline to stay proceedings on the basis of a jurisdiction agreement.[37] Where an action is brought in breach of a jurisdiction agreement, the trial court still has discretion whether or not to grant the application for a stay of proceedings. The law requires such discretion to be exercised by granting a stay unless strong cause for not doing so is shown. The party who has brought the action in breach of the jurisdiction agreement bears the burden of establishing grounds on which a stay should not be granted, and he or she must show 'strong cause' why the parties should not be held to their agreement.[38]

[33] *Sonnar (Nigeria) Ltd* v. *Partenreedri MS Nordwind* [1987] 1 All NLR (Part I) 396, [1988] LRC (Comm.) 191 (reversing *Sonnar (Nigeria) Ltd* v. *Partenreedri MS Nordwind* [1985] 3 NWLR 135).

[34] *Jammal* v. *Abdalla Hashem* 1975 (2) ALR Comm. 141, [1975] NCLR 141. See generally *Nahman* v. *Allan Wolowicz* [1993] 3 NWLR 443.

[35] *Comet Shipping Agencies (Nigeria) Ltd* v. *Panalpina World Transport (Nigeria) Ltd* [1990] LRC (Comm.) 206. Historically, some courts characterise such agreements as agreements to oust the jurisdiction of the courts and refuse to give effect to them. See *Ventujol* v. *Compagnie Française De L'Afrique Occidentale* [1949] 19 NLR 32; *Allied Trading Co. Ltd* v. *China Ocean Shipping Line* 1980 (1) ALR Comm. 146.

[36] *Unipetrol Nigeria Ltd* v. *Prima Alfa Enterprises (Nigeria) Ltd* [1986] 5 NWLR 532.

[37] *Sonnar (Nigeria) Ltd* v. *Partenreedri MS Nordwind* [1987] 1 All NLR (Part I) 396, [1988] LRC (Comm.) 191; *Adesanya* v. *Palm Line Ltd* 1967 (2) ALR Comm. 133.

[38] *Nika Fishing Co. Ltd* v. *Lavina Corp.* (2008) 1 All NLR 422 (reversing *Nika Fishing Co. Ltd* v. *Lavinia Corp.* [2001] 16 NWLR 556). See generally *Funduk Engineering Ltd* v. *McArthur* (1995) All NLR 157 at 165, where it was observed that the fact that an agreement states that it shall be interpreted in accordance with English Law (or any particular variety of law)

A Nigerian court will give effect to an arbitration agreement, including a *Scott* v. *Avery* clause.[39] Where parties to a contract have agreed to arbitration in a foreign jurisdiction, a defendant who has not taken steps in the foreign arbitration proceedings can, in a proceeding before the Nigerian court, apply for a stay of proceedings on the basis of the arbitration agreement.[40] The court is bound to stay proceedings unless satisfied that there is sufficient reason to justify refusal to refer the dispute to arbitration. It may refuse to order a stay of proceedings where the defendant establishes that he or she would suffer injustice if the case was stayed, that he or she cannot obtain justice from the arbitration tribunal, or that the agreement between the parties is null and void, inoperative or incapable of being performed. The onus is on the party seeking a stay to show that there is a strong reason why they must be permitted a discharge from their agreement and thus be allowed to settle their dispute through court proceedings instead of arbitration.[41]

Section 20 of the Admiralty Jurisdiction Decree, 1991 imposes limitations on the enforcement of jurisdiction and arbitration agreements.[42]

does not in any way amount to an ouster of jurisdiction of Nigerian courts to interpret or enforce the provisions of the said document.

39 *African Insurance Development Corp.* v. *Nigeria Liquified Natural Gas Ltd* [2000] 4 NWLR 494, [2000] 1 WRN 40. Nigeria is a party to the UN Convention on the Recognition and Enforcement of Foreign Arbitral Awards 1958. The Arbitration and Conciliation Act 1998 gives effect to the Convention. See further discussion of *Scott* v. *Avery* clause in Ch. 19.

40 Arbitration and Conciliation Act 1998, ss. 4 and 5.

41 *Owners of the MV Lupex* v. *Nigeria Overseas Chartering and Shipping Ltd* [2003] 15 NWLR 469, [2003] 43 WRN 123.

42 It provides that 'any agreement by any person or party to any cause, matter or action which seeks to oust the jurisdiction of the Court shall be null and void, if it relates to any admiralty matter falling under this Decree and if – (a) the place of performance, execution, delivery, act or default is or takes place in Nigeria; or (b) any of the parties resides or has resided in Nigeria; or (c) the payment under the agreement (implied or express) is made or is to be made in Nigeria; or (d) in any admiralty action or in the case of a maritime lien, the plaintiff submits to the jurisdiction of the Court and makes a declaration to that effect or the rem is within Nigerian jurisdiction; or (e) it is a case in which the Federal Military Government or the Government of a State of the Federation is involved and the Government or State submits to the jurisdiction of the Court; or (g) under any convention, for the time being, in force to which Nigeria is a party, the national court of a contracting State is either mandated or has a discretion to assume jurisdiction; or (h) in the opinion of the Court, the cause, matter or action adjudicated upon in Nigeria.'

An agreement which is inconsistent with the provisions of section 20 is null and void and the courts will not give effect to it.[43]

Sierra Leone

In an application for a stay of proceedings of an action brought in breach of a jurisdiction agreement, the Sierra Leonean court is not bound to grant a stay of the action – it has discretion as to whether to grant the application or refuse it as the case may be. The court will choose the forum in which the case can be tried more suitably in the interest of all the parties and for the ends of justice. The burden of proof lies on the defendant who is seeking a stay of the proceedings. He must not only show that the present forum is not the appropriate one: he must also show that the other forum is clearly more appropriate. In considering whether there is another forum which is more appropriate, the court will look for that forum with which the action has the most real and substantial connection (for example, in terms of convenience or expense, availability of witnesses, the law governing the relevant transaction, and the place where the parties reside or carry on business). In the instant case, the court held that despite the existence of an Italian jurisdiction agreement, Sierra Leone was the more appropriate forum to hear the action.[44]

South Africa

The South African courts have long acknowledged *lis alibi pendens* as a basis for staying proceedings in favour of litigation abroad. The courts appreciate that a costly confusion 'too ghastly to contemplate' may ensue if two actions are allowed to proceed pari passu in two jurisdictions.[45] It has been held that the principles applicable to the

[43] *MV Panormos Bay* v. *Olam Nigeria Plc* [2004] 5 NWLR 1; *Lignes Aeriennes Congolaises* v. *Air Atlantic Nigeria Ltd* [2006] 2 NWLR 49; *JSF Investment* v. *Brawal Line Ltd* [2010] 18 NWLR 495.

[44] *Technoscavi* v. *Civil Engineering Co.*, Case No. CC 424/2007 2007 T NO. 14 (High Court, Sierra Leone, 2007). See also *Samco Ltd* v. *Novel Commodities SA*, Case No. CC668/07 (High Court, Sierra Leone, 2008); *Transmarine Shipping and Trading Co. Ltd* v. *The Owners and / or Persons interested in the vessels "F/V Kawa" and others*, Case No. CC998/06 2006 T NO. 36 (High Court, Sierra Leone, 2007), where the court declined to give effect to a Greek jurisdiction agreement; *Leone Mining Co.* v. *Euro African Import and Export Co.*, Case No. CC1197/05 2005 L NO. 2V (High Court, Sierra Leone, 2007), where the court gave effect to a Spanish jurisdiction agreement.

[45] *Schlesinger* v. *Schlesinger* 1979 (3) SA 521; *Halfon* v. *Halfon* 1952 (4) SA 260. See generally *Melamed NO* v. *Munnikhuis* 1996 (4) SA 126 on the extent to which the exercise of

proper exercise of discretion in granting a stay of proceedings on the basis of *lis alibi pendens* are as follows.

In order to justify a stay, two conditions must be satisfied: one positive and the other negative. Firstly, the defendant or respondent must satisfy the court that there is another forum to whose jurisdiction he or she is amenable in which justice can be done between the parties at substantially less inconvenience or lower expense. Secondly, the stay must not deprive the plaintiff or applicant of the legitimate personal or juridical advantage which would be available if he or she invoked the jurisdiction of the local court. The court must weigh the advantage to the plaintiff against the advantage to the defendant, taking into account factors such as the availability of witnesses, the expense and inconvenience of all concerned, the speed of the judicial process, and the level of awards of damages and legal costs.[46] It is accordingly evident that there is no automatic right to stay on the basis of *lis alibi pendens* – even if all the requirements of the defence of *lis alibi pendens* existed, the court would have the discretion to stay or not to stay the proceedings before it.[47] The fact that one action is commenced first is not determinative,[48] but may afford a prima facie case for a stay in the absence of proof that injustice would be done if a stay was granted.[49] Considerations of convenience and fairness are decisive in determining whether or not to stay proceedings in such cases.[50]

The issue as to whether in actions *in personam*[51] there is a general discretion to stay proceedings on the basis of *forum non conveniens* is disputed in South African law,[52] but there have been occasional judicial

jurisdiction by a South African court may be influenced by the fact that the same issue will also feature in litigation before a foreign court.

46 *Berrange NO* v. *Hassan* 2009 (2) SA 339.

47 *HR Holfeld (Africa) Ltd* v. *Karl Walter & Co. GmbH* 1987 (4) SA 850; *Hubert* v. *Hubert* 1960 (3) SA 181.

48 *Van As* v. *Appollus en Andere* 1993 (1) SA 606; *HR Holfeld (Africa) Ltd* v. *Karl Walter & Co. GmbH* 1987 (4) SA 850.

49 *Kerbel* v. *Kerbel* 1987 (1) SA 562.

50 *Swanvest 234 (Pty) Ltd* v. *Nkwazi Resources Investments (Pty) Ltd*, Case No. 871/2010 (High Court, South Africa, 2010).

51 The doctrine of *forum non conveniens* is not totally unknown to the South African legal system. Its application in admiralty claims receives statutory imprimatur in s. 7(1)(a)(b) of the Admiralty Jurisdiction Regulation Act 1983. *MT Tigr Bouygues Offshore SA* v. *Owners of the MT Tigr* 1998 (4) SA 740; *Great River Shipping Inc.* v. *Sunnyface Marine Ltd* 1992 (4) SA 313; *Kandagasabapathy* v. *MV Melina Tsiris* 1981 (3) SA 950; *Magat* v. *MV Houda Pearl* 1982 (2) SA 37.

52 Forsyth, pp. 184–8; C. Schulze, '*Forum non-Conveniens* in Comparative Private International Law' (2001) 118 *South African Law Journal* 812 at 827–8.

references, both explicitly and implicitly, to the doctrine.[53] In *Bid Industrial Holdings (Pty) Ltd* v. *Strang*,[54] the Supreme Court of Appeal, after upholding a new basis for jurisdiction – mere presence – and being aware of the potential difficulties it can pose for a *peregrinus*, held that 'it is open to the defendant to contest, among other things, whether the South African court is the *forum conveniens* and whether there are sufficient links between the suit and this country to render litigation appropriate here rather than in the court of the defendant's domicile.'[55]

A foreign jurisdiction clause is not absolutely binding. The court in which an action is brought in breach thereof has the discretion to hear the matter itself and not to refer it to the chosen foreign court.[56] Where the parties have agreed that disputes are to be referred to a foreign tribunal, the onus rests upon the plaintiff in the South African court to show why the court should not stay the proceedings before it so as to give effect to the agreement between the parties.[57] The fact that, in the agreed forum, the plaintiff would have to pursue a different cause of action – in this instance an action *in personam* rather than an action *in rem* – or that the prospect of recovery in the agreed forum is poor, cannot justify the breach of a jurisdiction agreement.[58] However, a defendant who submits to an action brought in breach of a jurisdiction agreement will not succeed if he or she subsequently brings an action to stay the proceedings in favour of the foreign court.[59]

In South African law, an arbitration clause does not oust the jurisdiction of the court. If a party to an agreement seeks to rely on an arbitration clause when sued on that agreement, the court has discretion as to whether or not it should itself determine the dispute or whether it should order the proceedings to be stayed pending the arbitrator's decision.[60]

[53] See, e.g., *Moslemany* v. *Unilever Plc*, Case No. D102/06 (Labour Court, South Africa, 2006) at [35]; *Parry* v. *Astral Operations Ltd* [2005] 10 BLLR 989 at [35]; *Lane* v. *Dabelstein* 1999 (3) SA 150 at 171–2.

[54] 2008 (3) SA 355. [55] *Bid Industrial Holdings* v. *Strang* at 369.

[56] *Foize Africa (Pty) Ltd* v. *Foize Beheer BV* [2012] 4 All SA 387; *Butler* v. *Banimar Shipping Co. SA* 1978 (4) SA 753 at 761. See generally *Ind-Lex Investment CC* v. *Aqua-Terra (Pty) Ltd* [1991–2] 7 BSC 221.

[57] *MV Spartan-Runner* v. *Jotun-Henry Clark Ltd* 1991 (3) SA 803.

[58] *MV Achilleus* v. *Thai United Insurance Co. Ltd* 1992 (1) SA 324.

[59] *Ind-Lex Investment CC* v. *Aqua-Terra (Pty) Ltd*.

[60] Arbitration Act 1965, s. 6; Admiralty Jurisdiction Regulation 1983, s. 7(1). *Yorigami Maritime Construction Co. Ltd* v. *Nissho-Iwai Co. Ltd* 1977 (4) SA 682; *Polysius (Pty) Ltd* v. *Transvaal Alloys (Pty) Ltd* 1983 (2) SA 630; *MV Iran Dastghayb, Islamic Republic of*

Swaziland

A Swaziland court has discretion in upholding a jurisdiction agreement. The court will only allow the breach of a jurisdiction agreement in cases where there are strong and special reasons. In the instant case, in refusing to give effect to a South African jurisdiction agreement, the court took into account the close connection between the court and the substance of the case, convenience to the parties, the non-oppressive and non-vexatious nature of the proceedings, the fact that the law of South Africa and Swaziland is very similar and whether the respondent genuinely desires a trial in South Africa as opposed to merely seeking a tactical advantage.[61]

Tanzania

The pendency of a suit in a foreign court does not preclude the courts in Tanzania from trying a suit founded on the same cause of action.[62]

An agreement to refer disputes to arbitration is not void with regard to ousting the jurisdiction of the Tanzanian courts.[63] Submission to a foreign arbitrator does not of itself constitute ousting the jurisdiction of the court and neither does it amount to a violation of Tanzanian public policy.[64]

Where a party to an arbitration agreement commences legal proceedings against any other party to the agreement, a party to these proceedings may, at any time after appearance and before filing a written statement, or taking any other steps in the proceedings, apply to the court to stay the proceedings. The court, if satisfied that there is no sufficient reason why the matter should not be referred in accordance with the agreement and that the applicant was, at the time the proceedings commenced, and still remains, ready and willing to do all things necessary for the proper conduct of the arbitration, may make an order staying the proceedings.[65]

Iran Shipping Lines v. *Terra-Marine SA* [2011] 1 All SA 468, 2010 (6) SA 493. See generally *Intercontinental Export Co. (Pty) Ltd* v. *MV Dien Danielsen* 1983 (4) SA 275 (reversing *Intercontinental Export Co. (Pty) Ltd* v. *MV Dien Danielsen* 1982 (3) SA 534).

61 *Barlows Central Finance Corp. (Pty) Ltd* v. *Joncon (Pty) Ltd*, Case No. 2491/99 (High Court, Swaziland, 1999). See generally *Princess Nomcebo Dlamini* v. *Executive Financial Consultants Group*, Case No. 4/2011 (High Court, Swaziland, 2011).

62 This statement is contained in the explanatory note to s. 8 of the Civil Procedure Code 1908, but I have been unable to locate a case that directly applies it.

63 *Wendt* v. *Jiwan* [1921–52] 1 TLR 460.

64 *Motokov* v. *Auto Garage Ltd* [1970] EA 249.

65 Arbitration Act 1938, s. 6.

Uganda

A Ugandan court has the discretion to stay proceedings pending before it in favour of a foreign court.[66] An application for a stay of proceedings need not satisfy the court that continuance of the action against the defendant will work injustice because it would be oppressive or vexatious to him or her. However, the court must be satisfied that there is another forum to the jurisdiction of which he or she is amenable and where justice can be done between the parties at substantially less inconvenience or expense, and that the stay will not deprive the defendant of any legitimate, personal or juridical advantage available to him or her if they invoked the jurisdiction of a Ugandan court.[67]

Where parties have unequivocally submitted to the exclusive jurisdiction of a foreign court, the Ugandan courts will give effect to it. Thus, where a clause in one contract provided that the 'agreement shall be construed according to English Law and subject to the exclusive jurisdiction of the English Courts', it was held that the parties had not only chosen English law to govern their agreement, but had unequivocally submitted to the exclusive jurisdiction of the English Courts. Accordingly, the High Court of Uganda had no jurisdiction to adjudicate the dispute arising under the agreement.[68] On the other hand, a non-exclusive jurisdiction agreement constituted the named court as an 'alternative one' – it did not give the named court a 'monopoly to hear and determine disputes' arising from the contract.[69] The mere fact that the chosen law applicable to the transaction was foreign law would not of itself be grounds to shift the venue of trial abroad.[70] Such a clause constitutes a mere expression of the parties' choice of law to govern the contract.[71] It is not a decisive factor in determining whether a court has or should exercise jurisdiction to entertain a suit arising from the contract. What matters most is whether

[66] *American Express International Banking Corp.* v. *Atul* [1990–4] 1 EA 10. See also explanatory note to s. 6 of the Civil Procedure Act 1929.

[67] *American Express International Banking Corp.* v. *Atul*; *SC Baxi* v. *The Bank of India Ltd* [1966] EA 130.

[68] *Uganda Telecom Ltd* v. *Rodrigo Chacon t/a Andes*, Misc. Application 337/08 (High Court, Uganda, 2008).

[69] *Larco Concrete Products Ltd* v. *Transair Ltd*, Civil Appeal No. 3 of 1987 (High Court, Uganda, 1986).

[70] *Eastern and Southern African Trade and Development Bank* v. *Hassan Basajjabalaba*, HCT-00-CC-CS-0512-2006 (High Court, Uganda, 2007).

[71] *World Population Foundation* v. *Uganda Youth Anti-Aids Association* [2003] Kam. LR 287.

the parties had unequivocally submitted to the exclusive jurisdiction of a foreign court and whether it was proper and just for the court where proceedings were brought to entertain the action.[72]

A court before which proceedings have been brought in a matter subject to an arbitration agreement shall refer the matter back to arbitration unless it finds that the agreement is null and void, inoperative or incapable of being performed, or if the dispute falls outside the scope of the agreement.[73] It has been held that the fact that an applicant was poor did not constitute sufficient grounds for the court to deny an application to stay proceedings and give effect to an international arbitration agreement. Therefore, impecuniosity per se did not render an agreement to arbitrate incapable of being performed.[74]

Zambia

A court before which legal proceedings are brought in a matter which is the subject of an arbitration agreement shall, if a party so requests at any stage of the proceedings and notwithstanding any written law, stay those proceedings and refer the parties to arbitration, unless it finds that the agreement is null and void, inoperative or incapable of being performed.[75]

Zimbabwe

A Zimbabwean court has discretion to order or refuse a stay of proceedings on the grounds of *lis alibi pendens*. In exercising this discretion, it will have regard to the equities and balance of convenience in the matter – the fact that the defendant was the first to institute proceedings is of little weight in the circumstances.[76]

[72] *Larco Concrete Products Ltd* v. *Transair Ltd*, Civil Appeal No. 3 of 1987 (High Court, Uganda, 1986).

[73] Arbitration and Conciliation Act 2000, s. 5. This Act gives effect to the UN Convention on the Recognition and Enforcement of Foreign Arbitral Awards, 1958. See generally *Power & City Contractors Ltd* v. *LTL Project (PVT) Ltd*, HCT-09-CV-MA-0062-2011 (High Court, Uganda, 2012); *National Social Security Fund* v. *Alcon International Ltd*, Civil Appeal No. 02 of 2008 (Court of Appeal, Uganda, 2009); *Shell (U) Ltd* v. *Agip (U) Ltd* [1997] Kam. LR 250.

[74] *Fulgensius Mungereza* v. *PricewaterhouseCoopers Africa Central* [2004] Kam. LR 258.

[75] Arbitration Act 2000, s. 10(1).

[76] *Baldwin* v. *Baldwin* [1967] RLR 289.

Where an arbitration clause exists in an agreement, the court is required to give effect to it.[77] Thus, in *Bitumat Ltd* v. *Multicom Ltd*,[78] the court gave effect to an arbitration clause which provided for arbitration in Malawi under a contract governed by Malawi law. But an arbitration clause cannot completely oust the jurisdiction of the courts. The question of whether a dispute falls within the arbitration clause is primarily a question of interpretation of the agreement and arbitration clause, and the court can intervene to determine the existence of the dispute.[79]

Comments

The power of courts to decline to exercise jurisdiction in circumstances where they already have jurisdiction is an important feature of the rules on jurisdiction in most of the countries under study.[80] Arguably, this is part of the inherent jurisdiction of the courts[81] since in none[82] of the countries under study is this power directly provided for by legislation.

With the exception of South Africa, where its existence has been doubted, the doctrine of *forum non conveniens* has been invoked and applied in many cases. The overriding consideration has been the desire of courts to ensure that cases are tried in the most appropriate forum for the interests of the parties and for the ends of justice. To enable the courts to do this, they take into account all the circumstances of the case. No single factor is given a predominant place and the courts have not

[77] The Arbitration Act 1996 applies, with modifications, the Model Law on International Commercial Arbitration, 1985 and gives effect to the Convention on the Recognition and Enforcement of Foreign Arbitral Awards 1958.

[78] 2000 (1) ZLR 637. [79] *PTA Bank* v. *Elanne Ltd* 2000 (1) ZLR 156.

[80] See also *Sinco Anstalt* v. *Brown International* 1972 (1) ALR Comm. 439; *Misr Printing Press* v. *Kamil* [1959] SLJR 3.

[81] In respect of arbitration agreements, the jurisdiction to stay proceedings is provided for expressly by statute.

[82] The only exception – in the context of admiralty claims – appears to be the Admiralty Jurisdiction Regulation Act 1983, s. 7(1)(a)(b). It provides that 'a court may decline to exercise its admiralty jurisdiction in any proceedings instituted or to be instituted, if it is of the opinion that any other court in the Republic or any other court or any arbitrator, tribunal or body elsewhere will exercise jurisdiction in respect of the said proceedings and that it is more appropriate that the proceedings be adjudicated upon by any such other court or by such arbitrator, tribunal or body. A court may stay any proceedings in terms of this Act if it is agreed by the parties concerned that the matter in dispute be referred to arbitration in the Republic or elsewhere, or if for any other sufficient reason the court is of the opinion that the proceedings should be stayed.'

approached their analysis with any presumption in favour of one party. The factors taken into account in deciding applications to stay proceedings on the basis of *forum non conveniens* include: the connections between the forum and the transaction underlying the dispute; the location of witnesses; the applicable law and how it is similar to or different from the law of the forum; expense and convenience. An important factor considered in this regard involves the bargaining positions of the parties. In *Valentine Investment Co. Ltd* v. *Federal Republic of Germany*, the fact that 'the parties were negotiating not on level ground [and] the plaintiff was disadvantaged' was an important consideration in rejecting a German jurisdiction agreement.[83]

The party seeking a stay of proceedings on the basis of the doctrine has the burden of proof – it is a heavy burden, but the standard of proof is on the balance of probability. In general, the decided cases reveal a very balanced approach where all relevant factors are considered – there does not appear to be any implicit desire to keep cases in the forum. Indeed, there have been cases where, even though the factors arguably point to the forum as the more appropriate one, the courts have been prepared to allow for litigation abroad. Indeed, as noted in *Adel Kamel Barsoum* v. *Clemessy International*, 'the courts do not adopt or rely on pure sentimental approach in assuming jurisdiction merely because a person of its nationality is involved'.[84]

The fact that parties have agreed that, in the event of dispute, a named court shall have jurisdiction is an important consideration in deciding whether to stay proceedings. Historically, there were cases suggesting that such agreements attempt to oust the jurisdiction of the courts and are hence unenforceable. The dominant position is now that the courts have the discretion to give effect to such agreements. The courts have not imposed any requirement for a connection between the chosen forum and the dispute, but there has been no case where the sole connection was the jurisdiction agreement. The mere existence of a jurisdiction agreement is not enough to elicit

[83] [2006] eKLR. See also *Raytheon Aircraft Credit Corp.* v. *Air Al-Faraj Ltd* [2005] 2 KLR 47, in which the trial judge rejected an exclusive jurisdiction agreement on the grounds, inter alia, that the agreement was 'tinctured with oppression'. The Court of Appeal overturned the decision. On this point it held that the trial judge did not have sufficient material on which to decide the issue, but it did not expressly reject oppression as a ground for refusing to give effect to a jurisdiction agreement.

[84] [1999] 12 NWLR 516 at 526.

a stay of proceedings, but it appears that an exclusive jurisdiction agreement is given special privileges.[85]

Express statutory limitations on the enforceability of jurisdiction agreements are rare in the countries under study.[86] Subject to the discretion to refuse the enforcement of such agreements, it appears party autonomy in relation to jurisdiction agreements is well respected. However, a growing and recent 'threat'[87] to the enforceability of

[85] For example, in *Uganda Telecom Ltd* v. *Rodrigo Chacon t/a Andes*, Misc. Application 337/08 (High Court, Uganda, 2008), the court did not see any wisdom in including the exclusive jurisdiction clause in the contract or any economic sense in taking the case to the High Court of England, considering the costs likely to be incurred by the parties in litigating. It reasoned that there were competent courts in Uganda to handle the disputes; the agreement was performed in Uganda and most likely, the witnesses would be from Uganda. Furthermore, the applicant did not indicate in its application that it would be prejudiced or would suffer some form of injustice if this case was heard in Uganda. The court nonetheless held that given the 'natural and ordinary meaning' of the exclusive jurisdiction class, and in the absence of any reason why the clause should be set aside, its jurisdiction was 'ousted'. See also *Friendship Container Manufacturers Ltd* v. *Mitchell Cotts Ltd* [2001] 2 EA 338, [1995] LLR 1282, where the court upheld an exclusive jurisdiction clause contained in a bill of lading that vested jurisdiction in the South Africa courts even though the only connection of the contract with South Africa was that the defendant had its registered offices there.

[86] For an exception to this, see South Africa's Carriage of Goods by Sea Act 1986, s. 3(1), which provides that 'notwithstanding any purported ouster of jurisdiction, exclusive jurisdiction clause or agreement to refer any dispute to arbitration . . . any person carrying on business in the Republic and the consignee under, or holder of, any bill of lading, waybill or like document for the carriage of goods to a destination in the Republic or to any port in the Republic, whether for final discharge or for discharge or for discharge [sic] for further carriage, may bring any action relating to the carriage of the said goods or any such bill of lading, waybill or document in a competent court in the Republic'. See generally *Owners, Cargo Lately Laden on Board MV Kairos* v. *MV Alka* 1994 (4) SA 622.

[87] Although the invocation of constitutional provisions as a direct challenge to jurisdiction agreements has appeared only in recent cases, the use of constitutional/statutory language in this field has much deeper roots. See, e.g., Oputa JSC of the Nigeria Supreme Court in 1987; in *Sonnar (Nigeria) Ltd* v. *Partenreedri MS Nordwind* [1988] LRC (Comm.) 191 at 210, where Oputa JSC queried whether 'parties by their *private act* [can] remove the jurisdiction vested by our Constitution in our courts' and where it was held that, 'as a matter of public policy our court should not be too eager to divest themselves of jurisdiction conferred on them by the Constitution and by other laws simply because parties in their private contracts choose a foreign forum and a foreign law.' See generally R. F. Oppong, 'Choice of Law and Forum Agreement Survives a Constitutional Challenge in the Kenya Court of Appeal' (2007) 33(1) *Commonwealth Law Bulletin* 158–63; *Papco Industries Ltd* v. *Eastern and Southern African Trade and Development Bank* [2006] eKLR, in which a loan agreement provided that it shall be construed and governed in accordance with the law of England. The court held that Kenyan courts are obligated to uphold the Constitution and the laws of Kenya. It would therefore follow that it cannot construe the law of England in respect of the loan agreement.

jurisdiction agreements is the constitutional argument presented in some of the decided cases that they undermine the 'unlimited original jurisdiction' in all matters conferred on courts by national constitutions.[88] In all the cases where such an argument has been presented, it has been rejected.[89] It is trite to propose that a jurisdiction agreement does not purport to oust the jurisdiction conferred on the court by statute. Indeed, such jurisdiction can only be ousted by statute and not by private agreements. What jurisdiction agreements do is seek to influence the *exercise* of the court's jurisdiction by inviting the court to enforce, as it routinely does with other contractual agreements, the intention of the parties. The court must have jurisdiction over the parties – for example, through service of process on the defendants or attachment of the defendant's assets – before the question of enforcing a jurisdiction agreement arises. It is only when jurisdiction *exists* that the issue of *its exercise* arises, in which case the presence of a jurisdiction agreement becomes relevant.[90] Thus, as the Kenyan court rightly concluded in the *Raytheon Aircraft* case, these agreements do not challenge the jurisdiction conferred on the High Court by the Constitution; the existence of that jurisdiction is never an issue.

Apart from jurisdiction agreements, the pendency of an action before a foreign court often raises questions as to whether the proceedings of the forum should be stayed. The central issue here is often the relative significance to be given by a forum's court to the fact that concurrent proceedings are pending in another country, when deciding whether to stay proceedings. The decided cases suggest that the pendency of an action before a foreign court is not an automatic bar to the proceedings in the forum – as with jurisdiction agreements, the courts have the discretion to either order or refuse a stay of proceedings on the grounds of *lis alibi pendens*. *Lis alibi pendens* is an important additional element to be considered in *forum non conveniens* analysis. Considerations of justice and fairness are equally paramount here – the chronological order

[88] See, e.g., Constitution of the Republic of Kenya 2010, Art. 165(3)(a); Constitution of Republic of Uganda 1995, Art. 139; Constitution of Malawi 1994, Art. 108(1).

[89] Another threat is the invocation of domestic criminal law or criminal law processes to undermine the enforceability of contracts and arbitration agreements therein. See *Midland Finance & Securities Globetel Inc.* v. *Attorney General* [2008] KLR 650; *Nedermar Technology BV Ltd* v. *Kenya Anti-corruption Commission* [2008] KLR 476.

[90] In instances where the defendant is outside the territorial jurisdiction of the court, the existence of a foreign choice of law or forum clause may be a relevant consideration in deciding whether to allow leave for service out of the jurisdiction.

in which the proceedings were initiated is not conclusive. However, the fact that the foreign proceedings were initiated first may afford a prima facie case for a stay in the absence of proof that there would be an injustice if a stay was granted. Other factors which the courts have taken into account include: the enforceability of judgments arising from the proceedings; the cost and level of complexity of the proceedings; the location of witnesses; the disclosure of material facts; and the basis on which the foreign court has assumed jurisdiction.

The majority of the countries under study – Botswana, Ghana, Kenya, Lesotho, Nigeria, South Africa, Tanzania, Uganda, Zambia and Zimbabwe – are parties to the New York Convention and have enacted legislation to implement it. Gambia,[91] Malawi, Namibia, Sierra Leone and Swaziland are not parties to the Convention. The statutes on arbitration in the countries under study empower courts before which an action is brought in breach of an arbitration agreement to stay their proceedings in favour of arbitration. Putting aside New York Convention cases, it can be argued that while in some countries – Botswana, Malawi, Nigeria, South Africa and Tanzania – a stay of proceedings is discretionary, in others – Gambia, Ghana, Kenya, Uganda, Zambia and Zimbabwe – it is mandatory, unless certain defined conditions are present.

An important issue in the context of enforcing arbitration agreements – and indeed jurisdiction agreements – is the severability or separability of such agreements from the rest of the agreement in which they are embodied. The central question is whether the invalidity of the main agreement invalidates the arbitration agreement. In some of the countries under study, the principle separability of arbitration agreements is statutorily enshrined or has been judicially upheld. Under section 3(1) of Ghana's Alternative Dispute Resolution Act 2010, unless otherwise agreed by the parties, an arbitration agreement which forms, or is intended to form, part of another agreement shall not be regarded as invalid, non-existent or ineffective because that other agreement is invalid, or has not come into existence, or has become ineffective and shall for that purpose be treated as a distinct agreement.[92] Severability

[91] The UNCITRAL website does not list Gambia as a party to the Convention. However, the Alternative Dispute Resolution Act 2005 implements the Convention and lists it as the second Schedule to the Act.

[92] See generally *Attorney General* v. *Balkan Energy Ghana Ltd*, Reference No. J6/1/2012 (Supreme Court, Ghana, 2012), in which the court referred the constitutionality of the underlying contract for determination by the High Court, but held that the arbitration agreement is a 'separate transaction' which was unaffected by the constitutionality of the

enables an arbitration agreement to survive attacks to the underlying agreement. The uncertainty created by the fact that the issue is not legislatively dealt with directly in many of the countries under study and that there appears to be no direct decided case[93] on the subject is not good for the enforceability of the arbitration agreement.

underlying contract. In Kenya, see Arbitration Act 1995, s. 17; *Midland Finance & Securities Globetel Inc.* v. *Attorney General* [2008] KLR 650; *Nedermar Technology BV Ltd* v. *Kenya Anti-corruption Commission* [2008] KLR 476; *Nedermar Technology BV Ltd* v. *Kenya Anti-corruption Commission* [2006] 2 KLR 678.

93 In *National Insurance Co. Ltd* v. *Ngwira* [1993] 16(1) MLR 381, the court severed a *Scott* v. *Avery* clause from an arbitration agreement. The clause was found to be inconsistent with legislation and was hence invalid. The rest of the arbitration agreement and the contract were not affected by the invalidity of the clause. For a useful UK House of Lords decision on this point, see *Premium Nafta Products Ltd* v. *Fili Shipping Co. Ltd* [2007] UKHL 40.

6

Limitations on jurisdiction

There are instances in which express limitations are placed on the competence of a court to adjudicate a claim. The effect of such limitations on jurisdiction is to render the court incompetent to hear an action otherwise properly brought before it. The limitations are often grounded in public policy or in fulfilment of international obligations. The limitations may be in respect of parties to the action, the cause of action itself, or even the relief sought, and may be a creature of statute or the common law. This chapter explores limitations that are placed on the jurisdiction of courts to adjudicate claims.

Jurisdictional immunities

Botswana

The Diplomatic Immunities and Privileges Act 1969 gives effect to the Vienna Convention on Diplomatic Relations 1961. The Act empowers the President to extend the provisions of the Convention to international organisations and individuals. Botswana adheres to the restrictive doctrine of immunity.[1] In *Bah* v. *Libyan Embassy*,[2] the applicant sought severance pay, wages in lieu of notice, withheld wages and a certificate of employment from the respondent. The issue was whether the respondent, as an embassy of a foreign state, was capable of being sued for a breach of the provisions of the Employment Act, having regard to the provisions of the Act. In denying immunity in respect of this action, it was held that an action arising out of a breach of an employment contract involved a private law transaction and there was no reason why the respondent should be immune from a legal suit of this nature,

[1] *Republic of Angola* v. *Springbok Investments (Pty) Ltd* 2005 (2) BLR 159; *Dube* v. *American Embassy*, Case No. IC 897/2006 (High Court, Botswana, 2009).

[2] 2006 (1) BLR 22.

since the applicant was not challenging a governmental act, but merely seeking compliance with the statute. Indeed, to the court, it was the duty of a diplomatic mission to respect the laws of the receiving state, since to do otherwise could undermine the rule of law of the receiving state.

Ghana

Ghana is party to the Vienna Convention on Diplomatic Relations 1961, which was implemented under the Diplomatic Immunities Act 1962. It has been held that 'commercial activity' in Article 31 of the Convention means any commercial or business transaction entered into by a diplomat in his or her private capacity. Personal profit is not a key element in the commercial activities envisaged under Article 31. On the contrary, any private commercial transaction entered into by the diplomatic agent outside his or her official functions, whether or not for personal profit, represents a commercial activity within the meaning and intent of Article 31.[3] Furthermore, from a combined reading of Articles 31 and 42, a single isolated act of buying vehicles and other personal effects does not constitute an activity of a commercial nature – it should be a 'regular or frequent or repeated exercise in prosecution of an activity of a commercial nature'.[4]

A person who claims to be a diplomatic agent must provide proof to that effect. A letter from the Ministry of Foreign Affairs is admissible and conclusive proof of a person's diplomatic status in Ghana.[5] The relevant date at which a diplomatic agent's right to immunity from jurisdiction must exist is not the date on which the cause of action arises, but the time the action is brought.[6]

Immunity from jurisdiction can be waived.[7] However, a waiver of immunity is not to be lightly inferred. Thus, the fact that a diplomatic agent insures his or her car in compliance with the Motor Vehicles (Third Party Insurance) Act 1958 does not mean he or she has thereby

[3] See *Garcia* v. *Torrejoh* [1992] 1 GLR 143.

[4] *Torrenton* v. *Diez* [1992–3] GBR 1578 at 1582. The court, however, suggested that the presence of a 'profit-making motive or purpose' may convert an otherwise colourless activity into a commercial one.

[5] *Armon* v. *Katz* [1976] 2 GLR 115 (reversing *Katz* v. *Armon* [1967] GLR 624); *Garcia* v. *Torrejoh* [1992] 1 GLR 143; *Torrenton* v. *Diez* [1992–3] GBR 1578.

[6] *Armon* v. *Katz* [1976] 2 GLR 115.

[7] *Republic* v. *High Court (Commercial Division) Accra, Ex p. Attorney General, NML Capital and the Republic of Argentina*, Civil Motion No. J5/10/2013 (Supreme Court, Ghana, 2013); *NML Capital Ltd* v. *The Republic of Ghana*, Suit No. RPC/343/12 (High Court, Ghana, 2012).

expressly waived his or her diplomatic immunity. Such a waiver could validly be made only by his or her sending government – in this instance, the Israeli Government – under Article 32(1)(2) of the Convention.[8]

Diplomatic immunity protects foreign diplomats from the Ghanaian courts' jurisdiction; it does not protect a Ghanaian diplomat sued in Ghana for acts committed abroad. Thus, where an action was brought in the High Court of Ghana against a respondent, a Ghanaian chargé d'affaires at Ghana's embassy in Liberia at the time the alleged wrongs were committed, and the respondent pleaded immunity, it was held that the respondent was Ghanaian and a person sent by the Ghanaian Government to take charge of its embassy in Monrovia, and that the immunity he enjoyed under the Convention did not extend to an action brought against him before the courts of his own country.[9]

Kenya

The Privileges and Immunities Act 1970 gives effect to the Vienna Convention on Diplomatic Relations 1961 and the Vienna Convention on Consular Relations 1963. A Kenyan court will not entertain an action against certain privileged persons and institutions unless the privilege is waived and that person submits to the jurisdiction of the court.[10] Such persons include foreign sovereigns or heads of state and government, foreign diplomats, consular officers and representatives of international organisations. The courts will accept as conclusive proof a statement from the executive on the diplomatic status of a person.[11] A privileged person who submits to the jurisdiction of the courts loses the privilege to claim immunity from the courts' jurisdiction.[12] Similarly, a state which institutes an action against a person submits to the jurisdiction of the court and becomes amenable to remedies provided by the court. Accordingly, security for costs may be ordered against a state which brings an action before the Kenyan courts.[13]

It is not to all acts of a foreign sovereign or state that this principle applies – the immunity is not absolute, but restrictive. The test is whether

[8] *Armon* v. *Katz* [1976] 2 GLR 115. [9] *Kwarteng* v. *Sackey* [1984–6] 1 GLR 141.

[10] *Ministry of Defence of the Government of the United Kingdom* v. *Ndegwa* [1983] KLR 1, [1976–85] 1 EA 294; *Urbanus Mutiso* v. *Susan Kavanagh* [2012] eKLR.

[11] *Urbanus Mutiso* v. *Susan Kavanagh*.

[12] *Ijaz Hussein Gan Ijee* v. *Hussein M Aideed* [2005] eKLR.

[13] *State of Israel* v. *Somen* [2001] LLR 5932.

the foreign sovereign or government is acting in a governmental capacity – in which case it can claim immunity – or privately, in which case an action may be brought against it.[14] Thus, where an international organisation which had been granted immunity was sued over a contract of employment and it was found that the contract was necessary for the fulfilment of the defendant's purposes, it was held that the defendant was entitled to immunity.[15]

Nigeria

Although the Diplomatic Immunities and Privileges Act 1962 does not make express reference to the Vienna Convention on Diplomatic Immunity, Nigeria is a party to the Convention. Under the Act, every foreign envoy, foreign consular officer, the members of the families of those persons, the members of their official or domestic staff, and the members of the families of their official staff, shall be accorded immunity from suit and legal process to the extent to which they are respectively so entitled under the law in force in Nigeria immediately before the coming into operation of the Act.[16] It has been held that the Act provides protection only for diplomats rather than for the sovereign state itself. It is legislation that confers immunity on persons, both natural and artificial, who serve the state in another state, but it does not deal with the sovereign immunity of states.[17] Rather, the foundation of the doctrine of sovereign immunity is in common law as it existed in England before 1900. The common law has traditionally recognised a restrictive doctrine of sovereign immunity and the cases where this restrictive doctrine has been applied have largely been commercial as opposed to tort claims. Before applying the doctrine, the court must be cautious – it must be satisfied that from the plaintiff's claim, it is manifest that the defendant

[14] *Ministry of Defence of the Government of the United Kingdom* v. *Ndegwa* [1983] KLR 1, [1976–85] 1 EA 294. See also *Tononoka Steels Ltd* v. *Eastern and Southern Africa Trade and Development Bank* [2000] 2 EA 536.

[15] *Gerard Killeen* v. *International Centre of Insect Physiology and Ecology* [2005] 1 KLR 718. See generally *Joseph Kimani Gathungu* v. *Attorney General* [2010] eKLR on the immunity of the International Criminal Court.

[16] Diplomatic Immunities and Privileges Act 1962, s. 1. Like treatment is accorded to other named foreign officials under the Act. The laws in force before the Act included the Diplomatic Immunities and Privileges (Commonwealth Countries Republic of Ireland) Act and the Diplomatic Privileges (Extension) Act.

[17] *Oluwalogbon* v. *Government of United Kingdom* [2005] 14 NWLR 760.

acted in a manner inconsistent with its superior authority, something the plaintiffs failed to do in the instant case.[18]

The immunity conferred is immunity from jurisdiction. The existence of immunity does not negate the elements needed to constitute a cause of action. Accordingly, publication of a defamatory letter to the Israeli Ambassador at his residence in Lagos constituted publication in law such as could found a cause of action.[19] Diplomatic immunity may be waived.[20] A waiver is not to be presumed against a sovereign or an organisation that enjoys immunity. If anything, the presumption is that there is no waiver until evidence shows the contrary. A person in whose favour privilege of immunity is presumed must be shown to have waived it with full awareness of their action. A waiver of immunity must be expressly and positively carried out by the person in whose favour it exists.[21] It may take the form of submission to the jurisdiction of the court by conduct such as entering appearance and filing a statement of defence,[22] or through an appropriately worded jurisdiction[23] or arbitration agreement.[24] However, such a waiver does not affect the constitutional allocation of jurisdiction among national courts, nor does a person lose their diplomatic status by waiving a statutorily conferred immunity. Thus, where Article 251(1)(h) of the Nigerian Constitution granted the Federal High Court exclusive jurisdiction in civil causes and matters relating to diplomats, consular and trade representation and Article 272(1) vested in the State High Courts jurisdiction to hear and determine libel suits, it was held, in a libel action instituted by the plaintiffs, Bulgaria's Ambassador to Nigeria and the Bulgarian Embassy, that the action must be tried by the Federal High Court.[25]

Where the act complained of is an act of a commercial character, the fact that it was performed for governmental or political

[18] *Oluwalogbon* v. *Government of United Kingdom*. See also *AG Ishola Noah* v. *The British High Commission of Nigeria* [1980] FNLR 473.

[19] *Zabusky* v. *Israeli Aircraft Industries* [2008] 2 NWLR 109.

[20] Diplomatic Immunities and Privileges Act 1962, s. 2.

[21] *African Reinsurance Corp.* v. *Fantaye* [1986] 3 NWLR 811 (reversing *African Reinsurance Corp.* v. *Fantaye* [1986] 1 NWLR 113); *Dimitrov* v. *Multichoice Nigeria Ltd* [2005] 13 NWLR 575.

[22] *Grisby* v. *Jubwe* (1952–5) 14 WACA 637.

[23] *African Reinsurance Corp.* v. *JDP Construction (Nigeria) Ltd* [2007] 11 NWLR 224.

[24] *African Reinsurance Corp.* v. *Aim Consultants Ltd* [2004] 11 NWLR 223.

[25] *Dimitrov* v. *Multichoice Nigeria Ltd* [2005] 13 NWLR 575.

reasons by the department of a state does not attract sovereign immunity. A government department that enters into a commercial transaction – in this instance engaging the defendant to provide building consultancy services – is not immune from legal action instituted in respect of any dispute arising from the transaction.[26] In determining whether a transaction is commercial, the intrinsic nature of the transaction is the primary consideration. Thus, it has been held that a contract under which an embassy commissions a contractor to build a residence for an ambassador is not a purely commercial transaction.[27]

Sierra Leone

The Diplomatic Immunities and Privileges Act 1962 has regulated diplomatic immunity in Sierra Leone. To establish that a person has the status of a diplomatic agent, a letter or certificate to that effect from the Ministry of Foreign Affairs and International Cooperation will provide conclusive evidence of that fact.[28] Immunity may be waived. However, neither the fact that a person entered a conditional appearance, nor made an application to set aside the writ of summons for irregularity and jurisdiction, nor took out insurance in relation to the car involved in an accident, which is the subject matter of the suit in the instant case, amounts to a waiver of immunity.[29]

It is a well-settled principle of Sierra Leonean law that a foreign sovereign is not liable to be impleaded before its courts in relation to non-commercial transactions. However, there is nothing to prevent a foreign sovereign from appearing as a plaintiff in the Sierra Leone courts and if he or she does so appear, they are treated just like any other litigant in such matters as the discovery of documents and security for costs. A state which comes in as a suitor submits to the jurisdiction of the court and to all orders which may properly be made.[30]

[26] *African Reinsurance Corp.* v. *Aim Consultants Ltd.*

[27] *Kramer Italo Ltd* v. *Government of the Kingdom of Belgium* (2004) 103 ILR 299.

[28] *Representative of the World Health Organization* v. *Joseph Monrovia*, CC1215/2005 2005 F No. 51 (High Court, Sierra Leone, 2007).

[29] *Representative of the WHO* v. *Joseph Monrovia.*

[30] *Bank of Credit & Commerce International* v. *The Chargé D'affaires of the Ivory Coast Embassy*, Misc. App. No. 3/82 (Supreme Court, Sierra Leone, 1983).

South Africa

In relation to jurisdictional immunities, the Foreign State Immunities Act 1981[31] and the Diplomatic Immunity and Privileges Act 2001 are the two principal statutes. While the former focuses on foreign states and the extent to which they are immune from the jurisdiction of South African courts, the latter focuses on individuals and international organisations and gives effect to the Vienna Convention on Diplomatic Relations and the Vienna Convention on Consular Relations.

The Foreign State Immunities Act adopts the doctrine of restrictive immunity – it grants immunity to foreign states from the jurisdiction of the courts in relation to acts performed in the exercise of the sovereign authority of a foreign state, but not in relation to acts relating to commercial transactions undertaken by the state.[32] Indeed, the Act contains a number of specific subjects or issues for which, in defined situations, a foreign state shall not be immune from the jurisdiction of the South African court: these include commercial transactions, contracts of employment,[33] personal injuries and damage to property claims, ownership, possession and use of property claims, patents and trademark-related claims, actions ancillary to arbitration proceedings,[34] admiralty proceedings, taxes and duties. Given the nature and scope of the exceptions, it would be rare for a sovereign state to be immune from the jurisdiction of the South African court, especially in relation to transactions or causes of action arising in South Africa.

[31] The Act defines a foreign state, to include the head of state of that foreign state, in his or her capacity as such head of state, the government of that foreign state, and any department of that government. It excludes any entity which is distinct from the executive organs of the government of that foreign state and which is capable of suing or being sued; or any territory forming a constituent part of a federal foreign state. See *Lendalease Finance Co. (Pty) Ltd* v. *Corporacion de Mercadeo Agricola* 1975 (4) SA 397; *Banco de Mocambique* v. *Inter-science Research and Development Services (Pty) Ltd* 1982 (3) SA 330 (reversing *Inter-science Research and Development Services (Pty) Ltd* v. *Republica Popular de Mocambique* 1980 (2) SA 111); *The Shipping Corp. of India Ltd* v. *Evdomon Corp.* 1994 (1) SA 550.

[32] *KJ International* v. *MV Oscar Jupiter* 1998 (2) SA 130. This statutory position reflected the law which existed in South Africa prior to the Act: see *Banco de Mocambique* v. *Inter-science Research and Development Services (Pty) Ltd* 1982 (3) SA 330; *Kaffraria Property Co. (Pty) Ltd* v. *Government of the Republic of Zambia* 1980 (2) SA 709.

[33] The scope of this exception reserves the decision in *Prentice, Shaw & Schiess Inc.* v. *Government of the Republic of Bolivia* 1978 (3) SA 938.

[34] *The Akademik Fyodorov: Government of the Russian Federation* v. *Marine Expeditions Inc.* 1996 (4) SA 422.

Consistent with the immunity enjoyed by states, a South African court will not compel a state to be joined as a party to an action even if principle requires that the state should be a party to the action.[35] All property of a foreign state, including money held by it for public purposes in the area of jurisdiction of the court, and property it controls in the hands of its agents, is immune from attachment – an important basis of jurisdiction in South African law – under an order of the court.[36] Immunity may be waived under the Act.[37] A waiver must be expressed.[38] A state which, through its act, violates the forum state's sovereignty cannot claim sovereign immunity for the latter court in respect of that breach. It has thus been held that having violated Bophuthatswana's sovereignty, South Africa could hardly expect to enjoy the privilege of sovereign immunity in the courts of Bophuthatswana in respect of that very breach.[39]

The Diplomatic Immunities and Privileges Act 2001 gives effect to the Vienna Convention on Diplomatic Relations 1961 and the Vienna Convention on Consular Relations 1963. In relation to Article 31(1)(a) of the Vienna Convention, which denies immunity to a diplomatic agent in respect of 'a real action relating to private immovable property situated in the territory of the receiving State, unless he holds it on behalf of the sending State for the purposes of the mission', it was held that the mere claim of an interest in property by the government in question is not enough: the court has to be satisfied that the claim is not merely illusory or founded on a manifestly defective title.[40]

Tanzania

The Diplomatic and Consular Immunities Act 1986 gives the force of law to the Vienna Convention on Diplomatic Relations and the Vienna Convention on Consular Relations. The Tanzanian courts appreciate the

[35] *Leibowitz* v. *Schwartz* 1974 (2) SA 661.

[36] *Parkin* v. *Government of the Republique Democratique du Congo* 1971 (1) SA 259; *Lendalease Finance Co. (Pty) Ltd* v. *Corporacion de Mercadeo Agricola* 1975 (4) SA 397. Under s. 14(b)(i) of the Foreign States Immunities Act 1981, the property of a foreign state shall not be subject to any process for its attachment in order to found jurisdiction.

[37] Foreign States Immunities Act 1981, s. 3.

[38] *C G M Industrial (Pty) Ltd* v. *KPMG* 1998 (3) SA 738. See also Diplomatic Immunities and Privileges Act 2001, s. 8(3), which provides that a waiver must always be express and in writing.

[39] *Mangope* v. *Van der Walt* 1994 (3) SA 850.

[40] *Portion 20 of Plot 15 Athol (Pty) Ltd* v. *Rodrigues* 2001 (1) SA 1285.

distinction between the absolute and restrictive theory of immunity. It has been held that in deciding which theory to apply, a court should be free to exercise its judicial discretion on the basis of authorities and circumstances where the government of the receiving state takes no stance in the matter. However, where the government of the receiving state takes a definite stand on whether it adheres to either the absolute or restrictive theory of state and diplomatic immunity, the courts would do well to defer to such a pronouncement.[41] *Beysne* v. *Republic of Romania*[42] involved an action for damages for wrongful eviction under an agreement by which the Republic of Romania leased its premises to the plaintiff. The defendants claimed immunity under the Vienna Convention on Diplomatic Relations 1961. The Ministry of Foreign Affairs and International Cooperation informed the court that the defendants were not amenable to its jurisdiction. It held that, given the tone of the Ministry's letter, Tanzania still adhered to the absolute theory of immunity.

In respect of an international organisation which derives its immunity from its founding treaty, it has been held to be imperative that its claimed immunity is judged only on the basis of treaty provisions, and not on the customary international law doctrine of sovereign immunity. Thus, in such a case, where an interpretation of the relevant treaty provision led to the conclusion that the state parties intended to confer absolute immunity on the organisation, the fact that a restrictive approach to immunity now exists in customary international law is immaterial.[43]

Uganda

The Diplomatic Privileges Act 1965 gives effect to the Vienna Convention on Diplomatic Relations. In respect of international organisations, it has been held that on the basis of a strict interpretation of their founding treaties, the East African Development Bank and the International Finance Corporation enjoy absolute immunity under Ugandan law.[44] Accordingly, officers of both organisations cannot be orally examined before a court, since such examination is 'a form of legal process'.

[41] *Beysne* v. *Republic of Romania* [2000] 2 EA 322. [42] Ibid.

[43] *East African Development Bank* v. *Blueline Enterprises Ltd*, Civil Appeal No. 110 of 2009 (Tanzania, Court of Appeal, 2011). See also *Humphrey Construction Ltd* v. *Pan African Postal Union*, Misc. Comm. Case No. 8 of 2007 (Court of Appeal, Tanzania, 2008).

[44] *Nelson Dhibikirwa* v. *Agro Management (U) Ltd*, Misc. Application no. 651 of 2010 (High Court, Uganda, 2012).

Zimbabwe

The Privileges and Immunities Act 1972 gives effect to the Vienna Convention on Diplomatic Relations and the Vienna Convention on Consular Relations. It has been held that the doctrine of sovereign immunity is a question of international law. Zimbabwe adheres to the doctrine of restricted sovereign immunity which applies to *acta jure imperii*, i.e. acts of a purely governmental or public nature and not to *acta jure gestionis*, i.e. acts of a commercial or proprietary nature.[45] The courts distinguish *acta jure imperii* from *acta jure gestionis* by referring to the nature of the state transaction or the resultant legal relationships, and not to the motive or purpose of the state activity.[46] The International Organisation of the Red Cross enjoys immunity – albeit of a restricted nature – from suit and process. In the instant case, the court found that the contracts of employment which formed the basis of the respondents' claims for unlawful retrenchment were clearly acts of a private law character such as a private citizen might have entered into and for which the Red Cross did not enjoy immunity from suit and legal process.[47] It remains in doubt whether a court may *mero motu* raise the question of immunity.[48]

Comments

In the countries under study, the law on sovereign and diplomatic immunity is governed by a mixture of statute law, customary international law and international conventions.[49] Each of the countries under study is a

[45] *Barker McCormac Ltd* v. *Government of Kenya* 1983 (2) ZLR 72, 1983 (4) SA 817; *International Committee of the Red Cross* v. *Sibanda* 2007 (1) SA 476, 2004 (1) ZLR 27.

[46] *Barker McCormac Ltd* v. *Government of Kenya* 1983 (2) ZLR 72, 1983 (4) SA 817 (reversing *Barker McCormac Ltd* v. *Government of Kenya* 1983 (1) ZLR 137); *Barker McCormac Ltd* v. *Government of Kenya* 1985 (1) ZLR 18, 1985 (4) SA 197.

[47] *International Committee of the Red Cross* v. *Sibanda* 2007 (1) SA 476, 2004 (1) ZLR 27.

[48] In *Barker McCormac Ltd* v. *Government of Kenya* 1983 (1) ZLR 137, the court held that a proposal to sue a sovereign in the municipal courts of another state is a very serious action justifying action *mero motu* by the court. Although the Supreme Court reversed this decision in *Barker McCormac Ltd* v. *Government of Kenya* 1983 (2) ZLR 72, 1983 (4) SA 817, it found it 'unnecessary to rule on that issue'.

[49] Outside immunity from jurisdiction there may be special national rules, including notice requirements that apply to actions against foreign governments. See, e.g., *Maunga Seed Co. (T) Ltd* v. *Secretary to the Treasury, Ministry of Finance and National Planning: Government of the Republic of Zambia*, Civil Case No. 99 of 2003 (High Court, Tanzania, 2004), in which the action was dismissed because of failure to give notice to the Attorney General. There may also be immunity from other legal processes, such as being compelled to give evidence. See, e.g., *Tsatsu Tsikata* v. *The Republic* [2011] 1 SCGLR 1.

party to the Vienna Convention on Diplomatic Relations 1961 and has enacted legislation to implement it. They differ in the extent and mode of implementation of the Convention. However, all of them have given effect to Articles 31 and 32, which deal with jurisdictional immunity. Apart from Sierra Leone, which is a signatory, none of the countries under study is party to the UN Convention on Jurisdictional Immunities of States and their Property 2004, which is yet to come into force.[50]

A distinction is drawn between diplomatic immunity and sovereign immunity. Diplomatic immunity is well regulated, mostly by statute. Sovereign immunity is regulated by customary international law, which is considered as part of national law in the countries under study. In other words, the law of sovereign immunity in many cases is a reflection of the principles of customary international law, as ascertained by national courts and deemed to be part of national law. It is only in Malawi[51] and South Africa that sovereign immunity is regulated by statute.

It is often an issue whether a person or international organisation is entitled to immunity. On this issue, the courts have been prepared to give weight to an executive pronouncement on the subject. There is, however, divergence reflected in judicial decisions and legislation on the weight to be given to such evidence. Case law in Ghana and Sierra Leone, and legislation in Gambia, Botswana, Kenya, Malawi, Nigeria, Tanzania, Zambia and Zimbabwe, dictate that, where in any proceedings, a question arises over whether a person is entitled to the benefit of immunity, a certificate given by the Minister stating any fact relating to that question shall represent conclusive evidence of that fact.[52] In South Africa, such a certificate constitutes only prima facie evidence.[53]

[50] In addition, some countries are parties to specific organisational conventions, such as the General Convention on the Privileges and Immunities of the Organization of African Unity 1965; the Convention on the Privileges and Immunities of the United Nations 1946; the Convention on the Privileges and Immunities of the Specialised Agencies 1947.

[51] Immunities and Privileges Act 1984, ss. 3–19. These provisions are very similar to South Africa's Foreign States Immunities Act 1981. Both statutes are largely based on the English State Immunity Act 1978.

[52] Gambia – Diplomatic Privileges (Commonwealth and Foreign Missions) Act 1968, s. 5; Botswana – Diplomatic Immunities and Privileges Act 1969, s. 9; Kenya – Privileges and Immunities Act 1970, s. 16; Malawi – Immunities and Privileges Act 1984, ss. 19 and 32; Nigeria – Diplomatic Immunities and Privileges Act 1962, s. 18; Tanzania – Diplomatic and Consular Immunities and Privileges Act 1986, s. 20(2); Zambia – Diplomatic Immunities and Privileges Act 1965, s. 15; Zimbabwe – Privileges and Immunities Act 1972, s. 14.

[53] South Africa – Diplomatic Immunities and Privileges Act 2001, s. 9(3). In respect of sovereign immunity, a certificate from the Minister constitutes 'conclusive evidence' under s. 18 of the Foreign State Immunities Act 1981.

Regardless of whether one is dealing with diplomatic or sovereign immunity, it remains the case that the majority of the countries under study adhere to the restrictive doctrine of immunity. Tanzania appears to be a notable exception in this respect – it can be argued that the existing jurisprudence of its courts reveals a preference for the *absolute* doctrine. Under the *restricted* doctrine, immunity from the jurisdiction of national courts is granted with respect to acts *jure imperii* (governmental public acts), but not *jure gestionis* acts (commercial activities). The vexing question for courts has always been to draw the line of demarcation between public acts and commercial acts. Apart from South Africa's Foreign State Immunities Act 1981, the concept of commercial transaction remains largely undefined in the countries under study.[54] In this regard, each case has been largely decided on the basis of its own peculiar facts, and it is often difficult to rationalise the differences in outcome on the sole basis of the facts of the cases. Little guidance is provided in the cases for distinguishing between the two Acts. That said, the courts have noted that there must be a focus on the intrinsic nature of the transaction, that personal profit is not a conclusive determining factor, and that some level of continuity of activity may be required. However, it is submitted that the continuity of the activity should not be a significant consideration in deciding whether an activity is commercial. A diplomat or sovereign should not be able to avoid the jurisdiction of a municipal court merely because they sold or bought items on just one occasion. From the perspective of a plaintiff, whom the commercial activity exception aims to protect, the regularity or frequency with which the activity complained of was undertaken by the diplomat does not matter. Indeed, Article 31 specifically refers to 'commercial activity' and not commercial activities.

The statutes in the countries under study dealing with diplomatic immunity often contain provisions which allow for their extension to international organisations.[55] Nevertheless, it is not uncommon for

[54] Section 4(3) of the Act defines commercial transaction as: 'any contract for the supply of services or goods; any loan or other transaction for the provision of finance and any guarantee or indemnity in respect of any such loan or other transaction or of any other financial obligation; and any other transaction or activity or a commercial, industrial, financial, professional or other similar character into which a foreign state enters or in which it engages otherwise than in the exercise of sovereign authority, but does not include a contract of employment between a foreign state and an individual'.

[55] Gambia has a separate legislation dealing with international organisations. See Diplomatic Privileges (International Organizations) Act 1948.

the constitutive treaty of an international organisation to contain a specific provision conferring immunity on the organisation. Contrary to the approach adopted by the Kenyan courts,[56] Tanzanian and Ugandan courts have taken the position that, in relation to such an organisation, the existence or otherwise of immunity in proceedings instituted against it should be judged on the basis of an interpretation of treaty provisions and not on the customary international law doctrine of sovereign immunity.[57] The effect of this position is that an international organisation may enjoy absolute immunity from jurisdiction even though the prevailing position in customary international law is towards restrictive immunity. It is submitted that these two positions can be reconciled to the extent that courts are prepared to take into account existing customary international law on immunity when interpreting the relevant treaty provision. Such an approach to interpretation is more likely to be consonant with the intention of the states which created the organisation and the legislators who gave national force of law to the constitutive treaty of the organisation where its immunity is enshrined. It is unlikely that states will legislate to confer on a body any privileges above and beyond what the state enjoys before a foreign court.

In all the countries under study, immunity may be waived by the person entitled thereto. The existing jurisprudence indicates that waiver of immunity is not to be lightly inferred. Indeed, in some jurisdictions, such as South Africa, it must be undertaken in writing.[58] The presence of a jurisdiction agreement has been held to be an effective waiver of immunity. It is, however, doubtful whether a choice of law agreement would be similarly treated.[59]

An interesting question that has arisen in some cases is whether the issue of immunity may be raised *suo muto* by the court. In relation to sovereign immunity, section 2(2) of South Africa's Foreign State

[56] *Tononoka Steels Ltd* v. *Eastern and Southern Africa Trade and Development Bank* [2000] 2 EA 536. Contrast with *East African Development Bank* v. *Blueline Enterprises Ltd*, Civil Appeal No. 110 of 2009 (Tanzania, Court of Appeal, 2011).

[57] This approach appears to have been endorsed in the Ugandan case of *Nelson Dhibikirwa* v. *Agro Management (U) Ltd*, Misc. Application no. 651 of 2010 (High Court, Uganda, 2012), in which the court cited the Tanzania decision with approval.

[58] Diplomatic Immunities and Privileges Act 2001, s. 8(3).

[59] Under s. 3(2) of South Africa's Foreign State Immunities Act 1981 and s. 4(2) of Malawi's Immunities and Privileges Act 1984, a provision in an agreement that it is governed by South African or Malawian law shall not be regarded as a waiver.

Immunities Act 1981 expressly mandates the courts to 'give effect to the immunity conferred by this section even though the foreign state does not appear in the proceedings in question'.[60] There is a strong case to be made that, given the objective of immunity to protect harmonious relations between states, a court should, on its own, be able to raise the issue of immunity when the facts of a case dictate.

The Kenyan case of *Tononoka Steels Ltd* v. *Eastern and Southern Africa Trade and Development Bank*[61] raised an interesting issue of whether immunity was a question of procedure or substance. The case suggests that the *lex causae* may be a relevant consideration in determining the availability of immunity. In this case, the plaintiff sought damages for breach of contract against the defendant bank, a body corporate established by several African states under a multilateral treaty, and made an interlocutory application for an injunction. The bank claimed immunity from civil process under Kenya's Privileges and Immunity Act. It further contended that, by virtue of an arbitration clause in the contract, the applicable law was the law of England. The court held that under the Act, the bank enjoyed only qualified immunity. It further held that the defence of immunity was not available to the bank because the applicable law of the agreement was the law of England and, under that law, immunity did not extend to commercial transactions. Given that countries are still divided between restrictive and absolute immunity, this is a significant holding: if immunity is a question of substance, hence governed by the applicable law, it offers the possibility for parties to escape its effect through their choice of law agreements.

It has been decided that a state which through its act violates the forum state's sovereignty cannot claim sovereign immunity for the latter court in respect of that breach. However, it remains to be decided whether a state which acts in breach of international law, such as by violating fundamental human rights, would be immune from the jurisdiction of a court in respect of claims founded on such a breach. It is submitted that a breach of international law should attract immunity if the breach is the result of a public act. Arguably, the foundation of the doctrine of immunity is not in equity, or in the need to do justice in individual cases. Rather, it reflects the objective of maintaining harmonious relationships between states. The jurisdictional immunity of a state

[60] See also Malawi – Immunities and Privileges Act 1984, s. 3(2).

[61] [2000] 2 EA 536.

should prevail, even if the act complained of is allegedly a violation of international law.

Capacity to sue

The question often arises of whether a person has the capacity to invoke the jurisdiction of a court. This issue may arise in the context of persons such as alien enemies, foreign companies, foreign liquidators, trustees and other representatives. In Kenya, Tanzania and Uganda, an alien enemy residing in the country with the permission of the President (the government in Tanzania and Minister in Uganda) and alien friends may sue in the Kenyan, Tanzanian or Ugandan courts. However, no alien enemy residing in Kenya, Tanzania or Uganda without such permission, or residing in a foreign country shall sue in a Kenyan, Tanzanian or Ugandan court, respectively.[62]

The general position in the countries under study appears to be that a juristic person created by foreign law would be recognised as such by the forum's courts for the purpose of enabling that person to invoke the jurisdiction of the forum's courts. In Kenya, it has been held that when a foreign company has gone into voluntary winding up, or has been dissolved or wound up by the law of its domicile, Kenyan courts do not recognise it as an existing entity at all, but merely as a name, with no legal existence. Such an entity cannot therefore sue or be sued in Kenya.[63] In Ghana, it has been held that an unincorporated foreign firm not carrying on business in Ghana could not issue a writ of summons or sue in the firm's name.[64]

Nigerian courts have consistently held that a foreign corporation duly created according to the laws of a foreign state recognised by Nigeria may sue and be sued in its corporate name in Nigerian courts, except if it

[62] Kenya – Civil Procedure Act 1924, s. 56(1)(2); Tanzania – Civil Procedure Code 1966, s. 61(1)(2); Uganda – Civil Procedure Act 1929, s. 57(1)(2). The explanatory note to these provisions suggests that every person residing in a foreign country, the government of which is at war with Kenya or Uganda and carrying on business in that country without a licence in that behalf under the hand of the Minister, shall be deemed to be an alien enemy residing in a foreign country.

[63] *Shah* v. *Aperit Investments SA* [2002] KLR 1. See also *Fuhrmeister and Co.* v. *Abdel Ghani Ali Mousa* [1959] SLJR 38, which held that the question of whether a foreign corporation, firm or association can sue in its own name is governed by the law of its domicile. So long as that law gives it the status to sue, it can sue in Sudan.

[64] *Attorney General* v. *Levandowsky* [1971] 2 GLR 58.

can be shown that such a foreign corporation is voluntarily resident in an enemy or enemy-controlled territory, or that the foreign corporation is controlled by enemies.[65] Similarly, Namibian, Botswanan, Zimbabwean, South African and Swaziland courts have recognised the status of a foreign trustee,[66] judicial manager,[67] liquidator,[68] administrator[69] and curator.[70] The discretion to recognise the juristic personality conferred by foreign law is founded on comity and considerations of both equity and convenience.[71]

The capacity of foreign states to sue in Kenya, Tanzania and Uganda is regulated by statute. A foreign state may sue in any of these countries provided that the state has been recognised by Kenya, Tanzania or Uganda, as the case may be, and the object of the suit is to enforce a private right vested in the head of that state or in any officer of that state in his or her public capacity. [72]

[65] *Olaogun Enterprises Ltd* v. *Saeby Jernstoberi & Maskinfabrik* [1992] 4 NWLR 361. See also *Bank of Baroda* v. *Iyalabani Co. Ltd* [2002] All NLR 325, [2002] 13 NWLR 551, [2002] 40 WRN 13; *Saeby Jernstoberi Maskinfabric A/S* v. *Olaogun Enterprises Ltd* [2001] 11 WRN 179; *Edicomesa International Inc.* v. *Citec International Estates Ltd* [2006] 4 NWLR 114; *Companhia Brasileira de Infrastrututira* v. *Cobec (Nigeria) Ltd* [2004] 13 NWLR 376; *Nigerian Bank for Commerce & Industry Ltd* v. *Europa Trade (UK) Ltd* [1990] 6 NWLR 36; *Ritz & Co. KG* v. *Jechno Ltd* [1999] 4 NWLR 298; *Wema Bank Ltd* v. *Nigeria National Shipping Line Ltd* [1976] NCLR 68.

[66] *Bekker No* v. *Kotze* 1994 NR 373, 1996 (4) SA 1293; *Bekker No* v. *Kotze* 1994 NR 345, 1996 (4) SA 1287; *Oliver No* v. *Insolvent Estate D Lidchi* 1998 NR 31; *Ex p. Palmer NO: In re. Hahn* 1993 (3) SA 359; *Ex p. Steyn* 1979 (2) SA 309; *Lamonica* v. *Baltic Reefers Management Ltd* 2011 (3) SA 164.

[67] *Ex p. Lawton, No and Ruskin* 1950 (3) SA 129.

[68] *Ex p. Trakman* 1983 BLR 176; *Ex p. Shell Co. of Rhodesia Ltd* 1964 RLR 44, 1964 (2) SA 222; *Ex p. Meinke* 1954 (4) SA 391; *Liquidator Rhodesian Plastics (Pvt) Ltd* v. *Elvinco Plastic Products (Pty) Ltd* 1959 (1) SA 868; *Ex p. Gettliffe: In re. Dominion Reefs (Klerksdorp) Ltd* 1965 (4) SA 75; *Moolman* v. *Builders & Developers (Pty) Ltd* 1990 (1) SA 954 (reversing *Ex p. Moolman No: In re. Builders and Developers (Pty) Ltd* 1989 (4) SA 253); *Ward* v. *Smit* 1998 (3) SA 175; *Ex p. Groenewoud* [1963–9] Sw. LR 65.

[69] *In re. National Bank of Scotland Ltd* 1956 (3) SA 92; *Smith and Gilks* v. *The Master* 1957 (4) SA 582.

[70] *Ex p. Lang* 1963 (3) SA 733; *MTD (Mangula) Ltd* v. *Frost and Power* 1966 (2) SA 713; *Ex p. Nupen* 1957 (2) SA 450.

[71] *Bank of Baroda* v. *Iyalabani Co. Ltd* [2002] All NLR 325, [2002] 13 NWLR 551, [2002] 40 WRN 13; *Ex p. Trakman* 1983 BLR 176; *Ward* v. *Smit* 1998 (3) SA 175.

[72] Kenya – Civil Procedure Act 1924, s. 57; Tanzania – Civil Procedure Code 1966, s. 62; Uganda – Civil Procedure Act 1929, s. 58. Every court shall take judicial notice of the fact that a foreign state has or has not been recognised by Kenya, Tanzania or Uganda, as the case may be.

PART III

Obligations

7

Contract

An international contract can give rise to multiple private international law issues. Contracts are a fertile ground for choice of law problems. The diversity of potential connecting factors, the planned nature of contractual relations, the different issues that could arise, and the time lag between execution and performance all provide fodder for many problems of private international law in international contracts. Indeed, the fact that there are so many different types of contract often raises the issue of whether the same choice of law rules should be applied and, as we would discuss, special regimes often founded on international conventions have been created for some types of contract. This chapter discusses choice of law issues arising from international contracts. These include the status of party autonomy and the limitations thereon, the rules for determining the applicable law in the absence of choice of law by the parties, capacity and the scope of the applicable law.

Ascertaining the applicable law

Ghana

The proper law of a contract is the system of law by which the parties intend the contract to be governed or, where their intention is neither expressed nor can be inferred from the circumstances, that system of law with which the transaction has its closest and most real connection. It has been held that the mode of judicial ascertainment of the proper law of a contract is, in the absence of an express choice of law agreement, the objective and pragmatic application of the external standard of a reasonable man of business and then, a consideration of what the parties ought to have intended, had they considered the question of the proper law when the contract was made. In doing this, certain rebuttable presumptions, such as *lex loci contractus*, *lex loci solutionis*, *lex situs* for immovable property, and the law of the flag in contracts of affreightment, provide indications of the connections of the contract with specific legal systems. The presumptions provide prima facie inferences which may be rebutted by contraindications that suggest connection of the contract with a different legal system.[1] *Godka Group of Companies* v. *PS International Ltd*[2] involved a contract between an Indiana, US-registered company and a Ghanaian company. The contract was to be performed in Ghana by the delivery of goods to the defendants in Ghana. The goods were to be sold in Ghana and payment was also to be effected in Ghana. It was therefore held that the contract was governed by Ghanaian law. The parties' choice of governing law may be express or implied by the terms and nature of the contract and the general circumstances of the case.[3] It has also been held that the choice must be bona fide and not offend public policy.[4]

Kenya

The proper law of a contract is the system of law by reference to which, on consideration of all the facts of the case, the contract must have been made, or that with which the transaction has its closest and most real connection.[5]

Lesotho

In the absence of an agreed choice of law, a contract is governed by the law of the country with which the contract is most closely and substantially connected. The existence of a choice of forum clause in the contract offers a strong indication that the law of the forum chosen is the proper law.[6] In determining the proper law of a contract, it is essential to consider its written terms in order to arrive at the parties' natural or assumed intentions about the law that governs it. The parties' reliance on a contractual form in use within a particular country and references to the legislation of that country in the contract are particularly relevant.[7] It has been held that, in the absence of a choice of governing law by the parties, an employment contract concluded in

[1] *Société Générale de Compensation* v. *Ackerman* [1972] 1 GLR 413 (on appeal from *Ackerman* v. *Société Générale de Compensation* [1967] GLR 212); *Garcia* v. *Torrejoh* [1992] 1 GLR 143 at 151–3; *Fattal* v. *Fattal* [1999–2000] 1 GLR 331 at 351–2.

[2] [1999–2000] 1 GLR 409. [3] *Garcia* v. *Torrejoh* at 152. [4] *Fattal* v. *Fattal* at 351.

[5] *Karachi Gas Co. Ltd* v. *Issaq* [1965] EA 42, 1965 ALR Comm. 35. See generally *D. P. Bachheta* v. *Government of the United States of America* [2011] eKLR.

[6] *Khotle* v. *Metropolitan Life Insurance*, CIV/T/662/84 (High Court, Lesotho, 1985).

[7] *Western Credit (Africa) (Proprietary) Ltd* v. *Mapetla* 1965 ALR Comm. 361 at 364–6.

South Africa between a South African employer and the applicant, to be performed in Lesotho, was governed by Lesotho law.[8]

Nigeria

Parties to a contract have the autonomy to choose the law which will govern their transaction. It is that law chosen by the parties which will guide the court in the determination of their rights, provided the terms are not against public policy.[9]

South Africa

Where no express or tacit choice of law has been made by the parties to a contract, the proper law is determined by imputing an intention to the parties, or by looking for the legal system with which the transaction has its closest and most real connection.[10] In doing this, although counting the number of connective indicators is in itself unsatisfactory, a large number of indicators pointing one way offers a strong indication of the intention of the parties.[11]

Swaziland

The parties to a contract are free to choose the law applicable to that contract. The courts will give effect to their choice.[12] However, given that the court cannot apply two systems of law, a stipulation in a contract that it 'shall be governed by and construed in accordance with the laws of the Republic of South Africa and the Kingdom of Swaziland' will be disregarded – the court will apply the system of law with which the contract is most closely connected.[13]

[8] *Ingram* v. *Training and Rural Development Consultants (Pty) Ltd*, CIV/APN/181/98 (High Court, Lesotho, 1999).

[9] *JSF Investment* v. *Brawal Line Ltd* [2010] 18 NWLR 495. See also *Adesanya* v. *Palm Line Ltd* 1967 (2) ALR Comm. 133; *Sonnar (Nigeria) Ltd* v. *Partenreedri MS Nordwind* [1987] 1 All NLR (Part I) 396, [1988] LRC (Comm.) 191.

[10] *Improvair (Cape) (Pty) Ltd* v. *Establissements Neu* 1983 (2) SA 138; *Laconian Maritime Enterprises Ltd* v. *Agromar Lineas Ltd* 1986 (3) SA 509 at 524–30; *Guggenheim* v. *Rosenbaum (2)* 1961 (4) SA 21 at 30–1; *Roger Parry* v. *Astral Operations Ltd* 2005 (10) BLLR 989. E. Spiro, 'Failure to Choose the Applicable Law' (1984) 47 *Journal of Contemporary Roman-Dutch Law* 140.

[11] *Laconian Maritime Enterprises Ltd* v. *Agromar Lineas Ltd* 1986 (3) SA 509.

[12] *Barlows Central Finance Corp. (Pty) Ltd* v. *Joncon (Pty) Ltd*, Case No. 2491/99 (High Court, Swaziland, 1999).

[13] *Afinta Financial Services (Pty) Ltd* v. *Luke Malinga*, Civil Case No. 123/2001 (High Court, Swaziland, 2001).

Tanzania

In Tanzanian law, the validity of a contract depends on the law of the place where the contract was entered into – '*lex loci contractus*'. Where the contract is valid under the *lex loci contractus*, the fact that it may be invalid under Tanzanian law (for example, because it lacked consideration) is immaterial.[14]

Zimbabwe

Where the parties to a contract have not chosen the proper law of the contract, the court will determine it for them by looking for the system of law with which the transaction has its most real and substantial connection. In doing this, the court will take into account all the circumstances of the contract.[15]

Comments

The obligations created by a contract do not exist independently. For such obligations to be binding in law, a legal system must recognise them by attaching to them 'the force of law'. This gives rise to the need to ascertain the applicable law. Contracts come in various forms and can deal with diverse subject matter. Some may give rise to unique choice of law problems, often because of their subject matter and the nature of the relationships they create.[16] Indeed, in the countries under study, some contracts are regulated by specific statutes, which may influence determination of the law applicable to them. Although not examined in this chapter, two types of contracts notable in this regard are contracts for carriage by sea and carriage by air. Both are regulated by international conventions implemented in the countries under study.[17]

14 *Juma* v. *Mlinga*, Civil Appeal No. 10 of 2001 (Court of Appeal, Tanzania, 2002).

15 *Herbst* v. *Surti* 1990 (2) ZLR 269, 1991 (2) SA 75; *Cooper Bros & Co.* v. *HWJ Bottriell & Co. Ltd* 1971 (1) SA 22.

16 See, e.g., E. A. Fredericks and J. L. Neels, 'The Proper Law of a Documentary Letter of Credit (Part 1) and (Part 2)' (2003) 15 *South African Mercantile Law Journal* 63 at 207.

17 For jurisprudence in relation to carriage by air, see:

Gambia – *Ghana Airways* v. *Williams* [1994] GR 184.

Ghana – *Grippman* v. *Nigerian Airways* [1992] 2 GLR 80; *Sylvanus Juxon-Smith* v. *KLM Royal Dutch Airline*, Suit No. FTC 46/2002 (High Court, Ghana, 2003); *Sylvanus Juxon-Smith* v. *KLM Royal Dutch Airline*, Civil Appeal No. HI/18/2004 (Court of Appeal, Ghana, 2004); *Slyvanus Juxon-Smith* v. *KLM Royal Dutch Airline*, Civil Appeal No. J4/19/

Party autonomy, i.e. the freedom to choose the law governing a contract, is respected and upheld in most, if not all, of the countries under study.[18] Even though some doubts exist in South Africa,[19] the Supreme Court of Appeal has recently affirmed that 'where parties have made an express choice of law to govern such contract, their choice should be upheld'.[20]

In general, there is no express requirement in the cases decided that there must be any connection between the system of law chosen by the parties and their contract.[21] The parties' choice may be express or

2005 (Supreme Court, Ghana, 2006); *Madam Happy Akos Hloradzi* v. *Lufthansa German Airlines*, Accra Suit No. C. 801/2001 (High Court, Ghana, 2001); *Farmex Ltd* v. *Royal Dutch Airlines* [1987–8] 2 GLR 650; *Royal Dutch Airlines* v. *Farmex Ltd* [1989–90] 1 GLR 46.

Kenya – *Transworld Safari (K) Ltd* v. *Rateno* [2008] KLR 339; *Kihungi* v. *Iberia Airlines of Spain SA* [1991] KLR 1; *Akharali Karim Kurji* v. *British Airways Plc Ltd* [2005] eKLR; *Charity Wairimu Wanjau* v. *Ethiopian Airlines*, Civil Case No. 824 of 2003 (High Court, Kenya, 2004); *Ngunjiri* v. *British Airways World Cargo* [2003] KLR 222; *Alitalia Airlines* v. *Assegai* [1989] KLR 548; *VR Chande* v. *East African Airways Corp.* [1964] EA 78; *EMS* v. *Emirates Airlines* [2012] eKLR.

Lesotho – *S Carlos* v. *Government of Lesotho* [1999–2000] LLR-LB 139.

Nigeria – *African Continental Bank Ltd* v. *Swissair Air Transport Co. Ltd* 1968 (1) ALR Comm. 202; *Swissair Air Transport Co. Ltd* v. *African Continental Bank Ltd* 1971 (1) ALR Comm. 213, [1971] 1 All NLR 37, [1971] 1 NCLR 213; *International Messengers Nigeria Ltd* v. *Pegofor Industries Ltd* (2005) All NLR 234; *Cameroon Airlines* v. *Abdul Kareem* [2003] 11 NWLR 1; *UTA French Airlines* v. *Marie Fatayi-Williams* [2000] 14 NWLR 271; *Joseph Ibidapo* v. *Lufthansa Airlines* [1997] 4 NWLR 124; *KLM Royal Dutch Airlines* v. *Kumzhi* [2004] 46 WRN 59, [2004] 8 NWLR 231; *Joseph Ibidapo* v. *Lufthansa Airlines* [1994] 8 NWLR 355; *Oshevire* v. *British Caledonia Airways Ltd* [1990] 7 NWLR 489; *Kabo Air Ltd* v. *Oladipo* [1999] 10 NWLR 517; *Harka Air Services (Nigeria) Ltd* v. *Keazor* [2006] 1 NWLR 160; *Harka Air Services (Nig.) Ltd* v. *Keazor* [2011] 13 NWLR 321; *British Airways* v. *Atoyebi* [2010] 14 NWLR 561; *Cameroon Airlines* v. *Otutuizu* [2011] 4 NWLR 513.

South Africa – *Bafana* v. *Commercial Airways (Pty) Ltd* 1990 (1) SA 368; *KLM Royal Dutch Airlines* v. *Hamman* 2002 (3) SA 818; *Impala Platinum Ltd* v. *Koninklijke Luchtvaart Maatschappij NV* 2008 (6) SA 606; *Potgieter* v. *British Airways Plc* 2005 (3) SA 133.

Uganda – *Kenya Airways Ltd* v. *Ronald Katumba*, Civil Appeal No. 43 of 2005 (Court of Appeal, Uganda, 2006); *Ethiopian Airlines* v. *Olowu Motunrola*, Civil Appeal No. 30 of 2005 (Court of Appeal, Uganda).

Zambia – *Air France* v. *Mwase Import and Export* [2000] ZR 66; *Almaz Lulseged* v. *British Airways Ltd*, Appeal No. 99/06 (Supreme Court, Zambia, 2007).

Zimbabwe – *Barclays Bank of Zimbabwe Ltd* v. *Air Zimbabwe Corp.* 1992 (2) ZLR 377, 1994 (1) SA 639; *Roberts* v. *Air Zimbabwe Corp.* 2003 (1) ZLR 223.

[18] The separate but related issue of choice of forum and arbitration agreements is discussed in Ch. 5.

[19] Forsyth, p. 321; W. de Vos, 'Freedom of Choice of Law for Contracts in Private International Law' (1961) *Acta Juridica* 1.

[20] *Creutzburg* v. *Commercial Bank of Namibia Ltd* [2006] 4 All SA 327 at 330.

[21] But see *Sonnar (Nigeria) Ltd* v. *Partenreedri MS Nordwind* [1987] 1 All NLR (Part I) 396 at 414, [1988] LRC (Comm.) 191 at 210, where Justice Oputa observed: 'It is also

implied. However, it appears the courts have not been careful to distinguish situations of implied choice from cases where they are objectively looking for the legal system with which the contract is most closely connected.[22] A South African court has cautioned that a choice of law agreement 'should not be readily implied'.[23] Whatever the distinction, it remains unquestionable that the factors relevant to deciding whether there is an implied choice are equally significant in ascertaining the legal system with which a transaction is most closely connected.

There are *dicta* which support, to varying degrees, the position that different aspects of a contract may be governed by different proper laws, and the ability of parties to change the governing law. In *Improvair (Cape) (Pty) Ltd* v. *Establissements Neu*, Justice Grosskopf observed:

> An indivisible contract laying down reciprocal rights and obligations can, as a matter of logic, not be governed by more than one proper law. I exclude contracts where the parties have expressly agreed otherwise, or possibly some other exceptional cases, but in the ordinary contract which forms an organic whole, the parties' rights and obligations would be distorted if some were to be governed by one system of law and others, by another. The same logic applies in a temporal sense – the proper law which is assigned to a contract at the time of its formation should continue to apply until all rights and obligations thereunder are extinguished.[24]

conceded that when the intention of the parties to a contract, as to the law governing the contract, is expressed in words, this expressed intention *in general* and as a *general rule* determines the proper law of the contract. But to be effective the choice of law must be *real, genuine, bona fide, legal and reasonable.* It should not be capricious and absurd. Choosing German law to govern a contract between a Nigerian shipper and a Liberian "shipowner" is to my mind capricious and unreasonable. Luckily nowadays a choice of the proper law by the parties is not considered by the courts as conclusive . . . the proper law of the contract must have some relationship to, and must be connected with the realities of, the contract considered as a whole.'

[22] But see *Roger Parry* v. *Astral Operations Ltd* 2005 (10) BLLR 989 at [80]–[88].

[23] *Improvair (Cape) (Pty) Ltd* v. *Establissements Neu* 1983 (2) SA 138 at 145.

[24] 1983 (2) SA 138 at 147. *Karachi Gas Co Ltd* v. *Issaq* [1965] EA 42 at 50, 1965 ALR Comm. 35 at 47, where it was observed: 'I am of the view that it is not necessary for the determination of this case to decide what is the proper law of the whole contract as it appears to me that the parties intended that, in so far as the shipment and delivery of the goods were concerned, these were to be carried out in accordance with the law of Kenya, but, in so far as it concerned importation into Pakistan and the payment of the purchase price, this was to be governed by the law of Pakistan.' *Laconian Maritime Enterprises Ltd* v. *Agromar Lineas Ltd* 1986 (3) SA 509 at 529; *Shacklock* v. *Shacklock* 1948 (2) SA 40 at 51, which appear to suggest that a single contract would or might be governed by different proper laws merely because there is more than one *locus solutionis*.

It is worth mentioning that these observations were made in the context of cases where the parties failed to choose the proper law. There is no decided case in which parties have expressly agreed that specific parts of their contract should be governed by different laws. The propriety of doing so is doubtful, especially due to the legal challenges that multiple proper laws could give rise to. However, it is likely that if parties agreed different aspects of their contract were governed by different laws, then the courts would give effect to that agreement.[25]

An issue that remains judicially undecided is whether the parties' choice of non-state law as the proper law would be upheld. There is no legislation dealing with this issue. It is trite to assume that parties are free to include in their contract whichever terms they deem appropriate, including choosing non-state law as the law that governs their contract. The effectiveness or enforceability of such a term is a matter for national law. It is for national courts to decide whether they will give effect to such an agreement; however, in the countries under study, the legal position remains an open question. In Nigeria, it has been held that in order for the Uniform Customs Practice for Documentary Credits to be applicable, it must be incorporated in a contract.[26]

In cases where parties to a contract have not chosen the proper law, the courts have emphasised the objective and highly factual nature of their enquiries to determine the proper law. All factors demonstrating a connection of the transaction and the parties with a particular system of law have been held to be relevant. These include the place where a contract was made or was to be performed, the currency and place of payment, the place where the parties are resident, the language of negotiation and contract, the nature and purpose of the transaction, the presence of a choice of forum clauses, the agreed place of arbitration,

[25] The clauses in *Afinta Financial Services (Pty) Ltd* v. *Luke Malinga*, Civil Case No. 123/2001 (High Court, Swaziland, 2001) ('This agreement shall be governed by and construed in accordance with the laws of the Republic of South Africa and the Kingdom of Swaziland') and *Creutzburg* v. *Commercial Bank of Namibia* [2006] 4 All SA 327 ('This suretyship shall in all respects be governed by and construed in accordance with the law of the Republic of South Africa and/or the Republic of Namibia') are different in this respect.

[26] *Eagle Super Pack (Nigeria) Ltd* v. *African Continental Bank Plc* [2006] 19 NWLR 20 (on appeal from *African Continental Bank* v. *Eagle Super Pack (Nigeria) Ltd* [1995] 2 NWLR 590). See also *Nedermar Technology BV Ltd* v. *Kenya Anti-corruption Commission* [2008] KLR 476 at 499, where it was held *obiter* that the parties may choose 'transactional law (including general principles of law, international development law, the lex mercatoria, codified terms and practices and trade usages)'.

the use of particular forms of agreement, and references to national legislation in a contract. From the cases decided, it is evident that very considerable weight is given to the place of performance.

The Zimbabwean case of *Cooper Bros & Co.* v. *HWJ Bottriell & Co. Ltd*[27] suggests that, in addition to factual connections in ascertaining the proper law of a contract where no choice has been made by the parties, the court may take into account substantive considerations which could have 'affected [their] minds'[28] at the time they entered into the contract. In this particular case, the court was confronted with factual connections to both Zambia and Rhodesia (now Zimbabwe). On the issue of the proper law of the contract, the court was prepared to take into account the fact that the parties may have been influenced by the impact of Zambia's exchange control laws on their transaction. It is certainly the case that, in entering into contracts, parties are influenced by legitimate substantive considerations, such as cost, profit, efficiency, legal regimes and convenience. The parties to a contract are free to take all these into account and to choose a system of law that will meet their needs. However, where they have failed to choose the proper law, it is submitted that the above considerations should not materially affect judicial ascertainment of the proper law. The court should limit itself to factual connections and the terms of the contract, including the parties' use of terms which may be familiar in one legal system but not in another. A great deal of uncertainty would be introduced into this area if courts were to take into account considerations which may not necessarily be shared by the parties. It should not be the responsibility of the court to select the most efficient or business-appropriate law for the parties when they have failed to choose that law for themselves. Rather, the courts should focus on objectively determining the legal system with which the contract is most closely connected.

Limitations on party autonomy and application of the proper law

Even though parties to a contract are free to choose the proper law – and in many instances the courts will give effect to their choice – limitations do exist on this freedom. The limitations apply equally to cases where the parties have not chosen the proper law and the courts have decided on it for them, using the close connection test. In other words, whether the

[27] 1971 (1) SA 22. [28] *Cooper Bros & Co.* v. *HWJ Bottriell & Co. Ltd* 1971 (1) SA 22 at 24.

proper law is selected by the parties or by the courts, certain restrictions are placed on its application. The limitations are often imposed to protect certain interests of the forum, other countries, third parties or a party to the contract.[29]

Statutes are an important source of such limitations, and in this regard, consumers and employees appear to be notable 'protected classes'. Sections 38 and 39 of Zambia's Electronic Communications and Transactions Act 2009 illustrate this. The Act provides that 'the protection provided to consumers in this Part applies irrespective of the legal system applicable to the agreement in question'. In addition, 'any provision in an agreement which excluded any rights provided for in this Part is null and void'. Provisions with similar effect are to be found in statutes in other countries.[30] Furthermore, specific consumer rights have been enshrined in Article 46 of the Constitution of the Republic of Kenya 2010, which gives them added weight and importance.[31] These statutes aim to protect consumer rights and, in that light, where the proper law chosen by the parties or determined by the court is inconsistent with rights provided by the statutes, the latter will prevail. It is likely that similar legislation will be adopted in some of the countries under study.[32] The statutes do not limit the application of the law chosen by the parties if the latter affords better protection to the consumer. In other words, where the standards of consumer protection or consumer rights are higher in the system of law chosen by the parties, the court will give effect to the laws of that legal system.

Statutes also impose limitations on party autonomy in favour of employees. For example, Uganda's Employment Act 2006 does not generally apply to 'employment outside Uganda'.[33] However, as regards

[29] See generally G. Nnona, 'Choice of Law in International Contracts for the Transfer of Technology: A Critique of the Nigerian Approach' (2000) 44 *Journal of African Law* 78; E. Spiro, 'Autonomy of the Parties to a Contract and the Conflict of Laws: Illegality' (1984) 17 *Comparative and International Law Journal of Southern Africa* 197.

[30] See Botswana – Consumer Protection Act 1998, s. 18; Ghana – Electronic Transactions Act 2008, ss. 53 and 54; South Africa – Electronic Communications and Transactions Act 2002, ss. 47 and 48, Consumer Protection Act 2008, s. 51(3).

[31] Section 46 provides that consumers have the right to goods and services of reasonable quality; the information necessary for them to gain full benefit from goods and services; the protection of their health, safety and economic interests; and compensation for loss or injury arising from defects in goods or services.

[32] See, e.g., Kenya – Consumer Protection Bill 2007, s. 8; Namibia – Use of Electronic Transactions and Communications Bill 2010; Uganda – Electronic Transactions Bill 2008, s. 28.

[33] Employment Act 2006, s. 3(5).

employment in Uganda, the Act is very clear, in that 'any provision in an agreement, or a contract of service shall be void where it excludes or limits the operation of any provision of this Act to the detriment of the employee'.[34] Legislation to similar effect exists in other countries.[35] In addition, labour rights, such as the right to equal pay for equal work, fair remuneration, and the right to form or join trade unions, are often constitutionally protected.[36] These constitutionally protected rights are likely to be construed by the court as mandatory and not open to derogations outside those provided in the constitution. Indeed, as would be expected in the constitutions of all of the countries under study, the constitution is declared the supreme law of the land and any other law inconsistent with its dictates is void to the extent of inconsistency.

The courts have shown they are prepared to impose limitations on the proper law of contract in employment and insurance contracts. In *Roger Parry* v. *Astral Operations Ltd*,[37] the applicant sought damages for the breach of an employment contract with the respondent South African company. The applicant was responsible for the Malawi operations of the respondent and was located there. The central issue was the proper law for the contract. The South African court rejected the respondent's argument that the contract was governed by Malawi law, as it was the place of performance.[38] The court characterised South African labour legislation as mandatory and directly applicable to all employment contracts in South Africa. There was no choice of law clause in the contract. However, even if there had been a foreign choice of law clause, the court was prepared to be 'guided by' section 6 of the Rome Convention on the

[34] Employment Act 2006, s. 4(a).

[35] See, e.g., Botswana – Employment Act 1982, s. 37; Kenya – Employment Act 2007, s. 3(6); Namibia – Labour Act 2007, s. 9; Zambia – Employment Act 1965, s. 38(2) ('when a contract made within another country relates to employment in Zambia, the provisions of this Act shall apply to such contract'). Some statutes especially protect the freedom to form a trade union and declare invalid agreements to the contrary.

[36] See, e.g., Constitution of the Republic of Botswana 1966, Art. 13(1); Constitution of the Republic of the Gambia 1997, Art. 25(1)(e); Constitution of the Republic of Ghana 1992, Art. 24; Constitution of the Republic of Kenya 2010, Art. 41; Constitution of the Republic of Malawi 1994, Art. 31; Constitution of the Republic of Namibia 1998, Art. 21(1)(e); Constitution of the Republic of Sierra Leone 1991, Art. 26(1); Constitution of the Republic of South Africa 1996, Art. 23; Constitution of the United Republic of Tanzania 1977, Arts 22–3; Constitution of the Republic of Zambia 1991, Art. 21(1).

[37] 2005 (10) BLLR 989. See also *Kleinhans* v. *Paramalat SA (Pty) Ltd* [2002] 9 BLLR 879.

[38] The court held that the parties had by implication or tacitly chosen South African law as the proper law, or that in any case the contract was more substantially connected to South Africa.

Law Applicable to Contractual Obligations and to uphold that choice only if it did not deprive the employee of the protection afforded by the mandatory rules of South African law.

Lesotho courts have similarly demonstrated the need to allow employees to benefit from Lesotho's labour laws, regardless of the proper law of the contract.[39] In *Representative of Lloyds* v. *Classic Sailing Adventures (Pty) Ltd*,[40] it was held that South Africa's Short-Term Insurance Act was applicable even though the parties had chosen English law as the applicable law of their insurance contract. In the words of the court, 'the *ius cogens* (peremptory law) of the forum cannot be excluded. . . . peremptory (mandatory) rules of the forum – especially legislative provisions – apply. Complete party autonomy cannot prevail over the peremptory provisions of a statute'. In determining whether the *lex fori* should prevail over the applicable law, the courts will take into account the following factors: whether the statute is prohibitory or dispositive; whether it is designed to protect the weaker party in contractual negotiations; and whether the parties can waive or contract out of the application of the statute.

Public policy, which constitutes a channel for excluding the application of foreign law, can be used to limit the freedom of parties to choose the proper law of a contract. However, in the countries under study, there appears to be no case decided where a court has refused to enforce a choice of law agreement on the basis of public policy.

In addition to the above, international conventions, to which the countries under study are parties, may impose limitations on party autonomy or the enforceability of choice of law agreements. For example, under section 32 of the Convention for the Unification of Certain Rules Relating to International Carriage by Air 1929, 'any clause contained in the contract and all special agreements entered into before the damage occurred by which the parties purport to infringe the rules laid down by this Convention, whether by deciding the law to be applied, or by altering the rules as to jurisdiction, shall be null and void'.[41] Similarly, regardless of the applicable law, under Article VIII2(b) of the Articles of Agreement

[39] *Khotle* v. *Metropolitan Life Insurance*, CIV/T/662/84 (High Court, Lesotho, 1985); *Ingram* v. *Training and Rural Development Consultants (Pty) Ltd*, CIV/APN/181/98 (High Court, Lesotho, 1999); *Komane* v. *City Express Stores (Pty) Ltd*, LAC/CIV/A/5/2002 (High Court, Lesotho, 2006).

[40] 2010 (5) SA 90, [2010] 4 All SA 366.

[41] See also Montreal Convention for the Unification of Certain Rules for International Carriage by Air 1999, s. 49.

of the International Monetary Fund 1944, 'exchange contracts which involve the currency of any member and which are contrary to the exchange control regulations of that member maintained or imposed consistently with this Agreement shall be unenforceable in the territories of any member'.

Scope of the applicable law

In any contractual dispute, a number of issues, such as consent, terms, capacity, interpretation, performance, discharge, damages and interest, can arise.[42] There is a strong case for the view that all issues arising under a contract should be governed by one system of law – the proper law of the contract. However, judging by the decided cases, not all of these issues are currently governed by the proper law of the contract. Specific rules have been adopted to deal with issues like capacity, formal validity and performance.

Capacity and formal validity of contracts

Ghana

A person's capacity to enter into a contract is governed by the law of the country with which the contract is most closely connected. Thus, where a charter party, including an arbitration agreement, was determined to be governed by English law and, under that law, the respondent had no capacity to enter into the contract at the time it was signed, it was held that the arbitration agreement could not be enforced against the respondent.[43]

South Africa

In South Africa, it has been held that, in the case of an ordinary commercial contract, for example, a deed of suretyship, as in the instant case, contractual capacity is determined by *lex loci contractus.*[44] However,

[42] On the law governing interest on a contractual debt, see generally *Spirvin Bottling Co. (Pty) Ltd* v. *Lesotho Cash and Carry*, CIV/T/110/91 (High Court, Lesotho, 1992); *Royal Dutch Airlines* v. *Farmex Ltd (No. 2)* [1989–90] 2 GLR 682.

[43] *Jadbranska Slobodna Plovidba* v. *Oysa Ltd* [1979] GLR 129, 1978 (2) ALR Comm. 108 at 114–16.

[44] *Tesoriero* v. *Bhyjo Investments Share Block (Pty) Ltd* 2000 (1) SA 167 at 171–2.

in *Powell* v. *Powell*, an earlier case which dealt with the revocability of a donation between spouses, the court adopted the law of the country with which the contract was most closely connected.[45]

The South African courts adopt a facultative approach to the issue of the law governing the formal validity of contracts. This approach allows the formal validity of a contract to be determined by a system of law connected with the transaction, other than the place of execution. It ensures that a contract is not rendered invalid merely for lacking the form required by *lex loci contractus*, when it complies with some alternative system of law. Thus, it has been held that an antenuptial contract executed in accordance with the form required by either *lex loci contractus* or the proper law of the contract is formally valid.[46] However, the facultative approach applies to all contracts – it is not limited to antenuptial agreements. *Creutzburg* v. *Commercial Bank of Namibia Ltd*[47] dealt with the formal validity of a deed of suretyship executed in Namibia between the appellants, who were resident in South Africa, and a Namibian company. The deed contained a 'Republic of South Africa and/or the Republic of Namibia' choice of law clause. The deed was valid under Namibian law, but invalid under South African law. The court held that the formal validity of the deed was governed by *lex loci contractus*. The court discussed and endorsed the facultative approach to determining the formal validity of a contract.

Tanzania

A person is competent to enter into a contract if he or she is of the age of majority according to the law to which they are subject, and if they are of sound mind, and not disqualified from entering into a contract by any law to which they are subject.[48]

45 *Powell* v. *Powell* 1953 (4) SA 380.

46 *Ex p. Spinazze* 1985 (3) SA 650 (on appeal from *Ex p. Spinazze* 1983 (4) SA 751).

47 2006 (4) All SA 327.

48 Law of Contract Act 1961, s. 11(1). I have been unable to locate a Tanzanian conflict of laws case which interprets or applies this provision. Uganda and Kenya have had similar legislation (Indian Contract Act 1872, s. 11) – however, this has been repealed. Currently, the 'common law of England relating to contract' applies in Uganda and Kenya to determine the capacity to contract. See Uganda – Contract Act 1963, s. 2(1); Kenya – Law of Contract Act 1962, s. 2(1). Prior to the repeal, the Ugandan High Court interpreted s. 11 of the Indian Contract Act 1872 to mean that capacity to contract was determined by the law of the party's domicile. See *PB Damani* v. *Zangie* (1948) 6 ULR 179; *Kanji Naranji Lakhani* v. *Salim Mohamed Bin Name* [1960] EA 358.

Comments

The law that governs the capacity to enter into a commercial contract appears largely unsettled in the countries under study – there are cases and legislation which adopt the proper law of the contract, *lex loci contractus* and *lex domicilii.*[49] This state of affairs is consistent with the situation in other common law jurisdictions.[50] Furthermore, it is submitted that the proper law of a contract should determine the capacity to enter into a contract and this proper law should be objectively determined by the court, regardless of any choice of law agreement that the parties may have included in their contract, and despite the fact that the decided cases do not reflect this. In other words, although the courts should take into account the choice of law agreement included in the parties' contract, this should not be allowed to prevail or exclusively govern the issue of the capacity to enter into a contract. To allow parties to determine their own competence by using a choice of law agreement creates an incentive to evade national laws, under which they may otherwise be incompetent. The policy reasons that inform national laws on legal competence should not be sacrificed in favour of party autonomy.

Other systems of law which can determine the capacity to enter into a contract include the law of domicile, or place of residence of the parties: *lex loci solutionis* and *lex loci contractus*. Although each of these has its merits, their application can lead to arbitrary results. As Justice Wunsh observed, 'there could be valid objections to the rule that the *lex loci contractus* determines a person's capacity to enter into ordinary contracts since the place where a contract is concluded could be a matter of pure chance, especially if it is made by letter or telefax or over the telephone'.[51] Similarly, relying on *lex domicilii* or law of the place of residence raises

[49] See generally G. F. A. Sawyerr, 'Contractual Capacity and the Conflict of Laws in East Africa: A Study of Conflicts Method' (1968) 1 *Eastern African Law Review* 1; E. A. Fredericks, 'Contractual Capacity in Private International Law: Interpreting the Powell Case' (2006) 69 *Journal of Contemporary Roman-Dutch Law* 279. In the Ugandan case of *Bank of Uganda* v. *Banco Arabe Espanol* [2002] 2 EA 333, the issue of the capacity of the bank to enter into a contract was raised. The Supreme Court appears to have accepted that that issue was governed by Ugandan law even though the parties chose English law as the applicable law of the contract.

[50] *Cheshire, North & Fawcett*, p. 750, where they describe English jurisprudence as 'a matter of speculation'. S. G. A. Pitel and N. Rafferty, *Conflict of Laws* (Toronto: Irwin Law, 2010), p. 281, where they describe Canadian jurisprudence as 'inconsistent'.

[51] *Tesoriero* v. *Bhyjo Investments Share Block (Pty) Ltd* 2000 (1) SA 167 at 172.

difficult questions, such as: whose domicile or residence matters? Moreover, if the domiciles of both parties to the contract are in different countries, which prevails in a case of inconsistency? On the other hand, what happens if there is a change in domicile or residence? The proper law of the contract objectively determined by the court takes account of all connecting factors. It is more likely to lead to an outcome consistent with the expectations of the parties and the prevention of abuse.

Formal validity deals with the form which a contract should take in order to be valid. In many legal systems, requirements such as the need for writing, consideration and witnessing are imposed on the making of contracts. To date, it appears that the issue of the formal validity of contracts has been authoritatively decided only in South Africa.[52] The facultative approach adopted by South African courts has the merit of ensuring that a contract which would otherwise have been invalid under *lex loci contractus* is saved by looking at an alternative system of law.[53] However, the facultative approach is complicated by having to specify or limit one or more alternative systems of law. It is worth emphasising that the facultative approach is meant to facilitate the formal validity of a contract and should not be invoked to defeat it. Thus, where a contract is valid under *lex loci contractus*, then an alternative system of law should not be invoked to defeat its formal validity. In the words of Justice Mpati, 'if a contract is formally valid in terms of the *lex loci contractus* one need look no further'.[54] What is more, an international contract will often have connections with many systems of law. Selecting one system – such as *lex loci contractus* – over others can be difficult and, sometimes, arbitrary. There is a case for the view that formal validity should be

[52] The validity of a contract is separate from its enforceability in a particular country. A contract may be valid in essence and form under a country's private international law, but be unenforceable for lack of compliance with certain domestic requirements, such as registration and stamping. See generally *Continental Bakery (Pty) Ltd* v. *Giannakakis* 1956 (4) SA 324. *Syed Huq* v. *Islamic University in Uganda* [1997] Kam. LR 272 and *Thomas Robinson* v. *ACAV Commission* [1999] Kam. LR 836, both of which held that under s. 13 of the Employment Decree, a foreign contract of employment shall not be enforced unless it has been approved and attested in accordance with the provisions of the Decree.

[53] As discussed in Ch. 15, this apparently liberal attitude towards formal validity is also reflected in the law on wills in the countries under study. Thus, a case for adopting the facultative approach to the formal validity of contracts can be founded on the position in relation to the formal validity of wills, although, admittedly, the two instruments are different.

[54] *Creutzburg* v. *Commercial Bank of Namibia Ltd* [2006] 4 All SA 327 at 331.

determined by the proper law of the contract. Admittedly, logic dictates that the issue of formal validity precedes that of determining the proper law for a contract – a contract which is formally invalid is not a contract and so the issue of its governing law does not arise. The proper law of the contract takes into account all connections with various systems of law. It is particularly suitable in transactions where the place of contracting is uncertain.

Performance

Kenya

In Kenya, it has been held that where a contract is to be performed partly in one country and partly in another, the parties must be taken to have intended the performance to be carried out in accordance with the law of the first country, insofar as this is the place of performance, and with the law of the second, insofar as performance takes place there.[55]

Malawi

Where the performance of a contract would amount to a breach of the laws of a foreign country, a Malawian court will not enforce performance of the contract because this would be tantamount to a breach of international comity.[56]

South Africa

A South African court will not enforce contracts involving the perpetration of illegal acts in South Africa or in a foreign-friendly country.[57] Performance is governed by the proper law of the contract or *lex loci solutionis*. The mere fact that Exchange Control legislation is in force in the place where a party to the contract resides or carries out business, or in the state where he or she is a national, and that the performance of the contract is excused or made illegal by such legislation, is no defence to an action involving the contract, unless either the law to which the legislation belongs is the proper law of the contract, or the contract was to be performed in a place where the legislation was in force.[58]

[55] *Karachi Gas Co. Ltd* v. *Issaq* [1965] EA 42, 1965 ALR Comm. 35.
[56] *Mzumacharo* v. *Osman's Garage* [1978–80] 9 MLR 68.
[57] *Henry* v. *Branfield* 1996 (1) SA 244.
[58] *Cargo Motor Corp. Ltd* v. *Tofalos Transport Ltd* 1972 (1) SA 186.

Zambia

Where the performance of a contract is lawful under its proper law or place of performance, the fact that a foreign country legislates to render the performance of the contract unlawful will not affect its enforceability in the place of performance. Thus, in a case where a contract governed by English law provided that payment was to be made in sterling in London and the Rhodesian Government legislated to prohibit such payments, it was held that the Rhodesian legislation provided no defence against an action to enforce the contract in Zambia.[59]

Zimbabwe

A contract which is illegal and unenforceable under its proper law will not be enforced.[60] Similarly, a contract which is enforceable under its proper law will not be enforced in Zimbabwe if its enforcement would contravene Zimbabwe's public policy.[61]

Comments

As with the underlying contract, the performance of a contract may entail connections with many systems of law. Indeed, identifying what constitutes performance under a contract can sometimes be a challenge. It appears from the decided cases to have been accepted that performance is governed by the proper law of the contract and *lex loci solutionis*. It remains undecided which prevails in the case of inconsistency, such as where performance is legal under the proper law of the contract, but is illegal under *lex loci solutionis*. What is certain is that the courts will not enforce a contract which is illegal under *lex loci solutionis* or in the country where enforcement is sought. On the other hand, the mere fact that performance is illegal under the laws of any other country which has some connection with the contract, such as the place of residence, business, nationality or domicile of one party, will not prevent enforcement of the contract. Comity and public policy considerations which inform the non-enforcement of contracts for which performance is illegal under *lex loci solutionis*, the proper law of the contract or the place where enforcement is sought, have not been extended to countries with some

59 *Commonwealth Development Corp.* v. *Central African Power Corp.* (1968) ZR 70, 1968 (3) ALR Comm. 416.

60 *Herbst* v. *Surti* 1990 (2) ZLR 269, 1991 (2) SA 75. See generally *Cooper Bros & Co.* v. *HWJ Bottriell & Co. Ltd* 1971 (1) SA 22.

61 *Timms* v. *Nicol* [1967] RLR 386.

other connections with the contract. This is an appropriate stance because it prevents a situation arising where one party can rely on their own independent connections with a system of law to defeat performance under the contract.

Interpretation

There is very little direct authority on the issue of the law governing the interpretation of contracts. The few cases which exist affirm the proper law of the contract to be the law governing its interpretation. South African courts have held that the issue of the interpretation of a contract is governed by the proper law of the contract.[62] Similarly, in a case where a loan agreement provided that it 'shall be governed and construed in accordance with English law', it was held by a Ugandan court that the provision 'put the Ugandan laws out of application when interpretation of this agreement is in issue'.[63]

[62] *Polysius (Pty) Ltd* v. *Transvaal Alloys (Pty) Ltd* 1983 (2) SA 630 at 643; *Maschinen Frommer GmbH* v. *Trisave Engineering & Machinery Supplies (Pty) Ltd* 2003 (6) SA 69; *Shacklock* v. *Shacklock* 1949 (1) SA 91 at 100. See generally *Telkom Directory Services (Pty) Ltd* v. *Kern* [2011] 1 All SA 593, in which the court applied the principles of interpretation in Califonian law to a contract governed by that law.

[63] *Bank of Uganda* v. *Banco Arabe Espanol*, Civil Appeal No. 23 of 2000 (Court of Appeal, Uganda, 2000). The Supreme Court dismissed an appeal from this decision. *Bank of Uganda* v. *Banco Arabe Espanol* [2002] 2 EA 333.

8

Torts

As with contracts, complex private international law issues can arise from a tort, which is a type of non-contractual obligation.[1] This complexity is due to a number of factors. Firstly, as with contracts, different connecting factors can be raised by the facts of a given case, which creates problems when choosing the applicable law. Secondly, the diverse nature of tortious claims and issues raises the question of whether the same rules should be applicable to all torts or the issues arising thereunder. Thirdly, the fact that each tort often consists of elements (for example, for negligence, duty, breach and damage) and that different elements may occur in different countries raises serious definitional issues in some cases. This chapter addresses two principal issues in relation to foreign torts, namely, whether and when a court would assume jurisdiction over a foreign tort and, if it does so, the applicable law for determining issues arising from the tort. These issues include liability, capacity, defences and immunities, and remedies.

Ghana

In Ghana, it has been held that, in order to establish jurisdiction in a tort committed outside Ghana, the tort complained of must be actionable as a tort according to the law of Ghana and must be unjustifiable according to the law of the country where the tort was alleged to have been committed. However, if at the time the writ of summons was served, the defendant was within the jurisdiction of the court, then the court has jurisdiction in respect of any cause of action, regardless of where the cause of action arose.[2]

[1] Other forms of non-contractual obligations such as restitution and equitable obligations are not addressed in this chapter. In general, I was unable to identify any decided case or legislation in the countries under study relevant to the choice of law aspects of these claims. See generally Forsyth, p. 365.

[2] *Wachter* v. *Harlley* [1968] GLR 1069.

Kenya

An action will lie in Kenya for a libel published abroad if the libel is actionable both in Kenya and in the country of publication. If that is so, then provided the defendant is properly served, the Kenyan court has jurisdiction to hear the case.[3]

Lesotho

In Lesotho, it has been held that the law governing a tort allegedly committed abroad is the *lex loci delicti*.[4]

Nigeria

An action of tort will lie in a Nigerian court for a wrong alleged to have been committed abroad if two conditions are met: the wrong must be of a character that would have been actionable if it had been committed in Nigeria, and unjustifiable under the law of the place where the wrong was committed.[5]

It has been held in an inter-state dispute that, where a tort was committed in a state and action brought in another state, the law to be applied in such circumstances is the law of the state where the tort was committed.[6]

South Africa

In South Africa, provided a defendant is amenable to the jurisdiction by reason of residence or otherwise, an action is maintainable for the publication of defamatory matter in a foreign country.[7] It is, however, an open question whether the Roman-Dutch law requires that, in order to found an action in South Africa for a wrong committed abroad, it must be established that the wrong would be actionable if committed

[3] *Riddlesbarger* v. *Robson* [1958] EA 375. See generally *Rage Mohammed Ali* v. *Abdullahim* [2005] eKLR.

[4] *Lepota* v. *Hyland*, CIV/APN/280/87 (High Court, Lesotho, 1991).

[5] *Herb* v. *Devimco International* [2001] 52 WRN 19; *Zabusky* v. *Israeli Aircraft Industries* [2008] 2 NWLR 109 at 140–2. This rule applies equally to inter-state torts. *Amanambu v. Okafor* [1966] 1 All NLR 205; *Benson* v. *Ashiru* [1967] 1 All NLR 184; *Ajakaiye* v. *Robert Adedeji* [1990] 7 NWLR 192.

[6] *AO Agunanne* v. *Nigeria Tobacco Co. Ltd* [1979] 2 FNLR 13.

[7] *Rogaly* v. *General Imports (Pty) Ltd* 1948 (1) SA 1216.

in South Africa, but not have been actionable under the law of the place where it was committed.[8]

Until recently, the issue of the law governing a foreign tort remained *res nova* in South African law. It has been held that the law governing a foreign tort is the law of the country with the most significant relationship with the parties and the torts.[9] The *lex loci* should be used as one of the factors in the balancing test to decide which jurisdiction has the most significant relationship with the tort and parties.[10]

Comments

A foreign tort can have a connection with many countries. The question of what law governs liability in such a tort is an important one. The determination of which country's law should be applied in order to ascertain the rights and liabilities of the parties can be difficult. While some writers favour *lex fori* as the applicable law, others have proposed *lex loci delicti commissi* and the proper law of the tort as alternatives.

The law in many of the countries under study is uncertain on this issue. To the extent that there is case law on the subject – there is no legislation in the countries under study dealing with the issue – the countries are divided between the double actionability rule and the *lex loci delicti commissi* principle. The position taken by Ghana and Kenya is that a foreign tort is not actionable unless it is actionable both under *lex fori* and *lex loci delicti*. Lesotho has shown a preference for the *lex loci delicti commissi*. There is case law in Nigeria in favour of both the double actionability rule and the *lex loci delicti commissi* principle. And, recently, a South African court adopted the most significant relationship test, in which the place where the tort was committed is just one consideration.

[8] *Rogaly* v. *General Imports*.

[9] Admittedly, the decision is not very clear whether the court adopted the *lex loci delicti commissi* principle followed by consideration of whether it should be displaced in favour of another legal system with which there was a more 'significant relationship' or whether there should be a direct search for the jurisdiction with the most significant relationship with the parties and the delict. Forsyth, p. 364 expresses a preference for the former approach.

[10] *Burchell* v. *Anglin* 2010 (3) SA 48. It was also held that the law of the country with the most significant relationship so identified must pass constitutional scrutiny and therefore it was necessary to take into account in the choice of law process, moral values and public policy. See generally *Minister of Transport, Transkei* v. *Abdul* 1995 (1) SA 366.

The double actionability rule complicates litigation involving foreign torts. Indeed, the case law in Ghana and Kenya appears to treat the rule as a test of jurisdiction rather than what it truly is – a choice of law rule.[11] The paucity of cases dealing with this in the countries under study has masked the complexity of its application: a situation which has led to its modification and/or abandonment in some Commonwealth countries. In general, there is currently a trend in Commonwealth countries towards upholding the *lex loci delicti commissi* rule as the choice of law rule in torts.[12] Australian[13] and Canadian[14] courts, as well as the United Kingdom (by legislation)[15] have all adopted the *lex loci delicti commissi* principle, and abandoned the double actionability principle.[16] The *lex loci delicti commissi* principle is likely to meet the expectations of parties: for example, in an accident in Togo involving a Ghanaian trader and a Nigerian driver, it is likely that neither party would expect the law of either Ghana or Nigeria to have much to do with the accident. The *lex loci delicti commissi* principle also makes for certainty, especially when compared with the most significant relationship test. However, in some instances, deciding where a tort was committed could be difficult. An example of this would be a situation where the actions that occasioned harm are committed in one country, but the harm is suffered in another. In such a situation, the fundamental issue is whether the locus of the tort should be determined by reference to one of the places where the event giving rise to the damage occurred, or by reference to the place where the damage – actual or consequential – has been suffered. The facts of the decided cases in the

[11] It is submitted that, to the extent that the rules for assuming jurisdiction in an *in personam* action have been met, there is no need for the court to look further before assuming jurisdiction in a claim founded on tort committed abroad. Just as the courts will assume jurisdiction in a claim founded on breach of contract as long as the defendant has been served, and regardless of where the breach occurred, so too should they be prepared to assume jurisdiction in a claim founded on foreign torts, as long as the defendant has been properly served. Once jurisdiction is assumed, the separate and distinct issue of which law should govern the claim must be addressed. It is here that the double actionability rule becomes relevant.

[12] J. Kiggundu, 'Choice of Law in Delict: The Rise and Rise of the *Lex Loci Delicti Commissi*' (2006) 18 *South African Mercantile Law Journal* 97.

[13] *Régie National des Usines Renault SA* v. *Zhang* [2002] 210 CLR 491.

[14] *Tolofson* v. *Jensen* [1994] 120 DLR (4th) 289.

[15] Private International Law (Miscellaneous Provisions) Act 1995.

[16] J. Kiggundu, 'Choice of Law in Delict: The Rise and Rise of Lex Loci Delicti Commissi' (2006) 18 *South African Mercantile Law Journal* 97.

countries under study are very much 'localised' and so the courts were not compelled to decide this issue in the context of choice of law.[17]

It is submitted that no rigid rules can be developed here – while the place of the event giving rise to the damage may be significant in some contexts, in others, attention to the place where the damage has occurred may be better. It is submitted that in such cases, flexibility is required and the court should apply the law of the place which would afford the plaintiff the most effective remedy. This is consistent with the main function of tort law, which is to provide compensation to victims of torts.

From the decided cases, it appears that, for the purpose of determining the applicable law, the courts have not distinguished between various torts, such as defamation, inducing breach of contract and negligence.[18] The same approach to choice of law was adopted, regardless of the tort in question. It is submitted that such a unitary approach to choice of law in torts may not be entirely appropriate. Therefore, there may be the need to develop different rules for torts arising within specific contexts.

An interesting, but largely undecided, issue is whether the *lex loci* rule applies to all issues in tort, for example, liability, defences and damages. In *Burchell* v. *Anglin*,[19] the question of whether the law applied to prove the tort equally applied to prove that the issue of the quantum of damages was raised, but not decided.

17 For case law on the locus of a tort for jurisdictional purposes, see discussion in Ch. 8.

18 But see *Burchell* v. *Anglin* 2010 (3) SA 48 at 71, suggesting that all torts should not be treated alike.

19 2010 (3) SA 48 at 77.

9

Foreign currency obligations

Claims in foreign currency raise important private international law issues. Because of fluctuation in exchange rates and depreciation of currencies, the resolution of such issues may have serious financial implications for the parties. The private international law issues raised when there is a foreign currency claim include: whether a court has jurisdiction to give judgment in foreign currency; if it has such jurisdiction, what factors it would take into account in deciding to provide remedy in foreign currency as opposed to the currency of the court or some other foreign currency; if there is need for conversion of currencies (for example, for the purposes of execution), what date of conversion should be used; in what currency and by what method are interest on a foreign currency debt or judgment to be calculated; and the effect of domestic and international legislation on foreign currency claims. These issues are the subject matter of this chapter.[1]

Ghana

Ghanaian courts have jurisdiction to give judgment in foreign currency.[2] However, it has been held that it is inappropriate to exercise this jurisdiction in cases where the parties have not conducted their transactions

[1] The issues arising in the context of actions to enforce foreign judgments and arbitral awards are discussed in Chapters 17 and 19.

[2] *Royal Dutch Airlines* v. *Farmex Ltd* [1989–90] 2 GLR 632; *Royal Dutch Airlines* v. *Farmex Ltd* [1989–90] 1 GLR 46; *Hungarotex Foreign Trading Co.* v. *Boateng* [1984–6] 1 GLR 611. Historically, it was held that it is procedurally wrong for a Ghanaian court to award damages in foreign currency; *Société Générale de Compensation* v. *Ackerman* [1972] 1 GLR 413 at 433–4. See generally F. S. Tsikata, 'Actions in Respect of Foreign Currency Obligations' (1987–8) 26 *Review of Ghana Law* 234; R. E. Bannermah, 'Award of Damages in Foreign Currency: A Critical Look at the Judgments' (1993–5) 19 *Review of Ghana Law* 231.

with each other in foreign currency.[3] Where judgment is given in foreign currency, the rate of interest exigible on the amount is that of the foreign currency.[4] Similarly, where a judgment debt, money or damages is to be paid in a foreign currency, the rules governing monetary transactions in the foreign currency in the foreign country govern the rate of interest, unless the contrary is expressly provided for and agreed upon by the contracting parties.[5] Where judgment is given in foreign currency, the rate of exchange should be that prevailing on the date of payment and not on the date of judgment or date of breach.[6]

It has been held that, in the absence of clear statutory prohibition in the country of payment, parties to an international contract for goods or services can make a choice of law decision as regards the currency of payment, which may be different from the legal tender of the country where the transaction took place. However, where there is no contractual choice of currency provision, the currency of payment is presumed to be the legal tender of the place of transaction.[7]

Historically, the Exchange Control Act 1961, as amended by the Exchange Control (Amendment) Law 1986, imposed various limitations on making or receiving payments in foreign currency in Ghana.[8] The Exchange Control Act has now been repealed by the Foreign Exchange Act 2006. There is nothing in the Foreign Exchange Act that prevents parties to a contract from denominating their transactions in foreign currency.[9] Nevertheless, there are a few procedural restrictions on payments made in foreign currency. Under section 15(1) of the Foreign Exchange Act, payments in foreign currency to or from Ghana – between a resident and a non-resident or between non-residents – should be made through a bank. The transfer of foreign currency to or from Ghana should also be made through a person licensed to carry out money transfers.[10]

3 *Mensah* v. *National Savings and Credit Bank* [1989–90] 1 GLR 620; *Hungarotex Foreign Trading Co.* v. *Boateng* [1984–6] 1 GLR 611.

4 *National Investment Bank Ltd* v. *Silver Peak Ltd* [2003–4] SCGLR 1008; *Butt* v. *Chapel Hill Properties Ltd* [2003–4] SCGLR 636 at 661–3; *Royal Dutch Airlines* v. *Farmex Ltd (No. 2)* [1989–90] 2 GLR 682.

5 *Ghana Ports and Harbours Authority* v. *Issoufou* [1993–4] 1 GLR 24 at 50–2.

6 *Hungarotex Foreign Trading Co.* v. *Boateng* [1984–6] 1 GLR 611.

7 *Delmas America Africa Line Inc.* v. *Kisko Products Ghana Ltd* [2005–6] SCGLR 75 at 99–100.

8 For a discussion of some of its provisions, see *Sam Jonah* v. *Duodu-Kumi* [2003–4] SCGLR 50; *Takoradi Flour Mills* v. *Samir Faris* [2005–6] SCGLR 882.

9 See generally *Sam Jonah* v. *Duodu-Kumi* [2003–4] SCGLR 50.

10 Foreign Exchange Act 2006, s. 15(3).

Kenya

A person is entitled to discharge a monetary obligation using the actual currency in which it was assumed, regardless of any depreciation in the value of that currency. Thus, in a case where 1,000 Maria Theresa dollars were lent to the respondent, it was held that he was entitled to repay the loan with these actual dollars, despite the fact that the value of the dollar had fallen.[11]

The Kenyan courts have jurisdiction to give judgment in foreign currency.[12] However, this jurisdiction is to be exercised with caution. It has been held that, against the background of rapid fluctuation in the Kenyan shilling on the international money market, it would be contrary to public policy to allow a party to rake in supernormal profit using the judicial process.[13] Where a judgment is obtained in foreign currency, the rate of exchange is that which prevails on the day of payment and not at the time of judgment or when the cause of action arose.[14] However, in *Charles Thys* v. *Herman Steyn*,[15] it was held that a decision on the conversion of foreign currency (or not, or when) is a matter dependent on the 'facts of each case' as determined by the court, taking into account the merits of each claim, pertinent principles of law and considerations of public policy.

Nigeria

Historically, a Nigerian court had no jurisdiction to give judgment in foreign currency.[16] However, this is no longer the case – a Nigerian court now has jurisdiction to give judgment in foreign currency.[17] A party is

[11] *Abdurrehman* v. *Hamed* [1897–1905] EAP LR 11.

[12] *Beluf Establishment* v. *AG* [1993] eKLR. Historically the courts declined to give judgment in foreign currency; *Universal TPT Co. Ltd* v. *Tzortzis* [1973] EA 310 at 311, 1973 (2) ALR Comm. 323; *Life Insurance Corp. of India* v. *Valji* [1968] EA 225; *Intercontinental Greetings* v. *Kenya Litho Ltd* [1976–85] 1 EA 141.

[13] *Charles Thys* v. *Herman Steyn* [2006] eKLR.

[14] *Beluf Establishment* v. *AG* [1993] eKLR; *Ingra* v. *National Construction Corp.* [1987] KLR 652. But see *Universal TPT Co. Ltd* v. *Tzortzis* [1973] EA 310, 1973 (2) ALR Comm. 323, which held that, where a debt has to be converted from one currency to another, the conversion is calculated at the date when the debt became due.

[15] [2006] eKLR.

[16] *Aluminium Industries Aktien Gesellschaft* v. *Federal Board of Inland Revenue* 1971 (2) ALR Comm. 121 at 135, [1971] 2 NCLR 121 at 135.

[17] *Koya* v. *United Bank for Africa Ltd* [1997] 1 NWLR 251 at 276–89; *Saeby Jernstoberi Maskinfabric A/S* v. *Olaogun Enterprises Ltd* [2001] 11 WRN 179 at 196–7 (on appeal

entitled to make his or her claim in court, either in local or foreign currency if the basis of the contract is in foreign currency, and the court may order the specific performance of such a contract.[18] Indeed, there is generally no inhibition to a substantive claim being brought in foreign currency, particularly where the exchange rate is easily ascertainable.[19]

It has been held that, where a debt denominated in foreign currency or judgment is given in local currency, the exchange rate should be that prevailing on the date of payment.[20] Similarly, where an award is made in foreign currency, the judgment will be for the payment of the amount in foreign currency or its naira equivalent, converted for the purposes of enforcement at the time of payment.[21]

As a matter of law, if the claim of the plaintiff is in foreign currency and judgment has also been given in foreign currency, execution should also be carried out in the same foreign currency and it is only a matter of grace or special dispensation that a judgment-debtor can be allowed to pay his or her foreign debt in local currency. Moreover, if that is to be done, it has to be at the rate applicable on the date of exchange (that is, the date on which execution is sought to be levied).[22]

from *Olaogun Enterprises Ltd* v. *Saeby Jernstoberi & Maskinfabrik* [1992] 4 NWLR 361); *Afribank Nigeria Plc* v. *Akwara* [2006] 5 NWLR 619 at 644 and 656; *Erik Emborg Export* v. *Jos International Breweries Plc* [2003] 5 NWLR 505 at 533; *Nwankwo* v. *Ecumenical Development Co-operative Society* [2002] NWLR 513 at 543; *Tankereederi Ahrenkiel GmbH* v. *Adalma International Services Ltd* [1979] 2 FNLR 168 at 177–8; *Harka Air Services (Nigeria) Ltd* v. *Keazor* [2006] 1 NWLR 160 at 194 and 196–7; *Harka Air Services (Nig.) Ltd* v. *Keazor* [2011] 13 NWLR 321 at 355–6; *Co-operative and Commerce Bank (Nigeria) Ltd* v. *Onwuchekwa* [1998] 8 NWLR 375 at 123; *Broadline Enterprises Ltd* v. *Monterey Maritime Corp.* [1995] 9 NWLR 1. However, there are cases which cast doubt on the propriety of claims expressed in foreign currency or giving judgment in foreign currency: *Melwani* v. *Chanhira Corp.* [1995] 6 NWLR 438 at 461–9; *Savannah Bank of Nigeria Ltd* v. *Starite Industries Overseas Corp.* [2001] 1 NWLR 194 at 211; *Prospect Textiles Mills (Nig) Ltd* v. *ICI* [1996] 6 NWLR 668; *Wema Bank Plc* v. *Linton Industrial Trading Nigeria Ltd* [2011] 6 NWLR 479 at 511–12.

18 *Erik Emborg Export* v. *Jos International Breweries Plc* [2003] 5 NWLR 505 at 535; *Pan African Bank Ltd* v. *Ede* [1998] 7 NWLR 422 at 436–7; *UBA Ltd* v. *Ibhafidon* [1994] 1 NWLR 90 at 122.

19 *BB Apugo and Sons Ltd* v. *Orthopeadic Hospitals Management Board* [2005] 17 NWLR 305 at 338; *Momah* v. *VAB Petroleum Inc.* [2000] 2 SC 142, [2000] 4 NWLR 534.

20 *Erik Emborg Export* v. *Jos International Breweries Plc* [2003] 5 NWLR 505 at 535.

21 *Saeby Jernstoberi Maskinfabric A/S* v. *Olaogun Enterprises Ltd* [2001] 11 WRN 179 at 197; *Harka Air Services (Nigeria) Ltd* v. *Keazor* [2006] 1 NWLR 160 at 194.

22 *Salzgitter Stahl GmbH* v. *Aridi Industries (Nigeria) Ltd* [1996] 7 NWLR 192 at 201–2; *Union Bank of Nigeria Plc* v. *Eskol Paints Nigeria Ltd* [1997] 8 NWLR 157; *Akunne Patrick N Anyaorah* v. *Anyaorah* [2001] 7 NWLR 158. But see *Co-operative and Commerce Bank (Nigeria) Ltd* v. *Onwuchekwa* [1998] 8 NWLR 375 at 397 adopting the breach

In admiralty matters, the Admiralty Jurisdiction Decree 1991 gives the Federal High Court power to give judgment in any monetary currency (that is, accepted as legal tender by the laws of any other country), in which any of the parties has suffered loss or damage if: (a) the goods or consignment are paid for, or are to be paid for in that foreign currency; (b) the goods are insured in that currency and part of the amount so claimed is confined to that portion in foreign currency; or (c) the consideration or loss is derived from, accruing in, brought into or received (as the case may be) in the foreign currency, or for the benefit of the party making a claim before the court.[23] A judgment awarded by the court in any foreign currency is recoverable as if it were a judgment of the court awarded in naira.[24]

South Africa

The principle of currency nominalism is part of South African law. Accordingly, a debt sounding in money has to be paid in terms of its nominal value, irrespective of any fluctuation in the purchasing power of the currency.[25] It has been held that the doctrine of revalorisation – according to which the debtor's obligation in a case concerning repayment of a debt is not regarded as repaying the same amount, but repaying money of the same value – does not contravene South African public policy.[26]

A South African court has jurisdiction to give judgment in foreign currency.[27] Indeed, judgment may be given partly in one currency, and

date rule in assessing special damages for breach of contract on the basis of a statutory provision to that effect.

[23] Admiralty Jurisdiction Decree 1991, s. 17(1). [24] Ibid., s. 17(2).

[25] *SA Eagle Insurance Co. Ltd* v. *Hartley* 1990 (4) SA 833 at 839; *Radell* v. *Multilateral Motor Vehicle Accidents Fund* 1995 (4) SA 24.

[26] *Eden* v. *Pienaar* 2001 (1) SA 158. This case does not hold that the doctrine of revalorisation is part of South African law.

[27] *Standard Chartered Bank of Canada* v. *Nedperm Bank Ltd* 1994 (4) SA 747; *Skilya Property Investments (Pty) Ltd* v. *Lloyds of London Underwriting* 2002 (3) SA 765 at 815; *Barclays Bank of Swaziland* v. *Mnyeketi* 1992 (3) SA 425; *Elgin Brown and Hamer (Pty) Ltd* v. *Dampskibsselskabet Torm Ltd* 1988 (4) SA 671; *Murata Machinery Ltd* v. *Capelon Yarns (Pty) Ltd* 1986 (4) SA 671. Historically, the court declined to give judgment in foreign currency: *Carroll* v. *Carroll* 1978 (4) SA 714; *Voest Alpine Intertrading Gesellschaft Mbh* v. *Burwill and Co. SA (Pty) Ltd* 1985 (2) SA 149; *Malilang* v. *MV Houda Pearl* 1986 (2) SA 714.

partly in another.[28] The jurisdiction is discretionary and the discretion will be exercised in favour of a judgment in foreign currency where the relevant legal obligation has been incurred in a manner which contemplates quantification of the debt in such foreign currency,[29] or the loss has in fact been 'felt' in foreign currency.[30] The date on which the conversion from South African rand into foreign currency should be made is the date when payment is actually effected, not when payment is due.[31] The court may take judicial notice that a currency belongs to a named country. However, it cannot properly take judicial notice of the exchange rate which prevails between two currencies – proof of the exchange rate must be provided to the court.[32]

A South African court may in the exercise of its admiralty jurisdiction, and subject to the provisions of any law relating to exchange control, order payment to be made in such foreign currency where the circumstances of the case appear appropriate, and make such an order as seems just regarding the date upon which the calculation of the conversion from one currency to any other currency should be based.[33] Section 5(2)(g) confers discretion upon the court to choose an appropriate or just date upon which to convert the claims in foreign currency into rand. It has been held that the court will not lay down any general rule as to the manner in which this discretion is to be exercised.[34]

[28] See, e.g., *Elgin Brown and Hamer (Pty) Ltd* v. *Dampskibsselskabet Torm Ltd* 1988 (4) SA 671; *Radell* v. *Multilateral Motor Vehicle Accidents Fund* 1995 (4) SA 24.

[29] *Barclays Bank of Swaziland* v. *Mnyeketi* 1992 (3) SA 425; *Murata Machinery Ltd* v. *Capelon Yarns (Pty) Ltd* 1986 (4) SA 671.

[30] *Standard Chartered Bank of Canada* v. *Nedperm Bank Ltd* 1994 (4) SA 747; *Elgin Brown and Hamer (Pty) Ltd* v. *Dampskibsselskabet Torm Ltd* 1988 (4) SA 671; *Mediterranean Shipping Co. Ltd* v. *Speedwell Shipping Co. Ltd* 1989 (1) SA 164; *Macs Maritime Carrier* v. *Keeley Forwarding & Stevedoring (Pty) Ltd* 1995 (3) SA 377; *The MV Sea Joy* v. *The MV Sea Joy* 1998 (1) SA 487 at 509.

[31] *Murata Machinery Ltd* v. *Capelon Yarns (Pty) Ltd* 1986 (4) SA 671; *Skilya Property Investments (Pty) Ltd* v. *Lloyds of London Underwriting* 2002 (3) SA 765 at 815. Earlier, some courts had expressed a preference for the date of breach; *Voest Alpine Intertrading Gesellschaft Mbh* v. *Burwill and Co. SA (Pty) Ltd* 1985 (2) SA 149.

[32] *Barclays Bank of Swaziland* v. *Mnyeketi* 1992 (3) SA 425 at 427.

[33] Admiralty Jurisdiction Regulation Act 1983, s. 5(2)(g). *MT Argun; Master and Crew of the MT Argun* v. *MT Argun* 2003 (3) SA 149; *Mediterranean Shipping Co. Ltd* v. *Speedwell Shipping Co. Ltd* 1989 (1) SA 164; *Macs Maritime Carrier* v. *Keeley Forwarding & Stevedoring (Pty) Ltd* 1995 (3) SA 377.

[34] *Scallop Petroleum Co.* v. *The Fund Comprising the Proceeds of the Sale of The MV Jade Transporter* 1987 (1) SA 935.

Tanzania

A Tanzanian court can give judgment in foreign currency.[35] Historically, the courts have taken the position that they can only enter judgment in Tanzanian shillings.[36]

Uganda

A Ugandan court has jurisdiction to give judgment in foreign currency.[37] Accordingly, a claim in foreign currency is enforceable.[38] Where foreign currency has to be converted into Ugandan shillings, the rate of exchange should be the official Bank of Uganda exchange rate.[39]

Zambia

A Zambian court may give judgment in foreign currency. Where this is done, the rate of exchange applicable is the one prevailing at the time of enforcing the judgment.[40] Furthermore, in transactions expressed in kwacha, the court will disallow attempts to hedge against depreciation in the internal value of the kwacha through notionally storing the same in foreign currency at an earlier and more favourable exchange rate and then reconverting the foreign sum at the current rate.[41] To illustrate this, *Zambia Industrial Mining Corp.* v. *Lishomwa Muuka*[42] involved an action for breach of contract to sell a house worth 60,000 kwacha in 1975. The plaintiff argued that damages should be assessed at 125 million kwacha. This value was arrived at by converting 60,000 kwacha in 1975 into its US dollar equivalent and then reconverting the dollars back into kwacha at the current exchange rate. However, the court rejected this approach to assessing damages.[43]

35 *Attorney General* v. *Sisi Enterprises Ltd* [2007] 2 EA 33; *Transport Equipment* v. *Valambhia* [1993] TLR 91.

36 *Continental Agencies* v. *AC Berrill* [1971] EA 205.

37 *Interfreight Forwarders (U) Ltd* v. *East African Development Bank*, Civil Appeal No.33 of 1992 (Supreme Court, Uganda, 1993).

38 *Katatumba* v. *Uganda Cooperative Transport Union Ltd* [1994] V Kam. LR 138; *Willy Owacha* v. *Ringa Enterprises Ltd* [1995] Kam. LR 816.

39 *JK Patel* v. *Spear Motors Ltd* [1993] Kam. LR 145 at 157; *JK Patel* v. *Spear Motors Ltd* [1993] 1 Kam. LR 40 at 51.

40 *Zambia Export and Import Bank Ltd* v. *Mkuyu Farms Ltd* (1993–4) ZR 36 at 40.

41 *Zambia Industrial Mining Corp.* v. *Lishomwa Muuka* (1998) ZR 1.

42 (1998) ZR 1.

43 See also *Chinjavata* v. *The Administrator General* (2004) ZR 184; *Chibesakunda* v. *Mahtani* (1998) ZR 60.

Zimbabwe

A Zimbabwean court may make an order expressed in foreign currency and the date of conversion will be the date of payment, or when leave is given to enforce the judgment.[44] Where the courts have to convert foreign currency into Zimbabwean dollars and vice versa, they will apply the official rate of exchange and not the rate which prevails on the parallel market, regardless of the fact that one party may be seriously disadvantaged by using the official rate.[45] However, in appropriate cases and where no question of execution of judgment arises, the court may insist that a judgment given in foreign currency should also be discharged in foreign currency.[46] Indeed, where the parties specifically agreed that a loan would be repaid in foreign currency, the court will order that the performance must be *in forma specifica*, unless there is impossibility of performance.[47]

The court will look at the substance of the claim to see if the plaintiff has laid the foundation necessary to express its claim in foreign currency. In doing this, the plaintiff's motive, however laudable, is irrelevant in determining which currency reflects the true loss or damage it has suffered. In a claim in tort, the plaintiff must lay a foundation for the claim for judgment in foreign currency by demonstrating that it was in that currency that the loss was 'effectively felt or borne'.[48] The same applies in a contract claim.[49] Where a loss has been suffered and can be calculated in both the local and a foreign currency, the court has a discretion to award judgment in that currency that will redress the injury

[44] *Makwindi Oil Procurement Ltd* v. *National Oil Co. of Zimbabwe* 1988 (2) ZLR 482, 1989 (3) SA 191 (upholding *Makwindi Oil Procurement Ltd* v. *National Oil Co. of Zimbabwe* 1988 (2) SA 690 on this point). Historically this was not the case: see *National Food Distributors* v. *Weltman* 1985 (2) ZLR 310 at 311–12. See generally *Avacalos* v. *Riley*, HC 2022/06 (High Court, Zimbabwe, 2007).

[45] *Echodelta Ltd* v. *Kerr and Downey Safaris Ltd* 2004 (1) SA 508; *Zimbabwe Development Bank* v. *Zambezi Safari Lodges (Pvt) Ltd*, HC 703/2003 (High Court, Zimbabwe, 2006); *Lowveld Leather Products (Pvt) Ltd* v. *International Finance Corp. Ltd* 2003 (1) ZLR 78. However, the court may give effect to a contract discharged through the acquisition of foreign currency on the parallel market: *Meristem Investment (Pvt) Ltd* v. *NMB Bank* 2002 (2) ZLR 729.

[46] *Chiraga* v. *Msimuko* 2002 (2) ZLR 368, 2004 (1) SA 98.

[47] *Lowveld Leather Products (Pvt) Ltd* v. *International Finance Corp. Ltd* 2003 (1) ZLR 78.

[48] *Makwindi Oil Procurement Ltd* v. *National Oil Co. of Zimbabwe* 1988 (2) ZLR 482 at 494, 1989 (3) SA 191 at 199; *Muzeya* v. *Marais* 2004 (1) ZLR 326.

[49] *Watergate (Pvt) Ltd v. Commercial Bank of Zimbabwe*, Judgment No. SC 78/05 (Supreme Court, Zimbabwe, 2006).

suffered and adequately compensate the plaintiff for the loss. Thus, where the local currency has been rendered valueless by inflation and will not adequately compensate the plaintiff for their loss, the court may order judgment in the foreign currency.[50]

Where an award is made in foreign currency, interest should be claimed at the rate appropriate to the currency.[51] In this regard, the courts draw a distinction between the money of account[52] and the money of payment.[53] If the money of account is the same as the money of payment, the rate at which interest should be calculated is dependent on the money of account. But if the money of payment differs from the money of account, and unless a specific rate of interest is agreed upon, the rate of interest to be used should be the legal rate that applies to the money of payment.[54] Thus, where the money of account is in sterling and the money of payment is in Zimbabwean dollars, the rate of interest payable should be the rate prescribed in Zimbabwe.[55]

Comments

African economies are often susceptible to high inflation and currency depreciation. Thus, a claim involving a foreign currency raises concerns for the parties involved. The financial implications of a court's decision in such claims can be grave for the parties. This was brought out poignantly in the Zimbabwe case of *Echodelta Ltd* v. *Kerr and Downey Safaris*.[56] The plaintiff, a foreign company, sought repayment of a US$90,385.06 debt in the equivalent Zimbabwean dollars. The defendant consented to judgment and tendered payment of the amount in Zimbabwean dollars using the official exchange rate of 55:1. The plaintiff rejected the tender, and demanded payment at the parallel market exchange rate of about 300–350:1. To the plaintiff, justice required that it should not suffer loss

[50] *Fabiola* v. *Louis*, HC 6487/07 (High Court, Zimbabwe, 2009).

[51] *PTC* v. *Xan Zhong* 1999 (1) ZLR 525 at 527; *Industrial Equity Ltd* v. *Walker* 1996 (1) ZLR 85 at 108–9; *AMI Zimbabwe Ltd* v. *Casalee Hldgs (Successors) Ltd* 1997 (2) ZLR 77 at 86–7; *Nicholas* v. *Pearl General Insurance Co.* 1994 (1) ZLR 193 at 211; *Mawere* v. *Mukuna* 1997 (2) ZLR 361.

[52] The money of account is the currency in which the obligation is measured. It tells the debtor how much he or she has to pay.

[53] The money of payment is the currency in which the obligation is discharged. It tells the debtor by what means he or she has to pay.

[54] *Mawere* v. *Mukuna* 1997 (2) ZLR 361.

[55] *Chisese* v. *Garamukanwa* 2002 (2) ZLR 392.

[56] 2004 (1) SA 508.

by reason of the devaluation of the Zimbabwe dollar. The defendant argued that it was, by statute, illegal to acquire foreign currency from an unauthorised dealer or to pay anything above the official exchange rate. After accepting that, in appropriate cases, it had jurisdiction to give judgment in foreign currency, the court held that it could not order payment at any rate other than the official rate despite the reality of the parallel market. The defendant was ordered to pay the Zimbabwe equivalent of the debt at the official rate of 55:1.[57] The effect of this was that the plaintiff recovered only about US$18,000 of the original US$90,385.08 debt!

In an action where a foreign currency is involved, issues such as whether the court can give judgment in foreign currency, the exchange and interest rates to be used, the effect of exchange control laws and others may become relevant. This chapter examines how courts in the countries under study have approached some of these issues. Foreign currency claims arising in the context of actions to enforce foreign judgments, maintenance orders and arbitration awards are discussed in Chapters 17, 18 and 19, respectively.

The principle of nominalism[58] appears well entrenched in the countries under study. However, the cases decided – dating back to 1897 – have largely been in the domestic context.[59] There are pragmatic reasons for the principle – great difficulties and uncertainty would be occasioned if, in providing remedies, courts were invited to assess the real values or purchasing power of currencies. With persistent, high levels of inflation and the depreciation of currencies in Africa, it is arguable whether the philosophy underlying the principle has not been undermined. In the domestic context, it has been put forward that adherence to nominalism discourages reliance upon judicial institutions for remedies and could

[57] But see *Meristem Investment (Pvt) Ltd* v. *NMB Bank Ltd* 2002 (2) ZLR 729, where it was held that the respondent who acquired foreign currency on the parallel currency market for the applicant to enable the latter to discharge its pre-existing contractual obligation was entitled to debit the applicant's account with that amount.

[58] It holds that a debt expressed in any currency involves an obligation to pay the nominal amount of the debt in whatever is legal tender at the time of payment, according to the law of the country in whose currency the debt is expressed.

[59] M. Greig, 'Foreign Currency and Interest Awards in the Context of Fluctuating Inflation and Currency Rates' (2009) 126 *South African Law Journal* 124; H. J. A. N. Mensa-Bonsu, 'The Ghana Legal System in an Inflationary Economy' (1996–2000) 20 *Review of Ghana Law* 115; J. W. G. Van de Walt, 'Currency Fluctuations, Inflation and the Date with Regard to which Delictual Damage Must be Assessed: Towards a Clearer Understanding of the Issues Involved' (2002) 119 *South African Law Journal* 649.

undermine a legal system.[60] In the international context, it encourages the denomination of transactions in more stable currencies, which can put further pressure on the demand for such currencies. Indeed, it is not uncommon in some of the countries under study – Zimbabwe being the best and most recent example – for domestic transactions to be denominated and the value to be stored in foreign currency. This phenomenon has been encouraged by the elimination of exchange control regimes. Nevertheless, so deeply entrenched is the principle that, unless parties protect themselves in their transactions, they are unlikely to be helped by the courts to overcome adverse changes in the values of national currencies.

Historically, courts in most of the countries under study have declined jurisdiction to give judgment in foreign currency. The reason for this position is not difficult to find. As Justice Omolo aptly put it, 'the only reason I can think of is that that was the law in England and consequently that had to be the law in Kenya'.[61] However, in South Africa, after a careful historical inquiry, Justice Stegmann concluded that the English position, where a court could not give judgment in foreign currency, was 'entirely foreign to our law'.[62] When the position changed in England,[63] some courts in the countries under study did not enthusiastically embrace it. The existence of exchange control legislation, the need to conserve foreign currency, the persistent fluctuation in national currencies and the levels of national development were proffered as reasons for the reluctance to change.

However, it is now well settled that courts in many of the countries under study can give judgment in an amount expressed in foreign currency. The scope of this jurisdiction, which remains largely judge-made and not expressly provided for in statute,[64] is wide. In other words, the question of whether a court can give judgment expressed in foreign currency has been left largely to the courts to decide. Historically, some

60 Mensa-Bonsu, 'The Ghana Legal System in an Inflationary Economy' at 117–18.

61 *Beluf Establishment* v. *AG* [1993] eKLR.

62 *Barclays Bank of Swaziland* v. *Mnyeketi* 1992 (3) SA 425 at 435.

63 *Miliangos* v. *George Frank (Textiles) Ltd* [1976] AC 443. For a comprehensive and comparative discussion of how this case has been received in other jurisdictions, see V. Black, *Foreign Currency Claims in the Conflict of Laws* (Oxford: Hart Publishing, 2010).

64 There are a few statutes that expressly give the court jurisdiction to give judgment in foreign currency. See Nigeria – Admiralty Jurisdiction Decree 1991, s. 17; South Africa – Admiralty Jurisdiction Regulation Act 1983, s. 5(2)(g).

courts have sought to restrict their jurisdiction solely to claims to recover debt denominated in foreign currency or to the specific performance of contracts stipulating payment in foreign currency. However, this is now no longer the case. At present, jurisdiction has been exercised in actions to recover debt or damages for breach of contract and tort, and actions to enforce foreign judgments or arbitration awards.

The issue of the existence of jurisdiction to give judgment in foreign currency is distinct from whether, on the facts of a given case, it should be exercised. Even where the existence of the jurisdiction is well accepted, the circumstances in which it should be exercised continue to be debated in the decided cases. In general, the courts have emphasised that the parties should have transacted in a foreign currency or that their loss should have been felt in the foreign currency. For example, it has been suggested that it would be wrong to give judgment in foreign currency when parties have not 'conducted their transactions with each other in foreign currency'.[65] This approach to giving judgments in foreign currency is welcome – the jurisdiction to give judgment in foreign currency should not be invoked or exercised to enable a person to avoid the risks associated with holding a national currency.

In addition to the jurisdiction to give judgment in foreign currency, it has been held in some of the countries under study that execution of judgments may also be in foreign currency. In Nigeria, in admiralty matters, this position is enshrined in statute.[66] Where execution is allowed in foreign currency, it leaves 'no question of conversion into local currency'[67] and the prospect of foreign currency losses that can result from such conversion, even if conversion is carried out on the day of payment. This presents a great advantage to the judgment-creditor.

The courts have persistently held that, where there is a need to convert currencies, the rate of exchange should be the official exchange rate, which, in many of the countries under study, tends to be lower than the rate outside official circles. It has been held in South Africa and Zimbabwe that the courts will not take judicial notice of either exchange rates or the shortage of foreign currency,[68] respectively. In general, even

[65] *Mensah* v. *National Savings and Credit Bank* [1989–90] 1 GLR 620 at 625.

[66] Admiralty Jurisdiction Decree 1991, s. 17(2), which provides that a judgment awarded by the Federal High Court in any foreign currency shall be recoverable as if it were a judgment of the court awarded in naira.

[67] *Salzgitter Stahl GmbH* v. *Aridi Industries (Nigeria) Ltd* [1996] 7 NWLR 192 at 202.

[68] *Chiraga* v. *Msimuko* 2002 (2) ZLR 368, 2004 (1) SA 98.

though exchange control laws have largely been eliminated in the countries under study, some restrictions – mainly procedural – may be imposed on the transfer of foreign currency out of the jurisdiction.[69] Thus, even if the judgment-creditor is able to execute in foreign currency, he or she may encounter some restrictions transferring the amount outside the jurisdiction.

An important issue in any foreign currency claim is the date of conversion.[70] The need to convert may arise because judgment has been expressed in foreign currency but should be executed in the national currency, or that a claim for loss or debt has been made in the national currency but the loss was suffered, or the debt was denominated, in foreign currency. Irrespective of the source of this need, the sums that stand to be lost or gained are often very significant. In some of the countries under study, statute regulates this issue for defined subject matter, such as bills of exchange and actions to enforce foreign judgments, especially through registration. For example, under section 70(d) of South Africa's Bill of Exchange Act 1964, if a bill is drawn outside, but payable in South Africa, and the sum payable is expressed in a foreign currency, the amount shall, in the absence of an express stipulation to the contrary, be calculated according to the rate of exchange for sight drafts at the place of payment, and on the day the bill is payable.[71]

Apart from statutorily imposed conversion dates, the cases decided in the countries under study reflect wide acceptance of the payment date rule. In other words, where there is need for it, conversion of foreign currency into the national currency is carried out at the rate that prevails

[69] For example, under s. 15 of Ghana's Foreign Exchange Act 2006, payment in foreign currency, to or from Ghana between a resident and a non-resident, or between non-residents, shall be made through a bank. See also Nigeria – Foreign Exchange (Monitoring and Miscellaneous Provisions) Act 1995.

[70] A. V. Wyk, 'Judgments in a Foreign Currency' (1991) 3 *South African Mercantile Law Journal* 197.

[71] See also Botswana – Bills of Exchange Act 1964, s. 71(d); Ghana – Bills of Exchange Act 1961, s. 71(d); Kenya – Bills of Exchange Act 1927, s. 72(d); Malawi – Bills of Exchange Act 1967, s. 72(d); Namibia – Bills of Exchange Act 2003, s. 66(e); Nigeria – Bills of Exchange Act 1917, s. 72(d); Tanzania – Bills of Exchange Act 1931, s. 72(d); Uganda – Bills of Exchange Act 1933, s. 71(d); Zimbabwe – Bills of Exchange Act 1895, s. 71(d). These provisions are based on the now repealed s. 72(4) of the English Bills of Exchange Act 1882. This 1882 Act is still the law governing bills of exchange in Gambia and Zambia, but it is unclear whether the repeal of its s. 72(4) renders it inapplicable there. See also s. 442 of the Contract Law of Anambra State, which provides that, where damages for breach of contract are claimed which are prima facie calculable in a foreign currency, the amount claimed shall be converted into Nigerian currency at the date of the breach.

on the date of actual payment. It is an open question whether the payment date rule is a rigid one or may be departed from. In general, given the discretionary nature of the jurisdiction to give judgments in foreign currency, it is likely that, in appropriate cases, national courts may be prepared to depart from the payment date rule. Indeed, in South Africa, in admiralty claims, the court is empowered to make such order 'as seems just' as to the date conversion.[72]

Courts in some of the countries under study have grappled with the issue of interest on judgments in foreign currency. In general, interest rates in these countries tend to be considerably higher than those prevailing in most advanced economies. Accordingly, where judgment is given in foreign currency but the domestic interest rate is used, the judgment-creditor will end up over-compensated. Ghanaian and Zimbabwean courts have held that where judgment is given in foreign currency the applicable rate of interest should be that of the prevailing country to which the currency belongs. This approach is fair and makes commercial sense.[73]

[72] Admiralty Jurisdiction Regulations Act 1983, s. 5(2)(g).

[73] The contrary stance of the South African courts has been criticised: M. Greig, 'Foreign Currency and Interest Awards in the Context of Fluctuating Inflation and Currency Rates' (2009) 126 *South African Law Journal* 124.

10

Bills of exchange

A bill of exchange may be drawn in one country, accepted in a second and negotiated in a third. From a private international law perspective, this raises the issue of which country's law is to be used to determine the rights *inter se* of the holder and other parties to the bill, such as the drawer, drawee and endorser. In addition to issues related to the transfer of rights in a bill, there are other contractual issues related to a bill with private international law implications. These include the formal and essential validity of a bill, interpretation, duties of the parties and currency of payment. These issues are the focus of this chapter.

Botswana

Where a bill drawn in one country is negotiated, accepted or payable in another, the rights, duties and liabilities of the parties thereto are determined as follows: The validity of the bill as regards requisites in form is determined by the law of the place of issue, and the validity as regards requisites in form of every supervening contract, such as acceptance, endorsement or acceptance for honour *supra* protest, is determined by the law of the place where such a contract was made. However, where a bill is issued outside Botswana, it is not invalid purely because it is not stamped in accordance with the law of the place of issue. Furthermore, where a bill issued outside Botswana conforms, as regards requisites in form, to Botswanan law, it may, for the purpose of enforcing payment, be treated as valid as between all persons who negotiate, hold or become parties to it in Botswana.[1]

The interpretation of the contract of the drawer, endorser, acceptor or acceptor for honour *supra* protest of a bill is determined by the law of the place where such a contract is made. However, where a bill drawn and

[1] Bills of Exchange Act 1964, s. 71(a).

payable in Botswana is endorsed elsewhere, the endorsement shall be interpreted according to Botswanan law as regards the payer.[2] The duties of the holder with respect to presentment for acceptance or payment, and the necessity for, or sufficiency of, a protest or notice of dishonour (or otherwise) are determined by the law of the place where the act is performed or the bill is dishonoured.[3] Where a bill is drawn outside of, but is payable in, Botswana and the sum payable is not expressed in the currency of Botswana, the amount shall, in the absence of an express stipulation to the contrary, be calculated according to the rate of exchange for sight drafts at the place of payment on the day the bill is payable.[4] Where a bill is drawn in one country and is payable in another, the due date thereof is determined according to the law of the place where it is payable.[5]

Gambia

The UK Bills of Exchange Act 1882 remains in force in Gambia by virtue of section 2 of the Law of England (Application) Act 1953.[6] Section 72 of the 1882 Act deals with conflict of laws issues relating to bills of exchange. Except for the repeal of section 72(4), which deals with the rate of exchange for bills expressed in foreign currency, section 72 is similar to those provisions outlined in the country reports below; indeed, all the statutes in the countries under study are based on the 1882 Act. Section 72 is not outlined here.

Ghana

Where a bill drawn in one country is negotiated, accepted or payable in another, the rights, duties and liabilities of the parties thereto are determined as follows: The validity of a bill as regards requisites in form is determined by the law of the place of issue, and the validity as regards requisites in form of the supervening contracts, such as acceptance, or endorsement, or acceptance *supra* protest, is determined by the law of the place where such a contract was made. A bill issued outside Ghana is not invalid purely because it is not stamped in accordance with the law of the

[2] Ibid., s. 71(b). [3] Ibid., s. 71(c). [4] Ibid., s. 71(d). [5] Ibid., s. 71(e).

[6] It provides that subject to the provisions of this and any other Act, the common law, the doctrines of equity and the statutes of general application in force in England on the first day of November 1888 shall be in force in Gambia.

place of issue, and provided such a bill conforms, as regards requisites in form, to the law of Ghana, it may, for the purpose of enforcing payment there, be treated as valid as between all persons who negotiate, hold or become parties to it in Ghana.[7]

The interpretation of the drawing, endorsement, acceptance or acceptance *supra* protest of a bill is determined by the law of the place where such a contract is made, provided that where an inland bill is endorsed in a foreign country, the endorsement shall be interpreted according to the law of Ghana as regards the payer.[8] The duties of the holder with respect to presentment for acceptance or payment, and the necessity for, or sufficiency of, a protest or notice of dishonour (or otherwise) are determined by the law of the place where the act is performed or where the bill is dishonoured.[9] Where a bill is drawn outside of, but is payable in, Ghana and the sum payable is not expressed in the currency of Ghana, the amount shall, in the absence of an express stipulation to the contrary, be calculated according to the rate of exchange for sight drafts at the place of payment on the day the bill is payable.[10] Where a bill is drawn in one country and is payable in another, the due date thereof is determined according to the law of the place where it is payable.[11]

Kenya

Under Kenyan law, where a bill drawn in one country is negotiated, accepted or payable in another, the rights, duties and liabilities of the parties to it are determined as follows: the validity of a bill as regards requisites in form is determined by the law of the place of issue, and the validity as regards requisites in form of the supervening contracts, such as acceptance or endorsement or acceptance *supra* protest, is determined by the law of the place where such a contract was made. However, where a bill is issued outside Kenya, it is not invalid purely because it is not stamped in accordance with the law of the place of issue, and where a bill issued outside Kenya conforms, as regards requisites in form, to the law of Kenya, it may, for the purpose of enforcing payment thereof, be treated as valid as between all persons who negotiate, hold or become parties to it in Kenya.[12]

The interpretation of the drawing, endorsement, acceptance or acceptance *supra* protest of a bill is determined by the law of the place where

[7] Bills of Exchange Act 1961, s. 71(a). [8] Ibid., s. 71(b). [9] Ibid., s. 71(c).
[10] Ibid., s. 71(d). [11] Ibid., s. 71(e). [12] Bills of Exchange Act 1927, s. 72(a).

the contract is made, but where an inland bill is endorsed in a foreign country, the endorsement shall be interpreted according to the law of Kenya as regards the payer.[13] The duties of the holder with respect to presentment for acceptance or payment, and the necessity for, or sufficiency of, a protest or notice of dishonour (or otherwise) are determined by the law of the place where the act is performed or where the bill is dishonoured.[14] Where a bill is drawn outside of, but is payable in, Kenya and the sum payable is expressed in foreign currency, the amount shall, in the absence of an express stipulation to the contrary, be calculated according to the rate of exchange for sight drafts at the place of payment on the day the bill is payable.[15] Where a bill is drawn in one country and is payable in another, its due date is determined according to the law of the place where it is payable.[16]

Malawi

Where a bill drawn in one country is negotiated, accepted or payable in another, the rights, duties and liabilities of the parties to it are determined as follows: The validity of a bill as regards requisites in form is determined by the law of the place of issue, and the validity as regards requisites in form of the supervening contracts, such as acceptance, endorsement or acceptance *supra* protest, is determined by the law of the place where such a contract was made. However, where a bill is issued outside Malawi, it is not invalid solely because it is not stamped in accordance with the law of the place of issue, and where a bill issued outside Malawi conforms, as regards requisites in form, to the law of Malawi, it may, for the purpose of enforcing its payment, be treated as valid as between all persons who negotiate, hold or become parties to it in Malawi.[17]

The interpretation of the drawing, endorsement, acceptance or acceptance *supra* protest of a bill is determined by the law of the place where the contract is made, but where an inland bill is endorsed in a foreign country, the endorsement shall be interpreted according to the law of Malawi as regards the payer.[18] The duties of the holder with respect to presentment for acceptance or payment, and the necessity for, or sufficiency of, a protest or notice of dishonour (or otherwise) are determined by the law of the place where the act is performed, or where the bill is

[13] Ibid., s. 72(b). [14] Ibid., s. 72(c). [15] Ibid., s. 72(d). [16] Ibid., s. 72(e).
[17] Bills of Exchange Act 1967, s. 72(a). [18] Ibid., s. 72(b).

dishonoured.[19] Where a bill is drawn outside of, but is payable in, Malawi and the sum payable is expressed in foreign currency, the amount shall, in the absence of an express stipulation to the contrary, be calculated according to the rate of exchange for sight drafts at the place of payment on the day the bill is payable.[20] Where a bill is drawn in one country and is payable in another, its due date is determined according to the law of the place where it is payable.[21]

Namibia

If a bill drawn in one country is negotiated, accepted or payable in another, the rights, duties and liabilities of the parties to the bill are determined as follows: The validity of the bill as regards requisites in form is determined by the law of the place of issue, and the validity, as regards requisites in form of every supervening contract, such as acceptance, endorsement or signer of an aval, is determined by the law of the place where such a contract was made. But a bill issued outside Namibia is not invalid purely because it is not stamped in accordance with the law of the place of issue, and a bill issued outside Namibia which conforms, as regards requisites in form, to the law of Namibia, and is for the purpose of enforcing payment, may be treated as valid as between all persons who negotiate, hold or become parties to it in Namibia.[22]

The interpretation of the contract of the drawer, endorser, acceptor or signer of an aval of a bill is determined by the law of the place where such a contract is made, but if a bill payable in Namibia is endorsed outside Namibia, the endorsement must be interpreted according to the law of Namibia as regards the payer.[23] The duties of the holder with respect to presentment for acceptance or payment, and the necessity for, or sufficiency of, a protest or notice of dishonour (or otherwise) are determined by the law of the place where the act is performed or where the bill is dishonoured.[24] If a bill is drawn outside of, but is payable in, Namibia, and the sum payable is expressed in foreign currency, the amount, in the absence of an express stipulation to the contrary, must be calculated according to the rate of exchange for sight drafts at the place of payment on the day the bill is payable.[25] If a bill is drawn in one country and

[19] Ibid., s. 72(c). [20] Ibid., s. 72(d). [21] Ibid., s. 72(e).
[22] Bills of Exchange Act 2003, s. 66(a)(b). [23] Ibid., s. 66(c). [24] Ibid., s. 66(d).
[25] Ibid., s. 66(e).

is payable in another, the due date of the bill is determined according to the law of the place where it is payable.[26]

Nigeria

Where a bill drawn in one country is negotiated, accepted or payable in another, the rights, duties and liabilities of the parties thereto are determined as follows: The validity of a bill as regards requisites in form is determined by the law of the place of issue, and the validity as regards requisites in form of the supervening contracts, such as acceptance, endorsement or acceptance *supra* protest, is determined by the law of the place where such a contract was made. But where a bill is issued outside Nigeria, it is not invalid purely because it is not stamped in accordance with the law of the place of issue, and where a bill issued outside of Nigeria conforms, as regards requisites in form, to the law of Nigeria, it may, for the purpose of enforcing payment, be treated as valid as between all persons who negotiate, hold or become parties to it in Nigeria.[27]

The interpretation of the drawing, endorsement, acceptance or acceptance *supra* protest of a bill is determined by the law of the place where such a contract was made, but where an inland bill is endorsed in a foreign country, the endorsement shall be interpreted according to the law of Nigeria as regards the payer.[28] The duties of the holder with respect to presentment for acceptance or payment and the necessity for, or sufficiency of, a protest or notice of dishonour (or otherwise) are determined by the law of the place where the act is performed or where the bill is dishonoured.[29] Where a bill is drawn outside of, but is payable in, Nigeria and the sum payable is not expressed in the currency of Nigeria, the amount shall, in the absence of an express stipulation to the contrary, be calculated according to the rate of exchange for sight drafts at the place of payment on the day the bill is payable.[30] Where a bill is drawn in one country and is payable in another, the due date thereof is determined according to the law of the place where it is payable.[31]

South Africa

If a bill drawn in one country is negotiated, accepted or payable in another, the rights, duties and liabilities of the parties thereto are determined as follows: The validity of the bill as regards requisites in form is

[26] Ibid., s. 66(f). [27] Bills of Exchange Act 1917, s. 72(a). [28] Ibid., s. 72(b).
[29] Ibid., s. 72(c). [30] Ibid., s. 72(d). [31] Ibid., s. 72(e).

determined by the law of the place of issue, and the validity, as regards the requisites in form of every supervening contract, such as acceptance, endorsement or that of an aval, is determined by the law of the place where such a contract was made. But a bill issued outside South Africa is not invalid purely because it is not stamped in accordance with the law of the place of issue, and a bill issued outside South Africa which conforms, as regards requisites in form, to South African law, may for the purposes of enforcing payment thereof be treated as valid as between all persons who negotiate, hold or become parties to it in South Africa.[32]

The interpretation of the contract of the drawer, endorser, acceptor or signer of an aval of a bill is determined by the law of the place where such a contract is made, provided that, if a bill payable in South Africa is endorsed outside South Africa, the endorsement shall as regards the payer be interpreted according to South African law.[33] The duties of the holder with respect to presentment for acceptance or payment, and the necessity for, or sufficiency of, a protest or notice of dishonour (or otherwise) are determined by the law of the place where the act is performed or where the bill is dishonoured.[34] If a bill is drawn outside of, but is payable in, South Africa, and the sum payable is not expressed in foreign currency, the amount shall, in the absence of an express stipulation to the contrary, be calculated according to the rate of exchange for sight drafts at the place of payment on the day the bill is payable.[35] If a bill is drawn in one country and is payable in another, the due date thereof is determined according to the law of the place where it is payable.[36]

Tanzania

Where a bill drawn in one country is negotiated, accepted or payable in another, the rights, duties and liabilities of the parties are determined as follows: The validity of a bill as regards requisites in form is determined by the law of the place of issue, and the validity as regards the requisites in form of the supervening contracts, such as acceptance or endorsement, or acceptance *supra* protest, is determined by the law of the place where such a contract was made. A bill issued outside Tanzania is not invalid

[32] Bills of Exchange Act 1964, s. 70(a)(b). [33] Ibid., s. 70(c). [34] Ibid., s. 70(c).
[35] Ibid., s. 70(d). See *Tropic Plastic and Packaging* v. *Standard Bank of South Africa* 1969 (4) SA 108.
[36] Ibid., s. 70(e).

purely because it is not stamped in accordance with the law of the place of issue, but where a bill issued outside Tanzania conforms, as regards requisites in form, to the law of Tanzania, it may, for the purpose of enforcing payment, be treated as valid as between all persons who negotiate, hold or become parties to it in Tanzania.[37]

The interpretation of the drawing, endorsement, acceptance or acceptance *supra* protest of a bill is determined by the law of the place where such a contract is made.[38] Where an inland bill is endorsed in a foreign country, the endorsement shall, as regards the payer, be interpreted according to the law of Tanzania.[39]

The duties of the holder with respect to presentment for acceptance or payment, and the necessity for, or sufficiency of, a protest or notice of dishonour (or otherwise) are determined by the law of the place where the act is performed or where the bill is dishonoured.[40] Where a bill is drawn outside of, but is payable in, Tanzania, and the sum payable is not expressed in foreign currency, the amount shall, in the absence of an express stipulation to the contrary, be calculated according to the rate of exchange for sight drafts at the place of payment on the day the bill is payable.[41] Where a bill is drawn in one country and is payable in another, the due date is determined according to the law of the place where it is payable.[42]

Uganda

Where a bill drawn in one country is negotiated, accepted or payable in another, the rights, duties and liabilities of the parties are determined as follows: The validity of a bill as regards requisites in form is determined by the law of the place of issue, and the validity as regards the requisites in form of the supervening contracts, such as acceptance or endorsement, or acceptance *supra* protest, is determined by the law of the place where such a contract was made. A bill issued outside Uganda is not invalid solely because it is not stamped in accordance with the law of the place of issue, but if such a bill conforms, as regards requisites in form, to the law of Uganda, it may, for the purpose of enforcing payment, be treated as valid as between all persons who negotiate, hold or become parties to it in Uganda.[43]

[37] Bills of Exchange Act 1931, s. 72(1)(a). [38] Ibid., s. 72(1)(b). [39] Ibid., s. 72(2).
[40] Ibid., s. 72(1)(c). [41] Ibid., s. 72(1)(d). [42] Ibid., s. 72(1)(e).
[43] Bills of Exchange Act 1933, s. 71(a).

The interpretation of the drawing, endorsement, acceptance or acceptance *supra* protest of a bill is determined by the law of the place where such a contract is made, but where an inland bill is endorsed in a foreign country, the endorsement shall be interpreted according to the law of Uganda as regards the payer.[44]

The duties of the holder with respect to presentment for acceptance or payment and the necessity for, or sufficiency of, a protest or notice of dishonour (or otherwise) are determined by the law of the place where the act is performed or where the bill is dishonoured.[45] Where a bill is drawn outside of, but is payable in, Uganda and the sum payable is not expressed in foreign currency, the amount shall, in the absence of an express stipulation to the contrary, be calculated according to the rate of exchange for sight drafts at the place of payment on the day the bill is payable.[46] Where a bill is drawn in one country and is payable in another, the due date is determined according to the law of the place where it is payable.[47]

Zambia

The United Kingdom's Bills of Exchange Act 1882 remains in force in Zambia.[48] Section 72 of the Act deals with conflict of laws issues relating to bills of exchange. Except for the repeal of section 72(4), which deals with the rate of exchange for bills expressed in foreign currency, section 72 is similar to those provisions outlined in the above country reports.

Zimbabwe

Where a bill drawn in one country or territory is negotiated, accepted or payable in another, the rights, duties and liabilities of the parties thereto are determined as follows: The validity of a bill as regards requisites in form is determined by the law of the place of issue, and the validity as regards the requisites in form of every supervening contract, such as acceptance or endorsement, or acceptance *supra* protest, is determined by the law of the place where such a contract was made. Provided that where a bill issued outside Zimbabwe is not invalid solely because it is not stamped in accordance with the law of the place of issue, and if such a bill conforms as regards requisites in form to the law of Zimbabwe, it may,

[44] Ibid., s. 71(b). [45] Ibid., s. 71(c). [46] Ibid., s. 71(d). [47] Ibid., s. 71(e).
[48] See British Acts Extension Act 1923 and English Law (Extent of Application) Act 1963.

for the purpose of enforcing payment, be treated as valid as between all persons who negotiate, hold or become parties to it in Zimbabwe.[49]

The interpretation of the contract of the drawer, endorser, acceptor or acceptor *supra* protest of a bill is determined by the law of the place where such a contract is made. However, where a bill drawn and payable in Zimbabwe is endorsed elsewhere, the endorsement shall, as regards the payer, be interpreted according to the law of Zimbabwe.[50] The duties of the holder with respect to presentment for acceptance or payment, and the necessity for, or sufficiency of, a protest or notice of dishonour (or otherwise) are determined by the law of the place where the act is performed, or where the bill is dishonoured.[51] Where a bill is drawn outside of, but is payable in, Zimbabwe and the sum payable is not expressed in the currency of Zimbabwe, the amount shall, in the absence of an express stipulation to the contrary, be calculated according to the rates of exchange for sight drafts at the place of payment on the day the bill is payable.[52] Where the bill is drawn in one country or territory and is payable in another, the due date is determined according to the law of the place where it is payable.[53]

Comments

The nature of a bill is such that dealing with it often gives rise to conflict of laws problems. A bill may be drawn in one country and accepted or negotiated in another. The rules for resolving conflict of laws issues likely to arise in a transaction relating to a bill have largely been codified in statute in all the countries under study; the law in each of these has been inspired by the UK Bills of Exchange Act 1882. Indeed, Gambia and Zambia do not have an independent Act on the subject – the 1882 Act is still in force in those countries! However, it is uncertain whether subsequent amendments to the Act – and in this instance, there has been one – are also binding in Gambia and Zambia. It would be better for both countries to enact their own legislation.

The law in each of the countries under study does not purport to deal with all conflict of laws issues likely to arise in a transaction relating to a bill. The laws deal with five main subjects, namely questions of formal validity, interpretation, duties of the holder of a bill, the rate of exchange for bills drawn in foreign currency and the due date of payment. Subject

[49] Bills of Exchange Act 1895, s. 72(a). [50] Ibid., s. 72(b). [51] Ibid., s. 72(c).
[52] Ibid., s. 72(e). [53] Ibid., s. 72(f).

to named exceptions, in all the countries under study, the formal validity of a bill is governed by the law of the place of issue or contracting; interpretation is governed by the law of the country where the contract was made; the duties of the holder are governed by the law of the place where the act was performed or where the bill was dishonoured; the rate of exchange is the rate of exchange for sight drafts at the place of payment on the day the bill is payable, and the due date is governed by the law of the country where the bill is payable. From the preceding, it is evident that there is no single law, such as the proper law of the bill, which governs all contractual issues related to a bill.

The statutes do not address issues such as capacity, essential validity, discharge and the proprietary aspects of transferring bills. These issues are likely to be governed by the choice of laws rules applicable to contracts[54] and the transfer of movables.[55] Apart from some very old South African cases,[56] there appears to be a dearth of cases dealing with either the statutory rules or the rules applicable to issues outside the scope of those dealt with by legislation.

The fact that different laws govern different aspects of a bill means that the statutes do not provide a comprehensive code of the rules of choice of law relevant to bills, and the dearth of decided cases makes this area a very uncertain one. There is a need for greater certainty in this area of great commercial significance, especially on issues not yet addressed in the legislation.

[54] See Ch. 7. [55] See Ch. 14. [56] Forsyth, pp. 380–8.

PART IV

Family law

11

Marriage

The institution of marriage – from its creation to dissolution – is a fertile ground for private international law problems. Persons of different domicile, habitual residence or nationality may fall in love and marry in a country where they happen to be or choose. In addition to marital relations between persons of the opposite sex, same-sex relationships are increasingly becoming significant in Africa. The media is filled with news on such relationships, politicians and religious leaders have joined in the debate, and there have been attempts to legislate on the subject in some countries. Regardless of the nature of a marriage, questions relating to the formal validity of the marriage, the capacity of the parties to marry, the effect of the marriage on their property rights, and the recognition of the marriage celebrated abroad may arise. This chapter addresses these questions.

Nature of marriage

Although it is not a purely private international law issue, the question of 'what is a marriage' often raises significant private international law problems. Marriage relates to a person's status; a number of private international law issues turn on it. In some of the countries under study, marriage has been statutorily defined as 'the voluntary union of a man and a woman intended to last for their joint lives'.[1] In many of the countries, marriage is not expressly defined by statute; however, it can be argued that in a true and proper interpretation of the relevant statutes, they envisage only relationships between a man and a woman.[2] Both

[1] Kenya – Matrimonial Causes Act 1941, s. 2 (see also Marriage Bill 2007, s. 3); Sierra Leone – Matrimonial Causes Act 1950, s. 2; Tanzania – Law of Marriage Act 1971, s. 9(1).

[2] See, e.g., Botswana – Marriage Act 2001; Gambia – Civil Marriage Act 1938, Christian Marriage Act 1862 and Muslim Marriage and Divorce Act 1941; Ghana – Marriages Act 1884; Kenya – Marriage Act 1902; Malawi – Marriage Act 1903; Nigeria – Marriage Act 1990; Uganda – Marriage Act 1904; Zambia – Marriage Act 1918; Zimbabwe – Marriage Act 1964. When celebrating a marriage under many of these Acts, the

monogamous and potentially polygamous marriages, often referred to as 'African customary marriages'[3] (including those contracted abroad),[4] are recognised in the countries under study.

It still remains highly contentious in most of the countries under study whether associations between persons of the same sex[5] should be recognised as marriage. In Zambia, a marriage between persons of the same sex is void.[6] It is only in South Africa where civil unions solemnised either as a marriage or a civil partnership are recognised.[7] The constitutional foundations of South Africa's Civil Union Act 2006 and the judicial decisions which preceded it[8] can be found in the constitutions of

celebrating official is expected to declare and announce the parties as 'man and wife'. It is submitted that this would be interpreted to mean that only marriages between a man and woman are contemplated.

[3] See, e.g., Botswana – Marriage Act 2001, ss. 22–7; Kenya – Marriage Act 1902, s. 37; Malawi – Marriage Act 1903, s. 36; Nigeria – Marriage Act 1990, s. 35; South Africa – Marriage Act 1961, s. 28; Tanzania – Law of Marriage Act 1971, s. 25; Uganda – Marriage Act 1904, s. 36; Zambia – Marriage Act 1918, s. 34; Zimbabwe – Customary Marriages Act 1917. See also Gambia – Muslim Marriage and Divorce Act 1941. In some of these countries there is a requirement that customary marriages should be registered.

[4] See generally *Adegbola* v. *Johnson* [1921] 3 NLR 89; *Onikepe* v. *Goncallo* [1900] 1 NLR 41 and Zimbabwe – Customary Marriages Act 1917, s. 3(1)(d).

[5] There appears to be a customary practice in some of the countries under study which allows a woman to marry another woman. This has been described in the literature and case law as 'woman to woman marriage'. Cotran describes this marriage as: 'A woman past the age of [among the Nandi and Kipsigis] child-bearing and who has no sons may enter into a form of marriage with another woman. This may be done during the lifetime of her husband, but is more usual after his death. Marriage consideration is paid, as in regular marriage, and a man from the woman's husband's clan has sexual intercourse with the girl in respect of whom marriage consideration has been paid. Any children born to the girl are regarded as the children of the woman who paid marriage consideration and her husband.' E. Cotran, *The Law of Marriage and Divorce* (London: Sweet & Maxwell, 1968), vol. 1, p. 117. The woman who takes a wife becomes a man and (except for the absence of sexual intercourse with her wife) behaves in all social contexts exactly as would any ordinary man. The sole object of this relationship is to enable the female 'husband' to acquire a male heir for her property. R. Smith Oboler, 'Is the Female Husband a Man? Woman/Woman Marriage among the Nandi of Kenya' (1980) 19 *Ethnology* 69–88. Such a marriage has been recognised in Kenya for the purposes of inheritance in *The Matter of the Estate of Cherotich Kimong'ony Kibserea (Deceased)*, Succession Cause No. 212 of 2010 (High Court, Kenya, 2011). However, in Nigeria it was held in *Eugene Meribe* v. *Joshua C Egwu* [1976] 1 All NLR [Part 1] 266 that a custom which permits the marriage of a woman to another woman is contrary to public policy and ought not to be upheld by the court.

[6] Matrimonial Causes Act 2007, s. 27(1)(c).

[7] Civil Union Act 2006.

[8] *Minister of Home Affairs* v. *Fourie* 2006 (1) SA 524; *National Coalition for Gay and Lesbian Equality* v. *The Minister of Justice* 1999 (1) SA 6; *National Coalition for Gay and Lesbian Equality* v. *Minister of Home Affairs* 2000 (2) SA 1.

all the countries under study. These foundations include freedom of association and the right not to be discriminated against. It remains to be seen whether courts and legislators in other countries under study will follow a similar path. There is little prospect of this happening, despite growing international and domestic pressure on the countries to recognise such relationships. Indeed, there have been legislative attempts – often met with disapproval from human rights organisations – in countries such as Nigeria, Uganda, Malawi and Zimbabwe – to criminalise same-sex marriages.[9]

Formal and essential validity of marriage

Ghana

The essential validity of marriage is determined by the antenuptial *lex domicilii* of both parties. Accordingly, in a situation where a Sierra Leone domiciled man married a Ghanaian domiciled woman in Ghana, it was held that the validity of the marriage had to be determined not only by the law applicable in Ghana, but also by the law applicable in Sierra Leone.[10] However, a Ghanaian court may uphold a marriage as valid on grounds of public policy even though it is apparently void under the law of the domicile of one of the parties.[11]

Kenya

The formal validity of a marriage is determined by the *lex loci celebrationis* and the essential validity of the marriage determined by the *lex domicilii* of the parties or their matrimonial domicile.[12] Consent to marriage is a question of form and is determined by the *lex loci celebrationis.*[13]

[9] In December 2011, the Nigerian Senate voted to adopt the Same Gender Marriage (Prohibition) Bill 2011. The bill prohibits same gender marriage contracts and the recognition in Nigeria of such contracts entered into in foreign countries. Sex between persons of the same gender is already a crime in most of the countries under study.

[10] *Davis* v. *Randall* [1962] 1 GLR 1.

[11] *In re. Kariyavoulas (Deceased); Donkor* v. *Greek Consul-General* [1973] 2 GLR 52.

[12] *In re. an Application by Barbara Simpson Howison* [1959] EA 568 at 572–3.

[13] *In re. an Application by Barbara Simpson Howison* [1959] EA 568 at 573.

Lesotho

The *lex loci celebrationis* determines whether a marriage celebrated abroad is valid.[14] A marriage valid under the laws of the place of celebration will be recognised as valid in Lesotho.[15]

Malawi

The validity of marriage, insofar as formal requirements are concerned, is governed by the *lex loci celebrationis.*

In determining the essential validity of marriage, the law of the intended matrimonial home, as opposed to the law of the domicile of the parties, is to be preferred.[16]

Nigeria

A marriage is void if it is not a valid marriage under the law of the place where it took place, by reason of a failure to comply with the requirements of the law of that place with respect to the form of solemnisation of marriages.[17]

South Africa

The validity of marriage is tested by the *lex loci celebrationis.*[18] This rule applies to same-sex relationships celebrated abroad.[19]

Tanzania

A marriage contracted outside Tanzania is recognised as valid if: it was contracted in a form required or permitted by the law of the country

[14] *Mohapi* v. *Motleleng* (1985–9) LAC 316. On the facts it appears the court was dealing with the formal validity of the marriage.

[15] *Liaquat Anwary* v. *Geeti Ayub Saifee,* CIV/APN/172/90 (High Court, Lesotho, 1990).

[16] *Mndolo* v. *Mndolo* [1978–80] 9 MLR 101.

[17] Matrimonial Causes Act 1990, s. 3(1)(c).

[18] Forsyth, p. 280. *Pretorius* v. *Pretorius* 1948 (4) SA 144; *Santos* v. *Santos* 1987 (4) SA 150; *Chitima* v. *RAF* [2012] 2 All SA 632. This position is, however, not free from doubt since there are cases which appear to suggest that the essential validity of marriage is regulated by domicile. *Ex p. Cathrall* 1965 (2) SA 505 (decided under a repealed legislation). See generally: *Guggenheim* v. *Rosenbaum (2)* 1961 (4) SA 21, which held that the proper law of contract governs an action for breach of promise to marry.

[19] *AC* v. *CS* 2011 2 SA 360.

where it was contracted; each of the parties had, at the time of the marriage, capacity to marry under the law of the country of his or her domicile;[20] and both parties freely and voluntarily consented to the marriage or, where either party did not freely and voluntarily consent to the marriage, the parties have freely and voluntarily consummated the marriage.[21] Parental consent to marry is considered a question of form and is governed by the *lex loci celebrationis*.[22]

Zimbabwe

The form and ceremonies of entering into a contract of marriage are regulated by the *lex loci contractus* and the essentials of the marriage contract are regulated by the *lex domicilii*.[23] A marriage valid according to the *lex loci celebrationis* would be recognised as valid in Zimbabwe without a further requirement that it should be in compliance with Zimbabwean law.[24] However, such a marriage should not be contrary to Zimbabwean public policy, repugnant to moral principles within Zimbabwe, or lead to the laws and institutions of Zimbabwe being undermined.[25]

Comments

Most of the countries under study draw a distinction between the essential and formal validity of marriage. The main exception appears to be South Africa, where it has been suggested that the sole test for validity is the law of the place of celebration.[26] It appears well established that the formal validity of marriage is governed by the law of the place of celebration. It has been held in Kenya and Tanzania that consent to marriage is a question of form. It can also be inferred from the cases that

[20] Where either of the parties is a Tanzanian, or is domiciled in Tanzania, both parties should have capacity under Tanzanian law.

[21] Law of Marriage Act 1971, s. 36. Section 37 contains similar requirements for marriages contracted in foreign embassies.

[22] *Hasumati Chhaganlal* v. *Gulamali* [1983] TLR 320.

[23] *Mandimika* v. *Mandimika* 1997 (2) ZLR 352 at 355. But see *Chikosi* v. *Chikosi* 1975 (2) SA 644, where it was held that capacity to contract a valid and effective marriage is ascertained by reference to the *lex loci celebrationis*.

[24] *Bennett* v. *Master of the High Court* 1986 (1) ZLR 127.

[25] *Kassim* v. *Ghumran* 1981 ZLR 227, 1981 (4) SA 79; *Noratam* v. *Noratam* 1970 (1) RLR 84.

[26] There are *dicta* in the Zimbabwean case of *Kassim* v. *Ghumran* 1981 ZLR 227, 1981 (4) SA 79 supporting this position.

issues such as who has authority to celebrate a marriage, where it should be celebrated and how, would be characterised as questions of form.

The law that determines essential validity varies in the countries under study. The domicile of *both* parties, the matrimonial domicile, and the intended matrimonial domicile have been held as potential candidates for the law governing the essential validity of marriage.[27] There is authority in Ghana which suggests that public policy may be invoked to overcome the injustice that may be occasioned by the application of the dual domicile test as the law governing essential validity.

The distinction between formal and essential validity of marriage is sometimes difficult to draw. In South Africa, where the distinction is not drawn, it has been argued that not doing so tends to cut down on the number of limping marriages, with their attendant hardships and social undesirability. A rule that validity of marriage is governed by the *lex loci celebrationis* is also simple, clear and easy to apply – the *loci celebrationis* can be easily ascertained.[28] There is a lot to be said for adopting a simple rule that the validity of a marriage should be governed solely by the law of the place of celebration.[29] Such a rule can be subjected to a subsidiary rule that, in appropriate cases (such as where there has been a conscious effort by the parties to celebrate the marriage abroad to evade an essential requirement of the law of their domicile) public policy may be invoked to deny recognition to marriages validly celebrated abroad.[30]

Marriage and property rights of spouses

Botswana

In the absence of a special contract, the proprietary rights of spouses are governed by the law of the husband's domicile at the time of the marriage.[31] There is a presumption that community of property, community of profit and loss, and the marital power or any liabilities or privileges resulting from marriage shall not be attached to a marriage

[27] For an assessment of the merits and demerits of these approaches to essential validity, see *Cheshire, North & Fawcett*, pp. 896–9.

[28] Forsyth, p. 281.

[29] Indeed, this appears to have been the common law rule prior to 1861 when the distinction between formal and essential validity was introduced by the House of Lords in *Brook* v. *Brook* (1861) 9 HL Cas. 193.

[30] *Kassim* v. *Ghumran* 1981 ZLR 227, 1981 (4) SA 79.

[31] *Thebe* v. *Kemodisa* 2001 (2) BLR 263. See also *Mtui* v. *Mtui* 2001 (2) BLR 333; *Ljubica* v. *Dizdarevic*, MAHLB-000650-07 (High Court, Botswana, 2008).

solemnised between spouses whose matrimonial domicile is in Botswana, unless such spouses execute an instrument in writing to the contrary.[32]

Lesotho

The law governing the proprietary consequences of marriage is the law of the husband's domicile at the time of marriage.[33]

Malawi

Where Malawians marry abroad and purport to submit themselves to the matrimonial property regime of the country where the marriage was celebrated, and if they subsequently divorce in Malawi, evidence must be given of the law governing that property regime before it can control the division of their property. If no such evidence is presented, the court will apply Malawi law as the *lex fori*.[34]

South Africa

In the absence of an antenuptial contract,[35] the proprietary rights of spouses are governed by the law of the country where the husband was domiciled at the time of the marriage – the law of the country of any intended matrimonial home is irrelevant.[36] It remains to be decided whether and how this rule would apply to same-sex relationships celebrated abroad.[37] A subsequent change in the husband's domicile (even to a South African domicile) does not affect the law governing the proprietary consequences of the marriage.[38] Similarly, neither the Matrimonial Property Act 1984, nor the Marriage and Matrimonial Property Law Amendment 1988, were intended to displace the established principle that the *lex domicilii matrimonii* at the time of marriage

[32] Married Persons Property Act 1970, s. 1.

[33] *Mohapi* v. *Motleleng* (1985–9) LAC 316; *Lepelesana* v. *Lepelesana* [1977] LLR 190.

[34] *Maseko* v. *Maseko* [1973–4] 7 MLR 310. See also *Gouveia* v. *Gouveia* [1923–60] ALR Mal. 239.

[35] On what constitutes an antenuptial contract and the law governing it, see *Lagesse* v. *Lagesse* 1992 (1) SA 173; *Ex p. Spinazze* 1983 (4) SA 751; *Ex p. Spinazze* 1985 (3) SA 650.

[36] *Sperling* v. *Sperling* 1975 (3) SA 707; *Frankel's Estate* v. *The Master* 1950 (1) SA 220; *Estate of Frankel* v. *The Master* 1949 (2) SA 287; *Bell* v. *Bell* 1991 (4) SA 195; *Pitluk* v. *Gavendo* 1955 (2) SA 573; *Ex p. Wolfenden et Uxor* 1959 (2) SA 53.

[37] *AC* v. *CS* 2011 2 SA 360.

[38] *Anderson* v. *The Master* 1949 (4) SA 660; *Bell* v. *Bell* 1991 (4) SA 195.

determined its proprietary consequences.[39] When the South African rule of private international law prescribes that the proprietary consequences of a foreign marriage must be determined in accordance with the law of the matrimonial domicile, that reference should generally be to the entire law of the *lex causae*, including its transitional law.[40]

Uganda

If a person whose domicile is not in Uganda marries a person in Uganda whose domicile is in Uganda, neither party acquires by the marriage any rights in respect of property belonging to the other party that is not comprised in a settlement made previous to the marriage, and which he or she would not acquire by the marriage if both were domiciled in Uganda at the time of the marriage.[41]

Zimbabwe

The proprietary consequences of a marriage are governed by the law of the husband's domicile at the time of the marriage.[42] Subsequent conversion of the marriage from a polygamous to a monogamous one – even when performed abroad – does not change the applicability of this principle. Thus, where parties domiciled and married under customary law in Zimbabwe converted their marriage into a monogamous one in Nashville, United States, it was held that the position with regard to their proprietary rights once fixed by the valid customary marriage remained, by virtue of the domiciliary law of the husband, to govern their proprietary relationship, and the second marriage could not alter that.[43]

Comments

The laws in Botswana, Lesotho, South Africa and Zimbabwe appear unanimous that the proprietary consequences of marriage are governed

[39] *Esterhuizen* v. *Esterhuizen* 1999 (1) SA 492. [40] *Sperling* v. *Sperling* 1975 (3) SA 707.

[41] Succession Act 1906, s. 34. Under s. 3 of the Act, no person shall, by marriage, acquire any interest in the property of the person whom he or she marries, nor become incapable of performing any act in respect of his or her own property which he or she could have done if unmarried.

[42] *Lafontant* v. *Kennedy* 2000 (2) ZLR 280; *G* v. *G* 2003 (5) SA 396, 2002 (2) ZLR 408; *Beckford* v. *Beckford*, HC 3480/2003 (High Court, Zimbabwe, 2006).

[43] *Chikosi* v. *Chikosi* 1975 (2) SA 644.

by the law of the husband's domicile at the time of marriage.[44] South African and Zimbabwean jurisprudence firmly establish that neither a subsequent change in the husband's domicile, nor the conversion of the marriage, affects the law governing the proprietary consequences of the marriage, which is fixed at the time of marriage. Put differently, the principle of immutability is well entrenched in South African and Zimbabwean law as far as the law governing the proprietary consequences of marriage is concerned. Indeed, this position is likely to be accepted in Lesotho, Swaziland and Namibia, which closely follow South African law.

In the light of human rights imperatives and the fact that, at present, the law in some of the countries under study allows a married woman to maintain an independent domicile, it is open to question whether the principle that the proprietary consequences of marriage are governed by the law of the husband's domicile at the time of marriage is still valid. The rule has been criticised for its rigidity[45] and its validity questioned in a 'gender equal society'.[46] It is also incapable of application in cases of same-sex marriages. A potential alternative to the husband's domicile is the law of the intended matrimonial home, but the application of this could also lead to uncertainty.

The position is less clear in the common law countries, although it is likely they will adopt the domicile of the husband for determining the proprietary consequence of marriage.[47]

[44] Proprietary consequences of marriage deal with issues such as whether the marriage is one in or out of community and maintenance (*Hassan* v. *Hassan* 1998 (2) SA 589). On whether the right to donate property to the other spouse or for the prohibition of such donation is a proprietary right, see *Powell* v. *Powell* 1953 (4) SA 380. Depending on whether one accepts the characterisation, an important proprietary consequence of marriage in some of the countries under study is the rule which allows marriage to revoke the pre-marital wills of the spouses. See, e.g., Gambia – Wills Act 1992, s. 8(1)(a); Kenya – Law of Succession Act 1981, s. 19; Malawi – Deceased Estates (Wills, Inheritance and Protection) Act 2011, s. 10(1); Zimbabwe – Wills Act 1987, s. 16. Kenya is currently debating the Matrimonial Property Bill 2011. The bill contains no direct private international law-related provisions.

[45] Forsyth, pp. 295–302.

[46] *Sadiku* v. *Sadiku*, Case No. 30498/06 (High Court, South Africa, 2007).

[47] This approach was implicit in the Tanzanian case of *Juma* v. *Mlinga*, Civil Appeal No. 10 of 2001 (Court of Appeal, Tanzania, 2002).

12

Matrimonial causes

It is often said that everything that has a beginning has an end, or, certainly, associated problems on its path. The institution of marriage fares no better when it comes to this. Regardless of whether one is dealing with a petition for the divorce, nullity of marriage, judicial separation, presumption of death and dissolution of marriage difficulty questions of jurisdiction, choice of law, and recognition and enforcement of foreign decrees may arise. This chapter addresses these questions.

Jurisdiction in matrimonial causes

Botswana

A Botswanan court has jurisdiction to try an action instituted by one spouse against the other for divorce or judicial separation if, at the date of instituting the proceedings, either spouse is domiciled in Botswana[1] or, in the case of an action brought by a wife, the wife has been resident within Botswana for a continuous period of three years immediately preceding the date of instituting the proceedings.[2]

[1] Matrimonial Causes Act 1973, s. 7(1)(a). It has been held that this provision does not change the common law rule that a wife acquires the husband's domicile on marriage. *Nku* v. *Nku* 1998 BLR 187; *Egner* v. *Egner* 1974 (2) BLR 5. On domicile as a basis of jurisdiction, see generally: *Dance* v. *Dance (2)* 1976 BLR 43; *Dance* v. *Dance* 1975 (2) BLR 39; *Scarr* v. *Scarr* 1971 (2) BLR 44; *Jeffreys* v. *Jeffreys* 1973 (1) BLR 42; *Sergeant* v. *Sergeant* 1983 BLR 61; *Naude* v. *Naude* 2002 (1) BLR 30; *Ucanda* v. *Ucanda* 1989 BLR 21; *Kenyon* v. *Kenyon* 1974 (1) BLR 2.

[2] Matrimonial Causes Act 1973, s. 7(1)(b). Under s. 9 of the Act, a court with such jurisdiction shall have jurisdiction to hear an application by a wife for an order for maintenance *pendente lite*. Under s. 10, a court with jurisdiction to try an action for judicial separation shall also have jurisdiction to set aside an order of judicial separation insofar as it may be necessary to set aside such an order before a fresh action may be instituted or a divorce granted.

The High Court of Botswana has jurisdiction in proceedings for presumption of death and dissolution of marriage and for nullity, if the plaintiff was domiciled in Botswana at the date of the action or, in the case of an action brought by a wife, the wife was resident in Botswana at the date of the action and has been ordinarily resident in Botswana for the period of three years immediately preceding the date of the petition.[3]

Gambia

In cases of monogamous marriages,[4] a Gambian court has jurisdiction in a matrimonial cause where either party to the marriage is a citizen of Gambia, has been ordinarily resident in Gambia for at least three years immediately preceding commencement of the proceedings or is domiciled in Gambia.[5] Thus, in *Siwingwa* v. *Siwingwa*,[6] where it was found that the petitioner was domiciled in Tanzania, it was held that the court had no jurisdiction. For the sole purpose of determining jurisdiction in a matrimonial cause, the domicile of a married woman is determined as if the woman was above 21 years of age and not married.[7]

Ghana

A Ghanaian court has jurisdiction in a matrimonial cause where either party to the marriage is a citizen of Ghana, domiciled in Ghana, or has been ordinarily resident in Ghana for at least three years immediately preceding the commencement of the proceedings.[8] A court with such jurisdiction also has jurisdiction, where a party who may be ordered to make financial provision has assets in Ghana, to order that party to make financial provision not exceeding the value of those assets[9] or, to make child custody arrangements, whenever the child whose custody is in question is present in Ghana.[10] For the sole purpose of determining jurisdiction in a matrimonial cause, the domicile of a married woman shall be determined as if the woman was above 21 years of age and not married.[11]

[3] Matrimonial Causes Act 1973, s. 8.
[4] See Muslim Marriage and Divorce Act 1941.
[5] Matrimonial Causes Act 1986, s. 34.
[6] [1994] GR 276.
[7] Matrimonial Causes Act 1986, s. 35.
[8] Matrimonial Causes Act 1971, s. 31. *Abu-Jaudeh* v. *Abu-Jaudeh* [1972] 2 GLR 444; *Amponsah* v. *Amponsah* [1997–8] 1 GLR 43; *Simpson* v. *Simpson* [1960] GLR 105.
[9] Matrimonial Causes Act 1971, s. 33.
[10] Ibid., s. 34.
[11] Ibid., s. 32.

Kenya

Under the Matrimonial Causes Act 1941, subject to defined limitations, jurisdiction under the Act is to be exercised in accordance with the law applied in matrimonial proceedings in the High Court of Justice in England.[12] Notwithstanding this general provision, a court does not have jurisdiction to make a decree of dissolution of marriage or of nullity of marriage unless the petitioner is domiciled in Kenya at the time when the petition is presented.[13] Nor does it have jurisdiction to grant any other relief unless one of the parties to the suit has, at the time when the petition was presented, his or her usual residence in Kenya, or unless the marriage was solemnised in Kenya.[14]

Even where the husband is not domiciled in Kenya, the court shall have jurisdiction in proceedings by a wife for divorce, if she is resident in Kenya and has been ordinarily resident there for a period of three years immediately preceding the commencement of the proceedings.[15] In proceedings for a decree of presumption of death and dissolution of marriage, the court shall have jurisdiction if the petitioner is domiciled in Kenya or, in proceedings by the wife, if she is resident in Kenya and has been ordinarily resident there for a period of three years immediately preceding the commencement of the proceedings.[16]

Lesotho

The Lesotho High Court has jurisdiction to hear an action instituted by a wife against her husband for divorce, restitution of conjugal rights or judicial separation, if the wife has been ordinarily resident in Lesotho for

[12] Matrimonial Causes Act 1941, s. 3. This Act is currently being considered for amendment. See Marriage Bill 2007.

[13] Matrimonial Causes Act 1941, s. 4(a); *Schiratti* v. *Schiratti* [1976–80] 1 KLR 870; *Mageean* v. *Mageean* [1919] 8 EAP LR 154; *K* v. *K* [1917–18] 7 EAP LR 9; *Gulam Fatuma* v. *Gulam Mahomed* [1917–18] KLR 30.

[14] Matrimonial Causes Act 1941, s. 4(b). Where a wife has been deserted by her husband, or where her husband has been deported from Kenya, and the husband was immediately before the desertion or deportation domiciled in Kenya, the court shall have jurisdiction for the purpose of any proceedings under the Act, notwithstanding that the husband has changed his domicile since the desertion or deportation.

[15] Matrimonial Causes Act 1941, s. 5(1); *Ender* v. *Ender* [2008] 2 EA 105. This applies equally to proceedings for nullity of marriage. *Krishna Pyari* v. *Surjit Singh* [1964] EA 278.

[16] Matrimonial Causes Act 1941, s. 5(3). In determining whether a woman is domiciled in Kenya, her husband shall be treated as having died immediately after the last occasion on which she knew or had reason to believe him to be living.

a period of one year immediately preceding the date on which the proceedings were instituted.[17] This applies only if the husband has deserted the wife and has departed Lesotho or has been deported, and was, immediately prior to the desertion or deportation, domiciled in Lesotho, or, in an action for judicial separation, the husband was resident in Lesotho at the date of the proceedings.[18] The High Court also has jurisdiction to entertain an action instituted by a wife against her husband (who is not domiciled in Lesotho) for divorce or restitution of conjugal rights if, immediately prior to the marriage, the wife was domiciled in Lesotho, and she was ordinarily resident in Lesotho for one year immediately preceding the date when proceedings were instituted.[19]

Malawi

A Malawian court does not have jurisdiction to grant a decree of dissolution of marriage unless the petitioner is domiciled in Malawi at the time the petition is presented.[20] However, in proceedings for dissolution of marriage or judicial separation, where a wife has been deserted by the husband or the husband has been deported from Malawi, and the husband immediately before the desertion or deportation was domiciled in Malawi, the court has jurisdiction to grant a decree of divorce or judicial separation, notwithstanding that the husband has changed his domicile since the desertion or deportation.[21]

A Malawian court does not have jurisdiction to grant a decree of nullity of marriage unless the petitioner is domiciled in Malawi at the time the petition was presented or when the marriage was solemnised in Malawi.[22]

In general, the jurisdiction of the court under the Divorce Act is to be exercised in accordance with the law applied to matrimonial proceedings

[17] Matrimonial Cause Jurisdiction Act 1978, s. 2(1)(a); *Lotan* v. *Lotan* (1980–4) LAC 118.

[18] Matrimonial Cause Jurisdiction Act 1978, s. 2(1)(a)(i)(ii).

[19] Ibid., s. 2(1)(b); *Greenock* v. *Greenock*, CIV/APN/26/1985 (High Court, Lesotho, 1985); *Binns* v. *Binns* (1980–4) LAC 14, 1980 (1) LLR 18.

[20] Divorce Act 1905, s. 2(a). *Brown* v. *Brown*, Matrimonial Cause No. 9 of 2002 (High Court, Malawi, 2002); *Msindo* v. *Msindo*, Civil Cause No. 67 of 2006 (High Court, Malawi, 2006) (the court may *suo muto* raise the issue of domicile even where the parties fail to do so); *Kaunda* v. *Kaunda* [1993] 16(2) MLR 545; *Dorrington* v. *Dorrington* [1993] 16(1) MLR 73; *Whitelock* v. *Whitelock* [1978–80] 9 MLR 43; *Bond* v. *Bond* [1984–6] 11 MLR 87.

[21] Divorce Act 1905, s. 2(a).

[22] Ibid., s. 2(b).

in the High Court of Justice in England.[23] It has been held that this provision relates to the procedural aspects of English law and not the substantive law of divorce.[24] Once jurisdiction is established, the character of the foreign marriage does not matter. Accordingly, a Malawian court has jurisdiction to dissolve a marriage celebrated under the customary law of a foreign country.[25]

Namibia

A Namibian court has jurisdiction in a divorce action if the parties are, or either of the parties is, domiciled in the area of the court's jurisdiction on the date when the action is instituted,[26] or ordinarily resident in the court's area of jurisdiction on the said date, and have been ordinarily resident in Namibia for a period of not less than one year[27] immediately prior to that date.[28] This jurisdiction does not derogate from the jurisdiction which a court has in terms of any other law, including common law.[29]

Nigeria

Proceedings for a decree of dissolution of marriage, nullity, judicial separation, restitution of conjugal rights, and jactitation of marriage may only be instituted by a person domiciled in Nigeria.[30] A person domiciled in any state of the Nigerian Federation is domiciled in Nigeria and may institute matrimonial proceedings in the High Court of any state whether or not he is domiciled in that particular state.[31] For the purposes of the Matrimonial Causes Act, a deserted wife who is domiciled in Nigeria either immediately before her marriage, or immediately before the desertion, shall be deemed to be domiciled in Nigeria. In addition, a wife who is resident in Nigeria at the date of instituting proceedings under the Act and has been so resident for

[23] Ibid., s. 4. [24] *Chidzero* v. *Chidzero* [1978–80] 9 MLR 22.
[25] *Kalilombe* v. *Kalilombe* [1987–9] 12 MLR 170. [26] *Sauber* v. *Sauber* 1949 (2) SA 769.
[27] *Roeder* v. *Roeder* 1947 (2) SA 651. [28] Matrimonial Causes Jurisdiction Act 1939, s. 1.
[29] Ibid, s. 1(4).
[30] Matrimonial Causes Act 1990, s. 2(2). *Odiase* v. *Odiase* [1965] 2 All NLR 91; *Adeoye* v. *Adeoye* (1961) All NLR 821; *Jones* v. *Jones* [1938] 14 NLR 12; *Shyngle* v. *Shyngle* [1923] NLR 94; *Bhojwani* v. *Bhojwani* [1995] 7 NWLR 349; *Bhojwani* v. *Bhojwani* [1996] 6 NWLR 661; *Osibamowo* v. *Osibamowo* [1991] 3 NWLR 85; *Omotunde* v. *Omotunde* [2001] 9 NWLR 252; *Koku* v. *Koku* [1999] 8 NWLR 672.
[31] Matrimonial Causes Act 1990, s. 2(3); *Odiase* v. *Odiase* [1965] 2 All NLR 91.

a period of three years immediately preceding that date shall be deemed to be domiciled in Nigeria on that date.[32]

Sierra Leone

Notwithstanding the fact that the husband is not domiciled in Sierra Leone, a Sierra Leonean court has jurisdiction in proceedings by a wife for divorce or nullity of marriage if the wife is resident in Sierra Leone and has been ordinarily resident there for a period of three years immediately preceding the commencement of the proceedings.[33] In proceedings for a decree of presumption of death and dissolution of marriage, the court has jurisdiction if the petitioner is domiciled in Sierra Leone or, in proceedings by the wife, if she is resident in Sierra Leone and has been ordinarily resident for a period of three years immediately preceding the commencement of the proceedings.[34]

South Africa

A South African court has jurisdiction in a divorce action if either or both of the parties are domiciled in the area of jurisdiction of the court on the date when the action is instituted, or ordinarily resident in the court's area of jurisdiction on the said date[35] and have been ordinarily resident in South Africa for a period of not less than one year immediately prior to that date.[36] This jurisdiction does not derogate from the jurisdiction which a court has in terms of any other law, including common law.[37] Domicile provides a basis jurisdiction in this regard.[38] An agreement to

[32] Matrimonial Causes Act 1990, s. 7; *Mason* v. *Mason* [1979] 1 FNLR 148.

[33] Matrimonial Causes Act 1950, s. 30(1)(2). A change in the domicile of a husband following his desertion or deportation will not affect the jurisdiction of a court to hear a matrimonial cause instituted by the wife. See *Asiegbu* v. *Asiegbu* [1972–3] ALR SL 270, which held that a court may grant a decree of divorce on the cross-petition of a husband who is not domiciled in Sierra Leone, in proceedings brought by his wife over which the court has jurisdiction by virtue of the wife's ordinary residence in Sierra Leone.

[34] Matrimonial Causes Act 1950, s. 30(3). In determining whether a woman is domiciled in Sierra Leone, her husband shall be treated as having died immediately after the last occasion on which she knew or had reason to believe him to be living.

[35] *Eilon* v. *Eilon* 1965 (1) SA 703; *Massey* v. *Massey* 1968 (2) SA 199; *Hoosein* v. *Dangor* [2010] 2 All SA 55.

[36] Divorce Act 1979, s. 2(1). [37] Ibid., s. 2(4).

[38] *Ex p. Oxton* 1948 (1) SA 1011; *Locke* v. *Locke* 1950 (4) SA 240; *Locke* v. *Locke* 1951 (1) SA 132; *Sowry* v. *Sowry* 1953 (4) SA 629; *Holland* v. *Holland* 1973 (1) SA 897; *Rousalis* v.

waive the right to institute proceedings which could have been founded on the above basis of jurisdiction may not be enforced and may be regarded as contrary to public policy.[39]

Swaziland

In matrimonial causes, domicile provides a basis of jurisdiction for the Swaziland courts.[40] Although a wife acquires the domicile of the husband on marriage, where the full implication of adherence to this principle would lead to injustice, the court may be prepared to depart from it. Thus, in a case where a Swazi-domiciled woman married a South African domiciled man and their marriage was void under South African law, it being in violation of that country's Prohibition of Mixed Marriages Act 1949, the court was prepared to assume jurisdiction in an action for the restitution of conjugal rights.[41]

Tanzania

A person may petition the court for a declaratory decree[42] if that person is domiciled or resident in Tanzania, or where the decree sought relates to the validity of a ceremony which took place in Tanzania and purported to be a marriage.[43] A person may petition the court for a decree of separation if that person has been resident in Tanzania for at least one year immediately preceding the commencement of the proceedings and is present in Tanzania at the time of presenting the petition.[44] A person may petition the court for a decree of annulment or a decree of divorce if that person is domiciled in Tanzania,[45] or has been resident in Tanganyika[46] for at least one year immediately preceding the presentation of the petition.[47] Any person may apply to the court for maintenance, for

Rousalis 1980 (3) SA 446; *Ex p. Cathrall* 1965 (2) SA 505. The onus is on the plaintiff to establish jurisdiction. *Danks* v. *Danks* 1948 (4) SA 492.

[39] *Granoth* v. *Granoth* 1983 (4) SA 50. [40] *Bigalke* v. *Bigalke* [1970–6] Sw. LR 48.

[41] *Winters v. Winters* [1970–6] Sw. LR 49.

[42] Law of Marriage Act 1971, s. 91. Such a decree can relate to matters such as validity of marriage, nullity, legitimacy and the presumption of death of a spouse.

[43] Ibid., s. 77(1). [44] Ibid., s. 77(2).

[45] *Abdalla Hamid Mohamed* v. *Jasnena Zaludova* [1983] TLR 314; *Everard* v. *Everard* [1953–7] 2 TLR 375.

[46] *Partington* v. *Partington* [1962] EA 582; *Partington* v. *Partington* [1963] EA 77.

[47] Law of Marriage Act 1971, s. 77(3).

custody of infant children, or for any other matrimonial relief if that person is domiciled or resident in Tanzania, or both parties to the marriage are present in Tanzania at the time of the application.

Uganda

A Ugandan court does not have jurisdiction to grant a decree of dissolution or nullity of marriage unless the petitioner is domiciled in Uganda at the time when the petition is presented.[48] A decree of nullity may be granted where the marriage was solemnised in Uganda.[49] The jurisdiction of the court is to be exercised in accordance with the law applied to matrimonial proceedings in the High Court of Justice of England.[50]

Zambia

The Zambian High Court has jurisdiction in proceedings for divorce or for a decree of nullity of marriage if either party to the marriage is domiciled in Zambia[51] at the date of the commencement of the proceedings, or is resident in Zambia at the date of the commencement of the proceedings, and has been ordinarily so resident for a period of not less than twelve months immediately preceding that date.[52] A court has no jurisdiction to grant a decree of divorce when one of the parties to the marriage is dead.[53]

Zimbabwe

In cases where the wife is the plaintiff or applicant, the Zimbabwean High Court has jurisdiction to entertain an action for divorce, judicial separation or nullity of marriage: if the wife has been deserted by her husband and, immediately before the desertion, the husband was domiciled in Zimbabwe, notwithstanding that the husband has changed his domicile since the desertion; or if the marriage was celebrated in Zimbabwe and the wife has resided in Zimbabwe for a period of at least

[48] Divorce Act 1904, s. 1(a); *Joy Kiggundu* v. *Horace Awori* [2001] Kam. LR 374; *Satvinder Singh* v. *Saridner Kaur* [2002] Kam. LR 616; *Nawangwe Marina* v. *Nawangwe Barnabas* [2004] Kam. LR 495.

[49] Divorce Act 1904, s. 1(b). [50] Ibid., s. 3(3).

[51] *Tully* v. *Tully* (1965) ZR 165; *Dingle* v. *Dingle* [1949–54] NRLR 783.

[52] Matrimonial Causes Act 2007, s. 4(3).

[53] *Gumbo* v. *Land and Agricultural Bank of Zambia* (1968) ZR 50.

two years immediately before the date of commencement of the action and is still so residing, notwithstanding that the husband has never been domiciled in Zimbabwe, or if at the date of commencement of the action, the wife is a citizen of Zimbabwe and, immediately before that date, she has been ordinarily resident in Zimbabwe for a period of not less than two years and is still so residing.[54] This jurisdiction is without prejudice to any other basis of jurisdiction which the court has. Thus, it has been held that the jurisdiction of the court in matters of divorce depends on the domicile of the husband at the time the action is instituted.[55]

Comments

In the countries under study, the issue of jurisdiction in matrimonial causes is regulated mainly by statute.[56] Domicile is a basis of jurisdiction in all the countries under study. Nigeria stands out in its insistence on domicile as the sole basis of jurisdiction. However, it mitigates the hardship that could potentially result from this by *deeming* the pre-marital Nigerian domicile of a deserted wife or her residence for three years before presenting a petition as domicile. The other countries under study provide additional bases of jurisdiction or depart from the common law rules on determining the domicile of a wife in order to overcome the potential injustice that may be occasioned by having a wife's domicile tied to her husband's. For example, in Gambia and Ghana, for the sole purpose of jurisdiction in a matrimonial cause, the domicile of a wife is to be determined as if she were above 21 years of age and not married. In Kenya, the fact that the husband has changed his domicile since desertion or deportation does not affect the wife's domicile, and in Lesotho, a wife's Lesotho domicile prior to marriage provides a basis of jurisdiction.

[54] Matrimonial Causes Act 1986, s. 3(1)(a)(b)(c). *Braimah* v. *Braimah* 1996 (1) ZLR 571; *Mandlbaur* v. *Mandlbaur* 1983 (1) ZLR 26, 1983 (2) SA 213; *Kennedy* v. *Kennedy* 1978 (2) SA 698. See generally *Ex p. Pyke* 1948 (1) SA 526.

[55] *De Jager* v. *De Jager* 1998 (2) ZLR 419; *Boswinkel* v. *Boswinkel* 1995 (2) ZLR 58; *Latif* v. *Latif* 2004 (2) ZLR 102; *Latif* v. *Latif* 2002 (2) ZLR 466; *Juliet Chikwenengere* v. *George Chikwenengere*, HH 103–2005/HC 747/05 (High Court, Zimbabwe, 2005); *Howard* v. *Howard* [1966] RLR 182, 1966 (2) SA 718; *Nunes* v. *Nunes* 2003 (1) ZLR 14.

[56] As is the case in many aspects of the conflict of laws in the countries under study, the law on jurisdiction in matrimonial causes is heavily influenced by English law. Indeed, in Kenya, Malawi and Uganda, it is statutorily provided that the courts' jurisdiction is to be exercised in accordance with the law applied in matrimonial proceedings in the High Court of Justice of England.

Residence provides a basis of jurisdiction in many of the countries under study. While some jurisdictions such as Botswana and Lesotho allow this only for the wife, in others such as Gambia, Ghana, Namibia, Tanzania and Zambia, the residence of either party suffices. The duration of residence varies from one year (as in Lesotho and Namibia) to three years.

In addition to residence and domicile, nationality provides a basis of jurisdiction in Gambia, Ghana and Zimbabwe. Moreover, in Kenya and Tanzania, the fact that a marriage was solemnised in that country is a basis of jurisdiction.

The jurisdiction of the courts in matrimonial causes extends in most of the countries under study to both monogamous and polygamous marriages, and in South Africa, to civil unions. Historically – and that is still the case in Botswana[57] – some courts would decline jurisdiction in matrimonial causes founded on polygamous marriages.[58]

Choice of law in matrimonial causes

A matrimonial cause can give rise to choice of law issues, such as the grounds for divorce, maintenance and division of marital assets. The position taken in most of the countries under study is that such issues shall be determined in accordance with the law, which would be applicable thereto if both parties were domiciled in the forum at the time of the proceedings.[59] Applying the *lex fori* to all choice of law issues arising

[57] Matrimonial Causes Act 1973, s. 4, which provides that nothing in this Act shall authorise any court to pronounce a decree of divorce, nullity, judicial separation or presumption of death and dissolution of marriage, or to make any other order than an order dismissing an action unless the marriage to, or in respect of, which the decree or order relates, is a monogamous marriage.

[58] *Anyaegbunam* v. *Anyaegbunam* [1973] All NLR (Part I) 385; *Fatuma Binti Athuma* v. *Ali Baka* [1917–18] KLR 171; *Gulam Mahomed* v. *Gulam Fatima* [1917–18] KLR 102; *Sithole* v. *Sithole* (1969) ZR 92; *Mwiba* v. *Mwiba* (1980) ZR 175. Polygamous marriages were, however, recognised in respect of issues outside jurisdiction, such as succession and maintenance. *Kader* v. *Kader* 1972 (3) SA 203; *Estate of Mehta* v. *The Master of the High Court* 1958 R & N 570; *Coleman* v. *Shang* [1959] GLR 390. Parties can also convert a polygamous marriage into a monogamous one: *Chikosi* v. *Chikosi* 1975 (2) SA 644. On the other hand, an attempt to superimpose a monogamous marriage on a polygamous one has been held to be a nullity: *Oshodi* v. *Oshodi* [1963] 2 All NLR 214.

[59] Gambia – Matrimonial Causes Act 1986, s. 38; Ghana – Matrimonial Causes Act 1971, s. 35 (excludes in proceedings for a decree of nullity of a void marriage); Kenya – Matrimonial Causes Act 1941, s. 5(4); Lesotho – Matrimonial Cause Jurisdiction Act 1978, s. 2(2); Namibia – Matrimonial Causes Jurisdiction Act 1939, s. 1 (3); Sierra

in a matrimonial cause, aside from proceedings for nullity of void marriages, may be pragmatic: it is easier, less costly and less time-consuming to apply the *lex fori*. Indeed, the pro-*lex fori* rule may reflect the overwhelming importance attached by countries to their matrimonial laws – they treat them as mandatory rules that must be applied regardless of domicile. Historically, the existence of this rule posed little or no practical difficulty since the sole basis of jurisdiction in matrimonial cases was domicile.

As noted above, there has been a gradual expansion of the bases of jurisdiction. Furthermore, many issues can arise in matrimonial proceedings. It is open to question whether it will always be appropriate to determine all such issues as if the parties were domiciled in the forum. It is arguably inappropriate to allow parties to invoke the jurisdiction of the courts on residence or ordinary residence and then get a decree of divorce on grounds that would not have been available to the parties under the law of their real domicile.[60] Indeed, differences in national laws on issues such as financial relief and the division of matrimonial property may also encourage forum shopping.

Recognition of foreign decrees

Botswana

Decrees granted by the courts of the domicile of the parties at the time of their marriage may be recognised.[61] Similarly, where the foreign court exercised jurisdiction on a basis on which, given a similar circumstance,

Leone – Matrimonial Causes Act 1950, s. 30(5); South Africa – Divorce Act 1979, s. 2(3); Zimbabwe – Matrimonial Causes Act 1985, s. 3(3). In the United Kingdom, where a similar rule existed under s. 46(1)(b) of the Matrimonial Causes Act 1973, it was subsequently repealed by the Domicile and Matrimonial Proceedings Act 1973. See generally *Mtui* v. *Mtui* 2001 (2) BLR 333 on choice of law in the division of matrimonial property.

60 See, e.g., *Weng* v. *Weng*, CIV/T/351/99 (High Court, Lesotho, 1999), where the court appears to have ignored s. 2(2) of the Matrimonial Cause Jurisdiction Act 1978, in holding that the law applicable to the issue of whether a claim for divorce should succeed is the law of the husband's domicile (in this instance, the law of Taiwan). See also *Holland* v. *Holland* 1973 (1) SA 897; *Bassi* v. *Bassi* 1958 (1) SA 637; *Yanni Krithary* v. *Dasta* [1900–31] 1 SLR 91.

61 *Mtui* v. *Mtui* 2000 (1) BLR 406, affirmed in *Mtui* v. *Mtui* 2001 (2) BLR 333. See also *Mthethwa* v. *Lebang* (Practice Note) 1990 BLR 615; E. K. Quansah, 'Recognition of Foreign Divorce Decrees in Botswana' (1991) 23 *Botswana Notes and Records* 107–13.

the Botswanan court would have assumed jurisdiction, the Botswanan court will recognise a decree granted by such foreign court.[62]

Gambia

The court shall recognise as valid a decree of divorce, nullity, presumption of death and dissolution of marriage which is not contrary to natural justice and which has been granted by a tribunal with significant and substantial connection with the parties to the marriage, or else which was in accordance with the law of the place where both parties to the marriage were ordinarily resident at the time of the action dissolving or annulling the marriage.[63] The decree may emanate from a judicial process or otherwise.

Ghana

The court shall recognise as valid a decree of divorce, nullity or presumption of death and dissolution of marriage, obtained by judicial process or otherwise, which is not contrary to natural justice, and which has been granted by any tribunal with a significant and substantial connection with the parties to the marriage, or which is in accordance with the law of the place where both parties to the marriage were ordinarily resident at the time of the dissolution or annulment of the marriage.[64] The court will also recognise the validity of a decree of judicial separation pronounced by the courts of the domicile of the parties and decline jurisdiction to entertain a fresh petition for the same relief.[65]

Nigeria

A dissolution or annulment of a marriage effected in accordance with the law of a foreign country shall be recognised as valid in Nigeria where, at the date of the institution of the proceedings that resulted in the dissolution or annulment, the party at whose instance they were effected (or, if they were effected at the instance of both parties, either of those parties) was, in the case of the dissolution of a marriage or the annulment of a voidable marriage, domiciled in that foreign country.

[62] *Makgekgnene* v. *Makgekgnene* [2007] BLR 621.
[63] Matrimonial Causes Act 1986, s. 39. [64] Matrimonial Causes Act 1971, s. 36.
[65] *Khoury* v. *Khoury* (1958) 3 WALR 52.

In the case of the annulment of a void marriage, however, the party or parties instituting proceedings must be domiciled or resident in that foreign country.[66] A dissolution or annulment of a marriage effected in accordance with the law of a foreign country, outside the scope of the preceding, shall be recognised as valid in Nigeria if its validity would have been recognised under the law of the foreign country where, in the case of a dissolution, the parties were domiciled at the date of the dissolution, or where in the case of an annulment, either party was domiciled at the date of the annulment.[67] Furthermore, any dissolution or annulment of a marriage that would be recognised as valid under the rules of private international law shall be recognised as valid in Nigeria.[68]

A dissolution or annulment of a marriage shall not be recognised where, under the rules of private international law, recognition of its validity would be refused on the grounds that a party to the marriage had been denied natural justice, or that the dissolution or annulment had been obtained by fraud.[69]

Kenya

A decree of judicial separation has effect only within the limits of the territorial jurisdiction of the court pronouncing it. Accordingly, it cannot be the basis of a plea of *res judicata*.[70] However, a decree of nullity of marriage pronounced by a court of the petitioners' domicile (and not necessarily the domicile of both parties or domicile of the husband) will be recognised in Kenya.[71]

Lesotho

A Lesotho court will recognise a decree of divorce granted by the court of the domicile of the parties at the time the petition was made.[72]

South Africa

A South African court shall recognise the validity of a divorce order, or an order for the annulment of a marriage or for judicial separation

[66] Matrimonial Causes Act 1990, s. 81(2). [67] Ibid., s. 81(4). [68] Ibid., s. 81(5).
[69] Ibid., s. 81(6). [70] *De Souza* v. *De Souza* [1936–7] 17 KLR 78.
[71] *In re. a Notice of Marriage given by Sansone Banin* [1960] EA 532.
[72] *Adam* v. *Adam*, CIV/APN/327/94 (High Court, Lesotho, 1994).

granted in a court of a foreign country or territory if, on the date the order was granted, either party to the marriage was domiciled in the country or territory concerned (whether according to South African law or according to the law of that country or territory),[73] was ordinarily resident in that country or territory, or was a national of that country or territory.[74]

Swaziland

A Swaziland court shall not recognise a decree of divorce granted by a foreign court in relation to parties who are domiciled in Swaziland. Thus, where a US court, acting on residence as the basis of its jurisdiction, granted a decree of divorce in relation to a Swaziland-domiciled couple, it was held that that decree cannot be recognised as *res judicata* in Swaziland.[75]

Tanzania

Where a court of competent jurisdiction in any foreign country has passed a decree in any matrimonial proceeding, whether arising out of a marriage contracted in Tanzania or elsewhere, such a decree shall be recognised as effective for all purposes of Tanzanian law if the petitioning party was domiciled in that country or had been resident there for at least two years prior to filing the petition; or being a decree of annulment or divorce, it has been recognised as effective in a declaratory decree of a court of competent jurisdiction in the country of domicile of either or both parties.[76]

Specifically in relation to extra-judicial divorces, it is provided that such a decree of divorce shall be recognised as effective for all purposes of Tanzanian law if it was effective according to the law of the country of domicile of each of the parties at the time of the divorce, or if it has been recognised as effective in a declaratory decree of a court of competent jurisdiction in the country of domicile of either or both parties.[77]

[73] *De Bono* v. *De Bono* 1948 (2) SA 802; *Pink* v. *Pink* 1957 (4) SA 41; *Ex p. Stern* 1976 (2) SA 273.

[74] Divorce Act 1979, s. 13. See generally *Guggenheim* v. *Rosenbaum (2)* 1961 (4) SA 21; *De Sa Pessoa* v. *De Sa Pessoa* 1967 (4) SA 629; *Phelan* v. *Phelan* 2007 (1) SA 483.

[75] *Mamba* v. *Mamba*, Case No. 1451/09 (High Court, Swaziland, 2011).

[76] Law of Marriage Act 1971, s. 91.

[77] Ibid., s. 92.

Zambia

A dissolution or annulment of marriage effected in accordance with the law of a foreign country shall be recognised as valid in Zambia where, at the date of the institution of the proceedings that result in the dissolution or annulment of marriage, the party at whose instance it was effected, or if it was effected at the instance of both parties, either of those parties, was in the case of the dissolution of a marriage or the annulment of a voidable marriage, domiciled in that foreign country. In the case of the annulment of a void marriage, the party or parties should have been domiciled or resident in that foreign country.[78]

A dissolution or annulment effected in accordance with the law of a foreign country shall be recognised as valid in Zambia if its validity would have been recognised under the law of the foreign country where, in the case of a dissolution, the parties were domiciled at the date of the dissolution, or where, in the case of an annulment, either party was domiciled at the date of annulment. Furthermore, a dissolution or annulment that would be recognised as valid under the common law rules of private international law, but to which none of the preceding applies, shall be recognised as valid in Zambia.[79]

A dissolution or annulment shall not be recognised where a party to the marriage has been denied natural justice.[80]

Zimbabwe

In cases where the husband is not domiciled in the foreign country, a Zimbabwean court may recognise the validity of a decree or order of divorce, judicial separation[81] or nullity of marriage made in that country if the court is satisfied that the law of that country contains provisions which correspond substantially to the provisions of section 3 of the Matrimonial Causes Act 1986. In addition, the President may declare in a statutory instrument that the laws of a foreign country contain provisions which correspond substantially to the relevant

[78] Matrimonial Causes Act 2007, s. 86(1). This section relaxes the rules on domicile for wives who are victims of desertions, or who have been resident in the foreign country for at least three years.

[79] Ibid., s. 86(3).

[80] Ibid., s. 86(6).

[81] *Ex p. Pels* 1957 (1) SA 632, 1957 R & N 27; *Ex p. Pels* 1958 (1) SA 196. On the jurisdiction to set aside a foreign decree of judicial separation, see *Ex p. Worth* 1951 (3) SA 230.

provisions of section 3.[82] Such a proclamation is made on the basis of reciprocity[83] and may be revoked at any time.[84] The fact that the court of a foreign domicile, in an uncontested action, has granted a divorce in an action founded on alleged domicile in that country is not a bar to a divorce petition instituted in Zimbabwe.[85]

Comments

The recognition and enforcement of orders granted in foreign matrimonial proceedings is governed by statute in most of the countries under study. The statutes do not necessarily codify the common law on the subject[86] and there is relatively little or no reported case law interpreting or applying the statutes. None of the countries under study are a party to the Hague Convention of 1 June 1970 on the Recognition of Divorces and Legal Separations.[87]

Aside from legislation in Gambia and Ghana, which stipulate that orders can result from either judicial processes or otherwise, most of the statutory provisions are silent on this issue. However, even in these countries it is likely that both judicial and extra-judicial orders would be recognised and enforced.

In an action to enforce any foreign judgment, the foundation of the foreign court's jurisdiction is important, and as is the case in the enforcement of money judgments, it is open to scrutiny by the enforcing court. The countries under study differ on this issue: domicile, significant and substantial connection, residence and reciprocity are variously recognised as bases of jurisdiction. In addition, in Zambia and Tanzania, a dissolution or annulment of a marriage shall be recognised if its validity would have been recognised under the law of the domicile of the parties.[88]

It is an open question whether these bases for recognising foreign decrees are adequate to prevent limping marriages. Although almost all the countries under study have moved away from domicile as the sole

[82] Matrimonial Causes Act 1986, s. 12(1)(a)(b). Section 3 allows the domicile of a deserted husband, residence and nationality to be used as bases of jurisdiction.

[83] Ibid., s. 12(2). [84] Ibid., s. 12(3).

[85] *Moresby-White* v. *Moresby-White* 1972 (3) SA 222.

[86] The statutory provisions in Nigeria and Zambia expressly save the common law rules for recognition of foreign decrees.

[87] Egypt is the only African country that is party to the Convention.

[88] In Tanzania there must be a judgment from the court of the domicile recognising the foreign judgment. The mere fact that it would be recognised is not enough.

basis for recognising foreign decrees, there exists a strong case in arguing that a more flexible approach – always tempered by considerations of public policy – is preferable in this area of the law.

The courts in the countries under study are empowered to refuse recognition of a foreign order if one party to the proceedings is a victim of breach of natural justice and, in Nigeria, on the basis of fraud. Although none of the statutes expressly provides that a court may refuse to enforce a foreign order on grounds of public policy, it can be argued that it is a defence that is always available.

Enforcement of foreign maintenance orders

In many of the countries under study, foreign maintenance orders are expressly excluded from the statutory regimes for the enforcement of foreign money judgments.[89] It is also difficult to use the common law regime for enforcing foreign judgments to enforce such orders, given that they are often subject to variation and thus would fall foul of the finality requirement of the common law regime.[90] Accordingly, in many of the countries under study, specific legislation has been enacted to regulate the enforcement of foreign maintenance orders – both final and provisional – and the transmission abroad of domestic maintenance orders.[91]

Botswana

The Judgments (International Enforcement) Act 1981[92] allows for registration of maintenance orders from England, Wales, Ireland, the Island of Jersey and such other countries as the President may designate on a reciprocal basis.[93] A maintenance order made in such a country may be

[89] See a discussion of those regimes in Ch. 18.

[90] *Webb* v. *Murray, Ex p. Murray* [1961–3] ALR Mal. 205 at 207; *Knight* v. *Baldi* 1966 (3) SA 19. See generally *Walls* v. *Walls* 1996 (2) ZLR 117, which involved an application to vary a maintenance award when the parties were resident abroad.

[91] Botswana – Judgments (International Enforcement) Act 1961, ss. 17–18; Ghana – Courts Act 1993, ss. 92 and 93; Kenya – Maintenance Orders Enforcement Act 1964, ss. 4 and 5; Lesotho – Maintenance Orders Proclamation 1921, ss. 4 and 5; Zimbabwe – Maintenance Orders (Facilities for Enforcement) Act 1921, ss. 4 and 5.

[92] See also Judgments (Maintenance Orders (Facilities for Enforcement)) Rules 1923. *Mthethwa* v. *Lebang* (Practice Note) 1990 BLR 615.

[93] Judgments (International Enforcement) Act 1981, s. 14. Under the Judgments (Reciprocal Enforcement of Maintenance) Order 1922, the Act has been extended to: Lesotho; Swaziland; Zambia; Zimbabwe; Republic of South Africa; Zanzibar; New South Wales;

registered in court and shall then be of the same force and effect and be enforced as if the order had been an order originally given in that court on the date of registration. A certified copy of the order shall in the first instance be sent to the Minister of Justice for transmission to the appropriate court for registration.[94] The Act also empowers the courts to confirm provisional maintenance orders after a hearing.[95] During the hearing, it is open to the respondent to raise any defence he or she might have raised in the original proceedings had they been a party to it, but no other defence may be raised. A certificate from the court which made the provisional order stating the grounds on which the making of the order might have been opposed if the person against whom the order was made had been a party to the proceedings is conclusive evidence that those grounds are ones on which objection may be taken.[96]

Gambia

The enforcement of foreign maintenance orders is governed by the Maintenance Orders (Facilities for Enforcement) Act 1921.[97] The Act provides that, where a maintenance order has been made against a person by a court in the United Kingdom or Ireland,[98] and a certified copy of the order has been transmitted to the Minister of Foreign Affairs, he or she shall send a copy to the prescribed officer of a Gambian court for registration. On receipt of the certified copy, the order shall be registered and shall, from the date of registration, be of the same force and effect. Proceedings may be taken on the order, as if it had been an order originally obtained in the court in which it was registered, and that this court has power to enforce the order.[99] A Gambian court also has jurisdiction to enforce maintenance orders which are provisional only

Malawi; Western Australia; Uganda; Queensland; Kenya; New Zealand; Tasmania; South Australia; Victoria; Commonwealth of Australia; Cook Islands; India (except the State of Jammu and Kashmir); Bailiwick of Guernsey; Pakistan; and the Isle of Man.

[94] Judgments (International Enforcement) Act 1981, s. 15. [95] Ibid., s. 16.

[96] Ibid., s. 16(4).

[97] The Act should be read with the Maintenance Orders (Facilities for Enforcement) Provisional Rules.

[98] The President is empowered by s. 10 of the Act to extend its provisions to other Commonwealth countries on a reciprocal basis. The Act has been extended to Sierra Leone, Nigeria, New South Wales, the Commonwealth of Australia, Island of Jersey, Bailiwick of Guernsey and the Isle of Man.

[99] Maintenance Orders (Facilities for Enforcement) Act 1921, s. 3.

and have no effect until confirmed by a court. The enforcement of provisional orders is preceded by a hearing. At the hearing, the respondent may raise any defence he or she might have raised in the original proceedings had he or she been a party to them. The respondent is not allowed to raise any other defence. A certificate from the court which made the provisional order stating the grounds on which the making of the order might have been opposed if the person against whom the order was made had been a party to the proceedings, is conclusive evidence that those grounds are the ones on which objection may be taken.[100] The Act makes provision for the transmission to the United Kingdom and Ireland of final and provisional orders made in Gambia for the purpose of enforcing them.[101]

Ghana

The Ghanaian regime for enforcing foreign maintenance orders is regulated by the Courts Act 1993, especially sections 89 to 97. Under the Act, a maintenance order made in a designated country[102] may be registered in court, shall be of the same force and effect and may be enforced as if the order had been an order originally given in that court on the date of registration.[103] A certified copy of the order shall in the first instance be sent to the Minister of Justice for transmission to the appropriate court for registration.[104] The Ghanaian court may also confirm – with or without modifications and following a hearing – a foreign maintenance order which, under the law of the foreign country, is provisional only unless confirmed by a court in Ghana.[105] At the hearing, it is open to the respondent to state that he or she was not a party at the foreign hearing. He or she may also raise any defence which he or she might have raised in the original proceedings had he or she been a party to them, but no other defence shall be allowed. The certificate from the court which made the provisional order stating the grounds on which the making of the order might have been opposed if the person against whom it was made had been a party to the proceedings is conclusive evidence that

[100] Ibid., s. 6. [101] Ibid., ss. 4–5.

[102] Under the Foreign Judgments and Maintenance Orders (Reciprocal Enforcement) Instrument 1993, the following countries have been designated: Switzerland; United Kingdom; the following States in Australia (Queensland; Tasmania; Western Australia); the following Provinces in Canada (Alberta, British Columbia, Newfoundland, North-West Territories, Nova Scotia, Ontario, Prince Edward Island).

[103] Courts Act 1993, s. 90(1). [104] Ibid., s. 90(3). [105] Ibid., s. 91.

those grounds are ones on which objection may be taken.[106] A confirmed order has the same effect as if it were an order made by the court which confirmed it.[107]

Kenya

In Kenya, where a maintenance order[108] has been made against a person by a court in the United Kingdom or Ireland,[109] and a certified copy of the order has been transmitted by the Secretary of State to the Minister of Justice, they shall send a copy to the prescribed officer of a court in Kenya for registration. On receipt of the certified copy, the order shall be registered and from the date of registration, be of the same force and effect as an order from the registering court. Proceedings may be taken on the order, as if it had been an order originally obtained in the court where it was so registered, and that court shall have the power to enforce the order accordingly.[110] A Kenyan court is also given jurisdiction to enforce a maintenance order which is purely provisional and has no effect unless confirmed by a Kenyan court. Enforcement of such provisional orders shall be preceded by a hearing. At the hearing, the respondent may raise any defence which he or she might have raised in the original proceedings had he or she been a party thereto, but no other defence. A certificate from the court which made the provisional order, stating the grounds on which the making of the order might have been opposed if the person against whom it was made had been a party to the proceedings, shall be conclusive evidence that those grounds are grounds on which objection may be taken.[111]

Lesotho

The Maintenance Orders Proclamation 1921 allows the registration of maintenance orders from England or Ireland and such other countries

[106] Ibid., s. 91(4). [107] Ibid., s. 91(8).

[108] It has been held that such orders are not confined to orders made in separation and maintenance proceedings, but also include orders made ancillary to a decree of divorce. *In re. the Maintenance Orders Enforcement Ordinance* (1954) 27 KLR 94.

[109] The Minister of Justice is empowered by s. 10 of the Maintenance Orders Enforcement Act to extend its provisions to other countries on a reciprocal basis.

[110] Maintenance Orders Enforcement Act 1964, s. 3. See *In re. Ian Douglas Hunter* [1955] 28 KLR 120.

[111] Maintenance Orders Enforcement Act 1964, s. 6.

which the King may designate on a reciprocal basis.[112] A maintenance order made in such a country may be registered in court and shall then be of the same force and effect and may be enforced as if the order had been originally given in that court on the date of registration.[113] A certified copy of the order shall in the first instance be sent to the Minister of Justice for transmission to the appropriate court for registration. The Act also empowers the courts to confirm provisional maintenance orders after a hearing. At the hearing, it shall be open to the respondent to raise any defence which he or she might have raised in the original proceedings had he or she been a party thereto, but no other defence. A certificate from the court which made the provisional order, stating the grounds on which the making of the order might have been opposed if the person against whom it was made had been a party to the proceedings, shall be conclusive evidence that those grounds are grounds on which objection may be taken.[114]

Malawi

The enforcement of foreign maintenance orders is regulated by the Maintenance Orders (Enforcement) Act 1921.[115] Under the Act, where a maintenance order has been made against any person by any court of England or Ireland,[116] and where a certified copy of the order has been transmitted, the Registrar of the High Court shall send a copy of the order to the prescribed officer of a court in Malawi for registration. On

[112] Maintenance Orders Proclamation 1921, s. 12. The following countries and territories have been designated under the Application of Maintenance Orders Proclamation 1922: Botswana; Swaziland; Zambia, Zimbabwe; South Africa; New South Wales; Zanzibar; Malawi; Western Australia; Uganda; Queensland; Kenya; New Zealand; Tasmania; South Australia; Victoria; the Commonwealth of Australia; the Cook Islands; the Island of Jersey; India (except the State of Jammu and Kashmir); the Bailiwick of Guernsey; and Pakistan.

[113] Maintenance Orders Proclamation 1921, s. 3.

[114] Maintenance Orders Proclamation 1921, s. 6.

[115] This Act should be read with the Maintenance Orders (Enforcement) Rules 1922.

[116] The President is empowered to extend the Act to any country on a reciprocal basis. The Act has been extended to: the Seychelles, the State of New South Wales, Uganda, Zambia, Lesotho, Botswana, Swaziland, Southern Rhodesia, Kenya, the States of Victoria, South Australia, Queensland, Tasmania and Western Australia, the Territory for the seat of the Government of the Commonwealth of Australia, the Republic of India (excluding the State of Jammu and Kashmir), the Bailiwick of the Island of Guernsey, the Bailiwick of Jersey, the Isle of Man, Singapore, the Northern Territory of Australia, the Republic of South Africa, and the United Republic of Tanzania.

receipt of the order, the office shall register it in the prescribed manner, and from the date of such registration, the order shall be of the same force and effect as if it had been originally obtained in the court where it was so registered, and that court shall have the power to enforce the order accordingly.[117] It has been held that, with respect to such subsequently registered 'final' orders (in contrast with provisional orders) from foreign courts, the Malawi courts have no jurisdiction to vary them – that jurisdiction resides in the foreign court.[118]

The Act makes provision for the transmission of maintenance orders granted in Malawi to be sent to England and Ireland, or a reciprocating country, for enforcement.[119] It also provides for the enforcement of foreign provisional orders in Malawi.[120] In a hearing founded on a provisional order, it shall be open to the person affected by the order to raise any defence they might have raised in the original proceedings had they been a party thereto, but no other defence. A certificate from the court which made the provisional order, stating the grounds on which the making of the order might have been opposed if the person against whom it was made had been a party to the proceedings, shall be conclusive evidence that those grounds are grounds on which objection may be taken.[121] The court has jurisdiction to vary and amend a confirmed provisional order.[122]

Namibia

The enforcement of foreign maintenance orders is governed by the Reciprocal Enforcement of Maintenance Orders Act 1995.[123] The Act empowers the Minister of Justice to designate countries which should benefit from the enforcement regime established by the Act.[124] It also makes provision for the transmission of orders made by the Namibian court to the designated countries for enforcement.[125] Section 4 of the Act provides that, when a certified copy of a maintenance order made by a court in a designated country against a person resident in Namibia is transmitted to the Permanent Secretary by the administrative head of the

[117] Maintenance Orders (Enforcement) Act 1921, s. 3.
[118] *Webb* v. *Murray, Ex p. Murray* [1961–3] ALR Mal. 205.
[119] Maintenance Orders (Enforcement) Act 1921, s. 4. *McCall* v. *McCall* [1961–3] ALR Mal. 170.
[120] Maintenance Orders (Enforcement) Act 1921, s. 6. [121] Ibid., s. 6(3).
[122] Ibid., s. 6(6). [123] This Act should be read with the Maintenance Act 2003.
[124] Reciprocal Enforcement of Maintenance Orders Act 1995, s. 2. [125] Ibid., s. 3.

Department of Justice of that designated country, the Permanent Secretary shall transmit that copy to the maintenance court in whose area of jurisdiction the person against whom such order was made resides, or is alleged to reside, and such an order shall on receipt be registered by that maintenance court in the prescribed manner. The Act also makes provision for the registration of provisional maintenance orders after an inquiry.[126] An order from a designated country authorising any employer of a person mentioned in the order to make on behalf of such person any payments, required to be made in terms of a maintenance order, from the salary, wage or any other form of remuneration or allowance of such person may also be registered under the Act.[127]

Nigeria

The enforcement of foreign maintenance orders is governed by the Maintenance Orders Act 1921. The Act aims at facilitating the enforcement of maintenance orders from England and Ireland and, in the exercise of powers conferred on the President under section 11 of the Act, it has been extended to various reciprocating countries.[128] Section 3 of the Act provides that, where a maintenance order has been made against a person by an English or Irish court, and a copy has been transmitted to the President, the President shall send a copy to the prescribed officer of a Nigerian court for registration. The prescribed officer shall then register the order, and once registered, the order has the same force and effect as if it was originally in the court which registered it. The Act makes provision for the transmission to England, Ireland and other reciprocating countries of maintenance orders made in Nigeria.[129] The Nigerian courts are also empowered to give effect to foreign provisional orders after a hearing. At such a hearing, it shall be open to the defendant to raise any defence which they might have raised in the original proceedings had they been a party to them, but no other defence shall be entertained.[130]

[126] Ibid., s. 6. [127] Ibid., s. 9.

[128] These are: Gambia, Ghana, Sierra Leone, New South Wales, St Vincent, Grenada, British Guiana, Victoria, the Commonwealth of Australia, Northern Rhodesia, Western Australia, the Union of South Africa, New Zealand and the Island of Jersey. Maintenance Orders Proclamation 1954.

[129] Maintenance Orders Act 1921, s. 4. [130] Ibid., s. 6.

Sierra Leone

The Maintenance Orders (Facilities for Enforcement) Act 1921 governs the enforcement of maintenance orders in Sierra Leone. Under section 3 of the Act, where a maintenance order has been made against a person by a court in England or Ireland and a copy has been transmitted to the President, the President shall send a copy to the prescribed officer of a Sierra Leonean court for registration. The prescribed officer shall then register the order, and once registered, the order has the same force and effect as if it was originally in the court which registered it. The Act makes provision for the transmission to England, Ireland and other reciprocating countries of maintenance orders made in Sierra Leone.[131] The Sierra Leonean court is also empowered to give effect to provisional orders made by courts of summary jurisdiction in England or Ireland and these provisional orders shall be confirmed following a hearing. At such a hearing, it shall be open to the defendant to raise any defence which they might have raised in the original proceedings had they been a party to them, but no other defence shall be entertained.[132] A provisional order which has been confirmed may be varied or rescinded by the court.[133] The President is empowered to extend the Act to other Commonwealth countries.[134]

South Africa

The Reciprocal Enforcement of Maintenance Orders Act 1963 and, in relation to African countries, the Reciprocal Enforcement of Maintenance Orders (Countries in Africa) Act 1989[135] govern the enforcement of foreign maintenance orders in South Africa.[136] The Minister of Justice is empowered to designate the countries to which the Act

131 Maintenance Orders (Facilities for Enforcement) Act 1921, s. 4.

132 Ibid., s. 6(2).

133 Ibid., s. 6(5).

134 Ibid., s. 12. The Act has been extended to: the Colony of Gambia, the Colony of the Gold Coast, Ashanti and the Northern Territories of the Gold Coast (now Ghana), Nigeria, the territory of the seat of Government of the Commonwealth of Australia, and Gibraltar.

135 The provisions of the Act, especially as regards the procedure for registration, are largely similar to those of the Reciprocal Enforcement of Maintenance Orders Act 1963, and are accordingly not discussed here.

136 The common law provided very limited scope for enforcing foreign maintenance orders in South Africa, especially due to the finality requirement. See, e.g., *Estate Himovich* v. *Estate Himovich* 1951 (2) SA 156; *Estate H v. Estate H* 1952 (4) SA 168; *Hirschowitz* v. *Hirschowitz* 1965 (3) SA 407.

applies.[137] A certified copy of a foreign maintenance order made against any person by any court in a designated country should be transmitted to the Minister through diplomatic channels by an authority of such a country recognised for the purpose by the Minister. The Minister shall transmit a copy of the order to a maintenance court and the order shall, on receipt thereof, be registered by that court.[138] The Act also empowers the court to confirm provisional foreign maintenance orders after holding an inquiry.[139]

Tanzania

Under the Law of Marriage Act 1971, where a maintenance order has been made against any person in a court in a country to which the Act applies, and a certified copy of the order has been transmitted to the Minister of Foreign Affairs, the Minister shall send a copy to a court in Tanzania for registration and, thereupon, the order shall be registered in the prescribed manner.[140] A registered order may, from the date of registration, be enforced as if it had been an order made by the court where it is registered. The court and its officers are obliged to take steps to enforce the order.[141] Where a Tanzanian court makes a maintenance order against a person who is proved to be resident in a country to which the Act applies, the court shall send a certified copy of the order to the Minister for transmission to that country.[142]

Uganda

The enforcement of foreign maintenance orders is governed by the Maintenance Orders Enforcement Act 1921.[143] It provides that where a

[137] Reciprocal Enforcement of Maintenance Orders Act 1963, s. 2. See generally *Smit* v. *Smit* 1989 (3) SA 454, which held that a maintenance order made in the Supreme Court of South Africa is not enforceable in the Republic of Bophuthatswana, as the Republic of Bophuthatswana has not designated the Republic of South Africa as a proclaimed country in terms of the Reciprocal Enforcement of Maintenance Orders Act 1963.

[138] Reciprocal Enforcement of Maintenance Orders Act 1963, s. 3. A court has jurisdiction to suspend stay of execution of a judgment registering a foreign maintenance order. *Marendaz* v. *Marendaz* 1953 (4) SA 218. See also *Severin* v. *Severin* 1951 (1) SA 225, which held that registration is purely an administrative act and is in no way a judicial or quasi judicial act or a civil suit or proceeding.

[139] Reciprocal Enforcement of Maintenance Orders Act 1963, s. 4. The provision should be read with the Maintenance Act 1998.

[140] Law of Marriage Act 1971, s. 142(1). [141] Ibid., s. 143. [142] Ibid., s. 144.

[143] The Act should be read with the Maintenance Orders Enforcement Rules.

maintenance order has been made against any person by any court in England, Northern Ireland or the Republic of Ireland,[144] and where a certified copy of the order has been transmitted to the Minister, he or she shall send a copy to the prescribed officer of a court in Uganda for registration. On receipt of the certified copy, the order shall be registered and shall, from the date of registration, be of the same force and effect. Proceedings may be taken on the order as if it had been an order originally obtained in the court where it was so registered, and that court shall have the power to enforce the order accordingly.[145] A Ugandan court also has jurisdiction to enforce a maintenance order which is purely provisional and which has no effect until confirmed by a Ugandan court.[146] Enforcement of such provisional orders should be preceded by a hearing. At the hearing, the respondent may raise any defence which he or she might have raised in the original proceedings, had he or she been a party thereto, but no other defence. The certificate from the court which made the provisional order, stating the grounds on which the making of the order might have been opposed, if the person against whom it was made had been a party to the proceedings, shall be conclusive evidence that those grounds are grounds on which objection may be taken.[147]

Zambia

The enforcement of foreign maintenance orders is regulated by the Maintenance Orders (Enforcement) Act 1921.[148] Under the Act, where a maintenance order has been made against any person by any court of

[144] The Act empowers the Minister to extend the provisions of the Act to any Commonwealth Country. The Act has been extended to the following countries: the Seychelles, Sri Lanka, Mauritius, Malawi, Zambia, Lesotho, Botswana, Swaziland, New South Wales and its dependencies in the Commonwealth of Australia, Territory for the seat of Government of the Commonwealth of Australia, Kenya, Zanzibar, the Island of Jersey, India (excluding the State of Jammu and Kashmir), the State of South Australia, the Bailiwick of Guernsey, the State of Tasmania and its dependencies in the Commonwealth of Australia, the Isle of Man and New Zealand.

[145] Maintenance Orders Enforcement Act 1921, s. 2. [146] Ibid., s. 5(1).

[147] Ibid., s. 5(3).

[148] This Act should be read with the Maintenance Orders (Enforcement) Rules 1954 and the Affiliation and Maintenance of Children Act 1995. Although the Affiliation and Maintenance of Children Act 1995 provides that the Maintenance Orders (Enforcement) Act 'shall cease to apply to the maintenance of children or orders made in respect thereof', it does not provide for a separate regime to regulate foreign orders for the maintenance of children. It is submitted that the Maintenance Orders (Enforcement) Act continues to apply to such foreign orders.

England or Ireland[149] and where a certified copy of the order has been transmitted by a Secretary of State to the President, the President shall send a copy of the order to the prescribed officer of a court in Zambia for registration. On receipt of the order, the office shall register it in the prescribed manner, and from the date of such registration, the order shall be of the same force and effect as if it had been an order originally obtained in the court where it is so registered. That court shall then have the power to enforce the order accordingly.[150] The Act makes provision for the transmission of maintenance orders made in Zambia to be sent to England and Ireland[151] and also for the enforcing of provisional orders in Zambia.[152] In a hearing founded on a provisional order, it shall be open to the person affected by the order to raise any defence which he or she might have raised in the original proceedings had he or she been a party thereto, but no other defence. A certificate from the court which made the provisional order, stating the grounds on which the making of the order might have been opposed if the person against whom it was made had been a party to the proceedings, shall be conclusive evidence that those grounds are grounds on which objection may be taken.[153] The court has jurisdiction to vary and amend a confirmed provisional order.

Zimbabwe

In Zimbabwe, where a maintenance order has been made against any person by any court in a reciprocating country[154] and a certified copy of the order has been transmitted by the appropriate authority to the Minister of Justice, Legal and Parliamentary Affairs, the Minister shall send a copy of the order to the clerk of the maintenance court of the province or district where the person against whom the order was made is residing.[155] Upon receipt of such an order, the clerk shall register it.[156] Where there is an application to vary or discharge a registered order, and where the court at which it is registered is satisfied that it is necessary to refer the application to the court which originally made the order, the first-mentioned court may so refer the application and adjourn the

[149] Section 11 empowers the President to extend the Act to other Commonwealth Countries on a reciprocal basis. The Act has been extended to the Northern Territory of Australia, the Australian States of Queensland, South Australia and Tasmania.

[150] Maintenance Orders (Enforcement) Act 1921, s. 3(1).

[151] Ibid., s. 4. [152] Ibid., s. 6. [153] Ibid., s. 6(3).

[154] Maintenance Orders (Facilities for Enforcement) Act 1921, s. 10. [155] Ibid., s. 3(1).

[156] Ibid., s. 3(2).

proceedings for this purpose.[157] The Zimbabwean court is empowered to confirm and enforce a maintenance order made by a court in a reciprocating country which is expressed to be purely provisional, and of no effect unless and until confirmed by a court in Zimbabwe.[158] At the hearing to confirm or reject the order, it shall be open to the respondent to raise any defence which he or she might have raised in the original proceedings had he or she been a party thereto, but no other defence. The certificate from the court which made the provisional order, stating the grounds on which the making of the order might have been opposed if the person against whom it was made had been a party to the proceedings, shall be conclusive evidence that those grounds are grounds on which objection may be taken.[159]

Comments

There exists in each of the countries under study a statutory regime for registering foreign maintenance orders.[160] Unlike the statutory regime for enforcing foreign money judgments,[161] the regime for enforcing foreign maintenance orders is not expressed as exclusive. Accordingly, it is possible for a maintenance order that is either within or outside the scope of the regime to be enforced using the common law for enforcing foreign judgments.[162] However, because maintenance orders might be subject to variation by the foreign court – they are not final and conclusive – enforcing them at common law may be difficult.

None of the countries under study is a party to the UN Convention on the Recovery Abroad of Maintenance 1956,[163] the Hague Convention Concerning the Recognition and Enforcement of Decisions relating to Maintenance Obligations 1973 or the Hague Convention on the International Recovery of Child Support and Other Forms of Family Maintenance 2007.[164]

The statutory regimes operate on the basis of reciprocity. The President or the Minister of Justice is given the discretion to designate countries that should be beneficiaries of the regimes. Some countries

157 Ibid., s. 3(3). 158 Ibid., s. 6(1). 159 Ibid., s. 6(3).

160 Most of the statutes were enacted in 1921 and were modelled on the United Kingdom's Maintenance Orders (Facilities for Enforcement) Act 1920.

161 See Ch. 18. 162 See Ch. 17.

163 Burkina Faso; Cape Verde; the Central African Republic; Liberia; Niger; the Seychelles and Tunisia.

164 In Africa, only Burkina Faso has signed this convention.

restrict the states that can be designated solely to Commonwealth states. This is an undue restraint on the scope and applicability of the regime.

Apart from Namibia, South Africa and Zimbabwe, all of the other countries under study expressly exclude an 'order of affiliation' from the scope of their statutory regimes. The exclusion of orders of affiliation, which are orders that an illegitimate child be maintained by their father, could be problematic. This is because, under the constitutions and laws of some of the countries under study, every child, whether or not born in wedlock, is entitled to reasonable provision out of the estate of its parents.[165] It would be difficult to justify why a foreign maintenance order obtained against a man who fathers a child (perhaps now staying with a grandparent in one of the countries which exclude such orders) prior to marrying the mother, cannot be enforced against the assets of that person.

Each of the countries under study provides two distinct procedures for enforcing foreign maintenance orders. An order that is 'provisional only and has no effect unless and until confirmed' by the domestic court is registered only after a hearing or an inquiry. At a hearing, which should be held after notice of the proceedings has been given to the respondent, it is open to the respondent to raise any defence that he or she could have raised in the original proceedings, had he or she been a party to them. Most of the statutes in the countries under study are unanimous that no other defence is permissible.[166] A certificate from the foreign court, stating the grounds on which the making of the order might have been opposed if the person against whom the order was made had been a party to the proceedings, is conclusive evidence that those are grounds on which objection can be taken. In other words, although it is open to the respondent to raise a defence, his or her options are constrained to those that would have been available to him or her in the foreign court.

The fact that a respondent is limited to defences that would have been available to him or her in the foreign court is problematic. For example, it can be argued that it is not open to the respondent to argue that enforcement of the order would be against the enforcing country's public

[165] See, e.g., Constitution of the Republic of Ghana, Art. 28(2); Namibia – Children's Status Act 2006, s. 16(2); *Frans* v. *Paschke* 2007 (2) NR 520.

[166] The Namibian regime is generally silent on this issue of defences. However, under s. 6(6) of the Reciprocal Enforcement of Maintenance Orders Act 1995 and s. 13(3) of the Maintenance Act 2003, 'the person presiding at the maintenance court must conduct the maintenance enquiry in a manner that is aimed at ensuring that substantial justice is achieved between the parties as well as the beneficiary of the maintenance claim'.

policy. Many Africans emigrate to various jurisdictions with different values and legal systems. It is possible for such persons to become the objects of maintenance orders that are founded on bases that might be considered as offensive to domestic public policy. The fact that such persons would not be able to raise that defence before an enforcing court (because they definitely could not have raised it in the foreign court) is unacceptable. Indeed, without prejudice to the earlier observations, the fact that affiliation orders are excluded from the scope of the majority of maintenance order enforcement regimes suggests that not all foreign maintenance orders are acceptable in the countries under study. Significantly, international conventions on the enforcement of foreign maintenance orders recognise public policy as a basis for refusing recognition and enforcement.[167] Arguably, a defence that can be raised by a respondent in such proceedings is the lack of jurisdiction of the foreign court.

As regards provisional orders, the enforcing court has jurisdiction to confirm or refuse to register the order. In contrast, enforcement of foreign maintenance orders that are not expressed to be provisional is automatic and mandatory. On receipt of the copy of the order, which in many of the countries under study is transmitted through a member of the Executive, such as the Minister of Justice or the President, the prescribed officer of the court is obliged to – 'shall' – register the order. In other words, registration is mandatory. Registration renders the order domestically enforceable. Unlike provisional orders, the provisions applicable to orders which are not expressed to be provisional assume that the foreign court had jurisdiction – there is no provision for inquiring into or contesting the jurisdiction of the foreign court.[168] Indeed, there is no hearing prior to registration. However, given that proceedings may be taken on an order registering the foreign order, as if the latter was originally obtained in the court that registered it, a registered order is arguably open to appeal. Admittedly, this interpretation has been rejected in Malawi and Kenya. Courts in both jurisdictions have held that, where a foreign order which is not expressed as provisional is registered, the fact that it becomes an order of the registering court does not afford the respondent a right to appeal, either from the order itself or from the

[167] Hague Convention on the International Recovery of Child Support and Other Forms of Family Maintenance 2007, Art. 22(a); Hague Convention on the Recognition and Enforcement of Decisions Relating to Maintenance Obligations 1973, Art. 5(1).

[168] This may also be compared with the regimes for registering foreign money judgments which allow for the international competence of the foreign court to be examined.

registration of it, nor is the court empowered to discharge or vary the foreign order. An application to vary the order must be made to the foreign court.[169]

When compared to the regimes for enforcing foreign money judgments, the 'privileged' status given to foreign maintenance orders is difficult to rationalise. For example, *Re. Ian Douglas Hunter*[170] rationalises this position with an argument that matrimonial jurisdiction is founded on domicile and 'as the state of matrimony in the case of divorce has come to an end, it is necessary to embalm the deceased matrimonial domicile permanently in the pronouncing court'. However, the current state of the law on jurisdiction in matrimonial causes renders this position obsolete or indefensible. At present, in most of the countries under study, domicile is not the sole basis of jurisdiction in matrimonial matters.[171] Furthermore, an action for maintenance need not necessarily be preceded by granting a petition for divorce – it may be instituted in respect of a child within marriage. Furthermore, there are considerations to vary or discharge the order which relate to the inconvenience and cost of litigating in the foreign court. Indeed, in Zimbabwe, the courts have jurisdiction to discharge or vary registered orders which were not expressed as provisional, but they have the discretion to refer the matter to the foreign court.[172]

[169] *Webb* v. *Murray, Ex p. Murray* [1961–3] ALR Mal. 205; *In re. Ian Douglas Hunter* [1955] 28 KLR 120.

[170] [1955] 28 KLR 120 at 127. [171] See Ch. 12.

[172] Maintenance Orders (Facilities for Enforcement) Act 1921, s. 3(3).

13

Children

This chapter deals with the private international law aspects of orders concerning children and their status.[1] Specifically, it focuses on issues such as inter-country adoption, surrogacy, custody, international child abduction, legitimacy and illegitimacy of children. The substantive domestic laws on these issues are not examined here. These are issues dominated by statute with a significant body of case law, and where the impact of international law, especially international human rights law, is evident.

Adoption

Gambia

The Children's Court has jurisdiction to make an adoption order. A child need not be a citizen of Gambia to be adopted.[2] Gambian law allows for inter-country adoption in exceptional circumstances.[3] It further imposes conditions on adoption by foreigners. These include residence in Gambia for at least six months, fostering the child under supervision for at least thirty-six months, having no criminal record, and satisfying the court that the adopter's country of origin would respect and recognise the adoption order.[4] When an adoption order is made, all rights, duties, obligations and liabilities of the parents and guardians in relation to the future custody, maintenance and consent to marriage are extinguished. Furthermore, the order vests all such rights, duties, obligations and liabilities in relation to the future custody, maintenance and education of the child as if the adoptive parent is the natural parent.[5] The Children's Act 2005 is silent on whether and on what basis a Gambian court may recognise foreign adoption orders.

[1] The issue of domicile of children is discussed in Ch. 3. [2] Children's Act 2005, s. 109.
[3] Ibid., s. 111(1). [4] Ibid., s. 111. [5] Ibid., s. 115.

Ghana

The jurisdiction to make an adoption order with respect to children is conferred on the High Court, Circuit Court or Family Tribunals. No other institution is competent to make an adoption order in Ghana. An adoption order can be made only in respect of a child resident in Ghana.[6] Neither domicile nor nationality confer jurisdiction on the courts to make an adoption order with respect to a child. However, the fact that a child is not a Ghanaian does not prevent the courts from making a respective adoption order, provided he or she is resident in Ghana.[7] There are no statutory provisions dealing with the recognition of foreign adoption orders.

Ghanaian law allows a foreigner to adopt a child resident in Ghana. There are two categories of such adoptions – namely, adoption by a foreigner with a view to residing with the child in Ghana, and inter-country adoption. Inter-country adoption is the adoption of a child by a person who is not a citizen of Ghana, who resides outside Ghana and who intends to remove the adopted child from Ghana.[8] Ghanaian law imposes a number of constraints on foreign adopters. With respect to foreigners, an application for adoption should be made jointly by a husband and his wife.[9] The applicant and the child must reside in Ghana, and the child should have been continuously in the care and possession of the applicant for at least three consecutive months immediately preceding the date of the order.[10] Where the applicant for an adoption order is not a Ghanaian or where there is a joint application and one applicant is not a Ghanaian, the court must make an interim order for a period of not less than two years and should postpone the final determination on the application.[11]

Kenya

The jurisdiction to grant adoption orders is given to the High Court[12] and may be exercised in respect of any child who is resident within Kenya, regardless of citizenship or place of birth.[13] The Children Act

[6] Children's Act 2001, ss. 65 and 67(3). This Act should be read with the Adoption Rules 2003.

[7] Children's Act 2001, s. 80. See generally *In re. RF (An Infant)* [1972] 2 GLR 61; *Bulley-Neequaye* v. *Bulley-Neequaye* [1992] 1 GLR 165.

[8] Children's Act 2001, ss. 85 and 124. [9] Ibid., s. 66. [10] Ibid., s. 67(3).

[11] Ibid., s. 73.

[12] Children Act 2001, s. 154. See generally *In re. Baby PA (Infant)* [2005] eKLR; *In re. AW (a Child)* [2006] eKLR; *In re. EC (an Infant)* [2006] eKLR; *In re. AARE (a Child)* [2005] eKLR; *In re. EJ (An Infant)* [2004] eKLR; *In re. Baby Wayne Bakaria* [2004] eKLR.

[13] Children Act 2001, s. 157.

2001 allows an adoption order to be made in respect of a child upon the joint application of two spouses who are neither Kenyan citizens, nor resident in Kenya. Such applicants must: obtain the necessary consent; satisfy the court that the country where they ordinarily reside and where they expect to reside with the child immediately after the making of the adoption order will respect and recognise it and grant resident status to the child, and have been authorised and recommended as persons who are suitable (including being morally fit and financially capable) to adopt a foreign child by a competent government authority or court.[14]

A Kenyan court shall recognise an adoption order made by any court of law in the Commonwealth, or any court of competent jurisdiction in any other country. An order so recognised has the same effect as one validly made under the Children Act 2001.[15]

Malawi

The High Court has jurisdiction to make adoption orders.[16] Subject to statutorily defined conditions,[17] any person may apply for the authorisation to adopt a child.[18] This includes persons who are not citizens of Malawi.[19] An adoption order shall not be made in favour of any applicant who is not resident in Malawi, or in respect of any infant who is not so resident.[20] For this purpose, a person who is not a mere sojourner in Malawi, but has a targeted, long-term presence in the country, such as through regular visits and investment, is resident in Malawi.[21] An adoption order has the effect of extinguishing all rights, liabilities and obligations of the parents or guardian of the adopted child in relation to the future custody, maintenance and education of the adopted child. Such rights, liabilities and obligations become vested in the adopter.[22]

14 Ibid., s. 162. 15 Ibid., s. 176.

16 Adoption Act 1949, s. 9. On matters relating to children, see generally the Child Care, Protection and Justice Act 2010.

17 Adoption Act 1949, s. 3. 18 Ibid., s. 2(1).

19 *In the Matter of CJ (A Female Infant)*, Adoption Cause No. 28 of 2009 (Supreme Court of Appeal, Malawi, 2009), on appeal from *In the Matter of CJ (A Female Infant) of C/O Mr. Peter Baneti, Zomba*, Adoption Case No. 1 of 2009 (High Court, Malawi, 2009). See generally *In re. David Banda (A Male Infant)*, Adoption Cause No. 2 of 2006 (High Court, Malawi, 2008).

20 Adoption Act 1949, s. 3(5).

21 *In the Matter of CJ (A Female Infant)*, Adoption Cause No. 28 of 2009 (Supreme Court of Appeal, Malawi, 2009).

22 Adoption Act 1949, s. 6(1).

Sierra Leone

Adoption in Sierra Leone is governed by the Adoption Act 1989. The Act gives the High Court jurisdiction to make an order authorising an applicant to adopt a juvenile.[23] The Act does not exclude adoption by foreigners. However, where an applicant is not a citizen of Sierra Leone, the court is obliged to make an interim order for a period of not less than six months.[24] Conditions may be imposed in such orders and the time stipulated in the order generally serves as a probationary period.[25] An adoption order shall not be made in respect of a juvenile unless the applicant and the juvenile reside in Sierra Leone. When an adoption order is made, all rights, duties, obligations and liabilities of the parents of the juvenile, or of any other person, in relation to the future custody, maintenance and education of the juvenile are extinguished. They become vested in, exercisable by and enforceable against the adopter as if the juvenile was a child born to the adopter in lawful marriage.[26]

South Africa

Historically, there was an absolute proscription of the adoption of South African children by persons who were not South African citizens.[27] In 2000, this prohibition was declared unconstitutional – this opened up South Africa to inter-country adoption.[28] The South African courts have emphasised strict adherence to statutorily outlined procedures for adoption, including especially resorting to the appropriate court and seeking the right relief. They have cautioned against departing from such procedures, except in exceptional circumstances.[29] It has been held that the subsidiarity principle, which dictates that inter-country adoption should only be considered as a 'last resort', is not the ultimate governing factor in inter-country adoptions. Rather, it is the best interest of the child which is paramount in inter-country adoptions. Therefore, the subsidiarity principle itself is seen as subsidiary to the paramountcy principle, which means that each child has to be regarded as an individual when it comes

[23] Adoption Act 1989, s. 2(1). A juvenile is defined as a person who is under the age of 17 years.

[24] Ibid., s. 8. [25] Ibid., s. 7. [26] Ibid., s. 12. [27] Child Care Act 1983, s. 18(4).

[28] *Minister of Welfare and Population Development* v. *Fitzpatrick* 2000 (3) SA 422; *Fitzpatrick* v. *Minister of Social Welfare and Pensions* 2000 (3) SA 139.

[29] *AD* v. *DW* 2008 (3) SA 183; *De Gree* v. *Webb* 2007 (5) SA 184; *De Gree* v. *Webb* 2006 (6) SA 51.

to adoption.[30] It has been held that the effects of an adoption and the rights which it creates relate to status and, accordingly, are governed by the *lex adoptionis*.[31]

South Africa is a party to the 1993 Hague Convention on the Protection of Children and Co-operation in respect of Inter-country Adoption. The Children's Act 2005 gives the force of law to the Convention. The Convention complements existing South African laws on adoption and, in the event of conflict, supersedes them.[32] Under the Convention, the Act renders the Director-General the Central Authority for the purposes of inter-country adoption.[33] The Director-General is responsible for accrediting organisations to provide inter-country adoption services.[34] The Act also establishes substantively similar regimes for adoption by persons in either convention[35] or non-convention countries.[36] Both regimes demand trilateral relations between the foreign central authority, the South African central authority and the children's court in South Africa.[37] Among the facts the court is obliged to take into account before making adoption orders are: the best interests of the child; the child's presence in South Africa; that the child is not legally prevented from leaving South Africa; that arrangements for the adoption of the child are in accordance with the requirements of the Hague Convention on Inter-country Adoption and any prescribed requirements; that the central authority of the Convention country has agreed to the adoption of the child; that South Africa's Central Authority has agreed to the adoption of the child, and that the child has been placed on the Register of Adoptable Children and Prospective Adoptive Parents for at least 60 days and no fit and proper adoptive parent for the child is available in South Africa.[38]

Separate regimes have been created for the recognition of children of inter-country adoption in Convention and non-Convention countries. The adoption in a Convention country of a child habitually resident in that Convention country by a person habitually resident in South Africa (or in another Convention country) shall be recognised in South Africa if an adoption compliance certificate issued in that country is in force for the adoption. If an adoption compliance certificate has not been issued in the relevant Convention country, the South African Central Authority

[30] *AD* v. *DW* 2008 (3) SA 183. [31] *Board of Executors* v. *Vitt* 1989 (4) SA 480.

[32] Children's Act 2005, s. 256. [33] Ibid., s. 257. [34] Ibid., s. 259. [35] Ibid., s. 261.

[36] Ibid., s. 262. The Act also provides rules to regulate inter-country adoption by persons habitually resident in South Africa. See ss. 264 and 265.

[37] Ibid., s. 261. [38] Ibid., ss. 261(5) and 262(5).

may issue a declaration recognising the adoption.[39] As regards adoption from non-Convention countries, the South African Central Authority may issue a declaration recognising the adoption of the child if the adoption is in accordance with, and has not been rescinded, under the law of the country where the adoption order was made, and if the adoption in that country has the same effect it would have had if the order had been made in South Africa.[40]

An adoption order terminates all parental responsibilities and rights that any person, including a parent, step-parent or partner in a domestic life partnership, had in respect of the child immediately before the adoption. The order confers full parental responsibilities and rights regarding the adopted child upon the adoptive parent. However, adoption does not affect any rights to property acquired by the child before the adoption.[41]

Tanzania

The Law of the Child Act 2009 gives the High Court jurisdiction to grant adoption orders.[42] A child who is to be adopted should reside in Tanzania.[43] The Act allows persons who are not Tanzanians to adopt a Tanzanian child. Various restrictions are placed on adoption by such foreigners. These include residence in Tanzania for at least three consecutive years, absence of a criminal record in the country of origin and the need for the court to be satisfied that the prospective adoptive parents' country of origin would respect and recognise the adoption order.[44] Subject to the stipulated restrictions, the court is allowed to make an adoption order if it is in the best interests of the child.[45]

When an adoption order is made, the rights, duties, obligations and liabilities, including those under the customary law of the parents of the child, or of any other person of any nature whatsoever connected with the child, shall cease. Such rights, duties, obligations and liabilities are transferred to, and assumed by, the adoptive parent of the child.[46]

Uganda

An application for an adoption order may be made to a chief Magistrates' Court within the jurisdiction where the applicant or the child resides,[47] if

[39] Ibid., s. 266. [40] Ibid., s. 268. [41] Ibid., s. 242. [42] Law of the Child Act 2009, s. 54.
[43] Ibid., s. 56(3)(a). [44] Ibid., s. 74(1). [45] Ibid., s. 74(2). [46] Ibid., s. 64.
[47] On the meaning of residence, see *Re M (An Infant)* [1995–8] 2 EA 174, [1995] Kam. LR 450.

both the child and the applicant are citizens of Uganda, or to the High Court, where the child or applicant is not a citizen of Uganda.[48] A child need not be a Ugandan to be adopted.[49] The High Court has no jurisdiction to entertain an application for adoption where neither the applicant nor the child is a citizen of Uganda.[50]

In exceptional circumstances, a foreigner may adopt a Ugandan child if he or she has stayed in Uganda for a least three years, has fostered the child for at least thirty-six months,[51] does not have a criminal record, is able to produce appropriate recommendations to his or her suitability to adopt a child,[52] and the court is satisfied that his or her country of origin will respect and recognise the adoption order.[53]

An adoption order extinguishes all the rights, liabilities and obligations of the parents or guardian of the adopted child in relation to the future custody, maintenance and education of the adopted child. Such rights, liabilities and obligations become vested in the adopter.[54]

Zambia

An adoption order shall not be made in respect of an infant unless the applicant and the infant reside in Zambia.[55] However, in respect of a foreign infant, the infant should reside in Zambia and the applicant must be ordinarily resident in Zambia. Furthermore, the foreign infant should not be in Zambia under a temporary or visiting permit issued under the Immigration and Deportation Act.[56] Where an adoption order is made, all the rights, duties, obligations and liabilities of the parents or guardians of the infant in relation to his or her future custody, maintenance and education, including all rights to appoint a guardian and to consent or

[48] Children Act 1997, s. 44(1). See generally *In the matter of Deborah Joyce Alitubeera & Richard Masaba (infants)*, Civil Appeal No. 70 of 2011 (Court of Appeal, Uganda, 2012); *In re. Edith Nassaazi* [1997] 6 Kam. LR 42; *In re. Moses Kirabo Clay*, Adoption Cause No. 30 of 2004 (High Court, Uganda, 2004); *In re. Nsamba Isaac Dominic*, Adoption Petition No. 44 of 2006 (High Court, Uganda, 2005).

[49] Children Act 1997, s. 44(2).

[50] *Ayat Joy* v. *Jeneve Chenekan Obonyo*, Adoption Cause No. 52 of 2005 (High Court, Uganda, 2005).

[51] *In re. Cynthia June Robertson (An Infant)* [2004] Kam. LR 641, which held this requirement as not mandatory.

[52] *In re. Gorretti Nakasagga (An Infant)* [2002] Kam. LR 535, where a recommendation from a USA pastor was accepted.

[53] Children Act 1997, s. 46. [54] Children Act 1997, s. 51.

[55] Adoption Act 1956, s. 4(5). [56] Ibid., s. 4(6).

give notice of dissent to marriage, are extinguished. They become vested in, are exercisable by and are enforceable against the adopter, as if the infant was a child born to the adopter in lawful wedlock.[57]

Zimbabwe

The court with jurisdiction to make an adoption order is the court within the jurisdiction where the applicant or minor reside at the date of the application for the adoption order.[58] A court has jurisdiction in adoption proceedings, notwithstanding that the child is domiciled outside Zimbabwe.[59]

An adoption order shall not be made in favour of any applicant who is not resident and domiciled in Zimbabwe, or in respect of any minor who is not so resident. However, if the applicant and the minor are within the prohibited degrees of consanguinity, the adoption may be made in favour of an applicant who is not resident or domiciled in Zimbabwe.[60] Except in cases where the applicant and the minor are within the prohibited degrees of consanguinity, an adoption order cannot be made in favour of an applicant who is not a citizen of Zimbabwe without the consent of the Minister of Public Service, Labour and Social Welfare.[61]

The recognition of foreign adoption orders is governed by the Children's Act 1971. However, application of the Act does not limit the power of a Zimbabwean court to recognise or give effect to an adoption effected outside Zimbabwe under any other law.[62] The Act distinguishes between orders made in designated and non-designated countries.[63] The High Court is empowered to recognise an adoption order made in a designated country if it is satisfied that the order has been made by a competent authority there in respect of a person who was not born in Zimbabwe, and that it would not contravene public policy to recognise the adoption.[64] In respect of orders from non-designated countries, the

[57] Ibid., s. 14(1). [58] Children's Act 1971, s. 57(1).

[59] *Ex p. Egan* [1965] RLR 518, 1966 (1) SA 379. [60] Children's Act 1971, s. 59(5).

[61] Ibid., s. 59(7). The Act does not define which relationships fall within the scope of the 'prohibited degrees of consanguinity', but it appears this provision and s. 59(5) are aimed at facilitating adoption of family members. An example would be an uncle who has renounced his Zimbabwean citizenship and is now domiciled in and a citizen of South Africa and who wants to adopt a niece or nephew resident in Zimbabwe.

[62] Children's Act 1971, s. 75G.

[63] The Minister is empowered to designate countries. See Children's Act 1971, s. 75B.

[64] Ibid., s. 75C.

court must be further satisfied that the adopted person or the adopter was domiciled or permanently resident in the foreign country at the time the adoption order was made.[65] A recognised adoption order has the same effect, in all respects, as if it had been made in Zimbabwe.[66]

Comments

It is a well-known fact that there are instances where the only prospect of a child securing and living in a stable family is through adoption. Inter-country adoption is recognised in all the countries under study, with South Africa and Namibia[67] being the most recent to give non-nationals the right to adopt their nationals. However, in countries such as Uganda and Gambia, the adoption of nationals by foreigners is allowed only in 'exceptional circumstances' and in Zimbabwe the consent of the Minister of Public Service, Labour and Social Welfare is needed.

Inter-country adoption is mostly regulated by statute.[68] In some of the countries under study, customary law provides another regime for adoption. This regime is restricted to persons subject to customary law – it is not likely to be relevant in inter-country adoption. The customary law regime for adoption is expressly saved by some national legislation.[69]

Only Kenya, Lesotho and South Africa are parties[70] to the Hague Convention on the Protection of Children and Co-operation in Respect of Inter-country Adoption 1993.[71] With regard to inter-country

[65] Ibid., s. 75D. [66] Ibid., s. 75F.

[67] *Detmold* v. *Minister of Health and Social Services* 2004 NR 174; *NS* v. *RH* 2011 (2) NR 486.

[68] The above national reports have focused mainly on conflict of laws issues. There are certainly many other requirements which have to be satisfied under each country's adoption legislation as a matter of domestic law.

[69] See, e.g., Botswana – Adoption of Children Act 1952, s. 16.

[70] Burkina Faso, Burundi, Guinea, Madagascar, Mali, Mauritius and the Seychelles are also parties to the Convention.

[71] In the following: *NS* v. *RH* 2011 (2) NR 486; *In the Matter of Iren Najjuma*, HCT-00-FD-FC-079-2009 (High Court, Uganda, 2009); and *In the Matter of Michael, an Infant*, HCT-00-FD-FC-072-2009 (High Court, Uganda, 2009), the courts advocated for Namibia and Uganda to become a party to the Hague Adoption Convention. In the words of Ugandan Judge Egonde-Ntende: '[I]t is time to reform this aspect of our law by making inter-country adoption possible where there are no suitable local adoptive parents in order to ensure that all our children grow up in the loving care of their natural parents or adopted parents and are able to develop to their full potential. This would bring the law in line not only with our Constitution and International Obligations but also with international practice under the Hague Convention on the Protection and Co-operation in respect of

adoption, it can be said that the countries under study are principally 'states of origin', i.e. children resident in these countries are more likely to be adopted by foreigners with a view to taking the adopted children abroad. With over seventy contracting parties to the Convention, including all the major developed countries from which prospective adopters usually come, it can be argued that the countries under study stand to benefit from being party to it.

In the countries under study, an adoption order is made only after a judicial inquiry – only courts therefore have jurisdiction to grant an adoption order. Residence of the child provides the basis of jurisdiction in all the countries under study – the child's domicile or nationality are not bases of jurisdiction. The decided cases reveal a tendency to construe residence liberally. Indeed, as with other matters involving children, it has been held in Malawi and South Africa that the best interests of the child are the most important consideration: a consideration which prevails over the subsidiarity principle.[72]

None of the national legislation deals with choice of law issues that could potentially arise in adoption proceedings. It is arguable whether courts in the countries under study may pay attention to foreign law in adoption proceedings. As noted above, the domicile of a child is not a basis for the jurisdiction of the courts to make an adoption order – in most cases only residence in the country where the application is made is needed. However, at common law, questions of status are governed by the law of the domicile of a person. Adoption results in a fundamental change in the status of a child: old family ties are severed, new parents are acquired and new rights, including prospects for acquiring citizenship, accrue. That such a change can be effected without regard to the law of the prospective adopted child's domicile is against principle and could be problematic. Indeed, it is likely that an adoption order made in disregard of the law of the child's domicile will not be recognised in the country of the child's domicile or in the country to which the adopting parent is

Inter-Country Adoption of Children. It is time too for Uganda to sign up and ratify this convention for the benefit of its children and take advantage of the availability of a worldwide/international network of government agencies for the protection of children.' Section 24 of the African Charter on the Rights and Welfare of the Child and ss. 20–1 of the UN Convention on Rights of the Child Convention deal with adoption. All the countries under study are parties to both treaties.

72 This is the principle that inter-country adoption should be considered strictly as an alternative to the placement of a child with adoptive parents who reside in the child's country of birth.

taking the child. Although the national legislation is silent on the choice of law in adoption proceedings, it is submitted that, to the extent that the 'best interests of the child' might be affected if the law of his or her domicile is disregarded, courts would do well to pay attention to such law. They should refuse to make an adoption order if, after assessing all the relevant facts, including the law of the child's domicile and the place of their intended residence, it appears that it would not be in the best interests of the child.

Indeed, in adoption proceedings involving foreign domiciled children or non-nationals, it is not out of place if the embassy of the foreign country or the Attorney General is allowed to intervene in the proceedings to ensure the best interests of the child are protected. In addition, it may be important for the courts to invite submission from counsel on the law of the country where the prospective adopting parent is domiciled, is a citizen or intends to reside with the child. The courts must be satisfied that an adoption order made under domestic law will be recognised in that country. They must equally be satisfied with the rights that accrue to the child after such recognition. The prospects of citizenship, equality in treatment and entitlement to social benefits conferred on children by that country and the right to inherit the estate of the adopting parents are all worthy of consideration. These issues should be mandated by statute as material considerations in any inter-country adoption proceedings.[73]

Apart from Kenya, South Africa and Zimbabwe, there are no statutory provisions dealing with the recognition of foreign adoption orders. This is remarkable, since there are a number of issues that may arise where it may be necessary for a court to decide whether or not to recognise a foreign adoption order. These include the determination of rights to citizenship, succession to the estate of an adopting parent, and the domicile of an adopted child. In the absence of a statutory regime for recognising foreign adoption orders, one must arguably look to English common law. However, the position at common law remains unsettled, and a leading case on the subject[74] has been much criticised.[75] In general, it is recommended that an adoption order made in a jurisdiction where the child was resident, a national or domiciled should be recognised. In doing this, the courts should again pay attention to the best interests of

[73] In some national legislation, the court has to be satisfied that the adoption order will be recognised abroad.

[74] *Re. Valentine's Settlement* [1965] Ch. 831.

[75] *Cheshire, North & Fawcett*, pp. 1174–5; *Dicey, Morris & Collins*, para. 20–128.

the child; they should not be reluctant to recognise a foreign adoption order if denying recognition would result in material disadvantages to the child.

In South Africa, it has been held that the effects of an adoption and the rights which it creates relate to status and, accordingly, are governed by the *lex adoptionis*.[76] The effects of adoption are very similar in the countries under study. The order extinguishes all rights, duties, obligations and liabilities of the parents or guardians of the infant and vests them in the adopter.[77]

Surrogacy agreements

A surrogate mother is a woman who bears a child for another person – for or without remuneration – either through artificial insemination or by carrying until birth another woman's surgically implanted fertilised egg. Surrogacy therefore implies an underlying agreement – a contract. In simple terms, surrogacy is an arrangement in which a woman carries and delivers a child for another couple or person. Surrogacy is a reproductive arrangement. The extent to which it is prevalent in the countries under study remains to be investigated. But it cannot be doubted that informal arrangements for that purpose exist in some countries. Indeed, informal surrogacy, arrived at more often by private agreement between family members or people known to each other, is practised in many societies.

There appears to be a growing international trend to provide an adequate legislative basis to deal with surrogacy on a formalised basis. In a recent comparative judicial exploration of the subject, a North South African High Court[78] observed that while most countries prohibit commercial surrogacy, with India being the prominent exception, the responses of other countries have been varied, ranging from an outright prohibition of both altruistic and commercial surrogacy in some jurisdictions, to the recognition and legislative regulation of altruistic surrogacy in others.

In Africa, surrogacy as an institution formally regulated by the state appears to be a very recent addition to the legal landscape. In the countries under study, it appears that it is only in South Africa that surrogacy agreements are formally regulated by statutes. This is done under sections 292 to 303 of the Children's Act 2005. While its provisions

[76] *Board of Executors* v. *Vitt* 1989 (4) SA 480. [77] Adoption Act 1956, s. 14(1).
[78] *Ex p. WH* 2011 (6) SA 514; [2011] 4 All SA 630.

may be significant in some cases of international surrogacy agreements, they are largely domestic in orientation. They do not purport to address the many private international law problems that may be generated by surrogacy agreements. In other words, although surrogacy agreements are regulated in South African law, the private international law aspects remain largely unexplored either judicially[79] or in academic writings.[80]

The fact that private international law issues likely to be generated by surrogacy agreements have not attracted attention does not mean that African courts would not be confronted with such issues. In some countries around the world, surrogacy is recognised as a legal means of becoming a parent. Thus, it is not inconceivable for a Ghanaian couple to enter into a surrogacy agreement abroad and seek recognition of the child resulting from the agreement as their 'child' for the purposes of Ghanaian law.

Under South African law, no surrogate motherhood agreement[81] is valid unless, among other reasons: the agreement is entered into in the Republic; at least one of the commissioning parents, or where the commissioning parent is a single person, that person, is at the time of entering into the agreement domiciled in the Republic; and the surrogate mother and her husband or partner, if any, are at the time of entering into the agreement domiciled in the Republic.[82] As has been observed by Slabbert, this provision displays all the qualities of a unilateral conflicts rule.[83] It indicates *when* South African law applies to a surrogate motherhood agreement, instead of identifying a single connecting factor for the category of validity of a surrogate motherhood agreement that would point in the direction of the applicable law (for example, a surrogacy

[79] See generally *Ex p. WH*; *Ex p. Applications for the Confirmation of three Surrogate Motherhood Agreements* 2011 (6) SA 22.

[80] M. Slabbert, 'Legal Regulation of Surrogate Motherhood: South Africa' in K. Trimmings and P. Beaumont (eds.), *International Surrogacy Arrangements: Legal Regulation at the International Level* (Oxford: Hart Publishing, forthcoming).

[81] 'Surrogate motherhood agreement' means an agreement between a surrogate mother and a commissioning parent in which it is agreed that the surrogate mother will be artificially fertilised for the purpose of bearing a child for the commissioning parent and in which the surrogate mother undertakes to hand over such a child to the commissioning parent upon its birth, or within a reasonable time thereafter, with the intention that the child concerned becomes the legitimate child of the commissioning parent.

[82] Children's Act 2005, s. 292.

[83] Forsyth, pp. 7–10. A multilateral conflict rule exhibits no preference for any particular legal system. When applied to the facts of the dispute it indicates which legal system governs. An example is the rule that a contract shall be governed by the law chosen by the parties. Unilateral conflict rules on the other hand do not indicate which system applies; rather, they ordain when the legal system from which they come applies.

agreement is governed by the law chosen by the parties). In the light of this provision, it is very doubtful whether a South African court may recognise a foreign surrogacy agreement which does not meet the requirements of the Children's Act, but may otherwise be valid under the law of the place where it was executed.

In countries where there is no statute on the private international law aspects of surrogacy agreements, it is arguable that the private international law rules applicable to contracts should apply to surrogacy agreements. As discussed in Chapter 7, the position is that a contract is governed by the law chosen by the parties and in the absence of such choice the law of the country with which the contract has its most real and substantial connection.

Another important issue is the legal status of a child born under a surrogacy agreement and whether that status would be recognised abroad. Under South African law, any child born of a surrogate mother in accordance with the agreement is for all purposes the child of the commissioning parent or parents from the moment of birth. The child will have no claim for maintenance or of succession against the surrogate mother, her husband or partner or any of their relatives.[84] In Namibia, the status of children born of artificial insemination or in vitro fertilisation is also regulated by statute. Section 24(1) of the Children's Status Act 2006 provides that whenever the gamete or gametes of any person, other than a married woman or her husband, have been used with the consent of both such woman and her husband for artificial insemination or in vitro fertilisation, any child born as the result of such techniques is, for all purposes, deemed to be the biological child of such woman and her husband.

In the other countries under study, as regards commissioning parents, the question of whether the child borne out of the surrogacy agreement would be recognised as their child would depend on whether that status is conferred under the law applicable to the contract and whether surrogacy is recognised as a means of reproduction under the *lex fori*. It is arguable that considerations of public policy should be very relevant in such cases. Interestingly, while in some of the countries under study there are private international law rules for deciding whether a child is legitimate or illegitimate, there appears to be no decided case for determining the applicable law for the issue of whether a person is the child of another.

[84] Children's Act 2005, s. 297.

Custody, guardianship and abduction

Botswana

A Botswanan court has jurisdiction to hear an application for custody and order for the return to Botswana of a Botswanan citizen who, prior to his or her removal from the jurisdiction, was habitually resident in Botswana.[85] In such cases, the best interests of the child principle provides an overarching context within which the jurisdiction of the court is exercised.[86] However, the court would be slow to make an order which would be ineffective in practical terms. Accordingly, in a case where a mother and her children were in Mozambique – outside the court's jurisdiction – the court declined to make an order directing the mother to deliver custody of the children to the father, who was a foreigner domiciled in Botswana.[87]

Gambia

In addition to its jurisdiction in matrimonial causes, the Gambian High Court has jurisdiction to make child custody arrangements whenever the affected child is present in Gambia.[88] The parents of a child may also apply to the Children's Court for an order of custody in respect of the child. In such cases, there is no requirement that the child should be present in Gambia.[89]

Ghana

In addition to its jurisdiction in matrimonial causes, the High Court of Ghana has jurisdiction to make child custody arrangements whenever the child whose custody is in question is present in Ghana.[90] An application for custody may also be made under section 43 of the Children's Act 1998, which does not expressly impose a requirement that the child should be present in Ghana.

[85] *Sello* v. *Sello (No. 2)* 1999 (2) BLR 104 (on appeal from *Sello* v. *Sello* 1998 BLR 502). An application for custody may also be incidental to proceedings for divorce, nullity or judicial separation. See Matrimonial Causes Act 1973, s. 28 and, generally, the Children Act 1981.

[86] *Sello* v. *Sello (No. 2)* 1999 (2) BLR 104.

[87] *Verona* v. *Verona* 1983 BLR 9.

[88] Matrimonial Causes Act 1986, s. 37.

[89] Children's Act 2005, s. 146.

[90] Matrimonial Causes Act 1971, s. 34.

In questions of custody, including those involving the 'kidnapping' of children, the welfare and happiness of the child is the paramount consideration. The court looks at the facts from every angle and gives due weight to all relevant material. Accordingly, the mere fact that a foreign court has granted custody to one of the parties is not conclusive.[91] In *Fink* v. *Coelho*,[92] it was held that, even though in an action for custody of a child, a foreign custody order – in this instance an order from a German court – is not enforceable in Ghana, the court is entitled to admit and consider it for the purpose of determining the critical issues that affect the welfare and happiness of the child who is the subject matter of the custody action.

Malawi

The jurisdiction of the High Court of Malawi over the person of an infant is not limited to infants of Malawian nationality or domicile. The court is entitled to assume jurisdiction over an infant by virtue of his or her residence in Malawi and, having so assumed jurisdiction, it could order access to the child outside the country.[93] Similarly, a Malawian court, as the court of domicile, has pre-eminent jurisdiction to make an order for custody in respect of a Malawian-domiciled child and it could so order, despite the fact that the child is resident abroad, as in the instant case in the Netherlands.[94]

A Malawian court is not bound to recognise or enforce the decision of a foreign court on a matter such as the custody of children. A foreign custody award is not conclusive as to who is entitled to custody. The welfare of the children is the paramount consideration.[95]

South Africa

The South African court is the upper guardian of all minor children that are physically present or resident within its territorial jurisdiction.

[91] *Braun* v. *Mallet* [1975] 1 GLR 81. [92] [1999–2000] 2 GLR 166.

[93] *Pentony* v. *Rennie* [1975–7] 8 MLR 149. See also the Divorce Act 1905, s. 31 on the jurisdiction to order custody in proceeding for dissolution of marriage, nullity or judicial separation.

[94] *Van Genderen* v. *Van Genderen* [1968–70] ALR Mal. 170.

[95] *In re. Chitaukire* [1975–7] 8 MLR 38.

Accordingly, it has jurisdiction to determine the custody of such children.[96] In relation to custody matters, the jurisdiction of the court of the domicile of the child is not exclusive.[97] It has, however, been held that it is somewhat unusual for a South African Court to exercise jurisdiction in a custody case concerning a minor who is merely temporarily present in the country, particularly if the custody is already governed by an order of the foreign court of competent jurisdiction.[98] The general rule is that the pre-eminent jurisdiction in these matters rests with the court of the minors' domicile or permanent residence, and any decision as to the permanent custody of the minor would usually be left to that court. But this pre-eminent jurisdiction is not necessarily exclusive jurisdiction – the paramount consideration in these matters is the best interests of the child concerned. Thus, there might be occasion for the court to exercise jurisdiction in respect of a minor who is only temporarily in the country.[99] A South African court may assume jurisdiction to hear an application for custody of a child resident abroad if the respondent is subject to its jurisdiction.[100] The court may also, in appropriate cases and taking into account the best interests of the child, grant custody to a person to enable the latter to remove the child from the jurisdiction.[101]

A South African court is not bound by a foreign court's custody order. The function of the court is to determine the best interests of the child and to make a custody order accordingly. It must form an independent judgment on the evidence before it and, in the course of doing so, will give only such weight to a foreign custody order as the circumstances might justify.[102]

96 *Eilon* v. *Eilon* 1965 (1) SA 703; *Hubert* v. *Hubert* 1960 (3) SA 181; *Birkett* v. *Birkett* 1953 (4) SA 445; *Abrahams* v. *Abrahams* 1981 (3) SA 593, 1980–1 (2) BSC 97; *Ex p. Sakota* 1964 (3) SA 8; *Pretorius* v. *Pretorius* 1954 (4) SA 210.

97 *Hubert* v. *Hubert* 1960 (3) SA 181.

98 Other circumstances may justify leaving the issue of custody to be decided by a foreign court. See *Zorbas* v. *Zorbas* 1987 (3) SA 436.

99 *Littauer* v. *Littauer* 1973 (4) SA 290.

100 *Homan* v. *Bird* 1976 (2) SA 741. But see *Vandermaelen* v. *Vandermaelen* 1973 (4) SA 584; *Mashaoane* v. *Mashaoane* 1963 (3) SA 604 (on appeal from *Mashaoane* v. *Mashaoane* 1962 (1) SA 628). See generally *Martine* v. *Large* 1952 (4) SA 31; *Angelai* v. *Padayachee* 1948 (4) SA 718.

101 *Godbeer* v. *Godbeer* 2000 (3) SA 976; *Van Rooyen* v. *Van Rooyen* 1999 (4) SA 435; *H* v. *R* 2001 (3) SA 623; *F* v. *F* 2006 (3) SA 42.

102 *Martens* v. *Martens* 1991 (4) SA 287; *Riddle* v. *Riddle* 1956 (2) SA 739; *Abrahams* v. *Abrahams* 1981 (3) SA 593, 1980–1 (2) BSC 97; *Righetti* v. *Pinchen* 1955 (3) SA 338.

Tanzania

The Tanzanian High Court has jurisdiction to order the custody of a child on the application of a parent, guardian or relative.[103] The primary consideration in making such a determination is the best interests of the child.[104]

An order from a foreign court granting custody of a child to a person is not binding on a Tanzanian court, but may be of high persuasive value. Thus, where custody of a child was granted to a child's mother by a German court and the father took the child to Tanzania, it was held in an application for an order to return the child that although the German court's order was not binding, it was of high persuasive authority and custody was awarded to the mother.[105]

Zimbabwe

A Zimbabwean court has the jurisdiction to award the custody of a child who is physically present in Zimbabwe.[106] The domiciliary court is not the only court that has jurisdiction in respect of custody.[107] Where jurisdiction is being exercised on the basis of a child's physical presence within Zimbabwe, the court continues to have this jurisdiction until the final end or determination of the proceedings – it does not matter that the child is removed from Zimbabwe.[108] A Zimbabwean court has the jurisdiction to order a person resident abroad to return a child he or she has taken away from the jurisdiction of the court,[109] to order the immediate return of a child into the jurisdiction of a foreign court,[110] order that a child abroad be placed in the custody of a designated person abroad,[111] or restrain a person from removing a child from its jurisdiction.[112]

[103] Law of Children Act 2009, s. 37(1). See also Law of Marriage Act 1971, s. 125(1).
[104] Law of Children Act 2009, s. 37(4).
[105] *In re. Hofmann; Hofmann* v. *Hofmann* [1972] EA 100.
[106] *Dickinson* v. *Dickinson* 1971 (2) SA 507; *Dube* v. *Dube* 1969 (2) RLR 410, 1970 (1) SA 331; *McConnell* v. *McConnell* 1981 ZLR 12, 1981 (4) SA 300; *Ferrers* v. *Ferrers* 1954 (1) SA 514.
[107] *McConnell* v. *McConnell* 1981 ZLR 12, 1981 (4) SA 300.
[108] Ibid.
[109] *G* v. *G* 2003 (5) SA 396, 2002 (2) ZLR 408; but see *Handford* v. *Handford* 1958 (3) SA 378.
[110] *Ambala* v. *Ambala* 1981 ZLR 29.
[111] *Allan* v. *Allan* 1959 (3) SA 473.
[112] *Taylor* v. *Taylor* 1952 (4) SA 279.

In an application for custody, the primary consideration is the welfare of the child.[113] The court has to form an independent judgment on the evidence before it as to what these best interests are, but in so doing, it should give such weight to a foreign custody order as was justified in the circumstances.[114] The main factors which bear on the weight to be attached to such a judgment are whether a full inquiry was conducted by the foreign court, the foreign court's reasons for awarding custody to a particular parent, whether it recognises the same principles of Zimbabwean law, whether its judgment was a reasonable one, and whether there has been a substantial change in circumstances since the judgment.[115]

Comments

It is possible to distinguish between two types of custody application in the countries under study, namely those made incidental to a matrimonial cause[116] and those brought as independent actions. In respect of applications unrelated to a matrimonial cause, some jurisdictions, such as Gambia and Ghana, require that the child should be present in the country. The majority of the countries under study, however, impose no such restriction. On the other hand, a custody order in respect of a child resident abroad can create problems. Accordingly, jurisdiction should be exercised with caution since it involves a positive act affecting a child within a foreign state. The removal of the child from the foreign state as a result of the court's order is not likely to go unnoticed by the authorities of the foreign state, including its courts who, as guardians of children within the jurisdiction, can restrain such removal. Without diminishing the adverse impact such international custody battles can have on the child, the above situation also puts the removing parent in an insurmountable legal dilemma – each option he or she pursues may be visited with contempt of court proceedings. This is a recipe for

[113] In this regard, the court may take into account the prior conduct of the applicant, such as the previous removal of the child from its jurisdiction or declining to return the child following a court order. *Kuperman* v. *Posen* 2001 (1) ZLR 208.

[114] *Dube* v. *Dube* 1969 (2) RLR 410, 1970 (1) SA 331; *Ferrers* v. *Ferrers* 1954 (1) SA 514.

[115] *Jagoe* v. *Jagoe* 1969 (2) RLR 266, 1969 (4) SA 59.

[116] It was held in *Mehrunnissa* v. *Parvez* [1979] LLR 15 that an application for an order to allow the applicant, who had earlier been divorced, to take her child out of the jurisdiction did not raise a conflict of laws issue.

international judicial conflicts. Consequently, it is suggested that the considerations that underlie and encourage restraint in providing extra-territorial remedies relating to acts and things within a foreign state should be borne in mind in cases involving children.

The best interests of the child – the welfare principle – remain the primary or paramount consideration in all custody applications. This is encapsulated in the constitutions, statutes and judicial decisions of the countries under study. Jurisprudence in most of the countries under study affirms that one effect of the application of the principle is that a court is not bound by a decision of a foreign court awarding custody to a particular person.[117] Such a foreign decision is not conclusive and does not have a *res judicata* effect. The court will consider the application for custody afresh, but will give persuasive weight to the foreign custody decision.

Custody and abduction – Hague Convention cases

At present, only three of the countries under study – Lesotho, South Africa and Zimbabwe – are parties to the Hague Convention on the Civil Aspects of International Child Abduction 1980.[118] In countries that are not parties to the Convention, judicial responses to arguments inviting them to 'give effect' to the principles and spirit of the Convention have been mixed. Ghana is not a party to the Convention. However, it has been held that a Ghanaian court is permitted to make reference to the Convention when considering matters that affect the welfare and happiness of a child, especially in cases where the child is habitually resident in a country – in the instant case, Germany – that is party to the Convention.[119] In South Africa, the Convention was invoked at a time when the implementing legislation had not yet come into force.[120] In contrast, a similar invitation was rejected in Kenya[121]

[117] As regards Swaziland, see *Marques* v. *Marques* [1979–81] Sw. LR 200.

[118] South Africa's Children's Act 2005, ss. 274–80 and Zimbabwe's Child Abduction Act 1996 give effect to the Convention. Lesotho has not yet enacted legislation to give effect to the Convention.

[119] *Fink* v. *Coelho* [1999–2000] 2 GLR 166. [120] *K* v. *K* 1999 (4) SA 691.

[121] *AOG* v. *SAJ* [2011] eKLR. It was held that reliance on unratified treaties is not constitutionally sanctioned in Kenyan law and to do otherwise would also be inconsistent with binding judicial precedents. Earlier the trial court held that, subject to the best interests of the child principle, it was prepared to defer to an English court order that the child

and held unworthy of consideration in Zambia – for procedural reasons specific to the case.[122]

Early in the history of its implementation in South Africa, the constitutionality of the Convention was unsuccessfully challenged. In *Sonderup* v. *Tondelli*,[123] the respondent argued that the Hague Convention on the Civil Aspects of International Child Abduction Act 1996, which is the South African legislation implementing the Convention, obliged the courts to act in a manner inconsistent with Article 28(2) of the South Africa Constitution, which required that a child's best interests were of paramount importance in every matter concerning the child. The court rejected the challenge. It reasoned that the Convention clearly recognised and safeguarded the best interests of the child. Even assuming an inconsistency, it was prepared to hold that it could be justified under Article 36 of the Constitution, which required a proportionality analysis and the weighing up of relevant factors in deciding the justifiability of a limitation of fundamental rights. For countries which may potentially become parties to the Convention, the judgment is significant since provisions comparable to Articles 28(2) and 36 are found in the constitutions or statutes of other African countries.

The decision in *Sonderup* does not mean that the best interests of the child has no relevance in applications under the Convention. In *Senior Family Advocate, Cape Town* v. *Houtman*,[124] the court cautioned against blindly following foreign cases given the special dictates of the South African Constitution. The courts have, however, emphasised that in an application under the Convention, the best interests of the child analysis should not be pursued as in a custody application.[125] It has been reasoned that the Convention operates on the presumption that the best interests of the child are served by ordering the return of the wrongfully removed child to his or her place of habitual residence.[126] In general,

adbucted from the United Kingdom should be returned to the United Kingdom, and order the child's return. *Shabbir Ali Jusab* v. *Anaar Osman Gamrai* [2009] eKLR.

122 *Zanetta Nyendwa* v. *Kenneth Paul Spooner*, Judgment No. 20 of 2010 (Supreme Court, Zambia, 2010).

123 2001 (1) SA 1171. 124 2004 (6) SA 274.

125 In *Kuperman* v. *Posen* 2001 (1) ZLR 208, it was held that the conduct of an applicant for custody who previously removed the child in question from Zimbabwe to Israel, and who was subsequently ordered by the Israeli court to return the children to Zimbabwe, was a significant consideration in the determination of an application for custody on the child now residing in Zimbabwe.

126 *Sonderup* v. *Tondelli* 2001 (1) SA 1171.

there have been many instances in which the Convention has been invoked – not always successfully – to secure the immediate return of children who have been wrongly removed from their places of habitual residence.[127] Relatively fewer cases have been reported in Zimbabwe[128] and none in Lesotho.

A contentious issue considered in the cases is the degree of proof required of a party who wishes to rely on the Convention's Article 13 defences against the return of the child.[129] In *WS* v. *LS*,[130] the court held that the onus on a person opposing an application under the article was no greater than that ordinarily applicable in civil cases. The phrase 'grave risk' used in Article 13 did not introduce an onus above that normally applicable, but meant there had to be a serious or well-founded reason why the situation of the child would be intolerable if the application were granted. To the court, the high test of intolerability set by English courts was not required under South African law, given the country's Bill of Rights.[131]

It is open to discussion what the effect of the Convention or becoming a party to it is on the inherent jurisdiction of a country's

[127] *Pennello* v. *Pennello* 2004 (3) SA 100; *Central Authority* v. *H* 2008 (1) SA 49; *Central Authority* v. *B* 2009 (1) SA 624; *WS* v. *LS* 2000 (4) SA 104; *Smith* v. *Smith* 2001 (3) SA 845, [2001] 3 All SA 146; *Chief Family Advocate* v. *G* 2003 (2) SA 599; *Pennello* v. *Pennello* 2004 (3) SA 117; *Senior Family Advocate, Cape Town* v. *Houtman* 2004 (6) SA 274; *B* v. *S* 2006 (5) SA 540; *S* v. *H* 2007 (3) SA 330; *Central Authority (South Africa)* v. *A* 2007 (5) SA 501; *Central Authority* v. *Reynders (born Jones) (LS intervening)* [2011] 2 All SA 438; *Central Authority for the Republic of South Africa* v. *B* [2012] 3 All SA 95; *KG* v. *CB* [2012] 2 All SA 366, 2012 (4) SA 136; *B* v. *G* 2012 (2) SA 329; *Central Authority of the Republic of South Africa* v. *LG* 2011 (2) SA 386; *Central Authority of the Republic of South Africa* v. *B* 2012 (2) SA 296, [2012] 3 All SA 95; *KG* v. *CB* 2012 (4) SA 136, [2012] 2 All SA 366; *NF* v. *MC*, Case No. 17845/2012 (High Court, South Africa, 2012). For an updated list of South African cases decided under the Convention, see www.justice.gov.za/hague/case-law.html.

[128] *Secretary of Justice* v. *Parker* 1999 (2) ZLR 400; *G* v. *G* 2003 (5) SA 396, 2002 (2) ZLR 408; *Kuperman* v. *Posen* 2001 (1) ZLR 208; *Harris* v. *Harris*, HC 3110/08 (High Court, Zimbabwe, 2009); *Kumalo* v. *Kumalo* 2004 (1) ZLR 248.

[129] Under Art. 13, the judicial or administrative authority of the requested state is not bound to order the return of the child if the person, institution or other body which opposes its return establishes that: (a) the person, institution or other body having the care of the person of the child was not actually exercising the custody rights at the time of removal or retention, or had consented to or subsequently acquiesced in the removal or retention; or (b) there is a grave risk that his or her return would expose the child to physical or psychological harm or otherwise place the child in an intolerable situation.

[130] 2000 (4) SA 104.

[131] Compare *Secretary for Justice* v. *Parker* 1999 (2) ZLR 400.

courts. As discussed above, courts in the countries under study have jurisdiction in respect of custody application and some have in the exercise of that jurisdiction been willing to order the return of children taken abroad. The issue is whether, where they have jurisdiction in domestic law, they can make an *in personam* order against a person who has wrongfully removed a child to another Convention country for the return of the child, or whether they have to follow the Convention and leave it to the latter's court to order the return? In *B* v. *S*,[132] the court held that it had no jurisdiction to order a person resident in the United States to return to South Africa a child who had been removed from that country to the United States. To the court, such an order would be ineffective since the court could not enforce it and, under the Convention, the court which should order the child's return was the appropriate US court. It is submitted that this is an inappropriate limitation on the jurisdiction of the court. Indeed, it can be argued that Article 18 of the Convention, which provides that it does not 'limit the power of a judicial or administrative authority to order the return of the child at any time', implies national courts retain the jurisdiction under national law to order return of children from abroad, even in cases where the child has been taken to a Convention country. An example can be found in *G* v. *G*,[133] where, even though the United States is a party to the Convention, the Zimbabwe High Court ordered the defendant in an action for divorce to return to Zimbabwe children of the marriage whom she had unlawfully taken to California.

Admittedly, if this is the correct interpretation of Article 18,[134] it raises the prospect of conflicting judgments between courts in countries that are parties to the Convention and can adversely affect the operation of the Convention. The exercise of such a jurisdiction would be particularly important where the foreign court refuses to order the return of the child, but the domestic court has *in personam* jurisdiction over the person who removed the child to the foreign jurisdiction.

[132] 2006 (5) SA 540. [133] *G* v. *G* 2003 (5) SA 396, 2002 (2) ZLR 408.

[134] See generally Council Regulation (EC) No. 2201/2003 of 27 November 2003 concerning jurisdiction and the recognition and enforcement of judgments in matrimonial matters and the matters of parental responsibility, repealing Regulation (EC) No. 1347/2000, Art. 10, which supports this interpretation. Also, a reading of Elisa Perez-Vera's Explanatory Report to the Convention does not suggest a contrary interpretation.

The interaction between the Convention and national civil procedure rules,[135] especially the effect of the latter on the expedited return of wrongfully removed children, also deserves consideration. It was argued unsuccessfully in *Secretary for Justice* v. *Parker*[136] that in applications involving children, rule 249 of the Zimbabwe Rules of Court required appointment of a curator *ad litem* to investigate and submit a report for consideration.[137] Such a course would have delayed the proceedings, something which would have defeated a principal objective of the Convention. That one can appeal a decision ordering the return of a child, or apply for judicial review of a decision of a Central Authority to request a return, are additional examples.[138] Admittedly, the Convention does not purport to override national civil procedure rules on issues such as right of appeal and judicial review, which sometimes have constitutional foundations. In *Central Authority* v. *H*,[139] the South African court was troubled by the three-and-a-half years which had elapsed from the time of the wrongful retention. The delay was in part attributable to national procedural rules.[140] Compliance with such rules may, in large measure, be unavoidable. However, it is submitted that where there is discretion in enforcing such rules, it should be exercised to facilitate the expeditious return of the child as envisaged under the Convention.

135 See generally *GS* v. *AH*, Case No. 11592/05 (High Court, South Africa, 2006) on the inter-relationship between the Convention and national law.

136 1999 (2) ZLR 400.

137 *Secretary of Justice* v. *Parker*, at 403. However, the court accepted that there may be instances in Convention applications where they may be assisted by a specialist report, e.g. touching on the health of the minor.

138 An interesting comparative case in this respect is *Kolbatschenko* v. *King No* 2001 (4) SA 336. The underlying cause in this application was in criminal law. The ruling of the court has, however, relevance for international civil procedures, especially in instances where the state or its apparatus have to intervene in something outside their jurisdiction. A principal argument in the case was that as requests for international mutual assistance are directed to foreign states, the making of such requests is essentially a political act in the realm of international relations, and hence constitutes the non-justiciable conduct of foreign affairs by the Republic. The court held that the issue of letters of request is an administrative action and it is only in highly exceptional cases that a court will adopt a hands-off approach where discretion has been exercised or where an executive or administrative decision has been made which directly affects the rights of an individual applicant. This suggests that, potentially, a request by a Central Authority for the return of a child may be open to judicial review.

139 2008 (1) SA 49.

140 The court also found serious managerial, training and human resource shortfalls at the South African Central Authority. It directed that a copy of the judgment be sent to the Minister of Justice and Constitutional Development and the Director-General for attention.

Legitimacy and legitimation

Botswana

Any person who is a Botswanan citizen or whose right to be deemed a Botswanan citizen depends wholly or in part on his legitimacy or on the validity of any marriage, may, if he is domiciled in Botswana or claims any property situate in Botswana, apply to the High Court for an order declaring that he is the legitimate child of his parents, or that the marriage of his father and mother or of his grandfather or grandmother was a valid marriage or that his own marriage was a valid marriage.[141] Similarly, any person claiming that he or his parent or any more remote ancestor became or has become a legitimated person may apply to the High Court for an order declaring that he or his parent or more remote ancestor, as the case may be, became or has become a legitimated person.[142]

Ghana

The legitimacy of a person is considered one of status depending on the law of domicile of origin, i.e. the law of the place where the parents were domiciled at his birth and, where the parents have different domiciles, it is the domicile of the father which is relevant. Accordingly, where a child was born in Germany to a German-domiciled woman and a Ghanaian-domiciled man, it was held that the law of Ghana, as the *lex domicilii* of the child, should determine whether or not the child was legitimate.[143] A child legitimate by the law of the country where at the date of its birth the parents were domiciled is legitimate, whether or not he would be considered legitimate under Ghana law. Ghana law recognises the status declared by the law of domicile.[144]

Kenya

Where the parents of an illegitimate person marry, the marriage shall, if the father of the illegitimate person was or is at the date of the marriage domiciled in Kenya, render that person, if living, legitimate from the date of the marriage.[145] Where the parents of an illegitimate person marry and

[141] Matrimonial Causes Act 1973, s. 26(1). [142] Ibid., s. 26(2).
[143] *Republic* v. *Mallet, Ex p. Braun* [1975] 1 GLR 68.
[144] *Coleman* v. *Shang* [1959] GLR 390 at 406. [145] Legitimacy Act, s. 3(1).

the father of the illegitimate person was or is at the time of the marriage domiciled in a foreign country by the law of which the illegitimate person became legitimated by virtue of that subsequent marriage, that person, if living, shall in Kenya be recognised as having been so legitimated from the date of the marriage. This rule applies regardless of the fact that his father was not at the time of the birth of that person domiciled in a country in which legitimation by subsequent marriage was permitted by law.[146]

A person may petition the High Court for a declaration of legitimacy. Such a person need not be domiciled in or a citizen of Kenya.[147]

Namibia

A child born of parents who marry each other at any time after the child's birth is treated as a child born inside marriage in all respects as from the date of birth, regardless of whether the parents could not have legally married each other at the time of the child's conception or birth.[148] The status of any child conceived or born of a voidable marriage is not affected by the annulment of that marriage by a competent court.[149]

Nigeria

The legitimacy or illegitimacy of a child is to be determined by the law of the country in which its parents were domiciled at the time of the child's birth.[150]

Sierra Leone

Where the parents of an illegitimate person marry each other, the marriage shall, if the father or mother of the illegitimate person was or is at the date of the marriage resident in Sierra Leone, render that person, if living, legitimate from the date of the marriage.[151] Where the parents of an illegitimate person marry and the father of the illegitimate person was or is at the time of the marriage domiciled in a foreign country by the law

146 Ibid., s. 9(1). 147 Ibid., s. 4(1).
148 Children's Status Act 2006, s. 19. 149 Ibid., s. 22.
150 *Bamgbose* v. *Daniel* (1952–5) 14 WACA 111; *Bamgbose* v. *Daniel* (1952–5) 14 WACA 116.
151 Legitimacy Act 1989, s. 2(1).

of which the illegitimate person became legitimated by virtue of such subsequent marriage, that person, if living, shall in Sierra Leone be recognised as having been so legitimated from the date of the marriage. This is so regardless of the fact that his father was not, at the time of the birth of such person, domiciled in a country in which legitimation by subsequent marriage was permitted by law.[152]

Regardless of his domicile, a person claiming that he or his parent or any more remote ancestor became or has become a legitimated person may apply to the High Court for a decree declaring that the petitioner is the legitimate child of his parents.[153]

South Africa

A child born out of wedlock is legitimated by the subsequent marriage of his or her parents.[154] The courts of the domicile of the child[155] or the domicile of the applicant[156] have jurisdiction to declare whether a child is legitimate.

Tanzania

A person may petition the High Court of Tanzania for a declaratory decree if he or she is domiciled in Tanzania or if he or she is resident in Tanzania, or where the decree is sought as to the validity of a ceremony which took place in Tanzania and purported to be a marriage.[157] A declaration decree may be to the effect that the petitioner or either of his or her parents was born legitimate, or that the parents or grandparents were lawfully married.[158]

Zambia

Where the parents of an illegitimate person marry, the marriage shall, if the father of the illegitimate person is at the date of the marriage domiciled in Zambia, render that person, if living, legitimate.[159] In cases where a father is domiciled in Zambia (or if deceased was so domiciled before his death), the child of a void marriage is treated as

[152] Ibid., s. 8(1). [153] Ibid., s. 3(1). [154] *Ex p. J* 1951 (1) SA 665.
[155] *Von Wintzingerode* v. *Von Wintzingerode* 1964 (2) SA 618.
[156] *Ex p. Anastasio* 1969 (1) SA 36. [157] Law of Marriage Act 1971, s. 77(1).
[158] Ibid., s. 94(2)(b). [159] Legitimacy Act 1924, s. 3.

the legitimate child of his parents if at the time of the act of intercourse resulting in the birth (or at the time of the celebration of the marriage if later) both or either of the parties reasonably believed that the marriage was valid.[160] Where a decree of nullity is granted in respect of a voidable marriage, any child who would have been the legitimate child of the parties to the marriage if it had been dissolved, instead of being annulled, at the date of the decree shall be deemed to be their legitimate child notwithstanding the annulment.[161]

The High Court has jurisdiction to declare that an applicant is the legitimated child of his parents regardless of whether the applicant is domiciled in Zambia.[162] Where the father of an illegitimate person is, at the time of the marriage of both parents, domiciled in a country under whose law an illegitimate person becomes legitimated by virtue of subsequent marriage, the Zambian courts will recognise the legitimate status so conferred by the marriage, regardless of the fact that under the law of the domicile of the father at the time of birth legitimation by subsequent marriage was not permitted.[163]

Comments

Historically, legitimacy was very significant for the purposes of succession and inheritance. It can be argued that, at present, in the countries under study the distinction between legitimate and illegitimate children has become largely insignificant – judicial decisions, constitutional and statutory provisions have watered down the legal significance of the distinction.[164] Indeed, with the entrenchment of human rights in the constitutions of all the countries under study, it is doubtful whether the distinction between a legitimate and illegitimate child is still valid at all.[165] For example, under Article 23 of the Constitution of the Republic of Malawi, 'all children, regardless of the circumstances of their birth, are entitled to equal treatment before the law'. Similarly, under

[160] Ibid., s. 4. [161] Ibid., s. 5. [162] Ibid., s. 6. [163] Ibid., s. 12.

[164] See, e.g., Constitution of the Republic of Ghana 1992, Art. 28(1)(b); and the Children's Act 1998, s. 7. Both provide that 'every child, whether or not born in wedlock, shall be entitled to reasonable provision out of the estate of its parents'. Tanzania – Law of the Child Act 2009, ss. 5 and 10; *Frans* v. *Paschke* 2007 (2) NR 520; *Bhe* v. *Khayelitsha Magistrate* 2005 (1) SA 580; *In re. Asante (Decd.), Asante* v. *Owusu* [1992] 1 GLR 119 at 126.

[165] In this respect, it appears that customary law in some of the countries under study is far ahead of the modern human rights regime to the extent that it recognises no such distinction.

section 42(2) of the Constitution of the Republic of Nigeria, 'no citizen of Nigeria shall be subjected to any disability or deprivation merely by reason of the circumstances of his birth'.[166] Notwithstanding the above, the distinction remains germane for certain issues such as domicile of children.[167]

The bases upon which courts in the countries under study would have jurisdiction to entertain proceedings for a declaration of legitimacy appear not to have been expressly dealt with by legislation or case law in many of the countries. In the countries where the subject is addressed, such as Botswana, Kenya, South Africa, Sierra Leone, Tanzania and Zambia, the bases appear to draw on the bases of jurisdiction in matrimonial causes. In Botswana, South Africa and Tanzania, domicile provides a basis of jurisdiction for the court to declare that a person is legitimate, but no such requirement is imposed on the petitioner in Kenya, Sierra Leone and Zambia.

The legitimacy or illegitimacy of a child is a question of status and it appears that in most of the countries under study, it is governed by the law of the domicile of the father at the time of birth. Legitimation by subsequent marriage is statutorily recognised in most of the countries under study.[168] There are two aspects to this and on both aspects there appear to be variations in the law. Firstly, to become legitimated domestically, Kenya and Zambia require that the father – whose domicile the child acquires – should be domiciled in the country at the date of marriage. In Sierra Leone, the father should be resident in Sierra Leone at the date of marriage. South Africa and Namibia impose no such requirements – the subsequent marriage of the parents is enough to confer the domicile of the father on the child, but it remains unclear whether the child acquires the domicile of the mother or the father, especially in cases where the wife maintains her independent domicile despite marriage.

Secondly, in Kenya, Sierra Leone and Zambia, legitimation by subsequent marriage conferred by the law of the domicile of the father at the time of marriage will be recognised even though at the time of birth of the child the domicile of the father did not allow for legitimation by subsequent marriage. In other words, it need not be the case that the domicile of the father both at the time of the child's birth and also at the

166 See also Tanzania – Law of the Child Act 2009, s. 10.

167 See Ch. 3.

168 This also appears to be the case in the customary laws of some countries: see, e.g., *Mthembu* v. *Letsela* 2000 (3) SA 867.

time of the subsequent marriage allows for legitimation by subsequent marriage – the domicile of the father at the time of marriage is the sole criterion.

It is laudable that an illegitimate child may become legitimated by virtue of the subsequent marriage of the parents. The requirements imposed do not appear to be too onerous. However, the more liberal regimes in Namibia and South Africa are to be preferred. As in the case of domicile of married women, the rules here are heavily skewed towards the domicile of the father – they are not gender sensitive. As discussed in Chapter 3, a number of countries have reformed their law on domicile of married women and children to make it more balanced. This is an area where such reform is needed. It need not be the case that a child should always acquire the domicile of the father on birth. It may be appropriate in some instances for the child to acquire the domicile of the mother – of course, this assumes that the mother has an independent domicile and does not acquire the domicile of the husband on marriage, a position which is denied in some of the countries under study.

There are statutes that protect a child from becoming illegitimate when the parents' marriage is declared a nullity. For this purpose, most of the countries under study distinguish between void and voidable marriages, and restrict the privilege of continuing legitimacy despite annulment to only children of voidable marriages.[169] Indeed, in Malawi and Uganda the privilege is granted only for the purposes of inheritance and is limited to only two or three defined grounds of annulment.[170] However, in Gambia and Ghana, children of both void and voidable marriages benefit from the privilege.[171] It is uncertain in the countries which restrict the privilege to children of voidable marriage what happens when a void marriage is so declared. In Namibia, special

[169] See Botswana – Matrimonial Causes Act 1973, s. 22(6); Kenya – Matrimonial Causes Act 1941, s. 14(2); Namibia – Children's Status Act 2006, s. 22; Nigeria – Matrimonial Causes Act 1970, s. 38(2); Tanzania – Law of Marriage Act 1971, s. 98(1)(a); Zambia – Matrimonial Causes Act 2007, s. 33(2), Legitimacy Act 1924, s. 5; Zimbabwe – Matrimonial Causes Act 1986, s. 14.

[170] Section 13 of Uganda's Divorce Act 1904 allows the child of an annulled marriage to remain legitimate (and only for the purposes of succession) when the marriage has been annulled on grounds of insanity or when the marriage was entered into in good faith on the mistaken assumption that a former spouse was deceased. Section 13 of Malawi's Divorce Act 1905 adds another ground, namely that the respondent was at the time of the marriage suffering from venereal disease in a communicable form.

[171] Gambia – Matrimonial Causes Act 1986, s. 16; Ghana – Matrimonial Causes Act 1971, s. 14.

provision is made for such children. Under section 23(2) of Namibia's Children's Act 2006, in case of a void marriage involving a child the court must inquire into the best interests of the child and make provision for safeguarding the interests of the child born of that marriage. In general, it can be argued that a child born to a void marriage takes on the domicile of the mother since that is how the domicile of an illegitimate child is determined.[172]

[172] However, in Namibia, a child born outside of marriage is deemed to be domiciled at the place or in the country with which he or she has the closest connection. Children's Status Act 2006, s. 18.

PART V

Property, succession and administration of estates

14

Property

Property raises some of the most complex and difficult private international law issues. These issues span the fields of deciding whether a thing constitutes property and, if yes, what type of property, to ascertaining the rules applicable to the transfer of property and rights thereunder. Beyond the general treatment of the subject, specific contexts, such as marriage[1] and insolvency, often call for special treatment. This chapter deals with the nature of property, whether and when the courts would assume jurisdiction in respect of foreign property, choice of law regarding ownership and transfer of movables and immovables, and insolvency and bankruptcy.

Nature and legal *situs* of property

Namibia

The *situs* of an incorporeal right (in this instance, the rights in a Namibian judgment award and order for costs) do not only exist at the place where the debtor is, resides or is domiciled, but if the right can be enforced as effectively elsewhere, it may equally be deemed to exist there. In other words, the fact that the normal rule determines that an incorporeal right follows the person entitled to exercise it does not mean that is the only place where such a right can be enforced.[2] It has also been accepted that a patent is an incorporeal right which vests or is situated at the place where the inventor is domiciled.[3]

Nigeria

A simple contract debt is situated where the debtor resides, or is to be found, because it is there that the debt can be enforced against him or her

[1] The effect of marriage on the property rights of the spouses is addressed in Ch. 11.

[2] *Bourgwells Ltd* v. *Shepavolov* 1999 NR 410 (on appeal from *Bourgwells Ltd (Owners of MFV Ofelia)* v. *Shepalov* 1998 NR 307).

[3] *Gemfarm Investments (Pty) Ltd* v. *Trans Hex Group Ltd* 2009 (2) NR 477.

by process of law. This rule is not displaced by a stipulation for payment of the debt elsewhere.[4]

South Africa

The locality of an incorporeal property (in this instance, a claim for payment of costs) is the place where the debtor resides because that is where the debtor must be sued in order to obtain performance.[5] It has been held that the *situs* of incorporeals exists by virtue of the analogy between corporeals and incorporeals. Corporeals have only one *situs* and, by analogy, the same ought to apply to incorporeals.[6] Accordingly, it has been held that the contractual rights of a time charterer are not located wherever the vessel may happen to be from time to time, but are located where the disponent owner, from whom the vessel is chartered, resides.[7] Meanwhile, the *situs* of a share is clearly the place of registration of the shares.[8]

Comments

There are relatively very few cases on this subject. However, it cannot be doubted that all the countries under study distinguish between movable and immovable property for the purposes of applying their private international law rules. There does not appear to be direct judicial authority in the countries under study on the question of which law should determine whether a thing is movable or immovable.[9] It can be argued that, in the interest of uniformity of decision and consistency with approaches in other common law jurisdictions, the law of the place where the property is situated should decide whether a thing is movable or immovable.[10]

[4] *Aluminum Industries Aktien Gesellschaft* v. *Federal Board of Inland Revenue* 1971 (2) ALR Comm. 121, [1971] 2 NCLR 121.

[5] *Nahrungsmittel GmbH* v. *Otto* 1993 (1) SA 639 (*Nahrungsmittel GmbH* v. *Otto* 1992 (2) SA 748; *Nahrungsmittel GmbH* v. *Otto* 1991 (4) SA 414); *MV Snow Delta Serva Ship Ltd* v. *Discount Tonnage Ltd* 2000 (4) SA 746.

[6] *MV Snow Delta Serva Ship Ltd* v. *Discount Tonnage Ltd* 2000 (4) SA 746.

[7] *MV Snow Delta Serva Ship* v. *Discount Tonnage.*

[8] *Uniroyal Inc.* v. *Thor Chemical SA (Pty) Ltd* 1984 (1) SA 381.

[9] Although outside the scope of this study, it is worth mentioning that a Sudanese court once held that the right to distinguish between movables and immovables belongs exclusively to the Sudanese court, which holds that leaseholds are immovables. *Hanna Kattan* v. *John Y. Kattan* [1957] SLJR 35.

[10] Forsyth, p. 369.

The issue of where an incorporeal right is legally situated can be significant for both choice of law and jurisdictional purposes. The jurisprudence in Namibia, Nigeria and South Africa suggests that an incorporeal right, such as a debt, is located at the place where the debtor resides. The rule that a debt is situated in the country where the debtor resides is often appropriate, since, in most cases, that is the place where the right can be enforced. However, this can pose problems. In cases where jurisdiction is founded on the existence of property within the jurisdiction, the effect of the rule is that sometimes it is impossible to bring an action against the holder of the right other than in the country where he or she resides.[11] On the other hand, Namibian courts have been prepared to allow an 'exception' to the rule – they have held that where the right can be effectively enforced elsewhere, it is similarly located there. In the words of Justice Teek, 'it would amount to an extremely "ivory tower" and academic approach if the Court were to decline to exercise jurisdiction when it can do so effectively because of the rigorous enforcement of sterile legal formalisms'.[12] This approach of inquiring whether the right can be enforced at a place other than where the debtor resides is commendable. A debtor should not be able to evade recovery of the debt by changing residence or making it difficult or more onerous for the creditor to pursue their claim.

Jurisdiction over property

Botswana

The courts of the country where a child is domiciled have jurisdiction to adjudicate issues related to the transfer of immovable property owned by the child and situated in Botswana. In *In re. Estate Swart*,[13] the guardian of a minor applied for leave of the court to enable her to sell, on behalf of the minor, immovable property of the minor, situated in Botswana. The minor and her guardian were domiciled in South Africa. It was held that the South African court, being the court of the minor's domicile, was the proper court to exercise jurisdiction.

[11] In *MV Snow Delta Serva Ship Ltd* v. *Discount Tonnage Ltd* 2000 (4) SA 746 at 755, the court rejected an invitation to revise the rule. The court reasoned that the rule was not 'out of step with the international position' on the subject and also that holding otherwise would encourage litigation in South Africa on disputes which are 'unconnected to and between persons who have no relationship with [south Africa]'.

[12] *Bourgwells Ltd* v. *Shepavolov* 1999 NR 410 at 422.

[13] 1974 (1) BLR 88.

Ghana

A Ghanaian court has no jurisdiction to entertain proceedings principally concerned with a question of title to, or the right of possession of, immovable property situated outside of the jurisdiction. However, where there is evidence that a party has dealt most inequitably with immovable property situated abroad, a Ghanaian court may assume jurisdiction in equity.[14]

Kenya

A Kenyan court will not grant orders relating to land situated abroad.[15] However, where a contract relating to immovable property situated abroad has been entered into in Kenya, and where the relief sought is not a specific declaration as to the ownership of that property, nor does it represent damages for trespass to it, or any other relief which, if granted, would require execution by the courts of that foreign country, but is simply the payment or repayment of money arising from an alleged breach or repudiation of such contract, then, unless there are peculiar reasons which would make it difficult or impracticable for the Kenyan courts to assume jurisdiction to try the suit, the courts will assume such jurisdiction. This is so, notwithstanding that it may be necessary for the purpose of determining the suit to make a decision as to the ownership of such immovable property.[16] Accordingly, a suit to recover the purchase price of land in Tanzania is maintainable.[17]

Malawi

In proceedings under section 17 of the Married Women's Property Act 1882,[18] the court has jurisdiction to deal with property situated outside the jurisdiction. In this instance, the immovable property (a house) was in South Africa. The parties were domiciled in Malawi, the respondent was resident in Malawi at the time the summons were served and the court was satisfied that its order would not be ineffectual in South Africa.[19]

[14] *Akoto* v. *Akoto* [2011] 1 SCGLR 533.

[15] *Papco Industries Ltd* v. *Eastern and Southern African Trade and Development Bank* [2006] eKLR.

[16] *Singh* v. *Singh* [1955] 28 KLR 50.

[17] *Ladha* v. *Benbros Motors Ltd* [1975] 1 EA 1.

[18] This Act applies in Malawi by virtue of s. 4 of the Divorce Act 1905.

[19] *Cromar* v. *Cromar* [1991] 14 MLR 60.

Nigeria[20]

A Nigerian court has jurisdiction to entertain an action *in personam* in respect of immovable property situated outside the jurisdiction, on the grounds of either a contract or equity. However, it has no jurisdiction to entertain an action for determining title to, or the right to, the possession of, any immovable property situated abroad, or for the recovery of damages for trespass to such immovable property.[21] Accordingly, an action for the specific performance of a contract relating to land outside the jurisdiction is maintainable if the parties reside within the court's jurisdiction.[22] Similarly, a claim for a declaration nullifying a deed of mortgage of immovables situated outside the jurisdiction, executed within the jurisdiction by the parties who resided within it, and for a declaration nullifying the sale of the mortgage property by the mortgagee, were claims *in personam* which the High Court could adjudicate upon.[23] However, an action to recover damages for trespass of land situated abroad is not maintainable.[24]

South Africa

In respect of real actions directly raising the issue of title to property, the forum *rei sitae* is the only court which has jurisdiction.[25] Accordingly, where land located in Swaziland was, in one case, subject to sale, a South African court was not entitled to give any directions as to its transfer.[26] Nor will the court grant an injunction to restrain a person from fishing in foreign waters – for example, in the waters of Tristan da Cunha.[27] However, the court may grant an order confirming the purchase of property abroad by an administrator of estates.[28]

[20] The cases reported here dealt with intra-state conflict of laws problems in the Nigerian federation. The principles developed are, however, applicable to private international law issues.

[21] *Nigerian Ports Authority* v. *Panalpina World Transport (Nigeria) Ltd* 1973 (1) ALR Comm. 146, [1973] 1 All NLR (Part I) 486, [1973] NCLR 146.

[22] *British Bata Shoe Co. Ltd* v. *Melikian* [1956] 1 FSC 100.

[23] *Ashiru* v. *Barclays Bank of Nigeria* [1975] NCLR 233.

[24] *Lanleyin* v. *Rufai* [1959] 4 FSC 184.

[25] *Eilon* v. *Eilon* 1965 (1) SA 703 at 726–7.

[26] *Ex p. Erasmus* 1950 (3) SA 59. But see *Ex p. Barham* 1951 (2) SA 221: the court in appointing a *curator bonis* to the person and property of a patient with property, movable and immovable, situated in Southern Rhodesia made the order subject, in respect of such property, to its being confirmed or recognised by the High Court of Southern Rhodesia. See generally *Ex p. Maschwitz* 1965 (4) SA 356.

[27] *South Atlantic Islands Development Corp.* v. *Buchan* 1971 (1) SA 234.

[28] *Ex p. Southwood* 1948 (4) SA 785.

Zimbabwe

A Zimbabwean court has no jurisdiction to make an order declaring property situated outside its jurisdiction to be specially executable.[29]

Comments

The rule that the courts have no jurisdiction to adjudicate upon the right to property in foreign land, including an action for damages for trespass, is supported by authority in Kenya, Nigeria, South Africa and Zimbabwe. This so called 'Mocambique' rule and the case in which it was laid down[30] has been cited with approval in Kenya, Nigeria and South Africa. It can be justified on practical grounds – it is the court of the *situs* which is most likely to make an effective judgment. Indeed, even if a domestic court assumed jurisdiction to adjudicate a claim involving title to foreign land, its judgment would have to be enforced abroad. The mere fact that the court has jurisdiction over the person of the applicant does not ensure that such a judgment would be effective. Furthermore, it can be argued that comity demands that courts do not interfere with questions affecting title to foreign land. Indeed, issues affecting title to land are often so inextricably linked to a society's history, culture and socio-economic and political circumstances – this is certainly the case in Africa – that it would be almost always inappropriate for a foreign national court to assume it has the competence to deal with such issues.

The courts have acknowledged that where title is not directly an issue and that what is at stake is an *in personam* action arising from a contract or equity, they are prepared to assume jurisdiction. In other words, the courts would be prepared to adjudicate personal obligations arising from a contract or equity, even though such obligations may indirectly affect the foreign land. Statute – as is the case under Malawi's Divorce Act 1905 – may also provide an exception to the rule that courts will not assume jurisdiction over issues of title to foreign land.

It remains to be decided whether a foreign judgment in respect of title to land would be recognised and enforced. It is submitted that such a judgment should not be enforced by courts in Commonwealth Africa. The often complex and pluralistic legal regimes that govern title to land,

[29] *First National Bank of Namibia* v. *Kaure* 1999 (2) ZLR 269; *Johnston* v. *Cohen* 1957 R & N 185, 1957 (2) SA 277.

[30] *British South Africa Co.* v. *Companhia de Mocambique* [1893] AC 602.

the historical and colonial antecedents of land and land ownership in the countries under study, as well as the general importance of land, dictate that issues affecting title to such should be reserved for the courts of the *situs*.

A different approach is recommended in cases of judgments emanating from duly constituted regional or international courts. Accordingly, where it affected land purportedly expropriated, a duly constituted regional court held that the government should take all necessary measures to protect the possession, occupation and ownership of the land of the applicants,[31] it was inappropriate that a national court refused to recognise the judgment.[32]

Ownership and transfer of immovable and movable property

Ghana

The law applicable to a dispute involving land or real property is the *lex situs*, which prevails over any other laws. Accordingly, the fact that under English law, an undischarged bankrupt lacks the capacity to sue in his or her own right does not prevent them from litigating in Ghana, in relation to real property owned by the person and situated there.[33] In *Davies* v. *Randall*,[34] the letters of administration for the estate of Davies, who died intestate in Ghana while domiciled in Sierra Leone, were granted jointly to his widow and the registrar of the Divisional Court, Sekondi. The widow, as administratrix of the estate, but without the participation of the co-administrator, sold immovable property that was part of the estate to the first defendant, who leased it to the second defendant. In this action, the plaintiff, in his capacity as heir and successor to the late Davies, and as representative of Davies's other children, sought a declaration that the sale to the first defendant was invalid and passed no title that could be leased to the second defendant. The court held that,

[31] *Mike Campbell (Pvt) Ltd* v. *Republic of Zimbabwe*, Case No. SADC (T) 02/07 (South African Development Community Tribunal, 2007).

[32] *Gramara (Private) Ltd* v. *Government of the Republic of Zimbabwe*, Case No: X-ref. HC 5483/09 (High Court, Zimbabwe, 2010). This decision was based on public policy and not on the grounds that the court had no jurisdiction to adjudicate issues relating to title to foreign land – indeed that argument was neither presented to the regional tribunal nor to the domestic court.

[33] *Garrett* v. *Garrett* [1991] 1 GLR 32. This was because the status of an undischarged bankrupt is unknown to Ghanaian law.

[34] [1964] GLR 671.

although the deceased was domiciled in Sierra Leone at the time of his death, the property was situated in Ghana and all of the incidents to the property depended upon the law of Ghana. Accordingly, the law applicable to the transactions was the *lex situs*, and under Ghanaian law, the administratrix had no capacity to sell the property without the co-administrator's consent.[35]

Kenya

In cases of transferring land, power of attorney has to be construed for its effect in accordance with the law of Kenya.[36]

South Africa

Disputes concerning ownership, including the transfer of movables, are generally governed by the *lex situs* at the time of the transaction.[37] Accordingly, in a case where containers of goods were situated in South Africa and the dispute turned on a reservation of ownership clause, it was held that South African law governed the issue of whether the reservation of ownership clause was effective.[38] Similarly, in a claim analogous to the *rei vindication* in respect of property (shares) situated within the court's jurisdiction, the law to be applied is the *lex situs*.[39]

Tanzania

Under Tanzanian law, land and other immovable properties are governed by the *lex situs*, that is, the law of the place where the land is situated.[40]

[35] See generally *Youhana* v. *Abboud* [1974] 2 GLR 201.
[36] *Mayfair Holdings Ltd* v. *Ahmed* [1990–4] 1 EA 340.
[37] See generally *Antares International Ltd* v. *Louw Coetzee & Malan Inc.*, Case No. 11529/11 (High Court, South Africa, 2011).
[38] *Bominflot Ltd* v. *Kien Hung Shipping Co. Ltd* 2004 (2) SA 556; *Marcard Stein & Co.* v. *Port Marine Contractors (Pty) Ltd* 1995 (3) SA 663; *Ultisol Transport Contractors Ltd* v. *Bouygues Offshore* 1996 (1) SA 487.
[39] *Standard Bank of South Africa Ltd* v. *Ocean Commodities Inc.* 1983 (1) SA 276.
[40] *Juma* v. *Mlinga*, Civil Appeal No. 10 of 2001 (Court of Appeal, Tanzania, 2002).

Comments

A combination of the laws in Ghana and South Africa yield the principle that regardless of the character of the parties, questions involving the transfer of movable and immovable property are governed by the *lex situs*.[41] This rule is not difficult to apply when one is dealing with land. The *lex situs* determines the formal and essential validity of the transfer of immovables. In other words, those who qualify as parties to a transfer of immovable property, the question of whether the transfer should be in writing, the nature, scope and duration of the interest that can be transferred, and all other issues involving the transfer of immovable property, are governed by the *lex situs*. For the developing economies of the countries under study, the *lex situs* rule, which is in line with established, albeit criticised, common law principles,[42] serves a practical end. It can ensure that immovable properties are not dealt with in a manner detrimental to national laws or interests.

There is some merit in applying the *lex situs* rule to movables. In the words of Corbett:

> ... it would seem that the main reasons for the choice ... of the *lex situs* to govern the transfer of ownership in movable property are, briefly, (i) that the rule refers the passing of ownership to the system of law pertaining to the jurisdiction which has effective power over the property in question; (ii) that the rule is normally simple to apply and makes for certainty in that it does not lead to multiple solutions since the property can only be in one place at a time; (iii) that it satisfies the expectations of the reasonable man, for a party to a transfer naturally concludes that the transaction will be subject to the law of the country in which the subject-matter is at present situated; (iv) that property passes at the place where the goods themselves are; and (v) that commercial convenience imperatively demands that proprietary rights to movables shall generally be determined by the *lex situs*.[43]

Despite the above, considerable problems may be created when the *lex situs* principle is applied to movables. Invoking the principle raises the prospect that ownership of movable property may vary depending on the jurisdiction it is currently in, and additional problems result with respect to goods in transit or on the high seas. Alternatively, applicable laws that

41 The Ugandan case of *F.L. Kaderbhai* v. *Shamsherali Zaver Virji*, Civil Appeal No. 10 of 2008 (Supreme Court, Uganda, 2010) implicitly takes this position.

42 *Cheshire, North & Fawcett*, p. 1210.

43 *Marcard Stein & Co.* v. *Port Marine Contractors (Pty) Ltd* 1995 (3) SA 663 at 670.

have been suggested include the 'proper law of the transfer' and the 'domicile of the parties', but none of these is free of difficulties.

It remains undecided in many of the countries under study what the *lex situs* actually means in this context – is it restricted to the internal laws of the forum or does it encompass private international law rules? Here, the issue at stake may be relevant in deciding the meaning of the *lex situs*. While it may be appropriate to consider a reference to the *lex situs* as a reference to internal law when it comes to formalities surrounding an *inter vivos* transfer, it may not be entirely appropriate to restrict it in this way when the issue consists of the devolution of an estate. Indeed, in deciding a case involving the inheritance of land in Ghana, previously owned by a deceased Nigerian, the court held that 'the *lex situs* does not just mean the domestic law of the situs but the conflict of laws rule of the situs which may refer to some other system of domestic law'.[44]

Insolvency and bankruptcy

Botswana

The High Court of Botswana has jurisdiction over every debtor and with regard to the estate of every debtor who, at the date of the presentation of a petition for the sequestration of his or her estate, is possessed of, or entitled to, property within the jurisdiction, or who is domiciled, resides, has a dwelling-house, or place of business, or carries on business within the jurisdiction; or who at any time within the twelve months immediately preceding the presentation of the petition has ordinarily resided, had a dwelling-house or place of business, or carried on business within the jurisdiction, or has assigned that portion of his or her estate which lies within the jurisdiction of the court. However, where it appears to the court equitable or convenient that the estate of a person not domiciled in Botswana should be sequestrated elsewhere, the court may refuse or postpone the sequestration.

In addition to the jurisdiction to appoint a liquidator for an external company,[45] the Botswanan courts will recognise the status of a foreign

[44] *Youhana* v. *Abboud* [1974] 2 GLR 201 at 206. See also *Weytingh* v. *Bessaburo* (1906) 2 Ren. 427. (One of the questions which arose for determination was the claim to succeed a Dutchman who had died possessed of land in Cape Coast, Ghana. It was held that the claimant could only validly do so under Dutch law, not native law.)

[45] Companies Act 2007, s. 352.

liquidator in order to enable the latter to take possession of, and distribute the assets of, the insolvent. Thus, in *Ex p. Trakman*,[46] the applicants were appointed joint liquidators of a company in liquidation pursuant to an order of the Supreme Court of South Africa. The applicants applied for the recognition of their respective appointments in order to enable them to take possession of, and distribute the assets of, the insolvent company situated in Botswana. It was held that considerations of both equity and convenience demanded that the position of the foreign liquidators should be recognised, subject to the rights of local creditors and the operation of local laws.

Ghana

A body corporate incorporated outside Ghana may be wound up under the Bodies Corporate (Official Liquidations) Act 1963, although it has been dissolved, or has otherwise ceased to exist under, or by virtue of, the laws of the country where it was incorporated.[47] Where an order is made for the official winding-up of a body corporate incorporated outside Ghana, the High Court may, in the winding-up order, or on subsequent application by the liquidator, direct that the branch of that body corporate in Ghana shall be treated as a separate body corporate; that the assets and liabilities in Ghana shall be treated as the assets and liabilities of that body corporate for the purposes of the winding-up, and that the transactions by or with that branch shall be deemed valid, even where they occur after the date the body corporate is dissolved or has otherwise ceased to exist under the laws of its country of incorporation.[48]

Kenya

The High Court of Kenya has jurisdiction in bankruptcy.[49] In all matters of bankruptcy it is obliged to 'act in aid of and be auxiliary to every

[46] 1983 BLR 176. See also s. 352(2)(b) of the Companies Act 2007, which provides that where an external company goes into liquidation or is dissolved in its place of incorporation or origin, the liquidator appointed by the foreign court shall, until a liquidator for Botswana is appointed by the court, have the powers and functions of a liquidator for Botswana.

[47] Bodies Corporate (Official Liquidations) Act 1963, s. 62(1). See the Insolvency Act 2006 in relation to insolvency of natural persons.

[48] Bodies Corporate (Official Liquidations) Act 1963, s. 62(2).

[49] Bankruptcy Act 1930, s. 97.

Commonwealth court', elsewhere having jurisdiction in bankruptcy or insolvency.[50] A more elaborate regime for judicial co-operation in cross-border insolvency proceedings is established under sections 151 to 164 of the Bankruptcy Act 1930. The regime operates on the basis of reciprocity – the minister is empowered to designate countries which would benefit from the regime[51] – and deals with debtors 'having property in Kenya'.[52] A receiving order, an order of adjudication, or the appointment of a special manager or interim receiver undertaken in a reciprocating territory in bankruptcy proceedings against a debtor having property in Kenya is given the same effect as if it had been made in bankruptcy proceedings against the debtor in Kenya.[53] Similarly, where an order of adjudication is made by a reciprocating court, the property of the bankrupt situated in Kenya shall, by virtue of that order, be vested in the person from time to time discharging the office of trustee of the property of the bankrupt in the reciprocating territory, in the same manner as if the order of adjudication and the appointment of trustee had been made in Kenya.[54] Furthermore, any order, warrant or search warrant made or issued by a reciprocating court shall be enforced by the Kenyan court as if they had been issued by the Kenyan court.[55] The Act regulates concurrent bankruptcy proceedings. Subject to defined exceptions, a reciprocating court has sole jurisdiction in all matters arising out of any bankruptcy proceedings taken before that court against a debtor having property in Kenya – no Kenyan court shall entertain any action arising out of those proceedings.[56]

Where a company incorporated outside Kenya and which has been carrying on business in Kenya ceases to carry on business in Kenya, it may be wound up as an unregistered company under the Companies Act 1965, notwithstanding that it has been dissolved or has otherwise ceased to exist as a company under, or by virtue of, the laws of the country in which it was incorporated.[57]

Malawi

The High Court of Malawi is statutorily obliged to 'act in aid of and be auxiliary to every British court elsewhere having jurisdiction in bankruptcy or insolvency' in all matters of bankruptcy.[58] An elaborate regime

[50] Ibid., s. 115. *In re. Plantaniotis* [1958] EA 217. [51] Ibid., s. 151. [52] Ibid., s. 151.
[53] Ibid., s. 152. [54] Ibid., s. 153. [55] Ibid., s. 160. [56] Ibid., ss. 161–2.
[57] Companies Act 1965, s. 359. [58] Bankruptcy Act 1928, s. 113.

for international judicial co-operation in cross-border insolvency proceedings is established under sections 148 to 160 of the Bankruptcy Act 1928. The regime operates on the basis of reciprocity – the President is empowered to designate countries which would benefit from the regime – and deals with debtors 'having property in Malawi'.[59] A receiving order or order of adjudication or an appointment of a special manager or interim receiver made in a reciprocating territory in bankruptcy proceedings against a debtor having property in Malawi has the same effect as if it had been made in bankruptcy proceedings against the debtor in Malawi.[60] Similarly, where an order of adjudication is made by a reciprocating court, the property of the bankrupt situated in Malawi shall, by virtue of that order, be vested in the person from time to time discharging the office of trustee of the property of the bankrupt in the reciprocating territory, in the same manner as if the order of adjudication and the appointment of the trustee had been made in Malawi.[61] Furthermore, any order, warrant or search warrant made or issued by a reciprocating court shall be enforced by the Malawian court as if they had been issued by the Malawian court.[62] The Act regulates concurrent bankruptcy proceedings. Subject to named exceptions, a reciprocating court has sole jurisdiction in all matters arising out of any bankruptcy proceedings taken before that court against a debtor having property in Malawi – no Malawian court shall entertain any action arising out of those proceedings.[63]

A body corporate with assets in Malawi may be wound up under the Companies Act 1984.[64] Special provisions are made for external companies, i.e. a body corporate formed outside Malawi which establishes or maintains an established place of business in Malawi.[65] An external company may be wound up whether or not it has been dissolved or ceased to exist under the law of its country of incorporation.[66] Where an order is made to wind up an external company, it is treated for all purposes of the winding-up process as a Malawian incorporated company, and only the assets and liabilities situated in Malawi are deemed to be assets and liabilities of the company.[67] Transactions carried out in Malawi must be regarded as valid notwithstanding that they have occurred subsequent to the external company being dissolved, or ceasing to exist, under the law of the country of its incorporation.[68]

[59] Ibid., s. 148. [60] Ibid., s. 149. [61] Ibid., s. 150. [62] Ibid., s. 157.
[63] Ibid., s. 158. [64] Companies Act 1984, s. 305. [65] Ibid., ss. 306 and 319.
[66] Ibid., s. 319(1). [67] Ibid., s. 319(5). [68] Ibid., s. 319(6).

Namibia

The High Court of Namibia has jurisdiction over every debtor and in regard to the estate of every debtor who is domiciled, owns or is entitled to property situated within the jurisdiction; or who at any time within the twelve months immediately preceding the filing of the petition has ordinarily resided or carried on business within the jurisdiction of the court.[69]

This is effective from the date on which a petition is lodged with the registrar of the court for the acceptance of the surrender, or for the sequestration of their estate. It has been held that a sequestration order has no effect per se on immovable property situated in a foreign country. Such property remains vested in the insolvent. However, as regards movables, the position is different. A sequestration order granted by the court of the debtor's domicile *ipso facto* divests the insolvent of all his or her movable property, wherever situated, but a sequestration order granted by any other court has no operation per se on the debtor's assets, whether movable or immovable, that are situated out of such a court's jurisdiction. Thus, the necessity for recognition of the trustee of an insolvent estate will always exist if the insolvent has immovable property in a foreign jurisdiction, but, in the case of movables belonging to the insolvent there, this only applies if the order of sequestration has been granted by some court other than that of their domicile.[70] Accordingly, in the instant case, where the sequestration order was made by the court of the respondent's domicile, it was held that it vested his movables in the trustee and it was therefore not necessary to make an order recognising the appointment of the trustee.[71]

Nigeria

A creditor cannot present a bankruptcy petition against a debtor unless he or she demonstrates, among other things, that the debtor is ordinarily

[69] Insolvency Act 1936, s. 149. This is South African legislation with amendments up to 1979. See generally the Insolvency Amendment Act 2005.

[70] *Bekker No* v. *Kotze* 1994 NR 373, 1996 (4) SA 1293.

[71] *Bekker No* v. *Kotze* 1994 NR 373, 1996 (4) SA 1293. *Bekker No* v. *Kotze* 1994 NR 345, 1996 (4) SA 1287; *Oliver No* v. *Insolvent Estate D Lidchi* 1998 NR 31 at 38, where it was held that, although it is not strictly necessary for trustees laying claim to movable assets in a country other than the country of the insolvent's domicile where the sequestration was obtained, for recognition, such an application is invariably made and the need to apply for formal recognition has now been elevated into a principle. See also *Ex p. Lawton, No and Ruskin* 1950 (3) SA 129 on recognition of judicial managers appointed to a company placed under judicial management.

resident in Nigeria, or within a year before the date of the presentation of the petition, has ordinarily resided, had a dwelling-house or place of business in Nigeria, or has carried on business in Nigeria, either in person or by means of an agent or manager, or within the said period, has been a member of a firm or partnership of persons which has carried on business in Nigeria by means of a partner, partners, agent or manager.[72]

South Africa

The South African High Court has jurisdiction over every debtor and with regard to the estate of every debtor who, on the date on which a petition for the acceptance of the surrender or for the sequestration of his or her estate is lodged with the registrar of the court, is domiciled, owns or is entitled to property situated within the jurisdiction of the court, or who at any time within the twelve months immediately preceding the lodging of the petition, has ordinarily resided or carried on business within the jurisdiction of the court.[73] However, when it appears to the court equitable or convenient that the estate of a person domiciled in a state which has not been designated in terms of section 2 of the Cross-Border Insolvency Act 2000 should be sequestrated by a court outside South Africa, or that the estate of a person over whom it has jurisdiction be sequestrated by another court within South Africa, the court may refuse or postpone the acceptance of the surrender or the sequestration.[74]

Where the estate of an insolvent has been sequestrated by the order of a foreign court within whose jurisdiction the insolvent was domiciled at the time of sequestration, any movable property found in South Africa belonging to the insolvent would be vested in the trustee appointed by the order.[75] Formal recognition by the local courts of the foreign trustee to enable him or her to deal with the insolvent's movable property is not strictly necessary (since such property is governed by the *lex domicilii*). However, as a matter of practice, such an application is invariably made and the need for formal recognition has been elevated into a principle. On the other hand, formal recognition is required by a foreign trustee in order

[72] Bankruptcy Act 1979, s. 4(1)(d). Under s. 58 of the Companies and Allied Matters Act 1990, an exempted foreign company is deemed as an unregistered company under the Act and the provisions of the Act applicable to unregistered companies are applicable to such exempted foreign companies. Sections 532–6 provide for the winding up of unregistered companies.

[73] Insolvency Act 1936, s. 149(1)(a)(b).

[74] Ibid., s. 149(1).

[75] *Viljoen* v. *Venter No* 1981 (2) SA 152.

to deal with the insolvent's immovable property situated in South Africa, since such property is governed by the *lex situs*. Moreover, such recognition is necessary to demonstrate that the foreign court has exercised jurisdiction, based on the fact that the insolvent person was domiciled there.[76] In recognising a foreign trustee, a South African court will not make an order it is incapable of making in a South African insolvency.[77]

As is the case with natural persons, the liquidator of a foreign company requires recognition in South Africa before he or she has the power to deal with, or administer, assets situated in South Africa.[78] The legal permissibility of the recognition of a foreign trustee is not dependent upon the existence of legislative authorisation – this discretionary power finds its basis in the comity of nations.[79]

A South African court may issue letters of request, in terms of which it asks a foreign court to recognise a locally appointed liquidator and to allow this liquidator to institute such proceedings in the foreign court as may be necessary to enable the latter to carry out his or her duties of winding up a company.[80]

The Cross-Border Insolvency Act 2000 provides a mechanism for dealing with cross-border insolvency in accordance with the UNCITRAL Model Law on Cross-Border Insolvency. The Act applies only to states designated by the Minister of Justice. The Act also establishes a regime for co-operation between South African and foreign courts and foreign representatives,[81] as well as for regulating concurrent proceedings.[82] The Act allows foreign representatives and creditors to access the South African High Court, which is given jurisdiction under the Act.[83] A foreign representative may apply to the court for recognition of the foreign proceedings in which the representatives were appointed.[84] Such recognition is contingent on meeting a number of procedural[85] and

[76] *Ex p. Palmer NO: In re. Hahn* 1993 (3) SA 359. The judge noted that it may well be that English and Commonwealth courts have moved away from the exclusivity of domicile as a governing factor; there is, however, despite research, no similar trend to be found in our law.

[77] *Chaplin* v. *Gregory* 1950 (3) SA 555.

[78] *Liquidator Rhodesian Plastics (Pvt) Ltd* v. *Elvinco Plastic Products (Pty) Ltd* 1959 (1) SA 868; *Ex p. Gettliffe: In re. Dominion Reefs (Klerksdorp) Ltd* 1965 (4) SA 75; *Ward* v. *Smit* 1998 (3) SA 175; *Moolman* v. *Builders & Developers (Pty) Ltd* 1990 (1) SA 954 (on appeal from *Ex p. Moolman No: In re. Builders and Developers (Pty) Ltd* 1989 (4) SA 253); *Ex p. Meinke* 1954 (4) SA 391.

[79] *Ex p. Steyn* 1979 (2) SA 309; *Ward* v. *Smit* 1998 (3) SA 175; *Moolman* v. *Builders & Developers (Pty) Ltd* 1990 (1) SA 954.

[80] *Gardener* v. *Walters* 2002 (5) SA 796.

[81] Ibid., ss. 25–7.

[82] Ibid., ss. 28–32.

[83] Ibid., ss. 9–14.

[84] Ibid., s. 15(1).

[85] Ibid., s. 15(2)(3)(4).

substantive[86] requirements. Furthermore, recognition may be refused if it would manifestly contravene South African public policy.[87]

Tanzania

The court having jurisdiction in bankruptcy is the High Court.[88] The court is mandated to 'act in aid of every reciprocating court elsewhere having jurisdiction in bankruptcy or insolvency'.[89] An elaborate regime for international judicial co-operation in cross-border insolvency proceedings is established under sections 150 to 163 of the Bankruptcy Act 1930. The regime operates on the basis of reciprocity – the Minister responsible for legal affairs is empowered to designate countries which would benefit from the regime – and deals with debtors 'having property in Tanzania'.[90] A receiving order, order of adjudication, or the appointment of a special manager or interim receiver made in a reciprocating territory in bankruptcy proceedings against a debtor having property in Tanzania have the same effect as if they had been made in bankruptcy proceedings against the debtor in Tanzania.[91] Similarly, where an order of adjudication is made by a reciprocating court, the property of the bankrupt situated in Tanzania shall, by virtue of that order, be vested in the person from time to time discharging the office of trustee of the property of the bankrupt in the reciprocating territory, in the same manner as if the order of adjudication and the appointment of the trustee had been made in Tanzania.[92] In addition, any order, warrant or search warrant made or issued by a reciprocating court shall be enforced by the Tanzanian court as if they had been issued by the Tanzanian court.[93] The Act regulates concurrent bankruptcy proceedings. Subject to named exceptions, a reciprocating court has sole jurisdiction in all matters arising out of any bankruptcy proceedings taken before it against a debtor having property in Tanzania – no Tanzanian court shall entertain any action arising out of those proceedings.[94]

Where a company incorporated outside Tanzania, which has been carrying on business there, ceases to do so, it may be wound up as an unregistered company, notwithstanding that it has been dissolved or has otherwise ceased to exist as a company under, or by virtue of, the laws of the country where it was incorporated.[95]

[86] Ibid., s. 17. [87] Ibid., s. 6. [88] Bankruptcy Act 1930, s. 97. [89] Ibid., s. 115.
[90] Ibid., s. 150. [91] Ibid., s. 151. [92] Ibid., s. 152. [93] Ibid., s. 159.
[94] Ibid., s. 160. [95] Companies Act 2002, s. 427.

Zambia

The High Court of Zambia has jurisdiction in bankruptcy.[96] The court is statutorily obliged to 'act in aid of and be auxiliary to every court elsewhere in the Commonwealth having jurisdiction in bankruptcy or insolvency' in all matters of bankruptcy.[97] An elaborate regime for international judicial co-operation in cross-border insolvency proceedings is established under sections 149 to 162 of the Bankruptcy Act 1967. The regime operates on the basis of reciprocity – the Attorney General is empowered to designate countries which would benefit from the regime – and deals with debtors 'having property in Zambia'.[98] A receiving order, an order of adjudication, or an appointment of a special manager or interim receiver made in a reciprocating territory in bankruptcy proceedings against a debtor having property in Zambia has the same effect as if it had been made in bankruptcy proceedings against the debtor in Zambia.[99] Similarly, where an order of adjudication is made by a reciprocating court, the property of the bankrupt situated in Zambia shall, by virtue of that order, be vested in the person from time to time discharging the office of trustee of the property of the bankrupt in the reciprocating territory, in the same manner as if the order of adjudication and the appointment of the trustee had taken place in Zambia.[100] In addition, any order, warrant or search warrant made or issued by a reciprocating court shall be enforced by the Zambian court as if they had been issued there.[101] The Act regulates concurrent bankruptcy proceedings. Subject to defined exceptions, a reciprocating court has sole jurisdiction in all matters arising out of any bankruptcy proceedings taken before that court against a debtor having property in Zambia – no Zambian court shall entertain any action arising out of those proceedings.[102]

An external company[103] may be wound up under Zambian law, whether or not it has been dissolved or ceased to exist according to the law of the country of its incorporation.[104] The grounds on which an

[96] Bankruptcy Act 1967, s. 95(1). See generally the Preferential Claims in Bankruptcy Act 1995, which gives effect to the Protection of Workers' Claims (Employer's Insolvency) Convention 1992.

[97] Bankruptcy Act 1967, s. 112. [98] Ibid., s. 149. [99] Ibid., s. 150.

[100] Ibid., s. 151. [101] Ibid., s. 158. [102] Ibid., s. 159.

[103] A body corporate incorporated in a foreign country, not being a foreign company that has assets or an undertaking in Zambia.

[104] Companies Act 1994, s. 365(3).

external company may be wound up include: if it is in the course of being wound up, voluntarily or otherwise, in the country of its incorporation; if it is dissolved in the country of its incorporation, or has ceased to carry on business in Zambia, or is carrying on business for the sole purpose of winding up its affairs, and if the court is of the opinion that the company is being operated in Zambia for any unlawful purposes.[105] The court may, in the winding-up order, or on subsequent application by the liquidator, direct that all transactions in Zambia by, or with, the external company shall be deemed to be, or have been, validly performed, notwithstanding that they have occurred after the date the body corporate was dissolved, or has otherwise ceased to exist, according to its country of incorporation laws.[106]

Zimbabwe

The Zimbabwean High Court has jurisdiction over every debtor[107] and in regard to the estate of every debtor who: at the date of the presentation of a petition for the sequestration of their estate, is possessed of, or entitled to, property within Zimbabwe, or is domiciled, resides, has a dwelling-house or place of business, or carries on business in Zimbabwe; at any time within the twelve months immediately preceding the presentation of the petition has ordinarily resided, had a dwelling-house or place of business, has carried on business within Zimbabwe, or has assigned that portion of their estate which lies within Zimbabwe.[108] However, where it appears to the High Court equitable or convenient that the estate of a person not domiciled in Zimbabwe should be sequestrated elsewhere, the court may refuse or postpone the sequestration.[109]

Comments

The law in the countries under study distinguishes between bankruptcy proceedings involving natural and artificial persons. However, in general, most of them do not address the cross-border aspects and concomitantly,

[105] Ibid., s. 365(4). [106] Companies Act 1994, s. 365(5).

[107] In respect of the winding up of a foreign company (i.e. a company or other association of persons incorporated outside Zimbabwe which has established a place of business in Zimbabwe), see s. 337 of the Companies Act 1952.

[108] Insolvency Act 1975, s. 190(1). [109] Ibid., s. 190.

the private international law issues that may arise in bankruptcy proceedings.[110] Only South Africa has enacted legislation based on the UNCITRAL Model Law on Cross Border Insolvency 1997.

The jurisdiction in bankruptcy proceedings is given to the High Court in all the countries under study. However, the bases for exercising that jurisdiction are not clearly defined in countries such as Gambia, Ghana, Kenya, Malawi, Tanzania and Zambia. In Botswana, Namibia, South Africa and Zimbabwe, jurisdiction is clearly founded on domicile, existence of assets within the jurisdiction, ordinary residence and carrying on business within the jurisdiction at any time within the twelve months preceding the date the petition is made. In these countries, the courts have discretion to refuse or postpone sequestration where it appears equitable or convenient that the estate of a person domiciled in a foreign country should be sequestrated abroad. The mere presence of the debtor within the jurisdiction does not afford a basis of jurisdiction in any of the countries under study.

In all the countries under study, and from a domestic law perspective, when a debtor is adjudged bankrupt or a sequestration order is made on the property – movable and immovable – the bankrupt is vested in a trustee.[111] From a private international law perspective, this may prove inadequate to enable the trustee to deal with the property of the bankrupt abroad. For example, case law in Namibia and South Africa suggests that formal recognition is required by a foreign trustee in order to enable him or her to deal with the insolvent's immovable property situated in Namibia and South Africa, and also in respect of movables in Namibia and South Africa, in cases where the foreign court assumes jurisdiction on a basis other than the domicile of the insolvent. In Kenya, Malawi, Tanzania and Zambia, where an order of adjudication is made by a reciprocating court, the property of the bankrupt situated locally shall, by virtue of such an order, be vested in the trustee appointed in the reciprocating country, in the same manner as if the order of adjudication and the appointment of the trustee had been made domestically.

[110] See, e.g., Gambia – Insolvency Act 1992; Ghana – Insolvency Act 2006 and Bodies Corporate (Official Liquidations) Act 1963; Nigeria – Bankruptcy Act 1979.

[111] Botswana – Insolvency Act 1929, s. 20(1)(a); Ghana – Insolvency Act 2006, s. 37; Kenya – Bankruptcy Act 1930, ss. 20(1) and 57; Malawi – Bankruptcy Act 1928, ss. 20(1) and 54; Nigeria – Bankruptcy Act 1979, ss. 20(1) and 55; South Africa – Insolvency Act 1936, s. 20 (1)(a); Tanzania – Bankruptcy Act 1930, ss.20(1) and 57; Zambia – Bankruptcy Act 1967, ss. 20(4) and 55; Zimbabwe – Insolvency Act 1975, s. 23(1)(a).

There is jurisdiction to wind up[112] foreign companies in most of the countries under study,[113] but the position remains unclear in Gambia[114] and Sierra Leone.[115] Indeed, the fact that such a foreign company has been dissolved, or has otherwise ceased to exist as a company under the laws of the country in which it was incorporated, does not prevent the courts from winding up such companies. This suggests that, at least in respect of companies, the jurisdiction of the courts to wind up a company is not excluded by the fact that the company has been wound up by the court of a foreign country. In relation to proceedings involving individuals, and in respect of countries designated as reciprocating states, legislation in Malawi, Kenya, Tanzania and Zambia gives courts in those states sole jurisdiction in all matters in, or arising out of, any bankruptcy proceedings taken before such courts against a debtor having property in Kenya, Malawi, Tanzania and Zambia, subject to defined exceptions.

A regime for international judicial cooperation in insolvency proceedings is established by legislation in Kenya, Malawi, South Africa, Tanzania and Zambia.[116] The regimes are founded on reciprocity and provide for, among other things, the enforcement of non-money judgments resulting from insolvency proceedings – judgments which would otherwise not be enforceable at common law.

The courts may recognise foreign bankruptcy proceedings and representatives of the insolvent's estate appointed thereunder. The recognition

[112] Insolvency is only one of many reasons for which a company may be wound up in the countries under study. The focus here is mainly on the jurisdiction to wind up on grounds other than on which a company may be wound up.

[113] Lesotho's repealed Companies Act 1967, in s. 292, allowed for the winding up of external companies. This provision is absent in the new Companies Act 2011.

[114] Section 213 of the Companies Act 1955 gives the High Court 'jurisdiction to wind up a company registered in The Gambia', but it is silent on whether it has jurisdiction to wind up external companies.

[115] Section 349 of Sierra Leone's Companies Act 2009 gives the High Court jurisdiction to wind up any company incorporated or registered in Sierra Leone. There is no express provision giving it jurisdiction to wind up foreign companies. Rather, the Act obliges the local managers and agents of a foreign company that is being, or has already been, wound up to inform the Corporate Affairs Commission of this fact and cause such a fact to be recorded on all company invoices, documents and letters. It is also an offence for a person to carry on business on behalf of the company after the date on which it was dissolved or has otherwise ceased to exist in the country in which it was incorporated (Companies Act 2009, s. 490).

[116] D. A. Ailola, 'Recognition of Foreign Proceedings, Orders and Officials in Insolvency in Southern Africa: A Call for a Regional Convention' (1999) 32 *Comparative and International Law Journal of Southern Africa* 54.

accorded to such foreign representatives acknowledges the fact that he or she has been appointed as such in the foreign country. It also constitutes a declaration which entitles the representative to deal with the assets in the jurisdiction subject only to such conditions as the court may impose for the protection of local creditors, or in recognition of the requirements of local laws. In South Africa, in cases outside the scope of the Cross-Border Insolvency Act 2000, it has to be demonstrated that the foreign court has assumed jurisdiction on the basis of the domicile of the bankrupt. In other words, domicile provides the sole basis for the international competence of the foreign court.

Trusts

There is very little on the private international law aspects of a trust in the countries under study.[117] None of the countries under study is a party to the Hague Convention on the Law Applicable to Trusts and their Recognition 1985. The Zimbabwean case of *In re. Golding Trust*[118] involved an application to the court to consent on behalf of a minor beneficiary the varying of a trust executed in South Rhodesia relating to immovable property in South Rhodesia. The donor and all the beneficiaries were domiciled in the United Kingdom. On the issue of the court's jurisdiction to hear the application, it was held that by virtue of the domicile of the minor beneficiary, the English High Court had jurisdiction. And the fact that immovable property, the subject of the trust, was situated in South Rhodesia, and that all the parties concerned consented to the jurisdiction of the Rhodesian court, was not in the absence of special circumstances sufficient to justify the court assuming jurisdiction. In the instant case, the court found that the fact that the agreement to vary the terms of the trust deed was made subject to the approval of the court and that the deed was executed in South Rhodesia were special circumstances justifying its assuming jurisdiction.

It has also been held that a contract to create a trust is governed by its own proper law and the provisions of the trust, as with a contract, determine the law that governs it. In the absence of an express

[117] See, generally, Forsyth, pp. 388–92. In the common law countries, service out of the jurisdiction may be allowed where the action is for the execution (as to property within the jurisdiction) of the trusts of any instrument of which the person to be served is a trustee, which ought to be executed according to national law. See Ch. 4.

[118] 1964 RLR 249.

provision to the contrary, the governing law is that of the locus of administration.[119]

Intellectual property

Interesting private international law issues may arise in claims involving foreign intellectual property rights such as patents and copyrights. Most of the countries under study have specific legislation regulating intellectual property rights, but this legislation does not address private international law issues directly.

Apart from the South African decision of *Gallo Africa Ltd* v. *Sting Music (Pty) Ltd*,[120] there appears to be no case in the countries under study dealing with this subject. *Gallo* raised the issue of whether a South African court has jurisdiction to decide matters relating to an alleged breach of foreign copyrights. It was held that the court had no jurisdiction to deal with such an alleged infringement. The court reasoned that as a matter of principle intellectual property rights are territorial and are protected as such. Although the court appreciated the fact that a decision to not assume jurisdiction may entail litigating in many forums that could well last a year, it stated that this was an issue to be addressed through an international agreement.

[119] *Mnopf Trustees Ltd* v. *SA Marine Corp. (Pty) Ltd*, Case No. 9085/2008 (High Court, South Africa, 2010). See generally *Fattorini* v. *Johannesburg Board of Executors and Trustees* 1948 (4) SA 806.

[120] 2010 (6) SA 329, [2011] 1 All SA 449. This decision was inspired by an earlier English Court of Appeal decision which was overruled by the UK Supreme Court in *Lucasfilm Ltd* v. *Ainsworth* [2011] UKSC 39. See generally *Microsoft Corp.* v. *Franike Associates Ltd* [2012] 3 NWLR 301.

15

Succession

Regardless of whether a person dies testate or intestate a number of private international law issues may be generated in respect of the deceased's estate. In respect of a person who died testate, there may be questions as to the formal validity of the will he or she left, the capacity of the testator to make the will, the validity of the dispositions in the will, interpretation of the will, the capacity of named beneficiaries to take under the will and, in cases where the will is challenged, there may be a choice of law issue relating to revocation of wills. Regarding an intestate there may be issues as to what law governs succession to the movable and immovable parts of the estate and, when so determined, the scope of the applicable law. These issues are the subject matter of this chapter.

Testamentary succession

Formal and essential validity of wills

Botswana

A will shall be treated as properly executed if its execution conforms to the internal law in force in the territory where it is executed, or in the territory where, at the time of its execution, or of the testator's death, the latter was domiciled, or had his or her habitual residence, or in a state of which, at either of those times, he or she was a national.[1]

A will executed on board a vessel or aircraft is properly executed if its execution conforms to the internal law in force in the territory with which the vessel or aircraft may be taken to have been most closely connected.[2] A will which disposes of immovable property is properly executed if its execution conforms to the internal law in force in the territory where the property is situated.[3] In determining whether the execution of a will conforms to a particular law, regard shall be had

[1] Wills Act 1957, s. 10. [2] Ibid., s. 11(a). [3] Ibid., s. 11(b).

to the formal requirements of that law at the time of execution, but this shall not prevent taking into account an alteration of law affecting wills executed at the time, if the alteration enables the will to be treated as properly executed.[4]

Gambia

A will is properly executed if it conforms to the internal law in force in the territory where it is executed, or to the law in the territory where, at the time of its execution, or of the testator's death, the latter was domiciled, habitually resident or a national.[5]

A will for movable property is properly executed if its execution complies with the formalities prescribed by the law of the testator's domicile, or with the internal law of any system of law referred to by the domicile.[6] A will of land or an interest in land is properly executed if its execution complies with the requirements of the *lex situs*.[7] A will executed on board a vessel or aircraft is valid if its execution conforms to the internal law of the territory with which the vessel or aircraft is most closely connected.[8]

Where foreign law falls to be applied in relation to a will, any requirement of that law whereby special formalities are to be observed by testators or testatrixes answering a particular description, or witnesses to the execution of a will are to possess certain qualifications, shall be treated, notwithstanding any rule of that law to the contrary, as a formal requirement only.[9] In assessing the validity of execution, the court is to have regard for the formal requirements at the time of execution. However, the court may take into account subsequent alterations in foreign law if the alteration enables a will to be treated as properly executed.[10]

As regards essential validity, the Wills Act 1992 provides that, in relation to land, it shall be governed by the internal law of the *lex situs* and for any other property, the system of law intended by the testator.[11]

Ghana

A will is properly executed if its execution conforms to the internal law in force in the territory where it is executed, or in the territory where at the

[4] Ibid., s. 8(2). [5] Wills Act 1992, s. 24(1). [6] Ibid., s. 24(2). [7] Ibid., s. 24(3).
[8] Ibid., s. 24(4). [9] Ibid., s. 25. [10] Ibid., s. 26.
[11] Ibid., s. 27. This is a departure from the decision in *Theresa Saidie* v. *Saika Saidy* (1974) 18 *Journal of African Law* 190, which held that the essential validity of a will – in this instance the validity of the dispositions – is governed by *the lex domicilii*.

time of its execution, or of the testator's death, the latter was domiciled, or had his or her habitual residence, or in a state of which he or she was a national at either of those times.[12]

Without prejudice to the preceding, the following are all deemed to be properly executed: a will executed on board a vessel or aircraft of any description, if its execution conforms to the internal law in force in the territory with which the vessel or aircraft may be taken to have been most closely connected, having regard to registration, if any, and other relevant circumstances,[13] and a will so far as it disposes of immovable property, if its execution conforms to the internal law in force in the territory where the property is situated.[14]

Notwithstanding anything to the contrary under an applicable foreign law, any requirement in the foreign country where special formalities are to be observed by testators answering a particular description, or where witnesses to the execution of a will are to possess certain qualifications, is deemed to be purely a formal requirement.[15]

Kenya

A will, whether for movable or immovable property, shall be treated as properly executed if its execution conforms, either at the time of execution, or at the time of the testator's death, to the law in force in the state, i.e. where it was executed; where the property is situated; where, at the time of its execution or the testator's death, the latter was domiciled, or in a state of which the testator was a national, either at the time of its execution or on his or her death.[16]

Malawi

A will may be made outside Malawi in respect of any property in Malawi and a will so made shall be valid if made in accordance with the provisions of Deceased Estates (Wills, Inheritance and Protection) Act 2011 or of the law of the place where it was made, or the law of the place where the testator had his or her domicile when the will was made.[17]

[12] Wills Act 1971, s. 15(1); *In re. Lartey (Deceased); Lartey* v. *Affutu-Lartey* [1972] 2 GLR 488; *Kells* v. *Ako Adjei* [2001–2] 1 GLR 617.

[13] Wills Act 1971, s. 15(2)(a). [14] Ibid., s. 15(2)(b). [15] Ibid., s. 15(4).

[16] Law of Succession Act 1981, s. 16.

[17] Deceased Estates (Wills, Inheritance and Protection) Act 2011, s. 6(3); *In re. Osman Hussein; Ali* v. *Osman* [1923–60] ALR Mal. 276.

It has been held that the processor of this provision applied to both real and personal property in Malawi, and that the provision did not derogate from the common law rule that a will made domestically is formally valid if the formalities required by the law of the domicile of the testator at the time of his or her death are met.[18]

Namibia

The Wills Act 1953 of South Africa (see report on South Africa below) as amended in South Africa to November 1979 applies in Namibia. A will shall not be invalid merely by reason of its form, if such form complies with the internal law of the state or territory where: the will was executed; the testator was, at the time of the execution of the will, or at the time of his or death, domiciled or habitually resident, or where the testator was, at the time of the execution of the will or at the time of his or her death, a citizen.[19] These are independent requirements which should be read disjunctively. Accordingly, a will executed in Namibia by a German citizen which was invalid under Namibian law, but valid under German law, has been held formally valid.[20]

South Africa

A will shall not be invalid merely by reason of the form thereof, if such form complies with the internal law of the state or territory in which the will was executed;[21] in which the testator was, at the time of the execution of the will, or at the time of his or her death, domiciled or habitually resident, or where the testator was, at the time of the execution of the will, or at the time of his or her death, a citizen.[22]

So far as it disposes of immovable property, a will shall not be formally invalid if its form complies with the internal law of the state or territory where that property is situated.[23] A will shall not be formally invalid if it is executed on board a vessel or aircraft and its form complies with the internal law of the state or territory where such a vessel or aircraft was registered at the time of such execution, or with which it was otherwise most closely connected at that time.[24]

18 *In the Estate of Barretta* [1984–6] 11 MLR 110.
19 Wills Act 1953, s. 3bis(1)(a).
20 *Kalomo* v. *Master of the High Court* 2008 (2) NR 693.
21 This rule applies even if the will disposes of immovable property in South Africa. *Tomlinson* v. *Zwirchmayr* 1998 (2) SA 840.
22 Wills Act 1953, s. 3bis(1)(a). *Ex p. Estate Abbott* 1950 (3) SA 325.
23 Wills Act 1953, s. 3bis(1)(b). 24 Ibid., s. 3bis(1)(e).

Any requirement of the internal law of any other state or territory in terms of which a testator of a particular age or nationality, or who has any other personal qualification, is to observe special formalities in the execution of a will, or where a witness to a will is to possess certain qualifications, shall be construed as a requirement relating to form only.[25]

Zambia

A will is properly executed if its execution conforms to the internal law in force in the state where it is executed, or in the state where, at the time of its execution, or of the testator's death, the latter was domiciled, habitually resident, or was a national.[26]

A will executed on board a vessel or aircraft is properly executed if the execution of the will conforms to the internal law in force in the state with which the vessel or aircraft may be considered as having been most closely connected,[27] having regard to its registration, if any, and other relevant circumstances. A will which disposes of immovable property is properly executed if its execution conforms to the internal law in force in the state where the property is situated.[28]

Where a law in force outside Zambia falls to be applied in relation to a will, any requirement of that law where special formalities are to be observed by testators answering a particular description, or by witnesses to the execution of a will who are to possess certain qualifications, shall be deemed as purely a formal requirement, notwithstanding any rule of that law to the contrary.[29] In determining whether the execution of a will conforms to a particular law, the court must have regard to the formal requirements of that law at the time of execution, but this shall not prevent account being taken of an alteration of law affecting wills executed at that time, if the alteration enables the will to be treated as properly executed.[30]

Zimbabwe

A will is formally valid if its form complies with the internal law of: the country in which it is made; any country in which the testator is domiciled or ordinarily resident, either when the will was made or when he or she died, or any state or territory of which the testator was a citizen or national, either when he or she made the will or when he or she died.[31]

[25] Ibid., s. 3bis(2). [26] Wills and Administration of Testate Estates Act 1989, s. 7(1).
[27] Ibid., s. 7(2)(a). [28] Ibid., s. 7(2)(b). [29] Ibid., s. 7(4). [30] Ibid., s. 7(6).
[31] Wills Act 1987, s. 22(4)(a). *Ex p. Judd: In Estate Norhadian* 1963 R & N 667.

A will which disposes of movable property is valid if its form complies with the law of the country in which the property concerned is situated, either when the will was made, or when the testator died.[32] A will which disposes of immovable property is valid if its form complies with the law of the country in which the immovable property is situated.[33] Where a will is made on board a vessel or aircraft of any description, it is valid if its form complies with the internal law of the country with which, having regard to any relevant circumstances, the vessel or aircraft may be taken to have been most closely connected when the will was made.[34]

In determining the formal validity of a will, where under the law of any country a testator of a particular age, citizenship or nationality, or who possesses any other personal qualification or disqualification, is required to observe any special formality in the making of a will, or where a witness to a will is required to possess any particular qualification, such requirements shall be regarded as relating to the form of the will.[35] In determining whether or not the form of a will complies with a particular law, regard shall be had for the requirements of that law when the will was made, but this shall not prevent account being taken of a subsequent alteration in that law after that time if the alteration enables the will to be treated as properly made.[36]

The question of whether a testator has the capacity to make a will disposing of movable property shall be determined by the internal law of the country where he or she was domiciled when they made the will and, in the case of immovable property, by the internal law of the country in which the immovable property is situated. This question shall be determined according to the internal law which existed at the time the will was made.[37]

The capacity of a person to receive a benefit under a will disposing of movable property shall be determined by the internal law of the country where the beneficiary is domiciled on the date of the testator's death. This rule applies where the question of his or her capacity to receive the benefit arises because he or she is a minor, a married person, a body corporate or because of some similar personal or inherent characteristic. In any other case, the law of the country where the testator was domiciled at the date of his or her death is decisive.[38] In the case of immovable property, the capacity of a person to receive a benefit shall be determined by the internal law of the country where the immovable property is

[32] Wills Act 1987, s. 22(4)(b). [33] Ibid., s. 22(4)(c). [34] Ibid., s. 4(f).
[35] Ibid., s. 5(a). [36] Ibid., s. 5(b). [37] Ibid., s. 2. [38] Ibid., s. 22(3)(a).

situated, and in the case of a beneficiary that is a body corporate, additionally by the internal law of the country where the body corporate was constituted or established. This question shall be determined according to the internal law that existed when the testator died.[39]

The validity and effect of rights, interests and obligations created by the will, and the right of persons not specified in the will to receive any benefits thereunder, shall be determined according to the internal law of the country where the testator was domiciled when he or she died, to the extent that the will disposes of movable property, and to the extent that it disposes of immovable property, by the internal law of the country where the immovable property concerned is situated. This question shall be determined according to the internal law which existed when the testator died. However, the question of whether or not a person who has accepted a benefit under a will is obliged to divest themselves of any of their own property that has been disposed of to another person under the same will shall be determined according to the nature of the property accepted by them under that will and without regard to the nature of their own property disposed of under it.[40]

Comments

A significant body of the rules needed to resolve private international law issues that arise in relation to wills has been statutorily codified in many of the countries under study. To a large extent, the existing laws have been influenced by, or reflect, the provisions of the Hague Convention on the Conflict of Laws relating to the Form of Testamentary Dispositions.[41] Indeed, even countries that are not parties to the Convention, such as Ghana, Zambia and Zimbabwe, have provisions that are no doubt inspired by the Convention.

Each country provides multiple bases on which the formal validity of a will may be judged. Domicile, nationality, place of habitual residence and execution may all be used to decide the formal validity of a will. None of these connecting factors are defined in the respective statutes. This may create problems, for example, in cases where a person holds dual nationality. It is uncertain from the legislation which nationality would prevail,

[39] Ibid., s. 22(3)(b). [40] Ibid., s. 22(7).

[41] Botswana, Lesotho, South Africa and Swaziland are parties to the Convention. None of the countries under study has ratified the Convention providing a Uniform Law on the Form of an International Will 1973. Sierra Leone signed the Convention in 1973, but has never ratified it.

but it can be argued that given the underlying policy of the statutes – which is to prevent wills from becoming formally invalid – it should be enough if the will is formally valid under one of the dual national's national laws. Indeed, given the current state of the law in the countries under study, it will be rare for a will to fail on the basis of formal validity. Beyond the scope of the statutorily codified rules, South Africa and Zimbabwe leave room for the formal validity of wills to be tested by common law rules,[42] but given the breadth of the statutory rules, it is doubtful whether there will ever be the need to resort to common law. None of the statutes provides the governing laws to be invoked or applied in any particular order. Indeed, it has been held in Namibia that the connecting factors are disjunctive, which means the fact that a will is valid according to one governing law is enough to affirm its formal validity.

Most of the countries under study attempt to exclude *renvoi* in issues of formal validity. Internal law is defined to mean the law which would apply in a case where no question of the law in force in any other territory or state arises,[43] or as excluding the choice of law rules of that place.[44] *Renvoi*, however, operates in some cases. Thus, in Gambia, a will of movable property is properly executed if its execution complies with the formalities prescribed by the law of the testator's domicile, or by the internal law of any system of law referred to by the domicile.[45] An issue not clearly addressed in these attempts to exclude *renvoi* is the status of personal laws within an internal law. Many legal systems in the world are pluralistic, thus a reference to the internal law of a country often requires a subsidiary examination of which aspects of the internal law are applicable to particular issues. It is arguable that these attempts at excluding *renvoi* do not extend to the personal laws within the internal law.[46]

Compared to formal validity, the issues of capacity and essential validity of wills appear not to have engaged the attention of courts or

[42] South Africa – Wills Act 1953, s. 3bis(5); Zimbabwe – Wills Act 1987, s. 22(9).

[43] Botswana – Wills Act 1957, s. 8(1); Ghana – Wills Act 1971, s. 18; Zambia – Wills and Administration of Testate Estates Act 1989, s. 3; Zimbabwe – Wills Act 1987, s. 22(1).

[44] Gambia – Wills Act 1992, s. 2; South Africa – Wills Act 1953, s. 1.

[45] Wills Act 1992, s. 24(2).

[46] Indeed, s. 22 of Zimbabwe's Wills Act 1987 makes it clear that, if in any country there is in force a system of personal law applicable to wills made by persons, such as the testator in the case concerned, on the grounds of his race, tribe, religion, caste or other personal characteristic, that system of personal law shall be deemed to be the internal law of the country concerned in relation to that particular testator and his will.

legislators in the countries under study.[47] Only in Gambia and Zimbabwe do the issues receive legislative attention. The statutory provisions in Zimbabwe are more extensive with respect to the issues relating to the essential validity they cover. But Gambia's law is particularly noteworthy, since it allows for the essential validity of a will dealing with property other than land to be governed by 'the system of law intended by the testator'. This appears to allow the testator to choose the law governing the essential validity of their will, thus, arguably, enabling them to overcome any incapacity they may suffer from under the law of their domicile. The law constitutes a unique concession for party autonomy as regards the choice of law of succession in the countries under study.[48] However, it leaves many issues unaddressed in relation to this autonomy, including limitations on the freedom to choose.

In Zimbabwe, the capacity to make a will disposing of movable and immovable property is determined by the internal law of the country where the testator was domiciled and where the immovable property was situated, respectively. However, in both cases, it is the law at the time the will was made that is relevant. Subsequent changes in the domicile of the testator, or in the law of the place where the immovable property was situated, are immaterial. It is submitted that this position is appropriate. A will invalid at the time it was made should not become validated by subsequent changes in domicile or law.

Revocation, appointment and interpretation

Botswana

A will which revokes a will that under the Wills Act 1957 would be treated as properly executed, or which revokes a provision which would be treated as if included in a properly executed will, will be treated as

[47] See generally *Hanna Kattan* v. *John Y. Kattan* [1957] SLJR 35, which held that as regards movables, testamentary capacity (personal) is governed by the law of the testator's domicile at the time of the execution of the will. As regards immovables, testamentary capacity (personal) is governed by the *lex situs* – which is a reference to internal law. Proprietary capacity, i.e. whether the testator had unlimited or only limited power of disposition, is in the case of movables governed by the *lex domicilii* at the time of death, and in the case of immovables, by the *lex situs*. In *Evelyn-Wright* v. *Pierrepoint* 1987 (2) SA 111, the judge appears to have expressed preference for *lex ultimi domicilii*.

[48] Gambian law further allows for the construction of a will to be governed by the system of law intended by the testator, which shall be presumed to be the law of his or her domicile at the date of the execution of the will. Wills Act 1992, s. 28.

properly executed if the execution of the latter conforms to any law by reference to which the revoked will or provision would be treated as properly executed.[49]

Gambia

A will so far as it revokes a will which under the Wills Act 1992 would be treated as properly executed, or revokes a provision which under the Act would be treated as comprised in a properly executed will, is valid if the execution of the latter conforms to any law by reference to which the revoked will or provision would be so treated.[50]

To the extent that it exercises a power of appointment, a will is valid if its execution conforms to the law governing the essential validity of the power, and it shall not be treated as improperly executed by reason only that its execution was not in accordance with any formal requirements contained in the instrument creating the power.

The construction of a will is governed by the system of law intended by the testator, which shall be presumed to be the law of his or her domicile at the date of the execution of the will.[51]

Ghana

A will, so far as it revokes a will which, under the Wills Act 1971, would be deemed to be properly executed, or that revokes a provision which, under the Act, would be deemed as included in a properly executed will, will be treated as properly executed if the execution of the latter conforms to any law by reference to which the revoked will or provision would be so deemed.[52] A will shall not be held to be revoked or to have become invalid, and its construction shall not be altered, by reason of any subsequent change of domicile of the testator.[53]

A will, so far as it exercises a power of appointment, will be treated as properly executed if its execution conforms to the law governing the essential validity of the power.[54] A will, so far as it exercises a power of appointment, shall not be deemed to be improperly executed by reason only that its execution was not in accordance with any formal requirements contained in the instrument creating the power.[55]

[49] Wills Act 1957, s. 11(c).
[50] Wills Act 1992, s. 24(5).
[51] Ibid., s. 28.
[52] Wills Act 1971, s. 15(2)(c).
[53] Ibid., s. 16.
[54] Ibid., s. 15(2)(d).
[55] Ibid., s. 15(3).

Malawi

Subject to statutorily defined limits, the duty of a court, in construing a will, is to give effect to the intention of the testator so far as such intention can be ascertained from the wording of the will, and, in so doing, the court shall not be bound to follow any statutory provision, rule of common law or doctrine of equity.[56]

South Africa

So far as it revokes a will, or a portion of a will, which by virtue of the Wills Act 1953 is not invalid, a will shall not be formally invalid if its form complies with the internal law in terms of which, under the Act, the revoked will or portion is not invalid.[57]

So far as therein a power conferred by any instrument is exercised, or a duty imposed by any instrument is performed, a will shall not be formally invalid if its form complies with the internal law of the state or territory where the instrument was executed.[58] Where a testator domiciled in South Africa confers in his or her will the power of appointment on a person, there is an implied condition that that person's exercise of power should conform to South African law, even if the person exercising the power is not domiciled in South Africa.[59]

Zambia

A will which revokes a previous will, that under the Wills and Administration of Testate Estates Act 1989 would be treated as properly executed, is formally valid if the execution of that will conforms to any law, by reference to which the revoked will or provision would be so treated.[60]

A will, so far as it exercises a power of appointment, is properly executed if its execution conforms to the law governing the essential validity of the power.[61] A will, so far as it exercises a power of appointment, shall not be treated as improperly executed by reason only that its execution was not in accordance with any formal requirements contained in the instrument creating the power.[62]

[56] Deceased Estates (Wills, Inheritance and Protection) Act 2011, s. 11(1).
[57] Wills Act 1953, s. 3bis(1)(d). [58] Ibid., s. 3bis(1)(c).
[59] *Ex p. Reay No: In re. McGregor's Estate* 1982 (4) SA 27.
[60] Wills and Administration of Testate Estates Act 1989, s. 7(2)(c).
[61] Ibid., s. 7(2)(d). [62] Ibid., s. 7(3).

Zimbabwe

To the extent that a will expressly or implicitly revokes another will, or part of another will which is formally valid by virtue of the Wills Act 1987, that first mentioned will is valid if it complies with any law under which the revoked will, or part thereof, is formally valid.[63]

The question of whether or not a will has been wholly or partially revoked or rendered void by the dissolution or annulment of the testator's marriage, or by the testator's subsequent marriage, shall be determined according to the internal law of the country where the testator was domiciled, immediately after the dissolution or annulment of the marriage, or the subsequent marriage, as the case may be. The question of whether or not a will has been wholly or partially revoked, rendered void by the destruction of the will, or part thereof, or by the making of a subsequent will, shall be determined according to the internal law of the country where the testator was domiciled when the will was allegedly revoked or rendered void – to the extent that the will disposes of movable property – and of the country in which the immovable property concerned is situated, to the extent that the will allegedly revoked or rendered void disposes of immovable property. This question shall be determined according to such internal law as existed when the event or act allegedly revoking the will or rendering it void took place.[64]

To the extent that, in a will, a testator exercises the power of appointment, or other function conferred upon him or her by any instrument, the will is valid if its form complies with the law governing the essential validity of the instrument.[65]

The meaning of any word, expression or provision in a will shall be ascertained according to the internal law of the country where the testator was domiciled when he or she made the will, and in accordance with such internal law as then existed, unless a contrary intention appears from the terms of the will, or from any admissible extrinsic evidence.[66]

Comments

The countries under study are very much uniform in providing that a will which purports to revoke another will be treated as properly executed if its execution is consistent with the law under which the revoked will was considered properly executed. A will can be revoked by means other than

[63] Wills Act 1987, s. 22(4)(e). [64] Wills Act 1987, s. 22(8). [65] Ibid., s. 22(4)(d).

[66] Ibid., s. 22(6). *Kalshoven* v. *Kalshoven* 1966 (3) SA 466; *Ex p. Courteney Selous* 1956 R & N 14.

using another will, such as by tearing, other forms of physical destruction, or by operation of law (for example, on marriage). However, apart from Zimbabwe, none of the countries under study provides for the law governing whether such acts validly destroy the will. It has been suggested that it is the law of the testator's domicile which governs whether such an act validly revokes the will.[67] However, it is still an open question whether it is the domicile at the time of the will's destruction, or at the testator's death, which applies. Zimbabwean law opts for domicile (or *lex situs* in case of immovables) at the time of the will's destruction. Admittedly, whichever option is adopted, there are likely to be problems in some instances. But the domicile of the testator at the time the will is destroyed is to be preferred – it is more likely that a testator would legitimately expect that the validity, or otherwise, of an act of destroying his or her will would be determined by the law of the place of his or her domicile at the time this act was performed.

The law governing the interpretation of wills[68] is directly dealt with in Gambia, Malawi and Zimbabwe. Under Gambian and Zimbabwean law, interpretation is governed by the domicile of the testator at the time the will was made, but both allow for this rule to be displaced if there is evidence of a contrary intention on the part of the testator. In Malawi, the intention of the testator prevails over any rules of common law and equity. Arguably, this denies resort to private international law rules. The subject of the law governing the interpretation of wills is also dealt with indirectly in other jurisdictions, such as Ghana, where it is provided that the construction of a will shall not be altered by reason of any subsequent change of domicile of the testator. Compared to formal and essential validity, as regards the law governing the interpretation of wills, no distinction is made between movables and immovables.

Intestate succession

Ghana

In Ghana, intestate succession is governed by the Intestate Succession Act 1981. The law applies to the devolution of the estate of 'any person

[67] *Cheshire, North & Fawcett*, pp. 1275–6.

[68] See generally *Kershaw's Estate* v. *Commissioner of Inland Revenue* 1952 (2) SA 700, which holds that the rights which inure to the beneficiary of a will are determined by the law that governs the interpretation of the will.

who dies intestate'. However, its application is subject to the rules of private international law.[69] The law does not distinguish between movables and immovables; accordingly, it applies equally to both components of an intestate's estate.

Under Ghana law, succession to the movable property of an intestate is governed by the law of his or her domicile at the time of death.[70] This law determines issues such as the people entitled to succeed to the movables in the estate and the size of their entitlement. Where the deceased is a Ghanaian domiciled in Ghana, the Intestate Succession Act and those aspects of customary law incorporated into it will apply in determining these issues. Where the deceased is a foreigner who has become domiciled in Ghana, then, unless it is proved that he or she has become subject to a particular system of customary law, succession to his or her movable estate is to be governed by the Intestate Succession Act *without* the customary law aspects of the Act.[71] Where the deceased has been domiciled abroad, but has movables in Ghana, the law of his or her domicile applies to the devolution of those movables.[72]

Ghana adheres to the principle that succession to the immovable estate of a person who dies intestate is governed by the *lex situs*. In *Youhana* v. *Abboud*,[73] the court was emphatic that, where a person died intestate leaving immovable property, the incidence and course of succession to it should depend entirely on the *lex situs*. *Youhana* v. *Abboud*[74] is

[69] Intestate Succession Act 1985, s. 1(1). See *Amerley* v. *Otinkorang* [1965] GLR 656. It was held that where a domiciled Ghanaian dies intestate, succession to his property must be determined by his personal law and that English rules of private international law do not apply to the distribution of the estate of an intestate Ghanaian who dies in Ghana. See also *Ghamson* v. *Wobill* (1947) 12 WACA 181; *In re. Larbi (Deceased); Larbi* v. *Larbi* [1977] 2 GLR 506. The Intestate Succession Act has reduced the scope of the personal law (i.e. customary laws to which persons are subject) on issues of intestate success for domiciled Ghanaians.

[70] *Thompson* v. *Thompson* (1921–5) Div. Ct. 155; *Whittaker* v. *Choiteram* [1971] 2 GLR 267; *Ekem* v. *Nerba* (1948–51) Ghana DC (Land) 40.

[71] It is submitted that a Ghanaian who has lost or severed his association with the customary community into which he was born falls into this category and the principles here apply to him *mutatis mutandis*.

[72] *Thompson* v. *Thompson* (1921–5) Div. Ct. 155; *Whittaker* v. *Choiteram* [1971] 2 GLR 267.

[73] [1974] 2 GLR 201 (on appeal from *Youhana* v. *Abboud* [1973] 1 GLR 258). See also *Davies* v. *Randall* [1964] GLR 671; *Davies* v. *Randall* [1963] 1 GLR 382; G. Woodman, '*Youhana* v. *Abboud*: Choice of Law for Inheritance on Intestacy, and the Application of the Common Law' (1974) 11 *University of Ghana Law Journal* 97. But see *King* v. *Elliot* [1972] 1 GLR 54; *Elliot* v. *King* [1966] GLR 654.

[74] [1974] 2 GLR 201. See also *Thompson* v. *Thompson* [1981] GLR 537.

a classic illustration of the application of the law of the domicile of an intestate to the devolution of his immovable property in Ghana. The central issue was whether succession to immovables left in different parts of Ghana by two Lebanese who died domiciled in Lebanon should be governed by the customary law of the areas where the properties were situated, or by Lebanese law. The court rejected the argument that the *lex situs* refers only to the internal law of Ghana without its conflict of laws rules. It was observed that such an argument is 'delusively simple ... The *lex situs* does not just mean the domestic law of the *situs* but the conflict of laws rules of the *situs* which may refer to some other system of domestic law'.[75] In the instant case, it was held that the applicable law was Lebanese law. The application of the law of the domicile of an intestate to the devolution of his or her immovables in Ghana is subject to overriding provisions of the law of the place where the land is situated.[76] In following the 'law of the place in which the land is situated', both the customary laws of the community in which the land is located and Ghanaian law may be taken into account.[77]

Kenya

Succession to the immovable property of a deceased person in Kenya is governed by Kenyan law, regardless of the domicile of that person at the time of his or her death.[78] Succession to the movable property of a deceased person is regulated by the law of the domicile of the deceased at the time of death.[79] A person who, immediately before his or her death, was ordinarily resident in Kenya is presumed to have been domiciled in Kenya at the date of death, in the absence of proof of domicile elsewhere.[80]

[75] [1974] 2 GLR 201, at 205–6.

[76] Courts Act 1993, s. 54, r. 4. The *lex situs* also has no application in determining succession to immovable property upon the intestacy of a domiciled Ghanaian. *Yirenkyi* v. *Sakyi* [1991] 1 GLR 217.

[77] See *Garrett* v. *Garrett* [1991] 1 GLR 32 at 36.

[78] Law of Succession Act 1981, s. 4(1)(a).

[79] Law of Succession Act 1981, s. 4(1)(b). *In re. Estate of Naftali (Deceased)* [2002] 2 KLR 684.

[80] Law of Succession Act 1981, s. 4(2).

Lesotho

The law governing succession to immovables is the *lex situs* and the law govering movables is the *lex domicilii* of the deceased.[81]

Malawi

Historically, the persons entitled on the death of a non-domiciled person (a person whose place of domicile is outside Malawi) to such a part of the estate as consists of movable property, was to be ascertained in accordance with the law of the deceased person's country of domicile.[82] The Deceased Estates (Wills, Inheritance and Protection) Act 2011 does not address this issue.

Nigeria

The *lex situs* – i.e. law of Nigeria, including its conflict of laws rules – govern succession to immovables, in this instance, leasehold property. Thus, where the intestate, who appeared to have been domiciled in Lebanon, left immovable property in Nigeria, it was held that succession to the estate should be governed by the law of Lebanon.[83]

South Africa

The *lex situs* is the governing law for all questions that arise with regard to immovable property.[84]

Tanzania

Succession to the estate of an intestate who dies domiciled in Zanzibar is governed by Zanzibar law and, under that law, where a person dies intestate without any lineal relative and the deceased's estate has no

[81] *Mohapi* v. *Motleleng* (1985–9) LAC 316; *Maphathe* v. *Maphathe*, CIV/APN/479/02 (High Court, Lesotho, 2004).

[82] Wills and Inheritance Act 1967, s. 19; *In re. Osman Hussein; Ali* v. *Osman* [1923–60] ALR Mal. 276.

[83] *Kharie Zaidan* v. *Fatima Khalil Mohssen* [1973] 1 All NLR (Part II) 86.

[84] *Dhansay* v. *Davids* 1991 (4) SA 200.

legitimate claimants, the net estate of the deceased should go to the Government of Tanzania as *bona vacantia*.[85]

Uganda

Succession to the immovable property of a deceased person in Uganda is regulated by Ugandan law, wherever that person may have had his or her domicile at the time of death.[86] Succession to the movable property of a deceased person is regulated by the *lex domicilii* at the time of death.[87] A person can have only one domicile for the purpose of succession to his or her movable property.[88] If a man dies leaving movable property in Uganda, in the absence of proof of any domicile elsewhere, succession to the property is regulated by the law of Uganda.[89]

Comments

It appears to be well accepted in the countries under study that succession to movables is governed by the law of the domicile of the deceased at the time of death,[90] and that immovables are governed by the *lex situs*. The former rule reflects the unitary principle, which conveniently allows all movables of the deceased to be governed by one law – the law of domicile. The latter rule reflects the principle of scission, which necessarily leads to a situation in which different laws govern land situated in different countries. Admittedly, there is some ambiguity in how the Kenyan and Ugandan provisions are worded. They appear to deal purely with immovable property in Kenya and Uganda, which fails to address the question of which law governs immovable property outside Kenya or Uganda.

[85] *In re. Yusuf Bin Simbani (Deceased)* [1962] EA 623.
[86] Succession Act 1906, s. 4(1).
[87] Succession Act 1906, s. 4(2). For this purpose, a person dying intestate shall be deemed to have had his domicile in Uganda if – for a period of not less than two years preceding his or her death – they were ordinarily resident in Uganda; and they were survived by a spouse or child who was, at the time of their death, ordinarily resident in Uganda. *Suman Naresh Kara* v. *Bhatia* [1997] 4 Kam. LR 1.
[88] Succession Act 1906, s. 5.
[89] Ibid., s. 8.
[90] See generally *In re. Estate of Jacques Maqridis* [1932–40] 2 SLR 1; *Official Administrator* v. *Anba Bola Convent* [1900–31] 1 SLR 521: both cases support the *lex domicilii* as the governing law for succession to movables.

In Ghana and Nigeria it has been held that the *lex situs* includes their conflicts rules and under those rules the *lex domicilii* governs succession to immovables. Accordingly, in both countries, through a rather circuitous route, it appears that the whole estate of the deceased (movables and immovables) is governed by the *lex domicilii* – a position supported by leading authorities on the subject.[91]

[91] See *Dicey, Morris & Collins*, para. 27–018.

16

Administration of estates

The death of a person raises issues as to who is entitled to deal with the deceased's property. As discussed below, in the countries under study this role is entrusted to a person to whom a grant of probate or letter of administration is made by a judicial authority. The executor or administrator is entrusted with the responsibility of clearing the estate of liabilities and, assuming there is a residue after discharging all liabilities, distributing the residue among the beneficiaries according to the will or the rules of intestacy. This chapter deals with the jurisdiction of courts to grant probate and letters of administration or reseal foreign grants, the recognition of foreign administrators and executors, as well as the choice of law issues that may be generated in an application for a grant and the act of administration.

Botswana

The estate of all persons dying either testate or intestate shall be administered and distributed according to the law under letters of administration granted by the Master of the High Court.[1] The letters of administration shall be granted to the executors testamentary duly appointed by persons so dying or to such persons as executors dative to the deceased.[2] Letters of administration authorise the executor to administer the estate wherever situated.[3]

The Master is empowered to reseal grants of letters of administration for the estate of a deceased person from designated countries.[4] A letter so resealed has like force and effect and full operation in Botswana with respect to the whole estate in Botswana.[5]

[1] Administration of Estates Act 1972, s. 28(1). [2] Ibid., s. 28(2).
[3] Ibid., s. 28(3). [4] Ibid., s. 36.
[5] Ibid., s. 37. This provision applies to a foreign certificate of authority, s. 70.

Gambia

The jurisdiction to make an order authorising the administration of the estate of a deceased person is given to the High Court. This jurisdiction may be invoked by the Curator of Intestate Estates,[6] or by any other person.[7] Under section 5(3) of the Act, an order made authorising the administration of the estate of a deceased person gives 'power over all of the estate whatsoever situate'. This suggests that the jurisdiction is not limited only to property within Gambia.[8]

The Administration of Estates by Consular Officers Act 1940 empowers consular officers to apply for a letter of administration for the estate of the deceased person.[9] This power relates only to subjects or citizens of statutorily designated states[10] who die within Gambia or who die outside Gambia leaving property within Gambia, and for whom there are no persons rightfully entitled to administer their estate.[11]

Probate or letters of administration granted outside Gambia may be resealed there. Where a court of probate in any Commonwealth or British court in a foreign country has granted probate or letters of administration in respect of a deceased person's estate, the probate or letters so granted may be resealed in the High Court. When so sealed, the probate or letters have the same force and effect in Gambia as if granted by the Gambian court that resealed them.[12] Before resealing, the court may require evidence as to the domicile of the deceased person.

Ghana

On the death of a person, and regardless of their domicile, nationality or any other association with a foreign legal system, their movable and immovable property in Ghana devolves on their personal representatives[13] – that is, the executor or administrator, as the case

[6] Intestate Estates Act 1909, s. 4. [7] Ibid., s. 7.

[8] This position is strengthened by the fact that, in relation to the estate of a European officer – a person in the public service of Gambia who is not a citizen of a West African State – administration is expressly limited to assets, expenses and debt 'within the jurisdiction'. Intestate Estates Act 1909, s. 21(2).

[9] Administration of Estates by Consular Officers Act 1940, s. 2.

[10] i.e. Finland, Greece, Hungary, Japan, Thailand, Turkey and Yugoslavia.

[11] Administration of Estates by Consular Officers Act 1940, s. 2(1).

[12] Probate (Re-sealing) Act 1935, s. 3.

[13] Administration of Estates Act 1961, s. 1(1).

may be.[14] The grant of probate is necessary to entitle an executor to administer the estate of a testator; appointment as executor in a will is not enough.[15] The Circuit Court, District Courts and High Court have jurisdiction to hear applications for the granting of probate or letters of administration with respect to the estate of a deceased person, and to hear causes and matters relating to the succession to the property of that deceased person, who had, at the time of death, a fixed place of abode within the area of jurisdiction of the court. For the Circuit and District courts, the value of the estate in question should not exceed a defined amount.[16] Where the value of the estate exceeds that amount, the application must be made in the High Court, which has jurisdiction in all civil matters. These provisions suggest that the presence of assets in Ghana confers jurisdiction on the courts to grant probate or letters of administration, irrespective of the domicile of the deceased. The courts have jurisdiction to grant probate or letters of administration separately with respect to movable and immovable property.[17]

The Administration of Estates Act 1961 provides for the sealing of foreign probate or letters of administration to take effect in Ghana. Under section 84 of the Act, where a Court of Probate in a Commonwealth country, or in any country to which the section is applied, has granted probate or letters of administration with respect to the estate of a deceased person, the probate or letters so granted can, on being produced to and a copy thereof deposited with a Ghanaian court, be sealed with the seal of that court.[18] After sealing, the foreign probate or letters of administration have like force and effect and operate in the same way in Ghana as if they had been granted by the Ghanaian court. In *Gordon* v. *Essien*,[19] the deceased (a Nigerian domiciled in Nigeria) had immovable property in Ghana. Letters of administration were granted in Nigeria over his estate in Nigeria and were subsequently sealed in Ghana. It was

[14] Sections 66–73 of the Insolvency Act 2006 provide a special regime for the administration of the estate of deceased insolvents.

[15] Administration of Estates Act 1961, s. 61.

[16] Courts Act 1993, ss. 42(1)(a)(vii) and 47(1)(g). See also High Court (Civil Procedure) Rules 2004, Ord. 66, r. 1.

[17] Administration of Estates Act 1961, s. 75.

[18] Section 84(4) of the Administration of Estates Act 1961 empowers the President of Ghana to specify in a legislative instrument the countries to which the section should be applied. See *In re. Lartey (Deceased); Lartey* v. *Affutu-Lartey* [1972] 2 GLR 488, in which there was an attempt to reseal probate that had been granted in Liberia. The attempt was unsuccessful because there was no agreement between Ghana and Liberia.

[19] [1992] 1 GLR 232.

argued that the sealing did not give authority to administer the property in Ghana, since the Nigerian grant did not cover that property. In rejecting this argument, the court held that an interpretation of section 84(1) of the Administration of Estates Act that limits the effect of a sealing in Ghana to the property, with respect to which letters of administration have been granted in the foreign country, would render sealing a fanciful exercise. To the court, the purpose of the procedure of sealing in Ghana was to use letters of administration that had been sealed in administering the Ghanaian component of the deceased's estate, without the administrator going through the process of obtaining a fresh grant in Ghana.

Kenya

The Law of Succession Act 1981 gives the High Court and Magistrates' Courts jurisdiction to grant probate and letters of administration.[20] It has been held that the granting of letters of administration ought to be obtained from the domicile of the deceased at the time of death. Thus, where the deceased died in the Democratic Republic of Congo and was not domiciled in Kenya (the evidence showed that he was either domiciled in the Democratic Republic of Congo or Rwanda), it was held that the Kenyan court had no jurisdiction to grant letters of administration for his movable properties in Kenya.[21]

Where the deceased dies domiciled outside Kenya, the court may make a grant to the person entrusted with the administration of the estate by a court having jurisdiction at the place where the deceased died domiciled, to a person entitled to administer the estate by the law of the place where the deceased died domiciled, or to such other person as the court directs.[22]

Where a court or other authority, having jurisdiction in matters of probate or administration in any Commonwealth country, or in any other foreign country designated by the Minister by notice in the Gazette, has granted probate or letters of administration in respect of the estate of a deceased person, that grant may, when produced to the High Court, be sealed with the seal of the court. After that, the grant shall be of the same force and effect, and have the same operation in Kenya, as if granted and

[20] Law of Succession Act 1981, ss. 47–50B and 53.
[21] *In re. Estate of Naftali (Deceased)* [2002] 2 KLR 684.
[22] Law of Succession Act 1981, s. 28.

confirmed by that court.[23] Before sealing a grant, the High Court may require such evidence as it thinks fit concerning the domicile of the deceased person.[24]

It has been held that no suit can be brought against an administrator in his or her official capacity, except in the courts of the country from which he or she derives their authority to act by virtue of letters of administration granted to them.[25]

Lesotho

The estate of all deceased persons shall be administered and distributed according to law under letters of administration granted by the Master of the High Court. Such letters shall be granted to the executor testamentary or the executor dative.[26] Letters of administration authorise the executor to administer the estate, wherever it is situated.[27]

The Master is given jurisdiction to seal letters of administration granted in designated states.[28] A letter which is so sealed has like force and effect, and is fully operative in Lesotho in respect of assets there.[29]

Malawi

The High Court of Malawi has jurisdiction in all matters relating to probate and the administration of the estates of deceased persons, with the power to grant and revoke probate and letters of administration.[30]

The High Court also has jurisdiction to reseal grants of probate and letters of administration made by a court of probate in any country.[31] Where such foreign court of probate has granted probate or letters of administration to the estate of a deceased person, the Malawi court may seal the foreign grant with the seal of the Malawian court and thereupon the foreign grant shall be of the like force and effect and have the same

[23] Ibid., s. 77(1). [24] Ibid., s. 77(2).

[25] *National Bank of India Ltd* v. *The Administrator General of Zanzibar* [1924–6] 10 KLR 88.

[26] Administration of Estates Proclamation 1935, s. 31(1). [27] Ibid., s. 31(2).

[28] Ibid., ss. 40–1. See generally *Maphathe* v. *Maphathe*, CIV/APN/479/02 (High Court, Lesotho, 2004).

[29] Administration of Estates Proclamation 1935, s. 41.

[30] Deceased Estates (Wills, Inheritance and Protection) Act 2011, s. 20(1). The Magistrate courts also have jurisdiction limited by the value of the estate, s. 20(3).

[31] Ibid., s. 20(3).

operation in Malawi as if granted by the Malawian court.[32] Prior to resealing the court may require evidence of the domicile of the deceased.

In respect of a foreign national who dies within Malawi, or dies outside Malawi leaving property within Malawi, and there is no person present in Malawi at the time of his or her death who is rightfully entitled to administer the estate of such deceased person, the law empowers a consular officer of the foreign state of which the deceased is a national, within Malawi, to take possession of the property of such deceased person, and obtain from the court letters of administration of the property of such deceased person.[33]

Namibia

The Administration of Estates Act 1965 in South Africa (see report on South Africa below) as amended to 1979, also applies in Namibia. By virtue of the Estates and Succession Amendment Act 2005, the 1965 Act applies to the administration of all deceased estates, whether testate or intestate, of persons who died on or after 23 December 2005.[34]

Sierra Leone

The estate of every person dying intestate devolves upon the Administrator and Registrar-General. However, upon the grant of letters of administration, the estate is divested from the Administrator and Registrar-General and becomes vested in the person or persons to whom letters of administration have been granted.[35]

It has been held that there cannot be two original grants of probate of the same will and that, therefore, although a grant of probate by the Supreme Court of the Gold Coast (Ghana) has no immediate legal effect in Sierra Leone, the Sierra Leone courts will not make a fresh grant of probate in respect of property in Sierra Leone under the same will – it will give effect to the original grant by resealing it. Resealing applies to both personalty and realty.[36]

[32] Ibid., s 58. [33] Ibid., s. 21.

[34] Estates and Succession Amendment Act 2005, s. 3(1). Historically, the Administration of Estates (Rehoboth Gebiet) Proclamation 1941 applied to the administration of estates of persons who were members of the Rehoboth Baster Community.

[35] Administration of Estates Act 1946, s. 9(1).

[36] *In re. O'Reilly (Deceased); Williams* v. *McCormack* [1950–6] ALR SL 58. This decision was based on s. 3 of the Probates (British and Colonial) Recognition Ordinance.

Whenever a citizen of designated states[37] dies within Sierra Leone, or dies outside Sierra Leone leaving property within Sierra Leone, and no person, other than the Administrator and Registrar-General, is present in Sierra Leone at the time of his or her death, or is rightfully entitled to administer the estate of such a deceased person, the Consul, Vice-Consul or Consular Officer of such a state within Sierra Leone may take possession and have custody of the property of such a deceased person, and may apply the same in payment of his or her debts and funeral expenses, while also retaining the surplus for the benefit of the persons entitled thereto. The Consul, Vice-Consul or Consular Officer must apply for and is entitled to obtain from the court letters of administration for the property of the deceased person.[38]

South Africa

The jurisdiction to authorise the distribution of the estate of any deceased person is given to the Masters of the High Court.[39] Ordinary residence within the area of the jurisdiction of the High Court – as opposed to the presence of assets – to which the Master is appointed, is the most important criterion for the exercise of this jurisdiction.[40]

It is necessary for a foreign administrator to receive recognition of his or her appointment by a court of law.[41] In respect of letters of executorship granted from countries designated by the Minister,[42] the Master is empowered to sign and seal them with their seal of office on the application of the person in whose favour the letters are granted. After so sealing the letters, such a person shall, with respect to the whole estate

[37] Finland, Estonia, Hungary, Yugoslavia, Turkey, Romania, Thailand, Norway, United States, France, Sweden, Greece, Mexico, Italy and Germany.

[38] Administration of Estates by Consular Officers Act 1940, s. 2.

[39] Administration of Estates Act 1965, ss. 4 and 13.

[40] There, courts have expressed doubt as to whether there is jurisdiction to appoint an administrator over assets situated outside South Africa. See *Ex p. Barclays Bank* 1951 (3) SA 727. Moreover, the administrator's authority to collect or recover assets does not extend to assets outside South Africa. The authority to administer applies only to assets situated in South Africa and assets situated in a foreign country which have, in fact, come into possession of the South African executor in his capacity as such. There is no duty upon an executor to take steps to endeavour to recover property of the deceased situated out of this country. *Segal* v. *Segal* 1979 (1) SA 503.

[41] *Smith and Gilks* v. *The Master* 1957 (4) SA 582; *In re. National Bank of Scotland Ltd* 1956 (3) SA 92; *Ex p. Nupen* 1957 (2) SA 450.

[42] Administration of Estates Act 1965, s. 20.

of the deceased situated in South Africa, be deemed as an executor to whom letters of executorship have been granted by the Master.[43]

Tanzania

The High Court of Tanzania has jurisdiction in all matters relating to probate and the administration of a deceased's estates.[44] It has power to grant probates of wills and letters of administration to the estates of deceased persons and to alter or revoke such grants,[45] as well as to reseal grants of probate and letters of administration made by a court of probate in any part of the Commonwealth.[46] In respect of designated countries[47] and under defined conditions, the courts are allowed to make a grant to a consular officer in respect of the estate of a deceased national.[48] Furthermore, where any person, to whom letters of administration might be granted, is absent from Tanzania, letters of administration with the will annexed may be granted to his or her lawfully constituted attorney ordinarily resident in Tanzania.[49]

Where a court of probate in any part of the Commonwealth has granted probate or letters of administration in respect of the estate of a deceased person, the probate or letters may be sealed with the seal of the High Court. It shall then be of like force and effect and have the same operation in Tanzania as if granted by that court.[50] Before sealing, the court may require such evidence as it thinks fit as to the domicile of the deceased person.[51] Without resealing, the authority granted to the administrator or executor in the foreign court is ineffective in Tanzania. In *Bolton* v. *Salim Khambi*,[52] the plaintiff's son was killed in a motor accident in Tanganyika. The plaintiff, who lived in England, was granted letters of administration to his son's estate and, subsequently, without having the grant resealed in Tanganyika, commenced proceedings for

[43] Ibid., s. 21.

[44] Probate and letters of administration have effect over all the property, movable and immovable, of the deceased throughout Tanzania: Probate and Administration of Estates Act 1963, s. 70(a).

[45] Ibid., s. 3. Resident magistrates and district courts are also given jurisdiction in relation to small estates.

[46] Ibid., s. 4.

[47] Ibid., s. 7(6). The countries are: United States, France, Germany, Greece, Italy, Mexico, Norway and Sweden.

[48] Ibid., s. 7.

[49] Ibid., ss. 30–1; *Rajabali Mawji* v. *Remat Alibhai* [1921–52] 1 TLR 422.

[50] Ibid., s. 95.

[51] Ibid., s. 96.

[52] [1958] EA 360.

damages. It was held that a grant of administration in England does not authorise the administrator to sue as such in Tanganyika.

Uganda

Jurisdiction to grant probate and letters of administration is exercised by the High Court and a Magistrates' Court in accordance with the Administration of Estates (Small Estates) (Special Provisions) Act.[53]

Where the deceased person leaves property in Uganda, letters of administration shall be granted according to the Succession Act 1906, regardless of the fact that the deceased may have been domiciled in a country where the law relating to testate and intestate succession differs from Ugandan law.[54] There are special procedures fostering international judicial co-operation in cases where a person applying to the High Court for a grant of probate or letters of administration believes that the deceased has left property in Tanzania or Kenya.[55]

Letters of administration or probate may be granted to an attorney of an eligible personal representative who is absent from Uganda.[56] In defined circumstances, the court can appoint such a person as it thinks fit to administer the estate.[57]

Probate or letters of administration have effect over all the property and estate, whether movable or immovable, of the deceased throughout Uganda.[58] If the deceased was not domiciled in Uganda, the application of his or her movable property to the payment of his or her debts is to be regulated by Ugandan law.[59]

[53] Succession Act 1906, s. 235.

[54] Succession Act 1906, s. 207. In a decision which appears to be inconsistent with this provision, it was held that the High Court of Uganda has no jurisdiction to entertain an application for probate of a will executed outside Uganda by a person domiciled outside Uganda at the time of death and which will relates to movable properties situated in Uganda. *Suman Naresh Kara* v. *Bhatia* [1997] 4 Kam. LR 1.

[55] Succession Act 1906, s. 331. [56] Ibid., ss. 212–14. [57] Ibid., s. 224.

[58] Ibid., s. 242. See generally *Keshavlal Bhoja* v. *Tejalal Bhoja* [1967] 1 EA 217. The plaintiff, a resident of Uganda, brought an action in the High Court of Uganda for account against the defendant who was also resident in Uganda, as administrator of their deceased father's estate. The defendant had been granted letters of administration by the Kenyan court and the estate consisted solely of movable property situated in Kenya. The defendant objected that the Ugandan courts had no jurisdiction. It was held that the suit could not be maintained in Uganda as the defendant was accountable only to the Kenyan courts.

[59] Succession Act 1906, s. 284.

Zambia

The High Court of Zambia has original and unlimited jurisdiction in all matters relating to wills.[60] Subject to defined limitations, probate may be granted by a court only to an executor appointed by a will.[61] Where any executor, or the person to whom letters of administration might be granted, is absent from Zambia, and there is no other executor within Zambia willing to act, letters of administration may be granted to a lawfully constituted attorney of the executor or administrator who is ordinarily resident within Zambia.[62] A grant of probate or letters of administration entitles the personal representative to all rights belonging to the deceased as if the administration had been granted the moment after his or her death. Probate and letters of administration have effect over all the property of the deceased throughout Zambia.[63]

Where a court of probate outside Zambia has granted probate or letters of administration to the estate of a deceased person, the court may seal a grant with the seal of the court. After that, the grant has the same force and effect and has the same operation in Zambia as if granted by the court. The court may require evidence of domicile to be furnished in relation to an application for sealing.[64]

Zimbabwe

The estates of all persons dying either testate or intestate shall be administered and distributed according to law under letters of administration granted by the Master of the High Court to the testamentary executors duly appointed by such deceased persons, or to such persons as shall, in default of testamentary executors, be appointed executors dative to such deceased persons.[65]

The Master is empowered to sign and seal, with the seal of office, letters of administration granted in states designated by the President.[66]

[60] Wills and Administration of Testate Estates Act 1989, s. 66. In addition, there is the Intestate Succession Act 1989, which, under s. 2(1), applies to 'all persons who are at their death domiciled in Zambia and shall apply only to a member of a community to which customary law would have applied if this Act had not been passed'. The Intestate Succession Act, which is not discussed in this report, has its own regime for administering an intestate's estate. The regime in many respects is similar to that provided under the Wills and Administration of Estates Act.

[61] Wills and Administration of Testate Estates Act 1989, s. 29(1). [62] Ibid., ss. 37 and 38.

[63] Ibid., s. 44. [64] Ibid., s. 54. See also Probate (Resealing) Act 1936.

[65] Administration of Estates Act 1907, s. 23. [66] Ibid., s. 34.

When so sealed, the grant has the same effect and full operation in Zimbabwe as though it had been made by the Master.[67]

Upon the death of any person who is neither ordinarily resident within Zimbabwe, nor the owner of any property other than shares in a company, building society, stocks, moneys invested in participation bonds, moneys deposited with a bank, building society or finance house, or of any rights to interest in the preceding property, the Master may summarily and without observance of the usual and customary forms, and without requiring security or an account of the administration and distribution of the estate, sign and seal letters of administration produced to him or her to appoint a person registered under the Estate Administrators Act as executor dative for the administration of the estate of the deceased. The Master may also dispense with such an appointment and direct the manner in which the estate shall be administered.[68]

In addition, upon the death of any person domiciled in the United Kingdom whose only assets in Zimbabwe are shares, the Master or any other person appointed for the purpose by the Minister may, when the death certificate of such a person, or an officially certified copy of the probate or letters of administration in his or her estate, and an inventory showing that the only assets in such an estate in Zimbabwe consist of shares, is filed with him or her, authorise the transfer of such shares to the person entitled to them.[69]

Comments

Death and the concomitant need to control and distribute the assets of a deceased person can give rise to complex private international law issues. None of the countries under study is a party to the Convention concerning the International Administration of the Estates of Deceased Persons 1973.

In all the countries under study, the jurisdiction to grant probate or letters of administration in respect of a deceased person's estate is granted to the High Court or the Master of the High Court with a right of appeal to the High Court. In most of the countries under study, the presence of assets within the jurisdiction provides the basis of jurisdiction. The fact that assets should exist within the jurisdiction to found jurisdiction may be inconvenient in some cases. Where a person dies

[67] Ibid., s. 35. [68] Ibid., s. 67(2). [69] Ibid., s. 67(3).

domiciled in one country with assets in another, and the courts in the forum where the assets exist are unwilling to grant probate or a letter of administration because the deceased is domiciled elsewhere, it could lead to an impasse if the courts of the domicile are unwilling to grant probate because there are no assets within the jurisdiction. The prospect of this impasse is, however, slim, given that a person is unlikely to be considered domiciled in a jurisdiction where he or she does not have any assets.

Kenyan and Ugandan courts have held that letters of administration should be obtained from the court of the domicile of a deceased, regardless of the presence of movable property in Kenya and Uganda. The decisions appear to confuse questions over the administration of estates with issues concerning the distribution of the estate of a deceased person. Statute law in both countries is clear that succession to movables, i.e. the distribution of the movables of an intestate, is governed by the law of the domicile. This position, however, does not dictate that the court does not have jurisdiction to grant letters of administration for the estate of a deceased domiciled abroad.

A careful reading of the legislation in the countries under study suggests that there is no statutory prohibition on granting probate or letters of administration on the sole basis that the deceased was domiciled in the jurisdiction. However, because it is expressly provided in the relevant legislation that a grant is effective only over assets within the jurisdiction, the persons in whose favour the grant is made would have to reseal it in the forum where the assets are located in order to be able to administer the assets there. Unless an application to reseal a foreign grant of probate or letters of administration can be made, a foreign executor or administrator must apply to the courts of the country where the assets are located for a separate grant.

The resealing of grants made by foreign courts is provided for in all the countries under study.[70] To the extent that it is uncontested, it can be

[70] Bostwana, Lesotho and Zimbabwe's legislation only mention 'letters of administration' and it is unclear if resealing extends to foreign probate. However, it appears that the letters of administration are used broadly to encompass what is known as probate in some jurisdictions. This is because the statutes provide that the estates of all persons dying either testate or intestate shall be administered and distributed according to law under letters of administration to be granted by the Master. Botswana – Administration of Estates Act 1972, s. 28; Lesotho – Administration of Estates Proclamation 1935, s. 31; Zimbabwe – Administration of Estates Act 1907, s. 23. Futhermore, under s. 1 of Lesotho's Administration of Estates Proclamation 1935, 'letters of administration' is defined to encompass what is known as probate in some jurisdictions.

argued that resealing is largely an administrative exercise with the court or Master appending their signatures and seal to the foreign grant. In most of the countries under study, in addition to requirements, such as providing an authenticated copy of the grant, security for due administration[71] and stamping, the court may require evidence of the domicile of the deceased.

Apart from Malawi, the regimes for resealing apply only to grants made by designated countries.[72] The countries are designated on the basis of reciprocity. As with statutory regimes for enforcing foreign judgments,[73] it is remarkable that very few African countries have been designated in the regimes of the countries under study. In the Ghanaian case of *In re. Lartey (Deceased); Lartey* v. *Affutu-Lartey*,[74] the court decried the fact that the power to designate countries had not been exercised and extended, especially to African countries. The case involved an application to reseal probate that had been granted in Liberia. The attempt was unsuccessful because there was no agreement between Ghana and Liberia. The court observed:

> Section 84(1) of the Administration of Estates Act 1961, enables grants in Commonwealth countries and other countries to which the section has been applied, to be resealed in this country. It is our hope that the appropriate authorities will consider this matter and enter into agreements with other countries, especially African countries, to enable grants made abroad to be resealed here and vice versa. This is an area in which the aims and objectives of African unity can be demonstrated by action and with realism.[75]

[71] See *Ex p. Estate of Hayes-O'Sullivan* 1952 (2) SA 499; *Ex p. Barclays Bank* 1952 (4) SA 662. For a discussion of the formalities surrounding the registration of foreign wills, including issues such as whether a copy may be accepted, authentication requirements and the effect of registration, see Namibia – *Ex p. Gertenbach, No: In re. Estate Weigel* 1957 (1) SA 159; South Africa – *Ex p. Strydom* 1947 (3) SA 589; *In re. Estate Warren* 1948 (2) SA 461; *In re. Estate Van Eijken* 1948 (1) SA 1237; *Ex p. Patel* 1948 (2) SA 902; *Ex p. Estate Adams* 1953 (4) SA 305; *Ex p. Campbell* 1953 (4) SA 70; *Ex p. Bond* 1955 (2) SA 98; *In re. Estate Ram* 1955 (4) SA 334; *The Master* v. *Gray* 1958 (3) SA 524; Zimbabwe – *Ex p. Judd: In Estate Norhadian* 1963 R & N 667; *Ex p. Bonakis* 1950 (1) SA 838.

[72] Historically, the predecessor of Malawi's Deceased Estates (Wills, Inheritance and Protection) Act 2011 limited resealing to grants of probate and letters of administration made by a court of probate in any part of the Commonwealth, South Africa or any other country designated by the Minister, and it appears that only Denmark and the Republic of Ireland were so designated under the Act. See Wills and Inheritance Act 1967, ss. 21(2) and 58.

[73] See Ch. 18. [74] [1972] 2 GLR 488. [75] [1972] 2 GLR 488 at 501.

It is recommended that this judicial plea should be heeded in all the countries under study. Indeed, the regime for international judicial cooperation in the administration of estates, established under Section 331 of Uganda's Succession Act, 1906, can provide a model for cooperation in the administration of estates among the countries under study.

Except in Kenya, a significant issue which is not directly addressed in the statutes or case law is whether the courts should take account of the law of the domicile of the deceased in their selection of a personal representative. Under the existing legislation, it can be argued that the law states that, irrespective of the composition of the estate – movables, immovables or a mixture of both – the court is not bound to select as personal representative a person who would have been so entitled under the law of the domicile of the deceased. Nor is the court bound to select as a personal representative a person who, under the law of the domicile of the deceased, has a beneficial interest in the estate. The selection of a personal representative is within the courts' discretion, but the statutes in each of the countries under study provide a hierarchy of persons entitled to a grant.[76] For example, in Ghana, in granting administration, the court 'shall have regard to the rights of all persons interested in the estate',[77] and, in that regard, attention to persons who are so entitled under the law of the domicile of the deceased would be appropriate.[78]

In addition to individuals who may be selected as personal representatives, many of the countries under study expressly allow consular officers to apply for, and be appointed, personal representatives for the estates of deceased nationals.

[76] Ghana – Administration of Estates Act 1961, s. 79. See also Botswana – Administration of Estates Act 1972, s. 32; Kenya – Law of Succession Act 1981, ss. 56–66.

[77] Administration of Estates Act 1961, s. 79(2). See generally *In re. Kariyavoulas (Deceased); Donkor* v. *Greek Consul-General* [1973] 2 GLR 52; *Whittaker* v. *Choiteram* [1971] 2 GLR 267; G. Woodman, 'Whittaker v. Choiteram: Choice of Law in Cases Concerning the Rights of Children to be Maintained from the Estate of Their Deceased Fathers' (1972) 9 *University of Ghana Law Journal* 195.

[78] The High Court (Civil Procedure) Rules provide a 'priority list' of people entitled to probate or letters of administration. See Ord. 66, rr. 12 and 13. Justice Archer once observed: 'My own experience in the High Court at Accra, Cape Coast and Sekondi has been that when foreigners die in Ghana, e.g., Moshies, Wangaras, Yorubas or Ibos, possessed of immovable property, the affidavit supporting the application for letters indicates that according to their own law in their respective countries, the applicant is entitled to succeed to the estate. These applications have been granted without question.' *Youhana* v. *Abboud* [1974] 2 GLR 201 at 219.

In all the countries under study, probate or letters of administration have effect over the entire property and estate – whether movable or immovable – of the deceased, throughout the country where the grant was made. The grant has no effect on property situated abroad – the personal representative must obtain a separate grant in the foreign forum or have the grant resealed in order for him or her to have authority over the assets abroad. The duties of a personal representative in relation to the assets within the forum where the grant was made are well defined. The statutes in the countries under study are generally silent on his or her duties in relation to assets abroad.[79] There is, however, South African authority to the effect that there is no duty upon an executor to take steps to endeavour to recover the property of the deceased situated abroad.[80]

[79] There are specific statutory provisions regulating the transfer of assets to beneficiaries who are abroad as part of the process of administration.

[80] *Segal* v. *Segal* 1979 (1) SA 503.

PART VI

Foreign judgments and arbitration awards

17

The common law regime for enforcing foreign judgments

The effectiveness of the judgment of a court is territorially constrained. State sovereignty prevents the judgment of one country from having direct force or effect in the territory of another sovereign state. To be effective abroad such a judgment must obtain the approval of a public authority, usually the courts, within the country where that is sought. It is to facilitate this process that a regime for recognition and enforcement of foreign judgments is an essential feature of most legal systems.

There are two regimes for recognising and enforcing foreign judgments in the countries under study, namely the common law and statutory regimes. At present, none of the countries is party to any international treaty on the recognition and enforcement of foreign judgments. There are provisions in some regional economic integration treaties that could provide the legal bases for concluding such treaties.[1] However, to date, no such treaty has been negotiated. This chapter focuses on the common law regime for enforcing foreign judgments.

What is a foreign judgment?

The statutory regimes for enforcing foreign judgments often designate judgments from specific national courts as enforceable. That is not the case with the common law regime. The common law has not clearly defined where a foreign judgment should emanate from: should it purely be a judgment from national courts? Does it encompass judgments from other non-judicial, quasi-judicial and administrative institutions in a foreign country? What about judgments from regional or international courts? In *Gathuna* v. *African Orthodox Church of Kenya*,[2] it was held

[1] Revised Treaty establishing the Economic Community of West African States, 24 July 1993, 35 ILM 660, Art. 57(1); Treaty for the establishment of the East African Community, 30 November 1999, 2144 UNTS I-37437, Art. 126.

[2] [1982] KLR 1, [1982] LLR 1205.

that a judgment of the Holy Synod of the Apostolic and Patriarchal Throne of Greek Orthodox Patriarchate of Alexandria sitting in Alexandria was not a foreign judgment and was not enforceable as such in Kenya. Until recently, it appears that the courts have restricted themselves or have been asked to enforce only judgments from foreign national courts. This is affirmed by national statute. For example, under Kenya's Civil Procedure Act 1924, a foreign judgment is defined as the 'judgment of a foreign court', and a foreign court is defined as 'a court situated outside Kenya which has no authority in Kenya'.[3]

A significant issue likely to arise in future relates to enforcing judgments of international or regional courts (hereinafter, 'international judgments').[4] Some regional economic integration treaties establish regional courts[5] and allow individuals to directly litigate before them. The treaties envisage that national civil procedure would be used to enforce the judgments of the regional courts. Article 44 of the Treaty establishing the East African Community[6] provides that the execution of a judgment of the East African Court of Justice which imposes pecuniary obligation on a person shall be governed by the rules of civil procedure in force in the member state where the execution is to take place. Similar provisions are found in the treaties establishing the Court of Justice of the Common Market for Eastern and Southern Africa and the Southern African Development Community Tribunal.[7]

Currently, with the exception of Zimbabwe,[8] there are no national statutes for enforcing international judgments. The statutory regimes for enforcing foreign judgments have not been extended to international

[3] Kenya – Civil Procedure Act 1924, s. 1. See also Tanzania – Civil Procedure Code 1966, s. 1; Uganda – Civil Procedure Act 1929, s. 2.

[4] The author is currently researching this subject under a Social Sciences and Humanities Research Council of Canada funded project, entitled: 'Access to International Justice at the Post-adjudication Phase of International Dispute Settlement: The Role of National Courts'.

[5] e.g. East African Court of Justice, Court of Justice of the Common Market for Eastern and Southern Africa, and Court of Justice of the Economic Community of West African States. All of these courts are operational and active.

[6] The East African Community comprises Burundi, Kenya, Rwanda, Tanzania and Uganda.

[7] Treaty establishing the Common Market for Eastern and Southern Africa, 5 November 1993, 33 ILM 1067, Art. 40; Protocol to the Southern African Development Community Tribunal and Rules of Procedure Thereof, 7 August 2000, Art. 32(1)(2)(3).

[8] Civil Matters (Mutual Assistance) Act 1995, s. 3(2)(b), which allows the Minister of Justice, Legal and Parliamentary Affairs to extend the provisions of the Act to international tribunals established in pursuance of an international agreement or a resolution of the UN General Assembly.

judgments.[9] Accordingly, international judgments can only, if at all, be enforced using the common law regime. In a recent case, a Zimbabwean court was confronted with a request to register and enforce a judgment of the Southern African Development Community Tribunal.[10] The court routinely applied the common law regime without discussing whether it related to the enforcement of international judgments. Also routinely applying the common law regime, the South African Constitutional Court and Supreme Court of Appeal agreed to enforce a judgment for costs against Zimbabwe from the same Tribunal.[11] It remains to be seen whether other national courts will follow the South African and Zimbabwean examples, or whether they will decide to restrict the common law regime purely to judgments from national courts. If the latter option is taken, an alternative regime must be developed to enforce international judgments.

An attempt to extend the common law regime to international judgments raises many difficult questions: What should the relationship between national and international courts be – vertical or horizontal – and how would that affect the type of defences available in actions to enforce international judgments? To what extent should political considerations be important in such actions, given that enforcing international judgments may carry greater foreign policy implications than the judgments of foreign national courts? Are the principles on sovereign and diplomatic immunity enough to address the political aspects of enforcing international judgments? It is submitted that on this subject, legislation that gives national courts jurisdiction to enforce international judgments and which can deal with other issues that attend the exercise of such jurisdiction is particularly important and necessary.[12]

[9] Namibia's Enforcement of Foreign Civil Judgments Act 1994 and South Africa's Enforcement of Foreign Civil Judgments 1988 define a 'court' to include a 'regional court of that country'. This definition suggests that the references to regional court are not a reference to international courts.

[10] *Gramara (Private) Ltd* v. *Government of the Republic of Zimbabwe*, Case No. X-ref. HC 5483/09 (High Court, Zimbabwe, 2010).

[11] *Government of the Republic of Zimbabwe* v. *Louis Karel Fick*, Case CCT 101/12 (Constitutional Court, South Africa, 2013); *Government of the Republic of Zimbabwe* v. *Louis Karel Fick*, Case No. 657/11 (Supreme Court of Appeal, South Africa, 2012).

[12] See, e.g., United Kingdom – European Communities (Enforcement of Community Judgments) Order 1972, SI 1972/1590; Ireland – European Communities (Enforcement of Community Judgments, Orders and Decisions) Order 2007, SI 121 of 2007; Malta – European Communities (Enforcement of Community Judgments) Order 2007, LN 387 of 2007.

Nature and theoretical bases for enforcing foreign judgments

Courts are not bound to enforce foreign judgments. However, at common law, there has been a long-standing practice of the courts enforcing foreign judgments. The theoretical bases for doing this have not been thoroughly discussed in the judgments examined.[13] There have, however, been passing references to various bases for enforcing foreign judgments. A Kenyan court has held that the basic principle upon which foreign judgments are enforced is 'reciprocity and the advantage to be gained therefrom'.[14] Courts in Malawi, Tanzania and Zambia have held that foreign judgments are enforceable on the basis of the doctrine of obligation.[15] South African courts have made references to comity and acquired rights.[16] Other courts have found more pragmatic bases for enforcing foreign judgments by emphasising their role in facilitating international trade and commerce.[17]

The bases on which foreign judgments are enforced influence the scope of judgments that can be enforced. It can be argued that judgment enforcement regimes founded on comity or the need to facilitate international trade and commerce are more amenable to enforcing foreign judgments than regimes founded on reciprocity.[18] It is recommended that these broader bases for jurisdiction should inform African courts in their approach to foreign judgments. The ultimate goal should be that, while the rights and interests of the judgment-debtor should be protected (for example, through defences), rights legitimately created by foreign

[13] See generally *Laconian Maritime Enterprises Ltd* v. *Agromar Lineas Ltd* 1986 (3) SA 509 at 513–16, discussing the theoretical basis for one country's courts applying the law of another country.

[14] *Italframe Ltd* v. *Mediterranean Shipping Co.* [1986] KLR 54 at 62, [1985] LLR 236. This observation was made in the context of an application to register a foreign judgment under the Foreign Judgment (Reciprocal Enforcement) Act 1984.

[15] *Heyns* v. *Demetriou*, Civil Cause No. of 2001 (High Court, Malawi, 2001) – 'the power depends not on comity or reciprocity but on the defendant's duty to the court of the judgment and the contract'; *Willow Investment* v. *Mbomba Ntumba* [1996] TLR 377; *Mileta Pakou* v. *Rudnap Zambia Ltd* (1998) ZR 233.

[16] *Duarte* v. *Lissack* 1973 (3) SA 615 at 621; *Commissioner of Taxes, Federation of Rhodesia* v. *McFarland* 1965 (1) SA 470 at 471; *Laconian Maritime Enterprises Ltd* v. *Agromar Lineas Ltd* 1986 (3) SA 509 at 513–16.

[17] *Barclays Bank of Swaziland* v. *Koch* 1997 BLR 1294 at 1297; *Westdeutsche Landesbank Girozentrale (Landesbausparkasse)* v. *Horsch* 1992 NR 313, 1993 (2) SA 342.

[18] The term reciprocity is sometimes ambiguous. It could be a reference to the fact that both countries have the same bases of jurisdiction (jurisdictional reciprocity), or that both countries would in fact enforce each other's judgment, or have in fact done so in the past.

courts of competent jurisdiction in favour of a judgment-creditor should not be lightly defeated by constraining private international law, for example by limiting the bases of international competence[19] and restricting enforceable judgments solely to monetary judgments.

In the countries under study, a foreign judgment constitutes a debt.[20] The judgment-debtor's liability stems from an implied promise to pay the amount of the foreign judgment.[21] It has been held that the issue of whether that debt is due and payable is to be determined by the law of the place where the judgment was given.[22] A judgment-creditor cannot go into direct execution in the territory of another sovereign and independent state. He or she can only do that after the judgment has been recognised by the courts of that state.[23] On the other hand, foreign judgments are enforceable through action on the judgment. In Botswana, Lesotho, Namibia, South Africa, Swaziland and Zimbabwe, foreign judgments can be enforced through provisional sentence summons – foreign judgments are treated as liquid documents.[24] In Gambia, Ghana, Kenya, Malawi, Nigeria, Sierra Leone, Tanzania, Uganda and Zambia, the judgment-creditor has to bring an action of debt on the foreign judgment. A foreign judgment creates a new cause of action on which the judgment-creditor is entitled to sue. In Kenya and Tanzania no new cause of action arises in an action in Kenya or Tanzania on a foreign judgment.[25]

[19] *Grosvenor Casinos Ltd* v. *Ghassan Halaoui* [2009] 10 NWLR 309 at 338.

[20] Once it satisfies national laws on the admissibility of foreign evidence, such as laws relating to translation and authentication, a foreign judgment is treated as adequate proof of the existence of the debt. See *T Schouten's Imports (Pty) Ltd* v. *Wintercom Botswana (Pty) Ltd* 1984 BLR 111.

[21] *National Milling Co. Ltd* v. *Mohamed* 1966 RLR 279, 1966 (3) SA 22; *DTH Jethwa* v. *Mulji Bhanji* [1939] 6 EACA 28 at 33; *Heyns* v. *Demetriou*, Civil Cause No. of 2001 (High Court, Malawi, 2001); *Willow Investment* v. *Mbomba Ntumba* [1996] TLR 377; *Wide Seas Shipping Ltd* v. *Wale Sea Foods Ltd* [1983] 1 FNLR 530.

[22] *Premier Woodworking (Rhodesia) Ltd* v. *Hultman* 1960 R & N 275, 1960 (3) SA 174.

[23] *Ex p. the Registrar of the Supreme Court of Bophuthatswana* [1977–9] BSC 213, 1980 (1) SA 572.

[24] Provisional sentence has been characterised by courts as an 'extra-ordinary remedy'. Accordingly, they have emphasised the need for strict compliance with procedure. *Westdeutsche Landesbank Girozentrale (Landesbausparkasse)* v. *Horsch* 1992 NR 313, 1993 (2) SA 342; *Barclays Bank of Swaziland* v. *Koch* 1997 BLR 1294. A provisional sentence may also be appealed: *Jordaan* v. *Dijkhof*, Case No. 9967/2003 (High Court, South Africa, 2004). Foreign judgments can also be enforced by action or an application on notice of motion: see *Cosmopolitan National Bank of Chicago* v. *Steinberg* 1973 (4) SA 579.

[25] Kenya – Limitations of Actions Act 1967, s. 40(2); Tanzania – Law of Limitations Act 1971, s. 42(2). It is worth recalling here that s. 40(1) of Kenya's Limitations of Actions Act 1967 and s. 42(1) of Tanzania's Law of Limitations Act 1971 provide that where a foreign

Characterising a foreign judgment as a debt has a constraining effect on the type of judgments that are enforceable.[26] Such a characterisation excludes from the scope of foreign judgments enforcement regimes for non-money judgments. It is fictitious to argue that a judgment compelling a person to transfer assets to another person constitutes a debt. Characterising a foreign judgment as debt is an inappropriate legal fiction. A foreign judgment should be treated for what it is – a judgment.[27]

Jurisdiction to enforce foreign judgments

As with any claim involving foreign elements, a court has to have the jurisdiction to adjudicate an action in order to enforce a foreign judgment. A person who seeks to enforce a foreign judgment must satisfy the enforcing court's rules on jurisdiction in international matters. In many instances, this requirement would not be difficult to meet – the defendant may have assets or may be present or resident within the jurisdiction. As discussed in Chapter 4, all these are, to varying degrees, accepted bases of jurisdiction in the countries under study, but in a few cases, the jurisdiction of courts to enforce foreign judgments has been contested.[28]

Botswana

The courts in Botswana apply the same rules for assuming jurisdiction in claims involving a foreign element to actions for the enforcement of foreign judgments. In *Cloete* v. *Brink*,[29] the plaintiff sought to recover

law bars either the right or the remedy in respect of a cause of action arising outside Kenya/Tanzania which is sued upon a Kenya/Tanzania court, the action is barred. It appears that the provision that no new cause of action arises in an action in Kenya or Tanzania on a foreign judgment is meant to prevent it being argued that a cause of action arises in Kenya/Tanzania so as to circumvent a foreign rule preventing late execution of a judgment.

[26] As discussed below, it also has implications for the limitation period within which an action could be brought to enforce the judgment.

[27] Some Canadian courts have taken this position: *Girsberger* v. *Kresz* [2000] 47 OR (3d) 145; *Banque Nationale de Paris (Canada)* v. *Opiola* [2000] 78 Alta. LR (3rd Ed) 92; but see also *Lax* v. *Lax* [2004] 70 OR (3d) 520; *Canadian Mortgage & Housing Corp.* v. *Horsfall* [2004] 185 Man. R (2d) 151; *Pollier* v. *Laushway* [2006] NSSC 165.

[28] The issue of jurisdiction in actions to enforce foreign judgment against states is discussed below and more generally in Ch. 17.

[29] 1995 BLR 275 (also reported in 1996 BLR 224). See also *Pretorius* v. *Sweiger* 1979–80 BLR 124; *Pretorius* v. *Sweiger II* 1979–80 BLR 129.

from the defendant an amount due in terms of a judgment obtained against the defendant in South Africa. The defendant contested the jurisdiction of the High Court of Botswana to hear the case. The parties were peregrines, the cause of action arose in South Africa, and there was no clear indication of where the defendant actually resided. The court rejected the plaintiff's argument that the defendant had submitted to its jurisdiction by requesting the plaintiff to file a bond of security. In that request, the defendant expressly noted it would contest the court's jurisdiction. Accordingly, it was held that the court had no jurisdiction to hear the action to enforce the South African judgment.

Nigeria

The jurisdiction of a Nigerian court to hear an action to enforce a foreign judgment is unaffected by the nature of the cause of action litigated before the foreign court. The fact that a Nigerian court would not have had jurisdiction on the original cause of action does not affect its jurisdiction to enforce a foreign judgment founded on that cause of action. In *Wide Seas Shipping Ltd* v. *Wale Sea Foods Ltd*,[30] the applicant sought to register an English judgment under the Foreign Judgments (Reciprocal Enforcement) Act 1961. The respondent objected to the jurisdiction of the High Court of Lagos State to hear the application on the grounds that the suit in which the judgment was delivered was an admiralty matter and, under Nigerian law,[31] the proper court to hear the application was the Federal High Court. The court rejected this argument. It held that a foreign judgment is treated as an ordinary debt and the Act gave the State High Courts the jurisdiction to register such judgments. The nature of the original cause of action did not prejudice the unlimited jurisdiction of the High Court in a case of debt.

South Africa

A defendant's residence in South Africa gives a South African court jurisdiction to hear an action to enforce a foreign judgment given against him or her. *Zwyssig* v. *Zwyssig*[32] was an action to enforce a Florida judgment. The defendant challenged the jurisdiction of the South African court to hear the action on the grounds that he was neither domiciled nor

[30] [1983] 1 FNLR 530.
[31] Admiralty Jurisdiction Decree 1991, ss. 1 and 19.
[32] 1997 (2) SA 467.

resident in South Africa. The court rejected this argument and found that the defendant was resident in South Africa. The defendant owned a house, was present in South Africa six months a year, maintained a telephone line at the house and was a member of a local health club.

Comments

It is trite to declare that, in order to enforce a foreign judgment, the jurisdictional rules of the forum for dealing with claims involving foreign elements must be satisfied. In many instances, this would not be a problem. In Botswana, Lesotho, Namibia, South Africa, Swaziland and Zimbabwe, assets within the jurisdiction (the object of the action) could be attached. In Gambia, Ghana, Kenya, Malawi, Nigeria, Sierra Leone, Tanzania, Uganda and Zambia, residence and the presence of a defendant in the country can be the basis of jurisdiction.

However, the need to meet jurisdictional requirements can become particularly difficult for *peregrinus* plaintiffs in actions brought in Botswana, Lesotho, Namibia, South Africa and Swaziland if the defendant, the judgment-debtor, is also a *peregrinus*. As noted in Chapter 4, in these countries, where there are actions between two peregrines, unless there is a local *ratio jurisdictionis* (which is unlikely in the context of foreign judgments), the attachment of the defendant's assets to found jurisdiction is not possible and, accordingly, the court will not have jurisdiction to enforce the foreign judgment. Furthermore, except in Botswana,[33] unless there is a local *ratio jurisdictionis* in an action between two peregrines, submission by the defendant – which, in any case, is unlikely in an action to enforce a foreign judgment against him or her – is not enough to give jurisdiction to courts in Namibia,[34] South Africa and, perhaps, Lesotho and Swaziland. As a Botswanan court has observed, 'the time of the court should not be taken up with disputes, having nothing to do with Botswana, between persons neither domiciled nor resident here'.[35]

[33] *MAK (Pty) Ltd* v. *St Paul Insurance Co. SA Ltd* 2007 (1) BLR 210.

[34] *Argos Fishing Co. Ltd* v. *Friopesca SA* 1991 NR 106 at 111–12, 1991 (3) SA 255 at 260–1.

[35] *Pretorius* v. *Sweiger II* 1979–80 BLR 129 at 130. See also *Willow Investment v. Mbomba Ntumba* [1997] TLR 47 at 49, where, in an action to review an order enforcing a Zairian judgment, the court observed: 'surely the High Court of Tanzania cannot be and should not be an international judicial tribunal to which foreign litigants, all and sundry, can resort to'.

The above state of affairs is inappropriate. A second look should be taken at it – at least from the perspective of actions to enforce foreign judgments, which by their nature are often founded on causes of action unrelated to the country in which enforcement is sought. As Forsyth has perceptively observed, 'no country should be a haven for recalcitrant debtors adjudged as such by a court of competent jurisdiction, even if they and their creditors are peregrines'.[36]

In Gambia, Ghana, Kenya, Malawi, Nigeria, Sierra Leone, Tanzania, Uganda and Zambia, it is an undecided issue whether service outside the jurisdiction may be allowed in an action to enforce a foreign judgment. At present, there are no specific statutory grounds for allowing service outside the jurisdiction on the basis of an action to enforce a foreign judgment.[37] In Ghana, the High Court (Civil Procedure) Rules 2004 allow service outside the jurisdiction of notice of registration of a foreign judgment under the statutory regime, without leave of court.[38] It is unlikely this rule would be extended to writs issued to enforce foreign judgments at common law since the two regimes are very different. However, it may be argued that service could be allowed on the basis that the action relates to property within the jurisdiction.

If a judgment-creditor is unable to meet the jurisdictional requirements, he or she could arguably bring a new action on the original cause of action. This position is founded on the theory that a foreign judgment does not merge with the original cause of action. There are *dicta* which accept that a foreign judgment does not merge with the original cause of action and imply that a plaintiff retains the right to sue on their original cause of action.[39]

[36] Forsyth, p. 474.

[37] Compare United Kingdom – Civil Procedure Rules, para. 3.1(10) of Practice Direction 6B; *Tasarruf Mevduati Sigorta Fonu* v. *Demirel* [2007] 1 WLR 2508, [2007] 4 All ER 1014.

[38] High Court (Civil Procedure) Rules 2004, Ord. 71, r. 7(2).

[39] *Mileta Pakou* v. *Rudnap Zambia Ltd* (1998) ZR 233 at 236, where it was observed: 'In any event a foreign judgment constitutes a simple contract debt only and does not merge with the original cause of action. [Where such a judgment is not recognised the judgment-creditor] will have to sue on their original cause of action, if so minded'. *Willow Investment* v. *Mbomba Ntumba* [1996] TLR 377 at 380; *Steinberg* v. *Cosmopolitan National Bank of Chicago* 1973 (4) SA 564 at 577; but see also *Gabelsberger* v. *Babl* 1994 (2) SA 677 at 679, where it was observed that, where an internationally competent foreign court gives judgment, 'the matter is *res judicata* and the debt has been novated by [the foreign] judgment'.

Conditions for enforcing foreign judgments

International competence

At common law, it is a fundamental requirement for enforcing foreign judgments that the foreign court should be competent to hear the case in terms of the enforcing court's private international law. This is often technically labelled 'international competence'.

Ghana

Submission constitutes a basis of international competence in Ghana. Where a defendant does not appear at trial in a foreign country and a default judgment is given against him and he subsequently appeals against that decision, albeit unsuccessfully, he would be deemed to have submitted to the jurisdiction of the foreign court in an action brought to enforce the judgment in Ghana.[40] Similarly, a defendant who, upon being served with a writ issued for service abroad, makes an unconditional appearance in an English court and files a defence, but subsequently abandons further proceedings in this action, would be deemed to have submitted to the jurisdiction of the English court.[41]

Kenya

Residence and submission constitute bases of international competence in Kenya. However, merely purchasing goods from a foreign country does not amount to submission, which would lead to a Kenyan court enforcing a judgment given by the foreign court. This is so even if the defendant is resident in Kenya and is served with the writ but does not enter an appearance. Such a defendant would not be deemed to have submitted to the foreign court's jurisdiction.[42]

Namibia

In an action to enforce a foreign judgment in Namibia, it is essential to prove that the judgment has been given by a court of competent jurisdiction.[43] Submission constitutes a basis for international competence under Namibian law. Contractual submission gives the foreign court

[40] *John Holt & Co. Ltd* v. *Christoph Nutsugah* (1929–31) Div. Ct. 75.
[41] *Ashurst Morris Crisp* v. *Peter Awoonor Renner* (1931–7) Div. Ct. 107.
[42] *Ebramji* v. *Jivanji* [1917–18] KLR 89.
[43] *Westdeutsche Landesbank Girozentrale (Landesbausparkasse)* v. *Horsch* 1992 NR 313 at 314, 1993 (2) SA 342 at 344.

jurisdiction in the international sense, and it is irrelevant whether the parties have any other connection with the chosen forum.[44]

South Africa

In an action to enforce a foreign judgment in South Africa, it is not enough that the foreign court has jurisdiction according to its own law – it must also have jurisdiction under South African private international law.[45] Whether the foreign court is internationally competent is a question to be decided according to the principles recognised by South African municipal law.[46] The onus is on the plaintiff to prove that the foreign court has jurisdiction according to principles recognised by South African law with reference to foreign judgments.[47] A South African court will not review the merits of a foreign judgment. However, it is competent to adjudicate any jurisdictional fact necessary to establish international competence. Accordingly, it may inquire whether a document containing what appears to be a choice of forum clause forms part of the parties' contract.[48] A South African court will not necessarily recognise the judgment of a foreign court which applies jurisdictional principles exactly like its own. Accordingly, it refused to enforce a judgment from a Florida, US court which assumed jurisdiction on the basis that the cause of action arose there, i.e. the tort was committed there. This is not a basis for international competency under South African law.[49]

Submission constitutes a basis for international competence. Submission can be either express or implied, but it must be clear.[50] The fact that submission to jurisdiction must be clear does not mean that it must be proved 'as a matter of legal certainty'. What is required is proof on the balance of probability. In this regard, whether a provision in a contract amounts to submission to the jurisdiction of a foreign court is a question of interpretation, which must be decided in accordance with the ordinary canons of construction for the system of law applicable to

[44] *Argos Fishing Co. Ltd* v. *Friopesca SA* 1991 NR 106, 1991 (3) SA 255.
[45] *De Naamloze Vennootschap Alintex* v. *Von Gerlach* 1958 (1) SA 13.
[46] *Jones* v. *Krok* 1995 (1) SA 677 at 685.
[47] *Reiss Engineering Co. Ltd* v. *Insamcor (Pty) Ltd* 1983 (1) SA 1033.
[48] *Maschinen Frommer GmbH* v. *Trisave Engineering & Machinery Supplies (Pty) Ltd* 2003 (6) SA 69.
[49] *Supercat Inc.* v. *Two Oceans Marine CC* 2001 (4) SA 27.
[50] *Purser* v. *Sales* 2001 (3) SA 445; *Reiss Engineering Co. Ltd* v. *Insamcor (Pty) Ltd* 1983 (1) SA 1033; *Maschinen Frommer GmbH* v. *Trisave Engineering & Machinery Supplies (Pty) Ltd* 2003 (6) SA 69; *Standard Bank Ltd* v. *Butlin* 1981 (4) SA 158.

that contract.[51] Great care should be exercised in inferring submission from the conduct of a defendant.[52] However, a defendant who participates fully in foreign proceedings, raises no objection to the court's jurisdiction, and unsuccessfully asks the court to dismiss on its merits the claim brought against him or her submits to the jurisdiction of the court.[53] Neither the mere choice of a *domicilium citandi et executandi* in the foreign country,[54] nor the inclusion of a choice of law clause in a contract, constitutes submission to the jurisdiction of a foreign court.[55] However, it has been held that a provision in a contract which stipulates that it should be construed and governed by the laws of California, and that disputes arising under the contract should be tried by reference to the California Code of Civil Procedure, amounts to submission.[56] Similarly, a person who institutes action in a foreign court submits to the jurisdiction of the court in a counterclaim to that action. That person cannot deprive the foreign court of jurisdiction by subsequently withdrawing his or her original action.[57] Residence,[58] temporary presence[59] and domicile[60] within the jurisdiction of the foreign country also constitute bases of international competence.

Uganda

Submission constitutes a basis for international competence in Uganda. Although it could be inferred from conduct, the post-judgment conduct of a judgment-debtor does not amount to submission to the foreign court's jurisdiction. *Transroad Ltd* v. *Bank of Uganda*[61] was an appeal

51 In *Blanchard, Krasner & French* v. *Evans* 2002 (4) SA 144 at 148, it was held that the proper law of the contract should govern such an issue.

52 *Supercat Inc.* v. *Two Oceans Marine CC* 2001 (4) SA 27.

53 *Purser* v. *Sales* 2001 (3) SA 445.

54 *Standard Bank Ltd* v. *Butlin* 1981 (4) SA 158.

55 *Reiss Engineering Co. Ltd* v. *Insamcor (Pty) Ltd* 1983 (1) SA 1033.

56 *Blanchard, Krasner & French* v. *Evans* 2002 (4) SA 144 (reversing *Blanchard, Krasner & French* v. *Evans* 2001 (4) SA 86).

57 *Zwyssig* v. *Zwyssig* 1997 (2) SA 467.

58 *Zwyssig* v. *Zwyssig*.

59 *Richman* v. *Ben-Tovim* 2007 (2) SA 283 (reversing *Richman* v. *Ben-Tovim* 2006 (2) SA 591).

60 *Erskine* v. *Chinatex Oriental Trading Co.* 2001 (1) SA 817. The court held (reversing *Chinatex Oriental Trading Co.* v. *Erskine* 1998 (4) SA 1087) that the respondent had failed to prove that the appellant was domiciled in England at the time the summons was issued in the English action.

61 [1998] UGA J No. 12, [1998] Kam. LR 106 (on appeal from *Transroad Ltd* v. *Bank of Uganda* [1996] 6 Kam. LR 42). See also *Christopher Sales* v. *Attorney General*, Civil Suit

against a decision to register an English judgment in Uganda. Although the appellant was served with the process of the English proceedings, it did not appear or defend the suit; a default judgment was granted against it. The appellant unsuccessfully applied to the English court to set aside the judgment. However, it received a consent order discharging a garnishee order *nisi* issued in execution against the appellant's debts due and accruing from a bank in England. The appellant also entered into negotiations with the respondent with a view to paying the debt. In this appeal, the appellant contended that it did not submit to the jurisdiction of the English court. By a majority decision, the court held that the post-judgment conduct of the appellant could not be construed as submission to the jurisdiction of the English court.

Zambia

A Zambian court will not enforce a judgment from a foreign court unless the latter is internationally competent. Residence (or perhaps presence) and submission constitute bases for international competence. In *Mileta Pakou* v. *Rudnap Zambia Ltd*,[62] which was an action to enforce a judgment from Belgrade in former Yugoslavia, it was held that the court did not have jurisdiction because the defendant was not resident in Yugoslavia and did not submit to the jurisdiction of the court.

Zimbabwe

Zimbabwean courts will only enforce a foreign judgment if the foreign court has jurisdiction under Zimbabwean private international law. Submission, in this instance through a jurisdiction agreement, is a recognised basis for jurisdiction.[63] Similarly, a defendant who enters an appearance to defend a foreign action would be deemed to have submitted to the jurisdiction of the foreign court.[64] A Zimbabwean court can adjudicate any jurisdictional fact necessary to establish international competence.[65]

Public policy and natural justice may be relevant considerations in deciding whether the requirements of international competence have been satisfied. In *Steinberg* v. *Cosmopolitan National Bank of Chicago*,[66]

No. 91 of 2011 (High Court, Uganda, 2013), in which the court enforced a New York judgment.

62 (1998) ZR 233.

63 *Coluflandres Ltd* v. *Scandia Industrial Products Ltd* 1969 (2) RLR 431, 1969 (3) SA 551.

64 *Grauman* v. *Pers* 1970 (1) RLR 130.

65 *Coluflandres* v. *Scandia Industrial Products*.

66 1973 (4) SA 564.

an Illinois court assumed jurisdiction on the basis that the cause of action arose there and the defendant also had assets there, albeit insufficient. However, the defendant, an American, who was served in Rhodesia, could not be served in the United States. This was because he was a fugitive from justice with respect to criminal proceedings founded on the same facts that gave rise to the civil cause of action. It was held that, even though the defendant was neither resident nor domiciled in the United States at the time the Illinois action was instituted, the judgment should be recognised since it would either be against public policy to allow the defendant to rely on his own criminal act, or against natural justice to make the plaintiff re-litigate the matter in Rhodesia.[67]

Comments

The principle that a foreign court should be internationally competent before its judgment is enforced appears well entrenched in the countries under study.[68] Currently, presence, residence and submission are accepted bases of international competence.[69] Submission can be express, such as through jurisdiction agreements, or inferred from conduct. Accordingly, appearing to defend a case on its merits and appealing a trial court's decision have been held as equivalent to submission. An aspect of submission which is not immediately evident from the judgments is whether there are specific acts which do not amount to submission. Particularly noteworthy in this regard is post-judgment conduct, which, in Uganda, has been held not to constitute submission to the jurisdiction of a foreign court.[70] However, in South Africa, there is authority to the contrary.[71] In general, the cases reveal that the

[67] Because of the circumstances of the case, one of the judges was prepared to apply a legal fiction that the notice served in Rhodesia was in fact served in America.

[68] There are dicta in *Transvaal Lewendehawe Kooperasie Bpk* v. *Van Wyk* [1984–7] 4 BSC 228 at 232–3 which suggest that the internal jurisdiction or competence of a foreign court may also be relevant in determining whether to enforce its judgment.

[69] Some courts, citing the English case of *Emanuel* v. *Symon* [1908] 1 KB 302, have observed *obiter* that 'being a subject of the foreign country' is a basis of international competence. Given that this basis is uncertain in English law, it remains to be seen whether, when it comes up for decision, it will be accepted. See, e.g., *John Holt & Co. Ltd* v. *Christoph Nutsugah* (1929–31) Div. Ct. 75 at 76; *Heyns* v. *Demetriou*, Civil Cause No. of 2001 (High Court, Malawi, 2001). See also *Transvaal Lewendehawe Kooperasie Bpk* v. *Van Wyk* [1984–7] 4 BSC 228 at 230 ('this court probably would not recognise a foreign judgment based on a nationality principle').

[70] *Transroad Ltd* v. *Bank of Uganda* [1998] UGA J No. 12, [1998] Kam. LR 106.

[71] *Standard Bank Ltd* v. *Butlin* 1981 (4) SA 158 at 166, where it was observed: 'It is clear that, although the Court must ordinarily have jurisdiction when the litigation starts, a

assessment of whether a judgment-debtor has submitted to the jurisdiction of a foreign court is a highly factual inquiry. The courts will take into account all relevant facts before coming to a conclusion. This is especially so as regards submission through conduct.

The acceptance of mere presence as a basis of international competence in South Africa is problematic.[72] Writers in common law jurisdictions, such as Australia, Canada and England, have been very critical of presence as a basis for international competence, and there are cases doubting its appropriateness.[73] Jurisdiction founded on mere presence defeats the legitimate expectation of parties and is open to abuse. It does not provide enough evidence of a connection between a defendant and the foreign country to merit that courts in the latter adjudicate a dispute involving the former. It may even constitute a violation of human rights. Indeed, it is inappropriate for African courts to enforce foreign judgments on a basis which would not be accepted in many countries worldwide. It remains to be seen whether other African courts will follow the South African example.

It is open to question whether the existing recognised bases of international competence are adequate for the current international climate of increased international trade and transnational relationships. Canadian courts have experimented with another basis for international competence, namely real and substantial connection.[74] This ground was unsuccessfully invoked in the South African case of *Supercat Inc.* v. *Two Oceans Marine*.[75] In it, the counsel referred to several Canadian cases and argued that the traditional approach to the enforcement of foreign judgments was obsolete, and that the exigencies of international trade called for a new approach. The judge found

submission to such during its subsequent progress does as well as one which precedes the summons. Perhaps the same goes for the period after the judgment, at least while it remains unexecuted and its effectiveness untested. I shall take that to be so'.

[72] *Steinberg* v. *Cosmopolitan National Bank of Chicago* 1973 (4) SA 564 at 574 held that presence, plus the fact that the cause of action arose within the foreign jurisdiction, constitutes a basis for international competence.

[73] For a collection of some of these academic views and cases, see R. F. Oppong, 'Mere Presence and International Competence in Private International Law' (2007) 3 *Journal of Private International Law* 321.

[74] *Morguard Investments Ltd* v. *De Savoye* [1990] 3 SCR 1077; *Beals* v. *Saldanha* [2003] 3 SCR 416; *Club Resorts Ltd* v. *Van Breda* 2012 SCC 17. See generally J. Blom and E. Edinger, 'The Chimera of the Real and Substantial Connection Test' (2005) 38 *University of British Columbia Law Review* 373.

[75] 2001 (4) SA 27.

the Canadian cases 'informative,' but felt 'not inclined or, sitting as a single judge, entitled to ignore the considerable weight of judicial authority in this country.'[76]

In addition to real and substantial connection, an alternative way of broadening the bases for international competence is to adopt a test of jurisdictional equivalence. This test will allow enforcement of a foreign judgment if the foreign court assumes jurisdiction on a basis similar to that which the enforcing court would have done, given the same facts. The test can bridge the gap which currently exists between the rules on jurisdiction in international matters and those on international competence. Some cases have touched on or hinted at this possibility.[77] Indeed, as discussed in Chapter 18, the statutory regimes for enforcing foreign judgment recognise jurisdictional equivalence. However, at present, the position remains that the bases of international competence are not coterminous with the bases of jurisdiction in international matters.

An interesting issue raised in a couple of cases is the extent to which public policy considerations are material in determining whether a foreign court is internationally competent. Currently, the existing basis of international competence looks for factual relationships, which sometimes could be defeated by the conduct of defendants, such as when they flee the jurisdiction. Whether public policy should look unkindly on such conduct is controversial. In two cases, it was held that a person who changed his domicile and residence with evasive intent cannot rely on his absence from the foreign country to deprive its courts of international competence.[78] Including public policy consideration in the assessment of international competence could have either a constraining or expansive effect. However, it is recommended that such an approach should not be followed. It is likely to introduce a high level of uncertainty into decisions on international competence.

Where the competence of the foreign court is disputed, there is some divergence regarding who bears the burden of proof. In South Africa, the

[76] *Supercat Inc.* v. *Two Oceans Marine CC* 2001 (4) SA 27 at 31. Forsyth is also critical of it as a basis of international competence (Forsyth, pp. 437–8).

[77] *Supercat Inc.* v. *Two Oceans Marine CC*; *Grauman* v. *Pers* 1970 (1) RLR 130.

[78] *Steinberg* v. *Cosmopolitan National Bank of Chicago* 1973 (4) SA 564; *Chinatex Oriental Trading Co.* v. *Erskine* 1998 (4) SA 1087 at 1095. The appellate court in *Erskine* v. *Chinatex Oriental Trading Co.* 2001 (1) SA 817 reversed the trial court's decision, but did not comment on this issue.

burden 'falls squarely on the plaintiff'.[79] In Tanzania and Uganda, it appears that the burden falls on the defendant. This is because there is a rebuttable statutory presumption that a foreign court is internationally competent when a certified copy of the judgment is produced.[80]

Fixed sum judgments

There is no direct authority in the countries under study that a foreign judgment must be for a fixed sum of money before it will be enforced. Indeed, this is not discussed separately in some recent commentaries on the regime in South Africa and Botswana and, arguably, by extension, Lesotho, Namibia, Swaziland and Zimbabwe. However, in these countries, it could be proposed that such a requirement is implicit in the procedure for enforcing foreign judgments through provisional sentence summons,[81] which are proceedings on liquid documents.[82]

The only significant judicial pronouncement on the subject appeared in *Gramara (Private) Ltd* v. *Government of the Republic of Zimbabwe*,[83] which was an action to enforce a judgment of the SADC Tribunal – a regional court. It was contended that aspects of the judgment entailed administrative consequences and were not for the payment of a fixed sum of money.[84] The Zimbabwean High Court held that it would be 'contrary to principle to restrict the scope of recognition proceedings by reference to the specific remedies enjoined by a given foreign judgment'. In other words, the mere fact that a judgment did not entail the payment of money should not automatically lead a court to dismiss an application

[79] *Reiss Engineering Co. Ltd* v. *Insamcor (Pty) Ltd* 1983 (1) SA 1033 at 1037; *Erskine* v. *Chinatex* at 820.

[80] Tanzania – Civil Procedure Code 1966, s.12; Uganda – Civil Procedure Act 1929, s. 10.

[81] See *Westdeutsche Landesbank Girozentrale (Landesbausparkasse)* v. *Horsch* 1992 NR 313, 1993 (2) SA 342, where provisional sentence was described as an 'extraordinary remedy' that allows the judgment-creditor to obtain a provisional judgment speedily, and without resorting to the more expensive and dilatory machinery of an illiquid action.

[82] In *Jones* v. *Krok* 1995 (1) SA 677 at 685, it was defined as a written instrument signed by the defendant or his agent and evidencing an unconditional acknowledgement of indebtedness in a fixed sum of money.

[83] *Gramara (Private) Ltd* v. *Government of the Republic of Zimbabwe*, Case No. X-ref. HC 5483/09 (High Court, Zimbabwe, 2010).

[84] The respondent was directed to take all necessary measures, through its agents, to protect the possession, occupation and ownership of the applicants' lands, and to take all appropriate measures to ensure that no action is taken, directly or indirectly, whether by its agents or by others, to evict from, or interfere with, peaceful residence on the applicants' farms.

to enforce it. Whether this principle is restricted to enforcing judgments from regional courts, or extends to judgments from foreign national courts, remains to be decided.

As discussed in Chapter 18, almost all the statutory regimes for enforcing foreign judgments are restricted to money judgments. This may be taken as a reflection of the law in respect of the common law regime – to a large extent, the statutory regimes are codifications of the common law. The principle that only foreign judgments concerning money are enforceable is open to criticism. It takes a narrow view of the different remedies that courts provide. A foreign judgment might require the payment of money, but it might also demand the performance of an action, such as the transfer of shares, delivery of property, or specific performance of a contract. Rights accruing from such judicial remedies are also worthy of legal protection, even beyond the territorial jurisdiction of the courts that ordered them. Indeed, the judgment-for-a-fixed-sum principle excludes from the scope of foreign judgment enforcement some remedies that have become very important in international commercial litigation, such as Anton Piller orders, anti-suit injunctions and worldwide Mareva injunctions.

Comparatively, some countries have recognised the restrictive nature of the judgment-for-a-fixed-sum principle and have reformed it either through legislation[85] or case law. Following the lead of the Supreme Court of Canada in the *Pro Swing Inc.* v. *Elta Golf Inc.*,[86] where the court was unanimous that the principle should be changed, courts in Jersey and Cayman Islands have abandoned the rule.[87] In *Pro Swing*, the court noted that a change in the judgment-for-fixed-sum principle required caution and should be carried out incrementally. It should also be accompanied by judicial discretion that enables enforcing courts to consider relevant factors, so as to ensure that the structure and integrity of their legal system are not disturbed by the enforcement of non-money judgments. To the court in this case, the conditions for the recognition and enforcement of non-money judgments were generally expressed as follows: The judgment must be rendered by a court of competent

[85] See, e.g., New Zealand – Reciprocal Enforcement of Judgments Act 1934, s. 3B; Australia – Foreign Judgments Act 1991, s. 5(6).

[86] [2007] 273 DLR (4th) 663.

[87] *Brunei Investment Agency* v. *Fidelis Nominees Ltd* [2008] Jersey Law Reports 337; *Miller* v. *Gianne* [2007] Cayman Islands Law Reports 18. See also *Davis* v. *Turning Properties Pty Ltd* [2006 b] 222 ALR 267; *Pattni* v. *Ali* [2006] UKPC 51 at [27].

jurisdiction, it must be final, and it must be of such a nature that the principle of comity requires the domestic court to enforce it.[88]

It is recommended that future reforms of the common law regime in the countries under study should take account of these developments. Indeed, the South African Law Reform Commission has recommended that the 'rule specifying only judgments for fixed sums of money derives from technicalities of the English system and there is no reason why South African courts should not be free to enforce a wider range of foreign judgments, including those for specific performance (or non-performance, as the case may be)'.[89]

Finality of foreign judgments

Botswana

In an action to enforce a foreign judgment, it is necessary to allege and prove that the judgment is current (not superannuated) and final. A foreign judgment which has become superannuated cannot be enforced in Botswana.[90]

Kenya

A foreign judgment must be final before it is enforced in Kenya. Because a foreign maintenance order – in this instance an order from Southern Rhodesia – may be varied by the court which made it, it is not a final order. Accordingly, it cannot be enforced by an action at common law, unless it is proved to be a final order of the foreign court.[91] To be enforceable against a defendant, a foreign judgment should be one given on the merits of the case.[92]

88 *Pro Swing Inc.* v. *Elta Golf Inc.* [2007] 273 DLR (4th) 663 at [31] and [88]–[99]. See V. Black, 'Enforcement of Foreign Non-Money Judgments: *Pro Swing v. ELTA*' (2005) 42 *Canadian Business Law Journal* 81; R. F. Oppong, 'Enforcing Foreign Non-Money Judgments: An Examination of Some Recent Developments in Canada and Beyond' (2005) 39 *UBC Law Review* 257.

89 South African Law Reform Commission, *Consolidated Legislation Pertaining to International Co-operation in Civil Matters* (Pretoria: SALRC, 2004), p. 57.

90 *Accurist (SA) (Pty) Ltd* v. *Jan Jacob Van Zyl* 1982 (1) BLR 1. See generally *Design Unit (Pty) Ltd* v. *Tuli Lodge (Pty) Ltd* 1979–80 BLR 136 on certainty as to the parties to the foreign action.

91 *In re. the Maintenance Orders Enforcement Ordinance* [1954] 27 KLR 94.

92 *Singh* v. *Singh* [1936–7] 17 KLR 82 (it was also suggested in this judgment that 'a judgment in default of appearance is not, for the purposes of an action based on such judgment one given on the merits'); Civil Procedure Act 1924, s. 9(b).

Malawi

A foreign maintenance order ancillary to a divorce decree is an order *in personam*, which is not final. It cannot therefore be enforced in Malawi at common law.[93] Moreover, even though a foreign default judgment may be set aside by the foreign court, it may still be treated as final and conclusive in Malawi.[94]

Namibia

A Namibian court will not enforce a foreign judgment unless it is final. This is because a provisional order or judgment can be confirmed or discharged by the foreign court at a later date.[95] The question of whether a foreign judgment is final must be considered very carefully by a court when asked to enforce it, especially where neither party is an *incola* of the enforcing court's area of jurisdiction. Where there is insufficient proof that the judgment is final, the court should dismiss an application to enforce it.[96] In addition to establishing that the foreign judgment is final, it is required of the plaintiff to prove that it is enforceable according to the foreign law concerned.[97]

South Africa

A South African court will not disregard a foreign judgment by a court of competent jurisdiction merely because it was made without a full hearing of the case. In *Gabelsberger* v. *Babl*,[98] there was a settlement between the parties, subsequently recorded by a German court. Under German law, this entitled the plaintiff to execute in the same manner and just as effectively as if it had been a judgment given after a full hearing of the case. In enforcing the German court's judgment, it was held that there was no reason to disregard orders of foreign courts of competent jurisdiction made without determination of the merits, such as default judgments, judgments by consent or settlement orders in the form of

[93] *Webb* v. *Murray, Ex p. Murray* [1961–3] ALR Mal. 205. It is, however, enforceable under the Maintenance Orders (Facilities for Enforcement) Act 1920 and, subsequently, the Maintenance Orders (Enforcement) Ordinance.

[94] *Heyns* v. *Demetriou*, Civil Cause No. of 2001 (High Court, Malawi, 2001).

[95] *Bekker No* v. *Kotze* 1994 NR 345, 1996 (4) SA 1287; *Olympic Fruit* v. *Nagrapex Holdings*, Case No. A 278/2011 (High Court, Namibia, 2011).

[96] *Argos Fishing Co. Ltd* v. *Friopesca SA* 1991 NR 106, 1991 (3) SA 255.

[97] *Westdeutsche Landesbank Girozentrale (Landesbausparkasse)* v. *Horsch* 1992 NR 313, 1993 (2) SA 342.

[98] 1994 (2) SA 677. But see *Holz* v. *Harksen* 1995 (3) SA 521, disapproving *Gabelsberger*.

recorded settlements. An application to enforce a foreign judgment should allege that the judgment is final.[99] Only final judgments are enforceable.[100] Finality relates to the obligation to pay. Thus, where the obligation to pay is final, it is not undermined by the mere fact that one party is at liberty to apply for an adjustment to the execution of the court's order.[101]

A foreign judgment that is subject to appeal, or that has an appeal pending on it in the foreign country, is final, provided in all other respects, it is final and conclusive. Where, however, it is shown that the judgment is subject to an appeal, or that an appeal is pending, the court has discretion and may, instead of giving judgment in favour of the plaintiff, stay the proceedings pending the final determination of the appeal in the foreign country. This is done to prevent a 'most anomalous situation' where a judgment is discharged in one country, but fully enforced in another.[102] The onus of proving that a foreign judgment is final and conclusive rests on the party who seeks to enforce it.[103] Where the onus is discharged, it is up to the defendant to place before the court the facts relating to the impending appeal and such other relevant facts as may persuade the court to exercise its discretion in favour of granting a stay of proceedings. Among the factors that the court takes into account in exercising this discretion are: whether an appeal is actually pending; the consequences to the defendant if judgment is given in favour of the plaintiff and after (possibly after the judgment has been satisfied) the appeal succeeds in the foreign jurisdiction, and whether the defendant is genuinely pursuing the right of appeal with due diligence. However, the court should refuse to assess the merits and demerits of the appeal and its prospects of success.[104] Similarly, the possibility that a default judgment might be rescinded does not preclude it from being final, however remote the prospects of success may in fact be. A common-sense approach rather than adherence to rigid rules is needed in deciding whether a default judgment is final.[105]

[99] *Dale* v. *Dale* 1948 (4) SA 741.
[100] *Transvaal Lewendehawe Kooperasie Bpk* v. *Van Wyk* [1984–7] 4 BSC 228.
[101] *C Hoare & Co.* v. *Runewitsch* 1997 (1) SA 338.
[102] *Dale* v. *Dale* 1948 (4) SA 741 at 744.
[103] *C Hoare & Co.* v. *Runewitsch* 1997 (1) SA 338.
[104] *Jones* v. *Krok* 1995 (1) SA 677.
[105] *Blanchard, Krasner & French* v. *Evans* 2004 (4) SA 427.

Zimbabwe

A foreign judgment is enforced only if it is final.[106] The plaintiff has to plead and prove that the judgment is final under the laws of the country from which the judgment emanates.[107]

Comments

It makes practical sense that courts enforce only foreign judgments that are final. The public policy of ensuring that there is an end to litigation would be undermined if a foreign judgment enforced in one state is subsequently reopened – and, perhaps, even overturned – in the courts of the country where it was given. What constitutes a final judgment is, however, a matter of some debate. Even though there appears to be no direct authority on it, it is obvious from the decided cases that whether a foreign judgment is or is not final is to be determined by the law of the foreign country. In general, a final judgment is one which is unalterable by the court which pronounced it. It is possible to argue that this status is not achievable by any judgment: there always remains the possibility, even if very remote, that a judgment can be altered – for example, upon the discovery of new evidence. Such a theoretical possibility should, however, not be allowed to defeat reality and the need for justice. This has been recognised by the courts.

Aside from the need to offer the defendant a hearing (a breach of which affords the defendant a defence), the courts have not been prescriptive that the foreign court should follow a particular procedure in reaching its judgment. Thus, in one South African case, the court enforced a foreign judgment which was granted without a full hearing of the merits of the dispute. Besides, it is recommended that courts should be slow to enforce foreign judgments which have not been given on the merits of the parties' claim. Indeed, Kenya, Tanzania and Uganda statutes oblige courts to recognise only judgments given 'on the merits of the case'.[108]

[106] *Coluflandres Ltd* v. *Scandia Industrial Products Ltd* 1969 (2) RLR 431, 1969 (3) SA 551; *Knight* v. *Baldi* 1966 (3) SA 19.

[107] *Grauman* v. *Pers* 1970 (1) RLR 130.

[108] Kenya – Civil Procedure Act 1924, s. 9(b); Tanzania – Civil Procedure Code 1966, s. 11(b); Uganda – Civil Procedure Act 1929, s. 9(b). What constitutes a judgment on the merits is not defined in the statutes. In *Singh* v. *Singh* [1936–37] 17 KLR 82 at 83, it was held that a judgment is on the merits if the matter in controversy between the parties is 'the subject of direct adjudication'.

Default judgments pose a particular problem in terms of finality. In some countries, a defendant against whom a default judgment has been granted is entitled, either automatically or with leave (but often within a defined period), to apply for it to be set aside. However, there has been discussion in some cases whether default judgments are final. In South Africa, a common-sense approach has been recommended for making such a determination. A different view was taken in Namibia, where in *Argos Fishing Co. Ltd* v. *Friopesca*,[109] it was held that because an English default judgment could be set aside by the English court, it lacked finality. It is recommended that, on this subject, no rigid rules should be laid down. The common-sense approach adopted in South Africa is preferable. Accordingly, where the defendant has not demonstrated a genuine desire to apply for the judgment to be set aside, or where there is no defined period within which to apply for the default judgment to be set aside, it would be against the interests of justice not to treat such a default judgment as final. However, it should not be open to the enforcing court to investigate whether an application to set aside a default judgment is likely to succeed.

Conclusiveness and the *res judicata* effect of foreign judgments

In addition to enforcing a foreign judgment, a party can plead the judgment as *res judicata*. Such a plea may relate to either the cause of action as a whole or a specific issue decided by the foreign court. In both instances, the argument would be that the cause of action or issue has already been determined by the foreign court.

Botswana

A plea of *res judicata* should be founded on the same cause of action. Thus, where a foreign action consists of a claim for an alleged debt and the domestic action is for loss suffered by an alleged failure to perform in a subcontract agreement, it has been held that the averments to sustain the two claims are not the same and a plea for cause of action estoppel must fail.[110] A plea of issue estoppel can succeed even where a plea of cause of action estoppel has failed. Accordingly, where a foreign court has decided that a performance bond is qualified by a due cause letter,

[109] *Argos Fishing Co. Ltd* v. *Friopesca SA* 1991 NR 106, 1991 (3) SA 255.
[110] *MAK (Pty) Ltd* v. *St Paul Insurance Co. SA Ltd* 2007 (1) BLR 210.

that determination estops a party from reopening the debate on the issue of the interplay between the performance bond and the due cause letter.[111]

Gambia

In Gambia, where a foreign court has heard a case on its merits, the proper course open to a party dissatisfied with the judgment is to appeal in the foreign country. The foreign judgment can sustain a plea of *estoppel per rem judicatam* in an action between the same parties and on the same cause of action, if the party raising the plea satisfies the court that the foreign judgment is final and conclusive between the parties that it was given on the merits, and by a court of competent jurisdiction. Thus, where a Rotterdam court decided that the respondent was entitled to suspend delivery obligations under a contract and the appellant sought to enforce the contract in Gambia, it was held that the action was not sustainable.[112]

Kenya

Under Kenyan law, no court shall adjudicate any suit or issue which has been heard and finally decided by another court competent to try that action or issue. This rule applies to actions between the same parties, between parties under whom they or any of them claim, and between parties litigating under the same title.[113] Subject to defined exceptions, a foreign judgment shall be conclusive as to any matter which has been directly adjudicated upon between the same parties, or between parties under whom they or any of them claim, litigating under the same title.[114]

Nigeria

Under Nigerian law, a final and conclusive judgment of a foreign court against a plaintiff may be pleaded in estoppel. Estoppel is viewed as 'essentially a rule of evidence'.[115] It has been held that estoppel based

[111] Ibid. [112] *Bourgi Co. Ltd* v. *Withams H/V* (2002–8) 2 GR 38.
[113] Civil Procedure Act 1924, s. 7. [114] Ibid., s. 9.
[115] *Teleglobe America Inc.* v. *21st Century Technologies Ltd* [2008] 17 NWLR 108 at 133; *Master of MV 'Delos'* v. *Ocean Steamship Nigeria Ltd* [2004] 17 NWLR 88 at 104, [2005] 9 WRN 155 at 170.

on a foreign judgment should be treated with caution because of the uncertainties arising from procedural differences in foreign countries.[116] In *Teleglobe America Inc.* v. *21st Century Technologies Ltd*,[117] one issue which had to be decided was whether the issue of validity in the service of process of the foreign court on the judgment-debtor (raised and decided by the foreign court) could be reopened before the Nigerian court. It was held that it would be wrong to consider the issue, as it had been canvassed and determined by the foreign court.

South Africa

A South African court will not go into the merits of a case adjudicated upon by a foreign court, and will not attempt to review or set aside its findings of fact or law.[118] It was reasoned in *Gabelsberger* v. *Babl*[119] that 'the reason why there was no inquiry into the underlying cause of action of a foreign or any judgment is because the matter is *res judicata* and the debt has been novated by the judgment'. The novation of the debt terminates the *lis*. In South Africa, the rules of *res judicata* are procedural. Accordingly, whether a foreign judgment constitutes *res judicata* is a matter for South African law.[120]

Under the Protection of Businesses Act 1978, it shall be a defence to any action brought in a South African court if it is proved to the satisfaction of the court that the cause of action, which founds the action so brought, is the subject of a judgment given by a court in a foreign country. This shall be the case where: (a) in terms of the laws of the foreign country, the court which gave such judgment was competent to give that judgment; (b) in terms of such laws, such judgment is final and conclusive;[121] and (c) the parties to the proceedings in which such judgment was given, or their successors in title, are the same as the parties to the proceedings in South Africa.[122] It has been held that the

[116] *Master of MV 'Delos'* v. *Ocean Steamship Nigeria Ltd* [2004] 17 NWLR 88 at 106, [2005] 9 WRN 155 at 173.

[117] [2008] 17 NWLR 108.

[118] *Jones* v. *Krok* 1995 (1) SA 677 at 685.

[119] 1994 (2) SA 677 at 679.

[120] *Laconian Maritime Enterprises Ltd* v. *Agromar Lineas Ltd* 1986 (3) SA 509.

[121] *MV Silvergate; Tradax Ocean Transport* v. *MV Silvergate Properly Described as MV Astyanax* 1999 (4) SA 405 at 417–21.

[122] Protection of Businesses Act 1978, s. 1F. In *MV Silvergate* at 418, the court left open the question of whether this section applied to cases that fell outside s. 1(1)(a) read with s. 1

phrase 'the cause of action' should be understood as referring not to the cause of action in the strict sense, but to 'the same matter in issue'.[123]

Tanzania

Under Tanzanian law, no court shall adjudicate any suit or issue which has been heard and finally decided by another court competent to try that action or issue. This rule applies to actions between the same parties, between parties under whom they, or any of them, claim and between parties litigating under the same title.[124] Subject to defined exceptions, a foreign judgment shall be conclusive as to any matter which has been directly adjudicated upon between the same parties, or between parties under whom they or any of them claim, litigating under the same title.[125]

Uganda

Under Ugandan law, no court shall adjudicate any suit or issue which has been heard and finally decided by another court competent to try that action or issue. This rule applies to actions between the same parties, between parties under whom they or any of them claim, and between parties litigating under the same title.[126] Subject to defined exceptions, a foreign judgment shall be conclusive as to any matter it directly adjudicates upon between the same parties, or between parties under whom they or any of them claim, litigating under the same title.[127]

Comments

It is a fundamental principle accepted in the countries under study that a judgment pronounced by a foreign court of competent jurisdiction can found a plea of *res judicata*. However, there appears to be a degree of

(3) of the Act. It was submitted that the wording of s. 1F is too broad for it to admit of any such restriction on the scope of its application.

[123] *MV Silvergate* at 417; *Laconian Maritime Enterprises Ltd* v. *Agromar Lineas Ltd* 1986 (3) SA 509, which controversially held that an action to enforce an arbitration award in Alabama, United States was not dealing with the same subject matter as an action to enforce the same award in South Africa because the substantive laws of both countries in relation to the enforcement of the award (specifically in relation to limitation periods) were different.

[124] Civil Procedure Code 1966, s. 9.

[125] Ibid., s. 11.

[126] Civil Procedure Act 1929, s. 7.

[127] Ibid., s. 9.

uncertainty as to which law determines the competency of the foreign court. As discussed above, it is well accepted in the countries under study that, in actions to enforce a foreign judgment, the enforcing court determines the competence of the foreign court under the former's private international law. Does a different rule apply if a foreign judgment is pleaded as *res judicata*? Apart from South Africa, there is neither case law nor statute suggesting a clear affirmative response to this question. Under the South African Protection of Businesses Act, the foreign court should have been competent 'in terms of the laws of the foreign country'.[128] In Tanzania and Uganda, a court shall presume, upon the production of any document purporting to be a certified copy of a foreign judgment, that such judgment was pronounced by a court of competent jurisdiction, unless the contrary appears on the record. This presumption may be displaced by proving want of jurisdiction.[129] On the other hand, it is unclear whether 'want of jurisdiction' should be determined from the perspective of the private international law of Tanzania and Uganda, or from that of the foreign country. The wording and accommodating language of the provisions appear to suggest jurisdiction should be determined from the perspective of the laws of the foreign country.

It has been submitted that allowing the internal competence of a foreign court to suffice on a plea of *res judicata* is unsound. Such a position is inconsistent with the principle that, in an action to enforce a foreign judgment, the competence of the foreign court must be determined under the enforcing court's private international law. Neither does it afford equality of protection to disputing parties. The bases of international competence are very limited – there is often asymmetry between the bases of international competence and the bases of jurisdiction in international matters. Admittedly, in instances where the foreign judgment is pleaded as a defence, the domestic plaintiff will normally have been the plaintiff in the foreign proceedings, albeit unsuccessfully. His or her submission (through instituting the foreign action) is, in the countries under study, a basis of international competence. It is in cases outside the scope of this example where the asymmetry becomes truly material. A party that seeks to rely on a foreign judgment as *res judicata*

128 Protection of Businesses Act 1978, s. 1F.

129 Tanzania – Civil Procedure Code 1966, s. 12; Uganda – Civil Procedure Act 1929, s. 10. A similar provision in Kenya's Civil Procedure Act was repealed by the Evidence Act 1963.

should not be in a better position than one who seeks to enforce it: there should be equality of treatment. A person who raises the plea of *res judicata* and one who seeks to enforce a foreign judgment by action seek in essence the same thing in law, i.e. to give effect to the foreign judgment.

A foreign judgment which is final and which has been granted by a competent court is treated as conclusive. An instance of giving conclusive effect to foreign judgments is where the enforcing court will not review the merits of a judgment. It will neither examine the evidence upon which the foreign court has its judgment, nor reassess its findings on the evidence. However, to determine whether the foreign court was competent, the enforcing court may have to examine issues or evidence which could also have been examined by the foreign court. In such an instance, the enforcing court is not bound by the decision of the foreign court. A Zimbabwean court has observed that 'there is ample authority that, in proceedings to enforce a foreign judgment, the defendant cannot attack the judgment on its merits. On the other hand it would seem right in principle that the court which is called upon to enforce the foreign judgment should be entitled to determine for itself whether the facts upon which the jurisdiction of the foreign court is purported to be based really existed'.[130]

This is a sound position to take. An enforcing court is not expected to merely rubber stamp a foreign judgment. To compel a judgment-creditor to discharge obligations imposed by the judgment, it is appropriate that the enforcing court is satisfied that the foreign court based its decision to assume jurisdiction over the claim on a legitimate basis in order to gain the right to hear the dispute. This should not be based solely on the terms of the foreign court or the law of the foreign country.

Defences against the recognition and enforcement of foreign judgments

Kenya

Under Kenyan law, a foreign judgment shall be conclusive as to any matter directly adjudicated upon between the same parties or between

[130] *Coluflandres Ltd* v. *Scandia Industrial Products Ltd* 1969 (2) RLR 431 at 443, 1969 (3) SA 551 at 560; *Maschinen Frommer GmbH* v. *Trisave Engineering & Machinery Supplies (Pty) Ltd* 2003 (6) SA 69.

parties under whom they, or any of them, claim and who are litigating under the same title, except where: it was not pronounced by a court of competent jurisdiction; it was not given on the merits of the case; it appears on the face of the proceedings to be founded on an incorrect view of international law, or a refusal to recognise Kenyan law in cases where such law was applicable; the proceedings in which the judgment was obtained are opposed to natural justice; it was obtained by fraud; or it sustains a claim founded on a breach of Kenyan law.[131]

South Africa

A South African court will not enforce a foreign judgment which is contrary to South African public policy. Whether a foreign judgment is contrary to public policy depends largely on the facts of each case. Thus, it has been held that neither the fact that a judgment is founded on a cause of action unknown to South African law, nor that it requires the defendant to pay an additional sum to compensate for depreciation in currency, makes its enforcement contrary to South African public policy.[132] Similarly, it would be wrong in principle to refuse to enforce a foreign order of punitive damages merely because it was unknown in South Africa.[133] However, in one case where the punitive damages awarded were equivalent in real terms to granting the plaintiff double the amount of damages she had claimed and was awarded, it was held that the award was so excessive and exorbitant it contravened public policy in South Africa and, accordingly, was not enforceable.[134]

A South African court will not enforce a foreign judgment given in breach of natural justice – the defendant bears the burden of proving this.[135] The fact that a judgment is given on a wrong view of the law, or is in a wider sense unjust, will not per se amount to a failure of natural justice.[136] The term 'natural justice' is a reference to the procedure rather than to the merits of a particular case. Where the procedural rules of a competent court have been regularly observed in a *bona fide manner*, the

[131] Civil Procedure Act 1924, s. 9.

[132] *Eden* v. *Pienaar* 2001 (1) SA 158.

[133] *Jones* v. *Krok* 1996 (1) SA 504.

[134] Ibid.

[135] *Rubie* v. *Haines* 1948 (4) SA 998.

[136] *Lissack* v. *Duarte* 1974 (4) SA 560 (on appeal from *Duarte* v. *Lissack* 1973 (3) SA 615). However, there are dicta in *Jones* v. *Krok* 1996 (1) SA 504 at 510–15 to suggest that enforcement of an 'irrational' foreign judgment (e.g. one not based on evidence at all) would be denied on the grounds of violating natural justice.

judgment of that court will generally stand, unless those rules are so imperfect as to be repugnant to South African notions of natural justice. What the courts are vigilant of is that a defendant has not been unfairly deprived of an opportunity to present his or her side of the case. Thus, where judgment has been granted in a country against an absent defendant, the inquiry as to a possible failure of natural justice is to be answered with reference to all the circumstances of the case. The defendant's failure to timeously seek legal advice in the foreign country is only one of the relevant considerations.[137] The standard of natural justice expected and applied is that of South Africa – the country where enforcement is being sought.[138] Neither the fact that a foreign court has declined to grant an adjournment,[139] nor that it has refused to allow the judgment-debtor to raise a specific defence,[140] necessarily amounts to a breach of natural justice. However, in one instance, it was considered contrary to natural justice for a litigant to obtain judgment against one defendant and then seek judgment against another for the same sum and on the same grounds – the second judgment would not be recognised in South Africa.[141]

In addition to the above common law defences, a plaintiff can take advantage of the provisions of the Protection of Businesses Act 1978 to prevent the enforcement of foreign judgments relating to defined claims. The Act is seldom pleaded and to date has not been successfully invoked.[142] Under the Act, no foreign judgment arising from any act or transaction connected with the mining, production, importation, exportation, refinement, possession, use, sale or ownership of any matter or material, of whatever nature, whether within, outside, into or from South Africa, together with the directing of payment of multiple or punitive damages,[143] shall be recognised or enforced in South Africa.[144]

[137] *Lissack* v. *Duarte* 1974 (4) SA 560 (on appeal from *Duarte* v. *Lissack* 1973 (3) SA 615).

[138] *Corona* v. *Zimbabwe Iron & Steel Co. Ltd* 1985 (2) SA 423 at 426.

[139] *Rubie* v. *Haines* 1948 (4) SA 998.

[140] *Society of Lloyd's* v. *Romahn* 2006 (4) SA 23.

[141] *Corona* v. *Zimbabwe Iron & Steel.*

[142] *Jones* v. *Krok* 1996 (1) SA 504. See also *Chinatex Oriental Trading Co.* v. *Erskine* 1998 (4) SA 1087 (reversed on appeal – *Erskine* v. *Chinatex Oriental Trading Co.* 2001 (1) SA 817 – but the issue relating to the defence under the Act was not discussed); *Tradex Ocean Transportation SA* v. *M V Silvergate* 1994 (4) SA 119 at 121.

[143] This refers to an 'amount awarded as damages which exceeds the amount determined by the court as compensation for the damage or loss actually sustained by the person to whom the damages have been awarded'. Protection of Businesses Act 1978, s. 1A(2).

[144] Protection of Businesses Act 1978, s. 1A.

Tanzania

Under Tanzanian law, a foreign judgment shall be conclusive as to any matter directly adjudicated upon between the same parties, or between parties under whom they, or any of them, claim to be litigating under the same title, except where: it was not pronounced by a court of competent jurisdiction; it was not given on the merits of the case; it appears on the face of the proceedings to be founded on an incorrect view of international law or a refusal to recognise Tanzanian law in cases where such law was applicable; the proceedings in which the judgment was obtained are opposed to natural justice; it was obtained by fraud; or it sustains a claim founded on a breach of Tanzanian law.[145]

Uganda

Under Ugandan law, a foreign judgment shall be conclusive as to any matter directly adjudicated upon between the same parties, or between parties under whom they, or any of them, claim to be litigating under the same title, except where: it was not pronounced by a court of competent jurisdiction; it was not given on the merits of the case; it appears on the face of the proceedings to be founded on an incorrect view of international law or a refusal to recognise Ugandan law in cases where that law was applicable; the proceedings in which the judgment was obtained are opposed to natural justice; it was obtained by fraud; or it sustains a claim founded on a breach of Ugandan law.[146]

Zimbabwe

A defendant who alleges he or she did not receive notice of the trial in the foreign court bears the onus to show that the judgment resulting from the trial was vitiated by a failure of natural justice.[147] The standards of natural justice to be applied are those in force in Zimbabwe and not those which may pass muster in the procedure of another country.[148] In *Coluflandres Ltd* v. *Scandia Industrial Products Ltd*,[149] the defendant had notice of proceedings in a Belgian court. The notice gave him

145 Civil Procedure Code 1966, s. 11. 146 Civil Procedure Act 1929, s. 9.

147 *Coluflandres Ltd* v. *Scandia Industrial Products Ltd* 1969 (2) RLR 431 at 439, 1969 (3) SA 551 at 557.

148 *Steinberg* v. *Cosmopolitan National Bank of Chicago* 1973 (3) SA 885.

149 1969 (2) RLR 431, 1969 (3) SA 551.

adequate information of the case it was meant to address. The defendants chose to make their objections to the court's jurisdiction through a letter to a notary public and sheriff of the Belgian court, in the hope that the letter would be passed on to the court. In an action to enforce the Belgian judgment given in default of appearance, it was held that the defendant had failed to prove that the judgment was vitiated by a failure of natural justice. However, as a foreign judgment had been given without notice of the proceedings to the judgment-debtor, without them being afforded an opportunity to be heard, and without a period of notice that would have permitted them to appeal, and the judgment had in any case been entered against them, it was held that the proceedings – *cognovit* proceedings – were contrary to natural justice.[150]

Comments

It is open to a defendant to raise defences to an action for the recognition and enforcement of a foreign judgment. The courts have not placed a lid on the grounds upon which such defences may be founded. In some countries, statutes provide grounds – often imbued with nationalistic or protectionist undertones – which may not necessarily be available in others. The defence under South Africa's Protection of Businesses Act 1978 is a classic example. Similarly, in Kenya, Tanzania and Uganda, a foreign judgment would be denied recognition if the foreign court refused to recognise Kenyan, Tanzanian or Ugandan law as the applicable law.

In general, a refusal to recognise an enforcing country's law as applicable may constitute a violation of its public policy, especially in instances where those laws are considered mandatory in the country. However, under the Kenyan, Tanzanian and Ugandan statutes, it is unclear whether the applicable law is determinable by the private international law of the foreign court's country, or by the enforcing court's country, i.e. Kenya, Tanzania or Uganda. It has been submitted that the former interpretation is to be preferred. The latter would amount to nothing less than retrying the case. It would require the foreign court's choice of law rules to coincide with those of Kenya, Tanzania or Uganda. Although international harmonisation of choice of law rules may be a laudable objective, this is certainly not a legitimate way to pursue it. Indeed, it is submitted that these grounds for not recognising foreign judgments are

[150] *Steinberg* v. *Cosmopolitan National Bank of Chicago.*

too broad and should be repealed. Appropriate cases could be dealt with under the public policy defence.

Refusing to recognise a foreign judgment on the basis that it is founded on an incorrect view of international law constitutes other difficult grounds. It is unclear which international law this refers to. Can a Kenyan, Tanzanian or Ugandan court refuse to recognise a foreign judgment on the basis that it is founded on an incorrect view of a treaty to which Kenya, Tanzania or Uganda is not party? Can a foreign judgment which is inconsistent with a provision in the African Charter on Human and Peoples' Rights,[151] to which all the states under study are parties, be denied recognition on the basis that it violates international law? Assessing whether a foreign judgment is founded on an incorrect view of international law may also entail going into the merits of the case. This would potentially undermine the objective of ensuring that the process of enforcing foreign judgments is not protracted. With the spread of international human rights norms and their entrenchment in many African constitutions, these grounds may, however, become important.

The courts have generally restricted the natural justice defence to cases of procedural unfairness. However, some judgments suggest the courts look beyond the strictly procedural. Thus, in one case, the defence was successfully used to prevent the enforcement of a judgment given to a judgment-creditor who had sued two different persons in two different Zimbabwean courts on the same cause of action and sought to enforce one of the judgments in South Africa. In another case, the court left open the possibility that an irrational judgment may fall foul of the defence. However, the extension of the natural justice defence to cover cases of substantive justice in foreign judgments could be problematic. The principle that a foreign judgment shall not be reviewed on its merits necessitates, or at least renders appropriate, a restriction of the scope of the natural justice defence to cases of procedural unfairness. Apart from in exceptional circumstances, an action to enforce a foreign judgment should not be used as a forum to re-litigate a claim.

Default judgments have been a veritable object of attack under the natural justice defence. There are suggestions in a Malawian case that by submitting to the jurisdiction of a foreign court – in this instance through a jurisdiction agreement – a person becomes bound by the court's procedure and judgment, even though 'he may not have had notice

[151] African Charter on Human and Peoples Rights, 27 June 1981, (1982) 21 ILM 58.

of the proceedings'.[152] It has been submitted that this is inappropriate. A jurisdiction agreement reflects a desire by the parties to have their disputes resolved before the designated courts. It does not in any way deal with issues related to the procedures of trial. Even though linked in many respects, issues of jurisdiction and civil procedure are distinct, as jurisdiction agreements focus solely on the former.

Although it has been invoked in a number of cases, the public policy defence has rarely succeeded. In *Gramara (Private) Ltd* v. *Government of the Republic of Zimbabwe*, where the defence prevailed, Justice Patel perceptively observed that:

> ... what constitutes public policy in any given country is a matter that eludes precise definition. The notion is clearly not immutable and must perforce vary with time, place and circumstance, in tandem with changing social *mores*. Antecedent case authorities are obviously highly persuasive but may not always be germane or decisive ... public policy must be considered not only in the closed confines of the domestic sphere but also in the larger regional and international context.[153]

In general, especially in commercial cases, it is appropriate that the defence is given a highly restricted scope of application. Compared with subject matters, such as family and property law, national values tend not to overly dominate commercial matters.

A likely area for the successful invocation of public policy relates to foreign judgments given in breach of jurisdiction agreements. Should a Ghanaian court (or a court in any other African state) enforce a judgment given in a foreign country in breach of a Ghanaian choice of forum agreement? Because of negative perceptions about laws and judicial systems in Africa and imbalances in negotiating positions, parties to international contracts seldom choose African courts as their preferred forum for dispute settlement. Even in the rare cases where such choices are made, they are often challenged in foreign courts in the event of a dispute. It is important that parties are held to their bargain. An African court should decline to enforce a foreign judgment given in breach of an agreement that has selected the enforcing state as the choice of forum.[154]

[152] *Heyns* v. *Demetriou*, Civil Cause No. of 2001 (High Court, Malawi, 2001).

[153] *Gramara (Private) Ltd* v. *Government of the Republic of Zimbabwe*, Case No. X-ref. HC 5483/09 (High Court, Zimbabwe, 2010).

[154] A similar defence exists in English law: see Civil Jurisdiction and Judgments Act 1982, s. 32.

In future it is likely that constitutional norms may provide defences against the enforcement of foreign judgments, or influence how existing defences are interpreted. The natural justice defence is arguably just one aspect of the constitutionally entrenched right to a fair hearing.[155] Similarly, constitutional norms may shape the content of public policy.

Enforcing judgments against states

Enforcing foreign judgments against states or governments raises two principal issues, namely immunity from jurisdiction and immunity from execution or enforcement measures. The former is addressed in Chapter 6 of this book. In the countries under study, both issues are regulated mainly by statutes,[156] all of which, to varying degrees, give effect to the Vienna Convention of Diplomatic Relations[157] and/or the Vienna Convention on Consular Relations.[158] The relevant provisions of the conventions, which in many of the national implementing statutes have been listed as schedules, are not reproduced here. The country reports deal purely with decided cases.

Botswana

A Botswanan court will not order the attachment of assets necessary to maintain the diplomatic functions of a foreign government. In *Republic of Angola* v. *Springbok Investments (Pty) Ltd*,[159] the applicant brought an urgent application to set aside an attachment of funds standing to the

[155] See, e.g., Kenyan Constitution 2010, s. 50(1); South African Constitution 1996, s. 34. *Society of Lloyd's* v. *Romahn* 2006 (4) SA 23, where the enforcement of an English judgment was unsuccessfully challenged as a violation of the constitutional right to a 'fair public hearing'. As already discussed in Ch. 5, constitutional arguments have been unsuccessfully deployed to challenge the enforcement of choice of forum and choice of arbitration agreements. See *Raytheon Aircraft Credit Corp.* v. *Air Al-Faraj Ltd* [2005] 2 KLR 47; *Lerr Group Ltd* v. *Ballast Nedam Africa*, Civil Suit No: HC/269/09/CO/082/D2 (High Court, Gambia, 2010).

[156] Botswana – Diplomatic Immunities and Privileges Act 1969; Ghana – Diplomatic Immunities Act 1962; Kenya – Privileges and Immunities Act 1970; Namibia – Diplomatic Privileges Act 1951; Nigeria – Diplomatic Immunities and Privileges Act 1990; South Africa – Diplomatic Immunities and Privileges Act 2001, Foreign States Immunities Act 1981; Tanzania – Diplomatic and Consular Immunities and Privileges Act 1986; Uganda – Diplomatic Privileges Act 1965; Zambia – Diplomatic Immunities and Privileges Act 1965; Zimbabwe – Privileges and Immunities Act 1972.

[157] 18 April 1961 (1961), 500 UNTS 95.

[158] 24 April 1963 (1963), 596 UNTS 261.

[159] 2005 (2) BLR 159.

credit of the applicant's bank account and pursuant to a garnishee order obtained *ex parte* by the respondent. The applicant claimed that the account held sovereign balances which were used to operate its embassy in Botswana. Accordingly, the account was immune from execution on the bases of either sovereign or diplomatic immunity. It was held that the account fell within the category of accounts needed to maintain the applicant's diplomatic functions and dignity. It was, accordingly, immune under international law from attachment or garnishment.

South Africa

A South African court will not compel the government to offer diplomatic assistance to a judgment-creditor in order to secure the enforcement of a judgment. In *Roothman* v. *President of the Republic of South Africa*,[160] the applicant obtained a judgment against the Democratic Republic of Congo (DRC) in an action in South Africa where the DRC submitted to jurisdiction. The applicant was unable to obtain full satisfaction of the judgment debt, either within or outside South Africa. In this action, the applicant sought the aid of the South African Government to enforce the judgment on its behalf. The applicant relied on various constitutional arguments, including the right of access to justice, the rule of law and the duty of the state to ensure the effectiveness of its courts and assist its citizens in enforcing their rights. The applicant sought a declaratory order[161] that the state should take reasonable steps to assist him in ensuring compliance with the judgment. The respondent argued that the matter was governed by the private international law regime on the enforcement of foreign judgments, and it was from that regime which the applicant should seek remedy. The court held that the state has created mechanisms for the enforcement of judgments against commercial creditors. There was no reason for it to take additional steps in cases involving a commercial contract between a citizen and a foreign state. Thus, there was no duty on the part of the state to intercede on the applicant's behalf.

[160] [2006] South African Supreme Court of Appeal 80.

[161] In the trial court, the applicant sought a structural interdict directing the state to ensure compliance with the judgment.

Uganda

A Ugandan court will not order the attachment of the diplomatic premises of a foreign government. In *Emmanuel Bitwire* v. *Representative of Zaire*,[162] the plaintiff obtained judgment against the Embassy of the DRC in an action to recover rent arrears, interests, *mesne* profits and costs. It sought execution of the judgment on premises held in the name of the embassy and occupied by its accountant and his family. The court held that, for the premises to be immune from attachment in execution under Article 30(1) of the Vienna Convention on Diplomatic Relations of 1961, it must be shown that it is the private residence of a diplomatic agent. Staff, such as accountants, were not diplomatic agents. Accordingly, the premises were liable to attachment.

Comments

A judgment-creditor who seeks to enforce a foreign judgment against a state faces at least two legal challenges: immunity from jurisdiction and immunity from execution or enforcement measures. Currently, none of the countries under study has ratified the UN Convention on Jurisdictional Immunity of States and their Property,[163] which is not yet in force.[164] Sierra Leone is the only country within the scope of this study that has signed the Convention.[165]

As discussed in Chapter 6, almost all the countries under study have adopted the doctrine of restrictive immunity. Even if this was not so, it is submitted that without a specific statutory exemption for actions to enforce a foreign judgment – at present no such specific exemption exists – a state should not enjoy jurisdictional immunity in actions to enforce a foreign judgment. A foreign judgment merges the original cause of action. This renders irrelevant the character of the transaction or act constituting the cause of action in the foreign court. It is implausible (and therefore would be fictitious) to characterise the foreign

[162] [1998] 1 Kam. LR 21. [163] 3 June 2004, 44 ILM 803 (2005).

[164] See also UN Convention on the Law of the Sea, 10 December 1982, 1833 UNTS 3. Article 32 provides that 'nothing in this Convention affects the immunities of warships and other government ships operated for non-commercial purposes'. Except Swaziland, all the countries within the scope of this study are parties to the Convention. *NML Capital Ltd* v. *The Republic of Ghana*, Suit No. RPC/343/12 (High Court, Ghana, 2012) dealt with jurisdictional immunity and an Argentinian warship.

[165] Madagascar, Morocco and Senegal have also signed the Convention.

judgment as a 'governmental' or 'commercial' act or transaction of the state judgment-debtor. If anything at all, it is an act of the state from whence the judgment emanates; however, in an action to enforce a foreign judgment, the respective state is not on trial.

Admittedly, to argue that a foreign judgment is not the state judgment-debtor's governmental or commercial act or transaction creates a problem. It becomes an issue that is not expressly covered by the current regimes on immunity. Thus, national courts may be free to decide one way or the other. Furthermore, it appears that in some common law jurisdictions, when the issue of state immunity from jurisdiction has been raised, the courts have investigated the transactions which underlie the foreign judgment, in order to decide whether they fall within a commercial transactions exception. This approach, it is submitted, is inconsistent with the principle that a foreign judgment merges the original cause of action and that the courts will not investigate the merits of foreign judgments. In actions to enforce foreign judgments against states, national courts should err on the side of not granting immunity and if jurisdictional immunity is to be enjoyed, it should be specifically provided for by statute. In actions to enforce foreign judgments, the protection afforded to states should be at the execution and not the jurisdictional phase, especially in cases where the state has submitted to the jurisdiction of the foreign court.

Immunity from jurisdiction is not the same as immunity from execution. Immunity from execution is not absolute. However, the precise conditions under which it would be denied remain open. The purpose for which the property is being used, rather than the nature of the transaction which formed the basis of the foreign action, is paramount here. The existing cases and legislation suggest that the diplomatic premises or property of a government, and properties needed to perform a government's sovereign or diplomatic functions, are immune from execution.[166] Beyond these, the states under study have not specified which other properties of a foreign state are immune from execution. It may be argued that, consistent with the law on jurisdictional immunity – and this is the position in South African law[167] – property serving commercial purposes can be attached in execution.

[166] The foundations for this are Articles 22 and 30 of the Vienna Convention on Diplomatic Relations, 18 April 1961, 500 UNTS 95 and the Vienna Convention on Consular Relations, 24 April 1963, 596 UNTS 261.

[167] Foreign States Immunities Act 1981, s. 14(3)(b).

The distinction between property held for commercial and governmental purposes is, accordingly, crucial in a claim of immunity from execution. It is unclear from the decided cases who bears the burden of proof. The Botswanan and Ugandan courts appear to have placed the burden on the judgment-creditor to prove whether the property is being held for commercial purposes, or not being used for diplomatic ones. They also appear to give weight to statements or certificates issued from the relevant government stating the purpose for which the property sought to be attached is being used. A significant grey area in terms of this distinction is any money held by a country's central bank. At present in some countries,[168] this is excluded from execution: a position affirmed in Article 21(1)(c) of the UN Convention on Jurisdictional Immunity of States and their Property 2004.

Foreign judgments in foreign currency

As discussed in Chapter 9, the courts have jurisdiction to award judgments in foreign currency. This extends to actions to enforce foreign judgments at common law.[169] In instances where judgment-creditors have requested that awards be enforced in foreign currency, the courts have done so. In *Barclays Bank of Swaziland* v. *Mnyeketi*,[170] it was held that, when provisional sentence is sought on a foreign judgment for an amount in a foreign currency, the court has simply[171] to regard the foreign judgment as an obligation to pay the amount definitively quantified in the nominated currency in that judgment. The court should enter a provisional sentence for payment of the debt in the foreign currency in which the foreign judgment quantified the debt. However, the defendant should be left free to make payment in the currency which is legal tender in the jurisdiction of the court, in this instance South African rand.

[168] United Kingdom – State Immunity Act 1978, s. 14(4); United States – Foreign Sovereign Immunity Act 1976, s. 1611(b)(1); Australia – Foreign States Immunities Act 1985; Canada – State Immunity Act 1982.

[169] As discussed in Ch. 18, the statutory regimes for the registration of foreign judgments have their own rules on foreign currency obligations. In essence, they all require conversion of the foreign currency into the local currency, but vary on the date of conversion.

[170] 1992 (3) SA 425.

[171] It was reasoned that it was unnecessary to enquire whether or not the foreign judgment novated the cause of action and, if not, whether the cause of action was a contract which contemplated payment in the relevant foreign currency, or a delict requiring conversion of the debt to South African rand at such a rate of exchange as may have prevailed on the date appropriate to delictual damages.

To enforce a foreign judgment in foreign currency does not mean that it is to be executed in foreign judgments. Where the judgment-debtor seeks to discharge his or her obligation in the local currency, an interesting issue arises as to the date to be used in ascertaining the obligation. A number of options exist, including the date the foreign judgment was given, the date of the judgment enforcing the foreign judgment, and the date of payment or execution. Given that currencies fluctuate daily, whichever option is chosen will lead to some monetary loss to one party. In Zimbabwe, it has been held that the date for ascertaining the judgment-debtor's obligation was the date of the foreign judgment.[172] It is submitted that the date of payment or execution is the preferred date. Such a date will ensure that the judgment-creditor gets what is actually due to them.

Limitation of actions and foreign judgments

As discussed above in the countries under study, a foreign judgment is characterised as debt. In an action to enforce a foreign judgment at common law,[173] this characterisation becomes significant when a judgment-debtor argues that the enforcement of the foreign judgment is prescribed. In states where limitation of actions or prescription are characterised as procedural, this is a matter for the *lex fori*. The statutes dealing with limitation of actions in the countries under study do not devote specific provisions to foreign judgments. The courts have also shown a willingness to apply the limitation period applicable to debts in foreign judgments.[174] In Kenya and Tanzania, where action on a foreign judgment is barred in the foreign country, it is equally barred under their national law.[175]

[172] *Cosmopolitan National Bank of Chicago* v. *Steinberg* 1973 (4) SA 579; *Cosmopolitan National Bank of Chicago* v. *Steinberg* 1973 (2) SA 279.

[173] As discussed in Ch. 18, there exist designated time frames within which a foreign judgment can be registered under the statutory regimes.

[174] *Jethwa* v. *Bhanji* [1938–9] 18 KLR 11; *DTH Jethwa* v. *Bhanji* [1939] 6 EACA 28; *Society of Lloyd's* v. *Romahn* 2006 (4) SA 23.

[175] Kenya – Limitation of Actions Act 1967, s. 40; Tanzania – Law of Limitations Act 1971, s. 42.

18

The statutory regimes for enforcing foreign judgments

The statutory regime for enforcing foreign judgments[1] in Commonwealth Africa has a long history.[2] Currently, the regime exists in each of the countries under study.[3] Even though their scope of application is very limited, they remain an important complement to the common law regime, from which they derive many of their principles. Indeed, the statutory regimes, which are the subject matter of this chapter, could potentially form the starting point for regional or continent-wide conventions on the enforcement of foreign judgments.

Exclusivity of statutory regimes

In many of the countries under study, where the statutory regime applies, it is exclusive. A judgment enforceable under the regime cannot be enforced using the common law regime. However, a judgment which is not enforceable under the regime can be enforced using the common law regime.[4] As regards a foreign judgment that falls outside the scope of the statutory regime, the provisions which bar 'any other proceedings' on the judgment are not applicable to it.[5] Section 9 of Botswana's Judgments

[1] Foreign maintenance orders and decrees of divorce are discussed in Ch. 12.

[2] K. W. Patchett, *Recognition of Commercial Judgments and Awards in the Commonwealth* (London: Butterworths, 1984), pp. 18–21.

[3] I have been unable to access Malawi's British and Commonwealth Judgments Act 1922, Judgment Extension Ordinance 1922 and the Service of Process and Enforcement of Judgments Act 1957, which are the relevant legislation on the subject. See also *Heyns* v. *Demetriou*, Civil Cause No. of 2001 (High Court, Malawi, 2001), which was an action to set aside registration of a South African judgment.

[4] *NML Capital Ltd* v. *The Republic of Ghana*, Suit No. RPC/343/12 (High Court, Ghana, 2012). But see *Rosemond Salemi Akil* v. *Aristotle Kotey*, HI/82/2007 (Court of Appeal, Ghana, 2008), suggesting a judgment unenforceable under the statutory regime cannot be enforced at common law because that would amount to an evasion of the Act. It is, however, submitted that this position is wrong.

[5] *Shah Devsi Vardhaman* v. *TCN Haridas* [1958] EA 527.

(International Enforcement) Act 1981 is an example of such a provision. It provides: 'no proceedings for the recovery of a sum payable under a foreign judgment, being a judgment to which this Part applies, other than proceedings by way of registration of the judgment, shall be entertained by any court in Botswana'.[6]

What this and similar provisions in the other countries mean is that a judgment-creditor cannot seek to enforce a judgment registrable under the statutory regime by using the common law regime. As a Tanzanian court has observed, 'the effect of section 8 of the Ordinance . . . is merely that where a judgment is capable of registration under the Ordinance the judgment-creditor is barred from instituting any other kind of proceeding for its enforcement, such as an action upon the judgment or a suit on the original cause'.[7] In the elliptic words of Ghana's Justice Edusei, for a foreign judgment to which the Courts Act 1993 applies, the procedure of issuing a writ to enforce it is 'not open to [the plaintiff]'.[8] In *Yankson*, the plaintiff registered an English judgment in Ghana, but the registration was subsequently set aside for a period of time. The plaintiff then sought to recover the judgment debt by instituting action on the judgment. It was held that the action must fail. The court reasoned that, under the Courts Act 1971, the only recourse for the judgment-creditor was to have the judgment registered – in the instant case this was not an option open to him.

It is difficult to appreciate why the statutory regime is 'forced' on judgment-creditors to whose judgments the statutory regimes apply as the only means for enforcing their judgment. This position can occasion injustice. A judgment-creditor might have good reasons for not wanting to use the statutory regime, even if his or her judgment falls within its scope. The judgment might contain parts to which the statutory regime does not apply and the judgment-creditor might want to consolidate, rather than split, their enforcement.[9] He or she might also want to apply

[6] Botswana – Judgments (International Enforcement) Act 1981, s. 9. See also Ghana – Courts Act 1993, s. 85; Kenya – Foreign Judgments (Reciprocal Enforcement) Act 1984, s. 17(1); Tanzania – Foreign Judgments (Reciprocal Enforcement) Ordinance 1935, s. 8; Uganda – Foreign Judgments (Reciprocal Enforcement) Act 1961, s. 7; Zambia – Foreign Judgments (Reciprocal Enforcement) Act 1937, s. 8. The statutory regimes in Namibia, South Africa, Swaziland and Zimbabwe do not contain such provision.

[7] *Willow Investment* v. *Mbomba Ntumba* [1996] TLR 377 at 380.

[8] *Yankson* v. *Mensah* [1976] 1 GLR 355 at 357.

[9] Botswana – Judgments (International Enforcement) Act 1981, s. 5(7); Ghana – Courts Act 1993, s. 82(9); Kenya – Foreign Judgment (Reciprocal Enforcement) Act 1984, s. 6(5); Tanzania – Foreign Judgments (Reciprocal Enforcement) Ordinance 1935, s. 4(5);

for summary judgment, which is an equally expeditious means of securing the payment of a debt. They might want to avoid the mandatory currency conversion rules under the statutory regimes and explore the possibility of convincing a judge to follow common law and enforce the judgment in foreign currency. They might also have exceeded the six-year limitation period on applications to register foreign judgments and therefore wish to investigate whether the uncertainties in the common law regime on the issue of limitations and foreign judgments (as discussed in Chapter 17) could inure to their advantage. In international commercial litigation, the availability and possibility of exploring options are assets. The exclusivity provisions of the statutory regimes shut the door to these options.

These exclusivity provisions appear to have been borrowed from section 6 of the United Kingdom's Foreign Judgments (Reciprocal Enforcement) Act 1933. A brief account of the genesis of the English provision is apposite. According to Lord Justice Greer, the section represents the 'first time any restriction was placed upon the right of anyone to say that a foreign judgment created a debt which could be enforced in this country'.[10] He suggests that the section was 'introduced because the foreign countries with which we entered into negotiations required that it should be so provided in order to obtain their agreement to a convention with regard to the reciprocal obligation of this country and the foreign country for the enforcement of the judgment'.[11] From these observations, it can be surmised that the introduction of the section was contingent on the demands of that time. Those demands are not necessarily present today in the countries under study. Indeed, some Canadian provinces allow foreign judgment-creditors the option of registering or suing on a foreign judgment.[12]

On a strict interpretation of the provisions, it can be argued that there still remains the option to bring an action on the original cause of action. The provisions apply to proceedings 'for the recovery of a sum payable

Uganda – Foreign Judgments (Reciprocal Enforcement) Act 1961, s. 3(4); Zambia – Foreign Judgments (Reciprocal Enforcement) Act 1937, s. 4(5).

10 *Yukon Consolidated Gold Corp. Ltd* v. *Clark* [1938] 2 KB 241 at 253–4. No such provision is contained in the Administration of Justice Act 1920, which deals with similar matters.

11 *Yukon* v. *Clark* at 253.

12 Ontario – Reciprocal Enforcement of Judgment Act 1990, s. 8; Alberta – Reciprocal Enforcement of Judgment Act 2000, s. 7 (this section gives a judgment-creditor the right to bring action 'on the original cause of action'); Saskatchewan – Reciprocal Enforcement of Judgment Act 1996, s. 10.

under a foreign judgment'. It does not expressly bar an action on the original cause of action.[13] Admittedly, to do so would come at considerable expense to the judgment-creditor. The rules on jurisdiction in international matters must also be satisfied in such an action, which could be met with a plea of *res judicata*. Moreover, the exclusivity provisions do not bar an application to the court to recognise a foreign judgment for other purposes, such as using the judgment to support a plea of estoppel *per rem judicatam*, or as evidence of an outstanding debt that can set off a monetary claim by the judgment-debtor.

Power to make foreign judgments unenforceable

One of the most remarkable powers possessed by the Executive on a private international law issue in the countries under study is the power to render a foreign judgment unenforceable. This power exists under the statutory regime of many of the countries referred to in this study. Section 11 of Botswana's Judgments (International Enforcement) Act 1981 is an example. It provides that:

> . . . if it appears to the President that the treatment in respect of recognition and enforcement accorded by the courts of any country to judgments given in the superior courts of Botswana is substantially less favourable than that accorded by the courts of Botswana to judgments of the superior courts of that country, the President may by statutory instrument order that except in so far as the President may otherwise direct, no proceedings shall be entertained in any court of Botswana for the recovery of any sum alleged to be payable under a judgment given in a court of that country.[14]

To date, there is no recorded instance of this power being exercised. However, the power is enormous and merits careful scrutiny. Indeed, on a strict interpretation of the relevant provisions, the power extends to judgments enforceable only at common law. They direct that 'no

[13] *Cheshire, North & Fawcett*, p. 585; K. W. Patchett, *Recognition of Commercial Judgments and Awards in the Commonwealth* (London: Butterworths, 1984), p. 173. This option will be unavailable in countries which take the position that a foreign judgment merges the original cause of action.

[14] See also Ghana – Courts Act 1993, s. 87; Nigeria – Foreign Judgments (Reciprocal Enforcement) Act 1990, s. 12; Tanzania – Foreign Judgments (Reciprocal Enforcement) Ordinance 1935, s. 11; Uganda – Foreign Judgments (Reciprocal Enforcement) Act 1961, s. 10; Zambia – Foreign Judgments (Reciprocal Enforcement) Act 1937, s. 12. The power does not exist in the Kenyan, Lesotho, Namibian, South African, Swaziland and Zimbabwean statutes. Nigeria's Reciprocal Enforcement of Judgment Act 1961 does not contain such a provision.

proceedings' will be entertained in any court. Accordingly, it can be argued that both the statutory and common law regimes are affected.

It is significant that power is exercised in the direction of the courts; it commands and directs them as to which civil actions to entertain. The constitutions of the countries under study entrust judicial power to the courts. Thus, the constitutionality of the provisions is questionable.[15] The power to enforce judgments is 'judicial power' and, arguably, should not be subject to executive control or direction. Furthermore, the power is very broad; it directly targets a foreign judgment, regardless of the judgment-creditor. It is possible – albeit improbable – for nationals who obtain foreign judgments to be affected by the exercise of this power. It can be argued that a judgment-creditor whose judgment is denied enforcement as a result of the exercise of this executive power has had their property rights violated. A judgment that orders payment of money is 'property' – a choice in action. International human rights and national constitutions recognise a person's right to property. States should not make enjoyment of a judgment-creditor's property rights contingent on a state of affairs that the judgment-creditor had no hand in creating, i.e. the accordance of less favourable treatment of judgments from the country. A similar Australian statutory provision has been criticised as 'parochial'.[16] It is recommended that, in the countries where it exists, this provision should be repealed.

Description of each national statutory regime

Each of the countries under study has a statutory regime for enforcing foreign judgments. The governing statutes display remarkable similarities on a number of issues and, indeed, in their wording. However, there are also significant differences. The statutes usually deal with issues of private international law and national civil procedure.[17] In the reports below, I focus mainly on their private international law aspects.

[15] See *Rosemond Salemi Akil* v. *Aristotle Kotey*, HI/82/2007 (Court of Appeal, Ghana, 2008), in which this issue was raised but not discussed.

[16] Australia – Foreign Judgment Act 1991, s. 13; M. Tilbury et al., *Conflict of Laws in Australia* (Oxford University Press, 2002), p. 178, n. 25.

[17] These include issues such as whether an application to register should be *ex parte*, by originating summons or motion, or how the registration of the foreign judgment is communicated to the judgment-debtor. These are often addressed in the rules on procedure enacted under the Acts.

Botswana

The statutory regime for enforcing foreign judgments in Botswana is regulated by the Judgments (International Enforcement) Act 1981. The regime only applies to judgments from countries designated by the President of Botswana to benefit from the regime.[18] A judgment from a designated country must be final and conclusive between the parties to it.[19] There must be a sum of money payable under the judgment, which is not a sum payable in respect of taxes, fines or other penalties. In addition, the judgment must have been given after the coming into operation of the order extending the Act to that country.[20]

A judgment-creditor of a judgment to which the Act applies has six years within which they can apply to the High Court to register the judgment. Time starts running from the date of the judgment or, where there have been proceedings by way of appeal against the judgment given in those proceedings, after the date of the last judgment given in those proceedings.[21] The High Court is not bound to register a foreign judgment, although it 'may, subject to proof of prescribed matters, order the judgment to be registered'.[22] A judgment shall not be registered if it has been wholly satisfied,[23] or if it cannot be enforced by execution in the country where it was given.[24] A registered judgment is treated as if it is a judgment originally given by the registering Botswanan court and entered on the date of registration.[25] Where the sum payable under a foreign judgment is expressed in a foreign currency, it shall be registered as if it were a judgment for such a sum in Botswanan pula as is, on the basis of the exchange rate that prevails on the date of the judgment of the original court, equivalent to the sum so payable.[26]

[18] Judgments (International Enforcement) Act 1981, s. 3.

[19] A judgment is deemed final and conclusive even when an appeal is pending or if it is capable of being appealed. However, the court may set aside registration, or adjourn the application to set aside registration of a foreign judgment on either basis (Judgments (International Enforcement) Act 1981, ss. 8 and 3(3)).

[20] Judgments (International Enforcement) Act 1981, s. 3(2).

[21] Ibid., s. 5(1). [22] Ibid., s. 5(1).

[23] The sum of money payable under a foreign judgment includes any interest which, by the law of the country where the judgment was passed, becomes due under the judgment up until the time of registration. After registration, interest accrues as under Botswanan law on a Botswanan judgment: Judgments (International Enforcement) Act 1981, ss. 5(3)(a) and (8).

[24] Judgments (International Enforcement) Act 1981, s. 5(2).

[25] Ibid., s. 5(3). [26] Ibid., s. 5(5).

A judgment-debtor is allowed to apply to set aside the registration of a foreign judgment. There are mandatory and discretionary grounds for setting these foreign judgments aside. The registration of a judgment shall be set aside if the court is satisfied that: the judgment is outside the scope of the Act or was registered in contravention of the Act; the foreign court had no jurisdiction in the case; the judgment-debtor, being the defendant in the foreign court's proceedings, did not (notwithstanding that process may have been duly served on them in accordance with the law of the foreign country) receive notice of those proceedings in sufficient time to enable them to defend the proceedings and therefore did not appear; the judgment was obtained by fraud; enforcement of the judgment would contravene Botswana's public policy, or the rights under the judgment are not vested in the person applying for registration.[27] There is also a discretionary ground for setting aside the registration of foreign judgments. The registration may be set aside if the court is satisfied that the matter in dispute in the foreign court's proceedings had previously, and until the date of the foreign court's judgment, been the subject of a final and conclusive judgment in a court having jurisdiction in the matter.[28]

The jurisdiction of the foreign court is defined differently for three causes of action: actions *in personam*,[29] actions *in rem* (or with their subject matter as immovable property), and any other action. In the case of a judgment given in an action *in personam*, the foreign court is competent: if the judgment-debtor, being a defendant in the foreign court, submitted to its jurisdiction by voluntarily appearing in the proceedings for reasons other than to protect, or obtain the release of, property seized (or threatened with seizure) in the proceedings, or of contesting the jurisdiction of that court; if the judgment-debtor was a plaintiff in, or counterclaimed in, the proceedings in the foreign court; if the judgment-debtor, being a defendant in the foreign court, had before the commencement of the proceedings agreed, in respect of the subject matter of the proceedings, to submit to the jurisdiction of that court, or of the courts of the country; if the judgment-debtor, being a defendant in the foreign court, was at the time when the proceedings were instituted,

[27] Ibid., s. 7(1)(a). [28] Ibid., s. 7(1)(b).

[29] An action *in personam* does not include any matrimonial cause or proceedings in connection with matrimonial matters, administration of the estates of deceased persons, insolvency, winding up of companies, lunacy or guardianship of infants. Judgments (International Enforcement) Act 1981, s. 2(2).

resident in (or if a body corporate, had its principal place of business in) the country of that court, or if the judgment-debtor, being a defendant in the foreign court, had an office or place of business in the country of that court and the proceedings were in respect of a transaction effected through, or at, that office or place. In the case of a judgment given in an action where the subject matter was immovable property, or in an action *in rem* where the subject matter was movable property, the foreign court is deemed to have had jurisdiction, if the property in question was at the time of the proceedings in the foreign court situated in the country of that court. In any other action, the foreign court is deemed to have jurisdiction if its jurisdiction is recognised by Botswanan law.[30]

A foreign court shall not be deemed to have had jurisdiction if: the subject matter of the proceedings is immovable property outside the foreign country; bringing of the proceedings in the foreign court was contrary to a jurisdiction or arbitration agreement (unless there is submission to its jurisdiction), or the judgment-debtor, being a defendant in the foreign proceedings, was a person who under public international law was entitled to immunity from the jurisdiction of the foreign court and did not submit to its jurisdiction.[31]

Gambia

The recognition and enforcement of foreign judgments in Gambia are regulated by the Reciprocal Enforcement of Judgments Act 1922 and the Foreign Judgment Reciprocal Enforcement Act 1936.[32]

Under the 1922 Act, where a judgment has been obtained in the High Court in England or Northern Ireland, or in the Court of Session in Scotland, the judgment-creditor may apply to the High Court at any time within twelve months after the date of judgment, or such longer period as may be allowed by the High Court, to have the judgment registered in the High Court. When such an application is made, the High Court may, if in all the circumstances of the case it thinks it is just and convenient that the judgment shall be enforced in Gambia, order the judgment to be

[30] Judgments (International Enforcement) Act 1981, s. 7(2). [31] Ibid., s. 7(3).

[32] To date, the 1936 Act has been extended only to the Federal Republic of Nigeria and the following courts are deemed superior courts of Nigeria for the purposes of Part I of the Act: the Supreme Court of Nigeria; the High Court of Western Nigeria; the High Court of Northern Nigeria; the High Court of Eastern Nigeria; and the High Court of Lagos (Foreign Judgments Reciprocal Enforcement (Nigeria) Order 1956). The 1936 Act is not discussed in this report, but relevant provisions are referenced in the commentary.

registered.[33] The judgment shall not be registered if: the original court acted without jurisdiction; the judgment-debtor, being a person who was neither carrying on business nor ordinarily resident within the jurisdiction of the original court, did not voluntarily appear or otherwise submit, or agree to submit, to the jurisdiction of that court; the judgment-debtor, being the defendant in the proceedings, was not duly served with the process of the original court and did not appear – notwithstanding that he or she was ordinarily resident or was carrying on business within the jurisdiction of that court – or agree to submit to the jurisdiction of that court; the judgment was obtained by fraud; the judgment-debtor satisfies the High Court either that an appeal is pending, or that he or she is entitled and intends to appeal against the judgment, or the judgment was in respect of a cause of action which for reasons of public policy, or for some other similar reason, could not have been entertained by the High Court.[34]

Where a judgment is registered, the judgment is, as from the date of registration, of the same force and effect as if it had been a judgment originally obtained or entered upon the date of registration in the High Court and proceedings may be taken on it.[35] The High Court then has the same control and jurisdiction over the judgment as it has over similar judgments given by itself, but only insofar as it relates to the execution of the judgment.[36]

The Act empowers the Minister to extend the provisions of the Act to other parts of the Commonwealth.[37]

Ghana

The statutory regime for enforcing foreign judgments in Ghana is regulated by the Courts Act 1993, Order 71 of the High Court Civil Procedure

[33] Reciprocal Enforcement of Judgments Act 1922, s. 3(1). [34] Ibid., s. 3(2)(a)–(f).

[35] Ibid., s. 3(3)(a). [36] Ibid., s. 3(3)(b).

[37] Supreme Court of Sierra Leone; Supreme Court of the State of New South Wales; State of Tasmania and its dependencies in the Commonwealth of Australia and to judgments obtained in the High Court and Court of Appeal of the State of Tasmania and its dependencies. Australian Capital Territory and the Northern Territory in the Commonwealth of Australia and to judgments obtained in the High Court and Court of Appeal of the Australian Capital Territory and the Northern Territory and its dependencies. Orders of Extension 1924/1926 Reciprocal Enforcement of Judgments (State of Tasmania) Order 1975; Reciprocal Enforcement of Judgments (Australia Capital Territory and Northern Territory) Order 1975.

Rules 2004, and the Foreign Judgments and Maintenance Order (Reciprocal Enforcement) Instrument 1993.

The President of Ghana is empowered to designate countries to whose judgments the statutory regime should apply. This is done if he is assured that substantial reciprocity of treatment would be similarly accorded to Ghanaian judgments.[38] To date, only a few countries have been designated.[39] A judgment emanating from an undesignated country cannot be registered under the Act.[40] The regime applies only to judgments which are final and conclusive between the parties[41] and where a sum of money is payable other than in respect of taxes, fines or penalties. The judgment must also have been given after the relevant country was designated.[42]

A judgment-creditor of a judgment to which the regime applies is allowed to apply to the High Court to register the judgment. The application should be made within six years after the date of judgment, or where there has been an appeal, after the last judgment given in those proceedings.[43] It has been held that there is no jurisdiction to grant an extension of the six-year time frame.[44] Moreover, the High Court has discretion to register the judgment[45] and judgment shall not be registered if, at the date of the application, it has been wholly satisfied or it cannot be enforced by execution in the foreign country.[46] Once it is registered the judgment is treated as if it were the High Court's judgment. Accordingly, it carries interest from the date of registration and the registering court retains power on the execution of the judgment.[47]

Where the sum payable under a foreign judgment is expressed in foreign currency, the judgment should be registered as if it were a

[38] Courts Act 1993, s. 81(1).

[39] In the First Schedule to the Foreign Judgments and Maintenance Orders (Reciprocal Enforcement) Instrument 1993, the following countries and courts are designated: Brazil (Supreme Federal Court, Federal Court of Appeal, State High Court); France (*Cours De Cessation, Cours d'Appel*); Israel (Supreme Court); Italy (*Corte d'Appello, Corte di Cessazione*); Japan (Supreme Court of Japan); Lebanon (Court of Appeal, High Court); Senegal (*Cours Suprême, Cours D'Appel*); Spain (*Tribunal Supreme Audiencia Territorial Juez de Primera Instencia*); United Arab Republic (Court of Cassation, Court of Appeal); United Kingdom (High Court of England, High Court of Northern Ireland, Court of Session in Scotland); and any court to which an appeal from any of the foregoing courts lies.

[40] *Republic* v. *Mallet, Ex p. Braun* [1975] 1 GLR 68.

[41] A judgment shall be deemed to be final and conclusive notwithstanding an appeal may be pending against it or that it may still be subject to appeal in the courts of the country of the original court: Courts Act 1993, s. 81(3).

[42] Courts Act 1993, s. 81(2). [43] Ibid., s. 82(2).

[44] *Yankson* v. *Mensah* [1976] 1 GLR 355. [45] Courts Act 1993, s. 82(3).

[46] Ibid., s. 82(4). [47] Ibid., s. 82(5).

judgment for a sum in Ghanaian cedi, based on the exchange rate that prevails on the date of the judgment of the foreign court.[48] In *Broderick* v. *Northern Engineering Product*,[49] the plaintiff registered an English judgment under the Courts Act 1971 (predecessor of the Courts Act 1993), went into execution and realised part of the amount due. When the plaintiff sought to levy further execution, the defendants called for accounts. The issue that had to be determined was the rate of conversion of the cedi to pounds sterling, implemented in calculating the defendants' indebtedness. The choice was between the rate prevailing at the time of the English judgment and execution.[50] The plaintiff argued for the date of execution. At the time, the cedi had depreciated considerably against sterling. It was held that, given the volatility of exchange rates in Ghana, applying the rate prevailing at the time of execution would ensure that the plaintiff obtained what was properly due to him. However, under section 77(5) of the Courts Act 1971 (now section 82(7)), the exchange rate to be used in determining the value of a registered judgment was the rate prevailing at the time the foreign judgment was given. The court applied that rate accordingly, but, recognising the injustice it could occasion, called for reform of the law.

There are mandatory and discretionary grounds under which registration of a foreign judgment can be set aside. With regard to the mandatory grounds, it is provided that the registration shall be set aside if the court is satisfied that the judgment is outside the scope of the Act; the foreign court had no jurisdiction; the judgment-debtor, being the defendant in the proceedings in the foreign court, did not receive notice of these proceedings in sufficient time to enable him to defend the proceedings (notwithstanding that process might have been duly served on him in accordance with the law of the country of the original court) and did not appear; the judgment was obtained by fraud, or enforcement of the judgment would be contrary to Ghana's public policy.[51] Registration may be set aside if the court is satisfied the matter in dispute in the foreign proceedings had, prior to the date of the judgment in the foreign court, been the subject of a final and conclusive judgment by another court of competent jurisdiction.[52] A registered foreign judgment may

[48] Ibid., s. 82(7). [49] [1991] 2 GLR 88.

[50] Other options available, such as the date of registration, or when the original cause of action was accrued, were not discussed.

[51] Courts Act 1993, s. 83(1)(a). [52] Ibid., s. 83(1)(b).

also be set aside if the court is satisfied an appeal is pending or if the judgment-debtor is entitled and intends to appeal.[53]

The jurisdiction of the foreign court is defined differently for three causes of action: actions *in personam*, actions *in rem*, or with their subject matter as immovable property, and any other action. In the case of a judgment given in an action *in personam*, the foreign court is deemed to have had jurisdiction: if the judgment-debtor, being a defendant in the foreign court, submitted to its jurisdiction by voluntarily appearing in the proceedings, other than for the purpose of protecting or obtaining the release of property seized (or threatened with seizure) in the proceedings, or of contesting the jurisdiction of that court; if the judgment-debtor was plaintiff in, or counter-claimed in, the proceedings in the foreign court; if the judgment-debtor, being a defendant in the foreign court, had before the commencement of the proceedings agreed, in respect of the subject matter of the proceedings, to submit to the jurisdiction of that court, or of the courts of that country; if the judgment-debtor, being a defendant in the foreign court, was, at the time the proceedings were instituted, resident in (or if a body corporate, had its principal place of business in) the country of that court, or if the judgment-debtor, being a defendant in the foreign court, had an office or place of business in the foreign country and the proceedings in that court were in respect of a transaction effected through or at that office or place.[54] In the case of a judgment given in an action where the subject matter is immovable property, or in an action *in rem* where the subject matter is movable property, the foreign court is deemed to be competent if the property in question is, at the time of the proceedings in the foreign court, situated in the country of that court.[55] In any other action, the foreign court is competent if its jurisdiction is recognised by Ghanaian law.[56]

A foreign court shall not be deemed to have had jurisdiction if: the subject matter of the proceedings is immovable property outside the foreign country, the bringing of the proceedings in the court contravenes a jurisdiction or arbitration agreement (unless there is submission to its jurisdiction), or the judgment-debtor is a person who, under public international law, is entitled to immunity from the jurisdiction of the foreign court and has not submitted to its jurisdiction.

Ashurst Morris Crisp v. *Peter Awoonor Renner*[57] illustrates an unsuccessful attempt to set aside a registered judgment on the basis that the

[53] Ibid., s. 84(1). [54] Ibid., s. 83(2)(a). [55] Ibid., s. 83(2)(b). [56] Ibid., s. 83(2)(c).
[57] (1931–7) Div. Ct. 107.

foreign court lacked jurisdiction. The plaintiff obtained leave of the English court to serve a writ of summons, which was duly served on the defendant in the Gold Coast (now Ghana). Upon the defendant's instruction, his counsel entered an unconditional appearance and filed a defence, but subsequently abandoned further proceedings in the action. Judgment was given against the defendant and registered in the Gold Coast. In an application to set aside the registration, the applicant argued that, as a person neither carrying on business nor ordinarily resident in England, he did not submit to the jurisdiction of the English court. The court rejected this argument and held that the defendant, through his counsel, had submitted to the English court's jurisdiction.

Kenya

The statutory regime for enforcing foreign judgments in Kenya is regulated by the Foreign Judgments (Reciprocal Enforcement) Act 1984, the Foreign Judgments (Reciprocal Enforcement) (Extension of Act) Order 1984 and the Foreign Judgments (Reciprocal Enforcement) Rules 1984.

The regime applies only to judgments from designated countries.[58] The Minister of Justice is empowered to extend the Act to any country, if satisfied provisions which are substantially reciprocal will be or have been made by that country for the enforcement therein of judgments given by the superior or subordinate courts in Kenya,[59] or in order to give effect to an agreement between Kenya and another country.[60]

The scope of judgments to which the Act applies is quite broad. It encompasses both money and non-money judgments. Thus, a judgment whereby a sum of money is made payable; under which movable property is ordered to be delivered to any person; in criminal proceedings for the payment of a sum of money in respect of compensation or damage to an injured person, or for the delivery of movable property by way of restitution to an injured person, and in respect of an arbitration award, are all enforceable under the Act.[61]

[58] Under the Foreign Judgments (Reciprocal Enforcement) (Extension of Act) Order 1984, the following countries were designated: Australia, Malawi, Seychelles, Tanzania, Uganda, Zambia, the United Kingdom and Rwanda. See *In re. Lowenthal and Air France* 1966 (2) ALR Comm. 301, [1967] EA 75; *Italframe Ltd* v. *Mediterranean Shipping Co.* [1986] KLR 54, [1985] LLR 236.

[59] Foreign Judgments (Reciprocal Enforcement) Act 1984, s. 13.

[60] Ibid., s. 14.

[61] Ibid., s. 3(1).

Certain judgments – both money and non-money – are excluded from the scope of the Act on the bases of the proceedings from whence they emanate, or their character.[62] For example, the Act does not apply to a judgment to the extent where it provides for the payment of a sum of money by way of exemplary, punitive or multiple damages, nor to a judgment in bankruptcy proceedings, proceedings for the winding up or reorganisation of a corporation, or to proceedings for judicial arrangements, compositions or similar matters. Similarly, a judgment given in proceedings instituted in breach of a foreign jurisdiction agreement (except where the judgment-debtor has submitted to the jurisdiction) and a foreign judgment given in proceedings founded on, and to enforce, another foreign judgment – a judgment on a judgment – are excluded.[63]

The rules on international competence are similarly broad.[64] Submission (for example, through the judgment-debtor's voluntary appearance or a jurisdiction agreement[65]), habitual residence (or in the case of artificial persons: place of incorporation, place of business and location of headquarters) and, in defined situations, having a branch or agent, are all bases of international competence.[66] In the case of a claim arising from a contract, where the obligation was the subject of the proceedings and was, or was to be, wholly or mainly performed in a country, that country's courts are internationally competent.[67] In the case of an action to recover damages for physical injury or the death of a person, or for damage to tangible property, if the circumstances giving rise to injury, death or damage substantially occurred in a country, or the injury or damage was suffered in that country, the courts of that country are internationally competent.[68] In the case of a judgment given in an action *in rem*, or any other action to determine rights of ownership, use or possession of immovable property, or tangible movable property, the courts of the *situs* of the property in question at the time of instituting the proceedings are internationally competent.[69]

A court shall not be treated as internationally competent if the subject matter of the proceedings is, under Kenya's private international law, within the exclusive jurisdiction of another country's courts.[70] Nor is a

[62] Ibid., s. 3(3)(a)–(j). [63] Ibid., s. 3(3)(k) and (m). [64] Ibid., s. 4(1)(a)–(i).

[65] A jurisdiction agreement entered into as a result of a statutory requirement is not effective.

[66] *In re. Lowenthal and Air France* 1966 (2) ALR Comm. 301, [1967] EA 75.

[67] Foreign Judgments (Reciprocal Enforcement) Act 1984, s. 4(1)(g).

[68] Ibid., s. 4(1)(i). [69] Ibid., s. 4(1)(h). [70] Ibid., s. 4(2)(a).

foreign court internationally competent by reason only of the fact that the judgment-debtor, being the defendant in the original court, appeared (conditionally or otherwise) in the proceedings to contest the jurisdiction of the court, to invite the court in its discretion not to exercise its jurisdiction, or to protect, or obtain the release of, property seized or threatened with seizure in those proceedings.[71] Furthermore, a court is not internationally competent where the judgment-debtor is a person who, under public international law, is entitled to immunity from the jurisdiction of the foreign court and does not appear other than to contest the court's jurisdiction.[72]

In assessing where a foreign court is internationally competent, great weight is given to its findings of fact. Thus, its findings of fact, whether express or implied, shall constitute conclusive evidence of the fact found, and in any other case, be sufficient proof of that fact unless the contrary is shown,[73] if the judgment-debtor appeared in those proceedings and did not contest the jurisdiction of the court.

A judgment-creditor of a judgment to which the Act applies may apply to the High Court to register the judgment within six years of the date of the judgment or, where there have been proceedings by way of appeal against the judgment, of the date of the last judgment in the proceedings.[74] It is sufficient if the application to register is within the six-year time limit, even if the registration is not completed until after the six years has expired. In the words of Justice Lenaola, 'time stops running when proceedings are instituted and not when they are finalized or when they are ongoing'.[75] If the High Court is satisfied as to the proof of matters required under the Act, it shall order the judgment to be registered. However, the court shall not register a judgment if it considers that the judgment has been wholly satisfied or could not be enforced by execution in the foreign country.[76] A registered judgment is, for the purposes of execution, of the same force and effect as a judgment of the High Court entered at the date of registration.[77]

Where a sum payable under a judgment to be registered under this Act is expressed in foreign currency, the judgment may be registered as a

[71] Ibid., s. 4(2)(b). [72] Ibid., s. 4(2)(c). [73] Ibid., s. 4(3). [74] Ibid., s. 5(1).

[75] *Society of Lloyd's* v. *Larby* [2004] LLR 5919.

[76] Foreign Judgments (Reciprocal Enforcement) Act 1984, s. 6. *Herman Phillip Steyn* v. *Charles Thys* [2011] eKLR.

[77] Foreign Judgments (Reciprocal Enforcement) Act 1984, s. 8. *A Dewhurst* v. *GT Wilson* (1954) 27 KLR 42; *Pioneer General Assurance Society Ltd* v. *Zulfikarali Nimji Javer* [2006] eKLR.

judgment for a sum payable in equivalent sums in Kenyan shillings, based on the rate of exchange prevailing at the time of registration.[78]

There are a number of grounds on which registration of a foreign judgment may be set aside.[79] For example, these include where: the foreign court was internationally incompetent; the judgment-debtor did not appear in the foreign court and the jurisdiction of that court was based upon an agreement by the judgment-debtor to submit to its jurisdiction, which is invalid under Kenya's private international law; the judgment was given in breach of natural justice, or was obtained by fraud, or enforcement of the judgment would be manifestly contrary to Kenya's public policy.[80] A registered judgment may also be set aside if there is a binding and conclusive Kenyan judgment which is irreconcilable with the foreign judgment, and the Kenyan proceedings were instituted before the foreign proceedings.[81] Furthermore, a registered judgment may be set aside where there are Kenyan laws which, by virtue of Kenya's private international law, would have been applicable notwithstanding the choice of any other system of law by the judgment-creditor and the judgment-debtor, had the proceedings been brought in Kenya, and where the judgment disregards such Kenyan laws in some material respect.[82]

The Act allows the judgment-debtor to apply to set aside a registered judgment to the extent that its enforcement would require payment of sums in excess of monetary limits upon liability imposed by any Kenyan statute which applies under Kenya's private international law.[83] In addition, where

[78] Foreign Judgments (Reciprocal Enforcement) Act 1984, s. 7. *Ssebaggala* v. *Kenya National Shipping Line Ltd* [2000] LLR 931 (the date of conversion is when the judgment is registered and not when it was enforced).

[79] Foreign Judgments (Reciprocal Enforcement) Act 1984, s. 10. A decision not to set aside registration may be appealed: *Patel* v. *Bank of Baroda* [2000] LLR 3413. See also *Board of Governors of St Johns College* v. *John Nganyi Lugoyi* [2008] eKLR.

[80] *Patel* v. *Bank of Baroda* [2001] EA 189, [2000] LLR 3491 (public policy defence cannot be founded on a repealed statute). A default judgment may be registered. *Northern Executive Aviation Ltd* v. *Ibis Aviation Ltd*, Civil Suit No. 1088 of 1998 (High Court, Kenya, 2001).

[81] Foreign Judgments (Reciprocal Enforcement) Act 1984, s. 10(f). Under s. 10(e) of the Act, the existence of a prior final and conclusive judgment given by another foreign court on the same cause of action is also a basis for setting aside registration.

[82] Foreign Judgments (Reciprocal Enforcement) Act 1984, s. 10(i). Under s. 10(j) of the Act, a registered judgment may also be set aside if, in the foreign litigation, it was necessary for the court (in order to give its judgment) to decide a question relating to some specified matters, and if the decision of the foreign court is different from that which the High Court of Kenya would have reached by applying Kenya's private international law to that question.

[83] Foreign Judgments (Reciprocal Enforcement) Act 1984, s. 10(3).

the High Court is satisfied in an application made by a judgment-debtor that the sums, including costs, awarded under a registered judgment are substantially in excess of those which would have been awarded by the High Court on the basis of the findings of law and fact made by the foreign court (had the assessment of those sums been made in proceedings before the High Court), it may set aside the judgment to the extent of that excess.

A Kenyan court is barred from entertaining any proceedings brought by a judgment-debtor for the recovery of a sum payable under a foreign judgment, to the extent to which it is a judgment for exemplary, punitive or multiple damages.[84]

Lesotho

The statutory regime for enforcing foreign judgments in Lesotho is regulated by the Reciprocal Enforcement of Judgments Act 1922 and the Reciprocal Enforcement of Judgments Rules of Court 1923. The Act applies to money judgments obtained from the High Court in England or Ireland, or in the Court of Session in Scotland and arbitration awards.[85] The Act empowers the King of Lesotho to extend its provisions to other Commonwealth countries.[86]

A judgment-creditor has twelve months, or such longer period as the court may allow, within which to apply to the High Court of Lesotho for its judgment to be registered. On such an application, the court may, if in all the circumstances it thinks it is 'just and convenient' that the judgment should be enforced in Lesotho, order it to be registered.[87]

No judgment shall be registered if: the original court has acted without jurisdiction; the judgment-debtor did not submit to the court's jurisdiction, was not duly served with the process of the original court and did not appear, or has satisfied the court either that an appeal is pending, or that he or she intends to appeal against the judgment; the judgment was obtained by fraud, or was in respect of a cause of action which, for reasons of public policy or other similar reason, could not have been entertained by the High Court of Lesotho.[88] Registration may also be

[84] Ibid., s. 17(2). [85] Reciprocal Enforcement of Judgments Act 1922, s. 2.

[86] Ibid., s. 6(1). The Act has been extended to specific courts in: Swaziland, Southern Rhodesia (Zimbabwe), Northern Rhodesia (Zambia), Zanzibar Protectorate (Tanzania), Nyasaland Protectorate (Malawi), Kenya Colony and Protectorate (Kenya) and New Zealand. See Extension of Reciprocity, High Commissioner's Notice 96 of 1922.

[87] Ibid., s. 3(1). [88] Ibid., s. 3(2).

set aside if the judgment-debtor shows that it is 'not just or convenient that the judgment should be enforced in Lesotho or for other sufficient reasons'.[89] A registered judgment has the same force and effect as a judgment of the registering court.[90]

Before the court can order that a foreign judgment be registered under the Act, it must be satisfied that the application complies fully with the provisions of the Act. Accordingly, it is material for the applicant to show in his or her application for registration of a foreign judgment that the judgment was obtained in a superior court, which was sitting in part of Her Majesty's Dominions where there are similar legislative provisions to reciprocate for the judgment obtained from the Lesotho High Court.[91]

Namibia

Namibia's statutory regime for enforcing foreign judgments is governed by the Enforcement of Foreign Civil Judgments Act 1994. The regime applies only to judgments from designated countries. The Act empowers the Minister of Justice to designate any country with which Namibia has entered into an agreement providing for the reciprocal enforcement of foreign civil judgments as a beneficiary of the regime.[92] The Act applies only to final judgments or orders for the payment of money by a court in civil proceedings.[93] Such a judgment must be enforceable by execution in the country where it has been given. It does not include a judgment or order given or made for the payment of a tax, fine or other penalty, or for the periodical payment of sums of money towards the maintenance of a person.[94]

A judgment-creditor of a judgment to which the Act applies must lodge a certified copy of it with the clerk of an appropriate Namibian Magistrates' Court for its registration.[95] The clerk is obliged to register

89 Reciprocal Enforcement of Judgments Rules of Court 1923, s. 12.

90 Reciprocal Enforcement of Judgments Act 1922, s. 3(3).

91 *ABSA Bank Ltd* v. *Latela*, CIV/APN/466/01 (High Court, Lesotho, 2004).

92 Enforcement of Foreign Civil Judgments Act 1994, s. 2. To date South Africa is the only country that has been designated. See Government Gazette of the Republic of Namibia, No. 1095 of 15 June 1995.

93 The International Co-operation in Criminal Matters Act 2000 establishes a different regime for enforcing judgments resulting from criminal proceedings in designated countries.

94 Enforcement of Foreign Civil Judgments Act 1994, s. 1.

95 Unlike the High Court, there are monetary and territorial limitations of the jurisdiction of a Magistrates' Court. It is unclear from the Act whether a foreign judgment for a sum exceeding that which is within the jurisdiction of the Magistrates' Court can nonetheless be enforced by the court.

the judgment and notify the judgment-debtor of the registration.[96] A registered judgment has the same effect as a civil judgment of the court where it is registered.[97]

If the amount payable under a judgment to be registered is expressed in foreign currency, the judgment shall be registered as if it were a judgment for such an amount in Namibian dollars, calculated at the opening rate of exchange – as advised by the Bank of Namibia – on the date of registration.[98]

Grounds exist for setting aside the registration of a foreign judgment.[99] These include the fact that: the foreign court did not have jurisdiction in the circumstances of the case; the judgment was obtained in breach of natural justice or by fraud, or the enforcement of the judgment would contravene Namibia's public policy. Registration shall also be set aside if the court is satisfied that the matter in dispute in the proceedings had, prior to the date of the foreign judgment, been the subject of a final judgment by another court of competent jurisdiction in civil proceedings before such a court, or the judgment has become prescribed, either under Namibian law[100] or the law of the designated country concerned.

A foreign court shall be deemed to have had jurisdiction if the judgment-debtor submitted to its jurisdiction (by instituting proceedings, voluntary appearance or jurisdiction agreement), or was a defendant in the foreign proceedings and at the time the proceedings were instituted, was resident in, or being a juristic person, had their registered office or principal place of business in, such a designated country, or else at any time had an office or place of business in such a designated country through, or at which, the transaction relative to the proceedings was effected. In an action relating to immovable property, the foreign court has jurisdiction if, at the time the proceedings were instituted, the

[96] Enforcement of Foreign Civil Judgments Act 1994, s. 3(1)–(3). Under s. 8 of the Act, the notice operates as an interdict against the judgment-debtor on whom it is served, and against any person having knowledge of such notice, not to remove or dispose of any assets of the judgment-debtor if such removal or disposal would prejudice the execution of the judgment.

[97] Enforcement of Foreign Civil Judgments Act 1994, s. 4(1).

[98] Ibid., s. 3(4). Section 31(ii) of the International Co-operation in Criminal Matters Act 2000 also adopts the exchange rate which prevails on the date a foreign judgment is registered.

[99] Ibid., s. 5.

[100] The Prescription Act 1969 does not specifically stipulate a prescription period for foreign judgments. It lays down a thirty-year prescription period for 'judgment debts' and three years for 'any other debt'. Prescription Act 1969, s. 11(a)(ii) and (d).

property was situated in the designated country. In any other proceedings, the foreign court has jurisdiction if its jurisdiction is recognised by Namibian law.[101]

A foreign court shall be deemed not to have had jurisdiction in proceedings relating to immovable property situated outside the country where the court is located or, except in cases of submission, in proceedings instituted in contravention of a jurisdiction agreement, or else in proceedings where the person against whom the judgment is granted is entitled, under public international law, to immunity from the foreign court's jurisdiction and has not submitted to it.[102]

Nigeria

The statutory regime for enforcing foreign judgments in Nigeria is regulated by the Reciprocal Enforcement of Judgments Ordinance 1922 (hereinafter, 'Ordinance') and the Foreign Judgments (Reciprocal Enforcement) Act 1961 (hereinafter, 'Act').[103] For a long time confusion reigned as to the relationship between the Ordinance and the Act, especially regarding the enforcement of UK judgments. By a series of Supreme Court decisions, it is now well settled that the Ordinance was not repealed by the Act. The Ordinance still applies to the United Kingdom and to parts of Her Majesty's dominions to which it was extended by proclamation under section 5 of the Ordinance before the coming into force of the Act. The Act will become applicable to these countries only when they have been so designated under the Act by the Minister of Justice.[104] However, so far, no such country has been

[101] Enforcement of Foreign Civil Judgments Act 1994, s. 7(4)(a)–(c).

[102] Enforcement of Foreign Civil Judgments Act 1994, s. 7(5).

[103] This section focuses mainly on the Ordinance. Currently, no country has been designated under the Act. However, some courts have erroneously registered foreign judgments under it. See, e.g., *Teleglobe America Inc.* v. *21st Century Technologies Ltd* [2008] 17 NWLR 108 (registering a judgment from the Circuit Court of Fairfax County, Virginia, United States); and *Hyppolite* v. *Egharevba* [1998] 11 NWLR 598 (the court set aside the registration of a judgment from the Superior Court of Suffolk County, Massachusetts, United States on the grounds of a lack of international competence, but failed to appreciate that Massachusetts had not been designated under the Act).

[104] *Macaulay* v. *RZB of Austria* [2003] 18 NWLR 282, [2004] 4 WRN 1 (reversing *Macaulay* v. *RZB of Austria* [1999] 4 NWLR 599); *Witt & Busch Ltd* v. *Dale Power Systems Plc* [2007] 17 NWLR 1; *Grosvenor Casinos Ltd* v. *Ghassan Halaoui* [2009] 10 NWLR 309 (on appeal from *Halaoui* v. *Grosvenor Casinos Ltd* [2002] 17 NWLR 28); *Conoil Plc* v. *Vitol SA* [2012] 2 NWLR 50.

designated. Remarkably, even though no country has been designated under the Act, in some instances, courts have invoked its provisions or registered foreign judgments under it.[105] As the Supreme Court tersely observes, this is 'a mistake'.[106]

The Ordinance applies to money judgments obtained from the High Court in England or Ireland or in the Court of Session in Scotland.[107] The Act empowers the Governor-General (now President) to extend its provisions to other parts of Her Majesty's dominion outside the United Kingdom.[108] A judgment-creditor has twelve months, or such longer period as the court may allow, within which to apply for registration of the judgment.[109] In *Alhaji Risikatu Ramon* v. *Jinadu*,[110] an English judgment registered in Nigeria three years after it was given was set aside, because it was registered outside the twelve-month registration period and without leave of the court.

On an application to register a foreign judgment, the court[111] may, if in all the circumstances it thinks it is 'just and convenient' that the judgment should be enforced in Nigeria, order the judgment to be registered.[112] In *International Finance Corp.* v. *DSNL Offshore Ltd*,[113] there was an appeal against a decision to set aside the registration of an English judgment on the basis that it was not 'just or convenient' to register it as there were proceedings pending before a Nigerian court which, apparently, dealt with a different issue. In allowing the appeal, it was held that in setting aside the registration of a foreign judgment, a court must consider all relevant materials placed before it. It was inappropriate to only consider a pending Nigerian action and ignore other facts or materials placed before the court, such as the fact that there

105 See, e.g., *Teleglobe America Inc.* v. *21st Century Technologies Ltd* [2008] 17 NWLR 108; *Hyppolite* v. *Egharevba* [1998] 11 NWLR 598; *Momah* v. *VAB Petroleum Inc.* [2000] 2 SC 142, [2000] 4 NWLR 534; *Halaoui* v. *Grosvenor Casinos Ltd* [2002] 17 NWLR 28; *Macaulay* v. *RZB of Austria* [1999] 4 NWLR 599.

106 *Grosvenor Casinos Ltd* v. *Ghassan Halaoui* [2009] 10 NWLR 309 at 334.

107 Reciprocal Enforcement of Judgments Ordinance 1922, s. 3(1).

108 Ibid., s. 5(1).

109 *Marine & General Assurance Co. Plc* v. *Overseas Union Insurance Ltd* [2006] 4 NWLR 622 (reversing *Overseas Union Insurance Ltd* v. *Marine & General Assurance Co. Plc* [2001] 9 NWLR 92); *Macaulay* v. *RZB of Austria* [2003] 18 NWLR 282, [2004] 4 WRN 1.

110 [1986] 5 NWLR 100.

111 Any High Court in Nigeria has jurisdiction to register a foreign judgment – registration is not the preserve of the Federal High Court: *Wide Seas Shipping Ltd* v. *Wale Sea Foods Ltd* [1983] 1 FNLR 530.

112 Reciprocal Enforcement of Judgments Ordinance 1922, s. 3(1).

113 [2008] 9 NWLR 606.

was no appeal pending against the foreign decision in a foreign court and that the parties had agreed in their contract that any decision in an action brought on their contract should be conclusive and enforceable in any jurisdiction.

Under section 3(2) of the Ordinance, no judgment shall be registered if: the foreign court has acted without jurisdiction; the judgment-debtor has not submitted to the jurisdiction of the court,[114] was not duly served with the process of the original court and did not appear,[115] or has satisfied the court either that an appeal is pending or that they intend to appeal the judgment, that the judgment was obtained by fraud, or was in respect of a cause of action which, for reasons of public policy or other similar reason, could not have been entertained by the Nigerian court.[116] Even though the Ordinance does not expressly say so, these are also the grounds for an application to set aside registration.[117] Whether the registration of a foreign judgment is based on an *ex parte* application or on notice, the judgment-debtor is allowed to apply to set it aside. This is so even if the application to register the judgment is based on notice and is not opposed by the judgment-debtor.[118]

A registered judgment has the same force and effect as a judgment of the registering court.[119] The effect of registering a foreign judgment in a Nigerian court is, for all intents and purposes, to make it a judgment of the Nigerian court. The registering court has jurisdiction to set aside the registration and, when it does so, the validity of the foreign judgment is not affected.[120] Once a judgment has been registered, it can be enforced in any state in the Nigerian federation. It is not necessary to make a fresh application under section 3 of the Ordinance to register the judgment in

[114] *Grosvenor Casinos Ltd* v. *Ghassan Halaoui* [2009] 10 NWLR 309 (on appeal from *Halaoui* v. *Grosvenor Casinos Ltd* [2002] 17 NWLR 28); *Witt & Busch Ltd* v. *Dale Power Systems Plc* [2007] 17 NWLR 1 (on appeal from *Dale Power Systems Plc* v. *Witt & Busch Ltd* [2001] 8 NWLR 699, [2001] 33 WRN 62).

[115] *Shona-Jason Nigeria Ltd* v. *Omegar Air Ltd* [2005] WRN 123, [2006] 1 NWLR 1.

[116] *Conoil Plc* v. *Vitol SA* [2012] 2 NWLR 50 at 92–3 on the meaning of 'other similar reason'. The court held that the phrase ought to be confined to matters that are against public interest in the sense that they are injurious to public welfare or public good.

[117] Such an application should be made by a petition and not by way of motion on notice. *International Finance Corp.* v. *DSNL Offshore Ltd* [2008] 9 NWLR 606.

[118] *Shona-Jason Nigeria Ltd* v. *Omegar Air Ltd* [2005] WRN 123, [2006] 1 NWLR 1; *Consolidated Contractors (Oil and Gas) Co. SAL* v. *Masiri* [2011] 3 NWLR 283. It has been held that the only legally acceptable means of setting aside a registered foreign judgment is by petition and not by motion on notice: *Mudasiru* v. *Abdulahi* [2009] 17 NWLR 547.

[119] Reciprocal Enforcement of Judgments Ordinance 1922, s. 3(a).

[120] *Shona-Jason Nigeria Ltd* v. *Omegar Air Ltd* [2005] WRN 123 at 153, [2006] 1 NWLR 1 at 28.

a High Court in another state in Nigeria.[121] The registering court has the same control and jurisdiction over the judgment as it has over similar judgments given by it; however, this is insofar as it relates to execution under the Ordinance.[122]

South Africa

The statutory regime for enforcing foreign judgments in South Africa is governed by the Enforcement of Foreign Civil Judgments Act 1988. The Act empowers the Minister of Justice to designate countries to be beneficiaries of the regime.[123] There is no express requirement that this should be done on the basis of reciprocity. The Act applies only to final judgments or orders for the payment of money, given by a court in civil proceedings[124] and enforceable by execution in the country where they were given. It does not apply to judgments or orders for the payment of any taxes, fines or penalties, or for the periodical payment of sums of money towards the maintenance of any person.[125]

A judgment-creditor of a judgment to which the Act applies may apply to the clerk of an appropriate Magistrates' Court to register it. On receipt of a certified copy of the judgment, the clerk is obliged to register it and cause a notice of registration to be issued and served on the judgment-debtor.[126] A registered judgment has the same effect as a civil judgment given by the registering court.[127]

121 *Goodchild* v. *Onwuka* [1961] 1 All NLR 163.

122 Reciprocal Enforcement of Judgments Ordinance 1922, s. 3(b). See generally *Adwork Ltd* v. *Nigeria Airways Ltd* [2000] 2 NWLR 415, which held that, when a judgment has been registered in a foreign country, the original court which gave the judgment does not lose its jurisdiction in relation to the execution process just because the judgment has been registered in a foreign country. However, once it is recognised that the registering court has the same powers of execution as the original court, it becomes important to closely monitor what the registering court is doing in relation to the execution of the registered judgment in order to ensure there is no conflict in the exercise of the execution powers of either court.

123 Enforcement of Foreign Civil Judgments Act 1988. Currently, only Namibia has been designated.

124 A different regime for enforcing judgments resulting from criminal proceedings is established by the International Co-operation in Criminal Matters Act 1996.

125 Enforcement of Foreign Civil Judgments Act 1988, s. 1.

126 Ibid., s. 3(1)–(3). Under s. 8 of the Act, the notice operates as an interdict against the judgment-debtor on whom it is served, and against any person having knowledge of such notice, not to remove or dispose of any assets of the judgment-debtor if such removal or disposal would prejudice the execution of the judgment.

127 Ibid., s. 4(1).

Where the amount payable under a foreign judgment is expressed in foreign currency, the judgment shall be registered as if it were a judgment for such an amount in South African rand, calculated at the rate of exchange prevailing on the date of the judgment.[128]

There are grounds upon which registration of the foreign judgment shall be set aside on application by the judgment-debtor.[129] Where the foreign court does not have jurisdiction in the circumstances of the case, the judgment was obtained in breach of natural justice or by fraud, or enforcement of the judgment would be contrary to South Africa's public policy, the court shall set the registration aside. The registration shall also be set aside if the court is satisfied that the matter in dispute in the foreign proceedings had, prior to the date of the judgment, been the subject of a final judgment by another court of competent jurisdiction in civil proceedings before such a court, or the judgment has become prescribed under either South African law or the designated country's law.

A foreign court is deemed to have had jurisdiction if the judgment-debtor submitted to its jurisdiction (through instituting proceedings, voluntary appearance or a jurisdiction agreement). The foreign court also has jurisdiction if the judgment-debtor was a defendant in the proceedings before it and, at the institution of the proceedings, was resident in, or being a juristic person, had its registered office or principal place of business in, such a designated country, or at any time had an office or place of business there through, or at which, the transaction relative to the proceedings was effected. In an action relating to immovable property, the foreign court has jurisdiction if the property was situated in the designated country at the time the proceedings were instituted. In any other proceedings, the foreign court has jurisdiction if its jurisdiction is recognised under South African law.[130]

A foreign court is deemed not to have had jurisdiction in proceedings relating to immovable property situated outside the designated country or, except in cases of submission, in proceedings instituted in breach of a jurisdiction agreement, or else in proceedings where the judgment-debtor was entitled to immunity from the court's jurisdiction[131] under public international law and therefore did not submit to it.

[128] Ibid., s. 3(4). Section 32(b) of the International Co-operation in Criminal Matters Act 1996 adopts the rate which prevails on the date a foreign judgment is registered.

[129] Enforcement of Foreign Civil Judgments Act 1988, s. 5(1). See also the Protection of Businesses Act 1978.

[130] Enforcement of Foreign Civil Judgments Act 1988, s. 7(4).

[131] Ibid., s. 7(5).

Swaziland

The statutory regime for enforcing foreign judgments in Swaziland is regulated by the Reciprocal Enforcement of Judgments Act 1922 and the Reciprocal Enforcement of Judgments Rules 1923. The Act applies to money judgments obtained from the High Court in England or Ireland or in the Court of Session in Scotland and arbitration awards.[132] The Act empowers the Prime Minister to extend its provisions to other Commonwealth countries.[133] In *Mamba* v. *Mamba*, the court refused to register a judgment from Maryland, United States on the grounds that the United States was not on the list of countries that enjoy reciprocal enforcement of judgment arrangements with Swaziland.[134]

A judgment-creditor has twelve months, or such longer period as the court may allow, within which to apply to the High Court of Swaziland to register the judgment. On such an application, the court may, if in all the circumstances it thinks it is 'just and convenient' that the judgment should be enforced in Swaziland, order it to be registered.[135] It is provided that no judgment shall be registered if: the original court has acted without jurisdiction; the judgment-debtor did not submit to the jurisdiction of the court, was not duly served with the process of the original court and did not appear, or satisfies the court either that an appeal is pending or that they intend to appeal the judgment; the judgment was obtained by fraud, or was in respect of a cause of action which, for reasons of public policy or other similar reason, could not have been entertained by the High Court of Swaziland.[136] Registration of a foreign judgment may also be set aside if the judgment-debtor shows that it is 'not just or convenient that the judgment should be enforced in Swaziland or for other sufficient reasons'.[137] A registered judgment has the same force and effect as a judgment of the registering court.

[132] Reciprocal Enforcement of Judgments Act 1922, ss. 2 and 3(1).

[133] The Act has been extended to specific courts in Lesotho, Botswana, Southern Rhodesia (Zimbabwe), Zambia, Zanzibar, Malawi, Kenya, New Zealand, Western Australia, Tanzania (except Zanzibar), Uganda, New South Wales, Victoria, Territory of North Australia and Territory of Central Australia. See Notice No. 97 of 1992, reproduced in C. Schulze, *On Jurisdiction and the Recognition and Enforcement of Foreign Money Judgments* (Pretoria: UNISA Press, 2005), p. 277.

[134] *Mamba* v. *Mamba*, Case No. 1451/09 (High Court, Swaziland, 2011). The court also rejected a plea to enforce the judgment at common law. The court reasoned that to do so will be inconsistent with the Act.

[135] Reciprocal Enforcement of Judgments Act 1922, s. 3(1).

[136] Ibid., s. 3(2).

[137] See Reciprocal Enforcement of Judgments Rules 1923, s. 15.

Tanzania

The statutory regime for enforcing foreign judgments in Tanzania[138] is governed by the Foreign Judgments (Reciprocal Enforcement) Ordinance 1935, the Judgments Extension Ordinance[139] and the Foreign Judgments (Reciprocal Enforcement) Rules 1936.

The latter Ordinance empowers the Governor in Council (now President) to designate, on the basis of reciprocity, countries whose judgments will benefit from the regime,[140] or to direct that specific provisions of the Act apply to judgments from the United Kingdom and Her Majesty's dominions.[141] The Ordinance applies only to judgments which are final and conclusive and where there is payable under the judgment a sum of money, other than in respect of taxes, fines or penalties.[142]

A judgment-creditor of a judgment to which the Ordinance applies may apply to the High Court to register the judgment within six years after the date of the judgment, or where there have been proceedings by way of appeal against the judgment, after the date of the last judgment given in those proceedings. A court shall not register a judgment, if at the date of application it has been wholly satisfied, or it could not be enforced by execution in the foreign country.[143] In *FX Oliso-Emosingoit* v. *East*

138 A different regime applies to enforcing foreign judgments in Zanzibar, which is a semi-autonomous part of the United Republic of Tanzania. The regime is regulated by the British Judgments Decree and the Judgments Extension Decree: see W. B. Kapinga, 'Tanzania' in L. W. Newman (ed.), *Enforcement of Money Judgments* (New York: JurisNet LLC, 2006), vol. 3, p. 1.

139 This ordinance makes provision for the enforcement of judgments from the High Courts of Kenya, Uganda, Malawi and Zanzibar.

140 Foreign Judgments (Reciprocal Enforcement) Ordinance 1935, s. 3(1); *Willow Investment* v. *Mbomba Ntumba* [1996] TLR 377.

141 Foreign Judgments (Reciprocal Enforcement) Ordinance 1935, s. 9. See Foreign Judgments (Reciprocal Enforcement) (General Application) Order 1936 (extending Pt I of the Ordinance to the United Kingdom and Her Majesty's dominions); Foreign Judgments (Reciprocal Enforcement) (Extension of Part I) Order 1936 (extending the application of Pt I of the Ordinance to named superior courts in: Basutoland [now Lesotho]; Bechuanaland [now Botswana]; Ceylon [now Sri Lanka]; Mauritius; New South Wales; Northern Rhodesia [now Zambia]; Seychelles, Somaliland, Southern Rhodesia [now Zimbabwe]; Swaziland; and the United Kingdom). It was held in *Shah Devsi Vardhaman* v. *TCN Haridas* [1958] EA 527 that the effect of the General Application Order was merely to bring Her Majesty's dominions within the scope of s. 3 and that an order under s. 3 is required specifically, applying Pt I of the Ordinance to a particular territory before judgments of the courts of that territory can be registered under the Ordinance.

142 Foreign Judgments (Reciprocal Enforcement) Ordinance 1935, s. 3(2).

143 Ibid., s. 4(1).

African Community, the court observed that the fact that the 'Community had no property in England' would 'on that ground alone' have been enough to refuse registration.[144] A registered judgment has the same effect as a judgment originally given in the registering court and entered on the date of registration.[145]

Where the sum payable under a judgment to be registered is expressed in foreign currency, the judgment shall be registered as if it were a judgment for such a sum in Tanzanian shillings, based on the exchange rate that prevails on the date of the judgment of the foreign court.[146]

On an application by the judgment-debtor, the court is empowered to set aside the registration of a foreign judgment on defined grounds.[147] Registration of a foreign judgment shall be set aside if: it is proved the foreign court does not have jurisdiction; the judgment was obtained by fraud; natural justice has been breached; or its enforcement would be contrary to Tanzanian public policy.[148] On natural justice, it has been held that neither service in accordance with the laws of the foreign country, nor at a contractually agreed address, suffices: there must be actual notice to the judgment-debtor.[149] Registration of a foreign judgment may be set aside if the court is satisfied that the matter in dispute in the foreign proceedings had, prior to the date of the foreign judgment, been the subject of a final and conclusive judgment by another competent foreign court.[150]

In an action *in personam*, the foreign court is deemed to have had jurisdiction on the basis of the judgment-debtor's submission to the jurisdiction or residence therein. In the case of artificial persons, having a principal place of business, office or place of business in the country where

[144] [1982] TLR 155 at 166. It is submitted that this observation represents a misconstruction of the provision. Even though it is unclear whether the provision is referring to legal or factual impossibility of execution, the former is the preferred interpretation. The desire to register a judgment abroad is, in many instances, informed by factual difficulties, such as the judgment-debtor's lack of assets within the jurisdiction or his absence in the jurisdiction. See K. W. Patchett, *Recognition of Commercial Judgments and Awards in the Commonwealth* (London: Butterworths, 1984), pp. 110–11.

[145] Foreign Judgments (Reciprocal Enforcement) Ordinance 1935, s. 4(2).

[146] Foreign Judgments (Reciprocal Enforcement) Ordinance 1935, s. 4(3).

[147] The court may also decline to register a foreign judgment if the grounds for setting aside exist. See *FX Oliso-Emosingoit* v. *East African Community* [1982] TLR 155.

[148] Foreign Judgments (Reciprocal Enforcement) Ordinance 1935, s. 6(1)(a); *FX Oliso-Emosingoit* v. *East African Community.*

[149] *Ramus* v. *Donaldson* [1959] EA 355.

[150] Foreign Judgments (Reciprocal Enforcement) Ordinance 1935, s. 6(1)(b).

the foreign court is situated are recognised bases of international competence.[151] In the case of a judgment given in an action where the subject matter is immovable property, or in an action *in rem*, where the subject matter is movable property, a foreign court is deemed to have had jurisdiction if the property in question was, at the time of the proceedings in the foreign court, situated in the country of that court.[152] In any other case the court has jurisdiction if its jurisdiction is recognised by Tanzanian law.[153]

A foreign court shall not be deemed to have had jurisdiction if: the subject matter of the proceedings is immovable property outside the country of the foreign court; the proceedings before the foreign court were brought in breach of a foreign choice of forum agreement, or if the judgment-debtor is a person who, in public international law, is entitled to immunity from the jurisdiction of the foreign court and has not submitted to it.[154]

Uganda

The statutory regime for enforcing foreign judgments in Uganda is governed by the Foreign Judgments (Reciprocal Enforcement) Act 1961, the Reciprocal Enforcement of Judgments Act 1922,[155] the Judgments Extension Act 1908[156] and the Foreign Judgments (Reciprocal Enforcement) Rules.

The Foreign Judgments (Reciprocal Enforcement) Act 1961 empowers the Minister of Justice and Constitutional Affairs to designate on a reciprocal basis those countries whose judgments can benefit from the

151 Ibid., s. 6(2)(a). 152 Ibid., s. 6(2)(b). 153 Ibid., s. 6(2)(c). 154 Ibid., s. 6(3).

155 This Act makes provision for the enforcement of judgments from the United Kingdom and Republic of Ireland. It empowers the Minister to extend its provisions to judgments of Commonwealth countries on a reciprocal basis. The Reciprocal Enforcement of Judgments (Extension) Order, Statutory Instrument Nos. 21–2 extended the Act to Botswana, Lesotho, Mauritius, New South Wales, Seychelles, Sri Lanka, and Swaziland. The provisions of the Act are very similar to the Foreign Judgments (Reciprocal Enforcement) Act 1961, which is discussed in this section. A notable difference is that under the Act, the judgment-creditor should, subject to the discretion of the court to allow a longer time, apply to register the judgment within twelve months of it being granted by the foreign court: *In re. Sir John Bagaire* [1995] Kam. LR 681 (application to register a UK judgment dismissed for being out of time); *Transroad Ltd v. Bank of Uganda* [1996] 6 Kam. LR 42 (extension granted to apply to register a UK judgment).

156 This Act makes provision for the transfer and execution of judgments granted by the courts of Kenya, Malawi and Tanzania. In *In re. Michael Ndichu Mburu*, Miscellaneous Cause 09 of 2008 (High Court, Uganda, 2008), the court registered a Kenyan judgment by invoking the provisions of the Foreign Judgments (Reciprocal Enforcement) Act 1961. There was no reference to the Judgments Extension Act 1908.

regime established by the Act,[157] or direct the application of Part II of the Act to judgments from territories of the Commonwealth.[158]

A judgment-creditor of a judgment to which the Act applies may apply to the High Court to register the judgment within six years of the date of the judgment, or where there have been proceedings by way of appeal against the judgment, after the date of the last judgment given in those proceedings. However, a court shall not register a judgment if it was wholly satisfied at the date of application or if it could not be enforced by execution in the foreign country.[159] A registered judgment has the same effect as a judgment originally given in the registering court and entered on the date of registration.[160]

Where the sum payable under a judgment to be registered is expressed in foreign currency, the judgment shall be registered as if it were a judgment for such a sum in Ugandan shillings, based on the exchange rate that prevails on the date of the judgment of the foreign court.[161]

On an application by the judgment-debtor, the court is empowered to set aside the registration of a foreign judgment. A registered judgment shall be set aside if it is proved that the foreign court did not have jurisdiction, the judgment was obtained by fraud, there was a breach of natural justice, or its enforcement would be contrary to Uganda's public policy.[162] The court has discretion to set aside registration if it is satisfied the matter in dispute in the foreign proceedings had been the subject of a final and conclusive judgment by another foreign court with jurisdiction in the matter, prior to the date of the judgment.[163]

In an action *in personam*,[164] the foreign court is deemed to have had jurisdiction on the basis of the judgment-debtor's submission to the jurisdiction,[165] or their residence within the jurisdiction. In the case of

157 Foreign Judgments (Reciprocal Enforcement) Act 1961, s. 2.

158 Ibid., s. 8. See Foreign Judgments (Reciprocal Enforcement) (General Application) Order 2002 (which directs the application of Pt II of the Act to judgments from all Commonwealth territories) and the Foreign Judgments (Reciprocal Enforcement) (Grenada) Order 2002. A benefit of the country-specific order is that it enables the enforcement of arbitration awards which have become enforceable in the specified country.

159 Ibid., s. 3(1). 160 Ibid., s. 3(2). 161 Ibid., s. 3(3).

162 Ibid., s. 5(1)(a). 163 Ibid., s. 5(1)(b).

164 Under the Act, an action *in personam* shall not be deemed to include any matrimonial cause or proceedings in connection with matrimonial matters, administration of the estates of deceased persons, bankruptcy, winding up of companies, lunacy or guardianship of infants.

165 *Transroad Ltd* v. *Bank of Uganda* [1998] UGA J No. 12, [1998] Kam. LR 106; *Transroad Ltd* v. *Bank of Uganda* [1996] Kam. LR 697.

artificial persons, having a principal place of business, office or place of business in the foreign country are recognised bases of international competence.[166] In the case of a judgment given in an action where the subject matter is immovable property, or in an action *in rem* where the subject matter is movable property, a foreign court is deemed to have had jurisdiction if the property in question was at the time of the proceedings in the foreign court situated in the foreign country.[167] In any other case the court has jurisdiction if its jurisdiction is recognised by Ugandan law.[168]

A foreign court shall not be deemed to have had jurisdiction if: the subject matter of the proceedings is immovable property outside the country of the foreign court; the proceedings before the foreign court were brought in breach of a foreign choice of forum agreement, or the judgment-debtor is a person who is entitled to immunity from the jurisdiction of the foreign court under public international law and has therefore not submitted to its jurisdiction.[169]

Zambia

The statutory regime for enforcing foreign judgments in Zambia is regulated by the Foreign Judgments (Reciprocal Enforcement) Act 1937, the Foreign Judgment (Reciprocal Enforcement) Rules 1958 and, for judgments from Malawi and Zimbabwe, the Service of Process and Execution of Judgments Act 1957[170] and Service of Process and Execution of Judgments Regulations 1957.[171]

The Foreign Judgments (Reciprocal Enforcement) Act 1937 empowers the President to designate, on a reciprocal basis, those countries whose judgments will benefit from the Act.[172] The President can also direct that specific provisions of the Act apply to 'Her Majesty's dominions and to judgments obtained in the courts of the said dominions as it applies

166 Ibid., s. 5(2)(a). 167 Ibid., s. 5(2)(b). 168 Ibid., s. 5(2)(c). 169 Ibid., s. 5(3).

170 Service of Process and Execution of Judgments Act 1957, ss. 10–15. This Act is not discussed here. It is, however, worth noting that it provides for the almost automatic enforcement of Malawian and Zimbabwean judgments. The judgment-debtor is allowed to apply for a stay of proceedings to enable him to proceed and set aside the judgment in Malawi or Zimbabwe, as the case may be. Historically, the three countries constituted a federation – the Federation of Rhodesia and Nyasaland.

171 Service of Process and Execution of Judgments Regulations 1957, ss. 13–14.

172 Foreign Judgments (Reciprocal Enforcement) Act 1937, s. 3(1); *Mileta Pakou* v. *Rudnap Zambia Ltd* (1998) ZR 233.

to foreign countries'.[173] It has been held that section 9 of the Foreign Judgments (Reciprocal Enforcement) Ordinance (now Act) was meant for Her Britannic Majesty's dominions outside the United Kingdom. Therefore, in the Judgments (Reciprocal Enforcement) Order 1958, it was directed that Part II of the Foreign Judgments (Reciprocal Enforcement) Ordinance shall apply to those of Her Majesty's dominions that did not include the United Kingdom. Accordingly, at present, a judgment from the United Kingdom is not enforceable under the Act.[174]

The Act applies only to judgments which are final and conclusive[175] and where a sum of money is payable other than in respect of taxes, fines or penalties.[176] Accordingly, an order from an English court that a child should be returned to England is not enforceable under the Act.[177]

A judgment-creditor of a judgment to which the Act applies may apply to the High Court to register the judgment within six years of the date of the judgment or, where there have been proceedings by way of appeal against the judgment, after the date of the last judgment given in those proceedings. The court shall not register a judgment if, at the date of application, it has been wholly satisfied (i.e. the judgment has been paid in full), or if it could not be enforced by execution in the foreign country.[178] A registered judgment has the same effect as a judgment originally given in the registering court and entered on the date of registration.[179]

173 Foreign Judgments (Reciprocal Enforcement) Act 1937, s. 9(1). See Judgments (Reciprocal Enforcement) (Gilbert and Ellice Islands Colony) Order 1958; Judgments (Reciprocal Enforcement) (British Solomon Islands Protectorate) Order 1958 and Judgments (Reciprocal Enforcement) Order 1958. The last Order extended the application of Pt II of the Act to Her Britannic Majesty's dominions and to judgments obtained in the courts of those dominions. It is debatable whether courts will apply these orders to judgments from the independent states (e.g. Kiribati, Tuvalu, Solomon Islands) which succeeded the former colonies. The regime under Pt II of the Act is different in one material respect: the definition of foreign judgment is extended to include 'an award in proceedings on an arbitration if the award has, in pursuance of the law in force in the place where it was made, become enforceable in the same manner as a judgment given by a court in that place'. In other words, arbitration awards from the countries named in these Orders can be registered under the Act.

174 *Attorney General* v. *Frederick Chiluba*, Case No. 2007/HP/FJ/004 (High Court, Zambia, 2010).

175 *Claudio Ricagno* v. *Mario Rapetti* [1949–54] LRNR 735.

176 Foreign Judgments (Reciprocal Enforcement) Act 1937, s. 3(2).

177 *Zanetta Nyendwa* v. *Kenneth Paul Spooner*, Judgment No. 20 of 2010 (Supreme Court, Zambia, 2010).

178 Ibid., s. 4(1). 179 Ibid., s. 4(2).

Where the sum payable under a foreign judgment is expressed in foreign currency, the judgment shall be registered as if it were a judgment for such a sum in Zambian kwacha, based on the exchange rate that prevails on the date of the judgment of the foreign court.[180]

On an application by the judgment-debtor, the court is empowered to set aside the registration of a foreign judgment. Registration of a foreign judgment shall be set aside if it is proved that the foreign court did not have jurisdiction, the judgment was obtained by fraud, there is a breach of natural justice, or its enforcement would contravene Zambian public policy.[181] Registration of a foreign judgment may also be set aside if the court is satisfied the matter in dispute in the foreign proceedings had already been the subject of a final and conclusive judgment by another court of competent jurisdiction,[182] prior to the date of the judgment in the foreign court.

In an action *in personam*,[183] the foreign court is deemed to have had jurisdiction on the basis of the judgment-debtor's submission to the jurisdiction or residence therein. In the case of artificial persons, having a principal place of business, office or place of business in the foreign country are recognised bases of international competence.[184] In the case of a judgment given in an action where the subject matter is immovable property, or in an action *in rem* where the subject matter is movable property, a foreign court is deemed to have had jurisdiction if the property in question was, at the time of the foreign proceedings, situated in the foreign country.[185] In any other case, the court has jurisdiction if its jurisdiction is recognised by Zambian law.[186]

A foreign court shall not be deemed to have had jurisdiction if: the subject matter of the proceedings is immovable property outside the country of the foreign court; the proceedings before the foreign court were brought in breach of a foreign choice of forum agreement; or if the judgment-debtor is a person who is entitled to immunity from the jurisdiction of the foreign court under public international law and does not submit to its jurisdiction.[187]

180 Ibid., s. 4(3). 181 Ibid., s. 6(1). 182 Ibid., s. 6(1)(b).

183 Under the Act, an action *in personam* shall not be deemed to include any matrimonial cause or proceedings in connection with any of the following matters, that is to say, matrimonial matters, administration of the estates of deceased persons, bankruptcy, winding up of companies, lunacy or guardianship of infants.

184 Foreign Judgments (Reciprocal Enforcement) Act 1937, s. 6(2).

185 Ibid., s. 6(2)(b). 186 Ibid., s. 6(2)(c). 187 Ibid., s. 6(3).

Zimbabwe

The statutory regime for enforcing foreign judgments in Zimbabwe is governed by the Civil Matters (Mutual Assistance) Act 1995. The Act applies to judgments given by a court in a designated country or a designated international tribunal requiring the payment of money, including an award of compensation or damages to an aggrieved party in criminal proceedings.[188] The Act empowers the Minister of Justice, Legal and Parliamentary Affairs to designate countries and international tribunals as beneficiaries under the Act. There is no express requirement that this should be done on the basis of reciprocity. However, restrictions or conditions may be imposed, including in relation to the class of judgments enforceable under the Act.[189]

A judgment-creditor of a judgment given in a designated country may apply to the High Court or to an appropriate Magistrates' Court to register the judgment. The application can be made at any time within six years of the date of the judgment, or after the determination of any proceedings by way of appeal or review, where such proceedings have been instituted in respect of the judgment.[190]

The court before which the application is made shall direct the registration of the judgment if it is satisfied that it is 'just and convenient for the judgment to be enforced in Zimbabwe'.[191] The court can refuse registration on a number of more specific grounds.[192] Registration shall be refused if the foreign court does not have jurisdiction, the enforcement of the judgment would contravene Zimbabwean law or public policy, or the judgment was obtained by fraud or in breach of natural justice. Similarly, a foreign judgment which is not a final and conclusive judgment; cannot be enforced either wholly or in part by execution in the foreign country; has been set aside by a court of competent jurisdiction; has been wholly satisfied; has become prescribed under the law of the country where it was given; or is for the payment of a tax, duty, rate, fine penalty or maintenance of a person, shall be refused registration.[193]

[188] Civil Matters (Mutual Assistance) Act 1995, ss. 2 and 3(4)(a).
[189] Civil Matters (Mutual Assistance) Act 1995, s. 3(2)(3).
[190] Civil Matters (Mutual Assistance) Act 1995, s. 5. See generally *Harman* v. *Leaf* 1954 (2) SA 270.
[191] Civil Matters (Mutual Assistance) Act 1995, s. 6(1).
[192] It is significant to mention that, at this stage, the judgment-debtor will not have been notified that an application for registration has been made. Thus, the court is acting *suo motu*.
[193] Civil Matters (Mutual Assistance) Act 1995, s. 6(2).

When a judgment is registered, it has the same effect as a judgment of the registering court.[194] The judgment-creditor may go into execution after the time allowed for applying to set aside registration of the judgment.[195] The judgment-creditor of a registered judgment may apply for the attachment of assets of the judgment-debtor even though the latter has been ordered to pay the judgment by instalment in the foreign country, or where an appeal is pending against that order in the foreign country.[196]

After a foreign judgment has been registered, the judgment-debtor is given notice of the registration and any ancillary order[197] made by the court.[198] The judgment-debtor is allowed to apply to have the registration set aside.[199] Except with leave of the court, the judgment-debtor cannot apply to set aside registration of the judgment on grounds determined by the court in the application for registration.[200] However, if the court is satisfied that any of the above noted grounds for refusing registration of a foreign judgment exist, it should set aside the registration.[201]

There are a number of grounds on which a foreign court is deemed to have had jurisdiction.[202] These include submission, residence and having a principal place of business in the foreign country, or an office or place of business in the foreign country through, or at which, the transaction giving rise to the proceedings was effected. Where the proceedings relate to movable or immovable property, the foreign court has jurisdiction if the property was in the foreign country when the proceedings were instituted. In respect of any other proceedings, the foreign court has jurisdiction if its jurisdiction is recognised under Zimbabwean law.

Comments on national statutory regimes

Scope and application

In general, the statutory regime for enforcing foreign judgments has been designed to provide a much simpler and expedited procedure for

[194] Ibid., s. 7(1). [195] Ibid., s. 7(4).

[196] *Siwela Holdings (Pvt) Ltd* v. *Nyirongo* 1985 (1) ZLR 58. Sections 6(4) and 8(5)(b) of the Act empower the court to register the unsatisfied balance of a foreign judgment.

[197] This could include an order prohibiting the removal or disposal of any assets of the judgment-debtor. Civil Matters (Mutual Assistance) Act 1995, s. 6(3).

[198] Civil Matters (Mutual Assistance) Act 1995, s. 7(2).

[199] Civil Matters (Mutual Assistance) Act 1995, s. 8(1); *Vehicle Delivery Services (Zimbabwe) (Private) Ltd* v. *Galaun Holdings Ltd*, HC 8191/2002 (High Court, Zimbabwe, 2003).

[200] Civil Matters (Mutual Assistance) Act 1995, s. 8(3).

[201] Ibid., s. 8(4). [202] Ibid., s. 9(4).

enforcing foreign judgments. Rather than bringing a new action on the judgment, the judgment-creditor is allowed to register it, which in many instances can be done on an *ex parte* application. In practice, registration could turn out to be as complicated as bringing an action on the judgment. An application to set aside the registration of a foreign judgment could lead to protracted litigation.

The scope of judgments to which the statutory regimes apply is very limited. The regimes apply only to specific types of judgment emanating from specified courts in designated countries.

Apart from South Africa and Zimbabwe, the requirement of reciprocity lies at the heart of all the regimes. Even though a formal treaty is not required, it is likely that evidence of reciprocal treatment would be sought before a country is designated. The determination of whether reciprocal treatment exists is an executive decision in all the countries under study; the judiciary has no role to play in making that determination. Only judgments from countries designated after such determination are enforceable under the regimes. It is remarkable that relatively few countries – including African countries – have been designated by each of the countries under study. Indeed, for some countries, the list of designated countries is so outdated that some of these designated countries have ceased to exist or taken on a new name.

It is a damning indictment on African unity and Africa's economic integration that a judgment from the United Kingdom – a former colonial power – is more likely to be registered in the countries under study than judgments from other African states. After years of promoting economic integration and African unity, this is troubling. One would have expected African governments, in their 'determination to promote unity, solidarity, cohesion and cooperation among the peoples of Africa and African States',[203] to make the registration procedure for foreign judgments available to African judgments. Of the many African regional economic communities, it is only between the founding members of the East African Community – Kenya, Tanzania and Uganda – that judgments can be registered in each other's countries. To clarify, it is not being argued that a judgment from an African country should be automatically registered in another African country; there are factors that can justify the non-registration of an African judgment. What is being argued is that, in order to aid economic integration in Africa, judgments should be easily

[203] Constitutive Act of the African Union, 11 July 2000, (2005) 13 *African Journal of International and Comparative Law* 25, at Preamble.

enforceable among African states. Admittedly, to date, reported instances of attempts to register (or enforce at common law) judgments from African states in the countries under study are few. However, in the near future, this is unlikely to remain so. A strong case exists for easier circulation of African judgments. To this end, it is recommended that each African state should designate many more African states as beneficiaries of its statutory regime. A more ambitious and long-term project would be to conclude an African foreign judgment enforcement convention.

Even for designated countries, the statutory regimes do not apply to judgments from all courts. In many of the countries under study, the regimes have been expressly limited to judgments from superior courts of the designated countries. These courts are often named in the law designating the relevant country. For the designated courts, there is a further restriction in some countries. It is provided in the Gambian,[204] Botswanan, Ghanaian, Nigerian,[205] Tanzanian, Ugandan and Zambian statutes that only judgments 'other than a judgment of the court given on appeal from a court which is not a [designated] court' are within their scope. In other words, where a designated court in exercise of its appellate jurisdiction hears a case from a non-designated court, its appellate decision is outside the scope of the regime and hence unenforceable under it. This can be illustrated using Ghana's regime and judgments from England: a judgment from the High Court of England (which is designated) that affirms a judgment of a county court of England (which is not designated) does not qualify for registration under Ghana's statutory regime. However, it can be enforced at common law. On the other hand, a judgment from the High Court of England that is upheld by the Court of Appeal or Supreme Court (formerly the House of Lords) qualifies for registration under the regime.

The rationale for this limitation on the application of regimes is difficult to find or justify. It discriminates against courts of the same country. What is certain is that the provisions were borrowed from what is now section 1(2A)(a) of the United Kingdom's Foreign Judgments (Reciprocal Enforcement) Act 1933. There are statutes in some common law countries which allow for the extension of their respective statutory regimes to inferior or subordinate courts in foreign countries.[206] Such an

[204] Foreign Judgments Reciprocal Enforcement Act 1936, s 3(2).

[205] Foreign Judgments (Reciprocal Enforcement) Act 1961, s. 3(2).

[206] Australia – Foreign Judgment Act 1991, s. 5(3); New Zealand – Reciprocal Enforcement of Judgments Act 1934, s. 3A.

approach overcomes the limitations imposed on the scope of the statutory regime. Indeed, section 13(3) of Kenya's Foreign Judgment (Reciprocal Enforcement) Act 1984 empowers the Minister of Justice to designate 'subordinate courts' of foreign countries as beneficiaries of the regime. It is recommended that the current structure which discriminates between courts of the same country and judicial system is inappropriate and should be reassessed.

A further limitation on the scope and application of the statutory regimes is that, apart from the Kenyan regime, they apply only to money judgments.[207] The comments in Chapter 17 on the enforcement of non-money judgments at common law are equally applicable here. Other types of judgment and judgments on specific subject matters are also excluded from the scope of the regimes. For example, judgments for the payment of taxes, fines and penalties are commonly excluded. Kenya's regime specifically and uniquely excludes: judgments which provide for the payment of a sum of money by way of exemplary, punitive or multiple damages; a judgment enforcing another foreign judgment; and judgments given in proceedings relating to damage, death or injury caused by occurrences involving nuclear matters or the emission of ionising radiation. Generally, in Gambia,[208] Botswana, Ghana, Kenya, Nigeria,[209] Tanzania, Uganda and Zambia, proceedings in connection with matrimonial matters, the administration of estates of deceased persons, bankruptcy, winding up of companies, lunacy or the custody and guardianship of infants are excluded. In many of the statutory regimes, a judgment within their scope could arise from civil or criminal proceedings. Namibia and South Africa have separate regimes for enforcing judgments resulting from criminal prosecution.

From the above, it is obvious that the enforcement of most foreign judgments in Commonwealth Africa will have to be carried out through the common law regime.

[207] A few of the regimes could also be used to enforce foreign arbitration awards that have become enforceable in the designated country. See, e.g., Gambia – Reciprocal Enforcement of Judgments Act 1922, s. 2; Kenya – Foreign Judgments (Reciprocal Enforcement) Act 1984, s. 3(1)(f); Lesotho – Reciprocal Enforcement of Judgments Act 1922, s. 2; Nigeria – Foreign Judgments (Reciprocal Enforcement) Act 1961, s. 2(1), Reciprocal Enforcement of Judgments Ordinance 1922, s. 2; Swaziland – Reciprocal Enforcement of Judgments Act 1922, s. 2; Uganda – Foreign Judgment (Reciprocal Enforcement) Act 1961, s. 8(2); Zambia – Foreign Judgment (Reciprocal Enforcement) Act 1937, s. 10(a).

[208] Foreign Judgments Reciprocal Enforcement Act 1936, s. 2(2).

[209] Foreign Judgments (Reciprocal Enforcement) Act 1961, s. 2.

International competence

It is common to all the statutory regimes that the registration of a foreign judgment shall be set aside if the foreign court does not have jurisdiction.[210] The grounds which constitute jurisdiction in this sense are stipulated in the relevant statutes with remarkable similarity. Submission, residence and having a place of business or doing business in the foreign country are commonly accepted bases of international competence in the countries under study. Unlike at common law, it appears temporary presence is excluded. However, there is little or no guidance on how courts should interpret these bases of international competence, for example, how long residence should continue and what its character should be. In addition to this, Kenya's Foreign Judgment (Reciprocal Enforcement) Act 1984, the *lex loci solutionis* (in a claim arising out of a contract) and the *lex loci delicti* or *lex loci damni* (in an action to recover damages for physical injury, death or property damage) are bases of international competence.[211]

In causes of action not expressly provided for by the statutes, jurisdictional reciprocity is recognised in Gambia,[212] Botswana, Ghana, Namibia, Nigeria,[213] South Africa, Tanzania, Uganda, Zimbabwe and Zambia. In other words, the fact that, in hearing a case, the foreign court acted on a basis upon which the registering court would also have acted in similar circumstances suffices for international competence.

The above reveals a significant feature of the statutory regimes – they tend to recognise many more bases of international competence than does common law. As noted in Chapter 17, expanding the bases of international competence is something which should be encouraged. However, such expansion should be complemented with defences or laws aimed at ensuring that a judgment-debtor is well protected against potential abuse. For example, Kenya's regime, which contains two bases of international competence unknown to the other countries, also provides many more defences, even though, as discussed below, some of the defences can be criticised.

In the Gambian,[214] Botswanan, Ghanaian, Kenyan, Namibian, Nigerian,[215] South African, Tanzanian, Ugandan and Zambian statutes,

[210] See generally *Zakia Hanna Ibrahim* v. *Tawfik Ibrahim Mikael* [1932–40] 2 SLR 98; *Cairo Bank* v. *Mohamed Ali Bahaydar* 1966 (1) ALR Comm. 33.

[211] Foreign Judgment (Reciprocal Enforcement) Act 1984, s. 4(1)(g)(i).

[212] Foreign Judgments Reciprocal Enforcement Act 1936, s. 5(2)(c).

[213] Foreign Judgments (Reciprocal Enforcement) Act 1961, s. 6(2)(c).

[214] Foreign Judgments Reciprocal Enforcement Act 1936, s. 5(3).

[215] Foreign Judgments (Reciprocal Enforcement) Act 1961, s. 6(3).

international competence is expressly denied foreign courts which have heard claims in relation to immovable property situated abroad, in breach of a jurisdiction or arbitration agreement, and without regard for jurisdictional immunity in public international law. It is unclear what the scope of the immovable property provision is. It is likely to be restricted to cases involving questions of title to immovable property or rights of possession of such property.

Automaticity, registration periods and limitation of actions

There is no unanimity in the countries under study whether registration is as of right or discretionary. The Botswanan and Ghanaian statutes provide that the court 'may' order a foreign judgment to be registered subject to proof of prescribed matters. Statutes in Kenya, Namibia, South Africa, Tanzania, Uganda and Zambia provide that the court 'shall', subject to proof of prescribed matters, order a foreign judgment to be registered. And in Lesotho, Nigeria,[216] Swaziland and Zimbabwe, the court 'may' (or 'shall' in Zimbabwe) direct registration of the judgment if it is satisfied that it is 'just and convenient' for the judgment to be enforced in their respective countries.

At first sight, it appears that registration is not as of right, at least in Botswana, Ghana, Lesotho, Nigeria, Swaziland and Zimbabwe. However, it can be argued on a purposive interpretation of the relevant statutes that registration is as of right. Put differently, a judgment-debtor is entitled to have the judgment registered once existing formal and admissibility requirements – such as having a judgment that emanates from a designated country and court, authentication and translation – are met. This interpretation is consistent with the objective of the statutory regimes, which is to facilitate the enforcement of judgments. The burden is on the judgment-debtor on receipt of notice of registration to apply to set aside the registration. At that stage, the process becomes a full-blown legal contest. The court is then better placed to consider substantive issues, such as whether the foreign court was competent, whether the judgment was given in breach of natural justice, or obtained by fraud, or whether its enforcement contravenes public policy. The application for the registration stage should not be used as the forum for considering these substantive issues, except perhaps where the application is on

[216] Reciprocal Enforcement of Judgments Ordinance 1922, s. 3(1).

notice to the judgment-debtor. It is inappropriate for a court to 'look beyond' the foreign judgment (the document) at this stage. In Zimbabwe, courts are expressly allowed to consider the substantive issues during the application for registration stages. Indeed, once so considered, the judgment-debtor will only be allowed to reopen them for consideration with the leave of the court.[217]

Most of the statutes allow a judgment-creditor six years within which to apply for registration of a foreign judgment.[218] In Namibia and South Africa, no registration time frame is provided. However, registration shall be set aside if the judgment has become prescribed under Namibian or South African law, or the law of the country where the judgment was given. The six-year time frame relates to the time within which an application to register a foreign judgment must be made. It is argued here that this is independent of the issue of whether enforcement of the judgment is statute-barred or prescribed. The latter issue is not addressed in the statutes.[219] As an illustration, under South African law, enforcement of a South African judgment is prescribed thirty years after it is given. An application to register a South African judgment in Ghana was made seven years after it was given. This application should be dismissed (or if the judgment is registered, set aside) since it was brought outside the six years of the judgment. This is so, even though the judgment is still effective under South African law. Similarly, under Utopian law, the enforcement of a Utopian judgment is prescribed three years after it is given. If an application to register a Utopian judgment in Ghana is made four years after it is given, the application should also be dismissed (or if the judgment is registered, set aside) even though it has been brought within the six-year registration time frame. This is because, in Ghana and in the countries under study, a court should not register a foreign judgment if the judgment could not be enforced by execution in the foreign country at the date of the application. A judgment-creditor should not be able to circumvent legal

[217] See also *FX Oliso-Emosingoit* v. *East African Community* [1982] TLR 155.

[218] Some statutes provide a twelve-month period, which could be extended with leave of court. See, e.g., Gambia – Reciprocal Enforcement of Judgments Act 1922, s. 3(1); Lesotho – Reciprocal Enforcement of Judgments Act 1922, s. 3(1); Nigeria – Reciprocal Enforcement of Judgments 1922, s. 3(1); Swaziland – Reciprocal Enforcement of Judgments Act 1922, s. 3(1); Uganda – Reciprocal Enforcement of Judgments Act 1922, s. 2(1). None of these statutes provides any guidance on what courts should take into account before granting leave to apply to register a judgment outside the twelve-month period.

[219] See discussion on limitation of actions and foreign judgments in Ch. 17.

restrictions on the enforcement of a judgment in their country of origin merely by relying on a longer period for registration afforded in another country.

Foreign currency judgments

Apart from Lesotho, Nigeria,[220] Swaziland and Zimbabwe, it is a requirement in all the statutory regimes reported here that where (as would often be the case) a foreign judgment is in foreign currency, it should be registered in the currency of the registering court. Kenya's statute gives courts discretion on this. Given currency inconvertibility and fluctuating exchange rate problems, this issue is particularly important. As discussed in Chapter 9, the position in many of the countries under study is that courts can give judgments in foreign currency. In the absence of other exchange control restrictions, the courts' jurisdiction to give judgment in foreign currency inures to the benefit of a judgment-creditor who brings a common law action to enforce a foreign judgment or recover debts denominated in foreign currency. It is strange that, where a judgment-creditor seeks to register a foreign judgment, most of the statutory regimes mandate conversion of the judgment into the national currency. The mandatory currency conversion provisions are anachronistic – they were adopted at a time when courts did not have jurisdiction to give judgment in foreign currency.

Mandatory currency conversion provisions may be of great financial significance to both judgment-creditors and debtors, especially during times of fluctuating exchange rates which, unfortunately, always work to the detriment of one party. Some common law countries have recognised the potential hardship and injustice that can result, especially to judgment-creditors. Statutes in Australia and New Zealand give a judgment-creditor the option to state in their application for registration whether they wish the judgment to be registered in the currency of the original judgment.[221] This choice mitigates the potential hardship that

[220] Reciprocal Enforcement of Judgments Ordinance 1922. Section 4(3) of the Foreign Judgments (Reciprocal Enforcement Act) 1990, which requires currency conversion prior to registration, has not yet been extended to any country. See *Witt & Busch Ltd* v. *Dale Power Systems Plc* [2007] 17 NWLR 1 at 19–20, which held that, until the 1990 Act comes into force, 'there is no restriction for any superior court in Nigeria to register a foreign judgment in foreign currency'; *Momah* v. *VAB Petroleum Inc.* [2000] 2 SC 142 at 156–7, [2000] 4 NWLR 534 at 552.

[221] Australia – Foreign Judgments Act 1991, s. 6(11)(a); New Zealand – Reciprocal Enforcement of Judgments Act 1934, s. 4(3).

can be caused by fluctuations in exchange rates – at least from the perspective of the judgment-creditor. The discretionary language of Kenya's statute makes this option available to foreign judgment-creditors. It is recommended that future reform of the statutory regimes should incorporate a provision similar to the New Zealand and Australian statutes. Indeed, given that courts can now give judgment in foreign currency, there is no reason why they cannot similarly register a foreign judgment in the currency in which it was given.

Even though the countries under study are almost unanimous on the need for conversion, there is divergence on the equally important issue of when the conversion should be made. Gambia, Botswana, Ghana, Nigeria, South Africa, Tanzania, Uganda and Zambia opt for the date of the foreign judgment. Kenya and Namibia opt for the date of registration. On this issue, a number of potential conversion dates exist, such as the dates of the original judgment, registration, execution and when the original cause of action arose. There is unlikely to be one correct answer. Indeed, there is no international consensus on how the issue should be dealt with.[222] Whichever option is chosen is likely to lead to 'unintended' losses to one party. If there must be conversion – and as argued above, it should not be mandated – the conversion date which may work best for a judgment-creditor, and should be adopted, is a date as close as possible to the date of execution of the judgment or payment of the judgment debt.

Setting registration aside and 'nationalistic' provision

It is a characteristic of all the statutory regimes that the judgment-debtor of a registered judgment can apply to set aside the registration. There are many common grounds on which registration can be set aside. These include: lack of international competence, breach of natural justice, judgments obtained by fraud, the enforcement of the judgment being in contravention of public policy, and the existence of a prior conflicting judgment.

There are a number of unique provisions which arguably display nationalist undertones and merit discussion. In Gambia, Lesotho, Nigeria and Swaziland, a registered judgment can be set aside if the judgment was in respect of a cause of action which 'for reasons of public policy or other similar reason' could not have been entertained by the registering

[222] V. Black, *Foreign Currency Claims in the Conflict of Laws* (Oxford: Hart Publishing, 2010), pp. 193–8.

court. Registration in Kenya and South Africa stand out – perhaps alone – in this respect. In Chapter 17, we discussed provisions of South Africa's Protection of Businesses Act 1978 which prohibit the enforcement of judgments for multiple or punitive damages in defined transactions, or make prior permission from the Minister for Economic Affairs a condition precedent to enforcing some types of foreign judgment. The Act is equally applicable to judgments enforceable under the statutory regime.[223]

The most draconian of these nationalistic provisions is the power given to the Kenyan High Court to enforce foreign judgments for less than that which has been decreed by the foreign court. The High Court is allowed to do this where the sums, including costs awarded, are substantially in excess of those which would have been awarded by it on the basis of the findings of law and fact made by the foreign court, had the assessment been made in proceedings before the High Court. In addition to this, a judgment-debtor in Kenya may apply to set aside a registered judgment to the extent that its enforcement would require payment of sums in excess of monetary limits upon liability imposed by any Kenyan statute which applies under Kenya's private international law. Registration of a foreign judgment may also be set aside if there are provisions of Kenyan law which, by virtue of Kenya's private international law, would have been applicable, notwithstanding any choice of another system of law by the judgment-creditor and the judgment-debtor, had the proceedings been brought in Kenya, and where the judgment disregards those provisions in some material respect. The courts are also empowered to set aside a registered judgment if, in the foreign proceedings, it was necessary for the foreign court to decide a question relating to some defined matters[224] in order to give its judgment, and wherever its decision differs from that which the Kenyan High Court would have reached, after having applied Kenya's private international law to the question. These powers are not found in the statutory regime of any of the countries under study.

223 See Enforcement of Foreign Civil Judgments Act 1988, s. 5(1)(i), which allows registration of a foreign judgment to be set aside on the basis that it is a judgment which in terms of 'any law' may not be recognised or enforced in South Africa.

224 They include matrimonial causes, rights in property arising out of a matrimonial relationship, custody or guardianship of children, administration of the property or affairs of incompetent persons, succession to, or administration of, estates of deceased, social security or public assistance and bankruptcy, winding up or reorganisation of corporations, and proceedings relating to damage, death or injury caused by occurrences involving nuclear matter or the emission of ionising radiation.

Given that the statutory regimes operate on the basis of reciprocity, the presence of these provisions is worrying. It could potentially prevent countries with such statutes from being designated in countries without it. The provisions could also spread to other countries and, accordingly, limit the application of the statutory regimes.

The constraining effect these provisions could have on the enforcement of judgments is difficult to judge. There is no case invoking the Kenyan provisions in the law reports. The reported cases unsuccessfully invoking South Africa's Protection of Businesses Act 1978 have been under the common law regime. How courts interpret the provisions will be important in defining the effect they have. It is recommended that, without prejudice to the need to ensure that justice is served in individual cases when approaching such statutory provisions, courts should have the broader objective of facilitating the enforcement of the judgments in mind.

19

Recognition and enforcement of foreign arbitration awards

There are two principal regimes for enforcing foreign arbitration awards in the countries under study, namely the common law and statutory regimes.[1] The statutory regime has three manifestations, namely awards made under the Convention on the Recognition and Enforcement of Foreign Arbitral Awards 1958 (hereinafter, 'New York Convention')[2] or the Convention on the Settlement of Investment Disputes between States and Nationals of Other States ('ICSID Convention'),[3] and awards from countries to which the statutory regime for enforcing foreign judgments has been extended.

Status of international arbitration conventions

The majority of the countries under study are parties to the New York Convention. Gambia,[4] Malawi, Namibia, Sierra Leone and Swaziland are not parties to the New York Convention, whereas Botswana, Ghana, Kenya, Lesotho, Nigeria, South Africa, Tanzania, Uganda, Zambia and Zimbabwe are. Botswana, Kenya, Nigeria, Tanzania and Uganda entered

[1] A party may also seek only recognition of a foreign arbitral award, which can be granted at common law. See *Re. Ghelani Impex Ltd* [1975] 1 EA 197 (reversing *Re Ghelani Impex Ltd* [1974] 1 EA 532), which held that, although foreign awards may only be enforced in accordance with the Arbitration Act, such an award may be relied upon to show that a company is indebted for the purposes of winding up. This case is also reported as *M Hamburger & Sons Ltd* v. *Nyanza Impex Ltd* 1975 (1) ALR Comm. 90.

[2] UN Convention on the Recognition and Enforcement of Foreign Arbitral Awards, 10 June 1958, 330 UNTS 3.

[3] Convention on the Settlement of Investment Disputes between States and Nationals of Other States, 18 March 1965, 575 UNTS 159. The South African High Court has criticised the fact that South Africa is not party to the Convention: *Von Abo* v. *The Government of the Republic of South Africa* 2009 (2) SA 526 at 535–40.

[4] The UNCITRAL website does not list Gambia as a party to the Convention. However, the Alternative Dispute Resolution Act 2005 implements the Convention and reproduces it as the second schedule to the Act.

a reservation that they would apply the Convention only to the recognition and enforcement of awards made in the territory of another contracting state. Botswana and Nigeria entered an additional reservation that they would apply the Convention only to differences arising from legal relationships, contractual or otherwise, that are considered commercial under their national laws. The Protocol on Arbitration Clauses 1923 (hereinafter, 'Geneva Protocol')[5] and the Convention on the Execution of Foreign Arbitral Awards 1927 (hereinafter, 'Geneva Convention')[6] remain significant for a few of the countries under study.[7] The UNCITRAL Model Law on International Commercial Arbitration 1985 (hereinafter, 'Model Law')[8] has influenced arbitration statutes in some of the countries under study. According to information from UNCITRAL, Kenya, Nigeria, Uganda, Zambia and Zimbabwe have enacted statutes based on the Model Law.[9] The Organization for the Harmonization of Business Law in Africa (OHADA) adopted a Uniform Act on Arbitration Law in 1999. However, none of the countries under study is a member of OHADA.[10] With the exception of South Africa, all the countries under study are parties to the ICSID Convention.

Enforcement of arbitration awards at common law or with leave of court

Ghana

A Ghanaian court has jurisdiction to enforce a foreign arbitration award at common law. *Grinaker-LTA Ltd* v. *Stype Investment Ltd*[11] involved an

[5] 24 September 1923, 27 LNTS 157 (1924).
[6] 26 September 1927, 92 LNTS 301 (1929–30).
[7] Section 59(3) of Ghana's Alternative Dispute Resolution Act 2010 is based on Art. 2 of the Geneva Convention. Malawi implemented the Geneva Protocol and Geneva Convention in its Arbitration Act 1967. Tanzania has the Geneva Convention as a schedule to its Arbitration Act 1931. Zambia's Arbitration Act 2000 preserves the legal recognition and enforcement of foreign arbitral awards under the Geneva Protocol and Geneva Convention (Preamble and s. 33(4)). See, generally, *Kassamali Gulamhusein* v. *Kyrtatas Bros. Ltd* [1968] 1 EA 542.
[8] UNCITRAL Model Law on International Commercial Arbitration, 21 June 1985, 24 ILM 1302.
[9] www.uncitral.org/uncitral/en/uncitral_texts/arbitration/1985Model_arbitration_status.html.
[10] The members are: Benin, Burkina Faso, Cameroon, the Central African Republic, the Comoros, Congo-Brazzaville, Côte d'Ivoire, Gabon, Guinea, Guinea Bissau, Equatorial Guinea, Mali, Niger, Senegal, Chad and Togo. See, generally, B. Martor et al., *Business Law in Africa: OHADA and the Harmonization Process*, 2nd rev. edn (London: Kogan Page, 2007).
[11] *Grinaker-LTA Ltd* v. *Stype Investment Ltd*, Suit No. 34/2006 (High Court, Ghana, 2006).

action to enforce a South African arbitration award. The counsel for the defendant challenged the jurisdiction of the court on the grounds that South Africa was not a reciprocating state under the Arbitration (Foreign Awards) Instrument 1963. The court swiftly dismissed the objection and held that, in the absence of reciprocity, the award could be enforced by a common law action. Such an award should also be final and binding between the parties. Neither the fact that an appeal is pending nor the existence of a right to appeal will bar enforcement. However, where a foreign court has ordered 'a complete stay of execution' pending the conclusion of an appeal, it will bar the enforcement of the award.

Nigeria

It has long been acknowledged by the Nigerian courts that a foreign arbitration award may be enforced by a common law action on the award in the same way as a foreign judgment, even in the absence of a treaty or legislation guaranteeing reciprocal treatment of awards.[12] There is no need to bring a fresh action in Nigeria on the original or underlying cause of action. An arbitration award is enforceable at common law upon proof that the award was made pursuant to the provisions of an arbitration agreement and in an arbitration conducted in accordance with the agreement, and providing that it is a complete and final award valid according to the *lex fori* of the place where the arbitration was carried out and where the award was granted.[13]

South Africa

A South African court has jurisdiction to enforce a foreign arbitration award at common law. In *Benidai Trading Co. Ltd* v. *Gouws & Gouws (Pty) Ltd*,[14] an action to enforce a London arbitral award was dismissed for want of jurisdiction. On appeal, it was held that, as the respondent had not appealed against the award, it was conclusive against it and the award should be recognised and enforced.

[12] *Alfred C Toepfer* v. *Edokpolor* 1965 ALR Comm. 505, [1965] 1 All NLR 292 (reversing *Edokpolor* v. *Alfred C Toepfer* 1964 (1) ALR Comm. 322).

[13] *Murmansk State Steamship Line* v. *Kano Oil Millers Ltd* 1974 (3) ALR Comm. 192 at 197 (the decision was reversed in *Murmansk State SS Line* v. *Kano Oil Millers Ltd* 1974 (1) ALR Comm. 1, [1974] NCLR 1, [1974] 1 All NLR 402, but the court did not overrule this aspect).

[14] 1977 (3) SA 1020; *Laconian Maritime Enterprises Ltd* v. *Agromar Lineas Ltd* 1986 (3) SA 509 at 516–17.

Comments

A foreign arbitration award may be enforced at common law. This can be done by bringing action on the award as one would do with a foreign judgment. In addition, in some of the countries under study, statutes allow a person in whose favour an award has been made (hereinafter, the 'award-creditor') to enforce an award on an arbitration agreement in the same manner as a judgment, 'with leave of the court'.[15] This is a discretionary procedure.[16] Even though the provisions are often found in statutes or parts of statutes dealing with domestic arbitration, they serve as bases for enforcing foreign arbitration awards.

The 'with leave of court' provisions have their roots in a similar UK legislation that has been interpreted as thus empowering the courts.[17] In an action to enforce a Russian award, the Nigerian Supreme Court observed that the failure of the judgment-creditor to obtain leave of the judge or court before instituting action to enforce an award rendered the action incompetent.[18] Indeed, courts are likely to exercise the discretion to allow an award to be enforced as a judgment with caution, not least because it is only by judicial interpretation that the procedure has been extended to enforce foreign arbitration awards.

For a foreign arbitral award to be enforceable at common law, there must be submission to arbitration, the issues arbitrated should be within the scope of the arbitration agreement, and the award should be final and conclusive. In the cases examined, submission takes the form of an express written agreement to submit to arbitration. However, there is no reason why an oral agreement occurring before or after the dispute should not suffice.[19] It remains unsettled what defences are available in an action to enforce a foreign arbitral award at common law. In a Ghanaian case, the court relied on Article V of the New York Convention.[20] It is likely that,

[15] See, e.g., Botswana – Arbitration Act 1959, s. 20; Ghana – Alternative Dispute Resolution Act 2010, s. 57; Malawi – Arbitration Act 1967, ss. 27 and 37(1); Nigeria – Arbitration and Conciliation Act 1998, s. 31(3); South Africa – Arbitration Act 1965, s. 31.

[16] *Mauritius Steam Navigation Co. Ltd* v. *International Shipping Lines Ltd* 1969 (3) ALR Comm. 34, [1969] NCLR 174, which held that the application should be made by originating summons.

[17] Arbitration Act 1996, s. 66 (previously Arbitration Act 1950, s. 26, Arbitration Act 1889, s. 12). *Dalmia Cement Ltd* v. *National Bank of Pakistan* [1975] QB 9.

[18] *Murmansk State SS Line* v. *Kano Oil Millers Ltd* 1974 (1) ALR Comm. 1, 1974 NCLR 1, [1974] 1 All NLR 402.

[19] *Alfred C Toepfer* v. *Edokpolor* 1965 ALR Comm. 505 at 511, [1965] 1 All NLR 292.

[20] *Grinaker-LTA Ltd* v. *Stype Investment Ltd*, Suit No. 34/2006 (High Court, Ghana, 2006).

given its international acceptance, other courts will highly regard the defences provided in the Convention in actions to enforce foreign arbitration awards at common law.

The common law regime for enforcing foreign arbitration awards co-exists with other regimes that are discussed below. This raises a question as to the relationship between them.[21] It is submitted that the common law regime only applies to awards falling outside the scope of the regimes discussed below. However, where an award falls within the scope of any of these regimes, it should be enforced under that regime, and not at common law. Unlike in other jurisdictions,[22] statutes in many of the countries under study do not expressly confer or preserve the right to enforce a New York Convention award using common law,[23] or for the person in whose favour the award was granted to avail him- or herself of other remedies under national law, other than the enforcement of the award.[24] In general, as will be seen below, the New York Convention and ICSID Convention regimes afford better protection for awards than the common law regime. On the other hand, that is not the case when an award is enforced as a foreign judgment.

The common law regime is more likely to be relevant to enforcing awards from countries that are not parties to the New York Convention, and those few countries under study which do not have their statutory regime for enforcing foreign judgments extended to arbitration awards. The common law regime complements the other regimes – it should not be used as a substitute or allowed to supplant them.

[21] *Benidai Trading Co. Ltd* v. *Gouws & Gouws (Pty) Ltd* 1977 (3) SA 1020 at 1040. Counsel argued that invoking s. 31 of the Arbitration Act 1965 to give leave to enforce a foreign arbitration award rendered 'redundant' the Recognition and Enforcement of Foreign Arbitral Awards Act 1977, which implements the New York Convention. The court did not find it necessary to rule on this.

[22] See, e.g., United Kingdom – Arbitration Act 1996, s. 104.

[23] But see Uganda – Arbitration and Conciliation Act 2000, s. 44 (which provides: 'Nothing in this Part [dealing with enforcement of New York Convention awards] shall prejudice any rights which any person would have had of enforcing in Uganda of any award or of availing himself or herself in Uganda of any award if this Part had not been enacted'); Zambia – Arbitration Act 2000, s. 33(4), which preserves the right to have an award recognised or enforced under 'any other written law or rule of law'.

[24] See also *Re Ghelani Impex Ltd* [1975] 1 EA 197 (reversing *Re Ghelani Impex Ltd* [1974] 1 EA 532), which held that in addition to enforcing an award, there is nothing to prevent such an award from being used or relied on for the purpose of showing that a company is indebted.

Statutory schemes for enforcing arbitral awards

Arbitral awards enforceable as 'foreign judgments'

In some of the countries under study, the statutory regime for enforcing foreign judgments discussed in Chapter 18 can be used to enforce foreign arbitration awards.[25] Such awards are treated as a foreign judgment. The statutes provide that the award must have, under the laws in force in the country where it was granted, become enforceable in the same manner as a judgment given by a court in that country (hereinafter, 'arbitration award foreign judgment provisions').[26] In interpreting the equivalent Malawian provision, it has been held that it is enough if the award has reached the stage where it can be enforced by the courts in the country which granted it. It is not necessary for the registration of an award that the award-creditor should have instituted proceedings to enforce it in the country where it was granted, or to have obtained a judgment in the country enforcing the award.[27] A similar interpretation was recently adopted in Nigeria.[28] Indeed, if the award creditor has already obtained a judgment enforcing the award in the country where it was granted, then that judgment can be enforced as such – as a foreign judgment under the regimes discussed in Chapters 17 and 18.

The arbitration award foreign judgment provisions predate the New York Convention. They appear to have been instituted to create a regime for enforcing foreign arbitration awards akin to that which enforced foreign judgments within the British colonial empire. Even though in

[25] See, generally, K. W. Patchett, *Recognition of Commercial Judgments and Awards in the Commonwealth* (London: Butterworths, 1984), pp. 210–35.

[26] Botswana – Judgments (International Enforcement) Act 1981, s. 2; Gambia – Reciprocal Enforcement of Judgments Act 1922, s. 2; Kenya – Foreign Judgments (Reciprocal Enforcement) Act 1984, s. 3(1)(f); Lesotho – Reciprocal Enforcement of Judgments Act 1922, s. 2; Malawi – British and Commonwealth Judgments Act 1922, s. 2; Nigeria – Reciprocal Enforcement of Judgments Act 1958, s. 2, Foreign Judgments (Reciprocal Enforcement) Act 1990, s. 2; Swaziland – Reciprocal Enforcement of Judgments Act 1922, s. 2; Uganda – Foreign Judgment (Reciprocal Enforcement) Act 1961, s. 8(2); Zambia – Foreign Judgment (Reciprocal Enforcement) Act 1937, s. 10(a). These provisions have their historical root in s. 12(1) of the United Kingdom's Administration of Justice Act 1920. At present, Ghana, Namibia, Tanzania, South Africa and Zimbabwe do not have arbitration award foreign judgment provisions in their foreign judgment enforcement statutes.

[27] *Bauman, Hinde & Co. Ltd* v. *David Whitehead & Son Ltd*, Civil Cause No. 2107 of 1996 (High Court, Malawi, 1998); *Bauman Hinde* v. *David Whitehead*, MSCA Civil Appeal No. 17 of 1998 (Supreme Court, Malawi, 2000).

[28] *Tulip Nigeria Ltd* v. *Noleggioe Transport Maritime SAS* [2011] 4 NWLR 254.

many respects arbitration awards sometimes sit uncomfortably in the statutes drafted with 'foreign judgments' in mind, as Patchett has observed, 'there seems to be little doubt that the criteria in the statutes must be fulfilled mutatis mutandis in respect of the award before registration can be finalized'.[29] In other words, an application to register a foreign arbitration award is treated as an application to enforce a foreign judgment.

The arbitration award foreign judgment provisions rarely appear to be invoked. In *Bauman, Hinde & Co. Ltd* v. *David Whitehead & Son Ltd*, the court invoked sections 2 and 3 of the British and Commonwealth Judgments Act 1922 to register an award that was granted in the United Kingdom.[30]

In countries that have arbitration award foreign judgment provisions – Botswana, Gambia, Kenya, Lesotho, Malawi, Nigeria, Swaziland, Uganda and Zambia – the regime co-exists with the common law regime and, for countries that are parties, with the New York Convention regime. In Gambia, Lesotho, Nigeria and Swaziland, it is possible for award creditors to bring an action on the award at common law rather than seeking to register it under their respective Acts.[31] In other words, even though an award qualifies for registration as a foreign judgment in these countries, the award-creditor may choose to bring a common law action on the award. However, the disadvantage of choosing to bring a common law action on an award which could have been registered is that the plaintiff will be denied the costs of that action unless he or she has already failed in an application to register the award, or else the court decides otherwise.

It is arguable that in Botswana, Kenya, Nigeria, Uganda and Zambia, it is not possible to enforce an arbitration award falling within the scope of their respective statutes using the common law or New York Convention regime. This is so because under their statutes: 'No proceedings for the

[29] K. W. Patchett, *Recognition of Commercial Judgments and Awards in the Commonwealth* (London: Butterworths, 1984), p. 210.

[30] MSCA Civil Appeal No. 17 of 1998 (Supreme Court, Malawi, 2000). The Supreme Court affirmed the High Court decision, *Bauman, Hinde & Co. Ltd* v. *David Whitehead & Son Ltd*, Civil Cause No. 2107 of 1996 (High Court, Malawi, 1998). See also *Mauritius Steam Navigation Co. Ltd* v. *International Shipping Lines Ltd* 1969 (3) ALR Comm. 34, [1969] NCLR 174, in which the court noted the possibility that a foreign award may be registered using the Reciprocal Enforcement of Foreign Judgments Act 1958.

[31] Gambia – Reciprocal Enforcement of Judgments Act 1922, s. 3(4); Lesotho – Reciprocal Enforcement of Judgments Act 1922, s. 3(5); Nigeria – Reciprocal Enforcement of Judgments Act 1958, s. 3(4); Swaziland – Reciprocal Enforcement of Judgments Act 1922, s. 3(5).

recovery of a sum payable under a foreign [award], being [an award] to which this Part applies, other than proceedings by way of registration of the [award], shall be entertained by any court in the [forum]'.[32] This raises a difficult question, especially for states which are parties to the New York Convention, and which are also designated to benefit from the arbitration award foreign judgment enforcement provisions: what is the relationship between the two regimes?

This is a question of practical significance. The statutes under discussion contain an extensive list of defences and mandatory currency conversion rules which, compared with the regime provided by the New York Convention, could disadvantage either party to an arbitration award. For example, a party against whom a foreign award is given (hereinafter, the 'award-debtor') and for which enforcement is sought in Kenya, may, relying on section 10(3) of the Foreign Judgment (Reciprocal Enforcement) Act 1984, apply to 'set aside the [award] to the extent that its enforcement would require payment of sums in excess of monetary limits upon liability imposed by any statute of Kenya which applies under the rules of private international law of Kenya'. Such a defence is not open to an award-debtor under the New York Convention. Similarly, the award-creditor is compelled to convert and register the award in local currency. However, such a course is not mandated under the New York Convention.

The arbitration award foreign judgment provisions developed at a time when there was no international regime for enforcing foreign arbitration awards. The regime was deemed relevant to the British colonial empire – it facilitated the enforcement of awards in the colonies. With the adoption and worldwide acceptance of the New York Convention and the demise of the empire, the provisions have outlived their usefulness and should be repealed, especially in countries that are parties to the New York Convention. Applying the statutory regime for enforcing foreign judgments to the enforcement of foreign arbitration awards could, in some instances (such as the above-noted Kenyan example), amount to a breach of a country's international obligations. It is recommended that, in the countries with arbitration award foreign judgment provisions, the regime

[32] Botswana – Judgments (International Enforcement) Act 1981, s. 9; Kenya – Foreign Judgments (Reciprocal Enforcement) Act 1984, s. 17(1); Nigeria – Foreign Judgments (Reciprocal Enforcement) Act 1990, s. 8; Uganda – Foreign Judgment (Reciprocal Enforcement) Act 1961, s. 7; Zambia – Foreign Judgment (Reciprocal Enforcement) Act 1937, s. 8.

established by the provisions should be restricted to awards from countries that are not parties to the New York Convention, or as in the case of Botswana, Kenya, Nigeria and Uganda, countries for which no reciprocity exists under the Convention. Relying on Article III of the New York Convention, it can be argued that applying the regime created by the arbitration award foreign judgment provisions to New York Convention awards imposes 'substantially more onerous conditions ... than are imposed on the recognition or enforcement of domestic arbitral awards'.

The New York Convention and other foreign awards

Botswana

The enforcement of foreign awards in Botswana is governed by the Recognition and Enforcement of Foreign Arbitral Awards Act 1971, which gives effect to the New York Convention. An arbitral award made in any country which is a party to the Convention shall be binding and may be enforced in Botswana. The Act applies only to awards arising out of legal relationships, whether contractual or not, considered as commercial under the laws of Botswana. Furthermore, no award made in any country which is a party to the Convention shall be enforceable in Botswana unless a similar award made in Botswana would be enforceable in such a country. These provisions reflect the reservations Botswana made on becoming party to the Convention.

Gambia

The enforcement of arbitration awards is governed by the Alternative Dispute Resolution Act 2005. Two separate regimes are established by the Act, namely a regime for an 'award arising out of an international commercial arbitration'[33] and any other awards.

As regards 'award arising out of an international commercial arbitration', enforcement is governed by the New York Convention.[34] The award may have been made in Gambia or in any contracting state which has reciprocal legislation recognising the enforcement of arbitral awards made in Gambia, in accordance with the provisions of the Convention. The differences which form the foundation of the award must arise out of a legal contractual relationship.[35]

[33] The concept 'international commercial arbitration' is not defined in the Act.
[34] Alternative Dispute Resolution Act 2005, s. 56. [35] Ibid., s. 56(a)(b).

Concerning any other award, it is provided that an arbitral award, irrespective of the country in which it has been made, shall be recognised as binding and, on application in writing to the High Court, shall be enforced by entry as a judgment in terms of the award, or by action, subject to the defences outlined in the statute.[36] The party relying on an award, or applying for its enforcement, must supply the duly authenticated original award or a duly certified copy, and a duly certified translation into the English language, if necessary.[37] The court may refuse to recognise or enforce an arbitral award at the request of the party against whom it is invoked on proof that: a party to the arbitration agreement was under some incapacity, or the agreement is not valid under the law to which the parties have subjected it, or else, failing any indication on that question, under the law of the country where the award was made; the party against whom the award was invoked was not given proper notice of the appointment of an arbitrator or of the arbitral proceedings, or else was otherwise unable to present his or her case; the award deals with a dispute not contemplated by, or not falling within, the terms of the submission to arbitration, provided that, if the decisions on matters submitted to arbitration can be separated from those not so submitted, that part of the award which contains decisions on matters submitted to arbitration may be recognised and enforced; the composition of the arbitral tribunal, or the arbitral procedure, was not in accordance with the agreement of the parties, or failing such an agreement, was not in accordance with the law of the country where the arbitration took place, or the award has not yet become binding on the parties, or has been set aside or suspended by a court of the country in which, or under the law of which, that award was made.[38] The court may also refuse to recognise an award if it finds that the subject matter of the dispute is not capable of settlement by arbitration under Gambian law, or the recognition or enforcement of the award would be contrary to public policy.[39]

Ghana

The enforcement of foreign awards in Ghana is regulated by section 59 of the Alternative Dispute Resolution Act 2010. The High Court is given jurisdiction to enforce foreign awards. The court must be satisfied

[36] Ibid., s. 52(1). [37] Ibid., s. 52(2). [38] Ibid., s. 52(1)(a).

[39] Ibid., s. 52(1)(b). Under s. 52(3), an award is contrary to public policy if the making of the award was induced or affected by fraud, corruption or gross irregularity, or a breach of the rules of natural justice.

that: the award was granted by a competent authority under the law of the country where it was made; a reciprocal arrangement exists between Ghana and the country where the award was made;[40] or else that the award was made under the New York Convention or an international arbitration treaty ratified by Ghana.[41] A person who seeks to enforce a foreign award must produce original or duly authenticated copies of the award and agreement pursuant to which it was made.[42] There should be no appeal pending against the award in any court under the law applicable to the arbitration.[43] With respect to reciprocating states, the reciprocal arrangement must exist at the time of *application* for the enforcement of the award and not at the time the award was made.[44]

The High Court shall not enforce a foreign award if: it has been annulled in the country where it was granted; the award-debtor was not given sufficient notice to enable him or her to present his or her case; a party, lacking legal capacity, was not properly represented; it does not deal with the issues submitted to arbitration; or it contains a decision beyond the scope of matters submitted to arbitration.[45] An award may be denied recognition and enforcement under the New York Convention where the parties to the arbitration agreement are, under the law applicable to them, under some incapacity. *Jadbranska Slobodna Plovidba* v. *Oysa Ltd*[46] involved an application for leave to enforce a London arbitration award against the respondent. The award was obtained under an arbitration agreement in a charter-party. The applicant and respondent were Yugoslav and Ghanaian firms, respectively. The charter-party,

[40] Arbitration (Foreign Awards) Instrument 1963. The following countries are listed as reciprocating states for the purpose of enforcing New York Convention awards: Austria; Bulgaria; Byelorussian Soviet Socialist Republic; Cambodia; Central African Republic; Ceylon; Czechoslovakia; Ecuador; Federal Republic of Germany; Finland; France; Greece; Hungary; India; Israel; Japan; Madagascar; Morocco; Norway; Poland; Romania; Syria; Thailand; Ukrainian Soviet Socialist Republic; Union of Soviet Socialist Republics; and the United Arab Republic.

[41] Alternative Dispute Resolution Act 2010, s. 59(1).

[42] Ibid., s. 59(1)(d). [43] Ibid., s. 59(1)(e).

[44] *Strojexport* v. *Edward Nassar* [1965] GLR 591.

[45] Alternative Dispute Resolution Act 2010, s. 59(3). This provision appears to have been copied almost verbatim from Art. 2 of the Geneva Convention. The extent to which some provisions are consistent with the New York Convention, to which Ghana is party, is doubtful. For example, Art. 59(3)(c), which provides that the court shall not enforce a foreign award if 'a party, lacking legal capacity, was not properly represented', was taken from Art. 2(1)(b) of the Geneva Convention. This is very different from Art. V(1)(a) of the New York Convention.

[46] [1979] GLR 129, 1978 (2) ALR Comm. 108.

which contained the London arbitration agreement, was entered into prior to incorporating the respondent company. In dismissing the application, the court held that under English law – the law governing the respondent's capacity to enter into the charter-party – the respondent had no capacity to enter into the charter-party on the date on which it was signed.

Kenya

The enforcement of foreign awards in Kenya is regulated by the Arbitration Act 1995 and the Foreign Judgments (Reciprocal Enforcement) Act 1984.[47] Under the Arbitration Act, an arbitration is international if: the parties to an arbitration agreement have, at the time of the conclusion of that agreement, their places of business in different states; the parties have expressly agreed that the subject matter of the arbitration agreement relates to more than one state; or one of the following places is situated outside the state in which the parties have their places of business[48] – namely, the juridical seat of arbitration, as determined by or pursuant to the arbitration agreement, or any place where a substantial part of the obligations of the commercial relationship is to be performed, or the place with which the subject matter of the dispute is most closely connected.

An international arbitration award shall be recognised as binding and enforced in Kenya in accordance with the provisions of the New York Convention or any other convention to which Kenya is signatory and which relates to arbitral awards.[49] In addition to the defences available to an award-debtor under Article V of the Convention,[50] recognition and enforcement of an award may be refused if the granting of the arbitral award was induced or affected by fraud, bribery, corruption or undue influence.[51] A Kenyan court cannot be used to enforce foreign awards founded on illegal, void or immoral contracts. It is Kenya's public policy to enforce international arbitration treaties. However, the courts must balance the competing interests of the policy in favour of enforcing international awards with that of protecting the welfare of Kenyans. Accordingly, enforcement of an award for compensation for a contract,

47 Foreign Judgments (Reciprocal Enforcement) Act 1984, s. 3(1)(f).

48 If a party has more than one place of business, the place of business is that which has the closest relationship to the arbitration agreement. If a party does not have a place of business, reference is to be made to their habitual residence.

49 Arbitration Act 1995, s. 36(2).

50 These defences are repeated almost verbatim in s. 37 of the Act.

51 Arbitration Act 1995, s. 37(1)(a)(vii).

which, if performed, would have released onto the Kenyan market maize which had been officially certified as unfit for human consumption, was contrary to public policy.[52]

Malawi

A specific regime for enforcing foreign awards is created for any award made after 28 July 1924 in pursuance of an agreement for arbitration to which the Protocol on Arbitration Clauses 1923 applies and between persons of whom one is subject to the jurisdiction of a state designated by the Minister on a reciprocal basis as a party to the Convention on the Execution of Foreign Arbitral Awards 1927.[53] A foreign award shall be enforceable in Malawi either by action or by leave of court.[54] A foreign award which is so enforceable shall be treated as binding for all purposes on the persons as between whom it was made, and may accordingly be relied on by any of those persons by way of defence, set off or otherwise in any legal proceedings in Malawi.[55]

The party seeking to enforce a foreign award must produce: the original award or a copy duly authenticated in the manner required by the law of the country in which it was made; evidence proving that the award has become final; and such evidence as may be necessary to prove that the award is a foreign award and that the conditions for enforcement noted below are satisfied.[56] Where a required document is in a foreign language, it is the duty of the party seeking to enforce the award to produce a translation certified as correct by a diplomatic or consular agent of the country to which that party belongs, or certified as correct in such other manner as may be sufficient according to the law of Malawi.[57]

[52] *Glencore Grain Ltd* v. *TSS Grain Millers Ltd* [2002] KLR 1. On the definition of public policy, see generally *Christ for All Nations* v. *Apollo Insurance Co. Ltd* [1999] LLR 1635, where it was held in an application to set aside a local arbitration award that public policy is a broad concept that cannot be precisely defined. However, an award could be set aside as being contrary to Kenyan public policy if it is shown that it is: (i) inconsistent with the constitution or the laws of Kenya, whether written or unwritten; (ii) inimical to the national interests of Kenya; or (iii) contrary to justice or morality. Without claiming to be exhaustive, items included in the second category include the interests of national defence and security, good diplomatic relations with friendly nations, and the economic propriety of Kenya. In the third category are such considerations as whether the award was induced by corruption or fraud or was founded on a contract contrary to public morals.

[53] Arbitration Act 1967, s. 36. Malawi is not a party to the New York Convention.

[54] Arbitration Act 1967, ss. 37(1) and 27.

[55] Arbitration Act 1967, s. 37(2).

[56] Ibid., s. 39(1).

[57] Ibid., s. 39(2).

In order for a foreign award to be enforceable, it must have: been made in pursuance of an agreement for arbitration which was valid under the law by which it was governed; been made by the tribunal provided for in the agreement or constituted in a manner agreed upon by the parties; been made in conformity with the law governing the arbitration procedure; become final[58] in the country in which it was made; been in respect of a matter which may lawfully be referred to arbitration under the law of Malawi; and the enforcement of the award must not be contrary to the public policy or the law of Malawi.[59] A foreign award shall not be enforceable if the court is satisfied that: the award has been annulled in the country in which it was made; or the party against whom it is sought to enforce the award was not given notice of the arbitration proceedings in sufficient time to enable him or her to present his or her case, or was under some legal incapacity and was not properly represented; or the award does not deal with all the questions referred or contains decisions on matters beyond the scope of the agreement for arbitration.[60]

Nigeria

The enforcement of foreign awards in Nigeria is regulated by the Arbitration and Conciliation Act 1988, the Foreign Judgments (Reciprocal Enforcement) Act 1990 and the Reciprocal Enforcement of Judgments Ordinance 1922. Under section 57 of the Arbitration and Conciliation Act 1988, an arbitration is international if the parties to an arbitration agreement have, at the time of the conclusion of the agreement, their places of business in different countries;[61] or one of the following places is situated outside the country where the parties have their places of business: (i) the place of arbitration, if such a place is determined in, or pursuant to, the arbitration agreement; (ii) any place where a substantial part of the obligation of the commercial relationship is to be performed, or the place with which the subject matter of the dispute is most closely connected; or where the parties have expressly agreed that the subject matter of the arbitration agreement relates to more than one country, or where the parties, despite the nature of the contract,

[58] An award shall not be deemed final if any proceedings for the purpose of contesting the validity of the award are pending in the country in which it was made.

[59] Arbitration Act 1967, s. 38(1). [60] Ibid., s. 38(2).

[61] If a party has more than one place of business, the place of business shall be that which has the closest relationship to the arbitration agreement. If a party does not have a place of business, reference shall be made to their habitual residence.

expressly agree that any dispute arising from the commercial transaction shall be treated as an international arbitration.

An arbitral award shall, irrespective of the country in which it was granted, be recognised as binding and shall, upon application in writing to the court, be enforced by the court.[62] Any of the parties to an arbitration agreement may request the court to refuse recognition or enforcement of the award.[63] In other words, the party requesting denial of recognition or enforcement need not be the award-debtor; indeed, he or she need not even have been party to the arbitral proceedings. The court may refuse recognition and enforcement or set aside the award on grounds taken almost verbatim from Article V of the New York Convention.[64]

Without prejudice to the generality of the above, where recognition and enforcement of any award arising out of an international commercial arbitration is sought, the New York Convention shall apply to any award made in Nigeria or in any contracting state, provided that such a contracting state has reciprocal legislation recognising the enforcement of arbitral awards made in Nigeria in accordance with the provisions of the Convention. What is more, the Convention applies only to differences arising from a legal relationship which is contractual.[65] It has been held that an arbitration proceeding, like any proceedings of a tribunal, should observe the rules of natural justice, fair hearing and adherence to the principle of *audi alteram partem*. However, where a respondent has been served with proper notice of the arbitration proceedings, and in good time, and should have taken steps to present his or her defence but failed to do so, they cannot invoke a lack of proper notice as a defence.[66]

South Africa

The enforcement of foreign awards in South Africa is regulated by the Recognition and Enforcement of Foreign Arbitral Awards Act 1977.[67] A 'foreign arbitral award' is an award made outside South Africa, or else its enforcement is not permissible in terms of the Arbitration Act 1965,

[62] Arbitration and Conciliation Act 1990, s. 51(1). [63] Ibid., s. 52(1).

[64] Ibid., ss. 48 and 52(2). [65] Ibid., s. 54.

[66] *Michado & Co. Inc.* v. *Modak (Nigeria) Enterprises Ltd* [2002] 12 WRN 49.

[67] In 1998 the South African Law Reform Commission recommended that the Act should be repealed and replaced by legislation which deals expressly with both the recognition and enforcement of foreign arbitral awards and rectifies certain other defects in the Act. This recommendation has not been implemented. South African Law Reform Commission, *Arbitration: An International Arbitration Act for South Africa* (Pretoria: SALRC, Project 94, 1998).

but it does not conflict with the provisions of the 1965 Act.[68] The Act allows any court to make a foreign arbitral award an order of court and, thereafter, it can be enforced in the same manner as a judgment or order of the same effect.[69] It has been held that the Act invests any Provincial or Local Division of the Supreme Court of South Africa with jurisdiction to recognise any foreign arbitral award, including those between *peregrini*, subject only to the requirement of effectiveness provided by an attachment of property. It is immaterial that the cause of action or underlying transaction has nothing to do with South Africa.[70]

The court may refuse to grant an application to make a foreign award an order of court on grounds virtually identical to Article V of the New York Convention.[71] It is only in exceptional instances that a South African court will not give effect to an arbitration award.[72] Violation of South Africa's public policy is one such instance, i.e. in *Seton Co.* v. *Silveroak Industries Ltd*,[73] the respondent challenged the enforcement of a French award on the grounds of public policy, arguing that it was contrary to public policy to recognise an award obtained through fraud. Rejecting the challenge, it was held that the court will only refuse to recognise a foreign arbitral award where, on the face of the award and the arbitration agreement, it was clear that the award contravened public policy. There does not have to be any extraneous evidence to persuade the court of the illegality of the agreement in question. If extraneous evidence is necessary, as in the case of fraud, the court must first consider whether a remedy lies in the jurisdiction where the award was granted. If so, it would normally be appropriate to leave the respondent to pursue their remedy in that jurisdiction. However, a court will not refuse recognition of an award on the grounds of fraud where the respondent has not exhausted the available remedies in the foreign forum.[74] Where the agreement on the basis of which the foreign arbitral award was made is invalid, a South African court will not enforce the award.[75]

[68] Recognition and Enforcement of Foreign Arbitral Awards Act 1977, s. 1. [69] Ibid., s. 2.

[70] *Laconian Maritime Enterprises Ltd* v. *Agromar Lineas Ltd* 1984 (3) SA 233.

[71] Recognition and Enforcement of Foreign Arbitral Awards Act 1977, s. 4.

[72] *Seton Co.* v. *Silveroak Industries Ltd* 2000 (2) SA 215 at 229. See also *Telcordia Technologies Inc.* v. *Telkom SA Ltd* 2007 (3) SA 266, which involved an unsuccessful attempt to set aside an award on grounds of gross irregularity in the proceedings or excess of powers.

[73] 2000 (2) SA 215.

[74] This is an interesting, but, perhaps, unjustified approach compared to how the defence of fraud is treated in actions to enforce foreign judgments.

[75] *Phoenix Shipping Corp.* v. *DHL Global Forwarding SA (Pty) Ltd* 2012 (3) SA 381.

Enforcement of a foreign arbitration award may be excluded by the Protection of Businesses Act 1978. Under section 1 of the Act, no judgment or arbitral award made outside South Africa shall be enforced within South Africa without the consent of the Minister of Trade and Industry, where the judgment or award has arisen from an act or transaction connected with the mining, production, importation, exportation, refinement, possession, use, sale or ownership of any matter or material, regardless of its nature, and whether within, outside, into or from South Africa.[76]

Tanzania

Recognition and enforcement of foreign awards in Tanzania is governed by the Arbitration Act 1931. This Act has, as a schedule, the Geneva Convention on the Execution of Foreign Arbitral Awards 1927. However, given Tanzania is a party to the New York Convention, the Geneva Convention has 'ceased to have effect' between Tanzania and other contracting parties by virtue of Article VII:2 of the New York Convention. A foreign award shall be enforceable in the High Court.[77] Such an award shall be treated as binding for all purposes on the persons between whom it was made. It may accordingly be relied on by any of those persons by way of defence, set-off or otherwise in any legal proceedings.[78] In order for a foreign award to be enforceable, it must: be made in pursuance of an agreement for arbitration valid under the law that governs it; be made by the tribunal provided for in the agreement, or constituted in a manner agreed upon by the parties; be made in conformity with the law governing the arbitration procedure;[79] be final in the country in which it was made;[80] respect a matter which may lawfully be referred to arbitration under the law of Tanzania; and its enforcement must not contravene the public policy or the law of Tanzania.[81]

[76] In *Seton Co.* v. *Silveroak Industries Ltd* 2000 (2) SA 215 at 226, ministerial permission to enforce an award was sought and granted.

[77] In *Tanzania Cotton Marketing Board* v. *Cogecot Cotton Co.* [1997] TLR 165, it was held that under s. 11(2) of the Arbitration Ordinance, Ch. 15, an arbitration award need not be filed in court by the arbitrator himself. It is sufficient if he instructs somebody else to do it on his behalf.

[78] Arbitration Act 1931, s. 29.

[79] In *WJ Tame Ltd* v. *Zagoritis Estates Ltd* [1960] EA 370, it was held that a mistake as to the territorial law applicable in a dispute submitted to arbitration is such an error of law that justifies the court in setting aside an award.

[80] An award shall not be deemed final if any proceedings to contest the validity of the award are pending in the country in which it was made: Arbitration Act 1931, s. 32.

[81] Arbitration Act 1931, s. 30.

Uganda

The Arbitration and Conciliation Act 2000 makes provision for the enforcement of New York Convention awards.[82] Such an award shall be recognised as binding, and upon application in writing to the court, shall be enforced.[83] Where the court is satisfied that an award is enforceable, it shall be deemed a decree of the court.[84] An enforceable award is treated as binding for all purposes on the persons between whom it was made. Accordingly, it may be relied on by any of those persons by way of defence, set-off or otherwise in a Ugandan proceeding.[85] Even though the Act contains grounds on which an arbitration award can be set aside,[86] it does not contain grounds on which the recognition and enforcement of an award may be refused.

Zambia

Recognition and enforcement of foreign arbitral awards is governed by the Arbitration Act 2000. Under the Act, a New York Convention award is recognised as binding on the persons in relation to whom it was made and is enforceable in accordance with Articles 35 and 36 of the UNCITRAL Model Law on International Commercial Arbitration 1985.[87]

Zimbabwe

The Arbitration Act 1996 implements the UNCITRAL Model Law. Articles 35 and 36 of the Model Law deal with the recognition and enforcement of awards. Even though the law on the enforcement of foreign arbitration awards is based on the UNCITRAL Model Law, it has been held that decisions relating to the New York Convention's public policy defence afford persuasive guidance on interpreting the Model Law. However, in the event of direct conflict, the public policy of Zimbabwe must prevail.[88] Furthermore, it has been held that an award will contravene public policy if induced by fraud or corruption, or where

[82] Section 39 of the Arbitration and Conciliation Act 2000 defines it as an arbitral award made in pursuance of an arbitration agreement in the territory of a state (other than Uganda) which is party to the New York Convention.

[83] Ibid., ss. 35 and 42. [84] Ibid., s. 43. [85] Ibid., s. 41.

[86] Ibid., s. 34. The grounds provided are very similar to Art. V of the New York Convention. See generally *National Social Security Fund* v. *Alcon International Ltd*, Civil Appeal No. 15 of 2009 (Supreme Court, Uganda, 2013).

[87] Arbitration Act 2000, s. 31. The New York Convention is listed as the second schedule to the Act.

[88] *Zimbabwe Electricity Supply Authority* v. *Maposa* 1999 (2) ZLR 452.

a breach of natural justice has occurred, or where its substantive effect makes it contrary to public policy. The public policy defence is construed restrictively and is applicable only if some fundamental principle of law, morality or justice is violated. An award will not contravene public policy merely because the reasoning or conclusions of the arbitrator are wrong, either in fact, or in law. Where, however, the reasoning or conclusion in an award goes beyond mere faultiness or incorrectness and constitutes a palpable inequity so far-reaching and outrageous in its defiance of logic or accepted moral standards that a sensible and fair-minded person would consider that the conception of justice in Zimbabwe would be intolerably hurt by the award, then it contravenes public policy to uphold it. The same consequences apply where the arbitrator has not applied his or her mind to the question, or has totally misunderstood the issue, and the resultant injustice reaches the point mentioned above.[89] Granting full damages to a party in spite of its failure to meet all their obligations under a contract violates elementary justice and contravenes public policy.[90]

Comments

All the countries that are parties to the New York Convention – Botswana, Ghana, Kenya, Lesotho, Nigeria, South Africa, Tanzania, Uganda, Zambia and Zimbabwe – have enacted legislation to implement it.[91] Given that they are all dualist countries, as far as the relationship between international and national law is concerned, this is significant. Without legislation for implementation at a domestic level, the Convention will have no effect within their legal systems.[92]

However, when the implementing statutes are examined, it is sometimes doubtful whether they fully meet the obligations stipulated under the New York Convention. This can be illustrated through a number of provisions. Under Nigeria's Arbitration and Conciliation Act 1988, any parties to an arbitration agreement may request the court to refuse recognition or enforcement of the award in Nigeria. However, under the New York Convention, refusing to recognise and enforce an award should be at the 'request of the party against whom [the award] is invoked'. Similarly, under the Convention, the fact that an application to set aside an award is pending before a competent authority of the

[89] *Zimbabwe Electricity* v. *Maposa*. [90] *Pamire* v. *Dumbutshena* 2001 (1) ZLR 123.

[91] Gambia also implements the Convention in its Alternative Dispute Resolution Act 2005.

[92] *Transvaal Alloys (Pty) Ltd* v. *Polysius (Pty) Ltd* 1983 (2) SA 630 at 647.

country where, or under the law of which, the award was granted, does not automatically prevent the recognition and enforcement of the award – the court is given discretion to adjourn the enforcement proceedings. However, in Ghana's Alternative Dispute Resolution Act 2010, the fact that an 'appeal is pending against the award in any court under the law applicable to the arbitration' shall prevent the court from enforcing it. Concern has also been expressed that the use of 'may' in section 2(1) of South Africa's Recognition and Enforcement of Foreign Arbitral Awards Act 1977 could give the impression that recognition and enforcement is discretionary. Under Article III of the Convention, however, recognition and enforcement is not discretionary – there is an obligation to recognise and enforce the award subject to a very limited number of defences. Inspired by Article 19(1)(b)(iii) of the Model Law, Kenya's Arbitration Act 1995 allows for an award to be denied recognition and enforcement on the basis that the making of the award was 'induced or affected by fraud, bribery, undue influence or corruption'. The use of 'only if' in Article V of the New York Convention suggests the defences provided thereunder are exhaustive. To the extent that fraud, bribery, undue influence or corruption does not amount to a breach of public policy – a defence provided for in the Convention – it is unknown to the Convention.

The challenges which these apparently 'defective' implementation issues can present for the enforcement of New York Convention awards have not become evident in the countries under study. In part, this could be attributed to the very few cases that deal with the recognition and enforcement of awards.

The central issue in many of the cases decided under the Convention has been the scope of defences it provides. The defences of a lack of legal capacity, breach of natural justice and public policy have been discussed.[93] Delineating the scope and content of the relatively fluid concept of public policy is challenging. But the jurisprudence of the Kenyan, South African and Zimbabwean courts and national legislation offer guidance on this. Zimbabwe's Arbitration Act emphatically declares that 'an award is in conflict with the public policy of Zimbabwe if the making of the award was induced or effected by fraud or corruption, or a breach of the rules of natural justice occurred in connection

[93] In addition to these defences there are other procedural defences such as *res judicata* and limitation of actions. See *Laconian Maritime Enterprises Ltd* v. *Agromar Lineas Ltd* 1986 (3) SA 509.

with the making of the award'.[94] The courts have emphasised the need to narrowly construe the public policy defence and have used words and phrases such as 'clearly unacceptable' and 'offensive'[95] and 'only if some fundamental principle of the law or morality or justice is violated'.[96]

On the other hand, it is evident from the decided cases that what is at stake is domestic or concerns national public policy rather than 'international public policy'. In the words of the Zimbabwean Supreme Court, 'what has to be focused upon is whether the award, be it foreign or domestic, is contrary to the public policy of Zimbabwe. If it is, then it cannot be sustained no matter that any foreign forum would be prepared to recognise and enforce it'.[97] It is submitted that this position is consistent with Article V:2(b) of the Convention, which refers to 'the public policy of that country'.

ICSID Convention awards

As of 10 April 2013, Botswana, Gambia, Ghana, Kenya, Lesotho, Malawi, Namibia,[98] Nigeria, Sierra Leone, Swaziland, Tanzania, Uganda, Zambia and Zimbabwe are parties to the Convention on the Settlement of Investment Disputes between States and Nationals of Other States (ICSID Convention) 1965.[99] South Africa is the only country within the scope of this study that is not party to this Convention.[100] The Convention enjoins each contracting state to take such legislative or other measures as might be necessary for making the provisions of the

94 This was an elaboration to Art. 36(b)(ii) of the Model Law on which the Arbitration Act 1996 is modelled.

95 *Glencore Grain Ltd* v. *TSS Grain Millers Ltd* [2002] KLR 1 at 21.

96 *Zimbabwe Electricity Supply Authority* v. *Maposa* 1999 (2) ZLR 452 at 465.

97 *Zimbabwe Electricity* v. *Maposa* at 465.

98 Namibia only signed the Convention on 26 October 1998. It has not yet deposited its instrument of ratification and, thus, the Convention has not entered into force in its respect.

99 Convention on the Settlement of Investment Disputes between States and Nationals of Other States 1965, 575 UNTS 159.

100 The South African High Court has criticised the fact that South Africa is not party to the Convention: *Von Abo* v. *The Government of the Republic of South Africa* 2009 (2) SA 526 at 535–40. In 1998, the South African Law Reform Commission recommended that South Africa should ratify the Convention. This recommendation has not been implemented. South African Law Reform Commission, *Arbitration: An International Arbitration Act for South Africa* (Pretoria: SALRC, Project 94, 1998).

Convention effective in its territories[101] and many countries have enacted legislation to implement it at a domestic level.[102]

The ICSID Convention has a unique regime for enforcing awards made under it.[103] Article 53 of the Convention prevents national courts from modifying or setting aside an ICSID award. In other words, there can be no external review of an ICSID award. The Convention has its own self-contained procedures for reviewing awards. A party to an ICSID award cannot initiate action before a national court of a state that is party to the Convention to set aside or review the award: that court must dismiss any such action. This distinct feature of the Convention is important for the finality of ICSID awards. It provides a clear advantage over other international arbitration conventions or forums.[104] Significantly, and compared with other statutes for enforcing foreign arbitration awards, none of the ICSID Convention-implementing statutes in the countries under study contains a provision which allows the court enforcing an ICSID award to refuse its enforcement on any grounds. Consistent with the provisions of the Convention, what is provided is that the enforcing court should stay the enforcement proceedings for the parties to return to the ICSID and settle their differences as regards the award.

To date, there has not been a single reported case dealing with the enforcement of an ICSID award in any of the countries under study. In the prophetic words of Asouzu, 'it is unlikely that ICSID awards will be sought to be recognised or enforced in an African jurisdiction in the near future'.[105] The reasons for this state of affairs include adverse perceptions about the quality of African courts, the fact that many African states have

[101] ICSID Convention, Art. 69.

[102] See, e.g., Botswana – Settlement of Investment Disputes (Convention) Act 1970; Kenya – Investment Disputes Convention Act 1966; Lesotho – Arbitration International Investment (Disputes) Act 1974; Malawi – Investment Disputes (Enforcement of Awards) Act 1966; Nigeria – International Centre for Settlement of Investment Disputes (Enforcement of Awards) Decree 1967; Swaziland – Arbitration (International Investment Disputes) Act 1966; Uganda – Arbitration and Conciliation Act 2000, ss. 45–7; Zambia – Investment Disputes Convention Act 1970; Zimbabwe – Arbitration (International Investment) Act 1995. See generally A. A. Asouzu, *International Commercial Arbitration and African States: Practice, Participation and Institutional Development* (Cambridge University Press, 2001), pp. 368–408.

[103] ICSID Convention, Arts. 53–5.

[104] See C. H. Schreuer, *The ICSID Convention: A Commentary* (Cambridge University Press, 2001), pp. 1082–4.

[105] Asouzu, *International Commercial Arbitration and African States*, p. 367.

valuable and convertible assets outside the continent, and that parties generally tend to comply with awards without resort to litigation.

Arbitration awards in foreign currency

A foreign arbitration award will often be in foreign currency. As with foreign judgments, two important issues are: the currency in which foreign awards should be enforced; and if there is need for conversion, which date should be used.[106] As noted above, in Botswana, Gambia, Kenya, Lesotho, Nigeria, Swaziland, Uganda and Zambia, statutes on the enforcement of foreign judgments can be extended to the enforcement of arbitration awards from designated countries. The enforcement of awards under the Botswanan, Kenyan, Ugandan and Zambian statutes are governed by their currency conversion provisions.[107] The application of the statutory conversion provisions to foreign awards, especially awards made under the New York Convention, will not be inconsistent with the Convention, as the latter does not deal with the subject.

Apart from in Botswana, Kenya, Nigeria, Uganda and Zambia, it is only in South Africa that the issue is expressly and directly addressed by statute. Under the Recognition and Enforcement of Foreign Arbitral Awards Act 1977, where any amount payable in terms of an award is expressed in foreign currency, the award shall be made an order of court as if it were an award for such an amount in South African rand equivalent to the amount so payable, based on the exchange rate that prevails on the date of the award.[108] The South African Law Reform Commission has recommended repeal of this provision. The Commission reasoned that it undermines the effect of an arbitral award in a foreign currency if there is a substantial period between the date of the award and payment. Furthermore, the conversion of the foreign currency award into South African rand on the date of the award, instead of on

[106] See *Universal TPT Co. Ltd* v. *Tzortzis* [1973] EA 310, 1973 (2) ALR Comm. 323, which held in an application to register an English award that the correct date for conversion was the date the award was granted.

[107] Botswana – Judgments (International Enforcement) Act 1981; Kenya – Foreign Judgments (Reciprocal Enforcement) Act 1984, ss. 3(1)(f) and 7(1); Nigeria – Foreign Judgments (Reciprocal Enforcement) Act 1961, s. 4(3); Uganda – Foreign Judgment (Reciprocal Enforcement) Act 1961, ss. 8(2) and 3(3); Zambia – Foreign Judgment (Reciprocal Enforcement) Act 1937, ss. 10 (a) and 4(3). Gambia, Lesotho and Swaziland legislation contain no provision on currencies.

[108] Recognition and Enforcement of Foreign Arbitral Awards Act 1977, s. 2(2).

the date of payment, could indirectly affect the arbitral tribunal's award of interest, resulting in the advantage of one party and the detriment of the other.[109] Many countries do not have similar statutory provisions and even for those which have, a foreign award may fall outside their scope. It is recommended that, in such cases, the common law jurisdiction of the court to give judgment in foreign currency should be extended to the enforcement of arbitration awards.[110]

Limitation of actions and arbitration awards

In Ghana, Kenya, Tanzania and Uganda, an action to enforce an arbitration award shall not be brought after the expiration of six years from the date on which the cause of action arose.[111] This rule applies to both domestic and foreign arbitration awards.[112] In Kenya, it has been held that where an applicant has to reapply for recognition of an award after protracted litigation to enforce the award has been struck out on procedural grounds, the application may be accepted even though more than six years has elapsed since the award was made.[113]

In Kenya, 'where a submission contains a term that no cause of action shall accrue in respect of a matter, the cause of action, for the purposes of this Act and of any other written law relating to the limitation of actions (whether in their application to arbitration or to other proceedings),

[109] South African Law Reform Commission, *Arbitration: An International Arbitration Act for South Africa* (Pretoria: SALRC, Project 94, 1998), p. 151.

[110] Historically, the rule that prevented courts from giving judgment in foreign currency was extended to the enforcement of arbitral awards: *Universal TPT Co. Ltd* v. *Tzortzis* [1973] EA 310, 1973 (2) ALR Comm. 323.

[111] Ghana – Limitation Decree 1972, s. 4(1)(e); Kenya – Limitations of Actions Act 1967, s. 4(1)(c); Tanzania – Law of Limitations Act 1971, s. 3(1); Uganda – Limitations Act 1959, s. 3(1)(c). A similar six-year period is adopted in Nigeria, where each state in the federation has its own statute dealing with limitation of actions. As is the case in the enforcement of foreign judgment statutes in these countries, it would have been better if the issue of limitation of actions was dealt with in the statutes dealing with the enforcement of arbitration awards. Arguably, in the countries with the arbitration award foreign judgment provisions, this issue is addressed in the sense that the limitation period applicable to registering a foreign judgment will apply to an action to register an award. See, generally, A. Adaralegbe, 'Limitation Period for the Enforcement of Arbitral Awards in Nigeria' (2006) 22 *Arbitration International* 613; *Tulip Nigeria Ltd* v. *Noleggioe Transport Maritime SAS* [2011] 4 NWLR 254.

[112] Ghana – Limitation Decree 1972, s. 34; Kenya – Limitations of Actions Act 1967, s. 2(1); Tanzania – Law of Limitations Act 1971, s. 3(1); Uganda – Limitations Act 1959, s. 1(1)(b).

[113] *Glencore Grain Ltd* v. *TSS Grain Millers Ltd* [2012] eKLR.

accrues in respect of any such matter at the time when it would have accrued but for that term in the submission'.[114] Similar provision exists in Ghana, Tanzania and Uganda.[115] These provisions appear to be directed at instances where parties agree that arbitration should be a condition precedent to any action at law – what is often referred to as a *Scott* v. *Avery* clause.[116] Indeed, section 26(2) of Uganda's Limitations Act 1959 makes this explicit by including the condition 'until an award is made under the submission'. The effect of these provisions is to treat all arbitration agreements as the same for the purposes of limitation of actions. The provisions actually reversed the decision in *Murmansk State S.S. Line* v. *Kano Oil Millers Ltd*,[117] which held that, if the plaintiff expressly waives his right to sue as soon as a cause of action arises, as in agreeing that arbitration or an award shall be a condition precedent to any action, the limitation period runs from the date of the award, unless the defendant, for his part, waives his right to insist on the condition precedent. The provisions preserve what is implicit in the above decision, i.e. that limitation periods run from the date underlying the cause of action and not from the date of the award.[118]

The provisions appear to be founded on the view that an action to enforce an arbitration award is 'really one on the contract'.[119] The action to enforce the award is not an independent cause of action for which time runs from a date other than the date of the original breach of contract subject to arbitration.[120] The practical significance of these provisions is that, if enforcement of an award is envisaged in Ghana, Kenya, Tanzania and Uganda, a party to a *Scott* v. *Avery* clause is better off disregarding the need to arbitrate as a condition precedent to litigation and suing immediately there is a breach. This is because time starts to run from the date of the breach and not the date arbitration

114 Kenya – Limitations of Actions Act 1967, s. 34(2).

115 Ghana – Limitation Decree 1972, s. 28; Tanzania – Law of Limitations Act 1971, s. 40(2); Uganda – Limitations Act 1959, s. 26(2).

116 It derives its name from *Scott* v. *Avery* (1856) 5 HLC 809.

117 *Murmansk State SS Line* v. *Kano Oil Millers Ltd* 1974 (1) ALR Comm. 1, [1974] NCLR 1, [1974] 1 All NLR 402 (affirming *Murmansk State Steamship Line* v. *Kano Oil Millers Ltd* 1974 (3) ALR Comm. 192).

118 *City Engineering Nigeria Ltd* v. *Federal Housing Authority* [1997] 9 NWLR 224, (1997) All NLR 1.

119 *Murmansk State SS Line* v. *Kano Oil Millers Ltd* 1974 (1) ALR Comm. 1 at 8, [1974] NCLR 1 at 8, [1974] 1 All NLR 402 at 410.

120 A different position is expressed in the South African case of *Laconian Maritime Enterprises Ltd* v. *Agromar Lineas Ltd* 1986 (3) SA 509 at 525.

starts or when the award is granted. In this respect, the statutes appear to encourage breach of arbitration agreements.

On the other hand, a party to an arbitration agreement is better off initiating the arbitration process immediately a breach occurs and perhaps ensuring that the process does not drag on for too long – in any case, one of the virtues of arbitration is to ensure an expedited means of settling disputes. Delay in initiating and concluding arbitration proceedings could, in these countries, lead to a situation where the resulting award is unenforceable. Arguably, this is inconsistent with common sense and justice – a party to arbitration proceedings does not have sole control over their duration. To provide a party with the 'incentive' to delay proceedings by allowing them to rely on a delay to escape the enforcement of a resulting award is most inappropriate. The approach is also inconsistent with how foreign judgments are treated – an action to enforce a foreign judgment is an action on the judgment and not an action on the original cause of action. Admittedly, the juridical bases of a foreign judgment and of a foreign arbitration award are different. The former is founded on the jurisdiction of the foreign court, while the latter is founded on the consent of parties to the proceedings. However, as noted above, in some of the countries under study, Parliament has found it right to equate foreign arbitration awards with foreign judgments for the purposes of enforcement. It is submitted that the issue of limitation in actions to enforce foreign arbitration awards is an example of where the equality of treatment with foreign judgments is merited.

Botswana, Lesotho, South Africa and Zimbabwe's prescriptive statutes do not expressly address the issue of prescription in actions to enforce foreign arbitration awards.[121] However, it has been held that South Africa's Prescription Act 1969 is substantive in character. Accordingly, in an action to enforce a foreign arbitration award, whether the award is prescribed will be determined by the *lex causae* of the underlying contract.[122]

[121] Botswana – Prescription Act 1959; Lesotho – Prescription Act 1861; Namibia – Prescription Act 1969; South Africa – Prescription Act 1969; Zimbabwe – Prescription Act 1975.

[122] *Laconian Maritime Enterprises Ltd* v. *Agromar Lineas Ltd* 1986 (3) SA 509.

PART VII

International civil procedure

20

Remedies in support of or against foreign judicial and arbitral proceedings

Cross-border litigation is complex. While litigating in Utopia, a party may want to obtain relief from a court in another country to support proceedings in Utopia. They may want an order from the foreign court which will freeze the assets of the defendant within or even outside the jurisdiction, or else an order which will compel the defendant to produce or disclose certain documents. This applies equally to arbitral proceedings. A party may also want an injunction from the Utopian courts to restrain another party from litigating abroad or proceeding with arbitration. The issues involved in providing remedies in support of, or against, proceedings pending abroad are germane for the effective administration of justice. These issues are the focus of this chapter.

Botswana

A Botswanan court has jurisdiction to make an order for the attachment of assets of a defendant pending the determination of an action in a foreign court. Thus, in an instance where an application was made for the attachment of a grader, pending determination of an action to be brought in South Africa, it was held that the court had jurisdiction to grant an interim order of this nature, and it was so granted.[1]

The court has jurisdiction to grant a number of forms of interlocutory relief in support of arbitration proceedings. Thus, it has the power to order for the examination of a witness or witnesses before a special examiner, either in Botswana or elsewhere; for the discovery of documents and interrogatories; for another party to give security for costs in the same way as a litigant, and for an interim injunction or similar relief.[2]

[1] *Concorde Leasing Corp. Ltd* v. *TPR (Pty) Ltd* 1979–80 BLR 122.

[2] Arbitration Act 1959, s. 16. See generally *Cerimele Construction Co. (Botswana) (Pty) Ltd* v. *Joint Venture Morteo-Condotee SCRL* 1995 BLR 399. It is unclear from the decision whether the arbitration was to be held outside Botswana.

Ghana

A Ghanaian court has jurisdiction to grant an injunction restraining the pursuit of arbitration abroad. Thus, in *Attorney General* v. *Balkan Energy Co. LLC*,[3] the court granted an injunction restraining the defendant from proceeding with, or taking any further steps whatsoever in respect of, arbitration proceedings instituted before the Permanent Court of Arbitration.

Nigeria

In an appropriate case, a Nigerian court has jurisdiction to restrain a person from prosecuting an action in a foreign jurisdiction. However, this is a power that has to be exercised reluctantly, sparingly and with great circumspection. The relief should be granted where grave reasons and special circumstances have been established.[4] Thus, in the instant case, the court reversed an earlier decision of a Lagos High Court restraining the appellant from further prosecuting their case in the United States while the respondent's action against them was pending in Nigeria.[5]

In relation to admiralty proceedings, where it appears to a Nigerian court, where proceedings are pending, that these proceedings should be stayed or dismissed on the grounds that the claim concerned should be determined by arbitration (whether in Nigeria or elsewhere), or by a foreign court, and where a ship or other property is under arrest in the proceedings, the court may order that the proceedings be stayed on condition that the arrest and detention of the ship or property shall continue, or satisfactory security for their release be given, as security for the satisfaction of any award or judgment that may be made in the arbitration or foreign proceedings.[6] In staying proceedings, the court is also empowered to impose conditions with respect to the institution, prosecution of arbitration, or proceedings in the foreign court. It may also require that equivalent security be provided for the satisfaction of any award or judgment that may be made in the foreign proceedings.[7]

As regards relief in support of foreign arbitral proceedings, it has been held that a court cannot hear or determine a case on its merits where the

[3] Suit No. BDC/32/20 (High Court, Ghana, 2010).
[4] *United Bank of Africa Plc* v. *Ade Coker* [1996] 4 NWLR 239. [5] Ibid.
[6] Admiralty Jurisdiction Decree 1991, s. 10(1). [7] Ibid., s. 10(2).

only purpose of the action brought before it is for security in respect of arbitration proceedings abroad – in this instance in London. The court reasoned that given the actual controversy that gave rise to the demand for security was not before the court, it had no jurisdiction to deal with the ancillary issue. Thus, to order the arrest and detention of a vessel for the sole purpose of providing security for an award in arbitration proceedings pending in London is beyond the jurisdiction of the Federal High Court.[8]

South Africa

A South African court may, in the exercise of its admiralty jurisdiction, order any person to give security for costs or for any claim.[9] Such a claim includes claims pending before foreign arbitral or judicial bodies. The power to grant security in such cases has to be sparingly exercised. It should not be readily granted unless it is in order to assist a litigant with a firm claim against a defendant who might not otherwise satisfy a judgment.[10] Furthermore, a court may, in the exercise of its admiralty jurisdiction, order the arrest of any property for the purpose of providing security for a pending or prospective foreign arbitral or court proceeding, if the person seeking the arrest has a claim enforceable by an action *in personam* against the owner of the property concerned, or an action *in rem* against such property, or which would be so enforceable but for any such arbitration or proceedings.[11]

A claimant to an order for the arrest of a ship in terms of section 5(3)(a) of the Admiralty Jurisdiction Regulation Act 1983, with the aim of obtaining security in respect of a claim which is the subject of proceedings contemplated for a foreign forum, is required to satisfy the court that they have: a claim enforceable by an action *in rem* against the ship in question, or against a ship of which the ship in question is an associated

[8] *NV Scheep* v. *The MV S Araz* [2000] 15 NWLR 622, [2001] 4 WRN 105.

[9] Admiralty Jurisdiction Regulation Act 1983,.s. 5(2)(a).

[10] *The MV Leresti: Afris Shipping International Corp.* v. *MV Leresti* 1997 (2) SA 681. See also *The MV Zlatni Piasatzi: Frozen Foods International Ltd* v. *Kudu Holdings (Pty) Ltd* 1997 (2) SA 569; *The Yu Long Shan Guangzhou Maritime Group Co.* v. *Dry Bulk SA* 1997 (2) SA 454; *Devonia Shipping Ltd* v. *MV Luis (Yeoman Shipping Co. Ltd Intervening)* 1994 (2) SA 363.

[11] Admiralty Jurisdiction Regulation Act 1983, s. 5(3)(a). See *Katagum Wholesale Commodities Co. Ltd* v. *The MV Paz* 1984 (3) SA 261; *Babel Shipping Co. Ltd* v. *Grapsas t/a Nuova* 1995 (1) SA 716.

ship; a prima facie case in respect of such a claim, which is prima facie enforceable in the nominated forum or forums of their choice, and that they have a genuine and reasonable need for security in respect of the claim. If the claimant satisfies the above-mentioned requirements, then they are entitled to an order in terms of the section, unless the respondent ship-owner places countervailing material before the court by which it is proven that there are sound reasons for not granting the order. The respondent may show, for example, that the foreign court, despite having jurisdiction to adjudicate upon the claim, will nevertheless decline to do so for some particular reason, or that the defendant in the contemplated proceedings will not receive a fair hearing in the foreign court. The onus is a heavy one and the courts will require that the respondent proves and establishes their assertions in an objective manner by means of positive and cogent evidence.[12]

Zimbabwe

A Zimbabwean court may issue an order prohibiting a person within its jurisdiction from doing something outside the jurisdiction, but before doing so, the court must be satisfied that its order will be effective. Considerations to be taken into account in this regard include whether the respondent is an *incola* or a *peregrinus*. If the applicant satisfies the court that all the requirements for granting an interlocutory interdict are present, it is not a bar to an anti-dissipation interdict that the assets involved are held outside the country. In such a case, it does not necessarily have to be proved that the respondent has assets within the area of the court's jurisdiction. Where the person against whom a prohibitory interdict has been granted remains within the jurisdiction of the court, such a court can always enforce compliance with its order through the use of contempt of court proceedings.[13] In *Bozimo Trade and Development Co. Ltd* v. *First Merchant Bank of Zimbabwe Ltd*,[14] the applicant company applied for an anti-dissipation interdict in respect of assets situated outside Zimbabwe. It contended that its intent was to

[12] *Cargo Laden and Lately Laden on Board the MV Thalassini Avgi* v. *MV Dimitris* 1989 (3) SA 820. See *Imperial Marine Co.* v. *MV Pasquale Della Gatta* [2012] 1 All SA 491 on the prima facie case requirement.

[13] *Bozimo Trade and Development Co. Ltd* v. *First Merchant Bank of Zimbabwe Ltd* 2000 (1) ZLR 1.

[14] 2000 (1) ZLR 1.

commence legal proceedings against the first respondent in the United States and that the interdict was necessary to stop the respondents from dissipating assets in order to frustrate the execution of any judgment the applicant might obtain. Although the application was not successful, it was held that, where the relevant conditions are established, the court has jurisdiction to make such an order.

Comments

The complexity of international litigation is such that in prosecuting or defending judicial or arbitral proceedings in one country, a party may need the assistance of a foreign court to support an aspect of the proceedings. The courts in the countries under study have jurisdiction to grant remedies which may be usefully extended to assist a party to a foreign proceeding. These remedies include injunctions, for example, anti-suit and anti-arbitration injunctions, a Mareva injunction or an anti-dissipation interdict,[15] order security for costs, and order arrest *suspectus de fuga*.[16] Although these remedies are routinely deployed in domestic litigation, the courts of the countries under study have rarely been prepared to extend them to assist foreign proceedings, especially in cases where there is no direct statutory basis for the exercise of such jurisdiction.

Indeed, courts in the countries under study are generally reluctant to exercise 'extra-territorial jurisdiction' in the sense of providing remedies with extra-territorial reach and to assume jurisdiction over acts committed abroad. The South African case of *Ex p. Hay Management Consultants (Pty) Ltd*[17] involved an application for a prohibitory interdict against a *peregrinus* respondent. All the acts complained of were committed outside South Africa. The court held that, since it had no control over the

[15] See, e.g., Kenya – *Central Bank of Kenya* v. *Giro Commercial Bank Ltd* [2007] 2 EA 93; Malawi – *Investment and Development Bank of Malawi* v. *Gredean Africa (Pvt) Ltd* [1993] 16(2) MLR 531; South Africa – *Knox D'Arcy Ltd* v. *Jamieson* 1994 (3) SA 700.

[16] An arrest *suspectus de fuga* is aimed at preventing a debtor from fleeing the jurisdiction in order to avoid paying a debt. In South Africa, *Amrich* v. *Van Wesembeeck* 2010 (1) SA 117 held that the procedure of arrest *tamquam suspectus de fuga* was unconstitutional because it violates the debtor's right to personal freedom, as contained in s. 12 of the Constitution of the Republic of South Africa Act 1996. The procedure is, however, still available in some countries. See, e.g., Botswana – Rules of the High Court, Ord. 15; Lesotho – High Court Rules 1980, s. 7; Namibia – Rules of the High Court 1990, s. 9; Swaziland – High Court Rules 2010, s. 11; Zimbabwe – High Court Act 1981, s. 16.

[17] 2000 (3) SA 501.

respondent, or over the acts in question, it could not entertain the application. Similarly, in *B* v. *S*,[18] it was held that the South African courts had no jurisdiction to order a person resident in the United States to return to South Africa a child that had been removed from there to the United States. The court reasoned that such an order would be ineffective since they could not enforce it.[19] In *First National Bank of Namibia* v. *Kaure*,[20] the applicant bank sued for judgment on a mortgage bond securing a loan for the purchase of property in Namibia. It sought an order declaring the property in Namibia to be especially executable. The Zimbabwean court held that it had no jurisdiction to make such an order. Similarly, the Supreme Court of Namibia has also noted that 'the courts of a country may have power over the person of the defendant and yet not have power to give an effective judgment because the order prayed for by the plaintiff is one to be performed outside such country. In such a case the courts of such country will, in general have no jurisdiction to grant the order.'[21]

The South African case of *Metlika Trading Ltd* v. *Commissioner, South African Revenue Service*[22] was an appeal against a court order that the appellant take all necessary steps to procure the return of an aircraft to South Africa. The appellant challenged the order on the grounds that the aircraft was in a foreign country and that the court had no jurisdiction to order its return to South Africa. The appellant argued that such an order would infringe the sovereignty of the foreign country, and that the court would be unable to give effect to it. The court rejected these arguments. It held that with *incolae* respondents, it might assume jurisdiction to grant an *in personam* interdict (whether mandatory or prohibitory) no matter whether or not the act in question was to be performed or restrained outside the court's territory. The court reasoned that such an order did not affect the sovereignty of a foreign court; it was an *in personam* order against the respondent, subject to the court's jurisdiction and not against third parties. If not complied with, it would be domestically enforced against the respondent by contempt proceedings. We have already noted

[18] 2006 (5) SA 540.

[19] See also *Julie Brown* v. *Malcolm Clive Stone*, Case No. 489/05 (Supreme Court of Appeal, South Africa, 2005); *Di Bona* v. *Di Bona* 1993 (2) SA 682; and *South Atlantic Islands Development Corp*. v. *Buchan* 1971 (1) SA 234, where the court refused to restrain the respondent from fishing off the islands of Tristan de Cunha in the South Atlantic, outside the area over which the court exercised jurisdiction.

[20] 1999 (2) ZLR 269.

[21] *Parents' Committee of Namibia* v. *Nujoma* 1990 (1) SA 873 at 889.

[22] 2005 (3) SA 1.

Bozimo Trade and Development Co. Ltd v. *First Merchant Bank of Zimbabwe Ltd*,[23] where the applicant applied for an anti-dissipation interdict in respect of assets situated outside Zimbabwe, in anticipation of a prospective suit in the United States. The Zimbabwean court held that it might issue an order prohibiting a person within its jurisdiction from doing something outside the jurisdiction, but, before doing so, it must be satisfied that the order would be effective.

Most of the above cases do not involve invoking the jurisdiction of the forum's court to support foreign proceedings, but they give us a sense of the courts' attitude towards the exercise of extra-territorial jurisdiction. The courts have been concerned about the sovereignty of the foreign state and the effectiveness of any judgment, especially in the sense of an ability to enforce the judgment. Where the courts have exercised jurisdiction that, on the face of it, appears to be extra-territorial, they have always required some connection with the forum.

Leaving aside the above-noted legislation in South Africa and Nigeria that deals with arbitration and admiralty proceedings, the laws on arbitration in many of the countries under study allow courts to grant remedies or make orders in support of arbitration proceedings.[24] Such orders include orders for the examination of a witness; for the discovery of documents and interrogatories; for another party to give security for costs; for inspection, or interim preservation, or the sale of goods or property that constitute the subject matter of the arbitration; for the appointment of a receiver; for an interim injunction; and for an order securing the amount in dispute. Apart from the jurisdiction to stay proceedings in favour of arbitration in cases where there is an arbitration agreement, which, as discussed in Chapter 5, has been routinely granted in favour of foreign arbitration, there is little case law on the extent to which courts in the countries under study are prepared to grant remedies

[23] 2000 (1) ZLR 1.

[24] See, e.g., Botswana – Arbitration Act 1959, s. 16; Gambia – Alternative Dispute Resolution Act 2005, s. 13; Ghana – Alternative Dispute Resolution Act 2010, s. 39; Kenya – Arbitration Act 1995, s. 7, *Midland Finance & Securities Globetel Inc* v. *Attorney General* [2008] KLR 650 at 680, where the court described its role as 'supportive'. *Nedermar Technology BV Ltd* v. *Kenya Anti-corruption Commission* [2008] KLR 476; *Nedermar Technology BV Ltd* v. *Kenya Anti-corruption Commission* [2006] 2 KLR 678; South Africa – Arbitration Act 1965, s. 21 (s. 20 of the Act also allows an arbitration tribunal to, at any stage before making a final award, state any question of law arising in the course of the arbitration in the form of a special case for the opinion of the court); Uganda – Arbitration and Conciliation Act 2000, s. 6; Zambia – Arbitration Act 2000, s.11; Zimbabwe – Arbitration Act 1996, First Sch. S. 9.

in support of foreign arbitral proceedings. However, a purposive interpretation of the relevant statutory provisions suggests that the jurisdiction to grant interim orders in support of arbitral proceedings is not limited to domestic arbitration.[25] In Ghana, it appears that the parties may, by agreement, exclude the jurisdiction of the High Court to make certain interim orders in support of arbitral proceedings.[26]

[25] Indeed, Uganda's Arbitration and Conciliation Act 2000 defines arbitration to mean 'any arbitration whether or not administered by a domestic or international institution where there is an arbitration agreement'.

[26] Alternative Dispute Resolution Act 2010, s. 39(1).

21

International judicial assistance

In order to properly institute an action before a court, a plaintiff may have to serve legal process or documents on a defendant who is abroad, and when the action has been properly instituted, may find that there is the need to obtain evidence from witnesses abroad. How is the plaintiff to serve the legal process abroad? How can it be demonstrated that the defendant has been so served? How can a party to an action obtain evidence from a witness who is abroad and may not be able to come before the court to give evidence in person? These issues, which are the focus of this chapter, have been traditionally excluded from the scope of traditional private international law discourse. However, their significance is increasingly being recognised.

Service of domestic legal process abroad

A writ issued for service out of the jurisdiction must be served out of the jurisdiction. The civil procedure rules in the common law countries contain provisions for dealing with the procedures that serve the writ, or notice of the writ, out of the jurisdiction. The requirement, in some cases, that notice of the writ, instead of the writ itself, be served, originates in England. Under English procedure, the writ is a command from the sovereign. It was considered as more courteous, where the writ was to be served on a person who was neither a British subject liable to that command, nor a person resident in a country where the command could be enforced, to serve notice of the command rather than the command itself.[1] At present, in some of the common law countries, the decision over whether to serve notice of the writ instead of the writ itself is

[1] *Gohoho* v. *Guinea Press Ltd* [1962] 3 All ER 785. See also *Singh* v. *Singh* [1954] 27 KLR 62; *Leslie and Anderson* v. *Hoima Ginners Ltd* [1967] EA 44; *Nanjibhai Prabhudas Ltd* v. *Standard Bank Ltd* [1968] EA 670; *Aboud* v. *Mandi* [1920–36] ALR SL 240.

founded on whether the defendant is a national of the issuing state[2] or a citizen of a Commonwealth state.[3]

The rule as to whether the writ or notice thereof should be served on the defendant abroad is a technical rule, the foundations of which are difficult to sustain. It is unlikely that a sovereign state – with its many pressing socio-economic and political problems – will be too concerned with the fact that the writ itself, rather than notice of the writ, has been served within its jurisdiction. This does not deny that diplomatic courtesies are taken seriously by every country, irrespective of the domestic challenges involved. However, in the opinion of the present writer, what is important is that service is effected using the appropriate institutions in the respective state; it is the bypassing of a state's institutions to assume jurisdiction over its subjects, rather than the character of the document served, that is likely to be a cause for concern in the foreign state. Accordingly, it is submitted that, where a writ rather than the notice of the writ is served in a foreign state, this should be considered as a mere irregularity and should not render void the subsequent proceedings.

The civil procedure rules for each of the common law countries provide for how service of a writ (and other judicial documents) is to be effected outside the jurisdiction.[4] In general, in most of the common law countries, the document to be served is sealed by the court, forwarded to a branch within the executive (usually the Ministry of Justice or Ministry

[2] See, e.g., Sierra Leone – High Court Rules 2007, Ord. 11, r. 5; Zambia – High Court Rules, Ord. X, r. 18.

[3] See, e.g., Kenya – Civil Procedure Rules 2010, Ord. 5, r. 28; Uganda – Civil Procedure Rules, Ord. V, r. 27.

[4] Gambia – Rules of the High Court, Ord. VIII, r.10; *Joseph Sarjuka Jobe* v. *Jack Alderlifste* (2002–8) 2 GR 535; Ghana – High Court (Civil Procedure Rules), Ord. 8, rr. 5–11; Kenya – Civil Procedure Rules 2010, Ord. 5, rr. 27–30; Nigeria – Federal High Court (Civil Procedure Rules) 2000, Ord. 13, rr. 18–22, *Eimskip Ltd* v. *Exquisite Industries (Nigeria) Ltd* [2003] 4 NWLR 88, [2003] 14 WRN 77; Tanzania – Civil Procedure Code, Ord. V, rr. 28–33; Uganda – Civil Procedure Rules, Ord. V, r. 28.

Malawi is a party to the Hague Convention on the Service Abroad of Judicial and Extrajudicial Documents in Civil or Commercial Matters 1965: *Atupele Haulage Ltd* v. *Carbomoc* [1991] 14 MLR 18. Tanzania partially dispenses with the need for the intermediation of the executive arm of government in serving documents abroad. Under Ord. V, r. 29 of its Civil Procedure Code, where the defendant resides abroad, the court may, on the application of the plaintiff, order that service of the summons be effected by post (by the plaintiff or his agent) or through the courts of the country where the defendant is believed to reside. See *Willow Investment* v. *Mbomba Ntumba* [1997] TLR 47, in which the Tanzanian High Court directed service to be effected on the applicant in Zaire through DHL. Under Ord. V, r. 33 of the Code, executive intervention is envisaged where service is to be effected through the courts of the foreign country.

of Foreign Affairs) for transmission through diplomatic channels to the government of the foreign country, or directly to its courts.[5] The issue of who can properly effect service in the foreign country and how this should be done is left to the laws of that country and its courts. For example, in Ghana, the High Court (Civil Procedure) Rules outline the method by which notice of a writ is to be served out of the jurisdiction.[6] In countries where there is a civil procedure convention that provides for service in that country of processes of the courts of Ghana, the notice can be served through the judicial authorities of that country or through a Ghanaian consul there. In non-convention countries, notice can be served through the government of that country or through the Ghanaian consul in that country. Similarly, in Kenya, the notice to be served is sealed with the seal of the High Court. It is then forwarded by the Registrar to the Minister of Foreign Affairs, together with a copy thereof translated into the language of the country where service is to be effected, and with a request for the further transmission of the same through diplomatic channels to the government of the foreign country where leave to serve notice of the summons has been given.[7]

It is significant to note that, aside from Tanzania,[8] in none of the common law countries is a plaintiff expressly empowered by legislation to directly effect service on a defendant abroad. To a large extent, this is highly disempowering, and with the potentially bureaucratic nature of the currently existing judicial-executive led schemes for service abroad, it can also delay the dispute settlement process. In the Kenyan case of *Fonville* v. *Kelly III*,[9] the difficulties faced by parties in serving defendants abroad, and the consequences of trying to circumvent the often existing slow-moving procedures for service abroad, were brought to the fore. The case involved a dispute over a stock purchase agreement executed in the United States which purported to sell shares in Fonville Enterprises Incorporated, a company incorporated under the laws of Texas, and its two Kenyan subsidiaries. Three of the defendants were domiciled in the United States. The defendants had been served with a notice of summons via DHL, a private international courier company. They filed a defence under protest and argued, inter alia, that proper and lawful service of the

[5] A combined reading of Ord. 10 and Ord. 11, r. 6 or Sierra Leone's High Court Rules 2007 suggests that this approach is not required to serve a writ out of the jurisdiction.

[6] High Court (Civil Procedure) Rules, Ord. 8, rr. 5 and 6.

[7] Civil Procedure Rules 2010, Ord. 5, r. 29(a).

[8] Civil Procedure Code, Ord. V, r. 29(b).

[9] [2002] 1 EA 71, [1995] LLR 2636.

summons had not been effected upon them. The court held that the order of the court *a quo,* which gave leave to serve out of the jurisdiction through DHL, was a nullity. The correct procedure under Order V rule 27 was that the plaintiff should have made a formal request in the prescribed form. The Chief Justice would then have forwarded the notice of summons to the Minister of Foreign Affairs in the prescribed form for transmission through diplomatic channels to the US Government requesting service. The US Government would then have communicated service or acted otherwise through diplomatic channels.

An interesting issue discussed in the cases is whether substituted service can be ordered in cases where the plaintiff is unable to effect personal service on the defendant abroad.[10] In *Bruce* v. *Barrett,*[11] the defendant was outside the jurisdiction when the action was instituted. The writ was issued for service outside the jurisdiction, and an order was obtained for it to be so served, but the plaintiff failed to effect service on the defendant in London. The court ordered substituted service on the defendant's wife in London. In *Bawa* v. *Oyegoke,*[12] the plaintiff issued a writ in ordinary form against the first defendant, who was formerly resident in Ghana. At the time the writ was issued, he was resident in Nigeria. The plaintiff did not state the address at which he could be served. The plaintiff then brought an *ex parte* application for an order of substituted service of the writ on his wife, who was resident in Ghana. It was held that, where a writ was issued in the ordinary form for service within the jurisdiction against a person who, before the issue of the writ, had left the country and had since remained out of the jurisdiction, and where it did not appear that the defendant had gone out of the jurisdiction to avoid service of the writ, an order for substituted service could not be made. Where a writ cannot be directly served on a person, it cannot be served indirectly by means of substituted service. Gambian, Nigerian and Ugandan courts have similarly held that, where the defendant is out of the jurisdiction at the time of the issue of the writ and consequently cannot be served in law, then an order for substituted service cannot be made.[13]

[10] See also Zambia – High Court Rules, Ord. X, r. 17.

[11] (1931) 1 WACA 116. [12] [1977] 2 GLR 412.

[13] *Christel Brokmann* v. *Adama Saidy*, HC 596/09/CL/126 AO (High Court, Gambia, 2010); *Kida* v. *Ogunmola* [2006] 13 NWLR 377; *Ssesanga* v. *Greenland Bank Ltd (In Liquidation)*, Misc. App. No. 406 of 2010 (High Court, Uganda, 2010). See generally *Saihou O. Jim Drameh* v. *Alan Hayden*, Civil Suit No. HC/475/09/127/D2) (High Court, Gambia, 2010).

As discussed in Chapter 4, service is not the foundation of jurisdiction in the Roman-Dutch law countries. However, there is an explicit acknowledgment in their respective national laws that there may be circumstances where a defendant may need to be served with a legal process outside the jurisdiction. Accordingly, provision is made for service of legal process or documents abroad. The provisions in Namibia's Rules of the High Court 1990 are illustrative.[14] In Namibia, service of any process of the court or of any document in a foreign country shall be effected by any person who is, according to a certificate of designated officials (mostly diplomatic and consular officers), authorised under the law of such a country to serve such processes or documents; or Namibian diplomatic or consular officials if the law of such a country permits him or her to serve such a process or document, or if there is no law in such a country prohibiting such service and the authorities of that country have not interposed any objection thereto.[15] Special rules are created for service in South Africa and other designated countries. Thus, service of any process of the court or of any document may, in the Republic of South Africa, be effected by a sheriff authorised to serve the process of the relevant South African Court, and in Australia, Botswana, Finland, France, Hong Kong, Lesotho, Malawi, New Zealand, Spain, Swaziland, the United Kingdom of Great Britain and Northern Ireland and Zimbabwe by an attorney, solicitor, notary public or other legal practitioner in the country concerned and who is authorised to serve a process of court or documents under the law of that country.[16] Any process of court or document to be served in such a country shall be accompanied by a sworn translation thereof into an official language of the country where the process or document is to be served, together with a certified copy of the process or document and such a translation.[17] The process of court or document to be so served must be delivered to the Registrar, who then transmits it to the Permanent Secretary for Foreign Affairs or to a destination indicated by the Permanent Secretary for Foreign Affairs, for service in the foreign

[14] See also Botswana – Rules of the High Court 1970, Ord. 8, rr. 4–6; Lesotho – High Court Rules 1980, s. 5(6)–(9); South Africa – Uniform Rules of Court, s. 4(3)–(5); *Meyer* v. *Meyer* 1951 (4) SA 1; *Morcom* v. *Wagoner* 1948 (4) SA 542; *Newmarch* v. *Newmarch* 1950 (3) SA 591; *Star Shirt and Clothing Factory* v. *Kyoei Bussan Co. Ltd* 1958 (1) SA 717; Swaziland – High Court Rules 2010, s. 6(7)–(9); Zimbabwe – Civil Matters (Mutual Assistance) Act 1996, ss. 17–18; *Riseley* v. *Watt* 1965 (2) SA 664, [1965] RLR 82.

[15] Rules of the High Court 1990, s. 4(3).

[16] Ibid., s. 4(4).

[17] See the South African case of *Brumloop* v. *Brumloop (2)* 1972 (1) SA 503 on the impossibility or challenge of finding a translator.

country concerned.[18] In general, it appears that the courts may be prepared to waive non-compliances with the procedural rules on service abroad. Thus, it has been held that enactments regulating the procedure of the courts are usually imperative or mandatory. But, when not going to the jurisdiction of the courts, these may be waived by those for whose protection they were intended, unless public policy requires the observance of the provisions in question.[19]

The principal international agreement regulating the service of judicial documents is the Hague Convention on the Service Abroad of Judicial and Extrajudicial Documents in Civil or Commercial Matters 1965. Among the countries under study, only Botswana and Malawi are currently parties to the Convention. There is no African convention dealing with this issue.

Service of foreign process

Gambia

As regards the service of foreign processes, Gambian law distinguishes between processes from convention and non-convention countries. As regards processes from non-convention countries, the process must be transmitted to the Minister for Foreign Affairs, who then transmits it to the High Court. Two copies each of the letter of request and the process, all translated into English, are required. Service of the process is effected by an officer of the court, unless the court otherwise directs. Such service is effected by delivering to and leaving with the person to be served, one copy of the process and the translation thereof, in accordance with the rules and practice of the High Court regulating service. After service has been effected, the Registrar of the High Court forwards to the Minister for Foreign Affairs the received letter of request, together with evidence of service.[20]

In respect of foreign countries with which Gambia has a convention on service of documents, subject to any special requirements of that convention, the foreign process must be submitted to the Chief Justice. Service of the process is effected by an officer of the court, or by such method as the court may direct. The Chief Justice then transmits to the

[18] Rules of the High Court 1990, s. 4(5). *Hockeman* v. *Hockeman* 1954 (1) SA 37.
[19] *Van Zyl* v. *Van Zyl* 1961 (3) SA 472. But see *Walster* v. *Walster* 1971 (4) SA 442.
[20] Rules of the High Court, Ord. VIII, r. 13.

consular or other authority making the request, a certificate of service or must indicate the reasons for not being able to effect service.[21]

Ghana

The service of foreign documents in Ghana is regulated by Order 69 of the High Court (Civil Procedure) Rules 2004. Order 69 applies to the service of any process in connection with foreign civil or commercial proceedings. The law distinguishes between service of process from convention and non-convention countries. In non-convention countries, a letter from the foreign court requesting service of a process on a person in Ghana must be sent to the Ministry of Foreign Affairs for transmission to the Judicial Secretary. In general, service is effected by leaving a copy of the process with the person to be served. The Attorney General of Ghana can also apply for substituted service of the process. After service has been effected or unsuccessfully attempted, the Registrar of the court making or attempting service must forward to the Ministry of Foreign Affairs a certificate to that effect.

Convention countries are countries with which there is a Civil Procedure Convention that provides for service in Ghana of the process of courts of those countries. For such countries, a letter of request from a consular or other authority of the country must be addressed to the Judicial Secretary. For convention countries, the role of the Ministry of Foreign Affairs is dispensed with. The letter of request and two copies of the process to be served – these should be in English – must be submitted to the Judicial Secretary. After the process has been served or unsuccessfully attempted, the Registrar of the court making or attempting service must send a certificate to that effect to the consular or other authority that has requested service of the process.

Kenya

The service of foreign legal processes is regulated by Order 5 rules 32 to 34 of the Civil Procedure Rules 2010. Under rule 32, in any civil or commercial matter pending before a foreign court where there is a letter of request from the court for service of a process on any person transmitted to the High Court, with an intimation that it is desirable that

[21] Ibid., Ord. VIII, r. 15.

effect should be given to the same, the following procedure shall be adopted: the letter or request for service shall be accompanied by a translation thereof into English, together with two copies of the process of citation to be served, and two copies thereof in English. Service shall then be effected by delivering to and leaving with the person to be served, one copy of the process to be served, and one copy of the translation thereof, in accordance with the rules and practice of the High Court of Kenya regulating service to persons. After service has been effected, the process server shall return to the Registrar of the High Court one copy of the process, together with the evidence of service by affidavit of the person effecting the service, verified by a magistrate, and particulars of charges for the cost of effecting such service. The Registrar shall then return the letter of request for service received from the foreign country, together with the evidence of service and a certificate appended thereto, all duly sealed with the seal of the High Court for use out of the jurisdiction.

In relation to a process from a country with which Kenya has a convention, when a request for service is received by the Registrar of the High Court from the consular or other authority of such a country, service shall be effected by the delivery of the original, or a copy of the document, as indicated in the request, and the copy of the translation, to the party or person to be served, in person by the process server.[22]

Namibia

The service of foreign legal processes in Namibia is regulated by the Reciprocal Service of Civil Process Act 1994. The Act operates on the basis of reciprocity and empowers the Minister to designate countries which can benefit from its provisions.[23] In respect of a designated country, whenever any process other than a process relating to the enforcement of a civil judgment (purporting to be issued by an officer of a competent court of law in a designated country) is received from such an officer by any magistrate within whose area of jurisdiction such a process is sought to be served, such a magistrate shall, if he or she is satisfied that the

[22] Civil Procedure Rules 2010, Ord. 5, r. 34.

[23] Reciprocal Service of Civil Process Act 1994, s. 2: South Africa has been designated under the Act. But see also High Court Act 1990, s. 29(2) and s. 4(11)–(15) of the High Court Rules 1990, which allow for service of foreign legal process without a requirement that the foreign state should have been designated by the Minister.

process has been lawfully issued – notwithstanding the provisions of any other law relating to the service of process received from a foreign country – endorse such a process for service, whereupon it shall be served as if it were a process issued out of the court of that magistrate. Any process not drawn up in English must be accompanied by a sworn translation into English.[24]

Nigeria

In Nigerian law, in any civil cause or matter pending before a foreign court with which a convention on that behalf exists, a request for service of any document on a person within the jurisdiction is received by the Chief Judge from the consular or other authority of the country, and the following procedure shall, subject to any special provisions contained in the convention, be adopted: service shall be effected by the delivery of the original or a copy of the document (as indicated in the request) and the copy of the translation, to the party or person to be served in person by an officer of the court, unless the court directs otherwise. The Chief Judge shall then transmit to the consular or other authority making the request a certificate establishing the fact and date of the service in person, or indicating the reason for not being able to effect it.[25]

South Africa

The service of foreign legal processes in South Africa is regulated by the Reciprocal Service of Civil Process Act 1990. The Act operates on the basis of reciprocity and empowers the Minister to designate countries which would benefit from its provisions.[26] In respect of a designated country, whenever any process other than a process relating to the enforcement of a civil judgment (purporting to be issued by an officer of a competent court of law in a designated country) is received from such an officer by any magistrate within whose area of jurisdiction such a process is sought to be served, such a magistrate shall, if he or she is satisfied that the process has been lawfully issued – notwithstanding the provisions of any other law relating to the service of process received

24 Reciprocal Service of Civil Process Act 1994, s. 3.

25 Federal High Court (Civil Procedure) Rules 2000, Ord. 13, r. 23.

26 Reciprocal Service of Civil Process Act 1990, s. 2, but see Supreme Court Act 1959, s. 33 (2), which does not require designation.

from a foreign country – endorse such a process for service, whereupon it shall be served as if it were a process issued out of the court of that magistrate. Any process not drawn up in English or Afrikaans must be accompanied by a sworn translation into English or Afrikaans.[27]

Uganda

Where, in any civil or commercial matter pending before a foreign court, a letter of request from the court for service on any person in Uganda of any process concerning such a matter is transmitted to the High Court by the Minister with an intimation that it is desirable that effect be given to the letter of request, the following procedure shall be adopted: the letter of request for service shall be accompanied by a translation of the letter into English, two copies of the process of citation are to be served, and two copies of the process of citation are to be served in English. Service shall be effected by delivering to and leaving with the person to be served one copy of the process to be served, and one copy of the translation of it, in accordance with the rules and practice of the High Court of Uganda regulating the service of persons. After the service has been effected, the process server shall return to the Registrar of the High Court one copy of the process, together with evidence of service by affidavit of the person effecting the service, verified by a magistrate. The registrar shall then transmit the letter of request for service received from the foreign country to the authority who transmitted it to the High Court, together with the evidence of service and a certificate appended to it, duly sealed with the seal of the High Court.[28]

Zambia

Where, in any civil or commercial matter pending before a foreign court, a letter of request from such a court for the service on any person in Zambia of any process or citation in such a matter is transmitted to the Minister for Foreign Affairs and the Minister considers it to be desirable that effect should be given to the same, the following procedure shall be adopted: the letter of request for service shall be accompanied by a translation thereof into English, two copies of the process or citation are to be served, and two copies thereof in English. These shall be

[27] Reciprocal Service of Civil Process Act 1990, s. 3.
[28] Civil Procedure Rules, Ord. V, r. 30.

transmitted to the court by the Permanent Secretary at the Ministry of Foreign Affairs. Service of the process shall be effected by an officer of the court and effected by delivering to and leaving with the person to be served one copy of the process to be served and one copy of the translation thereof, in accordance with the rules and practice of the court regulating the service of process. After the service has been effected, the process server shall return to the Registrar one copy of the process, together with evidence of service by affidavit of the person effecting the service, verified by a person empowered to take oaths. Finally, the Registrar shall forward to the Permanent Secretary at the Ministry of Foreign Affairs, for transmission to the foreign country concerned, the letter of request for service received from the foreign country, together with the evidence of service.[29]

In respect of countries with which Zambia has a convention, where a request for service of any document on a person in Zambia is received by the court from the consular or other authority of such a country, service shall be effected by the delivery of the original or a copy of the document, as indicated in the request, and a copy of the translation to the party or person to be served, in person by an officer of the court. The Registrar shall transmit to the consular or other authority making the request a certificate establishing the fact and date of service in person, or must indicate the reason for not being able to effect it.[30]

Zimbabwe

Where any process purported to have been issued by an officer of a court in a designated country is received by a magistrate with a request to serve it within the province for which the Magistrates' Court is established, the magistrate shall, if he or she is satisfied that the process was lawfully issued, endorse the process for service. A process so endorsed shall be served as if it had been issued out of the court of the magistrate concerned. Any process not drawn up in English or in any other language commonly spoken within the area where the process is to be served, shall not be endorsed unless it is accompanied by a sworn translation into English or other appropriate language.[31]

[29] High Court Rules, Ord. X, r. 23. These rules should be read with the Service of Process and Execution of Judgments Act 1964, which makes provision for the service of process from Zimbabwe and Malawi.

[30] High Court Rules, Ord X, r. 24.

[31] Civil Matters (Mutual Assistance) Act 1996, s. 13.

Comments

A formidable challenge for the international administration of justice involves putting the wheels of justice in motion. The service of legal processes and documents is a key aspect of this challenge. Most of the countries under study have statutory regimes that allow the service of foreign processes on a person within their jurisdiction. The regimes discussed above deal with foreign proceedings for civil or commercial matters – criminal matters are dealt with under separate legislation.[32]

Very few African countries are parties to international conventions on this subject. Among the countries under study, only Botswana and Malawi are parties to the Hague Convention on the Service Abroad of Judicial and Extrajudicial Documents in Civil or Commercial Matters 1965.[33] The regimes in most of the countries under study are available to all foreign countries. However, there are regimes in Namibia, South Africa and Zimbabwe which operate on the basis of reciprocity. Countries such as Gambia, Ghana and Zambia have separate (but not too dissimilar) rules for processes from convention and non-convention countries, and it is also unclear with which countries they have a convention.

In all the countries under study, the procedure for serving foreign processes is governed by the *lex fori* – the law of the place from which the process emanates is largely irrelevant when it comes to serving the foreign document on a person within the jurisdiction. In the absence of an international convention to mandate it, it is unclear from the statutes whether any special direction as to the character or mode of service is to be upheld by the domestic courts. It is a requirement in all the countries under study that documents in foreign languages are to be translated into English (or Afrikaans in South Africa) before they can be served on a person within the jurisdiction.

[32] Botswana – Mutual Assistance in Criminal Matters Act 1990; Ghana – Mutual Legal Assistance Act 2010; Kenya – Mutual Legal Assistance Act 2011; Namibia – International Co-operation in Criminal Matters Act 2000; South Africa – International Co-operation in Criminal Matters 1996, *Falk* v. *NDPP* [2011] 1 All SA 354, *Thatcher* v. *Minister of Justice and Constitutional Development* 2005 (4) SA 543, *Kolbatschenko* v. *King No* 2001 (4) SA 336; *Tulip Diamonds FZE* v. *Minister for Justice and Constitutional Development*, CCT 93/12 (Constitutional Court, South Africa, 2013); *Tulip Diamonds FZE* v. *Minister of Justice and Constitutional Development* [2012] All SA 401; Zambia – Mutual Legal Assistance in Criminal Matters Act 1993.

[33] Botswana, Lesotho, Malawi, Namibia, South Africa and Swaziland are parties to the related instrument, the Hague Convention on Abolishing the Requirement of Legalisation for Foreign Public Documents. The interaction between this Convention and Namibian law was an issue in *S* v. *Koch* 2006 (2) NR 513.

There is no express statutory prohibition on persons in foreign countries from directly serving legal processes or documents on a defendant within the jurisdiction, but without resort to the regimes established by statute. Thus, to the extent that such service would be recognised as valid in the foreign country, a foreign plaintiff may serve processes directly on the defendant. Indeed, it can be argued that, with the ready availability of simple and apparently fast processes, such as service by post and email, individuals should be able to rely on these media to serve processes abroad, without the need for intermediation by institutions of the state in which the person to be served is present. That said, it is evident from the regimes in all the countries under study that the service of a foreign process is considered as an official act, carried out by state institutions (the executive and the courts) on behalf of the foreign court from which the process emanates.

Taking evidence for foreign courts[34]

Botswana

Where an application is made and it appears to the High Court that a foreign court of competent jurisdiction – before which any civil or

[34] This section focuses mainly on obtaining evidence for civil or commercial matters pending before foreign tribunals. Other issues related to evidence in domestic proceedings which may have foreign dimensions, such as obtaining evidence abroad for use in domestic proceedings, legalisation, authentication and the translation of documents and subpoena to attend foreign proceedings, are not addressed in this section. On these see generally: Botswana – Evidence (Commonwealth and Foreign Acts of State and Judgments) Act 1910; Evidence (Commonwealth Statutes) Act 1923; Foreign Documents Evidence Act 1934; Authentication of Documents Act 1967; Compulsion of Witnesses Act 1898; *Rakodu* v. *Attorney General of Botswana* 2007 (1) BLR 649.

Gambia – Foreign Affidavits Act 1915.

Ghana – High Court (Civil Procedure) Rules 2004, Ord. 39; *Kells* v. *Ako Adjei* [2001–2] 1 GLR 617.

Kenya – Civil Procedure Act 1924, ss. 52–4; Civil Procedure Rules 2010, Ord. 28; *Microsoft Corp.* v. *Mitsumi Computer Garage Ltd* [2001] KLR 470; *Pastificio Lucio Garofalo SPA* v. *Security & Fire Equipment Co.* [2001] KLR 483; *Premchand Raichand Ltd* v. *Quarry Services of East Africa Ltd* [1969] EA 514; *Batten* v. *Kampala African Bus Co.* [1959] EA 328; *O'swald* v. *Hussein Suleman* [1906–8] EAP LR 94; *Jaffer M Harji* v. *Dalgety & Co. Ltd* [1954] KLR 11.

Namibia – High Court Act 1990, s. 28; Foreign Courts Evidence Act 1995, s. 7; *S* v. *Lofty-Eaton (2)* 1993 NR 405; *Zhou* v. *Hong* 2006 (1) NR 85; *S* v. *Koch* 2006 (2) NR 513; *Sauber* v. *Sauber* 1949 (2) SA 769.

Nigeria – Federal High Court (Civil Procedure) Rules 2000, Ord. 41, rr. 12–13; *Melwani* v. *Five Star Industries Ltd* [2002] 3 NWLR 217, [2002] 10 WRN 1.

commercial matter is pending – desires to obtain testimony in relation to such matters from any witness in Botswana, the High Court may order the examination of the witness upon oath, upon interrogatories or otherwise, before any person named in the order. The court may order the attendance of any person for the purpose of being examined, or the production of specified writings or other documents, giving all such directions as to the time, place and manner of such examination, and all other matters connected therewith as the court thinks proper. Any order of the court may be enforced in the same manner as an order made in a cause pending in the High Court.[35] A person authorised to examine a witness by an order of the court may take all such examinations upon oath.[36] Every person so examined shall have the like right to refuse to answer questions that might incriminate him- or herself and other questions, as a witness in any cause pending in the High Court would be entitled to, and no person shall be compelled to produce under any order,

Sierra Leone – High Court Rules 2007, Ord. 32.

South Africa – Foreign Courts Evidence Act 1962, s. 7; *Minister of Water Affairs and Forestry* v. *Swissborough Diamond Mines (Pty) Ltd* 1999 (2) SA 345; Uniform Court Rules 1965, r. 38; *Fernandes* v. *Fittinghoff & Fihrer CC* 1993 (2) SA 704; *Jokl* v. *Alexander* 1947 (3) SA 542; *Alexander* v. *Jokl* 1947 (3) SA 550; *Hespel* v. *Hespel* 1948 (3) SA 257; *Princess Eugenie of Greece* v. *Prince Dominique Radziwill* 1949 (2) SA 259; *Grant* v. *Grant* 1949 (1) SA 22; *Segal* v. *Segal* 1949 (4) SA 86; *Storr* v. *Storr* 1950 (3) SA 331; *Hind* v. *Boswell Bros Circus (Pty) Ltd* 1952 (2) SA 158; *Scott* v. *Scott* 1955 (4) SA 153; *Guggenheim* v. *Rosenbaum (1)* 1961 (4) SA 15; *Hurwitz* v. *Southern Insurance Association Ltd* 1970 (3) SA 80; *Ex p. Wessels and Venter NNO: In re. Pyke-Nott's Insolvent Estate* 1996 (2) SA 677, 1996 (2) SA 677; *Ex p. Neubauer* 1947 (3) SA 736; *Ex p. Melcer* 1948 (4) SA 395; *Stift* v. *Stift* 1952 (4) SA 215; *Ex p. Heinmann* 1952 (3) SA 149; *McLeod* v. *Gesade Holdings (Pty) Ltd* 1958 (3) SA 672; *Friend* v. *Friend* 1962 (4) SA 115; *Caldwell* v. *Chelcourt Ltd* 1965 (2) SA 270; *Chopra* v. *Sparks Cinemas (Pty) Ltd* 1973 (2) SA 352; *Mountain View Hotel (Pty) Ltd* v. *Rossouw* 1985 (2) SA 73; *Maschinen Frommer GmbH* v. *Trisave Engineering & Machinery Supplies (Pty) Ltd* 2003 (6) SA 69; *Ex p. Wismer et Uxor* 1950 (2) SA 195.

Tanzania – Civil Procedure Code 1966, ss. 56–8; Civil Procedure Rules, Ord. XXVI.

Uganda – Civil Procedure Act 1929, ss. 53–5; Civil Procedure Rules, Ord. XXVIII; *Uganda Revenue Authority* v. *Toro & Mityana Tea Co. Ltd*, HCT-00-CC-CA-0004-2006 (High Court, Uganda, 2007); *Caspair Ltd* v. *Harry Gandy* [1962] EA 414.

Zambia – *Banda* v. *Zambia Newspapers Ltd* (1968) ZR 1; *Re. Margaret Mary Rowler, Deceased* [1949–54] NRLR 751; *Pietzsch* v. *Pietzsch* 1963 R & N 413.

Zimbabwe – Civil Matters (Mutual Assistance) Act 1996, s. 13; *Prosper Tawanda* v. *Tholakele Ndebele*, Case No. 1826/05 (High Court, Zimbabwe, 2006); *Electrical & Furniture Trading Co. Ltd* v. *M & N Technical Services (Zimbabwe) Ltd* 1988 (2) ZLR 265; *Pedregal* v. *Pedregal* 1958 (1) SA 436.

[35] Foreign Tribunal Evidence Act 1910, s. 2. See also Compulsion of Witnesses Act 1898, ss. 7–9, which applies to only designated countries.

[36] Foreign Tribunal Evidence Act 1910, s. 4.

any writing or other document that he or she could not be compelled to produce at a trial of such a cause.

Gambia

Gambian law makes provision for foreign courts to obtain evidence in Gambia.[37] Where any civil or commercial matter is pending before a foreign court and it is made to appear to the Gambian court by *commission rogatoire*, letter of request or other evidence, that the foreign court desires to obtain evidence in relation to such matters from a witness in Gambia, the court may, on an *ex parte* application, make an order for the examination of the witness.[38] The examination may be ordered to be taken by any person nominated by the person applying, or such a person as the court directs. On completion of the examination, the examiner is obliged to forward the examination to the Registrar of the High Court, who shall seal the disposition for transmission to the foreign court.[39]

Ghana

Obtaining evidence from a person resident in Ghana for use in an action abroad is regulated by sections 75 to 79 of the Courts Act 1993 and Order 70 of the High Court (Civil Procedure) Rules 2004. Under section 75(1) of the Courts Act, the High Court can order the examination of a witness within its jurisdiction on such terms as it considers necessary when an application is made by a foreign court or tribunal for that witness's testimony, with respect to criminal, civil or commercial matters before the respective foreign court or tribunal. The High Court can direct the witness to appear before any person named in its order. It can order the witness to be examined on oath, on interrogatories, or to produce specific documents. The order can be enforced in the same manner as an order made in a cause pending in the High Court.[40]

An application for an order for the examination of a witness in Ghana is made *ex parte* by a person duly authorised to make the application on behalf of the foreign court or tribunal. It must be supported by an affidavit.[41] The affidavit should be accompanied by a certificate or other

[37] Rules of the High Court, Ord. VII, rr. 32–7.
[38] Rules of the High Court, Ord. VII, r. 32.
[39] Rules of the High Court, Ord. VII, r. 34.
[40] Courts Act 1993, s. 75(2)(3).
[41] High Court (Civil Procedure) Rules 2004, Ord. 70, r. 1.

documents that evince the desire of the foreign court or tribunal to obtain evidence from the witness, for the purpose of a matter pending before the court or tribunal.[42] An ambassador, minister, diplomatic agent or consular officer can issue a certificate indicating that the foreign court or tribunal requires the evidence for a matter pending before it. In the absence of such a certificate, other evidence is admissible to show that the matter for which the evidence is required is pending before the foreign court or tribunal.[43] Every person examined under an order made under section 75 of the Courts Act has the same right to refuse to answer questions, including those questions that may incriminate him or her and other questions, as a witness in any cause pending in the High Court. Furthermore, no person will be compelled to produce any written or other document that he or she could not be compelled to produce at a trial of such a cause in Ghana.[44]

Kenya

Commissions issued by foreign courts for the examination of persons in Kenya shall be executed and returned in such a manner as may from time to time be authorised by the High Court.[45] It has been held that, in the absence of a certificate from an accredited diplomatic agent of a foreign power, the court may accept an applicant's affidavit as amounting to evidence sufficient to prove that a civil and commercial suit was pending before a foreign court desirous of obtaining the testimony of the named witness within the jurisdiction of the Kenyan courts.[46]

Namibia

If, upon an application to the Namibian High Court, it appears to it that a foreign court of competent jurisdiction, before which any civil proceedings are pending, desires to obtain evidence in relation to such proceedings of any witness within Namibia, the court may grant an order for the examination of such a witness before a person named in the order.[47] In addition, any magistrate shall, upon request of any judicial officer

[42] High Court (Civil Procedure) Rules 2004, Ord. 70, r. 2.
[43] Courts Act, s. 76(2). [44] Ibid., s. 79(1)(2).
[45] Civil Procedure Act 1924, s. 55. Civil Procedure Rules 2010, Ord. 28, r. 17.
[46] *Air Import* v. *The Newson Aeronautical Corp.* [1955] KLR 2.
[47] Foreign Courts Evidence Act 1995, s. 2(1). See also High Court Act 1990, s. 29(1).

performing the functions of a magistrate in any designated country, take the examination of any witness within their area of jurisdiction in connection with any civil proceedings pending in the court of such a judicial officer.[48]

The magistrate or person required to take an examination shall cause the person whose evidence is required to be summoned to appear and give evidence or produce any book, document or object before him or her; then upon such a person's appearance, shall administer an oath or affirmation to him or her (unless requested by the other country not to take such an oath or affirmation) and will take his or her evidence upon interrogatories or otherwise, as ordered or requested, as if he or she were a witness in a Magistrates' Court in proceedings similar to those in connection with which his or her evidence is required.[49] Upon completion of the examination, the person taking the examination shall transmit to the Registrar of the court granting the order for the examination, or to the judicial officer requesting it, the evidence certified by him or her as correct.[50] In connection with the giving of evidence or the production of any book, document or object at such an examination, the law relating to privilege as applicable to a witness giving evidence or summoned to produce a book, document or object in a Magistrates' Court in such proceedings shall apply.[51]

Nigeria

Where any civil or criminal matters are pending before a foreign court, and it is made to appear to the Nigerian court by *commission rogatoire*, or letter of request, or other sufficient evidence, that the foreign court desires to obtain the testimony in relation to the matter of any witness or witnesses within the jurisdiction, the court may, on the *ex parte* application of any person shown to be duly authorised to make an application on behalf of the foreign court, and on production of the *commission rogatoire*, letter of request or such other evidence as the court may require or consider sufficient, make such order or orders as may be required, considered sufficient or considered necessary to give effect to the intention of the *commission rogatoire* or letter of request.[52]

[48] Foreign Courts Evidence Act 1995, s. 3. South Africa has been designated under the Act.
[49] Ibid., s. 4. [50] Ibid., s. 4(4). [51] Foreign Courts Evidence Act 1995, s. 5(2).
[52] Federal High Court (Civil Procedure) Rules 2000, Ord. 41, r. 39.

Sierra Leone

Where a civil matter is pending before a foreign court, and it is made to appear before a judge by a *commission rogatoire*, letters of request or other evidence, that the court desires to obtain the testimony in relation to such matters, of any witness within the country, a judge may, on the *ex parte* application of any person shown to be duly authorised to make the application on behalf of the foreign court, and on the production of the *commission rogatoire*, letters of request, a certificate or such other evidence as a judge may require, make such an order as may be necessary to give effect to the request.[53] An order for the examination of a witness may order the examination to be taken before any fit and proper person nominated by the person applying for the order, before an examiner of the court or before such other qualified person as the court thinks fit.[54] The examiner before whom the examination is taken shall, on its completion, forward it to the Registrar of the High Court and on receipt, the Master shall append to it a certificate in an appropriate form, duly sealed with the seal of the court for use outside of Sierra Leone before forwarding the deposition so certified, the *commission rogatoire* or letters of request, to the Minister of Foreign Affairs and International Cooperation for transmission to the foreign court requiring the deposition.[55]

South Africa

If, upon an application in any provincial or local division of the Supreme Court of South Africa, it appears to the court or any judge that a foreign court of competent jurisdiction, before which any civil proceedings are pending, is desirous of obtaining the evidence in relation to such proceedings of any witness within the jurisdiction of such a

[53] High Court Rules 2007, Ord. 32, r. 1. Under Ord. 32, r. 4, a *commission rogatoire* or letters of request may be transmitted to the court by the Minister of Foreign Affairs and International Cooperation, with an intimation that it is desirable that effect be given to the *commission rogatoire* or letters of request without requiring an application to be made to the court by the agents in Sierra Leone of any of the parties to the action or matters in the foreign country. In such a case, the Master shall transmit it to the Attorney General who may, with the consent of the Minister of Foreign Affairs and International Cooperation, make such applications and take such steps as may be necessary to give effect to the *commission rogatoire* or letters of request.

[54] High Court Rules 2007, Ord. 32, r. 2.

[55] High Court Rules 2007, Ord. 32, r. 3.

division, the court or judge hearing the application may grant an order for the examination of such a witness before a person named in such an order.[56] In addition, a magistrate shall, upon the request of a judicial officer performing the functions of a magistrate in designated countries, take the examination of any witness within his or her area of jurisdiction, in connection with any civil proceedings pending in the court of such a judicial officer.[57]

A person required to take an examination shall cause any person whose evidence is required to be summoned to appear and give evidence, or to produce any book, document or object before him or her, and upon his or her appearance, shall administer an oath or affirmation to them and take their evidence upon interrogatories or otherwise, as ordered or requested, as if they were a witness in a Magistrates' Court in proceedings similar to those in connection with which the evidence is required. Any person to be so summoned shall be summoned in the same manner as a person subpoenaed to appear before such a court in such proceedings.[58] Upon completion of the examination, the person taking it shall transmit to the Registrar of the court which granted the order for the examination, or to the judicial officer who requested it, the evidence certified by him or her as correct.[59] In connection with the giving of evidence, or the production of any book, document or object at such an examination, the law relating to privilege, as applicable to a witness giving evidence or summoned to produce a book, document or object in a Magistrates' Court in such proceedings, shall apply.[60]

Tanzania

The provisions of the Civil Procedure Code 1966[61] as to the execution and return of commissions for the examination of witnesses apply to commissions issued by foreign courts for the examination of persons residing in Tanzania.[62]

[56] Foreign Courts Evidence Act 1962, s. 2(1). See also Supreme Court Act 1959, s. 33(1), and generally *Saunders* v. *Minister of Justice* 1997 (3) SA 1090.

[57] Foreign Courts Evidence Act 1962, s. 3. The following countries have been designated: Lesotho; Botswana; Swaziland; Malawi; Namibia and Zimbabwe.

[58] Ibid., s. 4. [59] Ibid., s. 4(4).

[60] Ibid., s. 5(2); *Cline* v. *Magistrate, Witbank* 1985 (4) SA 605.

[61] Civil Procedure Code 1966, ss. 56–8; Civil Procedure Rules, Ord. XXVI.

[62] Civil Procedure Code 1966, s. 59.

Uganda

Commissions issued by foreign courts for the examination of persons in Uganda shall be executed and returned in such a manner as may be from time to time prescribed.[63]

Zimbabwe

Where an application is made to the High Court or a Magistrates' Court for an order for evidence to be obtained in Zimbabwe, and the court is satisfied that the application is made in pursuance of a request issued by, or on behalf of, a court or tribunal exercising jurisdiction in a designated country, and where the evidence to which the application relates is to be obtained for the purposes of a civil case which has either been instituted before the requesting court or tribunal, or whose institution before that court or tribunal is contemplated; and in the case of an application made to a Magistrates' Court, where the evidence is to be obtained within the province for which the Magistrates' Court has been established, the court may make an order for obtaining evidence as the court considers will give effect to the request pursuant to which the application was made.[64]

The respective order may make provision for the examination of any witness (either orally or in writing), the production of any document and the inspection, photographing, preservation, custody or detention of any property, whether movable or immovable, together with the taking of a sample of any property, whether movable or immovable, and the carrying out of any experiment on or with any such property, as well as the medical examination of any person, including the taking and testing of a sample of their blood.[65] The order shall not require a person to state which documents relevant to the civil case and referred to by the application are, or have been, in their possession, custody or power; or to produce any document other than those specified in the order as appearing to the court making the order to be as, or likely to be, in their possession, custody or power.[66] A person shall not be compelled to give any evidence which he or she could not be compelled to give in a civil

[63] Civil Procedure Act 1929, s. 56; Civil Procedure Rules, Ord. XXVIII, r. 19.

[64] Civil Matters (Mutual Assistance) Act 1996, s. 20(1). The application may be made by, or on behalf of, any party to the civil case concerned, an officer of the requesting court or tribunal, or the Minister for Justice.

[65] Ibid., s. 21(2). [66] Ibid., s. 21(3).

case in Zimbabwe, or in a civil case in the designated country where the requesting court or tribunal exercises jurisdiction.[67]

Comments

A significant challenge in cross-border litigation is how to ensure that parties have access to all available evidence within and outside the jurisdiction so that they can make their case. International judicial assistance which enables parties to gather evidence abroad is important in this respect. Each of the countries under study has a regime which enables its courts to take evidence from persons abroad, and for their courts to assist foreign courts in gathering evidence from individuals within their jurisdiction.

Most of the statutes refer to 'courts or tribunals', but it is doubtful whether they could be extended to international arbitral tribunals (and, as discussed below, international or regional courts).[68] In other words, it is doubtful whether a *direct* request from a foreign arbitration tribunal for evidence to be taken from a witness in any of the other countries under study comes within the scope of the statutory regimes.[69] On the other hand, a request from an international arbitral tribunal which is channelled through a foreign court can be given effect under the regimes discussed above.

Although the ability to gather evidence abroad is a significant aspect of the international administration of justice, among the countries under study, only South Africa is a party to the Hague Convention on the Taking of Evidence Abroad in Civil or Commercial Matters 1970. Presently, there is no regional or continental convention on judicial co-operation that exists in Africa.

The regimes in most of the countries under study are open to any applicant, regardless of the country from which court the request emanates.

[67] Ibid., s. 22(1).
[68] See generally Ch. 20 on interim measures in support of arbitration proceedings.
[69] In the Canadian case of *BF Jones Logistics Inc.* v. *Rolko* (2004) 72 OR (3d) 355, the Ontario Superior Court of Judicature held that it had no jurisdiction, either at common law or under statute, to enforce a letter of request from a private arbitrator requesting an examination of a witness resident in Ontario. In *Viking Insurance Co.* v. *Rossdale* [2002] 1 Lloyd's Rep. 219, it was also held that the English court had no jurisdiction under the Evidence (Proceedings in Other Jurisdictions) Act 1975, to enforce a letter of request issued by a private arbitral tribunal. See generally M. Penny, 'Letters of Request: Will a Canadian Court Enforce a Letter of Request from an International Arbitral Tribunal?' (2001) 12 *American Review of International Arbitration* 249.

However, the regimes in Namibia, South Africa and Zimbabwe are founded on reciprocity – countries to benefit from the regime must be specifically designated under the Act. This leaves open the question of how requests from courts in non-designated countries will be treated. On the basis of comity and the need to ensure the proper administration of justice, it is submitted that a court should have jurisdiction to assist a foreign court in taking evidence from persons within the former's jurisdiction. Judicial assistance of this kind is closely related to enforcing a foreign judgment which the courts are permitted to do at common law.

In most of the countries under study, the application for the examination of a person within the jurisdiction of the court must be made by a person shown to be duly authorised to make the application on behalf of the foreign court. However, the regime in Sierra Leone allows an application to be made through the Attorney General. Unlike the regimes for serving foreign legal processes or documents on persons within the jurisdiction, the regimes on securing evidence for foreign courts do not provide that the request should be transmitted through diplomatic/executive channels to the courts. It most cases, a *commission rogatoire*, letter of request or other evidence must be produced and it must be demonstrated that the foreign court is desirous of obtaining evidence in relation to a civil matter pending before it from a witness within the jurisdiction. On the latter, an important role is given to consular officials in some of the countries under study. For example, in Ghana, an ambassador, minister, diplomatic agent or consular officer may issue a certificate that the subject of an application is a civil or commercial matter and that the foreign court requires the evidence for the matter pending before it.

When an order is made to examine a person within the jurisdiction, the examination is carried out largely in accordance with domestic procedures. However, the regimes in some countries, such as Gambia and Sierra Leone, specifically allow for the national court to direct that the examination should be conducted in such a manner as the foreign court may have requested, or by a person nominated by the person making the request. In general, the existing regimes are not very detailed on what can or cannot be done under an order to examine a witness. Zimbabwe's regimes are perhaps the most detailed on this subject.

Once the examination is complete, the procedure under most of the regimes is for the disposition to be transmitted to the executive (either the Ministry of Foreign Affairs or Ministry of Justice) for onward transmission to the foreign court.

Judicial assistance and African regional economic community courts

At present, there are a number of regional courts (hereinafter, 'community courts') in Africa.[70] These courts have been established under various regional economic integration treaties and given jurisdiction over what may be characterised as civil or commercial matters. Individuals also have *locus standi* before the community courts. As noted above, the legal framework for international judicial assistance with foreign courts in civil or commercial matters is regulated by national statutes. However, the same cannot be said of co-operation with community courts exercising their 'civil' jurisdiction.[71] Admittedly, when most of the national statutes were originally enacted, community courts were rare, especially in Africa. With the emergence of community courts, the importance of providing a legal framework to regulate judicial co-operation between community courts and national courts, and perhaps among community courts themselves, is evident.

There are a number of issues that could arise as regards co-operation between community and national courts for which no clear answers exist at present. Do national courts have jurisdiction to assist community courts to take evidence in member states? Do national courts have jurisdiction to assist community courts to serve documents on persons within the former's jurisdiction? What will be the legal basis and procedure for such co-operation? Do the legal basis and procedure provide an adequate regime to ensure efficient administration of justice at community level? Will a community court stay its proceedings if a similar issue is pending before a national court?[72] Will procedures adopted by national courts in co-operating with community courts be conducive to the effectiveness of community law?

Apart from Zimbabwe's Civil Matters (Mutual Assistance) Act 1995, there does not appear to be any statute in the countries under study that explicitly provides for judicial co-operation with community courts. Section 3(2) of the Act empowers the Minister of Justice to extend

[70] These include the Common Market for Eastern and Southern Africa Court of Justice; East African Court of Justice; the Court of Justice of the Economic Community of West African States; and the Southern African Development Community Tribunal.

[71] The regimes for judicial assistance in criminal matters in countries such as Botswana, Ghana, Kenya, Namibia, South Africa and Zambia make provision for co-operation with international criminal courts.

[72] *Richard Thomas Etheredge* v. *Minister of State for National Security Responsible for Lands, Land Reform and Resettlement*, Suit No. 3295/08 (High Court, Zimbabwe, 2008).

provisions of the Act to 'any international tribunal'. An international tribunal is defined as any court or tribunal which, in pursuance of any international agreement or any resolution of the General Assembly of the United Nations: (i) exercises any jurisdiction or performs any function of a judicial nature or by way of arbitration, conciliation or inquiry; or (ii) is appointed, whether permanently or temporarily, for the purpose of exercising any jurisdiction or performing any such function. This definition is broad enough to cover community courts in Africa,[73] but this ministerial power has not been exercised in respect of any international tribunal or community court.

With the emergence of the community courts, the importance of their co-operation with national courts for the effective administration of justice cannot be over-emphasised. Neither have the laws governing the community courts provided a clear legal framework for co-operation between them and national courts on issues such as taking evidence, summoning witnesses and serving documents. It appears that the only area where co-operation is explicitly anticipated, and a framework provided for, is the enforcement of the judgments of community courts.[74] Surely, judicial co-operation goes beyond the enforcement of judgments. The need for co-operation with national courts is important, especially as the community courts allow individuals to litigate directly before them and also provide them with jurisdiction to arbitrate disputes between individuals.

The lack of a legal framework on the issue of judicial co-operation between national and community courts in the community treaties is somewhat remedied by the rules of procedure in the community courts. Under Rule 74(1)(a) of the COMESA Court Rules,[75] the court may, *suo motu* or on application, stay its proceedings where the court and a

[73] This section appears to have been borrowed from some countries. United Kingdom: Evidence (Proceedings in Other Jurisdictions) Act 1975, s. 6(1); United States Code, ch. 28, s. 1782(a).

[74] See, e.g., Treaty establishing the East African Community, 30 November 1999, 2144 UNTS I-37437; Protocol to the Southern African Development Community Tribunal and Rules of Procedure Thereof, 7 August 2000, www.sadc.int/index/browse/page/163, Art. 32(1)(2)(3); Treaty on the Harmonization of Business Law in Africa, 1 November 1997, Official Journal of OHADA No. 4, p. 1, Art. 25; Treaty establishing the Common Market for Eastern and Southern Africa, 5 November 1993, 33 ILM 1067, Art. 40; Protocol A/P.1/7/91 on the Community Court of Justice of the High Contracting Parties as amended by Supplementary Protocol A/SP/.1/01/05 Amending the Protocol Relating to the Community Court of Justice, Art. 24.

[75] COMESA Legal Notice No. 6 of 2003, 8 April 2003.

national court are seized of a case where the same relief is sought, the same issue of interpretation is raised or the validity of the same act is called into question. As discussed in Chapter 5, from the perspective of national courts, the existence of *lis pendens* is a factor that weighs heavily in their decisions to stay proceedings, but they still retain the discretion not to do so under both common and statute law.

Under Rule 27 of the East African Court of Justice Rules of Procedure 2008 (EAC Court Rules), a national court may be requested to serve notice on a person. A national court to which a request for service of notification is sent *may*, upon receipt, proceed as if the notification had been issued by it, and then return the notification to the EAC Court, together with the record, if any, of its proceedings in this regard. In other words, national courts have discretion to serve the notification. What happens when discretion is exercised against the service of a notification is left unanswered. Article 74(1) of the Rules of the Court of Justice of the Economic Community of West African States (ECOWAS Court Rules) seems not to envisage the need to use national courts for serving documents.[76] It provides that, where the rules require a document to be served on a person, the Chief Registrar of the court should ensure that service is effected at that person's address, either by the dispatch of a copy of the document by registered post, with a form for acknowledgement of receipt, or by personal delivery of the copy against a receipt. It is very likely that such a process of serving documents will be considered as an infringement of state sovereignty.[77] Bypassing a state's institutions, including its courts, in order to assume jurisdiction over its subjects, is likely to be a cause for concern by the state. What is more, without the use of national legal processes, it is unlikely that any sanction can be imposed on an individual who does not acknowledge service from a community court.

Under Article 41(6)(7) of the COMESA Court Rules, the court may order that a witness or expert be heard by the judicial authority of his or her place of permanent residence. The order shall be sent for implementation to the competent judicial authority under conditions laid down in its rules of procedure.[78] Under Article 41(8), a member state

[76] Rule 43(5) provides that an order summoning witnesses shall be served on the parties and the witnesses, but there is no statement on how this service is to be made.

[77] It is envisaged under Art. 99(a) of the ECOWAS Court Rules that the court will adopt supplementary rules on letters rogatory.

[78] COMESA Court Rules, r. 41(7)(a).

shall treat any violation of an oath, or affirmation by a witness or expert, in the same manner as if the offence had been committed before one of its courts with jurisdiction in civil proceedings. At the instance of the court, the member state concerned *shall* prosecute the offender before its competent court. This provision is unlikely to sit well with constitutional provisions in member states which confer the discretion to prosecute criminal offences solely with the Attorney General. In the absence of legislation, it is unlikely that contempt of, or perjury before, a community court can be similarly treated and punished by a national court.[79]

The above suggests that the community courts envisage co-operation with national courts. However, it does not appear that careful thought has been given to the issue of whether the existing national laws have been tailored to facilitate this co-operation. To ensure effective co-operation, it is important for member states to enact statutes regulating co-operation between community and national courts. Pending such legislation, it is suggested that national courts should treat the community courts as foreign courts for the purposes of their civil procedure rules. However, it must be admitted that, in their current form, the definition of a foreign court in national statutes is a clear reference to foreign national courts.[80]

[79] See, e.g., South Africa – Rome Statute of the International Criminal Court Act 2002, s. 37.

[80] e.g. the Civil Procedure Acts in Kenya, Tanzania and Uganda define a foreign court as a court situated outside Kenya, Tanzania and Uganda, which has no authority in Kenya, Tanzania and Uganda, respectively. It remains an open question as to whether it can be argued that the COMESA Court and EAC Court, neither of which is geographically situated in either Kenya or Uganda, has no authority in either country. The EAC Court and COMESA Court are geographically situated in Tanzania and Zambia, respectively. See generally *Joseph Kimani Gathungu* v. *Attorney General* [2010] eKLR, discussing the place of the International Criminal Court in Kenya's legal system.

22

Security for costs

In the countries under study, a plaintiff, including a sovereign state,[1] may be required to deposit security for costs when prosecuting their claim.[2]

[1] *State of Israel* v. *Somen* [2001] LLR 5932.

[2] See generally:

Botswana – Rules of the High Court, Ord. 57; *Gaborone* v. *Lowrenco* 1999 (1) BLR 11; *Botswana Insurance Co. Ltd* v. *Matan Trucking Co. Ltd* 2003 (2) BLR 380; *Misroame* v. *Motsisi* 1994 BLR 313; *West* v. *Joubert* 2002 (1) BLR 329; *Sanders* v. *Hunt* 1976 BLR 19; *First National Bank of Botswana Ltd* v. *Buberwa* 2001 (2) BLR 34; *Worldview Botswana* v. *World University Services of Canada* 1996 BLR 527.

Ghana – High Court (Civil Procedure) Rules 2004, Ord. 24; *Mallet* v. *Braun* [1975] 1 GLR 78; *Gatco Chempharam* v. *Pharmdex (GH) Ltd* [1999–2000] 2 GLR 262.

Kenya – Civil Procedure Rules 2009, Ord. XXV; *State of Israel* v. *Somen* [2001] LLR 5932; *Parmex Ltd* v. *Austin & Partners Ltd* [2006] eKLR; *Fasco Trading Co. Ltd* v. *Goodearth Ltd* [2000] LLR 1236; *Healthwise Pharmaceuticals Ltd* v. *Smithkline Beecham Consumer Healthcare Ltd* [2001] LLR 1279; *Shah* v. *Shah* [1981] LLR 1206; *Indemnity Insurance Co. of North America* v. *Kenya Airfreight Handling Ltd*, Civil Case No. 531 of 1999 (High Court, Kenya, 2001); *Farrab Inc.* v. *Brian John Robson* [1957] EA 441; *Vallabhdas Hirji Kapadia* v. *Thakersey Laxmidas* [1960] EA 852.

Lesotho – High Court Rules 1980, s. 48.

Malawi – *Oliver* v. *Cadle* [1961–3] ALR Mal. 456.

Namibia – Rules of the High Court 1990, s. 47.

South Africa – Uniform Court Rules, s. 47; *Vanda* v. *Mbuqe* 1993 (4) SA 93; *Alexander* v. *Jokl* 1948 (3) SA 269; *Francis & Graham Ltd* v. *East African Disposal Co. Ltd* 1950 (3) SA 502; *Rapanos* v. *Rapanos* 1958 (2) SA 705; *Santam Insurance Co. Ltd* v. *Korste* 1962 (4) SA 53; *Banks* v. *Henshaw* 1962 (3) SA 464; *Drakensbergpers BPK* v. *Sharpe* 1963 (4) SA 615; *Sandock Austral Ltd* v. *Exploitation Industrielle et Commerciale–Bretic* 1974 (2) SA 280; *Seboko* v. *Moaki* 1978 (3) SA 639; *South African Television Manufacturing Co. (Pty) Ltd* v. *Jubati* 1983 (2) SA 14; *Minister of Police* v. *Magida* 1984 (3) SA 129; *Magida* v. *Minster of Police* 1987 (1) SA 1; *Protea Assurance Co. Ltd* v. *Januszkiewicz* 1989 (4) SA 292; *South African Iron and Steel Corp. Ltd* v. *Abdulnabi* 1989 (2) SA 224; *The Catamaran TNT Dean Catamarans CC* v. *Slupinski (No 1)* 1997 (2) SA 383; *Davies* v. *Starlauro Spa* 1997 (4) SA 779; *Majunga Food Processes Sarl* v. *South African Dried Fruit Co-operative Ltd* 2000 (2) SA 94; *MV Guzin S (No 2) Hamburgische Landesbank-Girozentrale* v. *Allied Sales Corp.* 2002 (6) SA 127; *Exploitatie-en Beleggingsmaatschappij Argonauten 11 BV* v. *Honig* [2012] 2 All SA 22.

Swaziland – High Court Rules 2010, s. 51; *Allison* v. *Swaziland Royal Insurance Corp. (Pty) Ltd* [1979–81] Sw. LR 4.

This is particularly so as regards plaintiffs who are not ordinarily resident in the jurisdiction, i.e. foreign plaintiffs. A court will not order a defendant to give security for costs at the instance of a plaintiff,[3] but a defendant who counterclaims (rather than who simply raises a defence to the action[4]) may, at the instance of the plaintiff, be ordered to give security for costs.[5] A defendant can apply to the court to have a plaintiff ordinarily resident outside the forum give security for the defendant's costs in defending the proceedings.[6] The rationale for this is to ensure that the defendant will have something within the jurisdiction to cover costs should the plaintiff be unsuccessful in their claim. In the words of Justice Francois in *Edusei* v. *Diners Club Suisse SA*,[7] 'the only hostage to fortune that the courts in their discretion impose is security for costs. This is only fair so that the party sued, if he won, would not be damnified in seeking relief from the plaintiff who was chasing a mirage in foreign claims.'

Tanzania – Civil Procedure Rules, Ord. XXV; *Uniliver Plc* v. *Hangaya* [1990–4] 1 EA 598.

Uganda – Civil Procedure Rules, Ord. XXVI; *Noble Builders Ltd* v. *Sandhu* [2004] EA 228, [2004] Kam. LR 253; *Rohini Damji Sidra* v. *Freny Damji Sidra*, Civil Appeal No. 60 of 1995 (Supreme Court, Uganda, 1997); *Serefaco Consultants Ltd* v. *Euro Consult BV*, Civil Application No. 16 of 2007 (Court of Appeal, Uganda, 2007); *Red Pepper Newspaper* v. *Chris Cotton & Karatis Karisimbi* [2004] Kam. LR 626; *Rohini Sidipra* v. *Freny Sidipra* [1995] Kam. LR 721; *Jubilee Insurance Co.* v. *Krediet Geneve Inc.* [2002] Kam. LR 560; *M/S Untorom Ltd* v. *M/S Kawsi & Co.* [1992] Kam. LR 109; *Shah* v. *Manurama Ltd* [2003] 1 EA 294.

Zambia – High Court Rules, Ord. XL, r. 7; *Darlington* v. *Mitchell Construction Co. Ltd* (1966) ZR 10; *Arthur Levinson* v. *Goodman Glasser* [1949–54] LRNR 381.

Zimbabwe – High Court Act 1981, s. 52; *Zendera* v. *McDade* 1985 (2) ZLR 18; *Africair (Rhodesia) Ltd* v. *Interocean Airways SA* 1964 R & N 61, 1964 (3) SA 114; *Graham* v. *Phillips* [1965] RLR 673, 1966 (1) SA 556; *Plagis* v. *Hubbard* 1975 (1) SA 469; *Gre Insurance Ltd* v. *Chisnall* 1982 (1) SA 387.

[3] *Botswana Insurance Co. Ltd* v. *Matan Trucking Co. Ltd* 2003 (2) BLR 380; *Sandock Austral Ltd* v. *Exploitation Industrielle et Commerciale–Bretic* 1974 (2) SA 280.

[4] *First National Bank of Botswana Ltd* v. *Buberwa* 2001 (2) BLR 34.

[5] *West* v. *Joubert* 2002 (1) BLR 329. In South Africa, a peregrine plaintiff may be ordered to pay security for costs of an *incola* defendant's counterclaim. See *Silvercraft Helicopters (Switzerland)* v. *Zonnekus Mansions* 2009 (5) SA 602; *B & W Industrial Technology (Pty) Ltd* v. *Baroutsos* 2006 (5) SA 135; *South African Iron and Steel Corp. Ltd* v. *Abdulnabi* 1989 (2) SA 224; C. Schulze 'Should a Peregrine Plaintiff Furnish Security for Costs for the Counterclaim of an Incola' (2007) 19 *South African Mercantile Law Journal* 393.

[6] In Tanzania, the court may, of its own motion, order the plaintiff(s) to give security for the payment of all costs incurred and likely to be incurred by any defendant. See Civil Procedure Rules, Ord. XXV, r. 1.

[7] [1982–3] GLR 809 at 816.

The defendant is not entitled to security for costs; rather the court has discretion to award security for costs in appropriate cases. The burden lies on the applicant to show sufficient cause why the respondent should be made to furnish security for costs. The courts take into account many factors in deciding whether to order the plaintiff to give security for costs. Among the factors taken into account in the decided cases are: the fact that the plaintiff has no assets or place of business in the jurisdiction; the existence of a reciprocal regime for the enforcement of judgments between the countries involved; impecuniosity and hardship for the plaintiff.

In the light of the numerous regional economic integration initiatives in Africa, it is heart-warming that residence in the economic region has also become a relevant consideration in applications for security for costs. In the Ugandan case of *Shah* v. *Manurama Ltd*,[8] the defendant brought an application seeking an order that required the plaintiff to pay security for costs. The plaintiff was resident in Kenya. The defendant argued that the fact that the plaintiff had been resident abroad provided prima facie grounds for ordering the payment of costs. The plaintiff argued that, given the re-establishment of the East African Community (EAC),[9] the question of residence for the purpose of ordering security for costs needed re-examination. The court denied the application. It reasoned that, in East Africa, there could no longer be an automatic and inflexible presumption for the courts to order security for costs with regard to a plaintiff's residence in the EAC. To the Ugandan court, the fact of EAC residence 'begs for a fresh re-evaluation of our judicial thinking' as regards the implementation of the law requiring plaintiffs to pay security for costs. Among the factors the court has considered in coming to its decision are the fact that the Treaty establishing the East African Community makes express provision for the unification and harmonisation of the laws of the partner states, including the standardisation of court judgments within the Community and the establishment of a common Bar (that is, cross-border legal practice) in the partner states, as well as the existence of a regime for the reciprocal enforcement of judgments among the member states. *Shah* can be contrasted with the Kenyan case of *Healthwise Pharmaceuticals Ltd* v. *Smithkline Beecham Consumer Healthcare Ltd*,[10] where the Kenyan court rejected the applicant's

[8] [2003] 1 EA 294.
[9] The EAC currently consists of Kenya, Uganda, Tanzania, Burundi and Rwanda.
[10] [2001] LLR 1279.

claim to be a resident of the EAC and, therefore, the defendant had no difficulties in recovering any costs awarded in the suit.

The deposit of security for costs can be a huge financial burden on foreign litigants. It can potentially force some to abandon litigation or to seek a settlement. It speaks ill of a legal system if foreigners believe that applications for security for costs are being used to obstruct legitimate claims. Accordingly, courts must exercise discretion to grant security for costs, to reasonably ensure that, while protecting the legitimate interests of domestic defendants against frivolous claims, an order for security for costs does not cause undue hardship to foreign plaintiffs in a manner that defeats the cause of justice. In this regard, the words of Justice Gyeke-Dako are apposite:

> Botswana like Ghana has a Constitution which expresses extensive democratic principles and respect for the rule of law. It eschews all forms of discrimination and provides equal and free access to the courts to all manner of persons living in the country. It is always a matter to be taken into account that a plaintiff should not be driven from the judgment seat, unless the justice of the case makes it imperative. In my view, the courts must be on their guard and consider whether the application for security is being used oppressively so as to try to stifle a genuine claim.[11]

[11] *Misroame* v. *Motsisi* 1994 BLR 313 at 324.

SELECTED BIBLIOGRAPHY*

Abraham, G., '"Yes . . . But Does It Have Personality?" The International Committee of the Red Cross and Sovereign Immunity' (2007) 124 *South African Law Journal* 499.

Adede, A. O., 'Loan Agreements with Foreign Sovereign Borrowers: Issues of Sovereign Immunity, Applicable Law and Settlement of Disputes' (1987) 3:2 *Lesotho Law Journal* 101.

Adeleke, F. A. R., 'Doctrine of Sovereign Immunity in Nigerian Law from Inception to Section 308 of 1999 Constitution' (2003) 7 *Journal of International and Comparative Law* 193.

Aden, M., 'The German Matrimonial Property Regime of Zugewinngemeinschaft in South African Private International Law' (1973) 90 *South African Law Journal* 160.

Agbede, I. O., 'Conflict of Laws in a Federation: The Nigerian Experience' (1973) 7 *Nigerian Law Journal* 48.

'Conflict of Laws: New Bases for Solution' (1977–80) 11 *Nigerian Law Journal* 75.

'Conflict of Tort Laws in Nigeria: An Analysis of the Rule in *Benson* v. *Ashiru*' (1972) 6 *Nigerian Law Journal* 103.

'Doctrine of Characterisation: Theory and Practice' (1988) 15 *Nigerian Journal of Contemporary Law* 41.

'Forum Law and Petroleum Contracts: Comments on Choice-of-law Provision of Decree 15 of 1969' (1986) *Nigerian Current Law Review* 122.

'The English Doctrine of Renvoi: Its Applicability in Common Law Africa' (1977) 2 *Nigerian Juridical Review* 55.

'Conflict of Torts Laws under the Received English Law in Common Law Africa: A Review' (1971) 3:1 *Zambia Law Journal* 64.

Agyemang, A. A., 'African Courts, the Settlement of Investment Disputes and the Enforcement of Awards' (1989) 33 *Journal of African Law* 31.

'African States and ICC Arbitration' (1989) 5:2 *Lesotho Law Journal* 217.

* A more extended form of this bibliography was first published in the *American Journal of Comparative Law*. See R. F. Oppong, 'Private International Law Scholarship in Africa (1884–2009) – A Selected Bibliography' (2010) 58 *American Journal of Comparative Law* 319–42.

'African States and ICSID Arbitration' (1988) *Comparative and International Law Journal of Southern Africa* 177.

Ailola, D. A., 'Recognition of Foreign Proceedings, Orders and Officials in Insolvency in Southern Africa: A Call for a Regional Convention' (1999) 32 *Comparative and International Law Journal of Southern Africa* 54.

'The UNCITRAL Model Law on Cross-Border Insolvency: Its Efficacy and Suitability as a Basis for a SADC Convention' (2000) 11 *Stellenbosch Law Review* 215.

Amerasinghe, C. F., 'Recognition of Foreign Nullity Decrees' (1963) 80 *South African Law Journal* 283.

Asante, S. K. B., 'The Perspective of African Countries on International Commercial Arbitration' (1995) *Nigerian Current Law Review* 42.

Asouzu, A. A., 'Some Fundamental Concerns and Issues about International Arbitration in Africa' (2006) 1 *Law for Development Review* 81.

Atilade, P., 'Is There One Nigerian Domicile or Different Regional Domicile in Regard to Divorce' (1964) 5 *Nigeria Bar Journal* 55.

G. Bamodu, 'In Personam Jurisdiction: An overlooked Concept in Recent Nigerian Jurisprudence' (2011) 7 *Journal of Private International Law* 273.

'Jurisdiction and Applicable Law in Transnational Dispute Resolution before the Nigerian Courts' (1995) 29 *The International Lawyer* 555.

'The Enforcement of Foreign Money Judgments in Nigeria: A Case of Unnecessary Judicial Pragmatism?' (2012) 12 *Oxford University Commonwealth Law Journal* 1.

R. E. Bannermah, 'Award of Damages in Foreign Currency: A Critical Look at the Judgments' (1993–95) 19 *Review of Ghana Law* 231.

Barrie, G. N., 'An Accurate Reflection of the Most Significant Relationship Test in the Private International Law of Delict' (1994) *Journal of South African Law* 851.

'Foreign Sovereign Immunity: Acta Iure Imperii or Acta Iure Gestionis' (1996) *Journal of South African Law* 591.

'Sovereign Immunity of States: Acts Iure Imperii and Acts Iure Gestionis – What is the Distinction' (2001) 26 *South African Yearbook of International Law* 156.

'The Approach of the Courts Regarding South African Custodian Parents Going into the Diaspora' (2009) *Journal of South African Law* 562.

Beck, A., 'Company Residence as a Jurisdictional Connecting Factor' (1985) 7 *Modern Business Law* 90.

'Jurisdiction over Peregrines, Consent, Attachment and Res Gestae' (1986) 103 *South African Law Journal* 14.

'The Convenience of Jurisdiction' (1983) 100 *South African Law Journal* 43.

Beck, A. C., 'Treasury Permission and the Jurisdiction of the Courts' (1982) 99 *South African Law Journal* 125.

'The Convenience of Jurisdiction' (1982) 15 *Comparative and International Law Journal of Southern Africa* 344.

Bennet, T. W., 'Cumulation and Gap: Are They Systemic Defects in the Conflict of Laws?' (1988) 105 *South African Law Journal* 444.

Bentwich, N., 'Private International Law in Ethiopia' (1951) 4 *International Law Quarterly* 111.

Booysen, H., 'Procedural and Jurisdictional Uncertainties in the Foreign States Immunities Act' (1987–88) 13 *South African Yearbook of International Law* 139.

'The Municipal Enforcement of Arbitration Awards against States in Terms of Arbitration Conventions, with Special References to the New York Convention – Does International Law Provide for a Municipal Law Concept of an Arbitrable Act of State' (1986–87) 12 *South African Yearbook of International Law* 73.

Bray, W. and Beukes, M., 'Recent Trends in the Development of State Immunity in South African Law' (1981) 7 *South African Yearbook of International Law* 13.

Brooks, P. E. J., 'Foreign Business Corporations and South African Private International Law' (1988) 21 *Comparative and International Law Journal of Southern Africa* 92.

'Matrimonial Property Regimes and Succession in South African Private International Law' (1978) 11 *Comparative and International Law Journal of Southern Africa* 289.

'Security Council Decisions and Private Contracts in Conflict of Law Situations' (1977) 3 *South African Yearbook of International Law* 33.

'The Effect of Changes to the Law Regulating Matrimonial Proprietary Regimes in South African Private International Law' (1976) 9 *Comparative and International Law Journal of Southern Africa* 99.

'The Status of Foreign Juristic Persons in South Africa' (1986) 8 *Modern Business Law* 91.

'The Wife's Residence and Domicile as Jurisdictional Factors in Divorce Actions' (1979) 42 *Journal of Contemporary Roman-Dutch Law* 103.

C. L. M., 'Effect of Foreign Custody Orders' (1970) 10 *Rhodesia Law Journal* 87.

Cheshire, G. C., 'Plea for a Wider Study of Private International Law' (1948) 65 *South African Law Journal* 213.

Couzens, M., 'A very Long Engagement: The Children's Act 38 of 2005 and the 1993 Hague Convention on the Protection of Children and Cooperation in respect of Intercountry Adoption' (2009) *Potchefstroom Electronic Law Journal* 54.

Davel, C. J. and Boniface, A., 'Cross Border Relocation of Children and Custodial Parent' (2003) 66 *Journal of Contemporary Roman-Dutch Law* 138.

de Vos, W., 'Freedom of Choice of Law for Contracts in Private International Law' (1961) *Acta Juridica* 1.

de Vos, W. L., 'International Aspects of Civil Procedural Law' (1996) 7 *Stellenbosch Law Review* 163.

du Toit, S. F., 'International Funds Transfer and Private International Law' (2006) 18 *South African Mercantile Law Journal* 53.

Edwards, A. B., 'Choice of Law in Delict: Rules or Approach' (1979) 96 *South African Law Journal* 48.

Eiselen, S., 'Goodbye Arrest ad Fundandam. Hello *Forum non Conveniens*?' (2008) *Journal of South African Law* 794.

'International Jurisdiction in Claims Sounding in Money' (2006) 18 *South African Mercantile Law Journal* 45.

'Laconian Revisited – A Reappraisal of Classification in Conflicts Law' (2006) 123 *South African Law Journal* 147.

Ekwere, F. N., 'Doctrine of Characterisation: Fact or Fiction' (1992–93) *Nigerian Current Law Review* 63.

'Is There Domicile of Dependence in Nigerian Conflict of Laws' (2000) 12 *African Journal of International and Comparative Law* 616.

Elbalti, B., 'The Jurisdiction of Foreign Courts and the Enforcement of their Judgments in Tunisia: A Need for Reconsideration' (2012) 8 *Journal of Private International Law* 195.

Erasmus, G., 'Execution of Judgments against Foreign States' (1983) 100 *South African Law Journal* 516.

Faris, J. A., 'Domicile and Residence – The Independent Grounds for Divorce Jurisdiction' (1993) 56 *Journal of Contemporary Roman-Dutch Law* 277.

Field, T.-L., 'What Law Determines the Money of Payment: Exploring a Recent Contribution to South African Conflict of Laws' (2001) 34 *Comparative and International Law Journal of Southern Africa* 365.

Forsyth, C., 'A Modest Defence of Renvoi' (2009) *Journal of South African Law* 135.

'Enforcement of Arbitral Awards, Choice of Law in Contract, Characterization and a New Attitude to Private International Law' (1987) 104 *South African Law Journal* 4.

'Exercise of Powers of Appointment in Foreign Wills' (1983) 100 *South African Law Journal* 172.

'Extinctive Prescription and the *Lex Fori*: A New Direction' (1982) 99 *South African Law Journal* 16.

'"Mind the Gap": A Practical Example of the Characterization of Prescription/Limitation Rules' (2006) 2 *Journal of Private International Law* 169.

'"Mind the Gap Part II": The South African Supreme Court of Appeal and Characterization' (2006) 2 *Journal of Private International Law* 425.

'Renvoi – Is there an Answer?' (1976) 1 *Natal University Law Review* 321.

'Submission as a Ground of International Competence and the Finality of Foreign Default Judgments' (1992) 109 *South African Law Journal* 1.

'The Growing Importance of the Conflict of Laws in South Africa' (1980) 43 *Journal of Contemporary Roman-Dutch Law* 77.
'The Impact of the Domestic on the International: Some Crucial Deficiencies in the South African Law of Jurisdiction with Their Regional and International Consequences' (2006) 18 *South African Mercantile Law Journal* 1.
'The Provenance and Future of Private International Law in Southern Africa' (2002) *Journal of South African Law* 60.
'What Happens When the Lex Causae Changes' (1975) 92 *South African Law Journal* 368.
Fredericks, E. A., 'Contractual Capacity in Private International Law: Interpreting the Powell Case' (2006) 69 *Journal of Contemporary Roman-Dutch Law* 279.
and J. L. Neels, 'The Proper Law of a Documentary Letter of Credit (Part 1)' (2003) 15 *South African Mercantile Law Journal* 63.
and J. L. Neels, 'The Proper Law of a Documentary Letter of Credit (Part 2)' (2003) 15 *South African Mercantile Law Journal* 207.
Greig, M., 'Foreign Currency and Interest Awards in the Context of Fluctuating Inflation and Currency Rates' (2009) 126 *South African Law Journal* 124.
G. R. J. H., 'The Enforcement of Foreign Judgments' (1970) 10 *Rhodesia Law Journal* 8.
'Domicil in Federated States' (1971) 11 *Rhodesia Law Journal* 5.
Hahlo, H. R., 'The Finality of Foreign Default Judgments' (1969) 86 *South African Law Journal* 354.
Heaton, J. and Schoeman, E., 'Foreign Marriages and Section 7(3) of the Divorce Act 70 of 1979' (2000) 63 *Journal of Contemporary Roman-Dutch Law* 141.
Hlophe, M. J., 'The Judicial Approach to Summary Applications for the Child's Return: A Move Away from "Best Interests" Principles' (1998) 115 *South African Law Journal* 439.
Idris, I., 'Ethiopian Law of Execution of Foreign Judgments' (1999) 19 *Journal of Ethiopian Law* 17.
Kahn, E., 'Choice of Law in Divorce Actions' (1973) 90 *South African Law Journal* 125.
'Choice of Law in Succession in the South African Conflict of Laws' (1956) 73 *South African Law Journal* 303.
'Choice of Law in Succession in the South African Conflict of Laws' (1956) 73 *South African Law Journal* 392.
'Choice of Law in Succession in the South African Conflict of Laws' (1957) 74 *South African Law Journal* 43.
'De Lege Ferenda: Jurisdiction and Choice of Law in Matrimonial Actions' (1953) 70 *South African Law Journal* 52.
'Divorced Abroad: Still Married Here' (1986) *Journal of South African Law* 1.
'Domicile: As Connecting and Jurisdictional Factor; Choice of Law' (1985) 102 *South African Law Journal* 407.

'Illegitimacy: Jurisdiction and Choice of Law' (1964) 81 *South African Law Journal* 283.

'International Contracts – I: What Legal System Governs Them?' (1990) 19 *Businessman's Law* 203.

'International Contracts – II: Is There a General Governing Legal System?' (1990) 19 *Businessman's Law* 259.

'International Contracts – III: The General Governing Legal System in Some Developed Countries' (1990) 20 *Businessman's Law* 35.

'International Contracts – IV: The General Governing Legal System in Other Developed Countries' (1990) 20 *Businessman's Law* 77.

'International Contracts – V: The General Rule in South Africa and the Issue of Capacity' (1991) 20 *Businessman's Law* 126.

'International Contracts – VI: A Potpourri of Problems' (1991) 20 *Businessman's Law* 147.

'Jurisdiction to Annul a Voidable Marriage' (1955) 72 *South African Law Journal* 410.

'Jurisdiction to Grant a Separation Order' (1965) 82 *South African Law Journal* 142.

'Legal Milestones (II). The Emergence of Private International Law (Conflict of Laws)' (1981) *De Rebus* 535.

'Multiple Domiciles' (1965) 82 *South African Law Journal* 147.

'Proving the Law of Our Friends and Neighbours' (1965) 82 *South African Law Journal* 133.

'Reform of the Law of Domicile: Time for some History' (1987) 12 *Journal of Juridical Science* 113.

'Ruminations of a Quondam Would-Be South African Conflicts Lawyer' (2002) *Journal of South African Law* 125.

'The Domicile of Choice of Immigrant and Deportee' (1948) 65 *South African Law Journal* 220.

'The Law Governing the Formal Validity of a Will Disposing of Movables' (1951) 4 *International Law Quarterly* 397.

'The South African Law of Domicile of Natural Persons' (1971) *Acta Juridica* 1.

'What Happens in a Conflicts Case When the Governing Foreign Law is Not Proved' (1970) 87 *South African Law Journal* 145.

Kallel, S., 'The Recognition and Enforcement of Foreign Arbitral Awards in Tunisia' (1992) 2 *Tilburg Foreign Law Review* 17.

Kane, T. G., 'Divorce Jurisdiction – What Basis' (1969) 1 *Review of Ghana Law* 235.

Kelbrick, R., 'The Incola Plaintiff, Consent and Arrest or Attachment to Found Jurisdiction' (1992) 25 *Comparative and International Law Journal of Southern Africa* 332.

Kelbrick, R. A., 'The Doctrine of Consent' (1986) 19 *Comparative and International Law Journal of Southern Africa* 130.

Kerr, A. J., 'Choosing a System of Law by the Exercise of Discretion' (1977) *Acta Juridica* 95.

'Judicial Notice of Foreign Law and of Customary Law' (1994) 111 *South African Law Journal* 577.

Kiggundu, J., 'Choice of Law in Delict: The Rise and Rise of *Lex Loci Delicti Commissi*' (2006) 18 *South African Mercantile Law Journal* 97.

'The Law of Domicile in Botswana: The Need for Reform' (1990) 2 *African Journal of International and Comparative Law* 626.

'The Problem of Child Abduction in Private International Law' (1991) 3 *African Journal of International and Comparative Law* 399.

'The Recognition of Foreign Divorces in Botswana' (1992) 25 *Comparative and International Law Journal of Southern Africa* 83.

'The Treatment of Foreign Polygamous Marriages in Private International Law' (2003) 17 *Speculum Juris* 214.

Kuforiji, A. A., 'Voluntary Submission in Actions *in Personam*: The Nigerian Solution' (1984) *Nigerian Current Law Review* 194.

Leon, P. S. G., 'Roma Non Locuta Est: The Recognition and Enforcement of Foreign Judgments in South Africa' (1983) 16 *Comparative and International Law Journal of Southern Africa* 325.

Leslie, R. D., 'The Non-enforcement of Foreign Revenue Laws' (1976) 93 *South African Law Journal* 46.

Lubuschagne, J. M. T., 'International Parental Abduction of Children: Remarks on the Overriding Status of the Best Interest of the Child in International Law' (2000) 33 *Comparative and International Law Journal of Southern Africa* 333.

Malan, F. R., 'Letters of Credit and Attachment Ad Fundandam Jurisdictionem' (1994) *Journal of South African Law* 150.

Malan, F. R., Neels, J. L., O'Brien, P. H., and Boshoff, A., 'Transnational Litigation in South African Law (1)' (1995) *Journal of South African Law* 106.

'Transnational Litigation in South African Law (2)' (1995) *Journal of South African Law* 282.

'Transnational Litigation in South African Law (3)' (1995) *Journal of South African Law* 460.

Martin, B., 'The Ascertainment of Foreign Law by Means of Judicial Notice' (1997) 8 *Stellenbosch Law Review* 377.

Martin, B. S. C., 'Judicial Notice of Foreign Law' (1998) 31 *Comparative and International Law Journal of Southern Africa* 61.

Mbanefo, I. D., 'Application of Foreign Law – A Minefield?' (1986) *Nigerian Current Law Review* 183.

Mendelsohn, J. M., 'The Choice of Law Rule for Goods in Transit: Bominflot Ltd v Kien Hung Shipping Co Ltd' (2007) 19 *South African Mercantile Law Journal* 387.

Mhone, K., 'Arbitration Law in Malawi and its Implications for the PTA/SADCC Organisations' (1990) 23 *Comparative and International Law Journal of Southern Africa* 234.

Mhura, N. D., 'The Making of Wills under the Law of Malawi: A Review of the Case of in the Estate of Guiseppe Pino Barretta and the Choice of Law' (1992) 25 *Comparative and International Law Journal of Southern Africa* 343.

Moodley, P., 'Unravelling the Legal Knots around Inter-Country Adoptions in *De Gree v. Webb*' (2007) *Potchefstroom Electronic Law Journal* 2.

Mosikatsana, T. L., 'www.buyababy.com: Inter-Country Adoption' (2003) 120 *South African Law Journal* 103.

Mosito, K. E., 'The UNCITRAL Model Law on International Commercial Arbitration and the Doctrine of the Party Autonomy' (1993) 9:2 *Lesotho Law Journal* 133.

Myburgh, P., 'Choice of Law in Maritime Delict: All at Sea' (1988) 10 *Modern Business Law* 25.

'Recognition of Foreign Maritime Liens' (1989) 106 *South African Law Journal* 263.

Namiseb, T., 'The Children's Status Act, 2006 (No. 6 of 2006)' (2009) 1 *Namibian Law Journal* 121.

Ndumo, M. E., 'Lesotho and the Cross-Border Protection of Children: A Focus on Inter-Country Adoption' (2006) 16:2 *Lesotho Law Journal* 377.

Neels, J. L., 'Classification as an Argumentative Device in International Family Law' (2003) 120 *South African Law Journal* 883.

'Falconbridge in Africa. Via Media Classification (Characterisation) and Liberative (Extinctive) Prescription (Limitation of Actions) in Private International Law – A Canadian Doctrine on Safari in Southern Africa (Hic Sunt Leones!); or: Simper Aliquid Novi Africam Adferre' (2008) 4 *Journal of Private International Law* 167.

'Private International Law of Succession in South Africa' (2005) 7 *Yearbook of Private International Law* 183.

'The Proprietary Effect of Reservation-of-Title Clauses in Private International Law' (2006) 18 *South African Mercantile Law Journal* 66.

'The Revocation of Wills in South African Private International Law' (2007) 56 *International & Comparative Law Quarterly* 613.

'Via Media Classification in Private International Law' (1994) 57 *Journal of Contemporary Roman-Dutch Law* 687.

Neels, J. L. and Fredericks, E. A., 'The Music Performance Contract in European and Southern African Private International Law (1)' (2008) 71 *Journal of Contemporary Roman-Dutch Law* 351.

'The Music Performance Contract in European and Southern African Private International Law (2)' (2008) 71 *Journal of Contemporary Roman-Dutch Law* 529.

Neels, J. L. and Wethmar-Lemmer, M., 'Constitutional Values and the Proprietary Consequences of Marriage in Private International Law – Introducing the Lex Causae Proprietatis Matrimonii' (2008) *Journal of South African Law* 587.

Nicholson, C., 'The Recognition and Enforcement of Foreign Custody Orders and the Problem of International Child Abduction' (1993) 34 *Codicillus* 4.

Nicholson, C. M. A., 'The Hague Convention on the Civil Aspects of International Child Abduction – Pill or Placebo?' (1999) 32 *Comparative and International Law Journal of Southern Africa* 228.

Niekerk, J. P. V., 'Commercial Law, Commercial Transactions and the Foreign States Immunities Act 87 of 1981' (1991) 3 *South African Mercantile Law Journal* 137.

Nnova, G., 'Choice of Law in International Contracts for the Transfer of Technology: A Critique of the Nigerian Approach' (2000) 44 *Journal of African Law* 78.

Obi, A. C., 'Divorce Jurisdiction in Nigeria Based on *Dr. Ogwurike v. Renate Ogwurike*' (1973) 11 *Nigeria Bar Journal* 146.

Olivier, M., 'Some Aspects of International Law in South African Cross-Border Insolvency Law' (2005) 38 *Comparative and International Law Journal of Southern Africa* 373.

Omoruyi, I. O., 'Enforcement of Foreign Judgments in Nigeria: An Appraisal' (2000) 1 *Nigeria Contemporary Law Journal* 28.

'The Determination of Applicable Law in International Contracts: A Nigerian Perspective' (2001) 5 *Modern Practice Journal of Finance & Investment Law* 582.

Oppong, R. F., 'Choice of Law and Forum Agreement Survives a Constitutional Challenge in the Kenya Court of Appeal' (2007) 33 *Commonwealth Law Bulletin* 158.

'Mere Presence and International Competence in Private International Law' (2007) 3 *Journal of Private International Law* 321.

'Private International Law and the African Economic Community: A Plea for Greater Attention' (2006) 55 *International & Comparative Law Quarterly* 911.

'Private International Law in Africa: The Past, Present and Future' (2007) 55 *American Journal of Comparative Law* 677.

'Recognition and Enforcement of Foreign Judgments in Ghana: A Second Look at a Colonial Inheritance' (2005) 31 *Commonwealth Law Bulletin* 19.

'Roman-Dutch Law meets the Common Law on Jurisdiction in International Matters' (2008) 4 *Journal of Private International Law* 311.

'The Hague Conference and the Development of Private International Law in Africa: A Plea for Cooperation' (2006) 8 *Yearbook of Private International Law* 189.

Osode, P. C., 'State Contracts, State Interests and International Commercial Arbitration: A Third World Perspective' (1997) 30 *Comparative and International Law Journal of Southern Africa* 37.

Peter, J., 'Attachment of Found Jurisdiction and the Effect of Consent' (1989) 106 *South African Law Journal* 27.

Pieterse-Spies, A., 'Inter-Country Adoption: A South African Perspective' (2008) 71 *Journal of Contemporary Roman-Dutch Law* 556.

Prevost, M. D., 'Does Immunity Attach to the State or Its Acts' (1996) 21 *South African Yearbook of International Law* 118.

Quansah, E. K., 'Determining Matrimonial Property Rights of Non-Domiciled Spouses: The Applicable Law in Botswana' (2004) 48 *Journal of African Law* 104.

Rantenbach, C., 'Formalities of "Foreign" Internet Wills in South Africa and the Netherlands: A Storm in a Teacup?' (2009) 72 *Journal of Contemporary Roman-Dutch Law* 240.

Reinhartz, B. E., 'International Matrimonial Property Law: Developments in the Netherlands, Europe and South Africa' (2009) *Journal of South African Law* 125.

Ringo, F. S., 'The Recognition and Enforcement of Foreign Arbitral Awards in the COMESA/SADC Region: Analysis of Legal Developments' (1993) 9:1 *Lesotho Law Journal* 185.

Roodt, C., 'Conflict of Law(s) and Autonomy in Antenuptial Agreements (1)' (2006) 69 *Journal of Contemporary Roman-Dutch Law* 215.

'Conflict of Law(s) and Autonomy in Antenuptial Agreements (2)' (2006) 69 *Journal of Contemporary Roman-Dutch Law* 367.

'Conflict of Law(s) and Autonomy in Antenuptial Agreements (3)' (2006) 69 *Journal of Contemporary Roman-Dutch Law* 546.

'International Regulation of Cultural Objects: The Options Facing South Africa' (1997) *South African Public Law* 99.

'Law Applicable to Certain Rights in Respect of Securities Held with an Intermediary: The Hague Securities Convention' (2006) 18 *South African Mercantile Law Journal* 83.

'Recognition and Enforcement of Foreign Judgments: Still a Hobson's Choice among Competing Theories' (2005) 38 *Comparative and International Law Journal of Southern Africa* 15.

'The Integration of Substantive Law Interests and Material Justice in South African Choice of Law' (2003) 36 *Comparative and International Law Journal of Southern Africa* 1.

'The Recognition and Enforcement of Foreign Judgments, Maintenance Orders and Arbitral Awards: A Proposal for Structural Reform' (2004) 45 *Codicillus* 64.

'Party Autonomy in International Law of Succession: A Starting Point for a Global Consensus?' (2009) *Journal of South African Law* 241.

Roodt, C. and Esser, I.-M., 'Venue in Transnational Litigation: Party Autonomy Adds New Impacts to the Judgment Project' (2006) 18 *South African Mercantile Law Journal* 13.

Sanders, A. J. G. M., 'The Expatriate Contract Worker and the Acquisition of a Domicile of Choice – The Botswana Position' (1983) 100 *South African Law Journal* 705.

Sawyerr, A. G. F., 'Contractual Capacity and the Conflict of Laws in East Africa: A Study in Conflicts Method' (1968) 1 *Eastern African Law Review* 1.

Schoeman, E., 'Choice of Law and Legitimacy: Back to 1917' (1999) 116 *South African Law Journal* 288.

'Domicile of Choice and Animus: How Definite is Indefinite?' (1999) 62 *Journal of Contemporary Roman-Dutch Law* 272.

'Domicile of Choice and Animus: How Definite is Indefinite? (Continued)' (1999) 62 *Journal of Contemporary Roman-Dutch Law* 325.

'Domicile, Status and Divorce in South African Conflict of Laws: A Historical Perspective' (1998) 4 *Fundamina: A Journal of Legal History* 1.

'The Abolition of the Wife's Domicile of Dependence: A Lesson in History' (1995) 58 *Journal of Contemporary Roman-Dutch Law* 488.

'The Connecting Factor for the Proprietary Consequences of Marriage' (2001) *Journal of South African Law* 74.

'The South African Conflict Rule for Proprietary Consequences of Marriage: Learning from the German Experience' (2004) *Journal of South African Law* 115.

'The South African Conflict Rule for Proprietary Consequences of Marriage: The Need for Reform' (2004) 24 *IPRax* 65.

Schulze, C., 'Electronic Commerce and Civil Jurisdiction, with Special Reference to Consumer Contracts' (2006) 18 *South African Mercantile Law Journal* 31.

'Formalistic and Discretionary Approaches to Characterization in Private International Law' (2006) 123 *South African Law Journal* 161.

'International Jurisdiction in Claims Sounding in Money: is Richman v Ben-Tovim the Last Word?' (2008) 20 *South African Mercantile Law Journal* 61.

'Practical Problems Regarding the Enforcement of Foreign Money Judgements' (2005) 17 *South African Mercantile Law Journal* 125.

'Should a Peregrine Plaintiff Furnish Security for Costs for the Counterclaim of an Incola Defendant?' (2007) 19 *South African Mercantile Law Journal* 393.

Schulze, H., 'The Recognition and Enforcement of Foreign Arbitral Awards in South Africa' (2000) 8 *Juta's Business Law* 66.

Schulze, H. C. A. W., 'Legal Aspects of Offshore Transactions' (1994) 27 *Comparative and International Law Journal of Southern Africa* 27.

'Private International Law and Jurisdictional Problems Relating to Offshore Joint Venture Agreements' (1995) 28 *Comparative and International Law Journal of Southern Africa* 383.

'Declining and Referring Jurisdiction in International Litigation: The Leuven/London Principles' (2000) 25 *South African Yearbook of International Law* 161.

'*Forum Non Conveniens* in Comparative Private International Law' (2001) 118 *South African Law Journal* 812.

'Conflicting Laws of Conflict in Cases of International Succession' (2001) 34 *Comparative and International Law Journal of Southern Africa* 34.

Schulze, W. G., 'Attachment Ad Fundandam Jurisdictionem of the Rights under a Documentary Letter of Credit – Some Questions Answered, Some Questions Raised' (2000) 63 *Journal of Contemporary Roman-Dutch Law* 672.

Sibanda, O., 'Jurisdictional Arrest of a Foreign Peregrinus Now Unconstitutional in South Africa: *Bid Industrial Holdings* v. *Strang*' (2008) 4 *Journal of Private International Law* 329.

'National Court Intervention in International Commercial Arbitration in South Africa' (2008) 12 *Vindobona Journal of International Commercial Law and Arbitration* 153.

Sigwadi, M., 'The Recognition and Enforcement of Foreign Judgments in South Africa' (2001) 13 *South African Mercantile Law Journal* 649.

Silberberg, H., 'The Determination of Matrimonial Property Rights and the Doctrine of Immutability in the Conflict of Laws' (1973) 6 *Comparative and International Law Journal of Southern Africa* 323.

Skeen, A. S. Q., 'The Mercenary Witness and the Grant of a Commission De Bene Esse' (1982) 99 *South African Law Journal* 338.

Smith, A., 'Some Aspects of Comity and the Protection of Local Creditors in Cross-Border Insolvency Law: South Africa and the United States Compared' (2002) 14 *South African Mercantile Law Journal* 17.

Spiro, E., 'Adoption and the Conflict of Laws' (1983) 16 *Comparative and International Law Journal of Southern Africa* 242.

'Autonomy of the Parties to a Contract and the Conflict of Laws: Illegality' (1984) 17 *Comparative and International Law Journal of Southern Africa* 197.

'Conflict of the Locus Regit Actum Rule and the Lex Causae' (1986) 49 *Journal of Contemporary Roman-Dutch Law* 139.

'Currency Problems in Transactions Extending Beyond One Legal Unit' (1985) 18 *Comparative and International Law Journal of Southern Africa* 377.

'Deportation and Domicile' (1964) 81 *South African Law Journal* 173.

'Domicile in South African Law' (1962) *Acta Juridica* 62.

'Domicile of Illegal Immigrant' (1963) 12 *International & Comparative Law Quarterly* 680.

'Effect of Adoption in South Africa' (1961) 78 *South African Law Journal* 318.

'Enforcement of a Foreign Judgment Sounding in Money against a Fugitive from Justice' (1974) 7 *Comparative and International Law Journal of Southern Africa* 339.

'Enforcement of Foreign Default Judgments' (1968) 1 *Comparative and International Law Journal of Southern Africa* 484.

'Failure to Choose the Applicable Law' (1984) 47 *Journal of Contemporary Roman-Dutch Law* 140.

'Foreign Acts of State and the Conflict of Laws' (1967) 16 *International & Comparative Law Quarterly* 145.

'Foreign Law' (1972) 5 *Comparative and International Law Journal of Southern Africa* 56.

'Foreign Order of Adoption' (1966) *Journal of Contemporary Roman-Dutch Law* 120.

'Forum Non Conveniens' (1980) 14 *Comparative and International Law Journal of Southern Africa* 333.

'Jurisdiction by Consent' (1967) 84 *South African Law Journal* 295.

'Kinds of Conflict Rules' (1979) 96 *South African Law Journal* 598.

'Legitimate and Illegitimate Children' (1964) *Acta Juridica* 53.

'Limitation of Action and the Conflict of Laws' (1988) 51 *Journal of Contemporary Roman-Dutch Law* 34.

'Must Foreign Law Be Applied?' (1979) 12 *Comparative and International Law Journal of Southern Africa* 319.

'Propriety Consequences of Marriage and the Conflict of Laws' (1976) *Journal of Contemporary Roman-Dutch Law* 22.

'Prorogatio Fori of Peregrini Parties' (1987) 20 *Comparative and International Law Journal of Southern Africa* 244.

'Recognition of Foreign Decrees of Divorce' (1974) 37 *Journal of Contemporary Roman-Dutch Law* 340.

'The Defence of *Lis Alibi Pendens*' (1976) 9 *Comparative and International Law Journal of Southern Africa* 89.

'The Evolution of the Closest (Most Significant) Connection in the Conflict of Laws' (1990) 53 *Journal of Contemporary Roman-Dutch Law* 74.

'The Incidence of Jurisdiction in the Recognition and Enforcement of Foreign Judgments' (1978) *Acta Juridica* 59.

Staniland, H., 'Is the Admiralty Court to be Turned into a Court of Convenience for the Wandering Litigants of the World' (1986) 103 *South African Law Journal* 9.

'Should Foreign Maritime Liens Be Recognized' (1991) 108 *South African Law Journal* 293.

Steyn, E., 'On the International Recognition of Gay Love' (2003) *Journal of South African Law* 340.

Taitz, J., 'Jurisdiction and Forum Conveniens – A New Approach?' (1980) 43 *Journal of Contemporary Roman-Dutch Law* 187.

'Jurisdiction and Forum Conveniens – A Reply' (1981) 44 *Journal of Contemporary Roman-Dutch Law* 372.

Tannock, Q., 'Public Policy as a Ground for Setting Aside an Award: Is Zimbabwe Out of Step?' (2008) 74 *Arbitration: The International Journal of Arbitration, Mediation and Dispute Management* 72.

Terblanche, P., 'Lex Fori or Lex Loci Delicti? The Problem of Choice of Law in International Delicts' (1997) 30 *Comparative and International Law Journal of Southern Africa* 243.

Teshale, S., 'Reciprocity with respect to Enforcement of Foreign Judgments in Ethiopia: A Critique of the Supreme Court's Decision in the Paulos Papassinous Case' (2000) 12 *African Journal of International and Comparative Law* 569.

'Towards Rationalizing Judicial Jurisdiction in Ethiopia' (2000) 8 *Tilburg Foreign Law Review* 195.

Thanawalla, S., 'Foreign Inter Partes Judgments: Their Recognition and Enforcement in the Private International Law of East Africa' (1970) 19 *International & Comparative Law Quarterly* 430.

Therion, S., 'The Validity of Marriages Solemnized in a Foreign Consulate' (1985) *De Rebus* 353.

Thomashausen, A., 'The Enforcement and Recognition of Judgments and Other Forms of Legal Cooperation in the SADC' (2002) 35 *Comparative and International Law Journal of Southern Africa* 26.

Thomashausen, A. E. A. M., 'Some Problems in the Application of South African Private International Law' (1984) 17 *Comparative and International Law Journal of Southern Africa* 78.

'The Matrimonial Property Act 1984: Some New Aspects for Marriages out of Community and Marriages Governed by Foreign Law' (1985) *De Rebus* 167.

Tiewul, S. A., 'The Enforcement of Arbitration Agreements and Awards' (1974) 11 *University of Ghana Law Journal* 143.

Tshosa, O. B., 'Immunity of Diplomatic Missions in Botswana in Light of *Amadou Oury Bah* v. *Libyan Embassy*' (2008) 7 *University of Botswana Law Journal.*

Tsikata, F., 'Proving Familiar Foreign Law' (1987–88) 16 *Review of Ghana Law* 249.

'Actions in Respect of Foreign Currency Obligations' (1987–88) 26 *Review of Ghana Law* 234.

Turpin, C. C., 'Characterization and Policy in the Conflict of Laws' (1959) *Acta Juridica* 222.

'Freedom of Choice in the Acquisition of a Domicile of Choice' (1957) 74 *South African Law Journal* 201.

Uys, J. F., 'The Continuation of Civil Proceedings in a Foreign Country' (1969) 2 *Comparative and International Law Journal of Southern Africa* 99.

Van Der Linde, K. and Van Der Merwe, T., 'Company Residence and Jurisdiction' (1994) 111 *South African Law Journal* 780.

van Loggerenberg, C., 'Changing the Matrimonial Property Regime in the Case of Spouses Married under a Foreign Domiciliary Law' (1987) *Obiter* 111.

Viejobueno, S., 'Private International Law Rules Relating to the Validity of International Sales Contracts' (1993) 26 *Comparative and International Law Journal of Southern Africa* 172.

Visser, C., 'Applicable Law in Online Copyright Disputes: A Proposal Emerges' (2004) 16 *South African Mercantile Law Journal* 765.

'Choice of Law in Internet Copyright Disputes' (1999) 11 *South African Mercantile Law Journal* 268.

Vrancken, P., 'Submission and Attachment to Found Jurisdiction' (1993) 110 *South African Law Journal* 208.

Vrancken, P. H. G., 'Continuance of Jurisdiction and Effectiveness' (1993) 56 *Journal of Contemporary Roman-Dutch Law* 320.

'Foreign Antenuptial Contracts and s 7(3) of the Divorce Act 1970 of 1979: *Lagesse* v. *Lagesse*' (1993) *Journal of South African Law* 180.

Walker, D. M., 'The Concept of Status' (1979) *Acta Juridica* 416.

Wesley, C., 'The Presumption that Foreign Law is the Same as the Local Law: An Absolute Tradition Revisited' (1996) 37 *Codicillus* 36.

Wyk, A. V., 'Judgments in a Foreign Currency' (1991) 3 *South African Mercantile Law Journal* 197.

Zajtay, I., 'The Application of Foreign Law: Science and Fictions' (1973) 6 *Comparative and International Law Journal of Southern Africa* 245.

INDEX